more
Richmond
Receipts
past & present

more Richmond Receipts

Recipts

past &
present

Jan Carlton

J & B EDITIONS

For
Virginia Wright Keller,
better known to her family as Muldie,
seven plus decades young and one savvy lady
and
the culinary devotees of the next generation
Stephanie and Ian McBride
and
J.P. and Jamie Carlton

Old Richmond Club, at
Third and Franklin Streets,
had side yard where little
girls could play.
**Richmond Times-
Dispatch,** Sunday
October 16, 1949

Acknowledgements

MY GRATEFUL APPRECIATION AND THANKS TO the many people who have contributed their time, efforts, and, of course, recipes to make this book a reality, including all recipe contributors and the following: Don Dale, Sarah Starke, Naomi Wilson and Renee King, The Virginia Museum of Fine Arts; Minor Weisiger; Rick Goodwin, Hyatt Richmond; Valentine Museum; Mary Jane Tayloe, Executive Mansion of Virginia; Floyd Sinkler, Crab Louie's Tavern; Elizabeth Daniel, Lewis Ginter Botanical Garden; Wilton Museum House; Carol Owen, The Reynolds Wrap Kitchens, The Reynolds Metals Company; Raymond L. Smith, Fanny's Restaurant, Holiday Inns; Su and Rick Young, Half Way House; David Bundy, Patti Loughridge, and Anne Burke, Museum of the Confederacy; Muriel McAuley, Barksdale Theater; Kevin Wade, The Omni Hotel; John Brown, Hollywood Cemetary; Sarah Shields, Robert E. Lee House; Monica Beach, Thalhimers; Women's Committee of the Richmond Symphony; Richmond Symphony; Virginia Division of Historic Landmarks, the Fan District; Peter Mooz; Mary Stuart Cruickshank, Jefferson Hotel; Ladies Missionary Society, Great Hope Baptist Church; Jan Alley and William Musgrave, Linden Row Inn; Terry O'Neill, Penny Lane Pub; Ruddee's on the James; Nate Johnson and Rick Giovanni, Stonewall Cafe; Sue Mullins, Strawberry Hill Races; Jackie Margoles, Greek Food Festival, St. Constantine and Helen Greek Orthodox Cathedral; Swift Creek Mill Playhouse; Anne Mitchell,

Sam Miller's Warehouse; Thierry Jugnet, Ridgewell's; Carrie and John Wong, Three Star Restaurant; Paul and Marie Antoinette Elbling, LaPetite France Restaurant; Sally Dunn, Miller & Rhoads; The Fairbrother Family, Thyme and Sage of Hanover; Rives Hardy, St. Christopher's School; Robin Dorsey, C.F. Sauer Co.; Richmond Culinary Guild; Sherrie Weiner, Science Museum of Virginia; City of Richmond, Department of Recreation and Parks; St. John's Episcopal Church; Jack Terry, Wakefield's Restaurant; Metro Richmond Visitors Center; Chef Frederick Christian, Sr. and Douglas Sinclair, Jefferson Lakeside Country Club; The Wickham-Valentine House and Museum; Carolyn Bess, Tobacco Company Restaurant; 17th Street Market; University of Richmond; Doug Brown, The Commonwealth Park Hotel; Virginia Commonwealth University; The Scottish Society of Richmond; Jack Boettcher, New York Deli; Bill Hartsock, The Country Club of Virginia; Alain and Sandra Vincey, La Maisonnette; James and Lynn News, Mr. Patrick Henry's Restaurant and Inn; Traveller's Restaurant; Martha and Ned Nielsen, Nielsen's 3N Restaurant; Edward, Jackie, and Paul Shibley, Paul's Place; Reference Librarians, Richmond City Library; Richard Carew, Strawberry Street Vineyard; Michel Zajur, Sr. and Michael Zajur, Jr., La Siesta Restaurant; Don Bleau and Judie Cohen, The Butlery Restaurant; John Marshall House; Homemades by Suzanne; The Commonwealth Club; Dale Wheary, Maymont; Jack Zehmer, Historic Richmond Foundation; Maymont Park; Douglas O. Tice; Kathryn Marshall Arnold; Deborah Woodward; Vince and Bruna Capocelli, Sorrento Restaurant; Ralph White, James River Park; Greg Kimball.

Special thanks go to Eliza Askin for her marvelous line drawings of Richmond landmarks which so enhance *More Richmond Receipts*, and to the Virginia Historical Society for making available many of the historical recipes to me for publication which have been included in *More Richmond Receipts*.

Special thanks go also to Shari Call for her typing expertise, to Vernelle Thomas for always being there ... my special sunshine, ... to Cheryl Guthrie for her always valuable help, ... and to Marion Peeschla, fondly known to me as Mimi, her many, many hours of tedious work, support, and friendship, a special thank you.

And to PUSSY CAT ... for always being special!

Table of Contents

Richmond Skyline

Introduction

Dear Readers,

Three years have passed since *Richmond Receipts* made its publication debut in 1987. With your warm support and response, I have been inspired to gather more recipes from a variety of Richmonders, as well as historical food folklore, anecdotes, and receipts of the area.

First, let's settle the question of *receipt* versus *recipe*. I've had quite a few chuckles concerning the word. Several readers have called my attention to a printing misspelling of *recipe* in the book title, *Richmond Receipts*. Not to worry! *Receipt* and *recipe* are interchangable words, resulting from the French word, *recipére* ... to take back or receive. Both words, referring to food preparation, date back to the fourteenth century. Chaucer, the great English literary master, makes reference to a receipt in his writing of 1386. My research shows the use of *receipt* over *recipe* appears more frequently prior to 1900. Sometime in the early part of the twentieth century, there seems to be a trend toward the use of recipe. As Skip Stockton of the Richmond Library pointed out, publishing came into its heyday in the 1920's and 30's. More food companies used recipes to promote their products, possibly resulting in *recipe* becoming the catch-word to describe a formula for food preparation. It's a bit like *to-(may)-toes* versus *to-(maw)-toes* ... take your pick ... either is acceptable.

The past three years has brought great change to the world. No doubt our food habits and culture in the United States will be influenced by these important global transitions. I suspect we Americans will be sampling more Russian, Polish, Hungarian and other Eastern European cuisines in the near future, resulting from the opening up of these countries to capitalism and democracy. As *More Richmond*

Receipts goes to press, the United States, as well as most of the world community, is involved in a Middle East crisis. With United States service men and women stationed in Saudi Arabia, there is bound to be a cultural influence of the region making its way to American shores ... probably with some of the food customs. Ethnic food influences have resulted in the American cuisine of the twentieth century with each war or major global military disturbance; i.e. World War I, World War II, Korea, and Vietnam. Just as our colonial ancestors and the nineteenth and early twentieth century immigrants, American men, and now women, have previously and will continue to bring back to the United States some of the food traditions they have experienced and tasted while they have been in foreign countries.

As I mentioned in *Richmond Receipts*, Richmond is a city steeped in American history and tradition. It retains much of its conservatism, but indeed, it has become more cosmopolitan and progressive in its make-up and attitudes over the past quarter century. At times in its history, this beautiful city has even had a few bawdy moments.

Founded in 1737 by William Byrd II, Richmond has known prosperity as well as adversity, severe hardship, and despair, as experienced by inhabitants during the later stage of the Civil War and the Reconstruction Era. From its humble beginnings as a muddy crossroads at the Falls of the James River, the city populace has always been a blend of various ethnic and cultural groups. Early on, persons of English, Scottish, German, French, Jewish, Scandinavian, and black African heritage formed a part of the nucleus of settlers. Today, Richmond boasts a potpourri of ethnic and cultural groups, expanding the metropolitan population to more than 750,000 persons. (The 1990 census not available at press time.) Richmond is ever changing, yet retains some of the cultural influences of the past which have contributed to the charm and uniqueness of the area. The traditional Southern foods are still to be found, but Richmonders are sampling the cuisines of foreign countries and other American regions.

What are the foods of the 1990's? With more than fifty percent of adult American women in the work force, foods and meals that are quick and easy in preparation are required. The specialties which require longer preparation are saved for special occasions. More men are sharing in household tasks and in doing so, experiencing the satisfaction of creative cooking.

The trend watchers suggest people are getting away form *haute* or *nouvelle* cuisine and returning to simpler foods. Yep, Grandma's meat loaf is back in style ... but perhaps with a different accent and perhaps a bit more healthy. Use the old fashioned, marvelous recipes of yesteryear, but include less salt, less sugar and less fat in their preparation.

Nutrition is top priority with many persons. Experts credit the 1990's to be the decade of complex carbohydrates ... whole grains breads, pasta, rice, barley, ... and fiber. We all have our weak points though. Many people will carefully limit the calories, salt, fat, and cholesterol intake ... and then splurge on a wonderful tasting, sinful dessert. However, if Americans have to make a choice between convenience and nutrition, convenience usually wins.

Fresh is best has become a by-word. Throughout the 1990's, more of us will use fresh fruits and vegetables when available. Leaner meats and more use of turkey and chicken have already influenced the culinary scene. With the trend toward using fresh food also comes the influence of using fresh herbs. Many people, Richmonders included, have become backyard or patio gardeners, growing a variety of herbs for use in cooking, as well as visual and fragrant appeal. Note the availability of fresh herbs such as basil, cilantro, dill weed, Italian parsley, thyme, and oregano in supermarket produce sections. They are excellent flavor enhancers.

Microwave cooking is finally coming into its own, although there are many holdouts who don't believe in such new fashioned cooking. Twenty-five years ago, I helped promote the Amana microwave oven, better known then as the *radar range*, and a pioneer in the field. What a difference in products and cooking results from then to now. The actual oven space was a tiny cavity housed in a huge, cumbersome box. And the culinary delicacies resulting ... in many instances, not worthy of remembrance.

Richmonders of the late twentieth century still favor the specialties of the area. Smithfield ham and tiny ham biscuits will never go out of style. That "pot o' greens" simmered slowly with fat back and the resulting "pot likker" still garners raves. Lemon chess pie and coconut cake remain favorites. Moist buttery pound cake is a year round specialty.

Locally grown fruits and vegetables find their way in summer to the colorful outdoor market stands, as well as the local supermarkets. No tomato of other regions will ever surpass the flavor of a succulent ripe Hanover tomato, oozing with sweet flavorful juice and goodness.

Peanut soup, crab or seafood bisque, oyster stew, and a Chesapeake Bay-style clam chowder made with neither milk or tomato base, but chock full of clams, potatoes, onions, and clam broth, retain their priority with Richmonders. So, too, is fried chicken, although lower caloric broiled or baked chicken has found its way into Richmonders' diets. Creamy poofy spoon bread or feather light biscuits dripping with melted butter win hands down over ordinary bread. Yes indeed ... the foods that made Southern cooking synonymous with warm hospitality and lip smackin' good tasting food are alive and well in Richmond, Virginia. But, like the up and coming New South, there are new trends and other food choices available.

I came to Richmond as a bride of a Virginia gentleman almost two decades ago. During those twenty years, I have learned to appreciate and love the beauty, culture, history, and people of the city and area. We who are living in this region are most fortunate for our bounty. The *recipes* or *receipts* of Richmond are a part of the American heritage and will be equally at home in Alburqurque or New York or Topeka. I invite you to sample the history, culture, hospitality and cuisine of this *fair lady.*

Bon Appetit!!

Jan Carlton

Facts &
Useful Information

Before You Begin!!!
Basic Information

Margarine may be substituted for butter unless otherwise specified. Lower calorie, reduced salt and cholesterol margarine may be used.

Flour is all-purpose unless otherwise indicated.

Sour cream denotes the commercial product.

Herbs and spices are dried and ground unless otherwise indicated, with the exception of parsley and chives which are fresh.

Canned soups are to be used undiluted.

When whipping cream, chill cream, bowl, and beaters thoroughly before using.

Use egg whites at room temperature for whipping.

Use very cold water or iced water when testing candy temperature.

When sauterne is called for, use the dry white domestic table wine known as sauterne rather than the sweeter French variety.

If fish or shellfish are purchased frozen, thaw and then proceed as recipe directs.

Preheat oven for 10 to 15 minutes before baking.

Insert meat thermometer into the thickest part of meat, away from fat and bone. Keep dial as far away from heat source as possible.

To heatproof the handle of a pot or skillet to be used in the oven, cover the handle loosely with two or three thicknesses of slightly crushed aluminum foil.

Undiluted evaporated milk may be substituted for light cream or half-and-half.

Vegetable cooking or salad oil refers to corn or safflower oil.

Commercial packaged pie crust mix, prepared as directed, or frozen pie shells may be substituted for handmade pastry crusts.

For Those Who Are Calorie, Fat, Cholesterol, and Salt Conscious

Salt to taste is usually recommended in a recipe. It may be omitted, if desired; however it does act as a flavor enhancer in many recipes.

A salt substitute may be used to taste in place of salt in recipes. Use a salt substitute sparingly as it may impart a bitter aftertaste if too much is used.

For foods requiring sautéing or browning, a skillet or frypan may be lightly coated with a reduced calorie vegetable-based cooking spray and the butter or margarine or shortening or oil indicated in a recipe reduced or omitted to help reduce the amount of calories and cholesterol consumed.

When using margarine, preferably use a safflower or corn oil base margarine. A reduced calorie and/or unsalted margarine may be used, if desired.

In recipes which do not require baking but do require sugar for sweetening, sugar may be reduced or honey used or a sugar substitute may be used, if desired. Follow directions of individual branded products for amount to use in place of sugar. Use sparingly as sugar substitute may impart a bitter aftertaste if too much is used.

For those recipes requiring baking and extensive heating on top of the range and sugar for sweetening, many recipes in the book, i.e., ...cakes, pie fillings, cookies, and other desserts...may use a sugar substitute in place of sugar; however, some experimentation with a recipe and the addition of a sugar substitute will be required. Again, in many recipes honey (fructose) may be substituted or sugar reduced; experimentation is suggested.

How to use a Recipe

Always read the recipe completely before you begin to cook...this means reading all the directions as well as the list of ingredients. Be sure that you are familiar with the cooking terms used; if you're not, check the procedure to see how to proceed.

Check the equipment you will need. When a specific size of pan is called for, the size given is the one that was used when the recipe was tested. Pan size and shape will affect the results of any dish; if you can't be exact, stay as close as possible to the size and shape described.

Assemble all the ingredients. Use the ones called for; they were chosen because they were best suited to the recipe. Don't alter amounts of key ingredients, such as flour, sugar, liquids, or shortening. Spices and seasoning may be varied. For best results in all recipes, butter, eggs, and milk should stand at room temperature a short time before you use them.

Assemble all the equipment. This will include measuring spoons and cups, mixing spoons and bowls, saucepans, and baking pans, depending on the recipe being prepared.

Measure accurately. Tested recipes are based on the use of standard measuring cups and spoons. Use dry weight measuring utensils for flour, sugar, etc., and liquid measuring utensils for water, milk, etc.; dry and liquid measurements of equal value are different.

Mix carefully. Follow directions exactly. Overmixing or undermixing, especially in baked goods, can give disastrous results.

Bake or cook as directed. Times and temperatures indicated in recipes should be carefully followed for complete success.

Tables of Measurements

This Measurement	Equals this Measurement
3 teaspoons	1 tablespoon
2 tablespoons liquid	1 ounce
4 tablespoons	1/4 cup
5 1/3 tablespoons	1/3 cup
6 tablespoons	3/8 cup
8 tablespoons	1/2 cup
16 tablespoons	1 cup
1 cup	8 ounces or 1/2 pint
2 cups	1 pint
4 cups	1 quart
1 pint	2 cups
2 pints	1 quart
1 quart	4 cups
4 quarts	1 gallon or 16 cups
8 quarts	1 peck
4 pecks	1 bushel
1 fluid ounce	2 tablespoons
1 pound	16 ounces or 453.60 grams
1 jigger	3 tablespoons or 1 1/2 fluid ounces
1 wine glass	1/4 cup
2 tablespoons fat or butter	1 ounce
1 stick butter	1/2 cup
1/2 pound butter, margarine, or lard.	1 cup
1 pound granulated sugar	2 to 2 1/4 cups (approximate)
1 pound brown sugar	2 1/4 cups (packed)
1 pound confectioners' sugar	4 1/2 cups (approximate)
1 pound all-purpose flour, sifted	4 cups
1 pound long-grain rice	2 to 2 1/2 cups
1 pound ground coffee	3 1/2 cups
1 pound pitted dates	2 cups
1 square chocolate	1 ounce
16 marshmallows	1/4 pound
1 pound rolled oats	5 1/3 cups
1 pound corn meal	2 2/3 cups
1 pound cornstarch	3 cups
1 pound diced cooked chicken	3 cups
1 pound cranberries	4 cups
1 pound chopped onions	3 cups
1 pound ground beef	2 cups
1 cup egg whites	8 to 12 whites (approximate)
1 cup egg yolks	13 to 14 yolks (approximate)
1 cup whole eggs	5 to 7 eggs
1 cup lemon juice	4 to 6 lemons

1 pound bananas................................	3 medium
1 pound potatoes..............................	3 to 4 medium
1 cup breadcrumbs............................	2 3/4 ounces
1/2 pound candied fruit or peel.........	1 1/2 cups chopped
1 pound shredded coconut...............	5 cups
1 gram..	0.035 ounces
1 kilogram...	2.205 pounds
1 liter...	35 fluid ounces, 1.056 quarts

Ingredient Equivalents

BEANS, DRIED

Kidney or Lima	1 pound	2 1/2 cups uncooked; 5 1/2 cups cooked
	1 cup uncooked	2 1/2 cups cooked, about
Navy	1 pound	2 1/3 cups uncooked; 5 1/2 cups cooked
	1 cup uncooked	3 cups cooked, about

BREAD, LOAF

	1 pound loaf	12 to 16 regular slices
Breadcrumbs, soft	1 sice	1/2 cup soft crumbs
Breadcrumbs, dry	1 slice	1/3 cup fine dry breadcrumbs

BROTH, CHICKEN OR BEEF

	1 cup	1 bouillon cube or 1 envelope powdered broth base dissolved in 1 cup boiling water

BUTTER, FATS, OILS

Butter or margarine	1 pound	2 cups
Hydrogenated shortening	1 pound	2 1/3 cups
Butter or margarine, whipped	1 pound	3 cups
Oils	1 pint or 1 pound	2 cups
Suet, chopped medium-fine	1 pound	3 3/4 cups

CEREALS

Corn meal

White	1 cup	4 cups cooked
		1 pound 3 to 3 1/2 cups
Yellow	1 pound	3 cups; 16 2/3 cups cooked
Farina	1 pound	3 cups; 16 2/3 cups cooked
Grits	1 pound	3 cups; 10 cups cooked
Hominy, whole	1 pound	2 1/2 cups; 16 2/3 cups cooked
Oats, rolled	1 pound	6 1/4 cups; 8 cups cooked
	1 cup uncooked	1 3/4 cups cooked

Rice

Long-grain	1 pound	2 1/2 cups; about 8 cups cooked
	1 cup uncooked	3 cups cooked
Precooked	1/2 pound	2 cups

CHEESE

Cheddar, American,

Swiss, Mozzarella	1 pound	4 cups grated or finely shredded
Cottage	1 pound	2 cups
Cream	8 ounces	1 cup
	3 ounces	6 tablespoons (about 1/3 cup)

5

FACTS and USEFUL INFORMATION

Parmesan	3 ounces	1 cup grated or finely shredded
CHOCOLATE		
Chips	6 ounces	1 cup
Unsweetened (bitter)	1 ounce	1 square
COCONUT, SHREDDED		
OR FLAKED	3 1/2 to 4-ounce can	1 1/4 to 1 1/3 cups
COFFEE, GROUND	1 pound	80 tablespoons
CRACKERS	18 small	1 cup coarsely crushed
	21 small	1 cup finely crushed
Graham	9 squares	1 cup coarse crumbs
	11 to 12 squares	1 cup fine crumbs
Vanilla wafers	26 to 30	1 cup fine crumbs
Zwieback	5 slices	1 cup fine crumbs
Potato chips	1 cup, firmly packed	1/2 cup potato chip crumbs
Pretzels	12 thin	1/2 cup pretzel crumbs
CREAM		
Light	1/2 pint	1 cup
Half-and-half	1 pint	2 cups
Heavy or whipping	1/2 pint	1 cup; 2 cups whipped
EGGS		
Whole	5 to 7	1 cup (approximate)
Whites, large	1 cup	8 to 10 whites (approximate)
Yolks, large	1 cup	12 to 14 (approximate)
FLOURS		
All-purpose, sifted	1 pound	4 cups
All-purpose, unsifted,		
spooned	1 pound	3 1/2 cups
Cake, sifted	1 pound	4 2/3 cups (approximate)
Cake, unsifted spooned	1 pound	4 cups (approximate)
Self-rising, sifted	1 pound	4 cups
Whole wheat	1 pound	3 1/3 cups
Rye, light, sifted	1 pound	5 cups (approximate)
Rye, dark, sifted	1 pound	3 1/2 (approximate)
FRUITS, CANNED		
Apples, sliced	20 ounces	2 1/2 cups
Apricots		
Whole	1 pound	8 to 12
Halved	1 pound	2 1/2 cups
Blueberries	14 ounces	1 1/2 cups
Cherries, red tart, pitted	1 pound	2 cups (approximate)
Cranberry juice	1 quart	4 cups
Cranberry sauce	1 pound	1 2/3 cups
Fruit juices		
(grapefruit, orange,		
pineapple)	46 ounces	5 3/4 cups
Fruit salad or cocktail	17 ounces	2 cups
Grapefruit, sections	1 pound	2 cups
Peaches		
Halves	1 pound	6 to 10 halves
Sliced	1 pound	2 cups
Pear, halves	1 pound	6 to 10 halves

6

Pineapple
  Chunks and tidbits   29 ounces   3 3/4 cups

Pineapple
  Chunks and tidbits   29 ounces   3 3/4 cups
  Crushed   29 ounces   3 3/4 cups
  Sliced   20 ounces   10 slices

FRUITS, DRIED
  Apricots
    Dried   1 pound   3 cups
    Cooked   1 pound   6 cups
  Currants   1 pound   3 1/4 cups
  Dates
    Whole   1 pound   60
    Pitted, cut   1 pound   2 1/2 cups
  Figs
    Whole   1 pound   44, or 2 1/4 cups
    Cut fine   1 pound   2 2/3 cups
    Cooked   1 pound   4 1/2 cups
  Peaches
    Whole   1 pound   2 3/4 cups
    Cooked   1 pound   4 1/2 cups
  Prunes
    Whole with pits   1 pound   2 1/2 cups
    Cooked   1 pound   4 to 4 1/2 cups
    Pitted   1 pound   2 1/4 cups
    Pitted and cooked   1 pound   4 to 4 1/2 cups
  Raisins, seedless
    Whole   1 pound   2 3/4 cups, 4 cups plumped
    Chopped   1 pound   2 cups

FRUITS, FRESH AND FROZEN
  Apples, fresh, whole   1 pound   3 medium; 3 cups cored and sliced or chopped
  Apricots, fresh   1 pound   8 to 12; 2 1/2 cups peeled sliced or halved
  Avocado   1 pound   2 1/2 cups peeled and cubed
  Bananas, whole   1 pound   3 to 4 medium; 2 to 2 1/2 cups peeled and sliced; 1 1/3 cups peeled and mashed
  Blueberries
    Fresh   1 pound   2 cups
    Frozen   10 ounces   1 1/2 cups
  Cantaloupe   1 medium   1 cup peeled and cubed
  Cherries, red   1 quart   2 cups, pitted
  Cranberries, fresh   1 pound   3 1/2 to 4 cups, about 3 to 3 1/2 cups sauce
  Grapes
    Seedless, fresh   1 pound   2 1/2 cups
    Tokay   1 pound   2 3/4 cups seeded
  Honeydew Melon   1 medium   1 cup peeled and cubed
  Kiwi   about 3   1 cup peeled and sliced
  Lemons
    Fresh   1 medium   3 tablespoons juice (approximate); 2 teaspoons grated peel

FACTS and USEFUL INFORMATION

Frozen juice (concentrate)	6 fluid ounces	3/4 cup
Limes, fresh	1 medium	2 tablespoons juice; 2 teaspoons grated peel
Nectarines	1 pound	4 medium (approximate), 2 cups sliced
Oranges, fresh	1 medium	1/3 to 1/2 cup juice (approximate); 2 to 3 tablespoons grated peel
Peaches, fresh	1 pound	4 medium; 2 cups peeled and sliced
Pears, fresh	1 pound	4 medium; 2 cups peeled and sliced
Pineapple		
Fresh	2 pounds	3 cups peeled and cubed
Frozen, chunks	13 1/2 ounces	1 1/2 cups
Plums	1 pound (8 to 20)	(about 2 cups) halved and pitted
Raspberries	1 pint	2 cups (approximate)
Rhubarb		
Fresh	1 pound	4 to 8 stalks; 2 cups cut up and cooked
Frozen, sliced	12 ounces	1 1/2 cups
Strawberries		
Fresh, whole	1 pint	2 cups (approximate)
Frozen, whole	1 pound	1 1/3 cups
Frozen, sliced	10 ounces	1 cup
Watermelon	1 pound	1 cup peeled and cubed
GELATIN, UNFLAVORED	1 ounce	1 envelope or 1 tablespoon
MACARONI, SPAGHETTI, NOODLES	8 ounces	4 cups cooked
	1 cup uncooked	2 cups cooked
MARSHMALLOWS	12 ounces	40 large marshmallows
MILK		
Whole, skim, buttermilk	1 quart	4 cups
Evaporated	13 ounces	1 cup plus 5 tablespoons; 2 1/2 cups plus 2 tablespoons reconstituted
NUTS		
Almonds	1 pound	In shells, 1 to 1 1/2 cups. Shelled, 3 1/4 cups
Macadamia	1 pound	Shelled, ? cups (approximate)
Peanuts	1 pound	In shells, 2 to 2 1/2 cups. Shelled, 4 cups
Pecans	1 pound	In shells, 2 1/4 cups. Shelled, 3 1/2 to 4 cups
Walnuts in shell	1 pound	2 1/2 cups
Walnut meats	4 ounces	1 cup chopped nutmeats
SUGARS		
Brown, light	1 pound	2 1/4 cups (packed)
Confectioners', unsifted	1 pound	4 1/2 cups (approximate)

Granulated	1 pound	2 to 2 1/4 cups (approximate)
Superfine	1 pound	2 1/3 cups (approximate)

SYRUPS

Corn Syrup	16 fluid ounces	2 cups
Honey	1 pound	1 1/3 cups
Maple syrup	12 fluid ounces	1 1/2 cups
Molasses, cane	12 fluid ounces	1 1/2 cups
Sorghum	1 pound	1 1/2 cups

VEGETABLE, FRESH, FROZEN, AND CANNED

Asparagus Spears
Fresh	1 pound	16 to 20 pieces, 2 cups cooked
Frozen	10 ounces	2 cups
Canned	15 1/2 ounces	2 cups

Green or Wax Beans
Fresh	1 pound	3 cups; 2 1/2 cups cooked
Frozen	9 ounces	1 1/2 cups
Canned	15 1/2 ounces	1 3/4 cups

Lima Beans
Fresh	1 pound	2 cups; 1 2/3 to 2 cups cooked
Frozen	10 ounces	1 3/4 cups
Canned	1 pound	2 cups

Beets
Canned	16 to 17 ounces	2 cups
Fresh (no tops)	1 pound	2 cups chopped; 2 cups cooked

Broccoli spears
Fresh	1 pound	2 cups cooked
Frozen	10 ounces	1 1/2 cups cooked
Brussel Sprouts	1 pound	4 cups cooked

Cabbage
Fresh, shredded	1 pound	3 1/2 to 4 1/2 cups; 2 cups cooked

Carrots
Fresh (no tops)	1 pound (7 to 8 medium)	3 cups; 2 1/2 cups shredded or diced, cooked
Canned	1 pound	2 cups

Cauliflower
Fresh	1 pound	1 1/2 cups; 1 1/2 cups cooked
Frozen	10 ounces	2 cups
Celery	1 pound	4 cups chopped (2 small stalks)
Corn	12 ounces	3 cups, cut
	12 ears	3 cups cut, about
Cucumber	1 medium	2 cups thinly sliced
	1 pound (about 2 to 3 large)	3 cups coarsely chopped 2 1/2 cups thinly sliced

Eggplant	1 pound	4 cups peeled and cubed or 8 thin slices
Green onion	about 3 bunches	1 cup chopped or thinly sliced
Green pepper or yellow or sweet red	1 medium	about 1 cup chopped
Greens (turnip, mustard, swiss chard or kale)	3 pounds	3 to 4 cups cooked (approximate)
Leeks	2	1 cup thinly sliced or 1 cup chopped
Lettuce	1 medium head	(about 6 to 8 cups) shredded or torn
Mushrooms		
Fresh, sliced	1 pound, 36 medium	2 to 3 cups sliced
Dried	3 ounces	1 pound fresh
Canned	4 ounces	2/3 cup
Okra		
Fresh	1 pound	2 1/4 cups cooked
Frozen	10 ounces	1 pound fresh
Canned	15 1/2 ounces	1 3/4 cups
Onions		
Fresh	1 pound	3 large, 2 to 2 1/2 cups chopped
Frozen, chopped	12 ounces	3 cups
Canned	16 to 17 ounces	2 cups
Parsnips	1 pound	(3 to 4 medium) 2 1/2 to 3 cups peeled and thinly sliced
Peas		
Fresh in pod	1 pound	1 cup shelled; 1 cup cooked
Frozen	10 ounces	2 cups; 2 cups cooked
Canned	1 pound	2 cups
Potatoes, white		
Fresh	1 pound	3 to 4 medium; 2 1/4 cups cooked; 2 1/2 cups peeled and cubed; 1 3/4 cups peeled and mashed
Frozen, French fries or puffs	9 ounces	3 to 4 servings
Canned, whole	16 to 17 ounces	8 to 12
Radishes	8 to 10	1 cup thinly sliced
Shallot	1	1 tablespoon minced
Spinach		
Fresh	1 pound	4 cups leaves; 1 1/2 cups cooked
Frozen	10 ounces	1 1/2 cups cooked
Canned	15 ounces	2 cups
Sweet Potatoes or Yams	1 large	3/4 pound (approximate), 3/4 to 1 cup cooked, peeled, and mashed (approximate)
Fresh	1 pound	4 cups; 1 1/2 cups cooked
Frozen	12 ounces	3 to 4
Canned	16 to 17 ounces	1 3/4 to 2 cups

Tomatoes		
Fresh	1 pound	3 to 4 small (approximate)
	2 pounds	1 1/2 cups cooked
Zucchini or summer squash	1 medium	1 cup thinly sliced
Winter squash	1 medium	1 1/2 cups peeled, cooked, and mashed

Handbook of Food Preparation (Sixth Edition, 1971). American Home Economics Association

About Herbs and Spices

Name	Description	Uses
Allspice	Miniature-sized fruit from a West Indian tree, named for its flavor which resembles a blend of cinnamon, cloves, and nutmeg.	Whole...pickling, preparation of meats, gravies, and fish.
Anise	An annual native to the Mediterranean region produces this licorice-flavored seed.	Used in vegetable soup, with sausages and roast pork, and in baked goods, particularly coffeecakes, and cookies
Balm, Lemon	A perennial of the mint family which grows to a height of two feet and bears purplish-white flowers.	The lemon-scented leaves are used as a seasoning as well as in herb tea, fruit cups, or salads.
Basil, Sweet	Herb of the mint family.	Good in stews, salads, soups, and sauces. Add to any tomato-base sauce.
Bay Leaves	The aromatic leaf of the laurel tree.	Used in pickling, stews, spiced vinegars, and soups. Excellent with fish and tomato dishes.
Capers	The unopened bud of the prickly caper bush.	Use sparingly in tomato and sea-food salads. Good with crabmeat and lobster.
Caraway Seed	Dried fruit of a hardy biennial of the parsley family.	A flavoring of rye bread, cakes, biscuits, cheese, applesauce, and cookies.
Cardamom	Tall perennial of the ginger family.	Whole is used in pickling spices. Ground is used in breads, coffeecakes, and pastries.

11

Cayenne	Finely ground hot red peppers.	Excellent with meats, fish, and sauces.
Celery Seed	Dried fruit of a biennial of the parsley family.	Used in soups, stews, and pickling, and with fish and salads.
Chervil	Small, low-growing annual of the parsley family.	Mainly used in fines herbes; chervil can be used alone with egg dishes, lamb, veal, pork, fish, and seafood.
Chives	A perennial of the lily family.	Use in any recipe requiring a mild onion flavor.
Cinnamon	Pungent bark of the cinnamon (laurel) tree.	Stick...pickling and preserving. Ground...baked goods.
Cloves	Dried nail-shaped flower bud of the clove tree.	Whole is used by studding pork and ham, pickled fruits and syrups. Ground is used in chocolate puddings, baked goods, stews, and soups.
Coriander (Also Called Cilantro)	Annual herb of the parsley family.	Whole seeds are used in mixed pickles, soups, cakes, cookies, and stuffings. Ground seeds are used in sausages and pork. An important ingredient in curry powder. Fresh leaves are used in salads, fish, and seafood dishes.
Cumin Seed	Small annual herb of the parsley family.	Used in meat dishes, especially chili, and with rice. Good with cheese, sausages, pickles, and soup.
Dill Seed and Weed	An herb of the parsley family with small feathery leaves and yellow flowers.	Used for pickling, sauerkraut, salads, gravies, fish and meat sauces, and spiced vinegars.
Fennel seed and Weed	Tiny seedlike fruit with flavor similar to anise.	Flavoring of fish sauces, soups, sweet pickles, and salads.
Garlic	The pungent bulb of a perennial plant of the lily .	Used for garlic butter and bread and in meat and marinades.
Ginger	A pungent rootstock.	Whole and grated is used to flavor syrups and pickling vinegar.

Ginger (continued)		Ground is used for gingerbread, desserts, and oriental meat dishes.
Horseradish	The root of a plant of the mustard family.	Grated is used in beef, oyster, and shrimp recipes, sauces, and dips.
Leek	An onion-like vegetable of the lily family	Used in vichyssoise and other soups and salads.
Mace	Dried outer covering of the fruit of the nutmeg tree. Orange-red in color.	Essential in fine pound cakes; valuable in all chocolate dishes. Used in oyster stews and stuffings for poultry.
Marjoram	Herb of the mint family.	Leaf is used with lamb and as a garnish. Dried herb is used for meats, liverwurst. some cheese, vegetables, soups, and sauces.
Mint	Perennials cultivated for their aromatic leaves.	Sprigs used in beverages. Chopped leaves used in mint sauce for roast lamb, stuffing for fish or garnish for vegetables.
Mustard Seed	Three mustards; white, yellow, and black or brown.	Whole mustard may be used in pickling and garnishing salads. Dry mustard flavors meats, sauces, and gravies.
Nutmeg	Glossy brown, oily seed from the nutmeg tree.	Used in baked goods and flavoring for meat products. Also, used in soups, sauces, preserves, eggnog, and puddings.
Oregano	A perennial of the mint family; it is closely related to marjoram and is often called "mild marjoram."	An excellent seasoning for pork dishes. Good for omelets, gravies, beef stew, lamb, and any tomato dish.
Paprika	There are many varieties, some mild and sweet, and others very hot.	Used extensively in Creole cooking, egg dishes, potato salads, salad dressings, and as a garnish.
Pepper	Prepared from the small berry of a woody evergreen climbing vine	Both black and white pepper are used in almost any type of food.

Rosemary	Small, spiky evergreen shrub of the mint family.	Fish and meat stocks, lamb and poultry dishes, potatoes, and other vegetables.
Saffron	Said to be the worlds most expensive spice, saffron is made from the dried stamen of the crocus plant.	An essential ingredient of Spanish and Mexican dishes.
Sage	Leaf of a low-growing evergreen shrub of the mint family.	Used in meat and poultry stuffings. Also in pork products.
Sesame Seed	Tiny honey-colored seed of an annual herb. Also called benne.	Sprinkle on bread, rolls, crackers, and biscuits. Also good on buttered noodles.
Shallot	A perennial bulb of the lily family, like garlic in shape, but milder in flavor.	Chopped shallots are used in chicken, fish, and vegetable soups, meat and fish stews.
Tarragon	The peculiar bittersweet flavor is produced by a small perennial plant of the sunflower family.	Use in soups, salads, stews, sauces, and vinegar. Good with chicken and lobster.
Thyme	Garden herb of the mint family.	Flavors clam and fish chowders, meats, sausages, poultry dressings, some fish sauces, and fresh tomatoes.
Turmeric	Perennial tropical herb of the ginger family.	Used in pickles and curried dishes.
Vanilla	The dried pod of a climbing plant of the orchid family.	Extract is used in ice cream, custards, cakes, sauces, puddings, and eggnog.

Blended Spices

Curry Powder
   There is considerable variation in curry powder blends. As a general rule, it contains a blend of six or more of the following ingredients: cumin, coriander, fenugreek, turmeric, ginger, pepper, dill, mace, cardamom, and cloves.

Fines Herbes
   Combination of three or more herbs ground fine and carefully blended. Herbs that may be used are parsley, chervil, tarragon, chives, sage, savory, and basil.

Italian Herb Seasoning
   Oregano, marjoram, thyme, savory, basil, rosemary, and sage generally make up this seasoning spice.

Pickling Spice
>A combination of cinnamon, bay leaves, coriander, mustard, ginger, allspice, cloves, dill, chili peppers, pepper, mace, and cardamom.

Poultry Seasoning
>Sage, onion, thyme, and marjoram are usually combined in poultry seasoning blends.

Pumpkin Pie Spice
>Usually consists of cinnamon, ginger, nutmeg, allspice, mace, and cloves.

Salad Herbs
>Basil, tarragon, and thyme make up this seasoning.

Salad Seasoning
>Usually consists of sesame seed, poppy seed, onion, garlic, and celery seed.

Helpful Hints

Baking Hints

When cutting cream pies, dip the knife in warm water, so none of the filling will stick to it.

If a bread or cake browns too quickly before it is done, place a pan of warm water on the rack above it in the oven.

Dredge dried fruits and nuts with some of the flour called for in a cake recipe to prevent them from sinking to the bottom of the pan when baking.

Crisp and freshen cookies or crackers which have become soft by placing them in a very low oven for 5 minutes.

For the best baked biscuits on meat pies, have the meat bubbling hot before the biscuits are placed on top. The biscuits will bake faster and be lighter and the bottoms will not get soggy. Use the same trick for fruit cobblers.

A few drops of vinegar added to ice water when making pastry will make it flakier.

Warming a pan before putting in the undercrust of a pie will keep the crust from becoming soft and soggy during baking.

Roll out pastry between two sheets of waxed paper; when the top sheet is pulled off, the pastry can be turned into a pie plate with little effort.

Coat pastry shells with egg white before baking to prevent a soggy crust.

To make a fine textured cake, add a few drops of boiling water to butter and sugar when creaming.

When a custard pie shrinks from the crust, it has been baked in a too hot oven.

Preferably use cake flour for preparing cakes. The flour is usually made with a softer wheat, needed for pastry flour. To duplicate the consistency of European pastry flour, one-third cup cake flour plus two-thirds cup of all-purpose flour equals 1 cup of pastry flour.

All-purpose flour varies from region to region. In the South, the blend of flours will be softer, resulting in optimum quick breads. The Northern product is more coarse, containing more gluten and producing best yeast bread results.

To melt chocolate over hot water, fit a piece of waxed paper in the top of a double boiler saucepan and place the chocolate on it. When the chocolate has melted, remove the paper, and transfer the chocolate with scraper to a mixing bowl. No pan to clean! Or, place chocolate squares in paper wrappers in a microwave oven; microwave at high power for 2 to 3 minutes or until melted. Add additional microwave time as needed in increments of 30 seconds.

A teaspoon of wine added to the waffle batter will prevent waffles from sticking to the waffle iron.

Beverage Hints

You can avoid cloudiness in iced tea by letting freshly brewed tea cool to room temperature before refrigerating it. If the tea becomes cloudy, pour a little boiling water into it until it clears.

16

When making lemonade, put the lemons through a meat grinder or food processor. The juice will go twice as far and have a better flavor.

A dash of salt added to coffee that has been overcooked or reheated will freshen the taste.

Bread Hints

To freshen French or Italian bread, hard rolls, etc., sprinkle the crust with cold water and place it in a preheated 350 degree F. oven for 5 to 10 minutes.

To make cutouts from bread slices, first freeze the bread to give it clean sharp edges.

Don't throw away a stale loaf of bread. Wrap it in a damp cloth for about 1 minute. Then place in a preheated 350 degree F. oven for about 20 minutes.

Serve warm. Or, microwave at high power for 30 to 60 seconds.

Egg Hints

To prevent an egg from cracking while cooking in simmering water, pierce both ends with a needle before putting in water.

When poaching eggs, add a dash of vinegar or lemon juice to the water to keep the white from spreading.

To cut hard-cooked eggs without breaking the yolks, dip the knife in water.

When frying eggs, sprinkle a little flour into the fat to prevent splattering.

A teaspoon of cold water added to egg whites while beating will almost double the quantity of stiffly-beaten egg whites.

Beat egg whites in a copper bowl to obtain the most volume of beaten egg whites.

To keep a puffy omelet from collapsing, add a pinch of cornstarch and a pinch of confectioners' sugar to the yolks before folding in the whites.

When hard-cooking eggs, add a tablespoon of salt to the water. This loosens the shells and they come off easily.

Before poaching eggs, rub the bottom of the pan with butter or margarine to prevent them from sticking and breaking. Or, spray pan bottom with vegetable cooking spray. It also makes the pan easier to wash.

Use a potato masher or pastry blender to chop hard-cooked eggs.

To prevent hard-cooked eggs from having unsightly dark tinged edges around the yolks, place eggs in a deep heavy saucepan and add water to cover completely and 1 tablespoon of salt. Bring to a beginning boil over moderate heat; immediately reduce heat, and simmer for no more than 20 minutes. Remove eggs and immediately immerse in cold water. Remove shell from eggs after they have cooled.

To cook perfect hard-cooked eggs, place clean eggs in a deep glass or ceramic oven-proof container. Add enough cool water to cover eggs completely and 1 tablespoon of salt. Bake, uncovered, in a moderate oven (350° F) for 50 to 60 minutes, depending upon number of eggs being cooked. Remove from container and immerse eggs immediately in cold water. Remove shell from eggs after they have cooled.

Fruit Hints

To ripen fruit, put it in a paper bag in a dark place for a few days. Or, place in a plastic fruit ripener, preferably with a banana, for 2 to 3 days.

For full flavor, always cook dried fruit in same water in which it was soaked.

If jelly does not set, place glasses in a drip pan half full of cold water, and bake in a moderate oven for 30 minutes.

If citrus fruits are warmed in the oven for a few minutes, they will give much more juice. Or, gently roll citrus fruits, pressing firmly with the heel of the hand before extracting juice.

To prevent apples and bananas used in salads from turning dark, sprinkle them with lemon juice or powdered fruit freshner (ascorbic acid).

To ripen avocados quickly, tuck them in a wool sock, and put in a dark place.

General Hints

One or two peeled potatoes simmered in oversalted soup for a little while will absorb excess salt. Discard the potato.

Boil several cloves in a cup of water to rid the house of objectionable food odors, especially seafood.

When doubling a recipe, never double the seasonings until you taste the finished product.

If you need a large amount of ice cubes for a party, remove them from trays and store them in plastic bags in the freezer.

If you have trouble cleaning a grater after grating cheese, rub raw potato over it before washing.

A few drops of ammonia dropped into greasy pans before hot water is added will make them much easier to clean.

To cook a hot dish in a hurry, place it in a pan of salted cold water. It will cook more rapidly than in plain cold water.

Lightly oil gelatin molds before filling. It makes for easier unmolding.

After peeling onions, wash hands in cold water; then rub with salt.

Don't discard the peel of grapefruits, oranges, or lemons. Grate them, put in tightly covered jars and store in refrigerator. They make excellent flavorings for cakes and frostings.

Green leaves on the outside of lettuce contain more vitamins than the inside leaves, so don't discard any more than necessary.

To prevent skin from forming on a pudding, cover it with waxed paper or clear plastic film while still hot.

If a boiled custard curdles, remove it from heat and beat it vigorously with a wire whisk. Or, place custard in a blender container; cover and blend at medium speed for a few seconds until custard is smooth.

A pinch of salt added to flour before it is mixed with a liquid helps keep gravy from becoming lumpy.

If a gravy does not brown, add a little coffee. There is no risk of the gravy taking on the coffee flavor.

To remove excess fat from gravy or stew, wrap an ice cube in a piece of cheesecloth and pull it back and forth over the surface. The fat will harden and stick to the cloth as it comes in contact with the ice. Or, use a skimmer.

A tablespoon of cold water beaten into Hollandaise which has curdled will often bring it back to a smooth texture.

Never let a soup or stew boil. It should barely simmer.

A little oatmeal or quick-cooking oats add flavor and thickening to stew.

Garnish soups with crisp croutons, paprika, finely cut chives, dill or parsley, grated cheese, and slivers of ham or chicken. Slices of avocado are excellent for consommé, green pea, or tomato soup. Dollops of sour cream or yogurt are good for consommé and chilled or hot cream soups.

Store the liquid from canned vegetables, mushrooms, etc., in a large container in the freezer. It is a valuable addition to soup stock.

Gelatin must be thoroughly dissolved before combining with other ingredients in order to achieve a gell.

Meat, Poultry, and Fish Hints

When baking a ham, slit the rind lengthwise on the underside before it is placed in the roasting pan. As it bakes, the rind will pull away and can be removed easily without lifting the ham from the pan.

Don't salt roasted meats until they are three-fourths cooked in order to retain juices and flavor.

When simmering tough meat, add a little vinegar to pot liquid to make it tender.

Before putting ground beef into the freezer, form the meat into patties. Place each patty on a square of waxed paper; wrap each in freezer paper. Seasonings may be added before or during cooking.

To clean shrimp, hold it under a slow stream of cold water, and run the tip of an icepick up the back of the shrimp. The shrimp is cleaned and remains whole.

Pour boiling water over clams, and they will open more easily.

Salad Hints

Celery ribs will be crisp and delicious if soaked in cold water containing 1 teaspoon sugar for about 1 hour.

Parsley keeps fresher longer if stored in a tightly closed jar in the refrigerator.

Storing Hints

To keep brown sugar soft, transfer it from the package to an airtight container. Store it in the refrigerator. Add a quartered apple to package. Hardened brown sugar may be softened in a ziplock plastic bag in the microwave for 30 seconds at high power.

Dampen a cloth; sprinkle it with vinegar and wrap it around cheese to keep it from hardening.

To keep cookies fresh and crisp, place a crumpled tissue in the bottom of the cookie jar.

To preserve the flavor of coffee after it has been ground, store it in an airtight container in the refrigerator or freezer.

Vegetable Hints

When cooking corn on the cob, add a little milk and a pinch of sugar to the cooking water.

Most vegetables are improved by adding a dash of sugar to the cooking water.

Rice grains will stay white and separated, if 1 teaspoon of lemon juice is added to each quart of water.

Never salt turnips while they are cooking; it extracts the sweetness.

To clean spinach quickly, wash it in fairly warm water.

Before baking potatoes, soak them in salted water for 20 minutes or in hot water for 15 minutes, and they will bake more rapidly.

Hot milk added to potatoes during the mashing will keep them from becoming soggy or heavy.

Add a teaspoon of baking powder to potatoes when mashing; then beat them vigorously to make them light and creamy.

For a crisper outer crust, rub skins of baking potatoes with butter before baking.

As soon as potatoes are baked, prick them with a fork to release steam, so that they will not get soggy.

Fresh tomatoes keep longer if stored with the stems down.

Bake tomatoes, stuffed green peppers, or apples in well-greased muffin tins. They will keep their shape better and be more attractive when served.

1 teaspoon butter added to water in which any greens are cooking will prevent them from boiling over.

When cooking fresh peas, add a few pods to the water to improve the flavor and color.

When cooking cauliflower, add a piece of white bread to eliminate odor.

Before cooking cauliflower, soak it, head down, for about 30 minutes in salted water to remove insects and grit.

Candy and Syrup Temperatures

Syrup	Temperature at Sea Level		Test for Doneness
	Fahrenheit	Centigrade	
Syrup	230° to 234°	110° to 112°	Thread stage: syrup spins a thread 2-inches long when dropped from spoon.
Fudge, Panocha, Fondant	234° to 240°	112° to 115°	Soft-ball stage: syrup forms a soft ball in very cold water that will flatten when removed from water
Caramels	244° to 248°	118° to 120°	Firm-ball stage: forms a firm ball when dropped into very cold water that will not flatten.
Divinity	250° to 266°	121° to 130°	Hard-ball stage: forms a ball hard enough to hold its shape in cold water.
Butterscotch, Taffy Popcorn balls	270° to 290°	132° to 130°	Soft crack stage: separates into hard brittle threads when dropped into very cold water.
Brittles	300° to 310°	149° to 154°	Hard crack stage: separates into very brittle strings that crack in cold water.

Note: As elevations increase 500 feet, cook syrups 1 degree F. lower than above temperature. When centigrade temperatures are used, cook syrup to 1 degree C. lower for each 900 feet elevation.

Deep-Fat Frying Temperatures

Food	Fry At		One-inch bread cube dropped in hot fat will brown in:
	Fahrenheit	Centigrade	
Chicken	350°	177°	65 seconds
Doughnuts, fish fritters, oysters, soft-shell crabs, scallops	350° to 365°	177° to 185°	60 to 65 seconds
Croquettes	370°	190°	40 seconds
French-fried potatoes, vegetables, onions	385° to 396°	196° to 201°	20 seconds

Handbook of Food Preparation (Sixth Edition, 1971). American Home Economics Association.

Oven Temperatures

Oven Temperature	Fahrenheit	Centigrade
Very slow	250 to 275	121 to 135
Slow	300 to 325	149 to 163
Moderate	350 to 375	177 to 190
Hot	400 to 425	204 to 218
Very hot	450 to 475	232 to 246
Extremely hot	500 to 525	260 to 274

Handbook of Food Preparation (Sixth Edition, 1971)American Home Economics Association.

Commercial Can Sizes

Size	Weight	Approximate Amount, in Cups
6 ounce	6 fluid ounces	3/4 cup
8 ounce	7 3/4 fluid ounces	1 cup
No. 1	10 1/2 ounces	1 1/4 cups
	9 1/2 ounces	1 2/3 cups
No. 303 or 1 1/2	1 pound	2 cups
No. 2	20 ounces	2 1/2 cups
No. 2 1/2	28 ounces	3 1/2 cups
No. 3	33 ounces	4 cups
46 ounce	1 quart-14 fluid ounces	5 3/4 cups
No. 10	106 ounces	12 to 13 cups

Reading antique recipes prepared in yesteryear can be amusing and often informative. Although not geared to today's methods and measurements for cooking, they often tell us about the culture and foods prepared and eaten by our ancestors. Through the years, we have borrowed from and changed many of these old American recipes which now have become an integral part of our life style and eating habits.

Emergency Substitutions

IF YOU DON'T HAVE THIS:	YOU CAN USE THIS:
BAKING POWDER	
1 teaspoon baking powder	1 teaspoon cream of tartar plus 1/2 teaspoon baking soda
BREADCRUMBS	
1 cup breadcrumbs	1 to 2 slices soft bread, crumbled
BUTTER	
1 cup butter	1 cup margarine or 1 cup shortening or lard plus 1/2 teaspoon salt
CHOCOLATE	
1 square (1-ounce) unsweetened chocolate	3 1/2 tablespoons cocoa powder plus 1 tablespoon shortening
CORNSTARCH	
1 tablespoon cornstarch	2 tablespoons flour
FLOUR	
For thickening—1 teaspoon flour	1/2 teaspoon cornstarch or 2 teaspoons quick tapioca
For baking—1 cup all-purpose flour	1 cup plus 2 tablespoons cake flour
1 cup sifted cake flour	1 cup minus 2 tablespoons all-purpose flour
1 cup pastry flour	2/3 cup cake flour plus 1/3 cup all-purpose flour
GARLIC	
1 clove	1/4 teaspoon garlic powder or 1/2 teaspoon minced garlic
HERBS	
1 tablespoon fresh minced	1 teaspoon dried
MILK	
1 cup sour or buttermilk	1 cup milk plus 1 tablespoon lemon juice or vinegar
1 cup whole fresh milk	1/2 cup evaporated milk plus 1/2 cup water
1 cup half-and-half	7/8 cup milk plus 3 tablespoons melted butter (combined well)

23

ONION

1/4 cup chopped

1 tablespoon dried minced onion or 1 teaspoon onion powder

SUGARS AND SYRUPS

1 cup honey

1 1/4 cups sugar plus 1/4 cup liquid

1 1/2 cups corn syrup

1 cup sugar plus 1/4 cup water

1/4 cup cinnamon sugar

1/4 cup granulated sugar plus 1 teaspoon cinnamon

YEAST

1 cake compressed yeast

1 package or 5 teaspoons active dry yeast

MISCELLANEOUS

1 teaspoon oregano

1 teaspoon marjoram

1/2 cup ketchup or chili sauce

1/2 cup tomato sauce plus 2 tablespoons sugar, 1 tablespoon vinegar, and 1/8 teaspoon ground cloves

Few drops of Tabasco or hot sauce

Dash of cayenne or red pepper

1 cup tomato juice

1/2 cup tomato sauce plus 1/2 cup water

1 cup chicken or beef stock

1 cup canned chicken or beef broth

1/2 pound mushrooms

4-ounce can mushroom caps

1 teaspoon Italian seasonings

1/4 teaspoon each oregano, basil, thyme, and rosemary plus dash of cayenne

1 teaspoon pumpkin pie spice

1/2 teaspoon cinnamon, 1/4 teaspoon ginger, 1/8 teaspoon each nutmeg and cloves

1 teaspoon allspice

1/2 teaspoon cinnamon plus 1/8 teaspoon cloves

1 large marshmallow

10 miniature marshmallows

Appetizers
and
Hors d'oeuvres

Tangy Cheese 'N Clam Spread

Yield: 8 to 10 appetizer servings

1 (6 1/2 to 8--ounce) can minced clams, drained (see note)
5 ounces sharp Cheddar cheese, at room temperature (see note)
1/4 cup minced green onion (include some green tops)
1/4 cup minced green pepper
1/2 tablespoon Worcestershire sauce
4 to 5 drops hot sauce or to taste
Paprika and/or minced parsley
Crisp potato chips, corn chips, or assorted crackers

In the top of a double boiler, combine the first 6 ingredients.Stir over boiling water until cheese melts, clams are tender, and mixture is bubbly hot. Spoon into the brazier of a chafing dish;sprinkle lightly with paprika and/or minced parsley. Serve hot accompanied with chips or crackers.

Note: 8 ounces shucked *little neck* (small) clams, drained and minced may be substituted.

Note: 1 (5-ounce) jar sharp Cheddar cheese food spread may be substituted.

Zesty Baked Artichoke Dip

Yield: about 2 cups

1 (14-ounce) can artichoke hearts, drained
1 (4-ounce) can chopped chiles (peppers), drained
1/2 cup mayonnaise
1/3 cup grated Parmesan cheese
Tortilla chips

Thinly slice artichoke hearts. In a bowl, combine artichoke pieces, chiles, mayonnaise, and Parmesan cheese, mixing well. Spoon into a greased 1-quart baking dish. Bake, uncovered, in a moderate oven (350 degrees F.) for about 30 minutes or until bubbly hot and top is lightly browned. Serve hot with tortilla chips.

Variation: Add 2 tablespoons minced pimento, drained, and 1/8 teaspoon dry mustard. Serve hot with assorted crackers or Melba toast rounds as spreaders. May omit chilles.

–Frances Miller (Mrs. Donald P)
–Virginia Cotrell (Mrs. Walker C., Jr.)

Cocktail Nibbles

Yield: about 4 1/2 cups

1/3 cup creamy-style peanut
  butter
2 tablespoons margarine
1/2 cup peanuts
2 cups crisp small rice
  cereal squares
2 cups crisp small wheat
  cereal squares

In a medium heavy saucepan, combine peanut butter and margarine together; melt over low heat. Add cereals and nuts, mixing well. Spread mixtures evenly over an ungreased 15 x 10 x 1-inch baking sheet. Bake in a moderate oven (375 F.) for 5 minutes. Remove and cool for several minutes before serving or storing in an airtight container.
–Nathalie Klaus (Mrs. Phillip)
Valentine Museum Guild

Old Dominion Crab Appetizer

Yield: 20 to 25 appetizer servings

2 pounds backfin crabmeat
1/2 cup butter or margarine
1/4 cup cream of mushroom
  soup, undiluted
1/4 cup dry white wine
1/2 teaspoon Worcester-
  shire sauce or to taste
Pinch of garlic powder or to
  taste
Melba toast rounds or crisp
  toast points

Pick over crabmeat; remove any shell or cartilage. In a large heavy skillet, melt butter over low heat. Stir in mushroom soup, wine, Worcestershire sauce, and garlic, blending well. Add crabmeat; stir gently in pan to warm, being careful not to break pieces of crabmeat. Carefully spoon into the brazier of a chafing dish. Garnish as desired and accompany with melba toast rounds or crisp toast points.

—Eddy Dalton (Mrs. John)
First Lady of Virginia, 1978 to 1982
Virginia State Senator, 1987 to ____

Separate dining rooms made their appearance during the eighteenth century in town as well as elegant country homes.

27

Piquant Fiesta Spread

Yield: about 4 cups

1 (8-ounce) package cream cheese, at room temperature
5 ounces air dried beef, shredded
1/2 cup minced peeled onion
1/2 cup sour cream
1/4 cup diced hot green chili peppers (see note)
1/4 to 1/2 teaspoon garlic salt
1 to 4 tablespoons milk, as needed
3 tablespoons butter or margarine, melted
Assorted crisp crackers or Melba toast rounds

In a medium bowl, beat cream cheese at medium speed of an electric mixer until smooth. Stir in dried beef, onion, sour cream, chili peppers, and garlic salt. Add enough milk to achieve desired consistency. Spoon into a lightly greased 1-quart casserole. Drizzle butter over top of cheese mixture. Bake, uncovered, in a moderate oven (350 degrees F.) for 20 to 25 minutes or until bubbly hot. Serve hot accompanied with assorted crisp crackers or Melba toast rounds.

Note: Fresh or canned chili peppers may be used.

Note: Spread freezes well. Baking time may be increased if casserole has been refrigerated or frozen in advance.

—Annette Knight

Curried Seafood Dip

Yield: 8 to 10 appetizer servings

8 ounces crabmeat or peeled, deveined, cooked small shrimp
1 (8-ounce) package cream cheese, at room temperature
1 tablespoon mayonnaise
2 teaspoons Worcestershire sauce
2 to 3 teaspoons curry powder
2 tablespoons minced peeled onion
Crisp corn chips

Pick over crabmeat, removing any remaining shell or cartilage; or, cut shrimp into bite-sized pieces. In a bowl, beat cream cheese until smooth. Beat in mayonnaise, Worcestershire sauce, and curry powder. Fold in crabmeat or shrimp and onion. Spoon into a lightly greased 1-quart casserole. Bake, uncovered, in a moderate oven (375 degrees F.) for 25 minutes or until bubbly hot. Serve accompanied with crisp corn chips as dippers.

Variation: Add 1 to 2 tablespoons chopped chutney to mixture and substitute green onion (include some green tops) in place of regular onion.

—Betty Wilton (Mrs. E. Carlton)

Chinese Chicken Walnut Fingers

Yield: 2 dozen appetizer servings

6 chicken breasts, skinned and boned
1 egg, beaten
About 1/2 to 3/4 cup cornstarch
About 1/2 to 1 cup finely chopped or coarsely ground English walnuts or pecans
Hot oil or shortening, melted, as needed
Wooden picks
Oriental Orange Sauce (see index)

Cut chicken breasts into narrow strips or bite-sized chunks (nuggets). Dip each chicken piece in egg. On a sheet of waxed paper, coat pieces thoroughly in cornstarch. On a second sheet of waxed paper, roll coated chicken pieces evenly in nuts. Deep-fry in hot oil (350 degrees F.) for 2 to 3 minutes or until golden brown and crispy. Drain well on absorbent paper. Serve immediately, piping hot, accompanied by wooden picks and Oriental Orange Sauce for dipping.

–Carol Nance
Assistant Attorney General
State of Virginia

Although appetizers and hors d'oeuvres are thought by many to be a creation of the twentieth century to accompany liquid libations during the cocktail hour, these nibble foods were known to the ancient Greeks as "provocatives to drinking." Such tidbits as marinated octopus, pistachio nuts, a form of goose liver pâté, caviar, oysters, roasted grasshoppers, and even a version of the popular dolmades of today might be offered. The ancient Romans also had their gustatio, or first course, to precede any banquet which could outshine the variety of foods presented on a colonial Virginia groaning board. The Italian antipasto refers to food eaten before the main course, mensae primae, appears. Literally, appetizer results from appetite or "to tease the palate for the good foods to follow." And, in some instances the palate is satiated rather than teased at late twentieth century cocktail buffets.

Crispy Chicken "Fingers" with Hot Plum Sauce

Yield: 14 to 16 appetizer servings

6 whole chicken breasts, skinned and boned (see note)
2 garlic cloves, peeled and minced or 1 teaspoon garlic juice
1 1/2 cups buttermilk
2 tablespoons lemon juice
1 tablespoon Greek seasoning powder
1 tablespoon soy sauce (see note)
2 teaspoons Worcestershire sauce
1 teaspoon paprika
1 teaspoon salt or to taste
1 teaspoon pepper
4 cups breadcrumbs (see note)
1/2 cup sesame seeds (optional)
1/2 cup butter or margarine, melted
1/2 cup shortening, melted
Hot Plum Sauce (see index)

Cut chicken into 1 1/2 x 2-inch strips. In a large bowl, combine the next 9 ingredients, mixing well. Add chicken pieces, coating each piece completely with the buttermilk mixture. Cover with clear plastic wrap and refrigerate several hours. Remove chicken pieces, draining thoroughly. Combine crumbs and sesame seeds on a sheet of waxed paper. Coat each chicken piece completely in crumb mixture. Arrange chicken pieces in two greased 13 x 9 x 2-inch baking dishes. Combine butter and shortening; brush chicken pieces with melted butter-shortening mixture. Bake, uncovered, in a moderate oven (350 degrees F.) for 35 to 40 minutes or until crisp and golden brown. Remove to a warm chafing dish and serve with wooden picks and Hot Plum Sauce for dipping.

Alternate Frying Method: Deep-fry crumb-coated chicken "fingers" in hot oil (350 to 375 degrees F. in at least 3 inches of oil) until crisp and golden brown. Drain well on absorbent paper.

Note: One skinned and boned whole turkey breast, or 3 boneless turkey filets or tenderloins, or 4 to 6 (1-pound) packages boneless turkey breast cutlets may be substituted for whole chicken breasts.

Note: May substitute reduced sodium (Lite) soy sauce, if desired.

Note: Cornflake crumbs or 2 cups cornflake and 2 cups breadcrumbs may be used in place of 4 cups breadcrumbs.

Variation: Cut the top lengthwise from a loaf of French bread. Hollow out the bottom portion of loaf, forming a container. Fill hollowed-out bread with crisp baked chicken "fingers." Cover with bread top. Wrap in aluminum foil. Keep warm in a slow oven (300 degrees F.). Serve chicken in bread "basket" with Hot Plum Sauce as accompaniment for dipping. When chicken is eaten, break off hunks of bread to dunk in sauce.

–Ann Tyler (Mrs. Hal)

Baked Clam Delights

Yield: 6 to 8 appetizer or 4 entreé servings

"These can be prepared several hours in advance, refrigerated, and baked just before serving. I usually serve four to five filled clam shells on a plate as an appetizer or first course."

1 pound shucked *little* or *top neck* (small) or *cherry stone* (medium) clams (see note)
2 cups chopped mushrooms
1/4 cup minced peeled onion
3 tablespoons butter or margarine, melted
3 tablespoons flour
1 cup reserved clam liquid (see note)
1 cup milk (see note)
1 tablespoon lemon juice
4 hard-cooked eggs, peeled and finely chopped
1/4 cup minced parsley
1/2 teaspoon salt or to taste
1/4 teaspoon pepper or to taste
5 to 6 drops hot sauce or to taste
1 1/2 to 2 cups buttered breadcrumbs (see note)
Paprika as needed

Drain clams, reserving 1 cup liquid, and mince with a sharp knife; set aside. In a medium heavy skillet, sauté mushrooms and onion in butter over moderate heat until tender but not browned. Sprinkle flour over mixture, mixing well. Gradually stir in clam liquid, milk, and lemon juice. Cook, stirring constantly, until mixture is thickened and bubbly hot. Add minced clams, eggs, parsley, salt, pepper, and hot sauce, mixing well. Adjust seasoning to taste. Spoon mixture into about 24 medium clam shells or 8 small or 4 large seafood baking shells or individual ramekins, dividing evenly. Sprinkle each with buttered breadcrumbs. Arrange filled clam shells or baking shells on ungreased baking sheets. Bake in a hot oven (400 degrees F.) for 10 to 15 minutes or until appetizers are bubbly hot and tops are lightly browned. Sprinkle each lightly with paprika. Serve immediately.

Note: 2 drained (7 1/2 to 8-ounce) cans or 3 (6 to 6 1/2-ounce) cans minced clams may be substituted for fresh clams. Reserve 1 cup clam liquid.

Note: Omit milk and use 2 cups clam liquid.

Note: Combine 1 cup breadcrumbs with 1/4 cup melted butter or margarine; toss lightly to mix.

–Shelly Bendheim (Mrs. Sam III)

Crab Streudel

Yield: 48 appetizers, about 16 appetizer servings

The Commonwealth Park Suites Hotel, a AAA Five Diamond Award Winner, boasts two fine restaurants. Maxine's, with an unsurpassed view of Capitol Square, serves breakfast and lunch, and The Assembly presents excellent continental cuisine in elegant and intimate surroundings.

1 pound crabmeat
1 (8-ounce) package cream cheese, at room temperature
1 teaspoon Worcestershire sauce
Few drops hot sauce to taste
3 tablespoons minced green onion (include some green tops)
1 (1-pound) package frozen phyllo or streudel leaves, thawed
1 cup butter or margarine, melted

Pick over crabmeat, removing any shell or cartilage. In a bowl, combine cream cheese, Worcestershire sauce, and hot sauce, beating until smooth. Fold in crabmeat and green onion, mixing well. Liberally brush each phyllo leaf with butter; stack leaves into 3 even layers. Cut layers into 7 narrow strips. Spoon 1 teaspoon crab mixture onto one end of each strip. Starting at filling end, fold each strip as a flag, end over end, to form a triangle. Arrange crab "triangles" on ungreased baking sheets. Bake in a moderate oven (375 degrees F.) for 20 minutes or until golden brown. Serve hot.

Note: These may be frozen until ready to bake. Do not thaw. Bake frozen, directly from freezer, in a preheated oven.

–The Assembly Restaurant
The Commonwealth Park Suites Hotel

Travelers in colonial Virginia often had to stop overnight at a wayside inn. No one was ever turned away. Sleeping arrangements were quite inconvenient and uncomfortable; some persons spent a night bedded on the floor. Food was served in a common room with no choice of victuals offered.

Jewell's Mushrooms

Yield: 36 to 42 mushroom snacks

8 ounces mushrooms, cleaned and minced
2 tablespoons butter or margarine, melted
1 tablespoon lemon juice
1/2 teaspoon curry power or to taste
1/2 teaspoon salt
Pinch black pepper
12 to 14 thin slices white bread
Additional melted butter or margarine as needed
Wooden picks

In a heavy skillet, saute mushrooms in 2 tablespoons butter over moderate heat. Blend in lemon juice, curry powder, salt, and pepper. Remove crusts from bread slices; with a rolling pin, roll each slice flat. Brush each slice with melted butter. Liberally spoon mushroom mixture onto each slice of buttered bread, spreading evenly to cover each slice. Roll each slice of bread, jelly-roll style; fasten securely with wooden picks. Brush rolls with additional melted butter and arrange on an ungreased baking sheet. Bake in a hot oven (425 F.) for 15 minutes or until rolls are lightly browned. Allow rolls to cool 3 to 5 minutes. Cut each roll into 3 pieces. Serve immediately and accompany with additional wooden picks as needed.

–Shirley Simmons (Mrs. Richard)

Early Virginians were known for their capacity to devour huge quantities of food at breakfast....foodstuffs such as fricasseed meats and hash, savory bacon and hams, game pies, hot grits, lavishly buttered biscuits and cornbread, local seasonal fruits such as strawberries or blackberries, a variety of egg dishes and a choice of coffee, tea, chocolate, cider...usually hard, or beer, and perhaps even a sweet of some kind.

Old Richmond Advertisement, circa 1909

APPETIZERS and HORS D'OEUVRES

Oriental Tidbit Snacks

Yield: 20 tidbit snacks

1/4 cup soy sauce (see note)
2 tablespoons light brown sugar, firmly packed
10 water chestnuts, halved
5 chicken livers, quartered
10 bacon slices, cut in half
Wooden picks

In a large bowl, combine soy sauce and brown sugar. Wrap a half slice of bacon around a piece of water chestnut and a piece of chicken liver; fasten with a wooden pick. Place tidbit snacks in soy sauce mixture, coating each tidbit well. Cover with clear plastic wrap and chill in refrigerator 4 hours, occasionally spooning soy mixture over snacks. Drain snacks from marinade and arrange on a rack in a broiler pan. Broil snacks, 6 inches from heat source, turning once, until crisp and lightly browned, about 3 minutes per side.

Note: Reduced sodium (Lite) soy sauce may be substituted for regular soy sauce. One teaspoon Lite soy sauce contains 100 milligrams of sodium.

–Suzanne Klein (Mrs. Edward)
Valentine Museum Guild

Hot Buttered Crabmeat w/Toast Points

Yield: 6 to 8 appetizer servings

1 pound lump crabmeat
1/2 cup butter or margarine, melted
Salt and pepper to taste
Ground nutmeg to taste
Few grains cayenne pepper
Brandy as desired
Minced fresh parsley for garnish
Hot buttered toast points

Pick over crabmeat, removing any remaining shell or cartilage. In a heavy saucepan, over low heat, combine melted butter and seasonings. Add crabmeat, so as not to break lumps. Heat mixture through, but brown. Sprinkle brandy, as desired, and parsley over mixture. Serve in the brazier of a chafing dish accompanied with hot buttered toast points. Or, spoon brandied crab mixture onto 6 to 8 appetizer plates, dividing evenly. Garnish each serving with minced parsley and accompany with hot buttered toast points.

Note: Use freshly ground nutmeg, if available.

–Sarah Baynes (Mrs. H. L.)
Valentine Museum Guild

34

The Fan

The Fan District, taking its name from its distinctive fan shape, is a very popular residential area in Richmond. Recently designated as a Virginia Landmark, it has been nominated to the National Register of Historic Places. Significant for its architectural cohesiveness, the development of The Fan highlighted the transformation of Richmond from a village to a city in the half century following the defeat of the Confederacy in the American Civil War The growing demand for better housing and improved city services by a new urban middle class spurred architects, builders, and real estate speculators to promote the construction and sale of entire blocks of residences in the area. The district conveys an agreeable feeling of harmony that depends not so much on uniformity of architectural style as on intrinsic qualities of good urban design. Today, this unique area is being continually revitalized by residents intent upon maintaining high quality standards and renaissance atmosphere. Neighborhood restaurants, shops, and boutiques add interest and variety to this charming area.

Cheesey Mushroom Sticks

Yield: 8 dozen

Cheesey Mushroom Sticks was one of the mushroom delicacies shared by noted mushroom authority and author, Hope Miller, at a special symposium on wild mushrooms growing in the Virginia area given at the Lewis Ginter Botanical Garden in Richmond in the Autumn of 1988.

1/2 cup butter or margarine, melted
2 garlic cloves, peeled and minced
1 small onion, peeled and chopped
1 small green pepper, cored, seeded, and chopped (optional)
1/2 cup sifted flour
1 teaspoon baking powder
3/4 teaspoon nutmeg
3/4 teaspoon salt
2 1/4 teaspoons minced fresh or 3/4 teaspoon dried basil
10 eggs
1 pound Monterey Jack or sharp Cheddar cheese, shredded
2 cups creamy-style cottage cheese, undrained

In a large heavy skillet, sauté mushrooms, garlic, onion, and green pepper, if desired, over moderate heat until tender but not browned; set aside. In a medium bowl, sift together flour, baking powder, nutmeg, and salt. Add basil, mixing well. In a large bowl, beat eggs until light and foamy; stir in flour mixture, blending well. Add cheeses, mixing well. Stir in mushroom mixture. Spoon into a lightly greased 17 1/4 x 11 1/2 x 1-inch baking sheet. Bake, uncovered, in a moderate oven (350 degrees F.) for 35 minutes or until a silver knife inserted in the center comes out clean. Cool at room temperature on a wire rack before cutting into 2 x 3/4-inch sticks. Baked mushroom sticks will keep, covered, in the refrigerator for up to two days. To serve, reheat, covered, in a moderate oven (350 degrees F.) for about 15 minutes or until heated through.

Note: Morel or shiitake mushrooms may be used, as well as the usual variety, *Agaricus campestris*, found in produce sections of grocery stores.

Note: Baked mushroom sticks freeze well for several months wrapped in heavy duty aluminum foil and sealed tightly. To serve, thaw and reheat as previously directed.

–Hope Miller

A Child of the '70s

Sunday was our favorite day, for it was then that we could be with our parents more than any other day of the week.

The dinner table there was laid with a shining damask cloth, pressed into folds, first this way and then that. At either end of the table stood the footed celery holders with green leaves frothing above the rims. Before each place was a little silver salt bowl. Under its base was enbedded a 25 cent piece as a weight. We had 24 of these salt bowls and thought our parents must be very rich indeed to have coins of such value hidden in mere tableware. Before Papa's place sat the steaming soup tureen. After it was removed and the roast brought in, Papa would whet his stag-handled knife and perform the carving with delicate skill. (Dear Grandmamma used to say that he could carve a ham thinner than any gentleman in the county). When he had finished, he would lay the tips of his carving tools across the backs of little silver goats, to avoid spotting the cloth.

When we had guests the children would eat in the breakfast room. The ladies and gentlemen would start their dinner with oysters which were shipped to us in an iced barrel and served on elegant oyster plates in which were realistic oyster-like depressions. Each plate was of a different color—cobalt blue, maroon, deep green—and was ornamented with painted oyster shells in relief and gold-flecked ribbons.

Yes, it was wonderful being a child in the 1870's.

Adelaide Stoddert
"Victorian Era Childhood
Held Own Special Charm,"
Richmond Time-Dispatch, Feb. 24, 1963

Sis's Mushroom Torte

Yield: 10 appetizer or 8 luncheon servings

Crust

2 cups sifted flour
1 teaspoon salt
3/4 cup butter or margarine,
  at room temperature
1/3 cup ice water

In a medium bowl, sift flour and salt together. With a pastry blender, cut in butter until mixture resembles coarse meal. Evenly sprinkle ice water over mixture and toss lightly with a fork. Form mixture into a ball; turn out onto a lightly floured board and knead 6 to 8 times. Roll out to an 11-inch diameter circle, 1/4-inch thick. Turn into a 10-inch pie plate, forming a standing ridge around the edge. Prick the bottom of the crust with the tines of a fork. Bake in a moderate oven (375 degrees F.) for 15 minutes or until lightly browned. Cool.

Filling

1 pound mushrooms, thinly
  sliced (about 6 cups)
2 teaspoons minced peeled
  shallots
5 tablespoons butter or
  margarine, melted and
  divided
3 tablespoons flour
3/4 cup milk
1/2 cup light cream or half-
  and-half
2 egg yolks, slightly beaten
1 teaspoon lemon juice
1/2 teaspoon salt
2 cups shredded Swiss
  cheese, divided

In a heavy skillet, sauté mushrooms and shallots in 3 tablespoons butter over moderate heat until tender but not browned; remove from heat and set aside. In a heavy saucepan, stir flour into 2 tablespoons butter until a smooth paste is formed. Gradually add milk and cream, blending well. Cook, stirring constantly, until thickened and bubbly hot. Gradually stir a small amount of mixture into egg yolk mixture, blending well. Stir egg yolk mixture into remaining sauce. Add mushroom mixture, 1 cup cheese, lemon juice, and salt, mixing well.

Spoon into baked pie shell; evenly sprinkle remaining 1 cup of cheese over mushroom mixture. Bake in a moderate oven (350 degrees F.) for 15 to 20 minutes or until cheese is melted and lightly browned on top. Cool for 5 to 7 minutes before cutting. Serve as a first course appetizer or luncheon entreé.

Note: Torte may be prepared in a 15 x 10 x 1-inch baking pan and cut into squares, if desired. Pass as hors d'oeuvres at a cocktail party.

–Libby Teeter(Mrs. James)

Bloemendaal

Lewis Ginter Botanical Garden at Bloemendaal Farm

Located on eighty acres of land in historic north Richmond, the Lewis Ginter Botanical Garden at Bloemendaal Farm was once property owned by Patrick Henry. The present day garden is the original location of nineteenth century Richmond philanthropist, Major Lewis Ginter's Lakeside Wheel Club. At the turn of the nineteenth/twentieth century, members would often bicycle from Richmond out to the Club for a day's outing. Portions of Bloemendaal House date back to the late 1800's.

Today the Botanical Garden, open to the public, is the site of Richmond's most extensive seasonal bedding displays. Botanical courses of study and events are conducted at the Garden throughout the year.

Wild Mushroom Strudel

Yield: 16 pastries

Delightful surroundings and distinctive cuisine afford visitors to Chardonnay's a premier dining experience. Located in the Richmond Mariott Hotel in downtown Richmond, adjacent to the renovated Sixth Street Market, the restaurant is open for dinner Monday through Saturday evenings.

1 1/2 pounds shiitake mushrooms
1 1/2 pounds oyster mushrooms
Mushroom essence
4 cups heavy cream, at room temperature
2 ounces shallots, peeled and chopped
1 cup butter or margarine, melted and divided
1 (8-ounce) package Boursin (herb and garlic) cheese, at room temperature
1 (16-ounce) package frozen phyllo dough thawed (16 sheets) (see note)
Breadcrumbs as needed

Remove stems from mushrooms and coarsely chop. Set aside mushroom caps. Place chopped stems in a large heavy saucepan; add water to pan to measure 2 inches above mushrooms. Cook, uncovered, over moderate heat until liquid is reduced by about three-fourths; strain liquid into a small heavy saucepan. Further reduce mushroom stock over moderate heat to 1 cup mushroom essence. In a medium heavy saucepan, reduce cream over moderate heat to 2 cups. Combine reduced cream and mushroom essence; consistency should be quite thick.

Coarsely chop mushroom caps. In a large heavy skillet, sauté chopped mushroom caps and shallots in 2 to 3 tablespoons butter over moderate heat until tender but not browned. In a medium bowl, combine mushroom mixture, cream-mushroom essence, and Boursin cheese, mixing well; cool thoroughly.

Brush each phyllo sheet liberally with remaining butter and lightly with breadcrumbs. Arrange buttered sheets in stacks, 3 sheets to a stack. Cut each stack vertically into 3 equal width strips. Spoon about 1 to 2 tablespoons mushroom mixture in the lower right corner of each strip. Working rapidly and keeping remaining phyllo strips covered with a damp cloth towel, fold each mushroom filled strip in the manner of folding a flag, ending with a triangle.

Arrange filled phyllo triangles, 1 inch apart, on ungreased baking sheets; brush each triangle with additional butter. Bake in a moderate oven (350 degrees F.) for 15 minutes or until pastries are golden brown. Arrange pastries, one each, on appetizer plates and garnish as desired. Serve immediately.

40

Note: Thaw phyllo dough in the refrigerator for 12 hours.

–Chef Jim Ertell
Chardonnay's
Richmond Mariott Hotel

Oysters Brookfield

Yield: 4 appetizer servings

Established in 1974, Hugo's has set a standard of fine dining for its patrons. Located in the Hyatt Richmond hotel off West Broad Street in the park-like Brookfield Complex, Hugo's offers a traditional menu specializing in fresh seafood, certified Black Angus beef, and grilled items. The chef features weekly specialties for those who are more adventuresome in their cuisine tastes. Hugo's is also known for some unusual after-dinner coffees, Cognac selections, and an extensive wine list.

24 *count* (large) oysters in the shell
8 ounces spinach
2 tablespoons shallots, peeled and minced
4 teaspoons minced peeled garlic
2 to 3 tablespoons butter or margarine, melted
6 ounces fully-cooked smoked Smithfield or Virginia country-style ham, cut into julienne strips (see note)
1/3 cup Pernod
Salt and pepper to taste
Hollandaise sauce for garnish (see index)

Shuck oysters, leaving individual oysters loose but in place on the half shells; set aside. Clean spinach, rinsing thoroughly to remove any grit or sand. Remove stems and finely chop leaves with a sharp knife. In a large heavy skillet, sauté spinach, shallots, and garlic in butter over moderate heat for 2 minutes. Add Pernod to mixture and ignite; when flame is extinguished, add ham and continue cooking for an additional 1 to 2 minutes. Cool. Top each oyster in shell with a small amount of spinach mixture, dividing evenly. Arrange oysters on a baking sheet or in an 11 x 7 x 2-inch baking pan evenly filled with rock salt. Bake, uncovered, in a moderate oven (350 degrees F.) for 10 to 12 minutes. Spoon a small amount of Hollandaise Sauce over each oyster. Arrange 6 glazed oysters on each of 4 heat-proof appetizer plates filled with a bed of hot rock salt, if desired. Garnish as desired.

Note: To julienne, cut ham with a sharp knife into *very* thin match-like strips.

–Hugo's
Hyatt Richmond

Coconut Batter Fried Shrimp
with Piquant Marmalade

Yield: 6 entreé or 10 appetizer servings

Casual Art Deco elegance and continental dining are presented at Benjamin's, located on West Broad Street near the Fan district of Richmond. Owners, and Virginians, include Ben and Rose Gill and Gary Edwards, former football star at Lee Davis High School and the University of Richmond during the late 1960's and early 70's. Opened in 1983, Benjamin's kitchen presents continental, as well as New Orleans-style cooking in its cuisine. To complete a dining occasion, nightly musical entertainment, including blues and jazz, is offered in the "Piano Bar" lounge.

2 1/2 pounds fresh or frozen medium shrimp, thawed (16 to 20 count) (see note)
3 cups orange marmalade
2 1/2 teaspoons grated peeled fresh horseradish
1 (12-ounce) can domestic beer
2 cups flour
Pinch salt and pepper
About 4 to 5 cups shredded coconut as needed
Hot peanut oil as needed
Minced parsley for garnish

Peel, devein, and wash shrimp; leave tails intact for easy dipping into marmalade. Dry shrimp on absorbent paper; set aside. In a small bowl, combine marmalade and horseradish, blending well; set aside. Heat oil in deep-fat fryer or large heavy skillet (3 inch depth) to 350 degrees F.. Pour beer into a medium bowl. Gradually beat in flour with a wire whisk. Beat in salt and pepper. Spread coconut evenly in one layer on a sheet of waxed paper. Dip shrimp in batter, allowing excess batter to drip back into bowl. Coat each batter-covered shrimp well in coconut. Immediately deep-fry or pan-fry shrimp after dipping in batter in peanut oil (350 degrees F.) for about 2 minutes or until shrimp are golden brown. Turn shrimp in skillet once. Drain well on absorbent paper. Arrange fried shrimp on an ungreased baking sheet and bake, uncovered, in a moderate oven (350 degrees F.) for 2 minutes. Spoon Piquant Marmalade into a serving bowl and garnish with minced parsley. Serve hot crisp fried shrimp with marmalade for dipping.

Note: 16 to 20 count refers to the number of shrimp per pound.

–Benjamin's Restaurant

Hot Pepper Jelly and Cheese Turnovers

Yield: 5 dozen appetizer turnovers

1 (5-ounce) jar sharp Cheddar cheese food spread, at room temperature (see note)
1/2 cup butter or margarine, at room temperature
1 cup flour
2 tablespoons water
1 (4-ounce) jar hot red or green pepper jelly

In a bowl, cut cheese and butter into flour with a pastry blender until mixture resembles coarse meal. Stir in water, mixing well; shape into a ball. Cover and refrigerate for several hours. On a lightly floured board, roll out dough very thin. Cut into circles with a lightly floured biscuit cutter, 2 inches in diameter. Place 1/2 teaspoon pepper jelly in the center of each biscuit circle. Fold circles in half and seal edges by crimping with the tines of a fork. Bake on ungreased baking sheets in a moderate oven (375 degrees F.) for 10 minutes.

Note: The turnovers can be frozen before or after baking.

Note: 5 ounces (1 1/4 cups) shredded sharp Cheddar cheese may be substituted for Cheddar cheese food spread.

–Libby Teeter (Mrs. James)

Baked Crab Puffs

Yield: about 16 to 20 servings (about 60 puffs)

1 pound lump backfin crabmeat
1 pound Swiss or Emmentaler cheese, shredded
1/4 cup dry white wine
About 1 tablespoon mayonnaise
2 to 3 drops Tabasco sauce
Salt to taste
Thin slices of party-style rye or pumpernickel bread
Minced parsley for garnish

Pick over crabmeat, removing any shell or cartilage. In a large bowl, combine crabmeat, cheese, wine, mayonnaise, and Tabasco sauce, mixing well. Season with salt to taste. Spoon 1 teaspoon crabmeat mixture onto each bread slice. Arrange bread slices on an ungreased baking sheet. Bake in a very hot oven (450 degrees F.) until cheese mixture becomes bubbly hot. Broil, 6 to 8 inches from heat source, for about 30 seconds to brown puffs lightly. Lightly sprinkle minced parsley over each puff. Serve hot.

–Sue and Rick Young, proprietors
Half Way House Restaurant

Thumbprints

Yield: 6 dozen appetizers
18 to 24 appetizer servings

1 cup milk, soured (see note)
3 cups sifted flour
4 teaspoons baking powder
1/4 teaspoon salt
2 cups (8 ounces) shredded sharp Cheddar cheese, at room temperature
1/2 cup butter or margarine, at room temperature
3/4 (12-ounce) package fully-cooked smoked sausage links
Grated Parmesan cheese for garnish

Prepare sour milk; set aside. In a bowl, sift together flour, baking powder, and salt. With a pastry blender, cut in cheese and butter until mixture is crumbly. Add soured milk, stirring to form a soft dough. Slice each of 6 sausage links, crosswise, into 12 equal pieces. Shape dough into 3/4 to 1-inch balls; arrange, 2 inches apart, on greased baking sheets. Press sausage piece into each ball; sprinkle each lightly with Parmesan cheese. Bake in a hot oven (425 degrees F.) for 12 to 14 minutes or until lightly browned. Serve hot. To freeze, cool on wire racks for 1 hour; wrap securely in aluminum foil and freeze. To serve, reheat, wrapped in aluminum foil, in a moderate over (375 degrees F.) for 12 to 15 minutes or until heated through.

Note: To sour milk, add 1 tablespoon lemon juice or vinegar to milk; let stand for 10 minutes.

–The Reynolds Wrap Kitchens
The Reynolds Metals Company

They Walked to Dances

Picnics, river and canal excursions were in vogue, and church lawn parties, lit by paper lanterns. Church fairs were prosperous....

Louisa Coleman Blair
"'Little Red Brick Town' In Era of Hoopskirts Was Friendly, Gossipy,"
Richmond Time-Dispatch, December 7, 1941

Avocado and Watercress Dip with Shrimp

Yield: 6 to 8 appetizer servings

Gallego's, located in the posh Omni Hotel in downtown Richmond adjacent to the contemporary James River Center and the historic Shockhoe Slip area, provides an opportunity to enjoy superbly prepared high quality food in an atmosphere of elegance and distinction.

2 ripe medium avocados, peeled, seeded, and cubed (see note)
3 tablespoons lemon juice
1/2 bunch watercress, chopped
2 tablespoons prepared horseradish
4 to 5 drops Tabasco sauce
Salt and pepper to taste
1 pound medium to large shrimp, cooked, peeled, and deveined (see note)

In the container of a food processor or blender, combine the first 5 ingredients; cover and process until mixture is a smooth thick pureé. Season with salt and pepper to taste. Spoon into a serving bowl, cover, and chill until ready to serve. Just before serving, arrange serving bowl of dip on a serving tray surrounded by shrimp and garnish as desired.

Note: Use fresh or frozen shrimp, as desired. Cook in boiling salted water to cover for about 3 minutes or until shrimp turn a coral pink and are opaque in color. *Do not overcook* as shrimp will become tough.

–Chef Kevin Wade
Gallego's Restaurant
The Omni Hotel

...The Spotswood, Exchange and American held beds at a high premium in the parlors, halls and even on the billiard-tables. All the lesser houses were equally packed, and crowds of guests stood hungrily round the dining-room doors at mealtimes, watching and scrambling for vacated seats. It was a clear case of "devil take the hindmost," for their cuisine decreased in quantity and quality in exact ratio to augmentation of their custom...(circa 1861-65)

DeLeon
Four Years in Rebel Capitals, 1890

Festive South-of-the-Border Dip

Yield: 12 appetizer servings

1 ripe large avocado
Lemon juice as needed
Salt and pepper to taste
2 cups sour cream
1 (8 1/8-ounce) jar hot taco
  sauce
1 1/2 cups shredded sharp
  Cheddar or Monterey Jack
  cheese
6 to 8 green onions, thinly
  sliced (include some
  green tops)
1/2 cup chopped peeled
  tomato
Crisp tortilla chips as
  needed

With a sharp knife, peel avocado; remove and coarsely chop. Immediately sprinkle avocado pieces liberally with lemon juice to retain clear green color. Arrange avocado pieces in a deep large clear glass serving bowl; sprinkle lightly with salt and pepper. Evenly spread sour cream over avocado and then spread taco sauce over sour cream. Sprinkle cheese over taco sauce layer. Top with a layer of thinly sliced green onions and then chopped tomatoes. Accompany with crisp tortilla chips for dipping.

– Kelly Yuhas (Mrs. Ken)

Curried Sesame Dip

Yield: 2 cups

"Curried Sesame Dip has been my favorite dip to serve with raw vegetables at parties for many years."

1/3 cup sesame seeds
2 teaspoons soy sauce (see
  note)
1/4 teaspoon curry powder
  or to taste
1/4 teaspoon ginger
1 cup sour cream
1/2 cup mayonaise
Assorted raw vegetable
  crudités

Spread sesame seeds over an ungreased baking sheet in one layer. Bake in a moderate oven (350 degrees F.) for about 7 to 10 minutes, stirring several times, until a golden brown; cool. In a small bowl, combine soy sauce, ginger, and curry powder, blending well. Gradually add sour cream and mayonnaise, blending well with a wire whisk. Stir in toasted sesame seeds. Cover and chill thoroughly in refrigerator for several hours to blend flavors. Spoon into a small serving bowl and serve accompanied with assorted raw vegetable crudités.

Note: Reduced sodium (Lite) soy sauce may be substituted for regular soy sauce. One teaspoon Lite soy sauce contains 100 milligrams of sodium.

–Vienna Taylor

Creamy Orange Fruit Dip with Assorted Fresh Fruits

Yield: about 2 to 3 cups

1 (8-ounce) container
unflavored yogurt
1 (8-ounce) container frozen
non-dairy whipped
topping, thawed
1 (3-ounce) can frozen
orange juice concentrate,
thawed
Thin apple, pear, or nectarine slices and/or pine-
apple chunks and whole
strawberries

In a small bowl, combine the first 3 ingredients, beating lightly until smooth. Cover and store in the refrigerator until ready to use. Serve as a dip for fresh fruit.

–Libby Teeter (Mrs. James)

Zola's Crab and Clam Dip

Yield: 10 to 12 appetizer servings

8 ounces crabmeat, fresh or
frozen, thawed and
drained
1 (8-ounce) package cream
cheese, at room tempera-
ture
1 (8-ounce) can minced
clams, drained (see note)
2 ribs celery, chopped
1 small green pepper, cored,
seeded, and chopped
About 1/2 cup mayonnaise
3 tablespoons lemon juice
1/2 to 1 teaspoon Worces-
tershire sauce or to taste
5 to 6 drops hot sauce
Parsley sprigs for garnish
Assorted crackers

Pick over crabmeat, removing any shell or carti-lage. In a bowl, beat cream cheese until smooth. Add crabmeat, clams, celery, green pepper, may-onnaise, lemon juice, Worcestershire sauce, and hot sauce, mixing well. Spoon into a serving bowl. Or, shape into a ball and arrange on a serving plate. Cover and chill until ready to serve. Garnish with parsley sprigs. Serve accompanied with as-sorted crackers.

Note: 8 ounces of fresh, shucked clams may be substituted for canned clams. Cook clams with liquid over low heat for 3 to 4 minutes or until tender; drain and finely chop.

47

Zesty Curry Dip with Vegetable Crudités

Yield: about 2 cups

1 cup sour cream
1/2 cup mayonnaise
2 tablespoons lemon juice
  (see note)
2 teaspoons prepared
  mustard
1 teaspoon curry powder or
  to taste
1/2 teaspoon paprika (see
  note)
Pepper to taste
2 tablespoons minced
  parsley
2 tablespoons minced
  peeled onion
2 tablespoons minced
  chives
Assorted raw vegetable
  crudités

In a bowl, combine the first 6 ingredients, blending well. Season with pepper to taste. Stir in parsley, onion, and chives, mixing well. Cover and refrigerate for 12 hours to blend flavors. Serve with assorted raw vegetable crudités as dippers.

Note: Use only freshly squeezed lemon juice.

Note: Regular paprika will give a more pungent flavor than sweet Hungarian paprika.

– Shep Blair (Mrs. John D.,III)

Crabmeat Soufflé Spread

Yield: 20 appetizer servings

1 pound crabmeat
1 tablespoon unflavored
  gelatin
3 tablespoons cold water
1 (10 1/2-ounce) can cream
  of mushroom soup
  (undiluted)
1 (8-ounce) package cream
  cheese (at room temperature)
1/2 teaspoon Worcester

Pick over crabmeat, removing any shell or cartilage. Soften gelatin in cold water. In a small heavy saucepan, stir mushroom soup over moderate heat until hot. Remove from heat and stir in gelatin until thoroughly dissolved. In a bowl, beat cream cheese until smooth. Stir in soup mixture and Worcestershire sauce. Fold in onion and celery. Spoon into a lightly oiled 2-quart mold. Chill in refrigerator until firm. Unmold onto a chilled serving plate and garnish with watercress sprigs or curly endive and cherry

sauce, or to taste
1 small onion, peeled and
minced
1 cup minced celery
Watercress sprigs or crisp
curly endive and cherry
tomatoes for garnish
Assorted crackers or raw
vegetable crudités

tomatoes. Serve with assorted crackers or raw
vegetable crudités.

–Jeanne Markow

Smoked Salmon Pâté

Yield: one 5-inch ball

1 (15 1/2-ounce) can red
salmon, drained and
flaked
1 (8-ounce) package cream
cheese, at room tempera-
ture
2 to 3 tablespoons minced
peeled onion
1 tablespoon lemon juice
1 teaspoon prepared
horseradish or 1/4 tea-
spoon grated peeled
horseradish root
1/2 teaspoon Worcester-
shire sauce
1/2 teaspoon liquid smoke
1/4 teaspoon salt 1/3 to
2/3 cup finely chopped
pecans Assorted crisp
crackers or toast points or
sliced party-or English
walnuts style rye or
pumpernickel bread

Remove any remaining bones or cartilage. In a
bowl, combine salmon and next 7 ingredients,
mixing well. Shape mixture into a ball. Cover with
clear plastic wrap and chill in refrigerator 2 hours
or until firm. On a sheet of waxed paper, roll ball
in chopped nuts, coating well. Arrange on a
serving plate, garnish as desired, and accompany
with crisp crackers.

Variation: Use 1 pound minced smoked salmon in place of canned salmon; omit
liquid smoke. Or, add 2 tablespoons sour cream, 1 additional tablespoon
lemon juice, 2 additional teaspoons prepared horseradish, 2 tablespoons
drained capers, and 1 1/2 teaspoons minced fresh dill weed to salmon
mixture. Spoon into a greased fish mold; chill until mixture is firm. Unmold
onto a serving plate and frost with sour cream. Garnish as desired.

–June Johnson (Mrs. Neville)

49

....Patrick Henry returned to the governorship in 1784, bringing his family to the wooden residence. From her windows Dolly Henry could see along the southwestern edge of the square, the soldiers' housing, with their chicken yards and their clotheslines filled with fluttering laundry....On May 1, 1785, the people of Richmond gathered in large number before the governor's house as the state's two most popular men sat down to dinner inside, Governor Henry and his guest George Washington.

William Seal
Virginia's Executive Mansion:
A History of the Goernor's House, 1988

Party-Time Triple Cheese Ball

Yield: one large or two small cheese balls

1 (8-ounce) package cream cheese, at room temperature
8 ounces sharp Cheddar cheese, shredded, at room temperature
4 ounces Roquefort or blue cheese, crumbled, at room temperature
1/2 cup butter or margarine, at room temperature
1/4 cup minced peeled onion
2 tablespoons minced green pepper
1 tablespoon Worcestershire sauce
1 teaspoon celery seed
Pepper to taste
1 to 1 1/2 cups minced parsley, or finely chopped pecans or English

In a large bowl, combine cheeses and butter, beating at medium speed of an electric mixer until mixture is smooth. Add onion, green pepper, Worcestershire sauce, celery seed, and pepper to taste, mixing well. Shape mixture into one large or two small balls. Wrap balls in clear plastic wrap and chill in the refrigerator until balls have become more firm. On a sheet of waxed paper, roll cheese balls in minced parsley, or finely chopped nuts, or toasted sunflower seeds. Rewrap coated cheeseballs in clear plastic wrap and refrigerate for at least 24 to 48 hours before serving to allow flavors to blend.

–Fran Lincoln

walnuts, or toasted sun-
flower seeds

Russian-Style Eggplant Butter

Yield: about 1 1/2 pints

"Russians use this like peanut butter. The Russians use the largest eggplants they can find and the authentic recipe I have calls for a 5-pound eggplant! I have halved it and it still makes quantities."

1 (2 1/2- to 3-pound)
    eggplant
1 large onion, peeled and
    minced
1/2 cup hot cooking oil
2 pounds tomatoes, peeled,
    seeded, and chopped
1/2 to 1 teaspoon sugar
Salt and pepper to taste
Toasted slices party-style
    rye bread, Melba toast
    rounds, or crisp crackers

Bake eggplant in a lightly greased baking pan in a moderate oven (350 degrees F.) until tender, about 1 hour. Remove core and peel; cut remaining eggplant into small pieces and mash thoroughly. In a large heavy skillet, sauté onion in oil over moderate heat until tender but not browned. Reduce heat, add tomatoes, and simmer, uncovered, for 20 to 25 minutes. Add eggplant, mixing well; continue to simmer, covered, for 1 hour, stirring occasionally. Add sugar and salt and pepper to taste. Chill, covered, in the refrigerator. Serve with toasted party-style rye bread, Melba toast, or crackers.

–Carol Nance
Assistant Attorney General
State of Virginia

When prohibition was introduced, the customary "cup that cheers" was stored away and during those "17 years in the desert," again only once was a member severely censored for "dancing under the influence of too much drink."...

During the early days of the German the dues were insufficient to serve dinner preceding the dances and at that time it was the general custom for individual ladies invited to the affair to entertain at informal supper parties. When the supper was first introduced into the organization, it was served shortly before midnight...

"First German Calls Virginia's '400',
Richmond Times-Dispatch, December 16, 1934

Smoked Oyster Roll

Yield: 8 appetizer servings

1 (8-ounce) package cream cheese, at room temperature
1 garlic clove, peeled and minced (see note)
2 tablespoons mayonnaise
1 (3 1/2-ounce) container smoked oysters, drained and chopped
1/2 cup finely chopped English walnuts
Minced parsley and chives for garnish
Assorted crackers

In a small bowl, combine cream cheese, garlic, and mayonnaise; beat at medium speed of an electric mixer until mixture is smooth. On a sheet of waxed paper, spread mixture into a 10 x 8-inch rectangle. Evenly sprinkle oysters and walnuts over cheese rectangle. Cover top with clear plastic wrap and refrigerate for several hours until firm. Remove plastic wrap. Using waxed paper as a guide, starting at narrow end, roll up lengthwise as a jelly roll. Remove waxed paper. Combine parsley and chives on a sheet of waxed paper; roll oyster "log" in parsley-chive mixture, coating well. Refrigerate until ready to serve accompanied with crackers.

Note: 1/2 teaspoon garlic juice may be substituted.

–Priscilla Alexander
Cheese Wedge Committee
St. Christopher's School

Roquefort Cheese Ball

Yield: 24 to 36 appetizer servings

1 (8-ounce) package cream cheese, at room temperature
8 ounces shredded sharp Cheddar cheese, at room temperature
3 ounces Roquefort cheese, at room temperature
1 garlic clove, peeled and minced (see note)
1 tablespoon Worcestershire sauce
1/2 cup finely chopped pecans, divided
1/2 cup minced parsley
Assorted crackers or Melba toast rounds

In a bowl, combine cheeses, garlic, and Worcestershire sauce, beating at medium speed of an electric mixer, until cheese mixture is smooth. Fold in 1/4 cup pecans. Shape mixture into 1 large or 2 small balls. On a sheet of waxed paper, roll balls in remaining pecans, coating evenly; then roll in parsley, coating well. Cover in clear plastic wrap and chill in refrigerator for 24 hours. Serve accompanied with assorted crackers or Melba toast rounds.

Note: 1/2 teaspoon garlic juice may be substituted.

–Leslie Stacks (Mrs. C. W.)
Cheese Wedge Committee
St. Christopher's School

Salmon Mousse

Yield: 6 to 8 servings

1 envelope (tablespoon) unflavored gelatin
1/4 cup water
1/2 cup boiling water
1/2 cup mayonnaise (see note)
1 tablespoon lemon juice
1 teaspoon salt
1/2 teaspoon hot sauce
2 tablespoons minced peeled onion
2 (7-ounce) cans pink or red salmon, drained, cartilage and bones removed, and flaked (see note)
1 tablespoon capers, drained
1/2 cup heavy cream, whipped
1 cup sour cream
2 tablespoons minced fresh or 2 teaspoons dried dill weed
Watercress sprigs and very thin lemon slices for garnish
Melba toast rounds or assorted crackers

In a small bowl, soften gelatin in cold water; stir in boiling water until gelatin is dissolved. Cool. Add mayonnaise, lemon juice, salt, and hot sauce, blending well. Stir in onion. Chill in the refrigerator until mixture starts to thicken. Add salmon and capers, mixing well. Fold in whipped cream. Spoon into a lightly greased 6-cup ring mold. Chill in the refrigerator until firm. Unmold onto a chilled serving plate. In a small bowl, combine sour cream and dill, mixing well. Fill cavity of salmon mousse with dilled sour cream. Surround mousse with watercress sprigs and garnish with very thin lemon slices. Serve with Melba toast rounds or assorted crackers.

Note: 1/2 cup imitation or calorie reduced mayonnaise may be substituted.

Note: 12 to 14 ounces poached fresh salmon fillet may be substituted for canned salmon. To cook salmon, arrange fish fillets in a medium shallow baking dish. Add enough water to just cover salmon. Bake, covered, in a moderate oven (350 degrees F.) for 20 to 25 minutes or until done. Fish is done when it turns opaque pink in color and flakes easily with a fork. Salmon may also be cooked in a microwave oven in a glass baking dish covered with clear plastic wrap at high power for 3 to 4 minutes or at three-fourths power for 6 to 7 minutes or until done. Add extra cooking time in increments of seconds. *Do not overcook as fish will become tough.* Drain cooked salmon well and flake into tiny pieces.

–Mary Tyler Cheek (Mrs. Leslie, Jr.)

> Nearly opposite to the present Exchange Bank stood a large wooden building, which, in my youthful days, was Mrs. Gilbert's Coffee House; not a news-room, but truly what its name imports; and here tea, coffee and chocolate were dispensed to customers, seated around the fire in winter, or at the open windows in summer. In after years, and under other occupants, it assumed the name of the Globe Tavern, and it closed its career a few years ago as an "oyster and beef-steak house, with other refreshments,"under a skilful mulatto woman, whose canvas backs, soras, and other delicacies of the season attracted many customers.
>
> Samuel Mordecai
> **Richmond in By-Gone Days**, 1856
> Reprint Edition, 1975

Easy Brie Appetizer

Yield: about 40 appetizer servings

1 (5.5-pound) whole Brie cheese wheel
1 cup minced fresh mixed herbs (equal amounts of thyme, chives, parsley, marjoram, and tarragon).
1/2 cup finely chopped pine nuts or English walnuts
Paprika as needed
Black peppercorns, coarsely ground, to taste, if desired
Extra virgin olive oil as needed
Crisp unseasoned crackers

Remove top rind of the cheese wheel, if desired. Arrange cheese wheel on a serving platter. Liberally cover the top of the cheese wheel with the minced mixed herbs. Evenly sprinkle nuts over herb coated cheese, slightly pressing nuts into the cheese. Sprinkle paprika and then freshly ground black peppercorns over nuts. Just before serving, evenly drizzle a small amount of olive oil over cheese wheel. Serve herbed cheese "wheel" at room temperature, accompanied with unseasoned crackers.

Note: A smaller 2- or 3-pound cheese wheel may be used. Decrease amounts of herbs to 1/2 to 2/3 cup and nuts to 1/4 to 1/3 cup. Use paprika, pepper, and olive oil as needed.

Variation: Omit nuts and substitute 1/4 cup minced green and sweet red pepper and 1/4 cup minced green onion, including some green tops, mixed together.

–Claudia Echols (Mrs. Steven)

54

Crab Stuffed Cherry Tomatoes

Yield: approximately 48 cherry tomatoes,
about 16 to 20 appetizer servings

1 cup flaked crabmeat
1 (8-ounce) package cream cheese, at room temperature
1/4 cup heavy cream 1 garlic clove, peeled and minced
2 teaspoons lemon juice
1 teaspoon Worcestershire sauce
1/4 teaspoon salt
About 48 ripe cherry tomatoes
Fresh parsley sprigs for garnish

Pick over crabmeat, removing any remaining shell or cartilage. In a medium bowl, combine the next 6 ingredients, beating until light and smooth. Fold in crabmeat. Scoop pulp from cherry tomatoes and stuff with crabmeat mixture. Arrange tomatoes on a tray, cover with clear plastic wrap, and refrigerate until serving. Transfer tomatoes to a chilled serving plate and garnish with parsley sprigs.

–Rosemary Davenport

..Passing out of the cut through the high bluff, just across the "Jeems" river bridge, Richmond burst beautifully into view; spreading panorama-like over her swelling hills, with the evening sun gilding simple houses and towering spires alike into a glory. The city follows the curve of the river, seated on amphitheratric hills, retreating from its banks; fringes of dense woods shading their slopes, or making blue background against the sky. No city of the South has a grander or more picturesque approach...(Spring, 1861)

DeLeon
Four Years in Rebel Capitals, 1890

Caviar Pie

Yield: 8 to 10 servings

8 hard-cooked eggs, peeled and grated
6 tablespoons butter or margarine, melted
1 cup sour cream
8 ounces black caviar (see note)
Watercress sprigs and very thin lemon wedges for garnish

In a bowl, combine eggs and butter, mixing well. Evenly press mixture over bottom and up sides of a greased 9-inch pie plate. Freeze until firm. Partially thaw and then spread sour cream over bottom of egg crust. Chill in freezer for several minutes to firm sour cream. Evenly spread caviar over sour cream. Refrigerate until ready to serve. Cut into wedges and garnish each serving with watercress sprigs and lemon wedges.

Note: Preferably use beluga or sevruga caviar

–Beth Buckle (Mrs. James)

Marinated Mushrooms

Yield: 6 to 8 appetizer servings

1 1/4 pounds large mushrooms
2 shallots, peeled and minced
1 small onion, peeled and minced
2 tablespoons minced chives
2/3 cup olive oil
1/4 cup tarragon vinegar
1/4 cup white wine
1 garlic clove, peeled and mashed (see note)
1 tablespoon grated lemon peel
Minced fresh parsley
Wooden picks
Thin slices of buttered dark

With a damp cloth or soft brush, gently wipe mushrooms, removing any dirt. Trim off any bad spots; remove stems. Thinly slice caps and stems and place in a large bowl. Add shallots, onions, and chives. In a small bowl, combine olive oil, tarragon vinegar, white wine, garlic, and lemon peel. With a whisk, beat mixture until well-blended. Pour marinade over mushroom mixture, tossing gently with two wooden spoons to mix well. Cover with clear plastic wrap, gently tossing mixture occasionally, and refrigerate at least 1 hour. Spoon mushrooms into a chilled serving bowl or onto 6 to 8 appetizer plates. Sprinkle with minced fresh parsley and serve with buttered dark bread. If serving mushrooms in a large serving bowl, accompany with wooden picks for skewering mushrooms.

Note: 1/2 to 1 teaspoon garlic juice may be used in place of garlic clove.

–Sarah Baynes (Mrs. H. L.)
Valentine Museum Guild

The Swan Tavern was kept by Major Moss, who probably also served in the Revolutionary war—this may or may not be. He also exhibited good breeding, good feeding, and good fellowship in his full figure and face. His house might have been called the Lincoln's Inn or Doctor's Commons of Richmond, for there assembled, in term time, the non-resident judges and lawyers, and though of unpretending exterior, the Swan was the tavern of highest repute for good fare, good wine, and good company. Here centred "the logic, and the wisdom, and the wit," nor was "theloud laugh" wanting.

Samuel Mordecai
Richmond in By-Gone Days, 1856
Reprint Edition, 1975

APPETIZERS and HORS D'OEUVRES

Jack Boettcher and his son Ken have been operating the New York Delicatessen Restaurant, a Richmond landmark located on Cary Street a few doors from the historic Byrd Theatre for almost two decades, since acquiring it in 1970.

Previous owners, the Brandeis family from Vienna, Austria, had opened a small grocery store in 1938 in the delicatessen location after fleeing to Richmond to escape the Nazi regime. Soon the grocery evolved into a delicatessen and served sandwiches and other knoshes to patrons. Although Jack and Ken have enlarged the restaurant and offer additional fare to the menu, the style of food and the ambiance of the deli have remained as during the Brandeis ownership.

Interestingly, Jack Boettcher came to the United States from Berlin in 1938 for identical reasons as the Brandeis family. Recently the Berlin city government invited him to return to visit his native city, which he had not seen in half a century.

Marinated Herring in Sour Cream Sauce

Yield: 8 to 10 appetizer servings

4 cups herring in white wine, drained (reserve marinade)
1 medium onion, peeled, very thinly sliced, and separated into rings
3 cups sour cream
2 to 3 tablespoons reserved herring wine marinade, as needed
Crisp lettuce leaves (optional)
Paprika for garnish
Thin lemon wedges for garnish

Cut herring into bite-sized pieces. In a large bowl, combine herring pieces, onion rings, and sour cream. Add wine marinade, as desired, to herring mixture, blending until smooth. Store in refrigerator, tightly covered, for up to three weeks until ready to serve. Spoon onto lettuce-lined appetizer or salad plates; sprinkle herring mixture with paprika and garnish with thin lemon wedges.

–Jack and Ken Boettcher
New York Delicatessen Restaurant

58

Strawberries and Pineapple in Champagne

Yield: 4 to 6 servings

Low calorie fresh fruit accented with wine and champagne serves equally well as an appetizer or desert course.

1 pint firm ripe strawberries, stems removed and sliced
1 1/2 cups cubed peeled ripe pineapple
2 to 3 tablespoons sugar or to taste
1/2 cup dry white wine
1 split (about 6 1/2-ounces) bottle brut champagne, chilled (about 3/4 cup)
4 to 6 whole firm ripe strawberries for garnish
Fresh mint sprigs for garnish

In a medium bowl, combine sliced strawberries, pineapple, and sugar, mixing lightly. Pour white wine over mixture. Cover and chill in refrigerator for several hours. Spoon fruit mixture into chilled crystal or glass goblets; add champagne to each glass, dividing evenly. Garnish each serving with a whole strawberry and a fresh mint sprig.

Variations: 3/4 cup halved seedless green grapes may be substituted for 1/2 cup of the cubed pineapple and 1/4 to 1/3 cup of sliced strawberries. One-half cup brandy or dry vermouth may be substituted for 1/2 cup dry white wine.

Like another famous Virginian, John Marshall, Thomas Jefferson preferred to do his own food marketing. While he was president of the United States, he would confer with Lemarie, his French chef, concerning the dinner menu. The two men would then visit the Georgetown market, with Jefferson personally making the selections of fresh fish, crisp fresh vegetables, properly aged meat, and succulent ripe fruit. Jefferson frequently spent as much as fifty dollars per day for provisions, indeed a very high amount for those days. Dinner was often served at four p.m., the fashionable hour for dining in the new republic.

Old First Market

The 17th Street market area has been a marketplace since the early history of Richmond. In 1742 authority was granted for holding yearly fairs on the grounds, or "commons," adjacent to Shockoe Creek. The two-day fairs were held on the second Thursday and Friday in May and the second Thursday and Friday in November for the sale of "all manner of cattle, victuals, provisions, goods, wares, and merchandise whatsoever." An ordinance passed July 19, 1782 designated the market house on the city commons as "The Market of the City of Richmond." The market house consisted of a roof supported by wooden posts and a wooden bridge spanned the creek. In 1794, a brick building with a colonnade was built to be replaced by a larger market in 1854. It was remodelled in 1903 and in 1930 it was again modernized. Richmonders frequent it today, especially during the summer months when seasonal fresh fruits and vegetables are brought to market daily by farmers from the surrounding area. Recently the market has again taken on a new look. In the summer of 1986, the old facilities were demolished and replaced with new quarters designed by Richmond architects Glave, Newman, Anderson in a contemporary outdoor market motif. A pair of antique terra cotta bull's heads, originally decoration at the old 6th Street Market, accent the Main Street entrance, reminding shoppers of years gone by. Seventy-six spaces are available for entrepreneurs to attractively display and sell their wares of farm fresh fruits, vegetables, plants, flowers, baked goods, eggs, and even a country cured Virginia ham. Each summer, one weekend at the market is transformed into a fair. Shoppers at the 17th Street Market not only find excellent value in produce, but an atmosphere reminiscent of shopping in bygone days prevails.

Soups
and
Stews

Soups and Stews

Soups and stews have developed together throughout the history of the world's cuisines, their origin lost to antiquity. One of the most widely accepted forms of food, the name, soup, derives from the Latin, suppa. In medieval times, hunks of bread or meat, called sop, were dipped into the stew broth. The number of sops in a serving was an indication to guests of the generosity or stinginess of their host. Before the latter part of the seventeenth century when Duc de Montausier is credited with inventing the soup ladle, each guest dipped into a common pot or soup tureen with his own wooden or pewter spoon. Slightly earlier, guests had drunk from a two-handled poringer passed around the table. Eventually the sop referred to the broth and transformed into our modern soup.

Iced Mint Bisque

Yield: 4 appetizer or 2 entree servings

3 tablespoons thinly sliced green onion, including tops
1 1/2 teaspoons crushed fresh or 1/2 teaspoon dried mint leaves
2 tablespoons butter or margarine, melted
1 (11 1/4-ounce) can green pea, or 1 (10 3/4-ounce) cream of asparagus or cream of chicken soup, undiluted
1 1/4 cups half-and-half or light cream (see note)
Fresh mint sprigs for garnish
Thin lemon slices for garnish

In a small heavy skillet, sauté onion and mint in butter over moderate heat until onion is tender. Place onion mixture in a blender container; cover and whiz until pureed. In a small heavy saucepan, combine onion mixture and soup. Gradually stir half-and-half into soup, blending well. Heat through. Cool, then chill several hours. Serve in chilled bouillon cups and garnish with fresh mint sprigs and lemon slices.

Note: For less calories, 1 1/4 cups of 2% or homogenized milk may be used in place of half-and-half or light cream.

Bisques

At one time bisque applied to a purée of wood pigeons or other poultry or game. Some authorities declare it to be of Provencal origin. Purists today confine the name to describe a thick shellfish soup, sometimes called a coules, usually made of lobster or crayfish. Others include a variety of foods. Often oyster bisque is served on New Year's Eve to celebrate the entrance of the New Year.

Seafood Bisque

Yield: 6 servings

1/4 cup finely chopped peeled onion
1/4 cup finely chopped celery
1/4 cup butter or margarine
2 tablespoons flour
1 teaspoon salt or to taste
1/4 teaspoon paprika
Pinch white pepper
4 cups milk or 2 cups milk and 2 cups half-and-half or light cream
2 cups cooked chopped shrimp or steamed crabmeat, flaked (see note)
Dry sherry to taste (optional)

In a large heavy saucepan, sauté onion and celery in butter until tender but not browned. Stir in flour and seasonings. Add milk gradually and cook until thick, stirring constantly. Fold in seafood. Heat through and serve at once. Dry sherry to taste maybe added to each serving, if desired.

Note: Pick over crabmeat, removing any remaining shell or cartilage.

Chilled Soups

Chilled soups are a pleasant and refreshing change from the more frequently served hot soups. They may be served in hot or cold weather and as an appetizer, main dish, or dessert and are a superb contrast to an accompanying hot dish. To taste best, all must be served ice cold and preferably in chilled cups.

Chilled Avocado Yogurt Soup

Yield: 6 servings

2 ripe medium avocados, peeled, seeded, and chopped
2 cups unflavored yogurt
2 cups chicken stock or broth (see note)
1 tablespoon lemon juice
1 teaspoon minced peeled onion
1/2 teaspoon celery salt
1/4 teaspoon salt or to taste
1/8 teaspoon white pepper
Few grains cayenne pepper
Minced chives for garnish
Thin slices of lemon peel for garnish

In a blender container, combine all ingredients together except chives and lemon peel. Cover and whiz until well-mixed. Chill thoroughly. Serve in chilled bouillon cups and garnish with minced chives and lemon peel.

Note: 2 chicken bouillon cubes dissolved in 2 cups of water or 1 undiluted (10 1/2-ounce) can chicken broth plus 3/4 cup water may be substituted for 2 cups of chicken stock or broth.

Variation: Some finely chopped pieces of avocado may be reserved to blend into soup just before serving.

Popular twentieth century casseroles or one-dish meals are adaptations or new interpretations of old time stews, ragouts, and hashes.

Chilled Curried Almond Chicken Soup

Yield: 4 servings

Curry powder adds a subtle pungency to the mild chicken and almond flavor of the soup. The origin of the word "curry" is obscure, but it probably comes from the Tamilkari, meaning sauce. Initially, it was used in Indian cooking for its medicinal and antiseptic properties rather than as a flavoring agent. Richmond enjoys a small population of Indians (from India) in its blend of people. Some of their cuisine has happily infiltrated the Southern cuisine of Richmond.

1 tablespoon butter or margarine, melted
1 tablespoon flour
1 tablespoon curry powder or to taste
3 cups chicken stock or broth (see note)
4 egg yolks, beaten
1 cup light cream or half-and-half
1/2 cup minced cooked chicken
1 cup finely chopped blanched almonds or pecans
Minced parsley for garnish

In a medium heavy saucepan, combine butter with flour and curry powder until smooth. Gradually blend in chicken stock. Simmer over low heat 10 minutes. Combine egg yolks and cream; blend into chicken stock. Add chicken. Simmer over low heat until mixture is slightly thickened. Chill thoroughly in refrigerator. Just before serving, add nuts. Ladle into bouillon cups and garnish with minced parsley.

Note: 2 undiluted (10 1/2-ounce) or 2 (13 3/4-ounce) cans chicken broth may be used.

Variation: For a slightly thicker soup, increase butter and flour each, to 2 table spoons.

About half a century before the war Virginia was in its prime, and Richmond was at the height of its social brilliance. In the winter many of the opulent planters would leave their stately homes in the counties of Virginia, and bring their families to Richmond for a month or more, thus swelling the ranks of society with beauty and wealth...

Ruth Nelson Robins
The Richmond News Leader, Date unknown

Eliza B. Askin 1990

The Virginia Museum of Fine Arts

The Virginia Museum of Fine Arts, located on the Boulevard in
Richmond, is one of the premier museums of America. Smaller
in scope than the National Gallery in Washington or the
Metropolitan in New York, the museum nevertheless is a "small
gem." Some fine collections,including the Sydney and Frances
Lewis collections of contemporary art and the decorative arts of
the late nineteenth and early twentieth centuries, Andrew
Mellon's collection of late nineteenth and early twentieth cen-
tury French paintings and sculpture, and the Lillian Pratt
Fabérge collection are in permanent residence. Begun in 1936,
the museum, the first state supported museum in the United
States, has expanded several times to its present status.

In addition to the fine arts, the museum boasts a charming
member's dining room featuring fine gourmet cuisine and
accented in decor with Boehm porcelains. A beaux arts café
located on the ground floor known for Ms. Naomi's famous
soups, attracts staff members and visitors to the museum.And
for those who enjoy the pleasure of tradition, after noon tea may
be enjoyed midst the antiquities and fountain of the Mediterranean courtyard.

Chilled Dilled Buttermilk Soup

Yield: 6 to 8 servings

7 1/2 cups buttermilk
3 tablespoons minced
 chives
1 large cucumber, peeled,
 seeded, and diced
3 tablespoons minced
 parsley
1 tablespoon minced fresh
 or 1 teaspoon dry dill
 weed
Salt, pepper, and cayenne
 pepper to taste
Paprika to taste
Fresh dill sprigs or minced
 chives for garnish (op-
 tional)

In a large bowl, combine buttermilk and 3 tablespoons minced chives, blending well; set aside for
30 minutes. Combine cucumber, parsley, and dill,
mixing well; stir into buttermilk. Add salt, pepper,
and cayenne pepper to taste. Cover and chill in
the refrigerator for several hours to blend flavors.
Spoon into soup cups and garnish each serving
with a sprinkle of paprika and additional chives or
a sprig of fresh dill for garnish, if desired.

−Naomi Wilson, Cafeteria Manager
Virginia Museum of Fine Arts

Chilled Cucumber Soup with Tarragon

Yield: 6 servings

*"This receipt came from a friend, Dame Mary Green, of London, England. We
serve it as a first course with homemade melba toast or prepare and take it to
the boat to be served at lunch. It's terrific on a hot day!"*

1 large cucumber, peeled
 and seeded
1 cup light cream or half-
 and-half
1 cup unflavored yogurt
1 cup chicken broth,
2 tablespoons tarragon
 vinegar
Garlic salt, salt, and pepper
 to taste
Whipped cream or addi-
 tional yogurt for garnish
Thin slices unpeeled
 cucumber and twists of
 lemon peel for garnish

Grate cucumber; set aside. In a large bowl, combine cream, yogurt, and chicken broth, blending
well. Add vinegar. Stir in cucumber. Season with
garlic salt, salt, and pepper to taste. Cover and
chill thoroughly in the refrigerator to blend flavors. Pour into chilled bowls and garnish with a
dollop of whipped cream or yogurt and thin cucumber slices and a twist of lemon peel.

−Doris Radcliffe (Mrs. Edward)

Gazpacho Blanco (White Gazpacho Soup)

Yield: 6 to 8 servings

A variation of the famous Spanish soup, White Gazpacho is made with cucumber, chicken stock, and sour cream in place of the traditional tomato base. Chopped tomatoes, sliced green onions, and minced fresh basil are used as a garnish.

4 medium cucumbers, peeled, seeded, and coarsely chopped
2 garlic cloves, peeled and chopped
4 cups chicken stock or broth
4 cups sour cream or unflavored yogurt
2 tablespoons white wine vinegar
Salt and pepper to taste
Chopped peeled tomatoes, thinly sliced green onions (include some green tops), and minced fresh basil for garnish

In a blender container, combine cucumbers, and garlic; cover and whiz until vegetables are puréed. In a large bowl, combine cucumber purée, chicken stock, sour cream, wine vinegar, and wine, blending well. Season with salt and pepper. Cover and chill thoroughly in refrigerator. Spoon into chilled soup cups or mugs and garnish each serving with chopped tomatoes, sliced green onions, and minced basil.

–Chef Robert Hamlin, proprietor
Jana Blue Hopper, proprietor
du Jour Restaurant and Caterers

Virginia Cookery Book, circa 1921

68

Mexican-Style Tomato Gazpacho

Yield: 6 to 8 servings

When the Zajurs moved from Mexico in the early 1960's, Papa Zajur opened an American style Restaurant in a small box car on Richmond's Jefferson Davis Highway. He soon added some original recipes from his homeland to the menu. Their immediate success led to a switch from American to Mexican cuisine and the formation of the new La Siesta Restaurant. La Siesta soon out grew its dining car and moved. The location has changed, now at 9900 Midlothian Turnpike, in with a charming south-of-the-border atmosphere, but the authentic Mexican recipes have stayed the same. La Siesta was named by The Very Best: Mexican Restaurants and Where to Find Them as "one of the very best Mexican Restaurants in the United States."

1 small tomato, peeled or unpeeled, chopped
1/2 medium cucumber, peeled or unpeeled, chopped
1/2 medium red or white (Bermuda) onion, peeled and chopped
1/2 (large) celery rib, chopped
1/2 ripe avocado, peeled, pitted, and thinly sliced or chopped and sprinkled with lemon juice
1/2 green chili pepper, chopped
1/4 cup minced fresh cilantro (coriander)
2 tablespoons lemon juice (see note)
1 1/2 teaspoons minced fresh or 1/2 teaspoon dried oregano
1/2 teaspoons salt
4 cups canned tomato juice
Fresh cilantro leaves for garnish

In a medium container, combine the first 11 ingredients. Add tomato juice, mixing well. Cover and chill thoroughly in the refrigerator. Garnish each serving with fresh cilantro leaves.

Note: Preferably use *only* freshly squeezed lemon juice.

–Michel Zazur, Jr., proprietor
La Siesta Mexican Restaurant

Chowders

Chowder takes its name from the French, la chaudiere, an enormous copper pot used in French coastal villages. Fishermen, returning with the day's catch, would toss part of the catch into la chaudiere and the community would prepare a soup to feast the safe return of the fishermen from the sea. A hearty thick soup, chowder can be made from a variety of foods often with a milk base.

New England clam chowder is made of clams, salt pork or bacon, milk, and seasonings while Virginia clam chowder uses water, clam broth, potatoes, onions, a variety of herbs, and spices. Milk may or may not be added to the chowder.

Old Dominion Clam Chowder

Yield: 6 to 8 servings

3 cups peeled cubed
  potatoes
Boiling water as needed
6 bacon slices
1 cup thinly sliced peeled
  onion
2 (8-ounce) cans minced
  clams, (including liquid)
  (see note)
1 1/2 teaspoons salt
1 teaspoon minced parsley
1 teaspoon celery salt
1/2 teaspoon monosodium
  glutamate (optional)
1/2 teaspoon pepper
2 cups milk, scalded
1/4 cup butter or margarine,
  at room temperature

In a heavy saucepan, cook potatoes in boiling water to cover over moderate heat until tender, about 10 to 15 minutes; drain well and very coarsely mash. In a heavy skillet, pan-fry bacon over moderate heat until crisp; drain well on absorbent paper, reserving drippings. Crumble bacon; set aside. Saute onion in hot drippings until tender but not browned. In a heavy saucepan, combine potatoes, bacon, onion, drippings, clams, clam liquid, and seasonings. Cook over moderate heat for 4 minutes. Reduce heat, add milk and butter and simmer for 2 to 3 minutes or until butter is melted and chowder steaming hot.

Note: 1 quart shucked fresh whole clams, finely chopped, may be substituted.

–Bebe Trice (Mrs. Robert)

Chowder: A Sea Dish

Take any kind firm fish, cut in pieces six inches long, sprinkle salt and pepper over each; cover the bottom of an oven with slices of salt pork, lay on the fish, stewing some chopped onion between. Cover with crackers that have been soaked in milk; pour over it two gills wine and two of water; stew it gently for one hour; take it out carefully and lay in a deep dish. Thicken the gravy, add some parsley, boil a few moments, and pour over the fish. Serve hot.

The Kitchen Queen, *1893*

Old Richmond Advertisement, circa 1895

71

Cream Soups

Cream soups may be prepared with a base of cream or milk, thick or thin in consistency, and served hot or cold. Sour cream may be added in some recipes. Eggs and/or flour are usually added for thickening and a variety of foods, herbs, and spices may be included in a cream soup to enhance the flavors.

Cream of Carrot Soup

Yield: 6 to 8 servings

The carrot comes from ancient lineage, originating in the Far East. Ancient Chinese and Japanese records refer to carrots. They are usually available year round, but the finest and sweetest tasting are the smallest. Generally speaking, the deeper the orange color of the carrot, the better the carrot.

1 pound carrots, peeled and sliced (about 8)
2 ribs celery, minced
3 cups chicken stock or broth (see note)
1 bay leaf, crumbled
1/2 teaspoon sugar
1/2 teaspoon salt
1/8 teaspoon white pepper
1 cup half-and-half or light cream
1 egg yolk, beaten
Minced parsley for garnish

In a 1 1/2-quart heavy saucepan, combine carrots, celery, chicken stock, bay leaf, sugar, salt, and pepper together. Simmer over low heat 30 minutes or until carrots are fork tender. Remove bayleaves. Put mixture through a food mill or puree in a blender container. Add half-and-half and egg yolk, blending well. Heat through. Serve immediately or chill thoroughly. Garnish with minced parsley.

Note: 3 cups water plus 3 mashed chicken bouillon cubes may be used in place of the chicken stock.

Note: For a thinner soup, increase half-and-half to 1 1/2 or 2 cups. For less calories, use 2% or whole milk.

Variation: Add 1/8 teaspoon nutmeg or ginger to soup.

Cream of Crab Soup

Yield: 6 servings

1 pound crabmeat
1/4 cup chopped peeled
  onion
1/4 cup butter or margarine,
  melted
2 tablespoons flour
1 teaspoon salt
1/4 teaspoon celery salt
Dash pepper
3 to 4 drops hot sauce or to
  taste
4 cups milk or 2 cups milk
  and 2 cups half-and-half
1 cup rich chicken stock
Dry sherry as desired
  (optional)
Minced parsley for garnish

Pick over crabmeat, removing any remaining shell or cartilage. In a large heavy saucepan, saute onion in butter over moderate heat until tender but not browned. Blend in flour and seasonings. Add milk and chicken stock gradually; cook stirring constantly until thickened. Gently fold in crabmeat, *being careful to not break up crabmeat*; heat through. Add dry sherry as desired to each serving. Garnish each serving with parsley.

Cream of Fresh Mushroom Soup

Yield: 6 servings

8 to 12 ounces fresh
  mushrooms, cleaned and
  chopped
2 teaspoons chopped
  peeled onion
1/2 cup butter or margarine,
  melted
1/3 cup flour
3 1/2 cups rich chicken
  broth or 2 (10 3/4-ounce)
  cans, undiluted
1/2 cup water
· 1/2 teaspoon salt or to taste
Dash white pepper
1 cup half-and-half or light
  cream

In a large heavy saucepan, sauté mushrooms and onion in butter, stirring constantly, over moderate heat for 3 to 4 minutes or until tender but not browned. Stir in flour and cook just until bubbly. Add chicken broth, water, salt, and pepper; continue cooking, stirring constantly, until mixture thickens. Reduce heat, add half-and-half, and heat through.

Creamy Fresh Broccoli Soup

Yield: 6 to 8 servings

Broccoli has been a favorite of gourmets throughout history and was highly esteemed by the Romans. A favorite vegetable of the first American gourmand, broccoli is low in calories and high in Vitamin C; it is also highly nutritious.

6 slices bacon
1/3 cup thinly sliced green onion
2 tablespoons reserved hot bacon drippings
1 1/2 pounds broccoli, cut into small pieces (about 3 cups) or 2 (10-ounce) packages frozen chopped broccoli
1 cup water
2 carrots, peeled and thinly sliced
1/2 cup chopped celery
2 chicken bouillon cubes, mashed
1 1/2 teaspoons salt
1/8 teaspoon white pepper
1/8 teaspoon paprika
2 to 3 drops hot sauce
2 tablespoons flour
1 egg yolk
4 cups half-and-half or light cream
Sour cream for garnish (optional)

In a large heavy skillet, pan-fry bacon over moderate heat until crisp. Drain well; crumble and set aside. Sauté onions in 2 tablespoons reserved bacon drippings until tender; drain well. In a small heavy saucepan, combine water, carrots, celery, and 1 bouillon cube. Cover and cook over moderate heat 10 minutes or until tender. Do not drain. Combine vegetables, 1 bouillon cube and seasonings together in a blender container. Cover and whiz 30 seconds. In a 2-quart heavy saucepan, blend a small amount of half-and-half into flour and egg yolk until smooth. Gradually add vegetable mixture and remaining half-and-half. Cook over moderate heat, stirring constantly, until slightly thickened and heated through. Ladle into individual serving bowls and garnish with crumbled bacon and sour cream, if desired.

Variation: Reserve some of the cooked vegetables. Do not combine in blender. Add just before serving.

During the Civil War, better known as the War Between the States in the South, dried beans were ground to brew as coffee. Potatoes were dried and ground to be used in place of wheat flour and peach leaves brewed into an infusion were substituted for almond flavoring. Recipes from this ear are almost unknown due to the scarcity of food and the temporary "receipts" improvised to prepare the available foods.

Easy Blender Fresh Asparagus Soup

Yield: 4 to 6 servings

As Thomas Jefferson did in Colonial times, Richmonders eagerly look forward to the first offerings of tender fresh asparagus of springtime.

2 pounds fresh asparagus
    spears
2 chicken bouillon cubes
1 cup boiling reserved
    asparagus cooking liquid
1 cup light cream or half-
    and-half or milk
1 to 2 teaspoons lemon
    juice (optional) (see note)
Salt and freshly ground
    pepper to taste
Pinch nutmeg or to taste
Sour cream or unflavored
    yogurt for garnish
Reserved cooked asparagus
    tips, cut in 1/2 to 1-inch
    pieces for garnish

Choose slender, tender, crisp asparagus spears. Rinse thoroughly to remove any sand or dirt. Remove the woody end of each spear at the point where the spear easily snaps or breaks. Very tender, young asparagus will not have to be trimmed.

In a large deep heavy saucepan, cook asparagus, uncovered, in salted boiling water to cover for 3 to 4 minutes after water returns to a boil or until asparagus are tender but crisp and firm. Drain thoroughly, reserving 1 cup boiling asparagus liquid. Rinse asparagus in *very* cold water; set aside. Dissolve chicken bouillon cubes in reserved boiling asparagus liquid. Trim 1/2 to 1 inch of top from cooked asparagus; reserve for garnish.

In a blender container, combine remaining cooked asparagus and chicken bouillon-asparagus liquid; cover and blend at medium to high speed until asparagus are pureed. Add cream and lemon juice, if desired; cover and blend until mixture is smooth. Season with salt, pepper, and nutmeg to taste. Refrigerate, covered, in the blender container or a clean 1-quart glass jar for 2 hours. Stir soup in a medium heavy saucepan over moderate heat until heated through. Ladle into soup cups or mugs and garnish each serving with a few pieces of reserved cooked asparagus tips and a dollop of sour cream or unflavored yogurt. Or, ladle *very* cold soup into chilled soup cups and garnish each serving as previously directed.

Note: Use *only* freshly squeezed lemon juice.

Old-Fashioned Cream of Tomato Soup

Yield: 4 to 6 servings

5 to 6 ripe medium toma-
   toes
1/2 cup chopped peeled
   onion
2 whole cloves
1 teaspoon salt or to taste
1 teaspoon sugar or to taste
1/8 teaspoon white pepper
   or to taste
3 tablespoons butter or
   margarine, melted
2 tablespoons flour
1 1/2 cups milk, scalded
1 cup half-and-half, at room
   temperature
Croutons for garnish
   (optional)
Whipped cream or sour
   cream for garnish (op-
   tional)
Minced chives for garnish
   (optional)

Peel, core, and chop tomatoes and combine with
the next 5 ingredients in a saucepan. Cover and
simmer over moderate heat until tomatoes are
just tender. Remove cloves. If a smooth soup is
desired, mix in a blender until smooth. In a
medium heavy saucepan, blend butter and flour;
gradually add milk and half-and-half, blending
well. Cook, stirring constantly, over moderate
heat until mixture is thickened and smooth. Add
hot tomato mixture gradually, stirring constantly.
Adjust seasoning, if desired. Serve at once topped
with croutons and whipped cream and minced
chives for garnish, if desired.

Variation: Add 1 tablespoon minced fresh or 1 teaspoon dried basil to the tomato
   mixture before simmering and omit cloves.

Quick N' Easy Company Tomato Soup

Yield: 4 to 6 servings

*Old fashioned flavor combined with modern know-how, gives this soup a
wonderful fresh quality. Preparation requires only about ten minutes and, the
soup is lower in salt (sodium) content!*

2 (10 3/4-ounce) cans salt-
   reduced cream of tomato
   soup, undiluted
1 (9 1/2-ounce) can no-

In a medium heavy saucepan, combine soup,
tomatoes, milk, and basil, blending well. Bring to
boiling over moderate heat, stirring occasionally.
Reduce heat and simmer for 3 to 5 minutes. Ladle

added salt diced toma-
toes, including liquid
1/2 cup milk or half-and-half
1 teaspoon minced fresh or
1/4 teaspoon dried basil
Sour cream for garnish

In a medium heavy saucepan, combine soup, tomatoes, milk, and basil, blending well. Bring to boiling over moderate heat, stirring occasionally. Reduce heat and simmer for 3 to 5 minutes. Ladle into individual soup cups and garnish each with a dollop of sour cream.

Variation: For lower calories, use 2% milk and unflavored yogart for garnish.

J.E.B. *Stuart Monument*

Gumbo

Gumbo, a thickened soup or stew served over hot cooked rice, is the crowning achievement of Creole cookery. Many varieties of fish and seafood, as well as ham and chicken, are used in preparing a tasty gumbo. Okra is usually the essential ingredient, although it is often omitted in New Orleans. The word gumbo, or gombo, is, indeed, a Creole patois corruption of the African word for okra. File powder is added for thickening just before serving. Flour has been used in place of file in some of the following recipes because file powder, a derivative of Sassafras leaves, is often unavailable. Gumbo has found its way up from New Orleans to Richmond. Although not as popular as in that Creole city, gumbo has many afficionados in the area.

Deluxe Gumbo

Yield: 12 to 14 servings

"I have combined food traditions of Pensacola, Florida, where I lived for many years, with those of Richmond. Hopefully, I have "married" the gumbo of the Gulf coast with Virginia crabmeat and ham. In Pensacola, tradition suggests the preparation of a gumbo to utilize the leftover Thanksgiving or Christmas turkey. Any combination of seafood is acceptable, depending upon personal taste and availability of products. Seasonings can also be altered for personal taste. Strive for a good rich roux with a pleasant and hearty blending of fowl, ham, and seafood."

2 pounds shrimp
1 meaty cooked turkey
  carcass (see note)
Water as needed
2 cups cut-up fully-cooked
  smoked Smithfield or
  country-style ham cut
  into bite-sized pieces
1/2 cup plus 2 tablespoons

Peel shrimp, cover, and refrigerate until needed. In a medium heavy saucepan, combine shrimp shells and water to cover; bring to a boil over moderate heat and continue boiling for 20 minutes. Remove shells and discard; reserve shrimp stock for gumbo.

In a large heavy pot or Dutch oven, combine turkey carcasses and 2 quarts of water. Bring to a boil over moderate heat; reduce temperature and

bacon drippings, divided
3/4 cup flour
4 ribs celery, including
  leaves, chopped
3 medium onions, peeled
  and chopped
3 garlic cloves, peeled and
  minced
1 large green pepper, cored,
  seeded, and chopped
2 small bay leaves,
  crumbled
1/2 cup chopped parsley
3 tablespoons minced fresh
  or 1 tablespoon dried
  basil
2 tablespoons minced fresh
  or 3 teaspoons dried
  thyme
1 tablespoon Pick-a-Peppa
  or Worcestershire or other
  desired hot sauce or to
  taste
1 teaspoon seafood seasoning (see note)
1 (28-ounce) can tomatoes,
  including liquid
4 to 6 uncooked blue crabs
1 to 2 cups cut-up cooked
  turkey, cut into bite-sized
  pieces
1 pound okra, sliced
  crosswise into 1/2 to 1-
  inch pieces (see note)
Salt and pepper to taste
2 tablespoons lemon juice
Gumbo filé as desired
6 to 7 cups hot cooked rice

simmer, cover ajar, for 1 1/2 hours. Strain stock to remove all bones; reserve any large chunks of turkey from carcass for gumbo and discard remaining carcass.

In a large heavy skillet, sauté ham over moderate heat until all fat has been rendered, but ham does not become crisp. Remove ham and reserve. Reduce heat and add 1/2 cup bacon drippings to hot rendered ham fat in skillet; with a wire whisk blend in flour. Cook, stirring constantly, over moderate heat until mixture is copper brown in color, about 20 to 25 minutes. *Do not scorch*. Stir in celery, onion, garlic, and green pepper; continue cooking for 30 minutes.*Mixture will be dry*. Add bay leaves, parsley, basil, and thyme, Pick-a-Peppa sauce, and seafood seasoning; continue to simmer for 10 minutes to release bouquet of seasoning flavors.

In a large heavy pot or Dutch oven, combine roux mixture, turkey stock, shrimp shell stock, reserved ham, and tomatoes. Bring to a boil over moderate heat; reduce temperature and simmer, uncovered, for 2 1/2 hours, stirring occasionally. While gumbo is simmering, clean crabs and sever claws from bodies; break crabs into two pieces. In a small heavy skillet, sauté okra in 2 tablespoons bacon drippings until *just* tender but crisp. Add reserved carcass meat, cut-up turkey, crab claws and body pieces, and okra, if desired, to mixture in pot; simmer for 30 minutes. Adjust seasoning to taste; add salt and pepper to taste (see note).Add shrimp and continue to simmer for 10 minutes. Add oysters and liquid and continue to simmer for 10 minutes. Stir in lemon juice and 1 to 2 tablespoons filé powder, as desired. Keep gumbo warm until ready to serve. Ladle mixture over rice in individual shallow soup bowls. Additional gumbo filé may be passed to sprinkle over each serving, if desired.

Note: Preferably use Old Bay brand seafood seasoning.
Note: 1 pound thawed frozen sliced okra may be substituted for fresh okra.
Note: Gumbo may be prepared in advance to this point; refrigerate for up to 48 hours or freeze until ready to use. Gumbo actually tastes better if the flavors are allowed to "ripen" in the refrigerator for 24 hours. Bring gumbo to a boil before proceeding with remaining part of the recipe.

—Marilyn Tipton (Mrs. Ray)

The John Marshall Hotel Seafood Gumbo

Yield: 6 servings

After a half-century of being a gracious Richmond landmark hotel which catered to dignitaries from the world over, as well as the hub of social and political activities of the city, the John Marshall Hotel sadly closed its doors in June, 1988. Opened to critical acclaim on October 30, 1929 at Fifth and Franklin Streets as a hotel that was "modern in every detail, offering all the luxuries and conveniences of the largest metropolitan hotels," it will long be remembered with fond memories by many.

1/4 cup minced peeled onion
1/4 cup minced peeled carrots
2 tablespoons minced celery
1 tablespoon minced parsley
2 1/2 to 3 tablespoons butter or margarine, melted
4 ounces codfish fillet, cut into bite-sized pieces
4 ounces peeled and deveined small shrimp
2 ounces bay or sea scallops
2 ounces shucked *little neck* (very small) clams
Simmering water as needed
1 (9 1/2-ounce) can diced tomatoes, including liquid
1/2 cup dry white wine
1/4 cup clam juice
3/4 teaspoon minced fresh or 1/4 teaspoon crushed dried rosemary
1 tablespoon butter or margarine, at room temperature
2 to 3 tablespoons flour
1 1/2 tablespoons heavy cream, at room temperature

In a large heavy saucepan, sauté onions, carrots, celery, and 1 tablespoonful parsley in melted butter over moderate heat until tender but not browned. In a separate large heavy saucepan, cook codfish, shrimp, scallops, and clams in 2 quarts *simmering* water for 3 to 4 minutes, or until *just* tender. *Do not over cook.* Drain well and set aside. In a large heavy saucepan, combine sautéed vegetables, tomatoes, 3 1/2 cups simmering water, wine, clam juice, and rosemary; simmer, uncovered, over low heat for 30 minutes. Blend flour into softened butter, forming a smooth paste; with a wire whisk, blend paste into stock mixture and continue simmering for 10 minutes. Add fish and seafood; bring to a boil over moderate heat. With a whisk, quickly blend in cream and add salt and pepper to taste. Ladle into individual soup bowls and garnish each serving with minced chives or additional minced parsley.

80

Salt and pepper to taste
Minced chives or additional
   minced parsley for
   garnish

The John Marshall Hotel

Ochra Soup

Get two double handsful of young ochra, wash and slice it thin, add two onions chopped fine, put it into a gallon of water at a very early hour in an earthen pipkin, or very nice iron pot: it must be kept steadily simmering, but not boiling: put in pepper and salt. At 12 o'clock, put in a handful of Lima beans, at half past one o'clock, add three young cimlins cleaned and cut in small pieces, a fowl, or knuckle of veal, bit of bacon or pork that has been boiled,and six tomatoas, with the skin taken off ..When nearly done:thicken with a spoonful of butter, mixed with one of flour. Have rice boiled to eat with it.

Mrs. Mary Randolph
The Virginia House-Wife or Methodical Cook
(first edition), 1824

Christmas Dinner of 1850

Cream chicken soup
Dried apricot johnny cake
Roast wild turkey
Pork and apple pie
Terrapin stew
Baked yams — samp.
Buttered squash — creamed onions
Cranberry jelly — watermelon rind pickle
Yellow tomato preserves
English plum pudding
Indian pudding
Cheese tarts
Raised raisin fritters
Almond cake
Great-grandma Gregory's crullers
1776 hard gingerbread
Cinder — apples — hickory nuts
Sugared popcorn
Coffee with cream and sugar.

Irene Bivens
"Yule Dinners Were Events In Old South,"
Richmond Times-Dispatch, Dec. 25, 1935

Tasty Beef-Barley Soup

Yield: 6 to 8 servings

Early colonists brought barley with them from England. Following the Indian instructions, barley was used in the making of soup, cereals, bread, and beer.

1 pound beef chuck, round, or stew meat, cut into 3/4 to 1-inch cubes
1 beef knuckle bone
2 tablespoons hot cooking oil or shortening, melted
8 cups water, divided
2 tablespoons barley
1 tablespoon Worcester-shire sauce or to taste
2 to 3 teaspoons salt or to taste
1 1/2 teaspoons minced fresh or 1/2 teaspoon dried basil
3/4 teaspoon minced fresh or 1/4 teaspoon dried rosemary
1/2 teaspoon minced peeled garlic
1/2 teaspoon minced fresh or 1/8 teaspoon dried oregano
1/4 teaspoon coarsely ground pepper
1/4 teaspoon crumbled bay leaves
3 to 4 drops hot sauce
1 cup canned tomatoes, including liquid
3 celery ribs, plus leaves, coarsely chopped
1/2 cup canned whole-kernel corn, drained
1/2 cup cut fresh or frozen green beans

In a large heavy pot, brown beef cubes and bone in oil or shortening, uncovered, over low heat. Add 6 cups water and barley. Simmer, uncovered, for 1 hour. Skim off excess fat and add seasonings. Continue simmering for an additional 2 1/2 hours. Add vegetables and remaining 2 cups water. Continue to cook for 30 minutes or until meat, barley, and vegetables are tender.

Savory Bean Soup

Yield: 8 servings (about 2 quarts)

When family members are tired of ham biscuits and ham sandwiches from the Christmas ham, prepare a pot of Savory Bean Soup to everyone's delight. It freezes well and makes a "souper"Sunday supper for family and/or friends.

1 (16-ounce) package dried navy or Great Northern beans
Cold water as needed
About 8 cups water
3 ribs celery, minced, including some leaves
2 small to medium onions, peeled and chopped
2 bay leaves, crushed
1 cooked meaty ham bone
1 dried hot red pepper, crushed
About 3 to 4 cups cubed fully-cooked smoked ham, cut in 1/2 to 3/4-inch cubes
2 tablespoons minced parsley
1 tablespoon Worcester-shire sauce
2 to 3 teaspoons salt or to taste
2 teaspoons garlic juice
1/2 teaspoon ground savory
Seasoned salt and pepper to taste
Additional minced parsley for garnish

Soak beans in cold water to cover for 12 hours; drain and rinse thoroughly. In a 4-quart pot, heat beans in about 8 to 10 cups cold water or to cover over high heat until foam gathers at water surface. Remove beans from heat, drain, and rinse thoroughly in cold water. Repeat process twice more to remove gas from beans.In a 4-quart heavy pot, combine degassed beans, about 8 cups water, and remaining ingredients. Bring to a boil over high heat, stirring occasionally. Reduce heat and simmer, uncovered, stirring frequently, for about 3 hours, or until beans are very tender and soup is slightly thickened. *Do not allow soup to burn.* Adjust seasoning to taste. Garnish each serving with minced parsley, if desired.

83

Hearty Company Soup

Yield: 8 servings

"Hearty Company Soup is delicious tasting and very satisfying. Perfect with buttered crispy French bread."

8 slices bacon
1 medium onion, peeled and coarsely chopped
About 6 thin, small to medium, meaty beef bones
1 pound beef round steak
12-ounce meaty ham hock
6 cups water
2 teaspoons salt
6 ounces mild or hot-spiced Polish sausage
4 medium potatoes, peeled and cubed
3 (15-ounce) cans garbanzo beans, undrained
1 large garlic clove, peeled and minced

In a large Dutch oven, pan-fry bacon over moderate heat until crisp; remove bacon drain well on absorbent paper, and crumble. Brown bones and round steak in hot drippings; revove from pan. Drain off all but 2 tablespoons bacon drippings from pan. Sauté onion in reserved hot bacon drippings until tender but not browned. Add beef bones, round steak, ham hock, water, and salt to Dutch oven. Reduce heat, cover, and simmer for 1 1/2 hours. Meanwhile, pan-fry sausage in a large heavy skillet over moderate heat until thoroughly browned. Remove from skillet, drain on absorbent paper, and cut into thin slices. Remove beef bones, steak, and ham hock from liquid in Dutch oven. Cut round steak into bite-sized pieces; discard bones. Skim fat from broth. Return round steak pieces to broth. Add potatoes, undrained garbanzo beans, and garlic to pot. Simmer, covered, over low heat for 30 minutes. Add reserved sausage and simmer, covered, for 15 minutes. Stir in bacon just before serving.

–Elizabeth Archer

Turtle Bean Soup

Soak 1/2 pint of black beans over night; put them into 3 quarts of warm water with a beef-bone, or small pieces of salt pork; boil 3 or 4 hours; strain and season with salt, pepper, cloves and lemon juice, and, if desired, slices of hard-boiled eggs, also small meat balls well fried. Serve with croutons. Add tomatoes to the soup.

Receipts for Luncheon and Tea, *1898*

"Oh Nothin' Soup"

Yield: 6 to 8 servings

One day when Vernelle Thomas was asked what was cooking that smelled so good, she replied, "Oh nothin'." The "nothin" turned out to be this delicious tasting soup.

3 to 4 chicken breasts or 1 (4- to 5-pound) stewing chicken, cut into serving pieces
About 12 cups water
3 chicken bouillon cubes
3 to 4 ribs celery, coarsely chopped
3 medium potatoes, peeled and cubed
2 medium carrots, peeled and thickly sliced
1 medium onion, peeled and cut into thin wedges
2 cups fresh or 1 (10-ounce) package frozen baby lima beans, thawed
Salt and pepper to taste
Pinch crushed dried hot red pepper or to taste
1/2 cup cold water
2 tablespoons flour
1 tablespoon minced parsley

In a *very* large heavy saucepan or Dutch oven, cook chicken and bouillon cubes, cover ajar, in water to cover over moderate heat for 1 hour or until chicken is almost fork tender. Remove meat from bone; cut chicken into cubes. Discard skin and bone. Return chicken to broth in pan. Add vegetables and seasonings and continue cooking for 20 minutes or until vegetables are tender. In a 1-cup measure, blend cold water into flour until smooth; stir flour mixture into soup. Continue cooking until soup is slightly thickened and bubbly hot. Add parsley to soup just before serving.

–Vernelle Thomas

Hare or Rabbit Soup

Cut up two hares, put them into a pot with a piece of bacon, two onions chopped, a bundle of thyme and parsley which must be taken out before the soup is thickened, add pepper, salt, pounded cloves, and mace, put in a sufficient quantity of water, stew it gentle three hours, thicken with a large spoonful of butter, and one of brown flour, with a glass of red wine; boil it a few minutes longer, and serve it up with the nicest parts of the hares. Squirrels make soup equally good, done the same way.

Mrs. Mary Randolph
The Virginia House-Wife, or Methodical Cook, *1830*

Mushroom Beef Noodle Soup

Yield: 6 to 8 servings

Mushrooms have long been thought to be food for the gods but have only been cultivated for human consumption since the seventeenth century. Thomas Jefferson, the great Virginia epicurean, thoroughly enjoyed them.

2 pounds beef, cut into
  1 1/2-inch cubes
3 tablespoons hot cooking
  oil
10 cups water
3 beef bouillon cubes,
  mashed
1 (8-ounce) package broad
  flat noodles
1 pound mushrooms, thinly
  sliced
1 tablespoon minced peeled
  onion
1/4 cup butter or margarine,
  melted
1/2 cup flour
1 teaspoon Worcestershire
  sauce
1 teaspoon salt or to taste
1/4 teaspoon pepper
3 to 4 drops hot sauce
3 to 4 drops browning and
  seasoning sauce, if
  desired
1 cup half-and-half or light
  cream

In a skillet, brown meat thoroughly in oil over moderate heat. Place meat and drippings in a 4-quart heavy saucepan; add water and bouillon cubes. Simmer over low heat 2 to 3 hours or until meat is tender. While meat is simmering, cook noodles according to package directions. Drain well; set aside. In a large heavy skillet, sauté the mushrooms and onion in butter over moderate heat for 3 to 4 minutes, stirring constantly. Stir in flour and cook until just bubbly. Blend mushroom mixture into beef. Add salt, Worcestershire sauce, browning and seasoning sauce, and hot sauce; cook, stirring constantly, until mixture thickens. Add cooked noodles.

Beef Tea

Take one pound of beef, free from fat; cut it into small pieces, and then submit it for three hours, each time in succession, to half its weight in water--half a pint of cold, of warm, and of boiling water. The fluids strained off from the first and second infusions are to be mixed with that strained off hot from the third, or boiling process, and the mixture should be just brought to a boiling heat to cook it; the fat should be skimmed off; a few drops of some acid (when admissible), with a very little salt, will improve the flavor.

Virginia Cookery-Book, *1885*

Soup of Any Kind of Old Fowl

(The only way in which they are eatable.)

Put the fowls in a coop and feed them moderately for a fortnight; kill one and cleanse it, cut off the legs and wings and separate the breast from the ribs, which, together with the whole back, must be thrown away, being too gross and strong for use. Take the skin and fat from the parts cut off which are also gross. Wash the pieces nicely, and put them on the fire with about a pound of bacon, a large onion chopped small, some pepper and salt, a few blades of mace, a handful of parsley cut up very fine, and two quarts of water if it be a common fowl or duck--a turkey will require more water. Boil it gently for three hours, tie up a small bunch of thyme, and let it boil in it half an hour, then take it out. Thicken your soup with a large spoonful of butter rubbed into two of flour, the yolks of two eggs, and half-pint of milk. Be careful not to let it curdle in the soup.

Mrs. Mary Randolph
The Virginia House-Wife, or Methodical Cook, *1830*

Pub-Style Onion Soup

Yield: 8 to 10 servings

This hearty soup has been adapted from a favorite recipe for one hundred portions served at the English-style Penny Lane Pub on 8th Street in downtown Richmond. Serve with mugs of ice-cold lager.

1 large Spanish (yellow) or other sweet onion, peeled and chopped
Water as needed
1 beef bouillon cube, mashed
Salt and pepper to taste
1/4 cup dry sherry
8 to 10 slices toasted party-style rye bread or about 1 cup croutons, divided
About 1 cup shredded Swiss or Emmentaler cheese

In a large heavy saucepan, combine onions and enough water to fill the pan three fourths full. Bring to a boil over moderate heat. Add bouillon cube and sherry. Add salt and pepper to taste. Reduce heat and simmer, uncovered, for 1 hour or until onion is tender and broth flavorful. Adjust seasonings to taste. Ladle soup into oven-proof soup bowls or mugs. Add 1 slice of toasted rye bread or about 2 tablespoons croutons to each serving. Sprinkle about 2 tablespoons shredded cheese over each soup-filled bowl. Arrange filled bowls or mugs on an ungreased baking sheet. Broil, about 8 inches from heat source, for 3 to 4 minutes or until cheese is melted and lightly browned. Serve immediately.

–Terry O,Neill, proprietor
John H. Mack, Jr., chef

87

Chicken Soup

For an invalid who needs plain, nourishing diet, but at the same time is not very sick, take a half-grown fowl, or spring chicken, and cut it up into eight pieces; put this meat into a stewpan of suitable size, and cover with cold water--about a quart will suffice; set it on the back part of the stove and let it simmer, but not boil, for two hours. Half an hour before it is needed add a gill of rice and put in salt to the taste; thicken with a very little flour made into a paste with cold water before putting it into the soup, and add a flavoring of parsley choppedup, or celery, whichever is preferred; skim off the grease very carefully. For a richer soup, the yolk of an egg beaten may be added to the thickening. Half this quantity will be enough to serve at one time.

Virginia Cookery-Book, *1885*

Sausage and Lentil Soup

Yield: 4 servings

Lentils were staples in the diet of the ancient Greeks and sausage a great favorite of the Romans. Known as "little bags of mystery" in Victorian times, sausage of the day was named for the inferior meat used in its preparation. Some authorities suggest that lentils may possibly have been a part of Essau's "mess of pottage." Together, they make a delightful marriage in flavors.

1/2 cup chopped bacon (about 5 to 6 slices)
12 ounces smoked Polish or other hot garlic-spiced pork sausage, diagonally sliced into 3/4-inch pieces
1 cup chopped peeled onion
1/2 cup chopped peeled carrots
1/2 cup chopped celery
1 (16-ounce) can tomatoes, chopped, including liquid
1 cup lentils, rinsed
2 tablespoons minced celery
1 bay leaf, crumbled
1/2 teaspoon salt or to taste
1/4 teaspoon majoram
1/8 teaspoon pepper

In a large heavy sauce pan, pan-fry bacon over moderate heat until done but not crisp. Remove bacon; set aside on absorbent paper. Drain off all bacon drippings, except 1 tablespoon, from saucepan. Add sausage and brown thoroughly over moderate heat. Remove sausage, drain well, and cut into bite-sized pieces; set aside. Skim off excess fat. Saute onions, carrots, and chopped celery in remaining drippings until tender. Reduce heat; add tomatoes and juice, water, lentils, bacon, sausage, minced celery, and seasonings. Cover and simmer over low heat 1 hour or until lentils are tender, stirring occasionally. Remove bay leaf before serving.

–Ann Tyler (Mr. Hal)

Savory Pumpkin and Mixed Vegetable Soup

Yield: 6 to 8 servings

2 medium tomatoes, peeled, seeded, and chopped
1/2 cup coarsely chopped green pepper
1/2 cup coarsely chopped peeled onion
1 tablespoon hot cooking oil
1 pound pumpkin, peeled, seeded, and cubed (see note)
1 (10 3/4-ounce) can cream of chicken soup, undiluted
1/2 cup chicken broth
1/2 cup chopped peeled turnip
1/2 cup chopped peeled carrot
1/2 teaspoon salt
1/4 teaspoon nutmeg (see note)
1/8 teaspoon crushed dried hot red pepper (optional)
1/2 cup milk or half-and-half
Sour cream for garnish

In a heavy saucepan, sauté tomatoes, green pepper, and onion in oil over moderate heat until tender. Add pumpkin, soup, broth, turnip, carrot, salt, nutmeg, and red pepper; bring to boiling.Reduce heat, cover, and simmer for 20 minutes or until pumpkin is tender. Pour half of the mixture into a blender container; cover and blend at medium speed until smooth. Repeat process with remaining pumpkin mixture. Return all of the puréed pumpkin mixture to the saucepan; add milk and heat through. Adjust seasonings to taste. Serve hot or chill in the refrigerator and serve garnished with a dollop of sour cream.

Note: 1 (16-ounce) can cooked pumpkin may be substituted. Simmer only for 10 minutes or until turnips and carrots are tender.

Note: Preferably use freshly grated nutmeg.

–Ann Epes (Mrs. Travis, Jr.)

Cream of Corn Soup

Cut the grains off 12 ears of corn, add 2 quarts of water, and let it boil until the corn is well done; then add 1 quart of milk, and let it come to a boil; put this through a colander, and put it on the stove to get warm; add to this pepper and salt and at ablespoon of butter, beat an egg until light, stirring all the time while pouring into the soup.

Mrs. Winn
Receipts for Luncheon and Tea, *1898*

Potato Soup with Avocado

Yield: 8 to 10 servings

"This soup is a specialty of my mother, Piedad Cornejo, in my native city Quito, Ecuador. I have served it to many friends here in Richmond who have requested the recipe."

1 cup chopped green onion
(include some green tops)
1/3 cup butter or margarine,
melted
12 medium potatoes,
peeled and quartered
(about 4 pounds)
3 teaspoons salt or to taste
1/2 teaspoon pepper
5 1/2 cups water
1 1/2 cups milk
2 eggs, beaten
2 cups grated Farmers' or
sharp Cheddar, or Monterey Jack cheese
1/2 teaspoon paprika (see
note)
Several drops hot sauce or
to taste (optional)
2 ripe avocados
Lemon juice as needed

In a large heavy saucepan, sauté onion in butter over moderate heat until tender but not browned. Add potatoes, salt, and pepper; stir for an additional 2 to 3 minutes. Add water to mixture. Bring to a boil and continue to cook on medium high temperature until potatoes are tender, about 20 to 25 minutes. Mash a few of the potatoes in the liquid. Gradually add milk, blending well. Bring mixture to a boil; reduce to simmering and gradually blend in eggs and cheese with a wire whisk. Add paprika and hot sauce, if desired. Peel and thinly slice avocados; lightly sprinkle slices with lemon juice. Ladle hot soup into soup bowls or mugs; garnish each serving with avocado slices. Add additional hot sauce to each serving, if desired.

Note: Although paprika is used in the United States, *achiote* is the seasoning used in Ecuador.

–Maria Teresa Taylor (Mrs. Richard)

Chicken Essence, or Tea

For a very sick person choose a full-grown fowl, the juice being more nutritious; chop it up fine with a meat-axe, bones and all, and put it into a wide-mouthed bottle closely stopped, with no water but what has adhered after washing; set the bottle into a pan of cold water, and let it boil around it for several hours. In some cases this is preferable to beef tea; but when to use one or the other it is the part of the physician to decide.

Virginia Cookery-Book, *1885*

Cheesy Potato Cabbage Soup

Yield: 6 servings

5 to 6 green onions, minced (including some green tops)

4 medium potatoes, peeled and cubed

1/2 medium cabbage, chopped

5 cups water

1 cup heavy cream, at room temperature

2 tablespoons butter or margarine, at room temperature

1 1/2 teaspoons salt or to taste

1/4 teaspoon pepper or to taste

Grated Parmesan cheese for garnish

In a heavy Dutch oven, combine green onions, potatoes, cabbage, and water; bring to a boil over moderate heat. Reduce temperature; cover and simmer for 25 to 30 minutes or until vegetables are tender. Stir in cream, butter, salt, and pepper; heat through. Ladle into individual soup bowls and sprinkle each serving liberally with Parmesan cheese.

–Ginny Moss (Mrs. John Simpson)

Blackeye-Pea Soup-No. 131.

1 quart peas, 1 tablespoon butter, 1 1/2 teaspoons salt,, 1/4 teaspoon black pepper, 4 quarts cold water, 1/2 pound sweet bacon, or one ham bone, 1 tablespoon browned flour, 1 gill walnut catsup, or, 1/2 gill Worcester sauce., To Make: Wash the peas well in cold water and soak them overnight; early in the morning drain off the water and cover with the cold water; boil until tender; press through a sieve; wash the kettle; return the soup to it and bring it to a boil; rub butter and flour together until perfectly smooth, and thicken the soup; add salt, pepper, and catsup, or Worcester sauce. Serve hot with croutons.

Instruction in Cooking with Selected Receipts, *1895*

Festive Pumpkin Soup

Yield: 8 to 10 servings

Festive Pumpkin Soup was served as the soup course at a Gourmet Holiday Journey hosted in Gallego's at a special dinner sponsored by the Women's Committee of the Richmond Symphony to benefit the Symphony prior to the 1988 holiday season.

2 medium carrots, peeled and minced
2 ribs celery, minced
1 small onion, peeled and minced
2 cups minced, peeled, and seeded fresh pumpkin
1/2 cup butter or margarine, melted
1/2 cup flour
8 cups hot chicken stock or broth (see note)
1/2 to 3/4 cup canned pumpkin
1/2 (3-inch) cinnamon stick or 1/4 teaspoon ground cinnamon
1/8 teaspoon nutmeg
Salt and pepper to taste
1/2 cup heavy or light cream
8 to 10 whole miniature pumpkins, seeds and pulp removed (see note) (optional)

In a large heavy pot, sauté carrots, celery, onion, and minced fresh pumpkin in butter over moderate heat until tender but not browned. Stir in flour, blending well. Gradually add hot chicken stock, blending well. Stir in canned pumpkin and seasonings. Reduce heat and simmer, cover ajar, for 1 to 1 1/2 hours, stirring occasionally. Pour about one-fourth to one-third of mixture into a blender container; cover and whiz until cooked vegetables are puréed. Strain mixture. Repeat process until all soup is puréed and strained. Return to pot, add cream, and adjust seasoning. Stir over low heat just until mixture begins to simmer. *Do not boil.* Ladle soup into individual miniature pumpkins or soup bowls. Garnish as desired and serve immediately.

Note: 4 1/2 undiluted (14-ounce) cans chicken broth may be substituted for chicken stock.

Note: While soup is simmering, cut a thin slice from the top of each miniature pumpkin. Scoop out pulp and seeds from pumpkins to form individual soup tureens, if desired.

–Chef Kevin Wade
Gallego's Restaurant
The Omni Hotel

Grandmother Garrett's Tomato-Potato Soup

Yield: 4 to 6 servings

Cloves, which can be overpowering and should be used with discretion, add a subtle pungent flavor to tomato-potato soup.

2 medium potatoes (1 cup grated potatoes)
Salted boiling water as needed
4 tablespoons butter or margarine, melted
4 tablespoons flour
1 teaspoon salt
1/8 teaspoon pepper
2 cups half-and-half or milk
1 (16-ounce) can tomatoes, including liquid
1 medium onion, peeled and chopped
3 whole cloves
1 teaspoon salt

Cook unpeeled potatoes in salted boiling water, to cover, 15 minutes, or until *just* tender. Remove and drain. Cool slightly, peel, and shred potatoes with a grater. In a medium heavy saucepan, combine butter, flour and salt, blending until smooth. Gradually add half-and-half or milk, blending well. Cook, stirring constantly, over moderate heat until thickened and bubbly hot; remove from heat and set aside. Combine tomatoes, onion, cloves, and salt together in a small heavy saucepan; simmer, uncovered, over low heat 25 to 30 minutes. Add potatoes to cream sauce and heat through. Remove cloves from tomato mixture; gradually add to cream sauce, stirring constantly to prevent curdling. Serve immediately.

Rice and Tomato Soup

A teacup of rice boiled fast in plenty of water; strain thoroughly. Wash ten large tomatoes, cut in quarters; boil with the skin on and pass through a sieve. Brown an onion and a slice of ham together. Put the rice, tomatoes, onion and ham into a saucepan with another onion and quarter-pound butter, one teaspoonful of whole allspice and thyme, two cloves, pepper and salt. Boil the spice, herbs and ham in a thin muslin bag. Add a few tablespoonfuls of white stock. Let the whole cook slowly, stirring frequently, and add some veal stock--say two or three quarts. It only requires cooling long enough to be well mixed with the seasoning.

Mrs. Dr. Stone
The Kitchen Queen, *1893*

Spring Garden Spinach 'N Leek Soup

Yield: 4 servings

12 ounces fresh spinach, divided
2 chicken bouillon cubes
1 cup reserved boiling spinach cooking water
1 cup half-and-half or light cream or milk
1/4 teaspoon salt
1/8 teaspoon white pepper
Pinch nutmeg
2 medium leeks, cleaned and minced (about 1 cup minced)
3 tablespoons butter or margarine, melted
1 1/2 tablespoons flour (optional)
Sour Cream for garnish (optional)

Thoroughly clean and dry spinach. With a French knife, mince 4 ounces of the spinach, set aside. In a medium heavy saucepan, bring 2 cups water to boil over moderate heat; add remaining 8 ounces spinach and return water to boil over moderate heat. Continue to cook spinach for 4 minutes; drain well, reserving 1 cup cooking water. Dissolve bouillon cubes in reserved liquid. Combine cooked spinach, reserved cooking liquid, half-and-half, salt, pepper, and nutmeg in a blender container; cover and blend until mixture is thoroughly puréed. In a medium heavy skillet, sauté 4 ounces minced spinach and leeks in butter over moderate heat until vegetables are tender but not browned.

Sprinkle flour over mixture, if desired, mixing well. Spoon three-fourths of spinach-leek mixture into blender container with other spinach mixture, cover and blend just until additional spinach-leek mixture is puréed but small bits of spinach are visible. Stir remaining spinach-leek mixture into soup. If flour is added to spinach, pour soup into a medium heavy saucepan and cook over moderate heat, stirring constantly, until soup is bubbly hot and slightly thickened. Store soup, tightly covered, in a 1-quart glass jar for up to 3 days in the refrigerator. Serve hot or chilled. Pour soup into cups or mugs and garnish each serving with a dollop of sour cream., if desired.

> ...The new icehouse was mounted over a cool, brick-lined pit dug deep into the ground and equipped with drains. Layers of ice were packed tightly in sawdust or straw, slowing the melting process to such an extent that the governor could enjoy ice year-round. (during construction of new Virginia Executive Mansion, 1812-1813)
>
> William Seal
> Virginia's Executive Mansion:
> **A History of the Governor's House**, 1988

St. John's Mews

Restored by the Garden Club of Virginia in 1966-67, St. John's
Mews has been transformed from a formerly ugly alley way into
a lonely community garden. Located on historic Churchill Hill
in Richmond, the alley way originally bisected Carrington
Square, terminating at St. John's Church. With an atmosphere characteristic of the late 18th /early 19th centuries,
original cobblestone paving and ironwork examples from early
Richmond foundries have been incorporated into the brick walls
and construction of the pavilion.

Spiced Crab Soup

Yield: 8 to 10 servings

The Pearce family. . . Bill, Cheryl, and son, W. Keith. . . has been involved in the catering business in Richmond for many years and resolve to uphold the high standard for which they have always been known.

1 pound backfin crabmeat
2 (15-ounce) cans Italian-style plum tomatoes (see note)
1 (5-ounce) can white corn, drained (see note)
1 (5-ounce) can very small lima beans, drained (see note)
4 cups cubed peeled potatoes, cut into 1/2 to 3/4-inch cubes
2 cups water
1/2 cup cross-cut fresh or frozen okra
1/2 cup minced peeled white onion
1/4 cup minced green pepper
3 tablespoons minced peeled garlic
3 tablespoons beef base or 3 beef bouillon cubes, mashed
3 tablespoons crab or seafood base or 3 shrimp bouillon cubes (see note)
3 tablespoons seafood seasoning (see note)
1 tablespoon sugar
1 tablespoon minced fresh or 1 teaspoon dried basil
1 tablespoon minced fresh or 1 teaspoon dried oregano
1 1/2 teaspoons minced fresh or 1/2 teaspoon dried dill weed
Cayenne pepper to taste

Pick over crabmeat, removing any shell or cartilage; set aside. Place tomatoes in a blender container; cover and whiz until tomatoes are puréed. Strain purée, removing seeds. In a medium heavy pot or Dutch oven, combine tomato purée and remaining ingredients, except crabmeat and cayenne pepper. Bring to a boil over moderate heat; reduce temperature and simmer uncovered, until vegetables are tender, about 30 to 35 minutes. Add crabmeat, stirring gently. Adjust seasonings. Continue to simmer until crab is heated through. Season with cayenne pepper to taste.

Note: 1 cup fresh or thawed frozen corn, and lima beans, may be used.

Note: Crab or seafood base or shrimp bouillon cubes are available in many local grocery stores.

Note: Preferably use Old Bay brand seafood seasoning.

–Chef W. Keith Pearce

Hot and Sour Soup

Yield: 4 to 6 servings

1 pound chicken bones
Water as needed
1 (10 1/2-ounce) package
   black bean curd (to-fu)
   (see note)
1 ounce dried Chinese lily
   flowers
1 ounce dried black fungus
4 ounces minced pork loin
   or tenderloin
1 ounce shredded bamboo
   shoots
2 teaspoons soy sauce (see
   note)
1 teaspoon hot red pepper
   oil
1/4 teaspoon white pepper
2 teaspoons white vinegar
Salt to taste
1 egg, slightly beaten
1 teaspoon corn starch
1 teaspoon sesame oil,
   divided
Thinly sliced green onions
   for garnish

In a 2-quart heavy pot, combine chicken bones and enough water to cover well. Bring to a boil over high heat; reduce temperature and simmer for 30 minutes. Discard bones. In a deep small bowl, soak dried lilies and fungus in hot water to cover for 15 minutes; drain well, wash flowers and fungus thoroughly. Cut off hard ends of flowers and discard. Pinch out knobs of fungus and discard.Add prepared lilies and fungus to hot broth. Stir in pork and bamboo shoots. Simmer, covered, for 10 minutes. Add soy sauce, red pepper oil, and white pepper. Sprinkle vinegar and salt over mixture; blend well. Gradually stir beaten egg into broth mixture. Combine corn starch with 3 teaspoons cold water until smooth; gradually stir into hot soup. Stir over low heat until soup is slightly thickened. Ladle soup into small bowls; blend a few drops sesame oil into each serving. Garnish each with thinly sliced green onions.

Note: Tofu is usually found as a block in the produce department of a grocery store or specialty Oriental grocery store.

Note: Reduced sodium (Lite) soy sauce may be substituted for regular soy sauce. One teaspoon Lite soy sauce contains 100 milligrams of sodium.

–Carrie and John Wong, proprietors
Three Star Restaurant

Kanawha Canal and Locks

An ambitious canal system linking the James and Kanawha Rivers was proposed by George Washington after the Revolution. By 1789, two canals around the falls cleared the James, creating the first canal system in America. Extending two hundred miles west to Buchannan, Virginia, it not only encouraged trade but was a link to the west to prevent uninhabited land from passing to the French or Spanish. Although a bustling area in the early nineteenth century, by 1880 the canal system had become a little used means of transportation, having been replaced by the "iron horse," the railroad. Today, a portion of the Canal has been preserved on the south side of the Shockoe Slip area. Visitors may tour the locks, built in 1859, and reflect over their historical role of lifting freight past the falls of the James River to move goods to and from the interior to foreign lands.

Goober Peas

Goober peas, better known as peanuts, were being raised by the Indians when colonists first arrived on the shores of Virginia. Indigenous to both the South and North American continents, peanut seeds were found in ancient Peruvian tombs.

Mrs. Dickinson's Peanut Soup

Yield: 6 to 8 servings

Mary Lou Dickinson, wife of Earl Dickinson, delegate from Hanover County to the House of Delegates of the Virginia Legislature, donated this peanut soup recipe, which originated with the Hotel Roanoke, to the recipe files of the Executive Mansion. It was served as the soup course for the formal dinner served to the justices of the Virginia Supreme Court and their spouses, November, 1987.

1/2 small onion, peeled and chopped
1 rib celery
1/4 cup butter or margarine, melted
1 1/2 tablespoons flour
4 cups hot chicken broth
1 cup creamy or crunch-style peanut butter
1/2 tablespoon lemon juice
1/2 teaspoon salt or to taste
1/8 teaspoon celery salt
Ground peanuts for garnish

In a large heavy saucepan, sauté onion and celery in butter over moderate heat until tender but not browned. Add flour, blending well. Gradually stir in chicken broth; cook, uncovered, for 30 minutes. Remove from heat and strain; return strained broth to saucepan. Add peanut butter, lemon juice, salt, and celery salt, blending well. Stir over low heat until soup is heated through. Ladle into soup bowls and garnish each serving with ground peanuts.

Quick Preparation Method : Combine 1 undiluted (10 3/4-ounce) can Cream of Chicken soup, with 1 1/4 cups milk, and 1/4 cup peanut butter together in a medium heavy saucepan; stir over moderate heat until heated through. Garnish each serving with ground peanuts.

–Virginia Executive Mansion

Virginia Peanut Soup

Yield: 10 servings

1 small onion, peeled and chopped
4 ounces celery ribs, chopped
4 ounces carrots, peeled and chopped
1/2 cup plus 2 tablespoons butter or margarine, melted and divided
4 cups chicken stock or broth
1 cup crushed unsalted peanuts
1/2 cup creamy-style peanut butter
2 ounces flour
2 cups heavy cream, at room temperature
1 tablespoon lemon juice
Salt and pepper to taste

In a Dutch oven or large heavy saucepan, sauté onion, celery, and carrots in 2 tablespoons butter over moderate heat until tender but not browned. Add chicken stock; bring to a boil. Reduce heat and stir crushed peanuts and peanut butter, blending well.Simmer, uncovered, for 30 minutes. In a small bowl, blend remaining 1/2 cup melted butter into flour until mixture is smooth. With a wire whisk, whisk flour-butter mixture into hot soup until well-blended. Continue cooking, stirring constantly,until mixture is slightly thickened. Stir in cream, lemon juice,salt and pepper. Continue simmering, uncovered, for 30 minutes.Serve immediately and garnish each serving as desired

Note: The soup base without the addition of cream may be frozen for future use. Add cream when reheating soup just before serving.

–The Jefferson Sheraton Hotel

Crab - Broccoli Soup

Yield: 4 to 6 servings

Crab and broccoli, with the addition of thyme, make an interesting flavor combination.

3 tablespoons butter or margarine, melted
1/2 cup chopped peeled onion
2 tablespoons flour
4 cups half-and-half or light cream

In a skillet, sauté onion in butter until tender; do not drain.Blend a small amount of half-and-half into the flour until smooth.In a 1 1/2 quart heavy saucepan, gradually blend the onions, flour mixture, and remaining half-and-half together, blending well. Add the bouillon cubes and seasonings. Cook over moderate heat, stirring constantly, until

2 chicken bouillon cubes,
mashed
3/4 teaspoon minced fresh
or 1/4 teaspoon dried
thyme
1/2 teaspoon salt
1/8 teaspoon white pepper
1/8 teaspoon cayenne
pepper or to taste
8 ounces fresh crabmeat or
(8-ounce) package frozen
Alaska King Crab thawed,
or (7 1/2-ounce) can
crabmeat (see note)
1 (10-ounce) package
chopped broccoli,
partially cooked and
drained

soup is thickened and smooth. Stir in crabmeat and broccoli; continue cooking until heated through.

Note: Pick over crabmeat, removing any cartilage or shell.

–Ann Tyler (Mrs. Hal)

Old Richmond Advertisement, circa 1905

Stews

An old saying suggests "a stew must smile, never laugh." It should tickle the palate, not jump down one's throat. Stews are hearty nutritious one-pot meals. Over a low temperature, the stew simmers until flavors are at their peak and the meat is tender.Stewing is a method of slow cooking by moist heat which can be done in a saucepan, stewpan, or casserole and on top of the range or in the oven. Thicker than soup in consistency, a stew may be made with meat, fish, or vegetables or a combination of them.

Stews can be classified into two categories, brown or white. In a brown stew, usually made of beef, the meat is browned before the vegetables and liquid are added. With the white stew, usually lamb, veal, or poultry, meat is put into the pot with cold water or stock and brought to a boil before the vegetables are added.Often there is a purpose for the creation of a dish ... so it is true with stew ... originally the stew provided a way of cooking a tough meat until it was tender, using available vegetables, and stretching a meal to include one or two extras.

History tells us that medieval meat was commonly stewed in broth, but no one drank the broth until the twelfth century. Possibly the broth was enhanced by any available spices used to disguise the flavor of the meat which was often tainted.

Oven Beef Stew with Guiness 'N Prunes

Yield: 6 to 8 servings

1 cup pitted prunes
Brandy
3 pounds boneless lean beef chuck, cut into 1/2 to 3/4-inch cubes
About 1/2 cup flour
2 to 3 tablespoons hot cooking oil
Salt and pepper to taste
2 small onions, peeled and quartered or 16 small boiler onions, peeled
2 bay leaves, crumbled

In a small deep bowl, combine prunes and enough brandy to cover fruit; allow to stand for at least 1 hour or until prunes are plumped. On a sheet of waxed paper, dredge beef cubes in flour, coating well. In a heavy skillet, brown beef thoroughly in hot oil over moderate heat. Season meat with salt and pepper to taste. Transfer meat with a slotted spoon to a Dutch oven or 3-quart casserole. Add onions, bay leaves, 1 1/2 cups water, and Guiness stout. Bake, partially covered, in a moderate oven (350 degrees F.) for 1 1/2 hours. Add more water to cover meat, if necessary. Add carrots and continue baking, partially covered,for 40 minutes.

About 1 1/2 cups water
1 (12-ounce) bottle Guiness stout or other ale or beer
6 medium carrots, peeled and cut into 1 1/2-inch pieces
1 (4-ounce) can whole mushrooms, drained (optional)
Minced parsley for garnish
Boiled small red new potatoes or Crispy Irish Potato Cakes (see index)

Add prunes, prune liquid and mushrooms; continue baking, partially covered, for 30 minutes. Add additional water, if needed. With a whisk, blend in 1 to 2 tablespoons flour if gravy is too thin. Continue baking until gravy is slightly thickened. Ladle into individual soup bowls and garnish each portion with minced parsley and serve with boiled red new potatoes or Crispy Irish Potato Cakes.

Beef Soup.

Take the hind shin of beef, cut off all the flesh of the leg-bone, which must be taken away entirely or the soup will be greasy. Wash the meat and lay it in a pot and sprinkle over it one small tablespoonful of pounded black pepper and two of salt, three onions cut small, six small carrots scraped, two small turnips cut fine; pour on this three quarts water; keep it boiling steadily five hours, taking off the scum carefully as it rises. When it has boiled, add a small bundle of thyme and parsley and a teaspoonful of celery seed. Put in some toasted bread cut in dice and serve.

Mrs. Mary Randolph
The Kitchen Queen, *1893*

Old Richmond Advertisement, circa 1909

Brunswick Stew

Early m'sick-quotosh, a combination of corn, kidney beans, squirrel meat, and sometimes wild turkey "sweetened" with bear fat, evolved into a famous Virginia specialty, Brunswick Stew. The succotash of today, consisting of corn and lima beans but minus the other flavorful ingredients, is a far cry from the original.

Brunswick-Style Stew

Yield: 10 to 12 servings

Brunswick Stew, originally prepared with squirrel and said to be invented in Brunswick County, Virginia, is a favored recipe of many Virginians, including Richmond residents. This version is slightly different than the traditional recipe, adding Italian sausage to the ingredients. It also is an excellent device to use left-over holiday turkey and ham.

1 (28-ounce) can tomatoes, including liquid
1 (13 3/4-ounce) can chicken broth, undiluted
1 (12-ounce) can whole kernel corn, drained
1 (10-ounce) package frozen baby lima beans
8 ounces mild-spiced Italian sausage, cut into bite-sized pieces
3 medium potatoes, peeled and cubed
2 garlic cloves, peeled and minced (optional)
2 chicken bouillon cubes, mashed
1 large onion, peeled and chopped
8 cups water

In a heavy 5-quart pot or Dutch oven, combine the first 14 to 15 ingredients. Add salt and pepper to taste. Bring to a boil over moderate heat; reduce temperature and simmer, cover ajar, for 45 to 60 minutes. Add okra and continue to simmer for 25 to 30 minutes, until flavors are well blended.In a 1-cup measure, gradually blend cold water into flour until mixture is smooth; stir mixture into hot stew.Increase heat to moderate and continue to cook for 7 to 10 minutes or until stew is thickened.

1 1/2 cups cubed cooked
  turkey
1 1/2 cups cubed fully-
  cooked smoked ham
1 1/2 cups chopped celery
1 1/2 cups chopped peeled
  carrots
1/4 teaspoon crushed dried
  hot red pepper or to taste
Salt and pepper to taste
2 cups fresh or thawed
  frozen sliced okra
1/4 cup cold water
3 to 4 tablespoons flour
Variation: 1 cup dry white wine may be substituted for 1 cup of the water.

Virginia Brunswick Stew

1 Large Frying Size Chicken or 2 Squirrels, 2 Slices Fat Salt Pork,, 1 Dozen Tomatoes,, 3 Cupsful Butter Beans,, 2 Medium Sized Onions,, Salt and Pepper,, 3 Large Potatoes,, 12 Ears Green Corn,, 1/4 Pound Lard,, 1/2 Pound Butter,, 1 Gallon Boiling Water,, 1 Table-spoonful Franklin Sugar., This stew is made in a variety of ways in the South, but this method is a favorite one in many parts of Virginia. The stew made in this way will of itself make a substantial meal. If chicken is used, cut in pieces and fry in lard until half done; then add the boiling water, pork, sliced onions,tomatoes (finely chopped), potatoes, which should be peeled and sliced, beans and butter. Cook slowly for four hours or a little less. In the meantime remove the corn from the cob by cutting off a small portion of the grain and scraping outthe pulp. About ten minutes before serving-time add the corn, which should thicken the stew. Next add the sugar and season plentifully with salt, cayenne and black pepper. A bunch of soup herbs may be added if you like.

Old Virginia Cooking, *circa 1909*

Brunswick Stew

Some slices of bacon, squirrel or chicken, one or two onions; put in one gallon water, and stew half an hour; then add one quart tomatoes, some potatoes (peeled), butterbeans, corn, pod of red pepper, and salt; stew all together until you can take out the bones. When done, add large spoonful of butter, and serve hot.

Governor Holliday
F. F. V. Receipt Book, *1894*

The Tredegar Works

During the Civil War, the Tredegar Works served as the "iron maker to the Confederacy," providing arms to confederate troops for use against the Union Forces. It was one of the few major sources of armaments available to the South.

Named after a similar ironworks located in Wales, Tredegar was started in the late 1830's. The addition of iron master Joseph Reid Anderson to the staff in 1838, and later chief company stockholder, helped to shape the destiny of the manufacturer. By the late twentieth century, the once great Tredegar was only producing spikes and connecting plates for railroads, finally closing in the late 1980's. In 1863, fire accruing at the Haxall flour mill located adjacent to the property threatened the Tredegar while an explosion of the munitions laboratory on the near by Brown's Island in the same year caused many deaths of female munitions workers. Again during the evacuation of Richmond by Confederate Forces in April 1865, fire came close to demolishing the ironworks; however, Anderson mustered workers into a brigade to eliminate the advancing flames. Today the once vast complex is a silent sentinel, overlooking the James River. Ethyl Corporation, with its corporate offices located just above the area on Gamble's Hill recently acquired the property, restoring the foundry...,
built during the Civil War to cast cannons... into a preserved historic attraction. The Valentine Museum and the corporation are presently engaged in forming a proposal to historically interpret this significant symbol of Richmond's past.

Irish Stew

There is no "true" recipe for Irish stew. Ingredients varied from one locale to another in Ireland, just as they do now in the United States. Kid (baby goat) and mutton were the most common meats used and bacon was sometimes added. Potatoes and onion were always included in those early recipes, while carrots and cabbage were later additions.

Irish Lamb Stew

Yield: 6 to 8 servings

The Irish of Ireland prefer mutton in their classic stew, but we Americans choose lamb. Introduced by Irish immigrants fleeing Ireland during the potato famine of the nineteenth century, Irish Stew is a favorite with Irish-Americans and others throughout the United States, including Richmond.

2 pounds lamb shoulder, cut into 3/4 to 1-inch pieces
2 tablespoons hot cooking oil, or shortening, melted
Water as needed
1 pound carrots, peeled, halved lengthwise, and cut into 2-inch pieces
8 small onions, peeled and quartered or 16 very small boiler onions, peeled
8 small potatoes, peeled
2 chicken bouillon cubes, mashed
2 teaspoons minced peeled garlic
1 teaspoon minced chives
1 1/2 teaspoons minced fresh or 1/2 teaspoon dried basil
1 1/2 teaspoons minced fresh or 1/2 teaspoon dried rosemary
1/4 teaspoon pepper
4 tablespoons flour
1/4 to 1/2 cup cold water

In a dutch oven, brown lamb thoroughly in oil over moderate heat. Cover lamb with water; simmer 40 to 60 minutes. Add carrots, onions, potatoes, bouillon cubes and spices. Reduce temperature and simmer over low heat for an additional hour or until meat and vegetables are fork tender. Add more water as needed to cover meat and vegetables. Remove from heat. Blend flour and cold water together until smooth; gradually add to stew. Continue cooking until stew is thickened.

Varation: Add 1 to 2 cups small fresh or partially thawed frozen peas about 10 minutes before stew is finished cooking. Reduce amount of carrots, onions, and potatoes. One cup sour cream may be stirred into stew just before serving, if desired. Garnish each serving with minced parsley, if desired.

Veal Stew

Yield: 6 to 8 servings

Although veal is not as popular or as plentiful as beef in the United States, veal, requiring moist heat to bring out the flavor and tenderness, is an excellent choice for a stew. It also is desirable as a meat for those requiring a low cholesterol diet.

3 tablespoons flour
2 teaspoons dry mustard
2 teaspoons minced peeled
  garlic, divided
2 pounds veal shoulder, cut
  into 3/4 to 1-inch pieces
2 tablespoons hot cooking
  oil or shortening, melted
1 (10 1/2-ounce) can onion
  soup, undiluted
1 cup chili sauce
2 tablespoons Worcester-
  shire sauce or to taste
1 1/2 teaspoons minced
  fresh or 1/2 teaspoon
  dried rosemary
1/2 teaspoon pepper
2 to 3 drops Tabasco sauce
  or taste
3/4 teaspoon minced fresh
  or 1/4 teaspoon dried
  basil
6 to 8 very small red-
  skinned new potatoes,
  peeled or peeled around
  the center of each potato
6 medium carrots, peeled,
  halved lengthwise, and
  cut into 2-inch pieces
3 tablespoons minced fresh
  or 1 tablespoon dried
  parsley

Mix together flour, dry mustard and 1 teaspoon garlic. Dredge meat on both sides in flour mixture. In a Dutch oven, brown meat thoroughly in oil over moderate heat. In a bowl, mix together onion soup, chili sauce, Worcestershire sauce, and remaining spices. Reduce heat; pour soup mixture over meat and cook, uncovered, for 1 1/2 hours. Add potatoes and carrots and continue cooking over low heat for 45 minutes or until vegetables and meat are tender. Add parsley just before serving.

Oyster Stew Magnifique

Yield: 4 to 6 servings

Oyster stew is favored by many Richmonders for a variety of special occasions or an ordinary lunch or supper. Oysters from the Rappahannock River and the Eastern Shore of Virginia are preferred.

2 ribs celery, minced
   (include some leaves)
1 to 2 tablespoons butter or
   margarine, melted
1 quart *select* (medium)
   oysters, including liquid
2 cups milk, scalded
1 cup light cream or half-
   and-half, scalded
1 to 2 teaspoons Worcestershire sauce or to taste
1 teaspoon celery salt or to
   taste
1/4 teaspoon white pepper
1/8 to 1/4 teaspoon seafood
   seasoning (optional) (see
   note)
4 to 5 drops hot sauce
   (optional)
2 teaspoons butter or
   margarine, divided and at
   room temperature
Paprika for garnish
Oyster crackers

In a small heavy skillet, sauté celery in melted butter over moderate heat until tender but not browned; set aside. In a medium heavy saucepan, cook oysters, including liquid, over moderate heat until edges of oysters begin to curl. Add scalded milk, cream, Worcestershire sauce, celery salt, pepper, seafood seasoning, and hot sauce, if desired. Stir in celery mixture; continue cooking for 1 to 2 minutes or until stew is heated through. *Do not boil.* Place 1/2 teaspoon butter in each soup bowl or mug. Ladle stew into individual bowls or mugs; sprinkle each lightly with paprika. Serve immediately accompanied with oyster crackers.

Note: Preferably use only Old Bay brand seasoning

–J. Robert Carlton.

Swedish Stew

2 1/2 Pounds Beef,, 1 Large Carrot, Sliced,, 2 Onions, Sliced,, 4 Cloves,, 3 Rounding Table-spoonsful Tapioca,, 1 1/4 Table-spoonsful Bread Crumbs,, 1 Table-spoonful Vinegar,, 1 Level Table-spoonful Salt,, Pepper,, Grated Nut-meg., Put into a baking dish or bean pot the beef, which should be of the stewing kind and cut in small pieces; add the carrot, onions, cloves, tapioca, bread crumbs, vinegar, salt, and a sufficient quantity of pepper and nutmeg. Cover tightly and bake in a hot oven five and one-half hours.

Old Virginia Cooking, *circa 1909*

Venison Stew

Yield: 10 servings

2 to 3 pounds boneless
  venison, cut into 3/4 to 1-
  inch pieces
3 to 4 tablespoons hot
  bacon drippings or
  cooking oil
Water as needed
1 lemon, thinly sliced, seeds
  removed
3 medium onions, peeled,
  thinly sliced, and divided
1 bay leaf, crumbled
1 teaspoon salt or to taste
1/8 to 1/4 teaspoon pepper
5 to 6 medium potatoes,
  peeled and quartered
4 medium carrots, peeled,
  halved lengthwise, and
  cut into 1 1/2-inch pieces
6 ribs celery, cut into 1 1/2-
  inch pieces
Boiling salted water as
  needed
Cold water as needed
1/4 cup flour
1/2 teaspoon curry powder,
  or to taste
2 to 3 medium tomatoes,
  peeled and cut into thin
  wedges

In a large heavy skillet or Dutch oven, brown venison thoroughly in bacon drippings over moderate heat. Add water to cover, lemon slices, two thirds of the onion slices, salt, and pepper. Simmer, uncovered, over low heat for 1 1/2 to 2 hours or until fork tender. In a large heavy saucepan cook potatoes, carrots, remaining onion and celery in boiling salted water to cover, until just tender. Remove from heat; drain and set aside. Remove lemon and onion slices and bay leaf from meat mixture. Blend a small amount of cold water into flour until smooth; add a small amount of meat broth to flour, mixing well. Gradually blend flour mixture into stew. Add curry powder and continue to simmer over low heat until thickened. Add prepared vegetables and tomatoes, if desired. Heat through.

Note: This stew may be prepared in advance and refrigerated for 2 to 3 days to allow flavors to blend. Do not add tomatoes until ready to serve.

> . . . the Jeffersons entertained small groups for dinner at home
> (at the rented "Palace," 1780, in Richmond). . .
>
> William Seal
> **Virginia's Executive Mansion:**
> **A History of the Governor's House**, 1988

Meats, Poultry, Fish, and Seafood

Savory He-Man Pepper Steak

Yield: 4 to 6 servings

"When I was the cook at Johnny's restaurant, located at 23rd and Marshall streets, this recipe was called Hungry He-Man's Quick Steak."

1 to 1 1/2 pounds beef round or cube steak, cut 1/4 to 1/2-inch thick
Meat tenderizer powder, as desired (optional)
2 tablespoons hot cooking oil or shortening, melted
1 medium to large firm ripe tomato, peeled and coarsely chopped or cut into thin wedges
1 medium onion, peeled and thinly sliced vertically into 2-inch pieces
1 medium green pepper, cored, seeded, and cut into thin 2-inch strips
2 to 3 teaspoons sugar
Salt or seasoned salt and pepper to taste

Sprinkle meat lightly with meat tenderizer; rub thoroughly into each side of steak, if desired. In a large heavy skillet, brown steak in oil over moderate heat, about 1 to 2 minutes per side. Add vegetables, sugar, salt or seasoned salt, and pepper. Reduce heat and simmer, cover ajar, for 10 to 15 minutes or until meat is tender and vegetables are crisp tender, but firm.

Note: Steak may be cut into thin 2 x 1/4-inch strips before browning in oil. Meat also may be dredged lightly in flour before browning.

Variation: 1 to 1 1/2 pounds thinly sliced (scallopine) veal or veal cutlets or fresh turkey breast cutlets or thinly sliced turkey tenderloin may be substituted for beef. The flavor will be substantially changed using veal or turkey.

–Vernelle Thomas

Beef Steak Pie

Cut nice steaks, and stew them till half done, put a puff paste in the dish, lay in the steaks with a few slices of boiled ham, season the gravy very high, pour it in the dish, put on a lid of paste and bake it.
The Virginia Housewife, *1831*

112

Grilled London Broil Teriyaki

Yield: 4 to 6 servings

2 garlic cloves, peeled and minced
1/2 cup soy sauce (see note)
1/4 cup dry white wine
2 tablespoons light brown sugar, firmly packed
1 teaspoon grated peeled ginger root
1 1/2 to 2 pounds boneless beef flank, sirloin tip, chuck, or top round steak, cut 1 to 1 1/4- inches thick

In a small bowl, combine the first 5 ingredients. Place beefsteak in a deep medium bowl or large ziplock plastic bag. Pour marinade over meat, coating well. Cover bowl or seal ziplock bag. Marinate beef at room temperature for 6 to 8 hours or refrigerate for 12 to 24 hours. Turn steak in marinade occasionally, basting well. Remove steak from marinade; drain well and arrange on a rack in a broiler pan. Broil, 4 to 6 inches from heat source, until desired degree of doneness, about 4 to 5 minutes per side for medium rare to medium. Or, arrange steak on a grill rack, 8 to 10 inches above medium charcoal coals (ash gray and glowing); grill about 10 to 14 minutes total, about 4 to 6 minutes per side for medium rare to medium. Brush steak liberally with remaining marinade frequently during broiling or grilling.With a sharp knife, cut steak diagonally across the grain into thin slices. Arrange steak slices on a heated platter and garnish as desired.

Note: Doneness of steak may also be determined by the touch test. With the forefinger, press the steak lightly. Rare steak will be very soft to the touch; medium rare, soft to firm to the touch; medium, springy firm to the touch, and well-done, hard (forget it!). When the steak is cut, the interior will be blood red for rare, red to pink for medium rare, light pink, no juices running for medium, and gray (sad) for well-done.

–Hal Tyler

No institution was more important in the social life of early Richmond than its taverns—also called inns or ordinaries, with the three terms used interchangeably. Men of the community gathered to eat or drink, to politick, to gossip, to play billiards, and to hear the latest news from travelers. After the capital was moved to Richmond, the local taverns incr
–Harry M. Ward and Harold E. Greer, Jr.
Richmond During The Revolution, 1775-83,
1977

Rolled Steak

Take a large, rather thin, sirloin steak. First fry a finely chopped onion in butter, lay the steak in this and fry quickly on both sides. Place on a large dish and cover with force meat made of minced fried onions, dry bread crumbs, a little sausage, oyster or chestnut dressing. Roll up tightly and tie with threads and fasten with skewers. Place in saucepan and cover closely. Add no water whatever, but set where it will slowly heat, and let it cook slowly for two hours. When ready to dish, thicken the gravy, which should be diluted with hot water, and remove the threads from the steak. Take out the skewers and pour the gravy over it.

–Old Virginia Cooking, *circa 1909*

The depot doors were forced open and a demoniacal struggle for the countless barrels of hams, bacon, whisky, flour, sugar, coffee, etc., etc., raged about the buildings among the hungry mob. The gutters ran whisky, and it was lapped as it flowed down the streets, while all fought for a share of the plunder. The flames came nearer and nearer, and at last caught in the commissariat itself...

Clement Sulivane, Captain, C.S.A.
"The Fall of Richmond,"
Battles and Leaders, 1887-88

Oriental Pepper Steak with Onions

Yield: 4 servings

Carrie and John Wong operated the Peking Restaurant in northern Virginia for thirteen years before moving to Richmond to open the Three Star Restaurant in August 1988 at 1600 Robin Hood Road in the near north side of Richmond near the Diamond baseball park. Specializing in mandarin and Cantonese cuisine, the restaurant has been enthusiastically received by local residents and visitors to Richmond.

1 pound boneless beef flank steak
4 teaspoons cornstarch, divided
3 1/2 teaspoons dry sherry, divided
4 teaspoons cooking oil, divided (see note)

With a sharp knife, cut beef across the grain into 1 1/2 x 1/2-inch strips. In a large bowl, combine 2 teaspoons cornstarch, 1 1/2 teaspoon sherry, 1 teaspoon oil, 1/2 teaspoon soy sauce, 1/2 teaspoon sugar, and 1/2 teaspoon salt, blending well. Add beef strips, coating meat well with marinade. Allow to marinate at room temperature for 30 minutes. Partially cook green peppers

2 1/2 teaspoons soy sauce, divided (see note)
1 teaspoon sugar, divided
1 teaspoon salt, divided
3 medium green peppers, cored, seeded, and cut into 2 x 1-inch pieces
1 garlic clove, peeled and minced
1/2 teaspoon minced peeled ginger root
4 teaspoons cold water
2 cups hot cooked long-grain rice (optional)

in a small amount of boiling water for 5 to 6 minutes or until tender but crisp; drain well and set aside. Heat a wok to a moderate high temperature (375 to 400 degrees F.); add 3 teaspoons oil and heat for 1 minute. Add garlic and ginger, stirring lightly. Add green pepper and onion; stir-fry for 20 seconds. Cover and cook for 3 minutes. Add 2 teaspoons sherry, 2 teaspoons soy sauce, 1/2 teaspoon sugar, and 1/2 teaspoon salt, blending well with the peppers and onion; stir-fry for 20 seconds. Drain beef and add to pepper-onion mixture. Stir-fry until beef strips are medium rare, browned on the outside but remain pink inside. In a cup; blend cold water into 2 teaspoons cornstarch until mixture is smooth; stir into meat mixture. Cook, stirring lightly, until sauce thickens slightly. Serve with hot cooked rice, if desired.

Note: Peanut oil is preferred for stir-fry cooking.

Note: Reduced sodium (Lite) soy sauce may be substituted for regular soy sauce. One teaspoon Lite soy sauce contains 100 milligrams of sodium

–Carrie and John Wong
Three Star Restaurant

Beef A-La-Mode

Take the bone from a round of beef, fill the space with a forcemeat made of the crumbs of a stale loaf, four ounces of marrow, two heads of garlic chopped with thyme and parsley, some nutmeg, cloves, pepper and salt, mix it to a paste with the yolks of four eggs beaten, stuff the lean part of the round with it, and make balls of the remainder; sew a fillet of strong linen wide enough to keep it round and compact, put it in a vessel just sufficiently large to hold it, add a pint of red wine, cover it with sheets of tin or iron, set it in a brick oven properly heated, and bake it three hours; when done, skim the fat from the gravy, thicken it with brown flour, add some mushrooms and walnut catsup, and serve it up garnished with force-meat balls fried. It is still better when eaten cold with salad.

Mrs. Mary Randolf
The Virginia Housewife, 1831

An Excellent Method of Dressing Beef

Take a rib roasting piece that has been hanging ten days or a fortnight, bone it neatly, rub some salt over it and roll it tight, binding it around with twine, put the spit through the inner fold without sticking it in the flesh-skewer it well and roast it nicely; when nearly done, dredge and froth it, garnish with scraped horse radish.

Mrs. Mary Randolph
The Virginia House-Wife *(first edition), 1824*

Antique Menu

(Cir. 1839)

Breakfast

Sliced Oranges
Bacon Griddle Cakes
Boiled Eggs
Coffee

Luncheon

Baked Potaoes (served with Butter and Milk)
Spring Onions Gluten Gems
Stewed Peaches
Cocoa

Dinner

Lamb Stew (made from ends of Sunday's forequarters)
Hash Browned Potatoes
Glazed Carrots
Fresh Tomato Salad
Cafe Frappe

Virginia Cook Book, 1839

In colonial days, a Dutch oven was not a heavy pot covered with a tight-fitting dome cover as we know it, but a portable metal box placed on the hearth with an open side turned toward the fire. It often contained metal shelves so that several food items could be baked at one time.

Tsmis

Yield: 6 to 8 servings

1 (4 to 5-pound) lean
  boneless beef chuck roast
About 3/4 to 1 cup flour,
  divided
1/4 cup hot cooking oil or
  shortening, melted
Salt and pepper to taste
1 teaspoon cinnamon,
  divided
20 pitted prunes
2 to 3 medium onions,
  peeled and quartered
2 medium lemons, thinly
  sliced and seeded
About 3 to 5 cups water,
  divided
6 to 8 medium carrots,
  peeled, halved length-
  wise, and cut into 2-inch
  pieces
4 medium white potatoes,
  peeled and quartered
4 medium yams or sweet
  potatoes, peeled and
  quartered
1/2 to 1 cup light brown
  sugar, firmly packed
1/2 cup cold water

Dredge meat thoroughly in 1/2 to 3/4 cup flour. In a Dutch oven or large heavy skillet, brown roast, all sides, in oil or shortening. Drain off fat. If using skillet, transfer meat to a roasting pan. Sprinkle roast lightly with salt and pepper and 1/2 teaspoon cinnamon. Add prunes, onions, and lemon slices. Pour about 3 to 4 cups of water over meat, prunes, and vegetables. Pot-roast, cover ajar, in a moderate oven (350 degrees F.) for 1 hour. Add carrots, white and sweet potatoes or yams to pan. Add additional 1/2 to 1 cup water, if necessary. Sprinkle brown sugar and remaining 1/2 teaspoon cinnamon over meat and vegetables. Continue to bake, cover ajar, in a moderate oven (350 degrees F.)for 2 hours or until meat and vegetables are fork tender. In a small bowl, blend cold water and 1/4 cup flour together until smooth. Gradually add to pan liquid, stirring lightly until blended. Continue cooking, uncovered, for 7 to 10 minutes or until gravy is thickened. Serve roast and vegetables with gravy.

–Sylvia Grossman (Mrs. Frank)

Beef Chuck Roast in Beer

Yield: 6 servings

2 shallots, peeled and chopped
1 medium onion, peeled and chopped
2 to 3 tablespoons hot cooking oil, divided
1 (4-pound) beef chuck roast
1 ripe medium tomato, peeled and chopped
1 (12-ounce) can beer
1/4 cup beef broth or consomme, undiluted
1 tablespoon minced fresh parsley or 1 teaspoon dried parsley flakes
1 tablespoon minced fresh or 1 teaspoon dried thyme
1 1/2 teaspoons minced fresh or 1/2 teaspoon dried rosemary
1 1/2 teaspoons salt or to taste
1/4 teaspoon nutmeg
1/4 teaspoon pepper
1/4 cup cold water
2 to 3 tablespoons corn-starch

In a Dutch oven, saute´ shallots and onion in 1 to 2 tablespoons oil over moderate heat until tender but not browned; remove shallots and onion with a slotted spoon. Add remaining tablespoon oil to pan. Brown chuck roast thoroughly in hot oil, about 2 minutes. Return shallots and onion to pan and add remainingingredients, except cold water and cornstarch. Bring to a simmer over moderate heat on top of the range; cover, remove from range,and bake in a slow oven (325 degrees F.) for 3 to 4 hours or until beef is fork tender, basting meat with pan drippings frequently. Remove from oven and skim or strain pan gravy to remove fat; pour drippings into a small heavy saucepan. Blend cold water into cornstarch until smooth, then blend mixture into pan gravy. Cook gravy, stirring constantly, over moderate heat until slightly thickened and bubbly hot. Cut roast into slices, arrange on dinner plates, and pass thickened beer gravy in a sauce boat.

–Linda M. Bourgeois (Mrs. Bruce)

Beef Steak and Radishes

Halve the radishes and fry in butter. Broil your steak, place on platter, surround with the fried radishes, arranging them as you would mushrooms, which they resemble.

Old Virginia Cooking, *circa 1909*

Easy Oven Barbecued Beef

Yield: 10 to 12 servings

1 (5-pound) boneless beef
  roast (see note)
4 beef bouillon cubes
5 to 6 cups water, divided
2 cups dry white wine or
  beer
1/2 cup Worcestershire
  sauce, divided
5 teaspoons chili powder,
  divided
2 bay leaves, crumbled
Salt and pepper to taste
2 garlic cloves, peeled and
  minced
1 cup chili sauce
1/2 cup cider vinegar
1/4 cup butter or margarine
2 tablespoons minced
  peeled onion
1 to 2 tablespoons light
  brown sugar, firmly
  packed
1 teaspoon prepared
  mustard
1 teaspoon paprika
1/4 teaspoon hot sauce
5 to 6 drops liquid smoke
  (optional)
10 to 12 hamburger buns or
  Kaiser rolls, split in half
  and buttered

Place beef in a large heavy roaster or Dutch oven. Combine bouillon cubes, 4 cups water, wine, 1/4 cup Worcestershire sauce, 2 teaspoons chili powder, and bay leaves in a small bowl; add to roaster. Bake, cover ajar, in a slow oven (325 degrees F.) for 3 hours or until fork tender, basting meat occasionally. When meat has browned, sprinkle lightly with salt and pepper to taste. While beef is pot-roasting, prepare sauce. In a medium heavy saucepan, combine garlic, chili sauce, 1 1/2 cups water, vinegar, 1/4 cup Worcestershire sauce, butter, onion, brown sugar, 2 to 3 teaspoons chili powder, mustard, paprika, 1/2 teaspoon salt, hot sauce, and liquid smoke. Bring to a boil over moderate heat, stirring constantly; reduce heat and simmer for 10 to 15 minutes.When meat is fork tender, remove from pan and shred with a fork. Remove bay leaves from pan; skim off fat from liquid (see note). Return meat to liquid in pan. Pour barbecue sauce over shredded meat, mixing well. Continue baking, uncovered, in a moderate oven(350 degrees F.) until mixture is thick, about 1 1/2 to 2 hours. Adjust seasonings to taste, if desired. Arrange buttered bun halves, buttered side up, on a rack in a broiler pan; broil, 6 to 8 inches from heat source, until bun halves are lightly toasted, about 2 minutes. Spoon barbecue onto one-half of the toasted bun halves, dividing evenly. Top each with a second toasted bun half.

Note: Use boneless chuck, or rump, or 7-bone, or cross-cut, or sirloin tip beef roast.

Note: If there is more than 2 cups liquid remaining in pan, use only 3 cups pan liquid with meat and sauce.

–Sarah Cardamone McBride (Mrs. Andrew S.)

119

In the South, where slavery existed to a much greater extent, the female head of the house was relieved of almost all manual labor. In its place was her share in the work of management of the plantation. True executive ability was required to care for both the family and the slave population with food, clothing, and medical attention. Domestic life was undoubtedly easier physically for the Southern woman.

In any colony most of the food was produced through every stage by the family itself. On farms, plantations, and even in small towns meat was raised, slaughtered, and cured at home. Wheat, oats, and corn were grown on home lands and, in the early days before grist mills, were made into flour and meal by the family. Fruit was dried or preserved, and herbs were grown, dried, and stored for later use.

A huge fireplace was the dominant feature of the Colonial kitchen and around it the life of every family seems to have centered. To start a fire required the uncertain use of flint and steel, so that it was kept alive, day and night, winter and summer, to avoid the chore of building a new one. If a fire died through inattention, live coals might be borrowed from another home to start a new fire.

Adelaide Hechtlinger
"Women in Early America,"
Early American Life, April 1973

Old Richmond Advertisement, date unknown

Barbecued He-Man Beef Brisket

Yield: 10 to 12 servings

1 large clove garlic, peeled,
and cut in half
1 (4 to 5-pound) boneless
beef brisket
1 tablespoon chili powder
1 teaspoon paprika
1 teaspoon salt or to taste
1/2 teaspoon sage
1/2 teaspoon cumin
1/2 teaspoon ground
oregano
1/2 teaspoon sugar
1/4 teaspoon cayenne
pepper or to taste
He-Man Barbecue sauce
10 to 12 Kaiser rolls or
onion buns, halved, but-
tered and toasted (op-
tional)

Rub garlic into brisket thoroughly. Combine chili powder, paprika, salt, sage, cumin, oregano, sugar, and cayenne pepper; rub thoroughly into brisket. Place a large sheet of aluminum foil in a shallow roasting pan. Arrange brisket in center of foil; close,sealing edges securely. Bake in a very slow oven (200 degrees F.)for 8 hours or until fork tender. Thinly slice brisket diagonally across the grain. Spoon barbecue sauce over each serving. Serve in toasted buttered Kaiser or onion rolls, if desired.

He-Man Barbecue Sauce

1 medium onion, peeled
and chopped
2 tablespoons butter or
margarine, melted
1/2 cup chili sauce
1/2 cup ketchup
1/2 cup water
1/4 cup cider vinegar
2 tablespoons Worcester-
shire sauce
2 tablespoons lemon juice
1 tablespoon molasses
2 teaspoons dry mustard
2 teaspoons salt or to taste
1/2 teaspoon pepper or to
taste
1/2 teaspoon paprika

In a heavy saucepan, saute´onion in butter over moderate heat until tender but not browned. Add remaining ingredients, blending well. Bring sauce to boiling; reduce heat and simmer, uncovered,for 30 minutes. Serve warm or at room temperature.

–Ginny Moss (Mrs. John Simpson)

121

The Mayor's Favorite Meat Loaf

Yield: 6 servings

2 slices white bread
Milk as needed
2 pounds lean ground beef
1/2 medium green pepper,
   cored, seeded, and
   chopped
1/2 medium onion, peeled
   and chopped
Salt and pepper to taste
1 (15-ounce) can tomato
   sauce, divided
1 cup water

In a large bowl, soak bread slices in enough milk to moisten bread thoroughly. Mash bread; add ground beef, green pepper, onion, and 1 tablespoon tomato sauce, mixing well. Season with salt and pepper to taste. Shape mixture into a round or oval loaf and place in a 1-quart casserole or 9 x 9 x 2-inch baking dish. In a 2-cup measure, combine tomato sauce and water, blending well; pour over meat loaf. Bake, uncovered, in a hot oven (400 degrees F.) for 10 minutes; reduce heat to slow (300 degrees F.) and continue baking for another 55 to 60 minutes or until meat loaf is done. Frequently baste meat loaf with sauce while baking. Allow meat to stand for several minutes before cutting into slices, spoon a small amount of sauce over each serving.

–Geline B. Williams
Mayor, City of Richmond, 1988 to 1990
Richmond City Council

Everybody Went to Work

Those who could cook, sold old-time dainties. Service was cheap, but for a while food prices were high. But a people who had faced starvation, with no bitterness or complaining, now thanked God for food....

Louisa Coleman Blair
"'Little Red Brick Town
In Era of Hoopskirts Was Friendly, Gossipy,"
Richmond Times-Dispatch, December 7, 1941

Flo's Mini Meat Loaves

Yield: 4 servings

1 pound lean ground beef
1 egg
1/4 cup soft breadcrumbs
   (see note)
1/4 cup milk
1 tablespoon minced peeled
   onion
1 teaspoon salt
1/4 teaspoon pepper

Sauce
1/2 cup ketchup or chili
   sauce
2 tablespoons Worcester-
   shire sauce
1 tablespoon vinegar
1 tablespoon chopped
   peeled onion
1/2 teaspoon chili powder

In a medium bowl, combine ground beef, egg, breadcrumbs, milk, 1 tablespoon minced onion, salt, and pepper, mixing well. Shape into 4 equal-sized individual loaves; arrange in a lightly greased 12 x 8 x 2-inch baking dish. In a small bowl, combine ketchup, Worcestershire sauce, vinegar, 1 tablespoon onion, and chili powder, blending well. Spoon sauce over meat loaves. Bake, uncovered, in a moderate oven (350 degrees F.) for 45 minutes, basting loaves frequently with sauce. Allow loaves to stand at room temperature for 5 to 10 minutes. With a sharp knife, cut loaves into slices. Spoon sauce over each serving.

Note: Prepare soft breadrumbs by crumbling day-old bread.

–Jane Hamlin (Mrs. Richard R.)

Virginia Cookery Book, circa 1921

Alice Bey's Spicy Pepperoni Meat Loaf

Yield: 4 to 6 servings

4 ounces (about 1 cup) thinly sliced pepperoni sausage (see note)
3 dried slices white bread, crumbled into crumbs
1 medium onion, peeled and chopped
1 egg, lightly beaten
2 tablespoons] commercially -bottled steak sauce (see note)
1 tablespoon milk
1 tablespoon dried minced onion
1 pound lean ground beef
1 1/2 teaspoons pepper or to taste
2 to 3 cups parslied buttered cooked noodles (optional)

In a large bowl, combine pepperoni, bread crumbs, chopped onion, egg, steak sauce, milk, dried onion, mixing well; allow mixture to stand for 2 minutes. Add ground beef, seasoned salt, and pepper, mixing well. Evenly pack mixture into a 9 x 5 x 3-inch loaf pan; smooth top of loaf. Bake, uncovered, in a moderate oven (350 degrees F.) for 45 minutes or until done. Drain off excess pan juices during baking. Cut meat loaf into medium slices and serve with hot parslied buttered cooked noodles, if desired.

Note: 4 ounces bulk pork sausage may be substituted for pepperoni, if desired. Brown sausage in a small heavy skillet over moderate heat; drain well.

Note: Preferably use A-1 steak sauce.

The Hotel Jefferson

The 3 o'clock dinner served each day in the week was something to be reckoned with. Sunday dinner, the table sparkling with cut-lass, was enough to knock anybody out.

Marcia Williams Sheerin
"Consider Lily: She Toiled Not,"
Richmond Times-Dispatch, Feb. 13, 1949

Cottage Pie

Yield: 8 to 10 servings

This typically English recipe, which might have been a favorite dish of early Virginia colonists, is adapted from a recipe for one hundred portions served at the popular Penny Lane Pub located in downtown Richmond, around the corner on Seventh Street from the Carpenter Center for the Performing Arts.

1 pound lean ground beef
Water as needed
1 beef bouillon cube mashed or 1 teaspoon beef base
Salt and pepper to taste
1 small onion, peeled and coarsely chopped
1 medium carrot, peeled and coarsely chopped
1/4 cup cold water
1 to 2 tablespoons flour
4 to 5 cups seasoned cooked mashed potatoes, divided
1 cup shredded sharp Cheddar cheese, divided

In a large heavy saucepan, brown ground beef over moderate heat, about 2 to 3 minutes. Add enough water to cover, and bouillon cube or beef base. Season to taste with salt and pepper. Bring to a boil over moderate heat; reduce temperature and simmer, uncovered, for 30 minutes. Add onion and carrots and additional water as necessary. Increase temperature to moderate and cook, uncovered, for about 12 to 15 minutes or until carrots and onions are tender but not mushy. Adjust seasoning. If a thicker gravy is desired, blend cold water and flour together until smooth; with a wire whisk blend flour mixture rapidly into meat mixture. Continue to cook, stirring constantly, until mixture is slightly thickened and bubbly hot. Spoon mixture into individual ramekins or casseroles, dividing evenly.

Fill a pastry bag with the seasoned cooked mashed potatoes; press mixture through pastry tube of bag in a decorative pattern around the edge of each filled ramekin. Sprinkle 2 tablespoons shredded sharp Cheddar cheese over the top of each casserole.

Arrange filled casseroles on an ungreased baking sheet. Bake in a moderate oven (350 degrees F.)for about 10 to 12 minutes or until cheese is melted and potato topping lightly browned. Or, broil, 8 to 10 inches from heat source, for 3 to 4 minutes or until cheese is melted and potato topping lightly browned. Serve immediately.

–Terry O'Neill, proprietor
John H. Mack, Jr., chef
Penny Lane Pub

Impossible Cheeseburger Pie

Yield: 6 to 8 servings

1 pound lean ground beef
1/2 to 1 cup chopped peeled onion
1/2 teaspoon salt or to taste
1/4 teaspoon pepper or to taste
3 eggs
1 1/2 cups milk
3/4 cup biscuit/baking mix
2 firm ripe medium tomatoes, thinly sliced (see note)
1 cup shredded sharp Cheddar, or Monterey Jack, or American cheese

In a medium heavy skillet, saute´ ground beef and onion over moderate heat until beef is browned and onion is tender but not browned; drain well. Spread mixture over the bottom of a greased 10-inch diameter pie plate. In a medium bowl, combine eggs, milk, and biscuit mix, beating until mixture is smooth; pour over ground beef. Bake in a hot oven (400 degrees F.) for 25 minutes. Arrange tomato slices over pie and sprinkle tomatoes evenly with cheese. Continue to bake for an additional 5 to 8 minutes, or until a silver knife inserted in center of pie comes out clean. Cool 5 minutes before cutting into wedges.

Note: If ripe tomatoes are unavailable, use one drained 16-ounce can of tomato wedges.

Variation: 8 ounces of crumbled mild or hot-spiced bulk sausage may be substituted for 8 ounces of the ground beef. Or, add 1 teaspoon commercial steak sauce, 1/2 teaspoon Worcestershire sauce, 1/2 teaspoon prepared Dijon-style mustard and 1/2 teaspoon garlic juice to beef mixture. Substitute seasoned salt for regular salt, if desired.

–Frances Williams

The Byrd and Shockoe warehouses used the Shockoe landing on the James River between what is today Fifteenth and Seventeenth streets. Shockoe landing was also known as the "Old Rock landing" because of a broad, flat rock located at the landing. The name "Shockoe" may come from the Indian word for stone—"Shacquonocan," as Capt. John Smith recorded it.

Harry M. Ward and Harold E. Greer, Jr.
Richmond During The Revolution, 1775-83, 1977

Ginny's Cheeseburgers

Yield: 4 to 6 servings

1/3 cup breadcrumbs
1/3 cup milk
1 pound lean ground beef
1 garlic clove, peeled and
minced (see note)
1 cup shredded sharp
Cheddar cheese
2 tablespoons chili sauce
1 teaspoon salt
1 teaspoon dry mustard
1 teaspoon Worcestershire
sauce
Hot toasted, buttered
hamburger buns or Kaiser
rolls

Combine breadcrumbs and milk for 5 minutes. Add ground beef, garlic, cheese, chili sauce, salt, mustard, and Worcestershire sauce, mixing well. Cover and refrigerate for 1 to 2 hours. Shape mixture into patties. Arrange patties on a rack in a broiler pan; broil, 4 to 6 inches from heat source, until cooked to desired degree of doneness, 3 to 4 minutes per side for medium rare and 5 to 6 minutes per side for medium, depending upon the thickness of the pattie. Or, grill on a rack over medium coals (ash gray and glowing) for 3 to 4 minutes per side for medium rare and 5 to 6 minutes per side for medium. Serve each in a hot toasted buttered bun with condiments.

Note: 1/2 teaspoon garlic powder or juice may be substituted for fresh garlic.

–Libby Teeter (Mrs. James L.)

127

Super Maid Rites

Yield: 6 to 8 servings

Teens, toddlers, and senior citizens alike love these satisfying, spicy ground beef sandwiches.

1 1/2 pounds lean ground beef
1 large onion, peeled and chopped
1 cup chili sauce
1/2 cup water
3 tablespoons light brown sugar, firmly packed
3 tablespoons Worcestershire sauce
1 teaspoon prepared mustard
4 to 5 drops hot sauce
Salt and pepper to taste
6 to 8 French or Kaiser rolls or onion buns, split in half and toasted
Sweet gerkins, pimento stuffed olives, and sweet cocktail onions for garnish

In a large heavy skillet, brown beef thoroughly over moderate heat; drain well, reserve drippings, and set aside. Saute' onion in reserved hot beef drippings until tender but not browned. Reduce heat and add chili sauce, water, brown sugar, Worcestershire sauce, mustard, and hot sauce, blending well. Stir in reserved ground beef. Add salt and pepper to taste. Simmer, uncovered, for 20 to 25 minutes or until mixture is bubbly hot and flavors blended. Spoon beef mixture onto one-half of each of 6 to 8 rolls or buns. Top each sandwich with a second roll half. Garnish each sandwich with sweet gerkins, pimento-stuffed olives, and sweet cocktail onions.

Swedish Meat Balls

1 1/2 lbs. round steak
2 eggs
1 1/2 lbs. fresh pork
2 onions (small)
1 cup bread crumbs
Salt, pepper
2/3 cup milk
Oil

Cut the meat in small pieces and chop fine. Beat eggs and milk together, add the bread crumbs and let soak. Peel and chop the onions fine, fry in some of the oil. Mix meat, soaked bread crumbs and onions, season to taste. Form balls and brown in hot oil, add some hot stock (made from bones and trimmings of the meat), cover and let simmer one-fourth hour. Remove the balls, add a spoonful of flour to the stock, stir well, add more stock if needed and pour over the balls.

Mrs. L. Aspegren
Virginia Cookery Book, *1921*

Going To Market As Richmond
Falls, April 3, 1865

Richmond was on fire. My first impulse was to go and see for myself what was happening in the lower part of the city. I was deterred, however, from carrying out this impulse at once by certain household duties. I had to go to market. Food was the scarce thing in Richmond towards the close of the war. Money, such as it was, was the most plentiful. It seemed to grow on trees. At the time of the evacuation, we had an unusual quantity of it, which, in consequence of its bulk, was kept in a box in a closet. Arming myself with the inconsiderable sum of $500, I sallied forth to make such purchases as I might be able to do for our day's need. When I arrived at the market-house I found only one butcher's stall open, and noticing here a piece of mutton about as big as my two fists, I asked the price. It was only after some persuasion that the kindly butcher let me have it for $250, which I paid at once. Then seeing a grocery store open on the next square, I went there, and offered to purchase several things, but could only get three quarts of blackeye peas, for which I paid $25 a quart. This closed my marketing operations for that day, and I went home with my mutton and peas in my basket, and $175 change in my pocket.

Richmond Dispatch February 3, 1902,
account of DallasTucker
In XXIX Southern Historical Society Papers

Savory 30-Minute Skillet Dinner

Yield: 4 servings

1 cup coarsely chopped
  peeled carrots
3/4 cup coarsely chopped
  celery
1 pound lean ground beef
1 cup coarsely chopped
  green pepper
1 cup coarsely chopped
  peeled onion
1/4 cup white or cider
  vinegar
1/4 cup chili sauce or
  ketchup
2 tablespoons sugar
1/2 to 1 teaspoon hot sauce
  or to taste
Salt and pepper to taste
2 to 4 cups hot cooked rice
  or noodles (optional)

In a small heavy saucepan, cook carrots and celery in boiling water to cover for 3 minutes; drain well. While carrots and celery are cooking, evenly brown ground beef in a large heavy skillet over moderate heat. Add green pepper and onion and continue cooking until vegetables are tender but not browned. Add partially cooked carrots and celery, vinegar, chili sauce, sugar, hot sauce, and salt and pepper to taste, mixing well. Reduce heat and simmer, uncovered, for 10 minutes. Serve over hot cooked rice or noodles, if desired.

–Vernelle Thomas

"Mookaws"

Yield: 4 to 6 entree or 10 to 12 appetizer servings

"This recipe has a most unusual flavor and receives raves from guests whether it is served as an entree over noodles or as an appetizer."

1 pound lean ground beef
1 egg, lightly beaten
2 slices day-old rye bread,
  crumbled
2 tablespoons grated peeled
  horseradish root
1 teaspoon caraway seeds
2 tablespoons butter or
  margarine, melted
1 1/2 tablespoons flour
1 (10 1/2-ounce) can beef

In a medium bowl, combine ground beef, egg, crumbled rye bread, horseradish, and caraway seeds, mixing well. Form into small balls, about 1/2 to 3/4-inch in diameter. In a medium heavy skillet or saucepan, brown meat balls evenly in butter over moderate heat. Reduce temperature and evenly sprinkle flour over meat balls and pan drippings, blending well. Gradually add beef broth, blending into flour-butter mixture. Bring to a boil over moderate heat. Reduce temperature and blend a small amount of thickened

130

broth or consomme´,
undiluted (see note)
1/2 cup sour cream
2 to 3 cups hot buttered
cooked noodles
Minced parsley for garnish

broth into sour cream. Stir broth-sour cream mixture into meatballs and sauce. Heat through. Serve over hot buttered noodles and sprinkle each portion with a small amount of parsley.

Variations: Add 1/2 to 1 teaspoon Dijon-style prepared mustard and salt and pepper to taste to sauce. Or, serve as an appetizer. Omit cooked noodles and minced parsley. Transfer meat balls and sauce to the brazier of a chafing dish to keep warm. Serve accompanied by wooden picks.

–Elizabeth Archer

....It was his habit to go to market every morning with his basket on his arm, and to return home with the marketing.... The Chief Justice had a decided convivial turn, and no one enjoyed more than himself the Saturday meetings of a famous club of which he was for many years, and to the time of his death, a member. This club was composed of the most eminent citizens—such men as Judge Marshall, John Wickham, Benjamin Watkins Leigh, Chapman Johnson, Daniel Call, Judge Nicholas, etc. There were skilful caterers among them, and their cooks were thorough masters of their art. The very pick of the market and the choicest liquors were provided for those occasions....They were held at Buchanan's Spring, then a nicely-shaded place at the head of Clay street (as now known). The long table stood under a frame structure, which sheltered it from sun and rain. It was there that those rare and dignified old gentry assembled once a week to drink, to eat, to pitch quoits, and to roll ten-pins. They threw off all ceremony and enjoyed themselves thoroughly—none more heartily than the good Chief Justice....

C. M. S.
William and Mary College
Quarterly Historical Magazine, January 1932

Chili

Richmonders vary on their Chili recipes, as do all Americans. One of America's favorite foods, it was originally named carne con chili (meat with chili peppers).

We can thank a German settler in New Braunfels, Texas at the turn of the nineteenth/twentieth century for our modern-day chili recipes. His invention of extracting the pulp from chili pods and mixing it with other spices led to the creation of chili powder.

One story suggests that nineteenth-century nuns living in San Antonio, Texas, prepared the dish made with minced meat, chili peppers, and beans. True chili afficionados do not add tomatoes or beans!

Red Hot Chili

Yield: 8 to 10 servings

2 pounds lean ground beef
1 medium onion, peeled and chopped
1 medium green pepper, cored, seeded, and chopped
1 garlic clove, peeled and chopped
1 (14 1/2-ounce) can tomatoes (including liquid)
1 (8-ounce) can tomato sauce
1 (12-ounce) bottle chili sauce
3 bay leaves, crumbled
1/4 cup chili powder
1 tablespoon prepared horseradish
2 teaspoons paprika
1 teaspoon lemon juice

In a Dutch oven or medium heavy pot, lightly brown ground beef over moderate heat. Add onion, green pepper, and garlic; continue to cook until vegetables are tender but not browned. Add remaining ingredients, except beans. Reduce heat and simmer, cover ajar, for 2 1/2 to 3 hours or until mixture is slightly thickened and bubbly hot. Add beans and continue to cook for 15 to 20 minutes. Chili may be cooled and then refrigerated for 24 hours to "ripen" and develop flavors.

1/2 teaspoon light brown
  sugar, firmly packed
1/2 teaspoon ginger
Salt to taste
4 (15-ounce) cans dark red
  kidney beans

–Rick Hamlin

Spicy Chunky Chili

Yield: 8 servings

3 pounds boneless beef
  chuck, cut into 3/4 to 1-
  inch cubes
2 tablespoons hot cooking
  oil
2 to 3 garlic cloves, peeled
  and minced
4 to 6 tablespoons chili
  powder
3 tablespoons flour
3 tablespoons minced fresh
  or 1 tablespoon dried
  oregano
2 teaspoons ground cumin
2 (13 3/4-ounce) cans beef
  broth or consomme´,
  undiluted and divided
1 teaspoon salt or to taste
1/4 teaspoon pepper or to
  taste
1 (15-ounce) can pinto
  beans, drained (optional)
1 cup sour cream for garnish
  (optional)
1 lime, cut into thin wedges
  for garnish (optional)

In a medium heavy pot or Dutch oven, brown beef cubes in oil over moderate heat about 2 to 3 minutes. In a small bowl, combine chili, flour, oregano, and cumin, mixing well. Sprinkle chili powder mixture over beef, stirring meat mixture with a wooden spoon to coat well. Stir in 1 1/2 cans soup, blending well with chili powder mixture. Add salt and pepper. Bring to a boil over moderate heat, stirring occasionally. Reduce heat; simmer, partially covered, for 1 1/2 hours, stirring occasionally. Add remaining broth; simmer an additional 30 minutes or until meat can be shredded with a fork. Cool thoroughly. Refrigerate, covered, for 12 hours to "ripen" flavors. Reheat chili in the top of a double boiler over boiling water or simmer in a heavy saucepan, stirring frequently, until chili is bubbly hot. Heat beans in a separate small heavy saucepan; drain and stir into chili, if desired. Garnish each serving with a dollop of sour cream and a lime wedge, if desired.

–Linda M. Bourgeois (Mrs. Bruce)

Orange Mustard Glazed Corned Beef

Yield: 8 to 10 servings

1 (5 to 6-pound) boneless corned beef brisket
Water
3 tablespoons pickling spice
About 3 to 4 tablespoons Dijon-style prepared mustard
About 1/2 cup light brown sugar, firmly packed
About 1 to 2 tablespoons orange juice
2 teaspoons grated orange peel

In a large heavy pot or Dutch oven, bring brisket to a boil in water to cover over moderate heat; reduce temperature, add pickling spice, and simmer, uncovered, for 3 1/2 to 4 hours or until fork tender. *Do not overcook.* Remove brisket from pot and allow to stand at room temperature for 15 minutes. Discard pot liquid.

Arrange cooked brisket in an 11 x 7 x 2-inch baking dish. Evenly spread mustard over top of brisket, coating well; allow to stand 10 to 15 minutes at room temperature until mustard flavor is absorbed by meat. In a small bowl, gradually blend about 1 to 2 tablespoons orange juice into brown sugar; glaze should not be too runny. Stir in orange peel. Evenly spread brown sugar mixture over mustard-coated brisket.

Bake, uncovered, in a moderate oven (375 degrees F.) for 15 to 20 minutes or until glaze is set. Allow corned beef to stand for about 15 minutes at room temperature before slicing. Serve warm or at room temperature. With a sharp knife, cut brisket across the grain into thin slices.

Variation: A 5 to 6-pound smoked pork shoulder may be substituted for the beef brisket. Arrange the pork shoulder on a rack in a shallow roasting pan. Insert a meat thermometer into the thickest part of the roast, being careful not to touch fat or bone. Bake, partially covered, in a moderate oven (350 degrees F.) until thermometer registers 160 degrees F., about 2 1/2 to 3 1/2 hours. Remove meat thermometer. With a sharp knife, remove layer of outside rind and fat from smoked shoulder. Arrange roast on a sheet of heavy-duty aluminum foil, shiny side turned in. Follow previous directions for mustard orange glaze. Loosely bring aluminum foil up around sides of smoked shoulder, leaving top uncovered. Spoon any glaze collecting in the bottom of the foil "container" over the top of the roast. A drained (11-ounce) can of mandarin oranges may be used to garnish the top of the smoked shoulder, if desired. Secure orange sections to the top of the smoked shoulder with wooden picks. Drizzle some of the glaze over the orange sections. Arrange foil enclosed roast on a baking sheet. Continue baking as previously directed for corned beef brisket with glaze.

Mustardy Beef Short Ribs

Yield: 4 servings

4 pounds beef short ribs, excess fat removed
Water as needed
2 1/2 teaspoons salt or to taste, divided
1/8 teaspoon pepper
1/2 cup cider vinegar
1/4 cup honey
1/4 cup minced peeled onion
2 tablespoons dry mustard
1 1/2 teaspoons minced fresh or 1/2 teaspoon dried tarragon
2 tablespoons chopped pitted green olives (optional)
2/3 cup sour cream

In a Dutch oven or large heavy saucepan, combine short ribs and 2 cups water. Cover and simmer over low heat for 1 hour, turning meat occasionally. Pour off drippings; season short ribs with about 2 teaspoons salt and 1/8 teaspoon pepper or to taste. Add 1/2 cup water to pan; cover and continue to simmer for 1 1/2 hours or until short ribs are fork tender.In a small heavy saucepan, combine vinegar, honey, onion, dry mustard, 1/2 teaspoon salt, and tarragon; simmer over low heat for 5 minutes, stirring frequently. Reserve 1/4 cup of the mixture for sour cream sauce. Remove meat from Dutch oven, draining well; arrange short ribs on a rack in a broiler pan. Brush meat liberally with glaze. Bake, uncovered, brushing short ribs with glaze frequently, in a moderate oven (350 degrees F.) for 20 minutes. In a small heavy saucepan, combine reserved 1/4 cup vinegar mixture and chopped olives; stir over low heat until bubbles begin to form. Gradually stir hot vinegar mixture into sour cream, blending well. Pass sauce in a sauceboat to serve with shortribs.

–Ladies' Missionary Society
Great Hope Baptist Church

Beef Olives

Cut slices from a fat rump of beef six inches long and half an inch thick, beat them well with a pestle; make a forcemeat of bread crumbs, fat bacon chopped parsley, a little onion, some shredded suet, pounded mace, pepper and salt; mix it up with the yolks of eggs, and spread a thin layer over each slice of beef,roll it up tight, and secure the rolls with skewers, set them before the fire, and turn them till they are a nice brown; have ready a pint of good gravy, thickened with brown flour and a spoonful of butter, a gill of red wine, with two spoonsful of mushroom catsup, lay the rolls in it, and stew them till tender;garnish with forcemeat balls.

The Virginia Housewife, *1831*

Roasted Leg O' Lamb with Tangy Glaze

Yield: 10 to 12 servings

1 (5 to 6-pound) leg of lamb *fat and fell removed* (see note)
Salt and pepper to taste
2 garlic cloves, peeled and minced
1 1/3 cups grape jelly or jam
1/2 cup cider vinegar
1 tablespoon minced fresh or dried thyme

Arrange leg of lamb on a metal rack in a roasting pan. Insert meat thermometer into thickest portion of roast, away from bone or fat; bake, uncovered, in a hot to very hot oven (425 to 450 degrees F.) until roast is lightly browned, about 25 to 30 minutes. Reduce heat to moderate (350 degrees F.), season roast with salt and pepper to taste, and bake, uncovered, 30 minutes per pound, until desired doneness, about 2 1/2 to 3 hours. Meat thermometer will register 140 to 150 degrees F. for medium rare,150 to 160 degrees F. for medium, and 170 degrees F. for well done. Cover roast loosely with aluminum foil, shiny side turned in, if roast becomes too brown. Baste roast liberally with glaze during the last 45 minutes of roasting. To prepare glaze, combine garlic, jelly, vinegar, and thyme in a small heavy saucepan; add salt and pepper to taste. Stir over low heat until jelly is melted. With a pastry brush, baste roast as previously directed.

Note: The "fell" is the thin paper-like material covering the fat of the roast. Removing the fell makes carving easier.

Note: Glaze may be reduced in half for use with a smaller roast.

–Leslie Davis Blackwell (Mrs. John D. Jr.)
Richmond TV personality

Baked Leg of Mutton

Take the flank off, but leave all the fat, cut out the bone, stuff the place with a rich forcemeat, lard the top and sides with bacon, put it in a pan with a pint of water, some chopped onion and cellery cut small, a gill of red wine, one of mushroom catsup and a tea-spoonful of curry powder, bake it and serve it up with the gravy, garnish with forcemeat balls fried.

Mrs. Mary Randolf
The Virginia Housewife, *1831*

Meats

All meats are better in winter for being kept several weeks, and it is well, in summer, to keep them as long as you can without danger of being tainted. IF it is not in your power to keep meat in an ice-house, in summer, keep it in a cool dark cellar, wrapped around with wet cloths, on top of which lay boughs of elderberry. The evaporation from the cloth will keep the meat cool and the elderberry will keep off insects.

If you should unfortunately be obliged to use stale meat or poultry, rub it in and out with soda, before washing it. Tough meats and poultry are rendered more tender by putting a little vinegar or a few slices of lemon in the water in which they are boiled. The use of an acid will save time and fuel in cooking them and will render them more tender and digestible.

If possible, keep the meat so clean that it will not be necessary to wash it, as water extracts the juices. When it is frozen, lay it in cold water to thaw, and then cook quickly, to prevent its losing its moisture and sweetness.

In roasting or boiling, use but little salt at first, as it hardens meat to do otherwise. In roasting, baste frequently, to prevent the meat from hardening on the outside, and try to preserve the juices. If possible, roast the meat on a pit before a large, open fire, after using salt, pepper, butter or lard, and dredging with flour. Where an open fire-place cannot be obtained, however, the meat may be well roasted in a stove or range. Mutton, pork, shote and veal should be well done, but beef should be cooked rare.

In boiling, put on salt meat in cold water, but fresh meat in hot. Remember also that salt meat requires more water and a longer time to cook than fresh. Boil slowly, removing the scum that rises when it begins to simmer. Keep a tea-kettle of boiling water at hand to replenish the water in the pot, as it boils.

Old Receipt
Source Unknown

Author's Note: The above recipe is as appropriate today as it was one hundred years ago.

Roast Leg of Lamb

Yield: 6 to 10 servings

1 (5 to 7-pound) leg of lamb, fat and *fell* removed (see note)
1 to 2 garlic cloves, peeled and halved
1/4 cup butter or margarine, at room temperature

Insert meat thermometer into thickest part of roast so it does not touch bone or fat. Rub meat with garlic and butter. If desired, cut garlic into small pieces; with a sharp knife, cut slits in the roast and insert garlic pieces. Roast, uncovered, in a slow oven (325 degrees F.), 30 to 35 minutes per pound or until meat thermometer registers 150 degrees F.(medium rare to medium) or desired degree of doneness. Remove from pan to hot platter; cover. Drain excess fat. Serve with Lamb Gravy or Mint Sauce.

Lamb Gravy
(Yield: 2 cups)
4 tablespoons reserved pan drippings
4 tablespoons flour
2 cups water
2 tablespoons Worcestershire sauce
1 teaspoon salt or to taste
3/4 teaspoon minced fresh or 1/4 teaspoon dried basil
1/4 teaspoon black pepper

Blend pan drippings with flour to form a smooth paste. Gradually add water and seasonings; cook over moderate heat, stirring constantly, until gravy thickens and begins to bubble. Reduce heat and simmer for 2 to 3 additional minutes.

Mint Sauce
(Yield: 1 1/2 cups)
2 tablespoons cornstarch
1 cup water
3/4 cup mint jelly
2 teaspoons lime juice
1 teaspoon lemon juice
1/4 teaspoon Worcestershire sauce
1/4 teaspoon salt
1/2 teaspoon minced fresh or 1/8 teaspoon dried mint or basil (optional)
1/8 teaspoon dried salad herbs (optional)

In a small heavy saucepan, blend cornstarch with small amount of water to form paste. Gradually add remaining water; cook, stirring constantly, until mixture is clear and thick. Remove from heat; add remaining ingredients. Continue cooking over low heat until jelly melts.

Note: The *"fell"* is the thin paper-like material covering the fat of the roast. Removing the fell makes carving easier.

Roasted Spiced Lamb

Yield: 6 to 8 servings

1 (4 to 5 pound) leg of lamb, fat and *fell* removed
1/2 cup soy sauce (see note)
1/4 cup tomato paste
1 1/2 tablespoons Worcestshire sauce
1 1/2 tablespoons lemon juice
1 1/2 tablespoons dry mustard or to taste
2 teaspoons sweet Hungarian paprika
1 1/2 teaspoons chili powder
3 tablespoons honey
3 tablespoons plum jam
About 1/4 cup chicken broth

Place lamb in a 13 x 9 x 2-inch baking dish. In a small bowl, combine the next 7 ingredients, blending well. Pour mixture over lamb; turn roast to coat all sides in marinade. Allow lamb to stand at room temperature, turning once, for 1 hour. Preheat oven to hot (400 degrees F.). Transfer roast to a metal rack in a large roasting pan; reserve marinade. Insert meat thermometer into the thickest part of the lamb, away from the bone. Reduce oven temperature to moderate (350 degrees F.); bake lamb, uncovered, for 1 hour. In a 1-cup measure, combine honey and jam, blending well. Liberally baste lamb with honey-jam mixture every 15 minutes until thermometer registers 150 degrees F. (medium rare to medium), about 1 hour. In a small heavy saucepan, gradually blend chicken broth into reserved marinade until desired consistency; stir over moderate heat until bubbly hot. With a sharp knife, cut lamb roast into thin slices, arrange on a platter, and garnish as desired. Pass hot marinade in a gravy or sauceboat to accompany meat.

Note: Reduce sodium (Lite) soy sauce may be substituted for regular soy sauce. One teaspoon Lite soy sauce contains 100 milligrams of sodium.

–Ann Tyler (Mrs. Hal)

Savory Grilled Leg of Lamb

Yield: 6 to 8 servings

1 (5 to 7-pound) leg of lamb, bone in (see note)
5 to 6 garlic cloves, peeled and cut into slivers
1 lemon, cut in half
Minced or dried fresh basil as needed
Salt and pepper as needed
Water-soaked hickory chips (optional)
Parsley-Orange Marinade
Thin orange slices and mint sprigs for garnish
Gravy

If desired, remove the thin paper-like covering of fat, called the "*fell*," to make carving easier. With a sharp knife, cut small slits into meat in several places and insert garlic pieces into slits. Rub outside of lamb with cut surface of lemon, then basil, salt, and pepper. Roast meat, uncovered, on a rack in a shallow baking pan in a slow oven (325 degrees F.) for 30 to 35 minutes per pound or until a meat thermometer registers 165 to 180 degrees F. Baste lamb occasionally with Parsley-Orange Marinade or marinate lamb in marinade for 1 to 2 hours prior to roasting. Transfer roast to a heated platter and garnish with thin orange slices and mint sprigs.

Note: Shank and aitch (H) bone may be removed from leg of lamb by butcher, if desired; roast should be rolled and tied.

Note: The "*fell*" is the thin paper-like material covering the fat of the roast. Removing the fell makes carving easier.

Gravy for Lamb: Drain off excess fat. Blend the meat drippings into 2 tablespoons flour and add enough water to equal 1 1/2 cups liquid; add salt and pepper to taste. Cook over moderate heat, stirring constantly, until slightly thickened and bubbly hot.

Parsley-Orange Marinade

1/2 cup butter or margarine, melted
1/4 cup orange juice
2 tablespoons minced parsley
2 tablespoons grated orange peel
1 tablespoon lemon juice

In a small sauce pan, combine all ingredients, blending well.

Rack of Lamb Sir Winston

Yield: 6 servings

The story goes that Sir Winston Churchill dearly loved the rack of lamb and mint sauce prepared by the renowned Chef, Jay Blair, at the Commander's Palace Restaurant in New Orleans shortly after World War II; however, Sir Winston sloshed the prepared dish liberally with Jim Beam bourbon! Jay decided to allow Mr. Churchill his Jim Beam as sippin' whisky and add a notable portion of the spirits directly to the sauce during preparation. As a protege of Jay's, Chef Stephen Hood was privileged to have Jay share the recipe with him.

6 seven-rib racks of lamb, about 1 pound each
Olive oil as needed
3 to 4 sprigs fresh rosemary, minced or 1 to 2 teaspoons dried rosemary
1/2 (16-ounce) loaf thinly sliced white bread (see note)
1 cup demi-glase (see note)
2/3 cup bourbon whisky (see note)
1/4 cup mint jelly
Additional sprigs of rosemary for garnish

Have a butcher remove the back bone from each lamb rack. With a sharp knife, remove layer of fat from outside area of lamb rack. With a smaller sharp knife, cut flesh away from between bones at opposite or boney side of lamb rack stopping 3/4 inch from loin area. Place prepared racks in a deep large bowl; add olive oil and rosemary to *just* cover lamb. Coat lamb racks well with marinade; allow to stand for at least 30 minutes or up to 1 1/2 hours. While lamb racks marinate, process dry bread slices in a food processor, blender, or mini chopper to make breadcrumbs. Or, roll bread slices, spread in one layer on a sheet of waxed paper and covered with a second sheet of paper, with a heavy rolling pin into crumbs. Remove lamb from marinade, draining well. To serve, cut through lamb racks between every other rib bone with a sharp knife. Arrange 3 cut-rib sections on each dinner plate; drizzle a small amount of warm sauce over each portion and garnish with a sprig of fresh rosemary, if desired.

Note: Allow bread slices to stand at room temperature for 24 hours if several-day-old bread is unavailable.

Note: Prepare 1 (1.2-ounce) package Demi-Glase (brown sauce) mix according to package directions. Or, prepare Basic Brown Sauce (see index).

Note: Preferably use Jim Beam bourbon whisky, as Sir Winston Churchill would have done.

Note: Use homemade or commercial mint jelly as desired.

–Chef Stephen Hood

La Petite France Restaurant

Restaurants come and go in Richmond; however, for the last two decades, one of the favorite dining choices remains La Petite France, " a little bit of France." Paul and Marie Antionette Elbling have indeed given Richmonders an excellent sampling of French cuisine as well as specialties utilizing food of Virginia. Paul, who presides over the kitchen, has won many awards, including gold medals as a member of the prestigious 1980 and 1984 Culinary Olympics held in Frankfurt, Germany. In addition, he finds finds time to act as an advisor, lecturer and teacher, and judge of culinary competitions, always with a mindful eye for maintaining high standards of his own kitchen.

While Paul orchestrates in the kitchen, Marie Antoinette takes charge in the dining room, reminiscent of a cozy, elegant private club.

Lamb Loin in Phyllo Pastry with Sweet Red Peppers

Yield: 4 servings

1 pound boneless lamb loin, cut into 4 equal pieces
About 2 to 3 tablespoons hot olive oil (see note)
8 mushrooms chopped
2 parsley sprigs, minced
1 medium sweet red pepper, cored, seeded, and chopped
1 medium onion, peeled and chopped
Salt and pepper to taste
Pinch of minced fresh or dried thyme

In a medium heavy skillet, lightly brown lamb pieces in olive oil over moderate heat; remove and set aside. Do not overcook. Add mushrooms, parsley, sweet red pepper, and onion to pan; stir in thyme, mixing well. Saute´ vegetable mixture in pan drippings over moderate heat until tender but crisp. Arrange a piece of lamb in the center of each phyllo pastry half sheet. Spoon one-fourth of the sauteed vegetable mixture onto each piece of lamb. Bring corners of each pastry sheet up and together; twist corners of pastry together to close and seal. Tie a leak stem around twisted portion of each pastry top. Lightly spray each lamb-in-pastry with vegetable cooking spray; arrange pastries on a baking sheet

142

2 phyllo pastry sheets, each cut in half (see note)
4 thin leek or green onion stems
Vegetable cooking spray
Julienne strips of desired vegetables and sprigs of fresh thyme for garnish

coated with vegetable cooking spray. Bake in a moderate oven (375 degrees F.) for 20 minutes. Arrange lamb pastries on each of 4 dinner plates. Garnish each plate with julienne strips of desired vegetables and a sprig of fresh thyme.

Note: Use a premium quality extra virgin olive oil. Extra virgin refers to the oil collected from the first press of the olives.

–Chef Paul and Marie Antionette Elbling
La Petite France Restaurant

Old Richmond Advertisement, circa 1909

Lamb Steak Marinade

Yield: 4 to 6 servings

4 to 6 lamb steaks, leg or
shoulder, cut 3/4 inch
thick
1 garlic clove, peeled and
halved
1 small onion, peeled and
thinly sliced
1 teaspoon Worcestershire
sauce
1/2 teaspoons minced fresh
or 1/2 teaspoons dried
thyme
3/4 teaspoons minced fresh
or 1/4 teaspoons dried
oregano
1 cup clear French dressing

Rub steaks with garlic. Add garlic, onion and spices to French dressing in shallow bowl. Place steaks in marinade, cover, and refrigerate several hours, turning frequently. Place steaks on a rack in a broiler pan, 6 to 8 inches from heat source; brush each liberally with marinade. Broil 5 minutes per side or to desired doneness.

To Harrico Mutton

a rich gravy out of the inferior parts, season it well with pepper, a little spice, and any kind of catsup you choose; when sufficiently done, strain it, and thicken it with butter and brown flour, have some carrots and turnips cut into small dice and boiled till tender, put them in the gravy, lay the chops in and stew them fifteen minutes; serve them up garnished with green pickle.

Mrs. Mary Randolf
The Virginia Housewife, *1831*

Old Richmond Advertisement, circa 1895

Lamb with Wine Sauce

Yield: 4 to 6 servings

1 1/2 pounds lamb shoulder, cut into 1-inch cubes
2 cups thinly sliced mushrooms
1/4 cup butter or margarine, melted
1 cup Thick White Sauce
3 tablespoons dry sauterne or other dry white wine
2 tablespoons Worcestershire sauce
1/2 teaspoon salt or to taste
1/2 teaspoon garlic juice
1/2 teaspoon sweet Hungarian paprika
1/8 teaspoon coarsely ground black pepper
1/8 teaspoon browning and seasoning sauce
1 (16-ounce) can very small potaoes, drained
1 (10-ounce) package frozen peas
1/3 cup chopped pimento, drained
Hot buttered noodles or rice (optional)
Minced parsley for granish

In a large heavy skillet, saute′ mushrooms in butter over moderate heat until tender. Drain mushrooms, set aside; reserve drippings. Brown meat in hot mushroom drippings. While meat is browning, prepare Thick White Sauce; reduce heat and add sauce to meat. Blend in wine, seasonings, mushrooms, pimento, peas and potatoes. Simmer over low heat 25 to 30 minutes. Serve with buttered noodles or rice if desired, and sprinkle with minced parsley.

Thick White Sauce
Yield: about 1 cup
Melt 3 tablespoons butter or margarine in a small heavy saucepan over low heat. Blend in 3 tablespoons flour to form a paste. Gradually add 1 cup milk, stirring constantly. Cook over moderate heat, stirring constantly, until sauce thickens and begins to boil. Remove from heat.

Apple 'N Honey Tagine
(Moroccan Lamb with Couscous)

Yield: 6 to 8 servings

2 pounds boneless lamb, cut into bite-sized pieces
2 tablespoons hot olive or other cooking oil
1 large onion, peeled and minced
2 teaspoons cinnamon
1 teaspoon salt or to taste
1/2 teaspoon coarsely ground black pepper
1/4 teaspoon crushed saffron
1/4 teaspoon ground ginger
Water as needed
2 pounds tart apples, peeled, cored, seeded, and chopped (see note)
1/4 cup honey
1 tablespoon sugar
1 (10-ounce) package couscous

In a Dutch oven or medium heavy pot, sear lamb in oil over moderate heat; add onion, cinnamon, salt, saffron, pepper, and ginger, mixing well. Add water to cover. Bring to a simmer; reduce heat and continue to simmer until lamb is very tender, about 1 1/2 to 2 hours. Add water as necessary so that pot does not become dry. Add apples, honey, and sugar; continue to cook until apples are tender, about 30 minutes. Cook couscous according to package direction. When apples are tender, correct seasonings to taste; pour meat mixture, including juice, into a serving bowl or tagine, Moroccan serving tureen. Serve with couscous.

Note: Use McIntosh, Winesap, Granny Smith, or other tart variety of apples.

–Elinor Kuhn (Mrs. Frank)
Buffet, catering firm
Richmond Culinary Guild

Luscious Lamb Casserole

Yield: 6 servings

1 1/2 cups sliced
  mushrooms
3 tablespoons butter or
  margarine
1 1/2 pounds ground lamb
1 (10 3/4- ounce) can cream
  of mushroom soup,
  undiluted
2 cups blanched cut fresh or
  1 (10-ounce) package
  frozen cut green beans,
  thawed
2 tablespoons
  Worcestershire sauce
3/4 teaspoon minced fresh
  or 1/4 teaspoon dried
  basil
1/2 teaspoon minced peeled
  garlic
1/2 teaspoon salt
1/8 teaspoon coarsely
  ground pepper
6 pimento slices, coarsely
  chopped and drained
1/4 cup slivered blanched
  almonds

In a large heavy skillet, sauté mushrooms in butter or margaine over moderate heat until tender but not browned; drain, and set aside. Brown meat in mushroom drippings over moderate heat. Reduce heat; add soup, green beans, seasonimgs, pimento, and almonds. Continue cooking over low heat until mixture is well blended and bubbly hot. Transfer mixture to a 9x9x2-inch baking dish and top with individual Curry Biscuits. Bake in a hot oven (450 degrees F.) 10 to 15 minutes or until biscuits are done and lightly browned.

Curry Biscuits

(Yield: 6 large biscuits)

1/2 teaspoon curry powder
3/4 teaspoon minced fresh
  or 1/4 teaspoon dried
  basil (optional)
2 cups biscuit/baking mix
3 tablespoons butter or
  margarine, melted
1/2 cup cold water
Paprika for garnish
  (optional)

In a medium bowl, combine biscuit/baking mix, curry powder, and basil, if desired, together, mixing well. Add melted butter and cold water; mix with a fork to form a soft dough. Spoon dough onto casserole forming individual biscuits. Sprinkle each biscuit lightly with paprika, if desired.

147

Saucy Lamb Patties

Yield: 4 servings

1 pound lean ground lamb
1 egg, slightly beaten
1/4 to 1/2 cup chili sauce
3 tablespoons
  Worcestershire sauce
1/2 teaspoon salt or to taste
1/2 teaspoon minced peeled
  garlic
1/8 teaspoon pepper or to
  taste
4 drops Tabasco sauce or to
  taste
6 bacon slices
Wooden picks

In a medium bowl, mix all ingredients, except bacon, together. Shape mixture into equal-sized patties; wrap bacon around patties and fasten with wooden picks. Arrange patties on a rack in a broiler pan, 8 to 10 inches from heat source. Broil about 5 to 7 minutes per side, according to desired degrees of doneness.

Note: If patties are of too "wet" a consistency, 1 to 2 tablespoons breadcrumbs may be added to meat mixture.

New Year's Day 1864 In A Well To Do Richmond Boarding House

My boarders during the last years of the war used to pay me about $900 a month, and we used to estimate the expenses of running our house at about $300,000 a year. Fancy this sum for household expenses, but you must remember that we were using Confederate money, and, as Mrs. Semmes used to say, we would send a whole basketful of money to market in exchange for provisions.

Thomas J. Semmes,
in **XXV Southern Historical Society Papers.**

Roasted Pork Loin with Herbed Apple Stuffing

Yield: 12 to 16 servings

1 (4-pound) boneless pork
    loin
2 cups herbed stuffing mix
1 tart medium apple,
    peeled, cored, seeded,
    and chopped (see note)
3/4 cup chopped celery
1/2 cup chopped peeled
    onion
2 tablespoons minced or 2
    teaspoons fresh sage
2/3 cup water
1/2 cup butter or margarine
1 egg, slightly beaten

If roast is rolled and tied, remove strings and open roast flat. (The roast may need to be slit lengthwise with a sharp knife 7/8 of the way through the meat to lay flat.) Or, the roast may be cut into two pieces lengthwise with a sharp knife, if desired.

In a medium bowl, combine stuffing mix, apple, celery, onion, and sage, mixing well. In a small heavy saucepan, melt butter in water over low heat; stir into stuffing mixture. Add egg, mixing well. Spread mixture over flattened roast; or if roast is in two pieces, spread mixture completely over one of the pieces. Arrange second piece of meat over the stuffing mixture, closing roast pieces together. Tie pieces of string around roast, about 2 to 3 inches apart, or secure roast pieces together with long wooden or metal skewers.

Arrange stuffed roast on a rack in a shallow roasting pan. Insert a meat thermometer into the center of the roast, away from fat. Bake, uncovered, in a moderate oven (350 degrees F.) until meat thermometer registers 170 degrees F., about 2 to 2 1/2 hours. Allow roast to stand, covered with aluminum foil, for 5 to 10 minutes before slicing. Remove strings or skewers and cut roast with a sharp knife into medium thick slices. Pan drippings may be used to prepare gravy, if desired.

Any leftover, uncooked dressing may be spooned into a greased 8 1/4 x 4 1/2 x 2 1/2-inch loaf pan and baked immediately, covered, in a moderate oven (350 degrees F.) for 40 to 45 minutes or until done. Cover may be removed during last 10 minutes of baking, if desired. Refrigerate, covered, until ready to serve; reheat, covered, in a moderate oven (350 degrees F.) for 15 minutes or until heated through.

Note: Use McIntosh, Winesap, Granny Smith, or other tart variety of apples.

Roast Pork with Savory Sauces

Yield: 6 to 8 servings

1 1/2 cups dry red wine
2 bay leaves, crumbled
1 1/2 teaspoons minced fresh or 1/2 teaspoon dried marjoram
1 teaspoon Worcestershire sauce
1/2 teaspoon minced peeled garlic
1 (2 to 3-pound) boneless pork loin, rolled and tied
Tomato Pepper Sauce or Herbed Wine sauce
Watercress sprigs for garnish (optional)

In a 2-cup measure, combine wine, bay leaves, marjoram, Worcestershire sauce, and garlic. Place pork loin in a deep medium bowl; pour marinade over roast, cover, and refrigerate for at least 12 hours, turning roast in marinade frequently. Remove roast from marinade and place in a 9 x 9 x 2-inch baking pan or small roaster; pour about 1/2 cup marinade over roast. Insert meat thermometer into center of roast. Reserve remaining marinade for Herbed Wine Sauce. Roast pork loin, uncovered, in a moderate oven (350 degrees F.) for 1 1/2 to 2 hours or until meat thermometer registers 160 degrees F. Baste with pan liquid frequently. Skim fat from pan drippings. If serving roast with Tomato Pepper Sauce, prepare sauce and spoon over roast. Continue baking roast, with either sauce, until meat thermometer registers 170 degrees F. With a sharp knife, cut roast into slices and arrange on individual plates. Spoon Tomato Pepper Sauce or Herbed Wine Sauce over each portion and garnish with a sprig of fresh watercress.

Tomato Pepper Sauce
(Yield: about 2 1/2 to 3 cups)
1 (16-ounce) can tomatoes, including liquid
1/2 small onion, peeled and coarsely chopped
1/2 small sweet red pepper, cored, seeded, and coarsely chopped
1/2 cup dry red or white wine
3 to 4 tablespoons roast pork pan drippings
2 to 3 teaspoons Worcestershire sauce
1 1/2 teaspoons minced

In a blender container, combine all ingredients; whiz at modertate to high speed until tomatoes, onion, and sweet red pepper are puréed. Strain and process as directed in recipe for roast pork loin. Or, serve with other meats. Pour sauce into a medium heavy saucepan and bring to a simmer over moderate heat. Reduce temperature and simmer, uncovered, for 15 to 20 minutes, or until sauce is slightly thickened and bubbly hot.

fresh or 1/2 teaspoon
dried marjoram
1/2 teaspoon minced peeled
  garlic
Salt and pepper to taste

Herbed Wine Sauce
(Yield: about 1 1/2 cups
  sauce)
1 cup reserved red wine
  marinade from pork roast
2 tablespoons chili sauce
2 tablespoons roast pork
  pan drippings (see note)
1 to 1 1/2 tablespoons flour
1/2 teaspoon prepared
  Dijon-style mustard
Salt and pepper to taste

Remove bay leaves from marinade. In a small heavy saucepan, combine 1 cup marinade, chili sauce, pan drippings, flour, and mustard, blending well with a wire whisk. Cook, whisking constantly, over moderate heat until sauce is slightly thickened and bubbly hot. Season with salt and pepper to taste.

Note: Roast beef or veal pan drippings may be substituted for pork pan drippings.

Variation: a (2 to 3-pound) pork tenderloin or boneless veal loin may be substituted for boneless pork loin. Pork tenderloin will only require about 1 hour of roasting as it is not as thick as a pork loin. Roast veal should be roasted in a slow oven (325 degrees F.) and partially covered to insure tenderness and moistness of roast. The meat thermometer should register 170 degrees F. for all roasts before serving.

Old Virginia Roast Pig

A fat pig about three weeks old is best for a roast. Wash it out thoroughly inside and out. Chop the liver finewith bread-crumbs, onions, parsley, pepper, salt, andpotatoes boiled and mashed. Make a paste with butter and egg. Put the stuffing into the pig and sew it up. Put in abaking pan with a little water and roast over a bright fire, basting well with butter; rub frequently, also, with a piece of lard tied in a clean rag. When thoroughly done, lay the pig back up on a dish, and put a red apple or pickled mango in the mouth, Make a sauce with some of the stuffing, a glass of wine, and some of the dripping. Serve with the roast pig, and also in a gravy boat.
                    (Old recipe, Highland Springs, date unknown)
                    The Williamsburg Art of Cookery, *1938*

Culinary Guild

In 1981, the Richmond Culinary Guild was formed as a means of establishing communication between people connected in some way with food in Richmond. Members include foodwriters, caterers, cooking school teachers, photography foodstylists, restaurant owners, and many non-professional devote's of the culinary arts. The Guild recruits nationally acclaimed culinary personalities to Richmond to present cooking schools and clinics. Such well-known culinary authorities as Jacques Pepin, Paula Wolfert, Richard Sax, Nina Simond, and Juliano Bugialli have demonstrated their talents to the members and guests. The Guild has co-sponsored with Historic Richmond Foundation, Taste of Virginia, a statewide food restaurant presentation and tasting in Richmond for the public. Members have been selected as judges for active food competitions held in the area. Vintage wine tastings have also been arranged and sponsored by the Guild to promote increased interest and awareness in food and wine excellence throughout the community. The Culinary Guild recently sponsored a $300 scholarship at the Johnson and Wales Culinary College in Norfolk, Virginia, designating the money be used toward the professional training of a deserving student of the culinary arts.

Pungent Pork Tenderloin

Yield: 10 to 12 servings

1 (3 to 3 1/2-pound) pork tenderloin, boned, rolled, and tied
3 tablespoons Dry Marinade, divided
1 garlic clove, peeled and minced
1 tablespoon olive oil
1 teaspoon crushed rosemary (see note)
1/2 medium onion, peeled

Wipe tenderloin with absorbent paper and slightly loosen string around roast. Using about one-half of the Dry Marinade, rub mixture into center and over the outside of the tenderloin, including ends. (Placing marinade on a sheet of waxed paper and rolling tenderloin in mixture works well.) Cover meat and allow to marinate in the refrigerator for 12 to 24 hours. About an hour before roasting, remove tenderloin from the refrigerator. In a 1-cup measure, combine garlic, olive oil, and rosemary; rub over tenderloin. Ar-

and thinly sliced
1 (13 3/4-ounce) can beef
consomme, undiluted
1/2 cup dry white wine
Turnip Cups, Sliced Sweet
Potatoes in Sherry, and
Buttered Brussel Sprouts
with Walnuts (optional)
(see index)

range tenderloin on a rack in a roasting pan or a 12 x 8 x 2-inch baking pan. Insert a meat thermometer into the center of tenderloin. Bake, uncovered, in a moderate oven, (350 degrees F.) about 25 to 30 minutes per pound until meat thermometer registers 170 degrees F.. Do not overcook. In a small heavy saucepan, combine onion, consommé, and wine; cook over moderate heat until liquid is reduced by half. Remove roast to a cutting board and cover with aluminum foil. Strain reduced liquid into roasting pan, discarding onion. Scrape pan, loosening bits and pieces of drippings. Pour liquid back into saucepan; simmer, uncovered, for 3 to 4 minutes. Remove string from tenderloin;separate loin. With a sharp knife, cut each half into thin slices. Arrange sliced pork on a heated platter or individual dinner plates. Skim fat from hot gravy and spoon a small amount over pork. Pass remaining gravy in a gravy boat or sauce boat. Serve with Turnip Cups, Sliced Sweet Potatoes in Sherry, and Buttered Brussel Sprouts with Walnuts, if desired.

Dry Marinade (see note)
20 bay leaves
1 whole star anise
2 tablespoons oregano
1 tablespoon toasted
Szechuan peppercorns
1 tablespoon whole cloves
1 tablespoon nutmeg
1 tablespoon thyme
1 tablespoon mace
1 tablespoon whole allspice
1 tablespoon black
peppercorns
1 tablespoon paprika
2 teaspoons cinnamon
2 teaspoons basil

Grind all ingredients together in a blender container or mini-chopper until powdery; store, covered, in an airtight container in a dry cool area. Dry marinade may be used with fresh pork or poultry recipes. It is an excellent salt substitute.poultry recipes. It is an excellent salt substitute.

Note: All herbs used in the recipe and marinade are crushed and dried. Whole spices are designated.

–Elinor Kuhn (Mrs. Frank)
Buffet, catering firm
Richmond Culinary Guild

Roasted Stuffed Pork Shoulder

Yield: 6 to 8 servings

1 (5 to 6-pound) fresh or smoked pork shoulder roast, boned (see note)
Salt and pepper to taste
5 bacon slices, crisp cooked, drained, and crumbled
1 1/2 cups breadcrumbs
1 1/2 cups chopped peeled apples
1 tablespoon minced parsley
1 large onion, peeled and chopped, divided
1 tablespoon minced green pepper
1/2 teaspoon minced fresh or 1/8 teaspoon dried marjoram
1/2 teaspoon minced fresh or 1/8 teaspoon dried thyme
1/2 teaspoon ground cloves
1/2 teaspoon nutmeg
Long thin metal or wooden skewers
1 rib celery, chopped
1 bay leaf, crumbled
1 1/2 cups cold water

Lay boned pork shoulder out flat; season lightly with salt and pepper to taste. In a medium bowl, combine bacon, breadcrumbs, apples, parsley, 1 tablespoon onion, green pepper, marjoram, thyme, cloves and nutmeg, mixing well. Pack mixture evenly over meat. Bring sides of roast together, closing tightly. Fasten with long metal or wooden skewers. Close ends allowing a small hole and fasten with skewers. Arrange stuffed pork shoulder on a rack in a shallow roasting pan. Insert a meat thermometer into the center of the roast. Add remaining chopped onion, celery, bay leaf, and water to pan. Bake, uncovered, in a very hot oven (450 degrees F.) for 25 minutes, turning roast frequently. Reduce heat to moderate (375 degrees F.) and continue baking for 2 hours or until meat thermometer registers 170 degrees F. and roast is fork tender, basting frequently with pan juices. Allow roast to stand, covered, at room temperature for several minutes before slicing. Garnish as desired.

Note: Butcher may remove bones from a bone-in roast, if desired. A 3 to 4-pound boneless, rolled, and tied pork loin may also be used.

–Linda M. Bourgeois (Mrs. Bruce)

Barbecues were popular in Colonial Virginia where sturgeons (long gone from local waters) and hogs were roasted over lice wood coals

Grilled Spicy Cranberry Picnic (Pork Shoulder)

Yield: 8 serving

1 (4- to 6-pound) fresh pork shoulder roast (see note)
2 cups sweetened or artifically sweetened cranberry juice (see note)
1/4 cup light brown sugar, firmly packed
1 tablespoon minced peeled onion
1 teaspoon chili powder
1/4 teaspoon ground cumin
1/4 teaspoon cinnamon
1/4 teaspoon salt
1/8 teaspoon pepper
2 teaspoons cornstarch (see note)

Place roast in a large deep glass or ceramic bowl.Combine cranberry juice, brown sugar, onion, chili powder, cumin, cinnamon, salt, and pepper, blending well. Pour marinade over meat, cover with clear plastic wrap, and refrigerate for 8 to 10 hours. Arrange 20 charcoal briquets on each side of barbecue firebox; place drip pan in center. Place greased grill 4 to 6 inches above drip pan. Remove picnic from marinade, draining well. Reserve 1 cup marinade for sauce (see note). Insert a meat thermometer into the center of the roast being careful not to touch fat or bone. Arrange meat on grill directly over drip pan and medium coals (ash gray and glowing). Cover barbecue, adjusting dampers according to manufacturer's directions. Or, cover meat loosely with heavy-duty aluminum foil, not touching meat thermometer and leaving ends open slightly. Roast, basting every 30 minutes with remaining marinade, for 3 to 3 1/2 hours or until meat thermometer registers 170 degrees F. Add 5 to 6 charcoal briquets on each side of fire every 30 minutes to maintain a constant temperature. In a small heavy saucepan, blenda small amount of the 1 cup reserved marinade into cornstarch until smooth. Gradually add remaining reserved marinade, blending well. Cook, stirring constantly, over moderate heat until mixture is thickened and bubbly hot. Slice roast and transfer to a heated platter. Spoon sauce over each serving.

Oven Method: Roast meat, uncovered, on a rack in a shallow baking pan in a slow oven (325 degrees F.) for 40 to 45 minutes per pound or until a meat thermometer registers 170 degrees F., basting with marinade as previously directed.

Note: Fresh indicates pork is not smoked.

Note: 1 cup orange juice may be substituted for 1 cup cranberry. Add 1 tablespoon grated orange peel to marinade. Or, use 1/2 cup cranberry juice and 1/2 cup orange juice in place of 1 cup cranberry juice.

Note: May increase marinade reserved for sauce to 2 cups and use4 teaspoons cornstarch, if desired.

Barbecue

Early English settlers in Virginia found Indians using a method of barbecuing as a manner of cooking meat. Unfamiliar with the techniques, the colonists soon copied their ideas. One method of cooking was to spit a haunch of meat on a stick suspended over an outdoor open fire. The stick was soon replaced by a grill. Another method evolved in which a trench was dug in the ground to contain the fire, whose heat would be confined and used more efficiently in cooking. Pork became the favored meat of the Virginians as pigs were fairly easy to transport by boat from the old to the new world. The early colonists could easily be described to have been eating high on the hog. William Byrd suggests that Virginians were eating so much pork they were becoming "extremely hoggish in their temper....and prone to grunt rather than speak." Today in Virginia, barbecue still denotes pork rather than beef or other meat.

Piquant Southern Barbecue

Yield: 12 to 16 servings

1 (3 to 4-pound) boneless pork loin, boned, rolled, and tied
Water as needed
1/2 cup cooking oil
1/2 cup lemon juice
1/2 cup red wine vinegar
1/4 cup soy sauce (see note)
2 tablespoons Worcestershire sauce
1 tablespoon dark corn syrup or to taste
2 teaspoons liquid smoke flavoring or to taste
Tabasco sauce to taste
Hamburger or onion buns,

In a large heavy pot or Dutch oven, combine pork loin and water to cover thoroughly; bring to a boil over moderate heat. Reduce temperature and simmer, cover ajar, for 2 1/2 to 3 hours or until meat shreds easily with a fork. Drain well and cool. With a fork, shred meat. In a small bowl, combine oil, lemon juice, vinegar, soy sauce, Worcestershire sauce, corn syrup, smoke flavoring, and Tabasco sauce. In a small roaster, combine shredded pork and barbecue sauce, mixing well. Bake, uncovered, in a moderate oven (350 degrees F.) for 2 to 3 hours or until pork mixture is reduced by one-half. Serve hot, on toasted buns, with Refrigerator Slaw, if desired.

split in half, buttered, and
  toasted (optional)
Refrigerator Slaw (see
  index) (optional)

Note: Reduced sodium (Lite) soy sauce may be substituted for regular soy
  sauce. One teaspoon Lite soy sauce contains 100 milligrams of sodium.

–Sylvia Reynolds (Mrs. A. Wayne)

THE
ROLLER
TRAY
TRUNK

THE MOST CONVENIENT TRUNK
EVER DEVISED.

Maple Glazed Pork Chops with Apricots

Yield: 6 servings

1 cup dried pitted apricots
  (see note)
1 cup warm water
1/2 cup flour
1/2 teaspoon salt
1/4 teaspoon thyme
1/4 teaspoon pepper
6 medium loin pork chops,
  each cut about 3/4-inch
  thick
3 tablespoons hot cooking
  oil or shortening, melted
1/4 cup maple syrup

In a deep small heavy saucepan, cook apricots in
water over moderate heat until tender; drain well.
On a sheet of waxed paper, combine flour, salt,
thyme, and pepper. Dredge pork chops in flour
mixture, coating each well. In a large heavy skillet, brown pork chops in oil over moderate heat,
about 2 minutes per side. Combine drained apricots and syrup; spoon mixture over pork chops.
Reduce heat; cover and simmer for about 1 hour
or until pork chops are fork tender. Adjust seasoning as desired.

Note: 1 cup dried pitted peaches or prunes may be substituted for apricots, if
  desired.

Variation: Add 1/4 teaspoon Dijon-style prepared mustard, if desired and/or 2
  tablespoons brandy to maple syrup.

–Linda M. Bourgeois (Mrs. Bruce)

157

Easy Pork Chop 'N Rice Casserole

Yield: 4 to 6 servings

4 to 6 medium pork chops, cut 1/2 to 3/4-inch thick
Seasoned salt and pepper to taste (optional)
3/4 cup uncooked rice
8 ounces mushrooms, thinly sliced
1 medium green pepper, cored, seeded, and thinly sliced lengthwise or into rings
1 medium onion, peeled, thinly sliced, and separated into rings
1 medium tomato, peeled and thinly sliced
About 1 cup chicken bouillon (see note)

In a large heavy skillet, brown pork chops thoroughly over moderate heat, about 2 minutes per side. Season each chop lightly with seasoned salt and pepper, if desired. Evenly spread rice over the bottom of a greased 12x8x2-inch baking dish. Arrange pork chops over rice; top each chop with mushroom slices, green pepper slices, onion rings, and tomato slices, dividing vegetables evenly. Sprinkle vegetable layers lightly with seasoned salt and pepper if desired. Pour bouillon over vegetables and meat. Bake covered, in a moderate oven (350 degrees F.) for 1 to 1 1/2 hours or until rice is cooked and pork chops are fork tender. Additional chicken bouillon may be added as necessary during baking if rice becomes too dry.

Note: Use undiluted commercially canned bouillon or 1 chicken bouillon cube dissolved in 1 cup water.

–Jane Rowe (Mrs. A. Prescott)

Fricatelli

Fresh Pork,
Salt and Pepper,
Bread,
2 Eggs,
2 Small Onions.

Chop the raw pork very fine; add the salt and plenty of pepper, also the onions finely chopped, and half as much bread as you have meat, after it has been soaked until soft; then your eggs. Mix thoroughly and make into little cakes; fry like oysters. These may be served for breakfast, and are equally nice for supper served with lemon sauce.

Old Virginia Cooking, circa 1909

The Hog Governor

During one of Thomas Jefferson's "hard-up" periods, he sent agents to intercept and purchase all the droves of hogs being sent to market at Richmond. Having cornered the hog market, he resold them to the capital's butchers at the price he was able to demand. The butchers did indeed buy from him; however, they let their feelings be known quite effectively by draping hog entrails over the fence surrounding his Richmond house. For some time after, the renowned Mr. Jefferson was referred to as "the hog governor."

Chalupa

Yield: 10 to 12 servings

1 pound dried pinto beans
3 pounds boneless pork loin
1 (6 1/2-ounce) can green chilies (optional)
2 garlic cloves, peeled and minced
2 tablespoons chili powder
1 tablespoon cumin
1 tablespoon salt
1 tablespoon minced fresh or 1 teaspoon dried oregano
Water as needed
Crisp corn chips as needed
Shredded sharp Cheddar cheese, shredded lettuce, chopped tomatoes, and onions
Hot sauce and sour cream for garnish

Rinse pinto beans and soak in water to cover for 12 hours; drain well. In a large pot, combine the first 8 ingredients; add water to cover. Simmer, cover ajar, over low heat for 6 hours, adding water as needed. Shred meat with a fork; cook, uncovered, for 1 hour. To serve, arrange crisp corn chips on individual plates and spoon pork mixture over chips. Top with cheese, lettuce, tomatoes, and onion. Sprinkle lightly with hot sauce and garnish with a dollop of sour cream.

–Mary and Ernie Swartz

Baked Sauerkraut 'N Country-Style Spareribs

Yield: 4 servings

4 pounds lean, meaty country-style spareribs, cut into serving pieces (see note)
1/2 to 1 cup flour (optional)
2 tablespoons hot cooking oil (optional)
Salt and pepper to taste (optional)
Water as needed
2 pounds sauerkraut (about 4 cups), undrained
1/2 cup light brown sugar, firmly packed
1 tablespoon bacon drippings, melted (optional)
2 unpeeled ripe tart medium apples, peeled, seeded, and thickly sliced (optional) (see note)
1 cup pitted dried small or medium prunes
1/2 cup dark seedless raisins

If desired, dredge ribs lightly in flour. In a Dutch oven, brown ribs thoroughly in hot oil over moderate heat, about 2 to 3 minutes (see note). Add enough water to cover ribs thoroughly; bring to a boil, cover ajar, over moderate heat. Reduce temperature and simmer 45 to 50 minutes. Drain off all liquid, returning ribs to Dutch oven. In a bowl, combine sauerkraut, including liquid, brown sugar, and bacon drippings, if desired, mixing well. Spoon mixture over ribs in Dutch oven. Baked, covered, in a slow oven (325 degrees F.) for 45 minutes. Add apples, if desired, prunes, and raisins, mixing into sauerkraut. Spoon pan liquid over sauerkraut and fruits. Continue baking, covered for 15 minutes. Remove cover and continue baking for 30 minutes until sauerkraut is lightly browned and apples tender.

Note: Regular spareribs or baby back pork ribs, cut into serving pieces, or 4 lean thick medium pork chops may be substituted for country-style spareribs, if desired.

Note: Use McIntosh, Winesap, Granny Smith, or other tart variety of apples.

Note: Ribs do not have to be dredged in flour and browned in hot oil, if desired. Ribs may be partially cooked in water as previously directed without doing those preparations.

Sweet 'N Sour Pork Loaf in Cabbage Leaves

Yield: 8 servings

"Serve lots of beer to wash down this sweet and sour German-style dish."

Water as needed
1 medium head cabbage (about 3 pounds), cored
2 slices bacon, chopped
1 garlic clove, peeled and minced
1 cup minced peeled onion
2 , ripe tart medium apples, cored, seeded, and chopped
3 tablespoons light brown sugar, firmly packed
2 1/2 tablespoons cider vinegar
1/2 teaspoon caraway seeds (optional)
1 1/2 pounds ground pork
2 eggs, beaten
1 cup pumpernickel bread crumbs (see note)
1 teaspoon salt or to taste

Fill a heavy saucepan halfway with water; bring to a boil over moderate heat. Add cabbage and blanche for 10 minutes. Drain and rinse cabbage in very cold water. Remove 10 large outer leaves from cabbage. Arrange 6 to 8 of the leaves, overlapping on bottom and around sides, in a greased 9 x 5 x 3-inch loaf pan; set aside. Reserve 2 to 4 remaining leaves. With a sharp knife, mince enough of the cabbage head to measure 3 cups. In a large heavy skillet, pan-fry bacon over moderate heat until partially cooked. Add garlic and onions; saute´until garlic and onions are tender and bacon is crisp. Add minced cabbage, apples, brown sugar, vinegar, and caraway seeds, if desired, mixing well. Cook for 5 minutes, stirring occasionally, until cabbage wilts. In a large bowl, combine minced cabbage mixture, ground pork, eggs, breadcrumbs, and salt, mixing well. Spoon mixture into cabbage-lined loaf pan. Top loaf with remaining whole cabbage leaves. Bake,covered, in a moderate oven (350 degrees F.) for 1 hour. Uncover and continue baking for an additional 30 minutes. Remove from oven and allow to stand for 10 minutes. Drain off excess liquid from pan, invert loaf onto a small serving platter. With a sharp knife, cut into 1/4-inch thick slices.

Note: To prepare pumpernickel bread crumbs, allow slices of pumpernickel bread to stand, uncovered, at room temperature for 48 hours. With a rolling pin, crush dried bread into crumbs.

–Vienna Taylor

....The Barbecue Club, to which a great many of the first gentlemen of the city belonged, was exceedingly popular. This club would meet at Buchanan's Spring, where a fine dinner would be laid under the great oaks. This dinner, with its cheerful accompaniment of toddy, punch, and mint-juleps, would be all the more enjoyed for being eaten in the open air. Before dinner the gentlemen amused themselves by pitching quoits, which was their favorite game....

Ruth Nelson Robins
The Richmond News Leader, date unknown

Apricot Glazed Ham

Yield: about 1 serving per 1/4 pound

1 whole or half boneless, rolled, fully-cooked smoked ham
1/2 cup light brown sugar, firmly packed
1/2 cup maple or maple-flavored syrup
1/2 cup apricot preserves
1/2 cup apricot nectar
1 teaspoon dry mustard
Maraschino cherries, halved and drained, for garnish

Arrange ham on a rack in a shallow roasting pan; insert a meat thermometer into the thickest part being careful not to touch fat. Bake, uncovered, in a slow oven (325 degrees F.) until meat thermometer registers 140 degrees F. Allow about 2 hours for a 6 to 8-pound half-ham and 3 hours for a 10 to 12-pound ham. While ham is baking, prepare glaze. In a heavy saucepan, combine brown sugar, maple syrup, apricot preserves, apricot nectar, and dry mustard, mixing well; simmer, stirring constantly, for 5 minutes. Thirty minutes before the end of the baking time, remove ham from oven and spoon half of the glaze over ham and arrange maraschino charry halves over glaze; return to oven to finish baking. Transfer ham to a heated platter and spoon remaining hot glaze over ham.

Note: If baking a cook-before-serving ham, meat thermometer should register 160 degrees F. before eating.

Note: Allow 1/4 to 1/2 pound boneless ham per serving.

Note: May garnish ham platter, if desired, with canned apricot halves filled with cream cheese and sprinkled with chopped English walnuts, arranged in nests of crisp greens.

Minced Ham

One pint of grated ham, the yolks of 6 eggs, 1/2 teaspoon of mustard, dash of red pepper. Take the grated ham, beat the yolks of eggs well, and add to the ham with the mustard and pepper; stir all over the fire until the eggs are cooked. Serve immediately on hot toast.

Receipts for Luncheon and Tea, *1898*

Jewel Glazed Holiday Ham

Yield: 3 to 4 servings

1 whole or half fully-cooked smoked ham, boned , rolled, and tied if desired
Whole cloves as needed (optional)
3/4 cup thick orange marmalade
2 tablespoon light corn syrup or honey
1 tablespoon grated orange peel
1/3 cup chopped mixed candied fruit
Pastry Christmas Trees (see below)
1 egg white, lightly beaten
Large gum drops

With a sharp knife, score top of ham in a diamond or X pattern. Insert a clove into the center of each X, if desired. Place ham on a rack in a shallow roasting pan and insert meat thermometer into the thickest part, away from fat and bone. Bake, uncovered, in a slow oven (325 degrees F.) until meat thermometer registers 140 degrees F. Allow about 2 to 2 1/2 hours for a 6 to 8-pound half ham and 3 hours for a 10 to 12-pound ham.

While ham is baking, prepare glaze. In a small heavy saucepan, combine marmalade, syrup or honey, and orange peel; bring to a simmer, stirring constantly, over moderate heat. Remove from heat at once. Thirty minutes before end of baking time, remove ham from oven and spoon half the glaze over top. Return ham to oven. Add candied fruit to remaining glaze and heat. Transfer ham to heated platter and spoon remaining hot glaze over ham. Garnish platter with pastry trees.

Pastry Trees

Use a prepared pie crust or prepare your own pastry for an unbaked 9-inch pie shell. Roll half the dough 3/8-inch thick on a lightly floured surface. Wrap remaining pastry in plastic and refrigerate for use at a later time. Cut dough with floured Christmas-tree cutter. Brush each tree lightly with beaten egg white. Sprinkle trees lightly with multi-colored candy decorations. Bake trees on ungreased baking sheets in a moderate oven (375 degrees F.) until done, about 8 minutes. Cool on wire racks. Stand trees upright; push tree stems into large gum drops which have been slit slightly with a sharp knife. Arrange trees on platter around ham.

163

Grilled Ham Apple-Yam Bundles

Yield: 8 servings

2 (1-pound) slices smoked fully-cooked ham, cut 3/4-inch thick
1 (21-ounce) can apple pie filling
2 tablespoons light brown sugar, firmly packed
1/2 teaspoon grated orange peel
1/4 teaspoon cinnamon
1/8 teaspoon ground cloves
1 (29-ounce) can yams or sweet potatoes, drained
2 tablespoons butter or margarine, cut into small pieces
Cashews, miniature marshmallows, orange slices or twists, and/or parsley sprigs for garnish

Place each ham slice on an 18-inch length sheet of heavy-duty aluminium foil. In a medium bowl, combine pie filling, sugar, orange peel, cinnamon, and cloves; top each ham slice with one-half of the yams, one-half of the apple mixture, and one-half of the butter. Bring four corners of the foil together in a pyramid shape. Fold the openings together loosely to allow heat circulation and expansion; seal by folding ends over and pressing to package. Grill each bundle over hot coals (ash gray and glowing) for 25 to 35 minutes or until heated through. Open each package and transfer to a heated platter. Garnish with cashews, miniature marshmallows, orange slices or twists, and/or parsley sprigs.

Oven Method: Follow above directions, except place foil bundles in a supporting pan. Bake in a moderate oven (350 degress F.) for 25 to 30 minutes. Or, omit foil; arrange each yam-apple topped ham slice in a 13x9x2-inch baking pan. Bake, covered, in a moderate oven (350 degress F.) for 25 to 30 minutes. Garnish as previously directed.

–The Reynolds Wrap Kitchens
The Reynolds Metals Company

....A dish of great antiquity is the boar's head which was to be found in all bills of fare for coronation and other festivities. In medieval England it was a custom to commence all great Christmas festivities with a solemn ceremony, bringing in the great boar's head as the initial dish. The head was wreathed with rosemary and laurel, and a lemon, symbol of plenty, was placed in the mouth....

Old Richmond Newspaper, Date unknown

Virginia Smithfield Ham

The distinctive, world-famous Virginia Smithfield hams enjoyed today are a legacy from the first English settlers at Jamestown. The secrets of smoking and curing meat were learned from the local Indians and have been passed down through the generations. The colonial way of curing ham made the name Virginia ham world famous.

Pigs were not native to the Jamestown area. Imported to the colony from England and Bermuda, they thrived, however, in the climate and in the rich, natural food of the land. Soon they became a nuisance and were rounded up in the town of Smithfield, named for the livestock center in London and also known as Hog Island.

Hogs were turned out to root in fields planted with peanuts which were to be harvested later as food for the plantation slaves. The hog fodder proved very influential in the distinctive flavor for which hams of the Old Dominion became known. After butchering, the meat of peanut-fed hogs was salted down and finally smoked very slowly over hickory or other hard wood and then hung to age for many months or years.

By the early part of the twentieth century, Smithfield ham had become so famous that the Virginia General Assembly passed a law in 1926 to protect it from imitation. Genuine Smithfield hams come from the hindquarters of peanut-fed hogs that have been cured, treated, smoked, and processed in the town of Smithfield, Virginia. They are usually long-shanked and have been aged at least six months.

One Smithfield ham even became famous as a "pet." In 1902, P.D. Gwaltney, Jr. cured a large Smithfiled ham. Since that time, it has reportedly never been refrigerated. Boasting a brass collar around it's shank that reads, "Mr. Gwaltney's Pet Ham," this unique ham was insured for a thousand dollars and chronicled in Ripley's "Believe It or Not."

From the smokehouse of the Jamestown settlement and aristocratic Tidewater plantations to grocery stores and restaurants of today, Smithfield ham is still a hallmark of Virginia hospitality and delicious eating

Crumb Topped Country Ham In A Bag

Yield: 20 to 28 servings

1 10 to 14-pound uncooked country-style smoked ham
Warm water as needed
1 tablespoon flour
4 cups water
Whole cloves as needed
1 cup fine breadcrumbs
1 cup light brown sugar, firmly packed

Soak ham in warm water to cover for 12 to 24 hours to remove salt. Use a stiff brush to remove surface mold from ham, if present. Sprinkle flour into a 23 x 19 1/2-inch cooking bag; place bag in a 2-inch deep large roasting pan. Place ham in bag, add water, and close tie of bag. Through a slit in the bag, puncture the thickest part of the ham with a knife and insert a meat thermometer. Bake in a slow oven (325 degrees F.) for 3 1/2 to 4 1/2 hours or until internal temperature of ham reaches 160 degrees F. Remove ham from oven, slit bag down center, and carefully remove ham. Discard bag and drippings; return ham to roasting pan. Increase oven temperature to (425 degrees F.). Trim skin and fat from ham, leaving a thin layer of fat. With a sharp knife, score fat in a criss-cross design; insert cloves into cuts. In a small bowl, combine breadcrumbs and sugar, mixing well; evenly pat mixture over top of ham. Bake in a hot oven (425 degrees F.) for 5 minutes more or until topping is golden brown. To serve, slice ham very thin.

–The Reynolds Wrap Kitchens
The Reynolds Metals Company

...One of the oldest taverns in town belonged to Abraham Cowley, who received his original license in 1737. His tavern occupied the southwest corner of Main and Twenty-third streets, near the county courthouse. In 1776 Cowley advertised his ordinary for rent, and described it as follows: "...the house is large, very commodious, a good kitchen, dairy, meethouse, new stable, that will contain 74 horses."

Harry M. Ward and Harold E. Greer, Jr.
Richmond During The Revolution, 1775-83, 1977

Old Dominion Deviled Ham

Yield: about 3 cups

1/4 cup butter or margarine, melted
1 tablespoon flour
1/2 teaspoon dry mustard
1/2 teaspoon Worcestershire sauce (optional)
3 to 4 drops hot sauce or to taste
1 cup heavy cream
2 cups minced or ground fully cooked smoked Smithfield or Virginia country-style ham
Assorted crisp crackers

In a medium heavy saucepan, combine butter and flour; add mustard, Worcestershire sauce, if desired, and hot sauce, blending well. Stir in cream and then ham, mixing well. Cook over low heat, stirring frequently, for about 10 minutes or until mixture is thick. Pack mixture into a lightly oiled 3-cup mold; refrigerate ham mixture in mold until firm. Unmold onto a serving plate, garnish as desired, and accompany with assorted crisp crackers as spreaders.

Virginia Cookery Book, circa 1921

Virginia Ham

"No Virginian ever failed to serve ham as well as another meat with his dinner."

Use a two-year-old ham. Soak for twenty-four hours. Then boil ham until done; put aside liquor to cool (not get cold), and skim. Remove skin from ham, and place in a shallow baking pan. Rub the fat well with a beaten egg and cover well with fine, stale bread crumbs, sprinkling a very little sugar over them. Bake in a slow oven for at least an hour, taking care not to brown too quickly. When well browned, pour over the ham a wine-glass of wine; remove from the oven and serve it up.

Virginia Cooking, 1939

Cheesy Ham 'N Broccoli Casserole

Yield: 6 servings

2 (10-ounce) packages
  frozen chopped broccoli,
  thawed
3 cups breadcrumbs
1/4 cup butter or margarine,
  melted
12 ounces shredded sharp
  Cheddar cheese
2 cups coarsely ground
  fully-cooked smoked ham
Medium White Sauce (see
  index)

Thoroughly pat dry broccoli between layers of absorbent paper, squeezing out as much water as possible. In a large bowl, combine breadcrumbs and butter, tossing lightly to mix. Add cheese, mixing well. Evenly spread one-half of the crumb mixture over the bottom of a lightly greased 12 x 8 x 2-inch baking dish. Evenly sprinkle ham over crumbs and spread broccoli over ham. Spoon Medium White Sauce over broccoli layer and evenly sprinkle remaining crumb mixture over top. Bake, uncovered, in a moderate oven (350 degrees F.) for 1 hour.

Note: 1 1/2 (10 3/4-ounce) cans cream of chicken soup, undiluted, may be substituted for Medium White Sauce.

–Crist Brown (Mrs. B. B.)

Ham 'N Artichoke Sandwich

Yield: 4 servings

8 thin slices white bread
  (see note)
Mayonnaise as needed
4 crisp lettuce leaves
8 very thin slices Swiss
  cheese
8 very thin slices boneless
  fully-cooked smoked ham
  (about 6 to 8 ounces) (see
  note)
1 (14-ounce) can artichoke
  hearts, drained and sliced
  crosswise
Salt and pepper to taste

Liberally spread one side of bread slices with mayonnaise. Arrange bread slices, mayonnaise side up, on individual plates. Layer a crisp lettuce leaf, two cheese slices, and two ham slices on four bread slices. Top each sandwich with sliced artichoke hearts and add salt and pepper to taste. Top each sandwich with a second slice of bread.

Note: 4 croissant rolls, split in half lengthwise may be substituted for white bread.

Note: Fully-cooked Virginia or Smithfield ham may be used.

–Elsie Mattingly Dickinson (Mrs. Alfred J., III)

Old Richmond Advertisement, circa 1909

Sausage has been made in Virginia since colonial days. Receipts (recipes) were brought by word of mouth with the earliest colonists from England and thereafter handed down from one generation to the next. This recipe is an updated version of an eighteenth-century Virginia pork sausage receipt which yields about fifty pounds.

Old Virginia Sausage

Yield: 2 1/2 pounds, 8 to 10 servings

2 pounds lean pork tenderloin or boneless pork loin, ground

8 to 12 ounces pork fat, ground

6 tablespoons minced fresh or 2 tablespoons dried sage

1 1/2 teaspoons salt or to taste

1 to 1 1/2 teaspoons mace or to taste

1 teaspoon black pepper

1 teaspoon ground allspice or to taste

3/4 to 1 teaspoon cayenne pepper or hot sauce

In a large bowl, combine pork, pork fat, and seasonings; with the hands, mix well. Cover with clear plastic wrap and refrigerate for 24 hours. Shape mixture, dividing evenly, into 20 small or 10 large patties, each about 1/4 inch thick. Pan-fry as many patties as desired in a cold large heavy skillet (lightly sprayed with vegetable cooking spray) over moderate heat until sausage is lightly browned, about 2 minutes per side. Reduce heat, cover, and simmer patties for about 5 to 6 minutes or until cooked through. Or, arrange patties on a rack in a broiler pan, about 8 inches from heat source. Broil about 3 minutes; turn patties and continue to broil for 3 minutes until patties are done and lightly browned. Drain well on absorbent paper. Serve immediately.

Note: Unused sausage may be wrapped in heavy duty aluminum foil or freezer paper, secured tightly, and stored in the freezer for up to three months.

W. A. HAMMOND, *
Florist,
* ̶ ̶107 East Broad Street,
PLANT DECORATIONS.
Choice Rosebuds, Cut Flowers, &c.   *RICHMOND, VA.*

Old Richmond Advertisement, date unknown

"Pigs in a Blizzard"

Yield: 4 to 6 servings

Old Virgina Sausage patties
(see index)
4 to 5 medium potatoes,
peeled and quartered
Salted boiling water as
needed
1/2 (8-ounce) package
cream cheese, at room
temperature
1/4 cup sour cream
1/2 teaspoon salt or to taste
1/8 teaspoon garlic salt
Pepper to taste
2 tablespoons minced
chives
2 tablespoons grated
Parmesan cheese
1 tablespoon butter or
margarine, at room
temperature
Paprika

Prepare sausage patties according to recipe directions through browning process; drain well and set aside. In a large heavy saucepan, cook potatoes, cover ajar, in salted boiling water to cover over moderate heat for 15 to 20 minutes, or until tender; drain well. Transfer potatoes to a large bowl and mash well. Add cream cheese, sour cream, salt, garlic, and pepper to taste; beat well at high speed of an electric mixer until mixture is smooth. Stir in minced chives. Arrange 4 to 6 well drained browned sausage patties in a lightly greased 11 x 7 x 2-inch or 9x9x2-inch baking dish. Evenly spread whipped potato mixture over sausage patties. Sprinkle potato topping with Parmesan cheese and then dot with butter. Bake, uncovered, in a moderate oven (350 degrees F.) for 20 minutes. Evenly sprinkle potato topping with paprika. Continue baking for about 10 minutes or until casserole is heated through and potato topping is golden brown.

–Marion Peeschla (Mrs. Ralf)

Pork Pot Pie

Chines and spare-ribs are generally used for this dish, but any part of lean pork will answer. Crack the bones and cut into pieces two inches long. Line the pot with pastry. Put in the meat, sprinkle with salt and pepper, then a layer of parboiled Irish potatoes, sliced, and so continue until the pot is nearly full. Then pour in a quart of cold water and put on the upper crust, cutting a small round hole out of the middle of the crust, through which you can pour hot water should the gravy boil away too fast. Put on the cover of the pot and boil about two hours. When done, remove the upper crust carefuly, turn out the meat and gravy into a bowl, and take out the lower crust. Put this upon a hot dish, put the meat and potatoes upon it, pour the gravy over it, and cover with the top crust. This can be browned by holding over it a red-hot oven lid or stove plate.

(Old Recipe, Richmond, Virginia, date unknown)
The Williamsburg Art of Cookery, *1938*

171

Dollar-Wise Sausage Casserole

Yield: 4 servings

1 pound medium spiced
  fresh bulk pork sausage,
  crumbled
2 medium apples, peeled,
  cored, seeded, and sliced
  (see note)
1 large onion, peeled and
  cut into thin wedges
1 garlic clove, peeled and
  minced
1 (15-ounce) can dark red
  kidney beans
1/2 cup tomato-vegetable
  cocktail juice
1/2 teaspoon chili powder
  or to taste
1/4 teaspoon ground cumin
  (optional)
1/4 teaspoon pepper
Salt to taste

In a heavy skillet, lightly brown sausage over moderate heat; drain well. In a medium bowl, combine sausage, apples, onion, garlic, beans, vegetable juice, chili powder, cumin, if desired, and pepper. Add salt to taste, mixing well. Spoon into a lightly greased 1-quart casserole or 8 x 8 x 2-inch baking dish. Bake, uncovered, in a very slow oven (250 degrees F.) for 1 1/2 hours.

Note: Use McIntosh, Winesap, Granny Smith, or other tart variety of apples.

Variation: In a medium bowl, combine 2 cups biscuit/baking mix, 2/3 cup milk, and 2 tablespoons melted butter or margarine, mixing just until dry ingredients are moistened and mixture blended. Drop by rounded teaspoonfuls, close together, over bubbling hot casserole. Increase oven temperature to hot (425 degrees F.); continue to bake, uncovered, for 10 to 12 minutes, or until biscuit topping is golden brown and done.

–Vernelle Thomas

Old Richmond Advertisement, circa 1909

Stuffed, Frenched Veal Chop Chardonnay's

Yield: 4 servings

4 (8-ounce) French-style
veal rib chops (see note)
2 tablespoons butter or
margarine
1/4 to 1/2 teaspoon minced
peeled garlic
1/4 cup pine nuts
1 small onion, peeled and
minced
8 ounces mushrooms,
chopped
2 ounces fully-cooked
smoked Smithfield or
Virginia country-style
ham, minced
2 ounces smoked
mozzarella or gouda
cheese, shredded
Wooden picks
About 1/2 cup flour
2 tablespoons clarified
butter, melted (see index)

Have butcher cut the veal chops in the French style. With a sharp knife, make a slit in each veal chop on the side opposite the bone to form a pocket, being careful not to puncture the meat anywhere else. Set chops aside. In a medium heavy skillet, melt butter over low to moderate heat; add garlic. When butter begins to brown, add pine nuts and sauté until nuts are golden brown. Remove nuts with a slotted spoon and set aside. Add onion and mushrooms to hot garlic butter in pan; saute mixture until vegetables are tender but not browned and mushroom volume is reduced by one half. Stir in ham and pine nuts. Add cheese and breadcrumbs, mixing lightly. Remove from heat. Pack 1/4 to 1/3 cup of mushroom mixture into each rib chop pocket. Secure tightly with wooden picks if desired. Dredge stuffed chops in flour, coating each very lightly. In a large heavy skillet, sear chops in clarified butter over moderate to high heat, about 1 minute per side. Transfer chops to an 11 x 7 x 2-inch baking pan and bake, uncovered, in a hot oven (400 degrees F.) for 12 to 15 minutes or until fork tender. Arrange one chop on each of 4 dinner plates and garnish as desired.

Note: A French-style chop is one in which the extra fat and gristle are cut away from the chop, as well as the non-meaty portion of the rib bone.

–Chef Jim Ertell
Chardonnay's
The Richmond Marriott Hotel

Old Richmond Advertisement, circa 1909

Women's Committee of the Richmond Symphony

The Women's Committee of the Richmond Symphony is a group of over four hundred dedicated women interested in the growth and development of the Richmond Symphony. Fund raising, through special events and projects, is one area in which members contribute their efforts. One such fund raiser includes the sponsorship of the Southern Living Cooking School Show biennially. Others include audience development, eduction, and hospitality. Membership is open to anyone who wishes to participate in the promotion and benefit of the Richmond Symphony

Apple and Apricot Stuffed Veal Loin with Madeira Sauce

Yield: 10 servings

Richmond Symphony patrons enjoyed this entreé at a gourmet fund raising dinner catered by Ridgewell's in the spring of 1988.

1 (5-pound) breast of veal
1 1/2 teaspoons minced fresh or dried sage, divided
1 1/2 teaspoon fresh or 1/2 teaspoon dried thyme, divided
Salt and pepper to taste
1 medium onion, peeled and minced
1 rib celery, minced
2 tablespoons unsalted butter, melted
1/4 cup Madeira wine
3 thick slices white bread, crusts removed, toasted, and cut into medium cubes

Have butcher bone-out and butterfly veal breast. Open veal breast out flat; rub meat, both sides, with half of the sage and thyme. Sprinkle with salt and pepper to taste. Cover lightly and refrigerate for 2 1/2 hours.

In a large heavy skillet, sauté onion and celery in butter over moderate heat until tender but browned. Add remaining herbs. Gradually add Madeira. Add bread cubes, apples, apricots, chicken stock, honey, and salt and pepper to taste, tossing lightly to mix. Cook stuffing mixture for 2 to 3 minutes, stirring constantly, over moderate heat. Remove from heat, transfer to a bowl, and chill, covered, in the refrigerator for 2 hours.

Lay the veal breast out flat; spread stuffing mixture evenly over one side of breast. Starting at the wide side, roll up meat jelly-roll-style,

174

2 tart medium apples,
  peeled, cored, and
  chopped (see note)
1 1/4 cups chopped dried
  plump apricots
1/4 cup chicken stock or
  commercial chicken
  broth, undiluted
2 tablespoons honey
About 2 cups water
Madeira Sauce

avoiding any air pockets. Seal both ends with aluminum foil and tie string around meat roll at several intervals. Arrange stuffed veal breast in a shallow roasting pan; bake, uncovered, in a hot oven (425 degrees F.) for 20 minutes. Reduce heat to moderate (350 degrees F.); add 2 cups water and continue baking an additional 1 hour, turning and basting every 15 minutes. Add more water to pan as necessary. Remove foil and string. With a sharp knife, cut meat crosswise into thin slices.

Note: Use McIntosh, Winesap, Granny Smith, or other tart variety of apples.

Maderia Sauce

(about 3 1/2 cups)

3 tablespoons unsalted
  butter
3 tablespoons flour
3 shallots, peeled and
  minced
2 cups veal stock or
  commercial beef
  consommé or beef broth
1 cup Madeira wine
Salt and pepper to taste

In a medium heavy saucepan, melt butter over low heat. With a wire whisk, add flour, blending thoroughly. Continue to whisk over low heat until mixture has turned a light brown. Add shallots and continue cooking, stirring occasionally, for 5 minutes. Gradually stir in veal stock and Madeira, blending well. Cook, stirring constantly, over moderate heat, until mixture is reduced by one-half. Add salt and pepper to taste. Strain sauce. Keep hot, covered, in the top of a double boiler over simmering water.

–Women's Committee of the
Richmond Symphony Fund Raising Dinner

Scotch Collops of Veal

They may be made of the nice part of the rack, or cut from the fillet, rub a little salt and pepper on them, and fry them a light brown; have a rich gravy seasoned with wine, and any kind of catsup you choose, with a few cloves of garlic, and some pounded mace, thicken it, put the collops in and stew them a short time, take them out, strain the gravy over, and garnish with bunches of parsley fried crisp, and thin slices of middling of bacon, curled around a skewer and boiled.

The Virginia Housewife, *1831*

Veal Piccata Jeanette

Yield: 4 servings

1 1/4 pounds *very* thinly
   sliced boneless veal,
   (scalloppine) cut 1/16 to
   1/8-inch thick
1/2 cup flour
1/3 cup butter or margarine,
   melted
1/4 teaspoon salt or to taste
1/8 teaspoon pepper or to
   taste
2 large lemons, quartered
   and seeded
2 to 3 teaspoons brandy
1 to 2 tablespoons minced
   fresh parsley for garnish
Thin lemon slices sprinkled
   with pakrika for garnish

If desired, pound veal with the flat side of a meat mallet. Dredge veal pieces in flour. In a large heavy skillet, saute' veal in butter until golden brown on both sides. Season with salt and pepper to taste. Extract juice from lemons and pour over meat. Reduce heat and simmer for 3 to 5 minutes. Pour brandy over meat just before serving. Sprinkle with parsley and garnish with lemon slices. Serve immediately.

Variations: 1 1/4 pounds boneless turkey breast cutlets may be substituted for veal, if desired.

Veal Cutlets from the Fillet or Leg

Cut off the flank and take the bone out, then take slices the size of the fillet and half an inch thick, beat two yolks of eggs light, and have some grated bread mixed with pepper, salt, pounded nutmeg and chopped parsley; beat the slices a little, lay them on a board and wash the upper side with the egg, cover it thick with the bread crumbs, press them on with a knife, and let them stand to dry a little, that they may not fall off in frying, then turn them gently, put egg and crumbs on in the same manner, put them into a pan of boiling lard, and fry them a light brown; have some good gravy ready, season it with a tea-spoonful of curry powder, a large one of wine, and one of lemon pickle, thicken with butter and brown flour, drain every drop of lard from the cutlets, layt hem in the gravy, and stew them fifteen or twenty minutes, serve them up garnished with lemon cut in thin slices.

The Virginia Housewife, *1831*

Veal of Hanover

Yield: 4 servings

Located in historic Hanover County, Thyme and Sage of Hanover exhibits a casual atmosphere, featuring antique church pews and chairs as part of the decor. Veal of Hanover, an entre specialty, is frequently requested by patrons.

2 pounds *very* thinly sliced
   boneless veal,
   (scalloppine)
About 1/2 cup flour
1 tablespoon clarified
   butter, melted (see index)
1 tablespoon hot cooking
   oil
1 cup thinly sliced
   mushrooms
1 tablespoon minced peeled
   shallots
1/4 cup dry white (chablis)
   wine
1/2 cup heavy cream, at
   room temperature
3 tablespoons browning and
   seasoning sauce
Salt and pepper to taste

Between sheets of waxed paper, flatten veal pieces, as desired, with a meat mallet. On a sheet of waxed paper, dredge veal pieces in flour, coating each well. In a large heavy skillet, saute' veal in butter and oil over moderate heat, about 30 seconds per side. Remove veal, draining well, and set aside. Add mushrooms and shallots to skillet; saute' vegetables in hot pan drippings, stirring frequently, until vegetables are tender. Add wine and continue cooking until liquid is almost gone. Add cream, and browning and seasoning sauce, blending well. Season with salt and pepper to taste; continue cooking for 30 seconds. Return veal to pan, spooning sauce over veal. Serve immediately.

Note: If sauce becomes too thick, a few drops of water may be added.

Variation: 2 pounds of boneless turkey breast cutlets may be substituted for veal. Proceed with recipe as previously directed.

–The Fairbrother family
Thyme and Sage of Hanover

Fricando of Veal

Cut slices from the fillet an inch thick and six inches long, lard them with slips of lean middling of bacon, bake them a light brown, stew them in well seasoned gravy, made as thick as rich cream, serve them up hot, and lay round the dish sorrel stewed with butter, pepper and salt, till quite dry.

The Virginia Housewife, 1831

Veal Saltimbocca

Yield: 4 servings

The Sorrento Restaurant, located at 4401 West Broad Street, opened in 1982 by its owners, Vince and Bruna Capocelli, originally of Italy. Patrons continue to award the restaurant many accolades. Pasta, made fresh each morning, and desserts, such as Espresso Pie are specialties of the house. Veal Saltimbocca is a favorite menu request of many regular patrons.

1 to 1 1/2 pounds very thinly sliced boneless veal, (scalloppine) cut into 12 equal pieces
About 3/4 to 1 cup flour
About 1/3 cup butter or margarine, melted
2 tablespoons hot cooking oil
About 6 to 8 tablespoons dry white wine
6 ounces prosciutto or fully-cooked Smithfield ham, cut into 12 *very* thin slices
About 10 to 12 fresh sage leaves, slightly crushed
Pepper to taste

With a meat mallet, flatten veal pieces to a thickness of 1/8 inch. On a sheet of waxed paper, dredge veal in flour, coating each piece well. In a large heavy skillet, saute veal in 1/3 cup butter and oil over moderate heat, about 2 to 3 minutes per side. Remove veal with tongs; set aside. Add wine to pan drippings. Saute prosciutto slices in wine butter, about 30 seconds per side. Add crushed sage leaves to pan. Return veal to pan, spooning wine butter over veal and prosciutto. Melt 1 to 2 tablespoons additional butter in pan, if necessary, spooning over meat. Season with pepper to taste. Cook for about 1 minute. Remove sage leaves from sauce before serving. Alternately arrange 3 slices of veal and 3 slices prosciutto on each plate; spoon wine butter over each portion, dividing evenly.

–Vince and Bruna Capocelli
Sorrento Restaurant

Baked Fillet of Veal

Take the bone out of the fillet, wrap the flap around and sew it, make a forcemeat of bread crumbs, the fat of bacon, a little onion chopped, parsley, pepper, salt, and a nutmeg pounded, wet it with the yolks of eggs, fill the place from which the bone was taken, make holes around it with a knife and fill them also, and lard the top; put it in a Dutch oven with a pint of water, bake it sufficiently, thicken the gravy with butter and brown flour, add a gill of wine and one of mushroom catsup, and serve it garnished with forcemeat balls fried.

The Virginia Housewife, 1831

Veal with Mushrooms

Yield: 6 servings

2 cups sliced mushrooms
2/3 cup chopped green
onions (include some
green tops)
3 tablespoons butter or
margarine, melted
6 veal cutlets
1 1/2 cups rich beef broth or
1 (10 1/2-ounce) can
consommé
1 cup dry white wine
2 tablespoons chili sauce
1 tablespoon
Worcestershire sauce
3/4 teaspoon minced fresh
or dried basil
1/4 teaspoon crumbled bay
leaves
1/4 teaspoon minced peeled
garlic
1/8 teaspoon pepper
2 tablespoons flour
2 tablespoons cold water
1 cup fresh or frozen peas,
thawed and drained

In a large heavy skillet, sauté mushrooms and onion in butter until tender. Remove with a slotted spoon, draining well. Brown cutlets on both sides in pan drippings; set aside. Reduce heat and add broth or consommé, wine, chili sauce, Worcestershire sauce, basil, bay leaves, garlic, and pepper to pan drippings. Blend flour and water together until smooth; gradually blend mixture into sauce. Continue cooking over low heat until sauce thickens, stirring constantly. Add meat, mushrooms, onions, and peas to sauce. Cook, uncovered, over low heat for 10 to 15 minutes or until meat is heated through and fork tender.

Common Patties

Take some veal, fat and lean, and some slices of boiled ham, chop them very fine, and season it with salt, pepper, grated nutmeg, and a small quantity of parsley and thyme minced very fine; with a little gravy make some paste, cover the bottoms of small moulds, fill them with the meat, put thin lids on, and bake them crisp; five is enough for a side dish.

The Virginia Housewife, *1831*

179

Virginia's Executive Mansion

180

Virginia Executive Mansion

The Virginia Executive Mansion, often referred to as the "Governor's Mansion or House," designed by New England architect, Alexander Parris, in the Greek Revival manner is the oldest continuously lived-in estate executive mansion in the United States. Built in 1812-13, the house also enjoys a reputation as one of the finest examples of neo-classical architecture in America.

Much folklore surrounds the history of the house. The first Virginia governor to live in the house, James Barbour, whose tastes were "exacting and expensive." made several changes to the original house plan. Important additions included a two-story kitchen/servant's quarters and a brick-lined icehouse equipped with gutters. Layers of ice were packed tightly in straw or sawdust, slowing the melting process considerably, allowing ice to be used year-round.

A tradition of hospitality also began under the stewardship of James and Lucy Barbour which was to be repeated for decades. Any legislator was welcome to make himself at home in the mansion while the state legislature was in session. As an inviting gesture, a large silver punch bowl located on the dining room sideboard was kept brimful with a strong whisky punch, always ready for a thirsty legislator to imbibe. The custom was not to change until the early twentieth century during William Hodges Mann's tenure. Much to Lucy Mann's delight, herself a temperance person, the punch bowl broke when it fell from a shelf.

Until recently, the mansion bore the exterior changes dictated during the later part of the nineteenth century. Although the interior of the mansion had been renovated with contemporary conveniences earlier in the twentieth century and the furnishings had been refurbished with period antiques of the early nineteenth century, the exterior of the house remained as it was in the Victorian era. In 1989 the exterior regained its original appearance with the restoration of the decorative panels between the windows, the balustrade above the front porch, and the parapet above the eaves.

Governors come and go, but hospitality is a byword at the Governor's Mansion. Visitors are always welcome.

Veal Oscar

Yield: 6 servings

Veal Oscar is reputed to be a creation named in honor of Oscar Tschirky, the renowned major domo of the Waldorf Astoria hotel in New York City at the turn of the century.

6 veal cutlets, about 4 to 6 ounces each
1 egg
1 tablespoon water
2/3 cup breadcrumbs
Salt and pepper to taste
About 1/4 cup flour
2 tablespoons butter or margarine, divided
2 tablespoons cooking oil
1/4 to 1/2 cup dry white wine
1 pound fresh asparagus spears, cleaned and woody stems removed or 1 (10-ounce) package frozen asparagus spears
Hollandaise Sauce (see index)

With a meat mallet, pound cutlets to a 1/4-inch thickness. In a small bowl, combine egg and water, beating lightly with a wire whisk. On a sheet of waxed paper, combine breadcrumbs and salt and pepper to taste. Dredge cutlets in flour, coating each well. Dip cutlets into egg mixture and then into crumb mixture, coating each well.

In a large heavy skillet, melt 1 tablespoon butter and heat 1 tablespoon oil over moderate heat; add half of the crumb-coated cutlets and saute´, turning once until done, about 5 minutes per side. Add half of the wine for the last two minutes of cooking time. Transfer sautéed cutlets to a warm platter and keep warm in a very slow oven (200 degrees F.). Prepare remaining cutlets as previously directed.

Cook fresh asparagus in a small amount of salted boiling water in a medium heavy saucepan, uncovered, for about 10 minutes or until crisp tender but not soft and mushy; drain well (see note). Prepare frozen asparagus according to package directions. Arrange cutlets on each of six dinner plates; top each cutlet with 3 to 4 asparagus spears. Spoon a small amount of Hollandaise Sauce over each serving. Garnish as desired and pass remaining Hollandaise Sauce in a sauceboat.

Note: To microwave, arrange asparagus spears in a 9 x 9 x 2-inch or 9 x 5 x 3-inch glass baking dish; add water to *just* cover asparagus. Cover with clear plastic wrap, allowing extra wrap for steam venting. Microwave at HIGH power for 4 minutes. Check doneness of asparagus. Continue microwaving at HIGH power in 30 to 60 second increments until asparagus are crisp tender but not soft or mushy. Drain well.

–Virginia Executive Mansion

Italian Sausages Rolled in Veal

Yield: 6 servings

3 hot-spiced Italian
  sausages, halved
Hot cooking oil as needed
6 boneless veal cutlets
1 garlic clove, peeled and
  minced
2 tablespoons grated
  Parmesan cheese
2 tablespoons minced
  parsley
1 teaspoon fennel seeds,
  crushed
About 3/4 to 1 cup flour
8 ounces mushrooms, thinly
  sliced, or 1 (4 to 6-ounce)
  can sliced mushrooms,
  drained
2 tablespoons butter or
  margarine
1 cup dry sherry
Additional minced parsley
  for garnish

Prick sausages lightly. In a large heavy skillet, brown sausage pieces in 1 tablespoon hot oil over moderate heat, about 2 minutes; reduce heat, cover, and simmer for about 15 minutes or until done. With a meat mallet; pound cutlets until flattened and each is large enough to enclose a piece of sausage without overlapping. In a small bowl, combine garlic, cheese, 2 tablespoons parsley, and crushed fennel seeds, mixing well. Spread a small amount of cheese mixture on each cutlet, dividing evenly. Arrange a sausage piece on the edge of each cutlet. Spread with the cheese mixture. Roll as a jelly roll; secure rolls with string tied around each roll in 3 places, spaced equally. Dredge stuffed veal rolls in flour, coating each well; shake excess flour from each roll. Add 3 to 4 tablespoons oil to skillet; saute' veal rolls in hot oil over moderate heat until done and golden brown, about 4 to 5 minutes. Drain rolls well and keep warm in a *very* slow oven (200 degrees F.). Add mushrooms to pan drippings; sauté over moderate heat until tender but not browned. Remove mushrooms with a slotted spoon; set aside. Reduce heat, add butter to skillet, and melt over low heat. Add sherry and continue simmering until sauce is thickened, about 5 minutes. Stir in reserved mushrooms. Arrange veal rolls on a heated platter. Spoon mushroom sauce over rolls and sprinkle with minced parsley.

–Frances Fox (Mrs. Paul)

Veal in Wine Sauce with Tiny Carrots and Onions

Yield: 6 to 8 servings

2 pounds boneless veal
  round steak, cut into
  serving pieces
1/2 cup flour
Salt
Sweet Hungarian paprika
Pepper
1/4 cup hot olive oil (see
  note) or cooking oil
8 ounces *very* small (pearl)
  white onions, peeled
18 to 24 *very* small carrots,
  peeled, or 4 to 5 medium
  carrots, peeled and cut
  into 4-inch strips
1 cup dry red wine
1/2 cup beef broth or
  consomme´ (see note)
1 bay leaf, crumbled
1 tablespoon minced fresh
  or 1 teaspoon dried
  thyme
Fresh thyme sprigs for
  garnish

Pound veal lightly with a meat mallet, if desired. In a small bowl, combine flour, 1 teaspoon salt, 1 teaspoon paprika, and 1/4 teaspoon pepper, mixing well. Dredge veal pieces in flour mixture, coating each well. In a deep large heavy skillet or Dutch oven, brown floured veal in oil over moderate heat, about 2 minutes per side. Add onions, carrots, broth, water, bay leaf, and thyme. Adjust salt, pepper, and paprika seasonings to taste. Reduce heat, partially cover, and simmer for 40 to 45 minutes until veal and vegetables are tender. Uncover, and continue simmering until sauce is reduced by one-third and slightly thickened. Arrange veal pieces and vegetables on individual dinner plates and spoon wine sauce over each serving. Garnish each with sprigs of fresh thyme.

Note: Use a premium quality extra virgin olive oil. Extra virgin refers to the oil collected from the first press of the olives.

Note: Undiluted commercially canned beef broth or consomme´ may be used.

Scrambled Brains

One pint or tray of brains; wash thoroughly and free them from all membranes, and sprinkle with salt and pepper; drop the brains in a spider on 2 tablespoonsful of butter, and stir constantly. When half cooked, add from 3 to 6 eggs, slightly beaten, and continue to stir until done.

Mrs. Anderson.
Virginia Recipes, *1890*

Baked Veal and Olives Au Gratin

Yield: 6 servings

3 tablespoons butter or
  margarine
4 tablespoons flour
2 cups milk
1/2 teaspoon salt or to taste
1/2 teaspoon nutmeg
1/4 teaspoon ginger
1/8 teaspoon pepper
1 (6-ounce) jar sliced
  mushrooms, drained
2 cups cubed cooked veal
  (see note)
3/4 to 1 cup medium
  pimento-stuffed olives,
  quartered
1/4 cup grated Parmesan or
  shredded mild Cheddar
  cheese
2 tablespoons breadcrumbs

In a small heavy saucepan, melt butter over low heat; with a wire whisk, blend in flour to form a smooth paste. Gradually add milk, blending well. Cook, stirring constantly, over moderate heat until sauce is thickened and bubbly hot. Stir in seasonings. In a small bowl, combine mushrooms, veal, and olives, mixing lightly; spoon mixture into a greased 8 x 8 x 2-inch baking pan. Spoon sauce evenly over veal mixture. Combine cheese and crumbs, tossing lightly; evenly sprinkle over sauce. Bake, uncovered, in a moderate oven (375 degrees F.) for 25 to 30 minutes or until bubbly hot and cheese mixture lightly browned.

Note: 2 cups cubed cooked pork loin or turkey or chicken may be substituted for veal.

–Linda M. Bourgeois (Mrs. Bruce)

After the capital was moved to Richmond, the local taverns increased in importance, providing board for members of the General Assembly and for other people who had business with the state. The Henrico County Court and the Richmond hustings court licensed fifteen men and one woman to keep taverns in Richmond during the years 1781,1782, and 1783.

–Harry M. Ward and Harold E. Greer, Jr.
Richmond During The Revolution, 1775-83,
1977

Veal Marengo

Yield: 8 to 10 servings

2 pounds boneless veal, cut into 3/4 to 1-inch cubes
4 to 5 tablespoons butter or margarine, melted and divided
4 to 5 tablespoons hot olive oil, divided
1 cup chopped peeled onion
2 tablespoons flour
2 cups canned tomatoes (including liquid) or 2 1/2 to 3 cups chopped peeled fresh tomatoes
1 1/2 cups dry white wine
1 tablespoon minced fresh or 1 teaspoon dried thyme
1 teaspoon garlic powder
Salt and pepper to taste
6 parsley sprigs and 1 crumbled bay leaf, tied in a cheesecloth bag
Chicken broth (see note)
16 *very* small (boiling) white onions peeled
8 ounces mushrooms, thinly sliced
1 cup small pitted green olives
Hot cooked noodles

In a Dutch oven, evenly brown veal cubes in 2 tablespoons butter and 2 tablespoons olive oil over moderate heat; remove with a slotted spoon and set aside. Saute' chopped onion in hot drippings until tender but not browned. Blend in flour and continue cooking for 3 to 4 minutes. Stir in tomatoes, wine, thyme, garlic powder, salt, and pepper to taste. Add veal cubes, parsley sprigs, and bay leaf. Add enough chicken broth to cover veal. Bake, covered, in a moderate oven (350 degrees F.) for 1 1/2 hours. In a heavy skillet, brown whole onions in 2 tablespoons butter and 2 tablespoons olive oil over moderate heat; remove with a slotted spoon. Saute' mushrooms in hot drippings until tender but not browned. Add onions, mushrooms, and olives to veal mixture; continue baking, covered, for 45 minutes. Discard parsley and bay leaf. Remove veal and vegetables with a slotted spoon; set aside. Reduce pan liquid to 3 cups over moderate heat; skim off fat. Return veal and vegetables to liquid, mixing well. Heat through. Serve over hot cooked noodles.

Note: Commercially canned chicken broth may be used, if desired.

Sherried Sweetbreads Elegante

Yield: 4 servings

"This delicious combination of flavors adds glamour to sweetbreads and makes a good entre'e to serve guests for a weekend brunch."

1 1/2 pounds veal sweetbreads, fresh or thawed frozen
Cold water as needed
1 1/2 tablespoons lemon juice
12 ounces *very* small mushrooms
7 1/2 tablespoons butter or margarine, divided
3 tablespoons flour
1 1/8 cups milk
3/4 cup chicken broth
6 tablespoons dry sherry
3/4 cup shredded Swiss cheese
1 1/2 teaspoons grated orange peel
1/4 teaspoon nutmeg
Salt and pepper to taste
Toast points or hot cooked rice
Minced parsley for garnish

In a medium bowl, soak sweetbreads in cold water to cover for 1 hour; drain well. Place sweetbreads in a 3 to 4-quart heavy saucepan; add water to cover, and lemon juice. Bring to a boil over moderate heat; reduce temperature, cover, and simmer for 20 minutes or until tender and white in color. Drain thoroughly, then immediately place cooked sweetbreads in cold water. Remove and discard membrane and tubes from sweetbreads; separate into small sections and pat dry with absorbent paper. In a large heavy skillet, melt butter over low heat. Add sweetbread sections and mushrooms; increase heat to moderate and saute mixture until sweetbreads are lightly browned and mushrooms tender. Remove with a slotted spoon or spatula and set aside. Melt remaining 4 1/2 tablespoons butter in skillet over low heat. Stir in flour, blending well, cook until mixture is bubbly hot. Gradually blend in milk, chicken broth, and sherry. Cook, stirring constantly,over moderate heat until mixture is thickened and bubbly hot. Reduce heat, add cheese, orange peel, and nutmeg; stir over low heat until cheese is melted. Add sweetbreads and mushrooms, mixing gently. Serve over toast points or hot cooked rice. Garnish each portion with minced parsley.

–Vienna Taylor

Galt's Tavern, referred to in later years as City Tavern, opened in 1775 and reported among its customers respectively, Arnold, Simcoe, Cornwallis and Lafayette, who made the tavern their headquarters. The Continental officer Feltman described in his journal playing billiards as Galt's Tavern and dining "very sumptuously upon Rock fish."

–Harry M. Ward and Harold E. Greer, Jr.
Richmond During The Revolution, 1775-83,
1977

WESTERN UNION TELEGRAPH CO.,

1217 East Main Street,

TELEPHONE NO. 186. RICHMOND, VA.

21,000 OFFICES IN AMERICA.

✹· Cable Service to all the World. ·✺

The above office is connected by telephone with the Southern Bell Telephone Company's Exchange. 'Phone subscribers can call up the Western Union Office—'Phone 186—and 'phone their messages, either from their residences or places of business, for transmission to any one of 21,000 offices in America, or to foreign points.

J. B. TREE, Superintendent.

At the corner of the Academic Square where now (1860's) stands the handsome mansion of Mr. Allen, was erected a Market House—the then New Market—but it did not thrive. It was occupied by live cattle and goats instead of beef and mutton. Hens, chickens and ducks volunteered their presence, without the fear of spit or frying-pan, and even laid their eggs in remote and dark corners, not likely to be visited by any other customers than prying school-boys or vagrant children. A few vegetables also volunteered their verdure; such as dandelions—an excellent salad—butter-cups, with roots more pungent than red pepper, chick-weed, for bird fanciers, and thistles—but not a good substitute for artichokes.

I don't assert that the fox made his hole and the wren built its nest in the market-house, but it is true that Fox & Wren occupied it and built coaches there. The Wrens now nestle elsewhere, cherished and cherishing—of the Foxes only one remains in quiet retirement.

The Market-house, guiltless of blood and slaughter, was demolished many years later.

Theatrical performances were afterwards held in the upper part of the old Market-house, on Main and Seventeenth streets, recently demolished and rebuilt;

Samuel Mordecai
Richmond in By-Gone Days, 1856
Reprint Edition, 1975

After returning to the United States from France, Thomas Jefferson, as secretary of state in George Washington's administration, frequently sent messages via the diplomatic pouch to William Short in France. Jefferson's former secretary while he was serving as U. S. Minister to France, was often requested to purchase and send the secretary of state such food delicacies as vanilla beans, Dijon mustard, and Parmesan cheese. Sometimes, Mr. Jefferson requested unusual tasks from Short...learning to prepare chicken in a "coffin" or enclosure of puff pastry, faire cuire un pouleten cassette.

Chicken Broccoli Casserole

Yield: 6 servings

1 (10-ounce) package frozen broccoli spears or cuts
5 tablespoons butter or margarine, melted and divided
1/2 cup flour
2 chicken bouillon cubes, mashed
2 cups water
2 3/4 cups cubed cooked chicken, cut into 1/2 to 3/4-inch cubes or bite-sized pieces
Salt and pepper to taste
1 1/4 cups grated mild Cheddar cheese
1/2 cup bread crumbs

In a medium heavy saucepan, partially cook broccoli for about 2 to 3 minutes; drain well. *Do not over cook.* In a large heavy saucepan, blend flour into 4 tablespoons butter to form a smooth paste. Add chicken bouillon cubes and water, stirring to dissolve bouillon well. Cook, stirring constantly, over moderate heat until mixture is thickened and bubbly hot. Add chicken, mixing well. Season with salt and pepper to taste. Arrange the broccoli spears or cuts in the bottom of an 11 x 7 x 2-inch baking dish. Pour chicken mixture over broccoli. In a small bowl, combine cheese, bread crumbs, and 1 tablespoon butter.

–Heilman Dining Center
University of Richmond
Food Services Department

189

Chicken Rice Casserole

Yield: 6 to 8 servings

1 (10 3/4-ounce) can cream of chicken soup, undiluted
1 (8-ounce) can sliced water chestnuts, drained
1 small onion, peeled and minced
2 cups cubed cooked chicken or turkey
2 cups cooked rice
1 cup chopped celery
3/4 cup mayonnaise
2 tablespoons lemon juice
1/2 teaspoon salt or to taste
1/8 teaspoon pepper or to taste
1 cup crumbled commercial stuffing mix
1/4 cup butter or margarine, melted

In a large bowl, combine the first 10 ingredients, mixing well. Spoon into a greased 2-quart casserole. In a small bowl, combine stuffing mix and butter, tossing lightly to mix; evenly sprinkle over chicken mixture. Bake, uncovered, in a moderate oven (350 degrees F.) for 40 minutes or until bubbly hot and topping is lightly browned.

Note: Casserole may be prepared and baked in advance, refrigerated for 24 hours, and then reheated, covered, in a moderate oven (350 degrees F.) for 15 to 20 minutes. Remove cover and continue reheating about 10 minutes or until bubbly hot. Casserole may also be prepared but refrigerated for 24 hours before baking.

–Mary Jo Banton (Mrs. Thomas)

Baked Chicken Salad (Casserole)

Yield: 6 servings

1 (10 3/4-ounce) can cream of mushroom soup, undiluted
2 cups cubed cooked chicken or turkey
1 cup chopped celery
1/2 cup mayonnaise
1/2 cup sliced water chestnuts, drained
1 tablespoon chopped pimento, drained
1 tablespoon lemon juice
1 teaspoon minced peeled onion
Salt and pepper to taste
Crushed crisp potato chips for garnish

In a medium bowl, combine the first 8 ingredients. Add salt and pepper to taste, mixing well. Spoon into a greased 1 1/2-quart casserole; top with crushed potato chips as desired. Bake, uncovered, in a moderate oven (375 degrees F.) for 30 minutes or until bubbly hot.

–Swift Creek Mill Playhouse

190

How to Clean and Dress Fowls-No. 287.

Cut off the head; remove every feather, taking the largest first. When all the feathers are off wash the fowl carefully and look to see that no feathers have been left on. If there are small feathers that cannot be removed with the fingers, use a pair of kitchen tweezers to draw them out. It is best to pick the fowls dry, though they are often dipped in boiling water to loosen the feathers. Having picked and cleaned the outside of the fowl, proceed to open and empty it. To do this, cut the skin on the back of the neck, turn it over on the breast, and cut off the neck; remove the crop, being particular to take out all the strings, membrane, etc; break the ligaments that hold the internal organs to the breastbone; cut the fowl open at the vent, beginning under the left leg; put the fingers in this opening and work around until the organs are loosened from the bones; draw all out at once, being careful not to break anything; return the fingers into the body of the fowl to see if anything is left there; cut the oil-bag from the tail and the feet off at the first joints of the leg. If there are any feathers or hairs around the tail or elsewhere singe the fowl, wash quickly in cold water, and prepare according to the way of cooking the fowl. Separate the liver and gizzard from the other internal organs, wash, open the gizzard, empty and clean it nicely.

Instruction in Cooking with Selected Receipts, *1895*

Baked Chicken 'N Onions

Yield: 4 servings

1 (3-pound) frying chicken, cut into serving pieces
Flour as needed
1/4 cup butter or margarine, melted
Salt and pepper to taste
1 medium onion, peeled and chopped (see note)
1 cup chicken broth or bouillon
Paprika and minced parsley for garnish

Dredge chicken pieces in flour, coating each piece well. In a heavy skillet, brown chicken in butter over moderate heat; season with salt and pepper to taste. Transfer chicken pieces, reserving drippings, to a greased 12 x 8 x 2-inch baking dish. Sauté onions in hot drippings until tender but not browned. Add chicken broth, blending well; bring to a boil and pour over chicken pieces. Bake, uncovered, in a moderate oven (350 degrees F.) for 1 hour or until tender. Sprinkle lightly with paprika and minced parsley for garnish.

Note: Onion may be thinly sliced and separated into rings, if desired.

–Libbie Davis (Mrs. Robert)

191

South-of-the-Border Chicken Pie

Yield: 6 to 8 servings

3/4 cup slivered blanched
  almonds
1 tablespoon butter or
  margarine, melted
1 tablespoon cornstarch
1 1/2 teaspoons Worcestershire sauce
1/2 teaspoon salt or to taste
1/4 teaspoon pepper or to
  taste
1 cup sour cream
2 cups cubed cooked
  chicken or turkey, cut into
  1/4 to 1/2-inch cubes
1 1/2 cups shredded sharp
  Cheddar or Monterey Jack
  cheese
2 tablespoons minced
  pimento, drained
2 tablespoons minced green
  pepper
3 to 4 drops Tabasco sauce
  or to taste
Pastry for Unbaked Pie Shell
  (9-inch) (see index)

Arrange almonds in one layer on a baking sheet; bake in a slow oven (300 degrees F.) for 8 to 10 minutes or until a very light ivory color. Combine toasted almonds and butter in a small bowl, tossing lightly; set aside. In a medium bowl, combine cornstarch, Worcestershire sauce, salt, and pepper. Add sour cream, blending until smooth. Stir in chicken, cheese, pimento, green pepper, and Tabasco sauce. Spoon mixture into pastry shell, spreading evenly. Bake in a hot oven (400 degrees F.) for 25 minutes. Evenly sprinkle almonds over pie. Bake an additional 5 to 10 minutes, until almonds are lightly browned and filling is set. A silver knife inserted in center will come out clean. Cool for 10 minutes on a wire rack before cutting and serving.

Variation: Stir 1 tablespoon minced green chili peppers into filling.

–Kelly Yuhas (Mrs. Ken)

Bird Pie

Line a baking dish with pie pastry; put in the bottom some thin slices of bacon, some hard-boiled eggs sliced up, and butter, pepper, and salt; parboil the birds, and cut them up; fill the dish with a layer of birds, eggs, and seasoning, and put in a little of the gravy in which the birds were parboiled. Cover the top with pastry, and bake for one hour.

F. F. V. Receipt Book, *1894*

Chicken Allouette

Yield: 4 servings

Thyme and Sage of Hanover, located near Ashland, Virginia on Leadbetter Road, just 10 miles north of Richmond, has caught many Richmonders' eyes. A family-operated restaurant, the Fairbrother family opened the restaurant of casual atmosphere and continental cuisine in Spring, 1987.Chicken Allouette is a frequently requested entrée.

4 (6 to 8-ounce) skinless
  boneless chicken breasts
1/2 cup Allouette cheese,
  divided
4 slices of fully-cooked
  smoked Dutch or Danish
  or other mild-flavored
  ham cut into 1/8-inch
  thick slices
Wooden picks (optional)
1/4 cup clarified butter, at
  room temperature(see
  index) or cooking oil
2 chicken bouillon cubes,
  mashed
1 cup heavy cream
4 teaspoons red wine
  vinegar
8 to 12 canned artichoke
  bottoms, drained, each
  cut in half
1/4 cup thinly sliced peeled
  roasted sweet red pepper
  or pimento, drained (see
  note)

Place chicken breasts between sheets of waxed paper or clear plastic wrap; flatten each breast to a 1/4 inch thickness with the edge of a small plate or meat mallet. Place 2 tablespoons cheese on each ham slice and roll each jelly-roll style; place a stuffed ham roll in the center of each chicken breast. Fold the sides of each breast inward and then roll forward to close around each ham roll, sealing with wooden picks, if desired. Stuffed chicken breasts may be wrapped in aluminum foil and frozen for use at a later date, if desired.In a medium heavy skillet, melt butter over moderate heat; continue to heat until a few drops of water dropped in butter sizzles. Add chicken breasts; saute breasts until lightly browned, about 2 to 3 minutes per side. Transfer chicken to a 9 x 9 x 2-inch baking pan. Bake, uncovered, in a moderate oven (350 degrees F.) for 10 to 15 minutes or until chicken breasts are fork tender. While chicken is baking, prepare sauce. In a heavy saucepan, combine bouillon cubes, cream,and vinegar, blending well. Stir over moderate heat until sauce begins to simmer; add artichokes and pepper, mixing lightly. Reduce heat and simmer for 2 minutes. Arrange a stuffed chicken breast on each of 4 dinner plates; spoon sauce over each portion, dividing evenly.

Note: To roast pepper, arrange pepper on a rack in a broiler pan. Broil, 6 to 8 inches from heat source.

–The Fairbrother Family
Thyme and Sage of Hanover

Baked Chicken Breasts with Apple Brandy

Yield: 4 to 6 servings

"This recipe was inspired by James Beard; however, I have adapted it to my tastes."

2 to 3 large chicken breasts, halved (see note)
1/4 cup butter or margarine, melted
1/2 cup plus 2 tablespoons apple brandy, divided
2 medium tart apples, peeled, cored, seeded, and chopped (see note)
1 medium onion, peeled and coarsely chopped
1 medium carrot, peeled, halved lengthwise, and cut into 1-inch pieces
1/2 cup coarsely chopped celery
1/2 cup chicken broth
1/2 teaspoon salt or to taste
1 1/2 teaspoons minced fresh or 1/2 teaspoon dried thyme
1 teaspoon cornstarch
2 egg yolks, beaten
1/2 cup heavy or light cream
1 tablespoon lemon juice or to taste
Pepper to taste (optional)
Fresh thyme or parsley sprigs for garnish

In a Dutch oven or oven-proof sauté pan, sauté chicken breasts in butter over moderate heat until lightly browned, about 2 minutes per side. In a small heavy saucepan, warm 1/2 cup brandy; then ignite. After flame has extinguished, pour over chicken. Add apples, onion, carrot, and celery to pan, scattering some of the mixture over chicken breasts. Add chicken broth and salt. Sprinkle evenly with thyme. Bring broth to boiling. Cover and transfer to a moderate oven (350 degrees F.); bake for 25 to 30 minutes or until chicken is fork tender. Remove chicken to a warm platter. Cover and keep warm. Continue to cook vegetables for an additional 10 minutes. Strain pan liquid by pressing vegetable mixture with a wooden spoon through a sieve. Discard any large pieces remaining in sieve. In a small heavy saucepan, blend 2 tablespoons apple brandy into cornstarch until smooth. With a wire whisk, blend in egg yolks, cream, and lemon juice. Stir in strained pan liquid. Stir over low heat *just* until mixture begins to simmer. Do *not* boil. Adjust seasonings, add pepper, if desired. Pour sauce over chicken, garnish with fresh thyme or parsley sprigs, and serve immediately.

Note: Boneless chicken breasts may be used. Reduce cooking time of chicken; remove from sauce when tender, keep warm, and continue to simmer sauce and vegetables longer to develop flavors before proceeding with recipe.

Note: Use McIntosh, Winesap, Granny Smith, or other tart variety of apples.

–Nancy Scoggins (Mrs. Robert)
Valentine Museum Guild

Chicken Breasts in Spiced Chutney Cream with Savory Curried Rice

Yield : 4 to 6 servings

3 chicken breasts, skinned, boned, and halved
About 1/4 cup flour
About 6 tablespoons butter or margarine, at room temperature and divided
2 green onions, minced (include some green tops)
3/4 cup chicken broth
1/3 cup Madeira or dry sherry
3 tablespoons chopped chutney (see note)
1/2 teaspoon minced peeled fresh ginger root
3/4 cup heavy cream, at room temperature
2 tablespoons chopped crystallized ginger for garnish
Savory Curried Rice (see index)
Cilantro (coriander) or parsley sprigs for garnish

Place chicken breast halves between sheets of waxed paper; flatten chicken pieces with a meat mallet until pieces are about 1/4-inch thick. On a sheet of waxed paper, dredge chicken in flour, coating each piece lightly. In a large heavy skillet, melt butter over moderate heat. Add chicken pieces and saute until lightly browned, about 2 to 3 minutes per side. Add additional butter to pan as needed. Transfer chicken pieces to a heated platter, cover, and keep warm in a *very* slow oven (200 degrees F.) Add green onions, chicken broth, Madeira, chutney, and fresh ginger root to pan drippings. Increase heat to high and cook, stirring constantly, until mixture is reduced in half, about 5 minutes. Add the cream and continue cooking, stirring constantly, until sauce is reduced to about 1 1/4 cups. Arrange chicken half breasts on individual plates; pour sauce over chicken, dividing evenly. Sprinkle chopped crystallized ginger over each portion. Accompany with Savory Curried Rice and garnish each serving with a sprig of cilantro or parsley.

Note: Preferably use Major Grey-style chutney

Variation: 1 1/2 to 2 pounds thinly sliced boneless veal (scallopine) or pork tenderloin may be substituted for chicken breasts.

–Vienna Taylor

Tender Chicken Breasts à la Wakefield

Yield: 6 servings

6 boneless whole chicken breasts, skinned
6 medium mushrooms
1 medium onion, peeled
1 medium zucchini squash
1 rib celery
1 pound broccoli, woody stems removed and separated into very small florets and tender stems
3 to 4 tablespoons hot olive oil (see note)
1 egg, lightly beaten
1 tablespoon water
About 1 cup fine cracker meal
Salt and pepper to taste
Hot corn or peanut oil as needed
Marsala Sauce (see index)
3/4 cup shredded Swiss cheese, divided

Separate each chicken breast into 2 halves; flatten each breast half with a meat mallet. With a sharp knife, cut vegetables, except broccoli florets, in a *julienne* (very thin match-like strips). In a large heavy skillet, sauté *julienne* vegetables and broccoli florets in olive oil over moderate heat until just crisp tender; *do not over cook.* Remove from heat and set aside. In a shallow bowl, combine egg and water, mixing well. Dip each chicken half breast in the egg wash and then dredge in cracker meal on waxed paper, coating each well. In a large heavy skillet, sauté breaded chicken breast halves in hot corn oil over moderate heat until golden brown, about 1 to 2 minutes per side. Spoon 2 tablespoons Marsala Sauce into each of 6 individual casseroles or ramekins. Arrange 2 chicken half breasts in each casserole. Top each serving with 1/2 cup sautéed *julienne*-style vegetables. Spoon 2 tablespoons additional sauce over each serving and sprinkle each with 2 tablespoons shredded Swiss cheese. Arrange casseroles on ungreased baking sheets. Bake, uncovered, in a moderate oven (350 degrees F.) for 8 to 10 minutes or until cheese melts and begins to brown. Serve immediately.

Note: Use a premium quality extra virgin olive oil. Extra virgin refers to the oil collected from the first press of the olives.

–Jack Terry, proprietor
Wakefields' Restaurant

...The ordinaries were tightly regulated by the county courts and subsequently by the Richmond hustings court. The court issued licenses to tavern keepers, and set all prices for "liquors, diet, lodging, provender, stablage, fodder, and pasturage...." Within one month after they were established, a table of the rates was to be "openly set up in the publick entertaining room of every ordinary."

Harry M. Ward and Harold E. Greer, Jr.
Richmond During The Revolution, 1775-83, 1977

Easy Chicken Divan

Yield: 4 to 6 servings

2 (10-ounce) packages
frozen broccoli spears
2 cups thinly sliced cooked
chicken
1 cup mayonnaise
1 teaspoon lemon juice
1/2 teaspoon curry powder
or to taste
1/2 cup shredded sharp
Cheddar cheese
1/2 cup bread or corn flake
crumbs
2 tablespoons butter or
margarine, melted

Partially cook broccoli according to package directions until just tender but firm; drain well. Arrange broccoli spears in a greased 11 x 7 x 2-inch baking dish. Evenly arrange chicken slices over broccoli. In a small bowl, combine mayonnaise, lemon juice, and curry powder, blending well; spoon over chicken, spreading evenly. Sprinkle with cheese. Combine breadcrumbs and butter, tossing lightly; evenly sprinkle over casserole. Bake, uncovered, in a moderate oven (350 degrees F.) for 25 to 30 minutes.

–Jidge Bates (Mrs. John, Jr.)

Old Richmond Advertisement, circa 1909

Mediterranean-Style Roasted Chicken

Yield: 6 to 8 servings

1 (3- to 4-pound) roasting chicken
2 tablespoons olive oil
1 tablespoon (about 6 to 8 leaves) minced fresh or 1 teaspoon dried basil
1 teaspoon minced peeled garlic
1 teaspoon grated lemon peel
1 teaspoon lemon pepper seasoning
1/4 cup lemon juice (see note)

Brush chicken with olive oil, coating well. Place half of the basil, half of the garlic, and half of the lemon peel in the cavity of the chicken. Secure wings behind chicken. Arrange chicken on a wire rack in a 9 x 9 x 2-inch baking pan or small shallow roaster. Sprinkle remaining basil, garlic, lemon peel, and all of the lemon pepper seasoning over the top and sides of chicken. Rub into chicken skin. Gradually pour lemon juice over chicken. Bake, uncovered, in a moderate oven (350 degrees F.) for 1 to 1 1/2 hours or until chicken is fork tender and golden brown. Baste chicken frequently with pan juices during roasting.

Note: Preferably use freshly squeezed lemon juice.

Chicken Pudding

"Oh! mickle is the powerful grace that lies in herbs,"-While four young chickens, cut up as for frying, and favored with "bundles of parsley and thyme," are gently stewing upon the fire, the housewife will make ready a thin batter. Take ten eggs; to these add a quart of rich milk, a quarter of a pound of melted butter, flour, pepper, and salt. When the chickens are nearly done, immerse the pieces in the batter, pour all into a deep dish and bake quickly. The remainder of the stew, after taking out the herbs, may be used as a basis for a white gravy. The flavor or the thyme, elusive and pungent, may intrigue your guest, but it cannot fail to please his palate.

GRANITE IRONWARE.   **Virginia Cooking,** 1939

Manufactured only by ST. LOUIS STAMPING CO.
ST. LOUIS, and For Sale Everywhere.

Old Richmond Advertisement, circa 1895

Coq Au Riesling

Yield: 6 to 8 servings

Chef Otto is a well respected Richmond culinary expert known for his wonderful recipes, especially pastries.

2 (2 1/2 to 3-pound) frying chickens, cut into serving pieces, skin removed (see note)
Flour as needed
3 tablespoons butter or margarine, melted
2 medium carrots, peeled and chopped
2 medium onions, peeled and chopped
2 ribs celery, peeled and chopped
2 garlic cloves, peeled and minced
2 tablespoons cognac or other brandy
8 cups water
4 cups dry white (Riesling) wine
4 bay leaves, crumbled
2 teaspoons salt or to taste
1 1/2 teaspoons minced fresh or 1/2 teaspoon dry thyme
1/2 teaspoon nutmet
2 cups heavy cream, at room temperature

On a sheet of waxed paper or in a ziplock plastic bag, dredge chicken pieces lightly in flour, coating each piece well. In a large heavy skillet, brown chicken thoroughly in butter over moderate heat; reduce temperature and simmer chicken, uncovered, for 8 minutes. In a medium heavy skillet, saute´ carrots, onions,celery, and garlic in cognac over moderate heat until vegetables are tender but not browned. Ignite brandy and flambé vegetable mixture until flame is extinguished. In a Dutch oven or medium heavy roasting pan, combine chicken pieces, vegetable mixture,water, wine, herbs, and nutmeg. Bake, covered, in a hot oven (400 degrees F.) for 40 to 45 minutes or until chicken is fork tender. Transfer chicken pieces and vegetables to a heated serving platter. Stir heavy cream into remaining sauce in pan. Spoon sauce over chicken and vegetables.

Note: Omit chicken pieces with backbone and livers.

Note: This recipe is more tasty if prepared 24 hours in advance of serving, refrigerated, and then reheated *just* before serving.

—Chef Otto Bernet

199

Linden Row Inn

Today historic Linden Row, a group of eight distinctive nineteenth century row houses, located between First and Second Streets on East Franklin Street, again takes its place in Richmond's rich heritage. Saved from the wrecking ball in the early 1950's by the well-known pioneer historic Richmond preservationist, Mary Wingfield Scott, the buildings have been restored and opened as a seventy-two room inn, including seven suites.

Originally known as Rutherford's Addition west of the city limits in the late eighteenth century, five row houses were built at the corner of Second and Franklin Streets in 1847 by Fleming James, followed by an additional five houses in 1853. Named for the Linden trees growing on the property, the buildings were home to three girls' schools in the last part of the nineteenth century. One early pupil of the Southern Female Institute recalled confederate President Jefferson Davis riding past Linden Row many days. The last school, Miss Jennie Ellett's (1895-1906), evolved into the well-regarded St. Catherine's Girls School, now located on Grove Avenue in the fashionable West End of Richmond.

One linden tree from that long ago era still graces the Inn's garden. Edgar Allan Poe, a neighbor during the nineteenth century, is said to have patterned his enchanted garden described in his poem, To Helen, after those long ago gardens ... known for the trees, old-fashioned roses, and jasmine growing there.

Decorated with Victorian antiques and reproductions, the Inn boasts a charming full-service dining room located in the former carriage house, offering specialties in good Southern cooking such as crab cakes, fried chicken, Kentucky Derby and pecan pies. Adjacent dependency buildings, originally nineteenth century servant's quarters and kitchens, have been turned into rooms decorated with reproduction cottage furniture.

Managed by Great Inns of America, governed by the covenants of the Historic Richmond Foundation, and registered as an historic landmark, Lindow Row is now a delightful place for Richmonders and city visitors to sample a touch of history and Southern hospitality and food.

Mrs. Pegram's Chicken

Yield: 4 servings

This recipe is dedicated to Mrs. Virginia Pegram who founded a girl's school which was located in the Linden Row buildings on First and Franklin Streets from 1856 to 1866. Mrs. Pegram. the widow of General James Pegram, hero of the Mexican War, also handled the boarding facilities and taught music instruction in the Southern Female Institute, located in the row houses.

4 boneless whole double chicken breasts, each about 6 ounces, skinned (see note)

8 *very* thin slices fully-cooked smoked Smithfield or Virginia country-style ham (about 2 ounces)

4 (1-ounce) slices provolone cheese

1/2 to 1 cup flour

Salt and pepper to taste

1 egg, beaten

1 tablespoon water

About 1/2 to 1 cup breadcrumbs

1/4 cup butter or margarine, melted

Apple Mustard Sauce (see index)

Remove any remaining skin or gristle from chicken breasts. Open chicken breasts out flat and pound each to a 1/2 inch thickness. Arrange 2 ham slices on one-half of each breast; top ham with a cheese slice. Fold remaining half of each chicken breast over cheese to form a stuffed breast. On a sheet of waxed paper, combine flour, salt, and pepper, mixing well. In a shallow bowl, combine egg and water, beating lightly. Dredge stuffed breasts in seasoned flour, coating each well. Dip each floured breast in egg wash, then roll in bread crumbs, coating each well. In a large heavy skillet, sauté breaded chicken breasts in butter over moderate heat until lightly browned, about 2 minutes per side. Transfer to an 11 x 7 x 2-inch baking pan; bake, uncovered, in a moderate oven (350 degrees F.) for 25 to 30 minutes or until chicken is fork tender. Arrange each chicken breast on a dinner plate and spoon a small amount of Apple Mustard Sauce over each portion. Garnish as desired.

–Linden Row Dining Room
Linden Row Inn

Executive Mansion Chicken
with Basil Tomato Sauce

Yield: 4 servings

Adapted from a recipe of Time-Life books, this recipe is a popular dining offering at the Virginia Executive Mansion.

2 cups chicken stock or
  broth (see note)
2 cups loosely packed fresh
  basil leaves, divided
2 (1-pound) chicken breasts,
  skinned, boned, and
  halved
1 garlic clove, peeled
1/2 cup water
2 tablespoons mayonnaise
  (see note)
1 firm ripe medium tomato,
  peeled, seeded, and
  chopped
Sprigs of fresh basil for
  garnish

In a small Dutch oven or shallow heavy small roaster or baking pan, combine chicken stock and 1/2 cup basil leaves. Bring mixture to simmering over moderate heat; reduce temperature and continue simmering for 5 minutes. Add boneless chicken half breasts to stock, cover, and poach over low heat for 8 minutes. Turn chicken pieces over and continue poaching for about an additional 4 minutes or until chicken breasts are firm but springy to the touch. Place garlic in a food processor or blender container; cover and process until garlic is finely chopped. Add the remaining 1 1/2 cups basil leaves and water; cover and puree mixture. Strain purée, lightly pressing mixture through a sieve with the back of a wooden spoon to remove all liquid. To prepare sauce, combine strained purée, mayonnaise, and half of the chopped tomato, blending well. Remove chicken half breasts from poaching liquid and pat dry with absorbent paper. Cut each half breast diagonally into thin slices, dividing evenly, and arrange slices in a fan design over additional fresh basil leaves on individual serving plates. Spoon about 2 tablespoons tomato sauce over each serving and sprinkle each with chopped tomato, dividing evenly.

Note: 1 (13 1/2-ounce) can commercial chicken broth plus 2 1/2 ounces of water may be substituted for chicken stock.

Note: Preferably use Homemade Mayonnaise (see index).

–Virginia Executive Mansion

Zesty Bar-B-Q'd Chicken

Yield: 4 servings

1 (2 1/2 to 3-pound) frying chicken, cut into serving pieces
Tillman's Bar-B-Q Sauce (see index)

In a deep medium bowl, combine chicken pieces and Tillman's Bar-B-Q Sauce, coating chicken pieces well. Cover and refrigerate for 2 to 3 hours, basting chicken with sauce frequently. Drain chicken and arrange pieces in a 12 x 8 x 2-inch baking pan. Reserve marinade for basting chicken during baking. Bake chicken, uncovered, in a moderate oven (350 degrees F.) for 1 hour or until chicken is fork tender and lightly browned, basting frequently with the sauce. Or, arrange chicken pieces bone side down, on a grill rack lined with aluminum foil, shiny side turned up, 8 to 10 inches above medium coals (ash gray and glowing); grill for 10 to 15 minutes, basting chicken frequently with sauce. Turn chicken, bone side up, and continue grilling for 10 to 15 minutes or until chicken is fork tender, basting frequently with sauce. Chicken may be covered during grilling, if desired. For gas grills, follow manufacturer's directions.

–Laurie Brickham (Mrs. Bruce)

Virginia Cookery Book, circa 1921

Hot and Spicy Skewered Chicken

Yield: 6 entrée or 12 appetizer servings

3 chicken breasts, skinned
and boned
6 to 8 green onions, minced
(include some green tops)
1 cup crunch-style peanut
butter
3/4 cup hot-spiced salsa
1/3 cup minced parsley
1/4 cup light brown sugar,
firmly packed
1/4 cup soy sauce (see note)
1/4 cup lemon juice
3 tablespoons minced
peeled garlic
1/2 teaspoon cayenne
pepper
Long thin wooden or metal
skewers
2 sweet red or yellow or
green peppers, cored,
seeded and cut into 1 to
1 1/2-inch squares (see
note)

With a sharp knife, cut chicken into long narrow strips. In a deep medium bowl, combine green onions, peanut butter, salsa, parsley, brown sugar, soy sauce, lemon juice, garlic, and cayenne and black peppers, mixing well. Place chicken strips in marinade, coating strips well with mixture. Cover and refrigerate for 3 to 12 hours, as desired, in the refrigerator. Turn chicken pieces occasionally in marinade. Remove chicken from marinade. Thread one end of a chicken strip on skewer, then thread a pepper square on skewer, loop loose end of chicken strip over pepper square and thread to the skewer; repeat process until all chicken strips and pepper squares are used. Arrange kabobs on a metal rack in a broiler pan. Broil, 6 to 8 inches from heat source, turning once, for about 5 minutes per side. Or, arrange kabobs on a grill rack, 8 to 10 inches above moderate coals (ash gray and glowing). Grill, turning once, about 5 minutes per side or until chicken is fork tender and lightly browned on the outside and the inside is white in color. Serve immediately.

Note: Reduced sodium (Lite) soy sauce may be substituted for regular soy sauce. One teaspoon Lite soy sauce contains 100 milligrams of sodium.

Note: Peppers may be blanched in boiling water for 2 to 3 minutes after water returns to a boil, if desired. Remove peel from blanched peppers, if desired.

–Hal Tyler

Chicken Guillaume

Yield: 4 servings

"My son, Bill Crowell, invented this recipe after eating in a Philadelphia French restaurant...thus the name. It can be prepared early in the day and reheated at dinner time. It's even better because the flavors meld."

2 pounds mild spiced bulk
  pork sausage or Italian-
  style sausage links, cut
  into 1-inch pieces
4 chicken breasts, skinned,
  boned, and cut into bite-
  sized pieces
1 pound mushrooms, thinly
  sliced
1 (20-ounce) can tomatoes,
  drained
1 (16-ounce) package frozen
  very small white onions
1 cup dry white wine
1 teaspoon minced peeled
  garlic
1 tablespoon minced fresh
  tarragon or 1 teaspoon
  dry
Salt and pepper to taste
Hot cooked long grain rice

In a large heavy skillet, lightly brown sausage over moderate heat. Add chicken and mushrooms and sauté until chicken and mushrooms are lightly browned, about 10 minutes. Add tomatoes, onions, wine, garlic, and tarragon. Season with salt and pepper to taste. Reduce heat and simmer for 15 minutes or until onions are tender and mixture bubbly hot. Serve over hot cooked rice.

–Sue Crowell (Mrs. Robert)

205

> A small elegant hotel in the English manner, The Berkley Hotel opened in the spring of 1988 at the corner of Cary and 12th Streets in historic Shockoe Slip. Although the construction is new, the architecture of the building has been designed to blend into the surrounding area. The intimate Berkley Restaurant and cocktail lounge located at street level with windows overlooking the historic scene, provides an excellent place "to see and be seen" while enjoying a pleasant drink or dinner.

Chicken Balsamic

Yield: 4 servings

4 boneless chicken breasts, skinned, each about 8 ounces
About 1/2 cup flour
Salt and pepper to taste
3 to 4 tablespoons clarified butter, melted (see index)
1 garlic clove, peeled and minced
1 cup julienne peeled red onion (see note)
1/4 cup chicken stock or broth
1/4 cup dry white wine
1/4 cup balsamic vinegar
1/4 cup unsalted butter, at room temperature
1/4 teaspoon sugar or to taste (see note)
4 canned artichoke hearts, drained and quartered

With a meat mallet, pound chicken breasts lightly. On a sheet of waxed paper, combine flour with salt and pepper to taste, mixing well. Dredge chicken breasts in seasoned flour, coating each well. In a large heavy skillet, sauté chicken in 3 to 4 tablespoons clarified butter over moderate to high heat until golden brown, about 2 to 3 minutes per side. Add garlic and onion and continue to sauté for 30 to 60 seconds. Remove chicken breasts; set aside. Add chicken stock, wine, and balsamic vinegar to skillet, blending well with garlic and onion. With a wire whisk, blend in unsalted butter. Add sugar, and salt and pepper to taste. Return chicken breasts and add artichoke hearts to sauce; continue to cook, uncovered, until sauce is reduced and slightly thickened. Arrange chicken breasts on each of 4 dinner plates; spoon a small amount of sauce and vegetables over each serving. Garnish as desired.

Note: To julienne onions, cut into narrow, lengthwise, matchstick-like strips.

Note: The addition of sugar is used just to cut the bite of the sauce flavor.

–Chef Kevin Goodrich
The Berkeley Restaurant
The Berkeley Hotel

Sautéed Chicken Livers, Onions, 'N Mushrooms in White Wine

Yield: 2 servings

1 medium onion, peeled, thinly sliced, and separated into rings
4 ounces mushrooms thinly sliced
2 tablespoons butter or margarine, melted
1/2 cup flour
1 teaspoon salt
1/4 teaspoon pepper
1/8 teaspoon paprika
1/8 teaspoon garlic powder
1 pound chicken livers
3 tablespoons hot cooking oil
3/4 cup dry white wine
Hot cooked buttered rice
Additional paprika for garnish
Minced parsley for garnish

In a large heavy skillet, sauté onion and mushrooms in butter over moderate heat until tender but not browned; remove, drain, and set aside. In a bowl or ziplock plastic bag, combine flour and spices, mixing well. Add chicken livers, coating each well in the flour mixture. Saute livers in remaining hot drippings and cooking oil over moderate heat until lightly browned. Reduce temperature and add mushroom-onion mixture. Gradually blend in wine; simmer, covered, over low heat for 10 minutes. Do not over cook; the inside of the chicken livers should be slightly pink in color. Adjust seasoning to taste. Serve over hot buttered rice and sprinkle lightly with additional paprika and minced parsley for garnish.

–Elinor Hart (Mrs. Charles)

207

Chicken Paprika with Parsley Dumplings

Yield: 4 servings

1 1/2 tablespoons butter or margarine
1 1/2 tablespoons cooking oil
1 cup chopped peeled onion
2 tablespoons sweet Hungarian paprika
2 cups chicken stock or broth (see note)
1/2 teaspoon salt or to taste
1 (2 1/2 to 3-pound) chicken, cut into serving pieces
2 teaspoons flour
1 cup sour cream
Parsley Dumplings

In a Dutch oven or large heavy pot, melt butter and heat oil to about 325 to 350 degrees F. Add onions and paprika, mixing well; simmer, stirring constantly, until onion is tender but not browned. Add chicken stock and salt. Increase heat to moderate and bring mixture to a full boil. Add chicken; reduce heat and simmer, covered, for about 1 hour or until chicken is fork tender. Stir flour into sour cream; gradually add mixture to pot liquid, blending well. Continue to simmer for about 5 minutes until sauce is thickened and smooth. *Do not boil.* Serve at once with Parsley Dumplings.

Note: 1 1/2 (10 1/2-ounce) undiluted cans chicken broth may be substituted for chicken stock or broth.

Parsley Dumplings
Yield: 4 servings
1 1/2 cups sifted flour
1/2 teaspoon salt
1/4 teaspoon baking powder
3 tablespoons minced fresh or 1 tablespoon dried parsley
2 eggs, beaten
1/2 cup water
About 3 quarts boiling water or simmering chicken broth

In a medium bowl, sift together the first 3 ingredients. Add parsley, mixing well. Stir in eggs and water, mixing only until ingredients are thoroughly moistened. Drop by rounded tablespoonfuls into a large deep pot of boiling water or chicken broth. Cook, cover ajar, about 12 minutes for boiling water and about 15 to 20 minutes for simmering chicken stock.

Note: The dumpling dough may be dropped by rounded tablespoonfuls into hot Chicken Paprika broth and cooked for 15 to 20 minutes. Then add sour cream to broth mixture.

–Paige Curtis (Mrs. Jeffrey)

Chicken & Dumplins

Cut and joint a large chicken. Cover with water and let boil gently until tender. Season with salt and pepper and thicken the gravy with two tablespoonfuls of flour mixed smooth in a piece of butter the size of an egg. Have ready nice light bread dough about an inch thick; cut with a biscuit-cutter. Drop into the boiling gravy, having previously removed the chicken to a hot platter; cover and let these boil from one half to three quarters of an hour. To ascertain whether they are done stick them with a fork; if it comes out clean they are done. Lay them on the platter with the chicken; pour the gravy over and serve.

(Old Recipe, Highland Springs, VA,
The Williamsburg Art of Cookery
date unknown)1938

Chicken Livers with Rice

Yield: 4 to 6 servings

3 tablespoons minced
  peeled onion
1/2 cup butter or margarine,
  melted and divided
1 1/2 cups uncooked rice
Boiling water as needed
8 ounces chicken livers
Flour as needed
1 (10 3/4-ounce) can cream
  of chicken soup, undi-
  luted
1/2 cup milk
1 tablespoon minced
  parsley
1 teaspoon minced fresh or
  1/4 teaspoon dried basil
Salt and pepper to taste

In a small heavy saucepan, sauté onion in 1 tablespoon butter over moderate heat until tender but not browned. In a medium heavy saucepan, cook rice in boiling water according to package directions; drain well. Stir in sautéed onion. Dredge chicken livers lightly in flour. In a medium heavy skillet, sauté chicken livers in remaining melted butter over moderate heat until chicken livers are browned on the outside and pink inside. *Do not over cook.* Cut livers into bite-sized pieces, if desired. In a medium bowl, combine cooked rice mixture, chicken livers, soup, milk, parsley, and basil. Season with salt and pepper to taste.Spoon mixture into a greased 1 1/2-quart casserole. Bake, uncovered, for 20 to 30 minutes or until bubbly hot.

–Ladies' Missionary Society
Great Hope Baptist Church

Chicken Polynesian

Yield: 4 to 6 servings

"This is one of my favorite recipes. Serve with broccoli and tomatoes. Pretty plate, too."

4 chicken breasts, skinned
2 to 3 tablespoons hot
   cooking oil
1/2 small onion, peeled and
   chopped
1 tablespoon butter or
   margarine, at room
   temperature
Hot water as needed
1/2 tablespoon chicken
   stock base or 1/2 chicken
   bouillon cube, mashed
3 to 4 pieces (about 1 to
   1 1/2-inches in diameter)
   crystallized ginger,
   divided
1/4 to 1/2 teaspoon ground
   coriander or to taste
1/8 teaspoon cayenne
   pepper or to taste
2/3 cup sour cream
2 to 3 tablespoons grated
   orange peel
Salt and pepper to taste
2 to 3 cups hot cooked rice
Minced fresh cilantro
   (coriander) for garnish
   (optional)

In a Dutch oven or medium heavy pot, thoroughly brown chicken breasts in oil over moderate heat; remove chicken and set aside.Saute onion in hot pan drippings until tender but not browned.Return chicken to pan and add butter and enough hot water to *just* cover chicken. Add chicken stock base, half of the crystallized ginger, pinch or coriander, and cayenne pepper. Reduce heat and simmer, cover ajar, for 40 minutes. Remove chicken from stock and remove bones from chicken. Discard bones, cut chicken into bite-sized pieces, and return chicken to broth. Stir in sour cream, orange peel, and remaining preserved ginger. Season with salt and pepper to taste. Simmer over low heat until heated through. Do *not* *boil*. Serve over hot cooked rice and garnish each serving with minced fresh cilantro, if desired.

–Pat Boschen

Chicken Dressed with Tomatoes

Fry the fowls a light brown; put them into a dish; then pour into the pan in which they were fried one quart boiling water, one onion chopped fine with parsley, four large tomatoes a little stewed, one tablespoon of butter, rolled in, one tablespoon flour; let it stand for fifteen minutes and then pour it upon the fried chicken to serve. This receipt is for two chickens.

The Kitchen Queen, 1893

Southern Fried Chicken with Country Gravy

Yield: 4 to 6 servings

In these days of diets shunning fat and cholesterol, Southern Fried Chicken, a traditional southern recipe, should probably be banned...but my, oh my, it certainly is "fingerlickin' good." The trick is to brown the chicken first over a high temperature and then cook slowly over a low temperature to seal in the flavor. Southerners in the past would only use corn meal as a coating, but today many people prefer a lighter coating of flour.

1 to 2 (2 1/2 to 3-pound) frying chickens, cut into serving pieces
1 to 1 1/2 cups flour or sifted *very fine* corn meal
Salt or seasoned salt and pepper to taste
About 2 cups shortening, cooking oil, or bacon drippings (or a combination), divided
Country Gravy (see index)
Paul's Place Buttermilk Biscuits or Flaky Sour Cream Biscuits (optional) (see index)
Butter or margarine. at room temperature (optional)
Honey as desired (optional)

On a sheet of waxed paper, dredge chicken pieces in flour, coating well. Sprinkle each lightly with salt or seasoned salt and pepper to taste. Add about half of the shortening, oil, or bacon drippings to a large heavy skillet; heat to moderate (350 to 375 degrees F). Brown chicken pieces, a few at a time, thoroughly in hot fat, turning once, about 3 minutes per side. Add remaining fat as necessary to brown chicken. Remove browned pieces with tongs and set aside. Drain off excess drippings, reserving about 1/4 cup for gravy. Return chicken pieces to skillet; reduce heat and simmer, cover ajar, for 20 to 25 minutes or until chicken is fork tender. Uncover, increase heat to 350 degrees F. and continue cooking until outside of chicken becomes crispy, about 2 minutes per side. Transfer to a warm platter and keep warm in a *very* slow oven (150 to 200 degrees F.) while gravy is prepared. Pour gravy over chicken, garnish as desired, and serve immediately. Serve with Paul's Place Buttermilk Biscuits or Flaky Sour Cream Biscuits, butter, and honey, if desired.

Note: Usually, 1 (3-pound) chicken will yield 4 servings; however, appetites may dictate larger portions for this recipe.

–Vernelle Thomas

Fried Chicken

Divide the chicken into breast, wings, legs, back and scrag; dust with salt, pepper, and flour; put into boiling grease, and keep over the hot fire until all the pieces are a light brown, then reduce the heat and cook until thoroughly done. Serve hot, with or without cream gravy, and on toast, or fried bread, or fried mush. It can be served alone, without bread of any kind.
Instruction in Cooking with Selected Receipts, 1895

Cornish Hens Wellington
with Piquant Currant Sauce

Yield: 6 servings

"This variation of a famous beef recipe, named for the English Duke of Wellington, is a delightful choice for holiday entertaining presented on a silver tray and garnished with spiced crab apples and crisp greens."

6 Rock Cornish hens, each about 1 pound
Twine or heavy string
1 1/2 teaspoons salt or seasoned salt, divided
Pepper or seasoned pepper, to taste
1 egg, separated
1 (6-ounce) package long grain and wild rice
1/4 cup grated orange peel
3 (8-ounce) packages refrigerated crescent rolls
Piquant Currant Sauce
Spice crab apples and watercress sprigs for garnish

Rinse Cornish Hens in cold water; wipe dry with absorbent paper. Tie legs of hens together with twine; place wings behind backs of hens turned akimbo. Sprinkle each hen with salt or seasoned salt and pepper. Brush each hen with eggwhite. Refrigerate hens while rice is cooking. Prepare rice according to package directions; add orange peel, mixing lightly. Unwrap package of crescent rolls; unroll one half of the dough package. Press the two triangles of dough together at the perforated seams to form a 6 inch square of dough. Roll square on a lightly floured board with a lightly floured rolling pin into an 8 inch circle. Place one rice stuffed hen on dough circle, breast-side down on dough. Press dough up around hen, pressing edges together to seal. With a wide spatula, transfer dough covered hen to a 15 x 10x1 inch baking pan; turn breast side up. Repeat process until all the hens are covered with dough. Brush each dough covered hen lightly with beaten egg yolk. Bake, uncovered, in a moderate oven (350 degrees F.) for 1 hour or until a metal tester can be inserted easily into thigh. Transfer hens to individual heated plates; garnish each serving with spiced crab apples and watercress sprigs. Pass hot Piquant Currant Sauce in sauceboat.

Piquant Currant Sauce
Yield: about 3 cups
2 (10-ounce) jars currant jelly 1/4 cup lemon juice
3 tablespoons red port wine
1 tablespoon prepared Dijon-style mustard

In a small heavy saucepan, combine jelly, lemon juice, portwine, and mustard. Stir over low heat until bubbly hot.

–Vienna Taylor

Grilled Breast of Duck with Apples, Wild Mushrooms, and Lettuce

Yield: 4 servings

Chef Paul would carve the apples into attractive duck-image garnishes. You may wish to try your hand at this culinary feat!

4 (7 to 8-ounce) boneless, skinned duck breasts
Salt and pepper to taste
2 tablespoons butter or margarine
2 1/2 tablespoons minced peeled shallots
3 ounces oyster mushrooms, thinly sliced
3 ounces shiitake mushrooms, thinly sliced
3 ounces chanterelle mushrooms, thinly sliced
1/2 head Boston lettuce, cut into a julienne (see note)
1 to 2 ripe tart apples, cored, seeded, and thinly sliced (see note)

Lightly sprinkle duck breasts with salt and pepper. In a teflon-coated large heavy skillet, saute duck breasts over moderate heat, about 5 minutes, turning once. Remove from heat and keep warm in a *very very* slow oven (200 degrees F.). Melt butter in a hot skillet; add shallots and saute until tender but not browned. Add mushrooms and lettuce to pan; saute mixture for 1 minute. Season with salt and pepper. Spoon mushroom mixture onto 4 dinner plates, dividing evenly. Arrange duck breasts a top bed of mushrooms and garnish with apple slices or as desired.

Note: To julienne, cut lettuce into narrow, lengthwise matchstick-like strips.

Note: Use McIntosh, Winesap, Granny Smith, or other tart variety of apples.

—Chef Paul and Marie Antoinette Elbling
La Petite France Restaurant

To Roast Partridges

Clean the birds as for stuffing. Rub with butter, salt and pepper. Put in sheets of letter-paper and allow to cook in this way.

Mrs. George M. West
The Kitchen Queen, 1893

Hickory Smoked Duckling
with Raspberry Cumin Sauce

Yield: 4 servings

1 package hickory chips
Water as needed
2 (2 1/2-pound) fresh or
   frozen domestic duck-
   lings, dressed
Salt and pepper to taste
Charcoal as needed
1 1/2 cups fresh raspberries,
   divided
1 cup water
Pinch ground cumin
Cooked wild rice
Mr. Patrick Henry's Baked
   Granny Smith Apples
   (see index)

Thaw frozen ducklings and remove giblets from duck cavities. In a large container, soak hickory chips in water to cover for about 1 to 2 hours. Arrange dressed ducklings on wire racks in a roasting pan. Liberally sprinkle outside of birds with salt and pepper. Bake, uncovered, in a hot oven (425 degrees F.) for 1 1/2 hours. While duck-lings are baking, start charcoal fire in the firebox of a charcoal smoker or covered grill. Arrange charcoal to one side of firebox; ignite coals. When coals are ash gray in color and glowing, spread hickory chips over charcoal. Arrange ducklings on grill rack *opposite* the hickory chips and charcoal. Cover and smoke for 1 1/2 to 2 hours. Add addi-tional charcoal briquets as needed to outer oven of fire box to warm first, before adding to main fire. While ducklings are smoking, prepare sauce. To prepare Raspberry Cumin Sauce, combine rasp-berries and 1 cup water in a small heavy saucepan; blend in cumin. Reduce mixture by one fourth over moderate heat, stirring constantly. Remove from heat and fold in 1/2 cup additional raspber-ries. Remove ducklings from smoker/grill; carve, removing bones, if desired, and serve with cooked wild rice, berry sauce, and Mr. Patrick's Henry's Baked Granny Smith Apples.

Note: 1 thawed (10-ounce) package frozen raspberries, including liquid, may be substituted for fresh raspberries. Omit water. Combine with cumin and prepare as previously directed.

–Chef James and Lynn News, proprietors
Mr. Patrick Henry's Restaurant and Inn

Breast of Duck

Cut the breast of wild duck free from the bone; put it into a chafing-dish; add butter, little red pepper and salt; cook it for eight minutes, and serve hot with currant jelly. Wine may be added if desired.
Mrs. Philip Dandridge

F. F. V. Receipt Book, 1894

Science Museum

The Science Museum, located at 2500 West Broad Street, attracts a multitude of Virginians from youngsters to advanced senior citizens. Once the Broad Street Station, former railroad station of the Richmond, Fredericksburg, and Potomac Railroad in bygone years, it is listed on the register of historic places. Opened in 1976, the museum offers hands-on displays and important exhibitions featuring aerospace, astronomy, electricity, light and vision, crystal illusions, computers, and many other science related subjects. A major planetarium and a renowned space theatre, Universe, provide interactive programs and spectacular films, surrounding a visitor with action. Aurora a winter festival of lights, culminates each year's schedule of activities presented from the end of November to the early part of January. This celebration of the winter solstice includes dome lighting and ceremonies and customs from varied cultures.

215

Roast Duckling with Olive Sauce

Yield: 4 servings

1 (4 1/2 to 5-pound) fresh or frozen duckling, dressed (see note)
Salt to taste
Salted cold water as needed (optional)
2 medium tart apples, quartered (optional) (see note)
Olive Sauce (see index)

Thaw frozen duckling, remove giblets from duck cavity and reserve for preparation of duck stock. Remove all loose fat from the cavity around neck and the back at the base of the tail. Sprinkle salt lightly over inside cavity of duck.

Cook duck by one of the three following methods: 1) Place duck in a large heavy pot filled with enough salted cold water to cover duck. Prick neck skin all over to allow release of fat while cooking. Bring to a simmer over moderate heat; reduce temperature and continue simmering, uncovered, for one half the cooking time. Plan 1 hour 15 to 20 minutes total cooking time for medium rare (juices will be slightly red in color) and 1 hour 25 to 35 minutes total cooking time for well-done ducks (juices will be yellow). Remove duck from liquid, draining well. Arrange partially cooked duck on a metal rack in a roasting pan. Bake, uncovered, in a hot oven (400 degrees F.) for the remainder of the cooking time.

Or, 2) sprinkle salt over inside of duck cavity and stuff bird with apple quarters and celery ribs, allowing celery to protrude from end of duck cavity. Duck need not be trussed. Prick duck skin lightly all over to allow the release of fat while the duck is roasting. Arrange duck on a metal rack in a roasting pan; add a small amount of water to pan. Bake, uncovered, in a moderate oven (350 degrees F.) for the desired degree of doneness (see previous instructions).

Or, 3) prepare duck as previously directed in cooking method 2. About halfway through the roasting time, remove pan juices from roasting pan. Separate the fat from the stock (see note); reserve stock for Olive Sauce and discard fat. To serve, cut duck into quarters with a sharp knife or kitchen shears. Garnish each portion with a small amount of Olive Sauce and pass remaining sauce. If duck is large enough, the breast may be sliced and the remaining portion cut into serving piece; i.e. wings, thighs, and back quarters.

Note: Use McIntosh, Winesap, Granny,Smith, or other tart variety of apples.

Note: If a fat separating measuring cup is available, pour juices into cup. Fat will rise above the juices and juices can be poured out the spout leaving the fat in the cup.

Note: Wild ducks may be substituted for domestic ducks; however, the ducks are usually lighter in weiight and two may be required for 4 servings. Soak wild ducks in cold salted water to cover for 24 hours to remove gamey flavor. A tablespoon of white vinegar may be added to water, if desired. Drain and thoroughly rinse ducks in fresh water before cooking.

Note: Duck can be kept, covered lightly with aluminum foil, in the oven turned to off for about 15 to 20 minutes before serving, if desired, after roasting time is completed. Do not hold too long as skin will become soft, not remaining crisp.

Duck Stock: To prepare duck stock, combine duck neck, giblets, and about 5 cups lightly salted water in a medium heavy saucepan. Cook, cover ajar, over moderate heat for about 1 to 1 1/2 hours or until giblets and neck meat are tender and broth is flavorful. Add more water to pan as necessary. Do not use liver as the flavor is undesirable. Skim off fat; strain before using, if desired.

—Doris Roberts (Mrs. Irving)

Nice Way to Cook Rabbit

Lay the rabbit in salt and water for half an hour; pour boiling water over it and wipe dry; season with pepper and salt; lay it on a gridiron over clear coals; let it cook thoroughly, but not become hard; make a gravy of one tablespoonful of vinegar, two teaspoonfuls of made mustard, one tablespoonful of butter, and pour over it. Serve very hot.

F. F. V. Receipt Book, *1894*

Barbacued Hare

Have pan hot, put in one tablespoon butter, rub rabbit with black and red pepper and salt, gash it down back one inch apart. Put well in pan on side. When nearly done put in one cup vinegar, put pan on back of stove and cover andl et cook five or six minutes. If you like much gravy, add a little boiling water after taking rabbit out.

Mrs. Augustine Royal
Virginia Cookery Book, *1921*

217

Holiday Roast Goose with Giblet and Mushroom Corn Bread Dressing

Yield: 6 to 8 servings

Chef Kevin Wade suggests serving a roasted goose, such as early Virginian colonists of English ancestry might have done, for the next winter holiday feast. Many supporters of the Richmond Symphony were treated to this special goose recipe at a holiday gourmet feast presented at the Omni Hotel by the Women's Committee of the Richmond Symphony to benefit the Symphony.

1 (5 to 6-pound) goose (domestic or wild) (see note)
1 tablespoon minced fresh or 1 teaspoon dried rosemary
1 tablespoon minced fresh or 1 teaspoon dried thyme
Salt and pepper to taste
1/2 cup cooking oil
1 medium orange, cut into 8 wedges
1 medium lemon, cut into 8 wedges
Giblet and Mushroom Corn Bread Dressing (see index)

Rinse goose thoroughly and pat dry with absorbent paper. Rub rosemary and thyme thoroughly over outer skin of goose; sprinkle lightly with salt and pepper. Place orange and lemon wedges, and some of seasonings in cavity of goose. Brush oil over skin of goose. Lock wings behind the back, akimbo, and tie drumsticks to bird with heavy string or twine. Arrange goose on a rack in a roasting pan, breast side up. Bake, loosely covered, in a moderate oven (375 degrees F.) for 2 to 3 hours until done, alternately turning goose on each side, and the breast up, every 30 minutes. Do *not turn goose breast side down.* Goose will be done when drum stick can be moved or "wiggled" easily. A meat thermometer inserted into fleshiest part of goose should register 170 to 180 degrees F. *Do not over bake.* Drain off fat from goose; remove orange and lemon wedges. Allow goose to stand for several minutes before carving. Arrange slices of goose on heated dinner plates, garnish as desired, and serve with Giblet and Mushroom Corn Bread Dressing.

Note: Soak a wild goose in salted water for 24 hours to remove wild or gamey flavor; rinse and drain well. Some culinary authorities soak a wild goose in milk in the refrigerator for 24 hours. Prepare a wild goose that has been immediately "dressed" after shooting to insure a less gamey flavor.

Note: Orange and lemon (citrus) wedges, added to the goose cavity assists in breaking down the large quantity of fat found in a goose.

–Chef Kevin Wade
Gallego's Restaurant
The Omni Hotel

Wild Goose 'A La Orange

Yield: 6 servings

1 (6-ounce) can frozen orange juice concentrate, thawed
1 (1 1/8-ounce) package Hunter sauce mix
1 cup hot water
1/4 cup flour
2 tablespoons English-style marmalade (see note)
2 tablespoons sugar
1 1/2 teaspoons salt
1 (6-pound) wild goose, dressed

Place a large 20 x 14-inch oven bag in a roasting pan. Add orange juice concentrate, Hunter sauce mix, water, flour, marmalade, sugar and salt to the bag; mix well. Add goose to bag; turn well to moisten with liquid. Tie top of bag securely; make six 1/2 inch slits in top of bag. Bake in a moderate oven (375 degrees F.) for 2 to 2 1/2 hours or until fork tender. Pour sauce into a bowl; skim off fat. Remove goose from bag, carve, and arrange on a heated platter. Pour sauce into a sauce dish and serve with goose.

Note: English-style marmalade has a slightly bitter flavor.

Variation: Two wild ducks may be prepared at one time in this manner. Reduce baking time to 2 hours.

–Ann Epes (Mrs. Travis, Jr.)

Roast Goose

1 Young Goose, 6 Potatoes, Mashed, 2 Table-spoonsful Butter, 1 Table-spoonful Onion Juice, 1 Teaspoonful Salt, 1/2 Teaspoonful Pepper, 1 Tea-spoonful Powdered Sage, Flour, Cress or Celery., After washing and cleaning the goose wipe it dry. Mix the potatoes with the butter, onion juice, salt and the pepper, also the sage, using this for the dressing. Sew and tie the goose in the same way you do the chicken. Steam it for half an hour and draw out the oil, after which place it in pan, dredge with pepper, salt and flour, place in oven and roast, pouring a little hot water over it when it begins to brown, basting often. Draw off the oil in the pan and make a brown gravy with flour and water the same as you do for turkey. Garnish the goose with watercress or celery tops. Serve with apple sauce or cider. If better suited to your taste you may substitute a dry dressing as is used for other fowls.

Old Virginia Cooking, *circa 1909*

219

Stewed Pigeons

Take six fat young pigeons, put them in a pot, with a slice of pork beneath them, cut the thickness of a silver dollar, and two table-spoonfuls of butter, but no water at all. Let them remain over a gentle fire for two hours, keeping the pot well covered; during this time put in a handful of chopped onions and parsley; stir now and then, to prevent burning; after two hours put in the pot half a tumbler of claret, with a little red pepper, salt, and cloves. Let the pigeons stew for half an hour longer, then take a little of the gravy from the pot and thicken it with a teaspoonful of flour; return this to the pot, and stir well. Have ready some slices of hot buttered toast on a dish, and upon these lay the birds; pour the gravy over the whole. Mutton-chops cooked in the same way are very good.

Virginia Cookery-Book, *1885*

Turkey A La Daub

Bone a turkey, season with pepper and salt on the inside, fill it with force meat and mushrooms, well seasoned with butter, salt, and pepper; sew it up and boil until done; cover it with currant jelly, and serve.

F. F. V. Receipt Book, *1894*

Carrying the Key Basket in the Elegant '80's

At that time (1880's) flour sold for $6.75 a berrel. Other items were:

Coffee, 4 lbs.	$1.00
Rice, 6 lbs.	.50
Sugar, 10 lbs.	.75
Butter, 2 lbs.	.70
Eggs	.25
Claret	.69

Lucy Cole Durham
"Diary of Young Matron Reveals Strange Notations,"
Richmond Times-Dispatch (Condensed), Fedbuary 13, 1938

Wilton

Located on Wilton Road in the far west end of Richmond, Wilton, an eighteenth century mansion completed in 1753 by William Randolph III and moved ten miles up the James River in 1933 to its present location high atop a bluff overlooking the James River, is one of the historic attractions of Richmond. Now a private museum open to the public and considered to be one of the most beautiful examples of Georgian architecture in the United States, the interior is fully panelled throughout. Each room is authentically furnished with period antiques according to the Randolph inventory.

After attending the famous gathering of Virginians in April 1774 at St. John's church in Richmond where author Patrick Henry gave his famous speech, George Washington stopped at Wilton as a overnight guest of the Randolph family. Later, in 1781, the Marquis de Lafayette camped with his troops on the premises enroute to the final encounter of the Revolutionary War at Yorktown.

Classic Turkey Pot Pie

Yield: 4 servings

Sadly a Richmond tradition ... indeed an institution and way of life ... closed in January 1990. After more than a century of business, the renowned department store of Miller & Rhoads closed its doors forever. Before its final days ended, however, many Richmonders, men and women alike, experienced a last meal at the famed tearoom in the downtown store. Many matrons from near and far donned their hats and white gloves of a past era to reminisce at one last lunch of delightful times experienced in The Tearoom.

A downtown Richmond landmark for more than the past half century, the Miller & Rhoads Tea Room debuted in 1917 as the Colonial Tea Room on the 3rd floor of the 6th and Grace Streets store. In 1924, it was moved to larger quarters when the Miller & Rhoads department store, originating in Richmond in 1885, completed and expanded its store on Grace Street between 5th and 6th Streets. Originally divided into three sections, English, Italian and Colonial, the three rooms were later combined into one large tea room. Unfortunately, a customer fell into the fountain in the Italian Room causing its closing. Prior to 1939, a musical trio entertained lunch patrons; however, one day the leader became so intoxicated that Mr. Rhoads fired him on the spot. Walking across the street to the Lowe's Theatre, he returned with Eddie Weaver in tow. Some fifty years later, the last day of tearoom service, Eddie was still charming an enormous crowd of lunch patrons with his musical talent.

According to Sally Dunn, former Miller & Rhoads Director of Food Service, peas were included in the Turkey Pot Pie in cycles. "About every six months the pea issue came up ... put them in, take them out, put them back in."

20 to 24 very small white onions, peeled

4 medium carrots, peeled, cut in half lengthwise, and then cut into 1/2-inch pieces

4 ribs celery, thinly sliced

4 small potatoes, peeled and cubed

About 1/4 cup shelled fresh peas, blanched, or frozen peas, thawed

3 tablespoons butter or margarine, melted

3 tablespoons flour

1 chicken bouillon cube, mashed

In a medium heavy saucepan, cook onions and carrots in boiling water to cover until just tender, about 8 to 10 minutes. In a small heavy saucepan, cook celery in a small amount of boiling water until just tender, about 5 to 7 minutes. In a medium heavy saucepan, cook potatoes in boiling water to cover for 10 to 15 minutes or until just tender. Drain all vegetables thoroughly. In a medium heavy saucepan, blend butter, flour, and mashed bouillon cube together until a smooth paste is formed. Gradually add broth, blending well. Cook, stirring constantly, over moderate heat until sauce is thickened and bubbly hot. Add vegetables and turkey, mixing lightly. Season with salt and pepper to taste, as desired. Spoon mixture into individual 10-ounce heat-proof glass baking cups or metal tart pans, dividing evenly.

1 to 1 1/2 cups chicken or turkey broth (see note)
6 ounces cubed cooked light turkey
6 ounces cubed cooked dark turkey
Salt and pepper to taste
Unbaked pastry for 1 crust pie (9 to 10 inch)

Roll out pastry dough to a 1/8-inch thickness. Cut into 4 even circles, about 1 inch larger in diameter than diameter of baking cups or tart pans. Top each filled baking cup or tart pan with pastry circle; tuck pastry edges under, sealing to edge of cup or pan, and flute or pinch around edge of pastry with the fingers. With a sharp knife, cut a slit in each pit crust to allow steam to escape. Bake pies in a moderate oven (350 degrees F.) for 20 to 25 minutes or until crust is golden brown and filling is bubbly hot.

Note: Homemade rich chicken or turkey broth or 1 undiluted (14-ounce) can chicken broth may be used.

Note: One egg white with a few drops of water and lightly beaten with a fork or wire whisk may be brushed over the pastry crusts before baking.

—Miller & Rhoades Tearoom

LIGHT FEASTS

M&R Marinated Pork Tenderloin Sampler 3.95
Medallions of marinated pork grilled and sliced chilled. Served with hot, hot mustard and sesame seeds for dipping. A perfect snack or light meal. Served with apples marinated and glazed with calvados.

Grilled Chicken with Raspberry Vinaigrette 5.65
Marinated and grilled breast of chicken sliced atop a bed of tossed romaine and bibb lettuce. Laced with walnuts and accompanied by award-winning Corryell's Crossing fine raspberry jam.

Ratatouille Au Gratin 4.25
A melange of seasonal vegetables in a spicy tomato basil sauce topped with melted monterey jack cheese and accompanied by our crispy cheese biscuits.

Chunky Chicken Salad 4.95
Generous chunks of chicken blended with lemon mayonnaise and surrounded by strawberries and honeydew melon. Served with muffins or crispy cheese biscuits.

Virginia Sampler 5.50
Combine a cup of steaming she-crab soup with a sample of turkey waldorf salad and traditional ham biscuits for a real taste of Virginia's best!

Chicken Marietta Salad 4.85
A light, but rich blend of breast of chicken, rotini pasta, fresh parsley onions and cucumber in a piquant creamy dressing. Served with muffins or crispy cheese biscuits.

Boarshead Breast of Turkey on Four Grain Roll 4.50
Smoked breast of turkey with lettuce, tomato and monterey jack cheese on our own four grain roll. Served with Corryell's Crossing award-winning fine raspberry jam.

Roast Beef and Boursin on French Roll 4.50
Thinly sliced roast beef on our own French roll dressed with the fine herbs and creamy smoothness of boursin cheese.

HEARTY FARE

Chicken and Virginia Ham Shortcake 5.65
Chunks of chicken and slowly cured country ham in a savory sauce served over toasted cornbread and complemented by Corryell's Crossing award-winning fine raspberry jam.

Savory Grill 5.50
Marinated breast of chicken grilled and topped with tart Granny Smith apples and melted cheddar cheese on a braided poppy seed roll. Served with cole slaw and Corryell's Crossing fine raspberry jam.

Filet of Chicken Sandwich 3.95
Lightly breaded and fried filet of chicken with lettuce, tomato and mayonnaise on braided roll. Served with our natural style french fries.

Chesapeake Crab Cake Sandwich 6.25
Imperial style blend of Chesapeake crab, seasonings and mornay sauce. Broiled to a golden brown and served with cole slaw and our natural style french fries.

CLASSICS

Turkey Pot Pie 4.75
Chunks of turkey and garden vegetables in a rich fricassee sauce, topped with a pastry crust and accompanied by a house salad.

Deviled Crab 5.65
Our own golden blend of crab, country eggs and special spices. Served with our own cole slaw and sliced tomatoes.

Missouri Club 4.95
Virginia ham, turkey, bacon and tomato topped with cheddar cheese sauce and complemented by our own mustard pickles and a house salad.

Tea Room Club 4.25
A triple-layer creation with ham, turkey, bacon, lettuce and tomato complemented by your choice of potato chips or sorbet and fresh fruit.

Our Great Hamburger 4.50
A juicy 6-ounce burger topped with mushrooms, Swiss cheese and bacon on a grilled onion roll with natural style fries.

Classic Burger 4.00
Perfect by itself! A 6-ounce burger on a grilled onion roll with lettuce and tomato served with our natural style fries.

Custom Cheeseburger 4.30
You choose Swiss, cheddar, monterey jack or bleu cheese to top your juicy burger on a grilled onion roll. Served with lettuce, tomato and natural style fries.

Barbecued Turkey Breast with Orange

Yield: 8 to 10 servings

2 (6-ounce) cans tomato paste
1 large garlic clove, peeled and minced
1 1/2 cups orange marmalade (see note)
1/2 cup orange juice
1/4 cup butter or margarine
1/4 cup honey
3 tablespoons Worcestershire sauce
1 teaspoon salt or to taste
1 teaspoon chili powder
1 teaspoon soy sauce (see note)
1/2 teaspoon pepper or to taste
1 (4- to 7-pound) fresh or thawed frozen whole turkey breast
Cooking oil as needed

Combine all ingredients, except turkey and oil in a large heavy saucepan; simmer, uncovered, over low heat for 15 to 20 minutes, set aside. Turkey will be done when thermometer registers 170 degrees F. Meat will turn from pink to white and become fork tender. Add briquets as necessary to maintain medium hot coals, about 8 to each side at end of each hour of cooking.

Note: Preferabley use English-style.

Note: Reduced sodium (Lite) soy sauce may be substituded for regular soy sauce. One teaspoon lite soy sauce contains 100 milligrams of sodium.

Baked Turkey-Best Way

2 Teaspoonsful Salt,, 1/2 Cupful Boiling Water,, Butter,, Fat., After the turkey has been drawn and trussed stand it in a shallow pan, adding to the pan the salt and boiling water. Put it at once in a very hot oven. When the turkey is thoroughly brown remove it from the oven, brush it over with butter and return to the oven, reduce the heat of the oven and bake slowly for twenty minutes to each pound. See that there is sufficient fat in the pan for basting. Do not add any more water to the pan. Just before the turkey is done baste the breast thoroughly with fat, dusting it thickly with flour, then brown.

Old Virginia Cooking, *circa* 1909

Deviled Turkey

Half cup tomato catsup, teaspoonful dry mustard, a little red pepper, a tablespoonful of butter. Melt and pour hot on the turkey when boiled.

Miss Whitcomb.
Virginia Recipes, *1890*

Deviled Turkey Leg for Breakfast

Slash the leg of a cold turkey, put in a pan, with gravy made of half a cup of vinegar, a little mustard, red pepper, and tablespoonful of butter; let it get boiling hot and serve.

Virginia Cooking, 1939

Wild Turkey

Prepare the turkey as usual; make a stuffing of chopped celery, bread-crumbs, butter, pepper, and salt; sprinkle a little salt and pepper over the turkey and put some bits of butter on it; stuff it, and lay in a pan in a hot oven; baste it often with the gravy made of hot water (or stock is better), a little butter and pepper. When well done, serve with celery sauce.

F. F. V. Receipt Book, *1894*

Boaning A Turkey

The height of elegance was to have the famous caterer John Dabney perform his miracles, the greatest of which was to bone a turkey ... He shut himself up with the turkey and perfomred the rigt, and when you next saw the noble bird there was not a break in the bronze gold skin, but all its bones were on another dish. When the glorious fowl was carved, the knife glided clear through.

Helena Lefroy Caperton
"Time Gambols Withal"
The Richmond News Leader, 1931

Creamed Turkey with Toasted Almonds 'N Raisins Over Toast Points

Yield: 6 servings

1 tablespoon minced peeled onion
3 tablespoons butter or margarine, melted
4 chicken bouillon cubes, mashed
3 tablespoons flour
1 1/4 cups half-and-half or light cream
1 cup water
1 bay leaf, crumbled
1 whole clove
1/4 cup toasted slivered blanched almonds
1/4 cup chopped dark seedless raisins
Salt and white pepper to taste
12 thin slices cooked turkey or chicken
6 slices white bread, crusts removed, toasted, buttered, and quartered
Parsley sprigs for garnish

In a medium heavy saucepan, sauté onion in butter over moderate heat until tender but not browned. Blend in bouillon cubes and flour until smooth. Gradually stir in half-and-half and water. Add bay leaf and clove. Cook, stirring constantly, over moderate heat until thickened and bubbly hot. Remove bay leaf and clove from sauce. Stir in almonds and raisins. Season with salt and pepper, as desired. On each heated plate, arrange 2 slices of turkey over 4 buttered toast points. Spoon sauce over each serving, dividing evenly, and garnish with parsley sprigs.

–Virginia Cottrell (Mrs. Walker C., Jr.)

Turkey Au Poivre in Cognac Sauce

Yield: 4 servings

1 pound turkey breast cutlets or tenderloin (see note)
About 3/4 cup flour
5 tablespoons butter or margarine, divided
8 ounces thinly sliced mushrooms

With a sharp knife, cut tenderloin across the grain into thin slices. On a sheet of waxed paper, dredge turkey slices or cutlets lightly in flour. In a large heavy skillet, melt 2 to 3 tablespoons butter over moderate heat. Sauté turkey pieces in butter over moderate heat, about 2 to 3 minutes per side. Remove cutlets or slices; set aside. Melt remaining butter in hot pan drippings. Add

1 (10 3/4-ounce) can chicken broth, undiluted (see note)

1/2 cup heavy cream, at room temperature

3 tablespoons cognac or brandy

2 tablespoons green peppercorns, slightly crushed (fresh or canned)

1 tablespoon Worcestershire sauce

1/2 teaspoon coarsely ground pepper or to taste

Salt to taste

1 tablespoon minced parsley

mushrooms and sauté over moderate heat until tender but not browned. Add chicken broth, cream, cognac, green peppercorns, Worcestershire sauce, pepper, and salt to taste. Cook, uncovered, over moderate to high heat until sauce is reduced to two-thirds its original amount. Reduce heat; return turkey to skillet, spoon sauce over cutlets, and simmer, covered, until turkey is heated through. Sprinkle parsley over turkey and sauce just before serving.

Note: 1 pound very thinly sliced veal scalloppine may be substituted for turkey.

Note: 1 (10 3/4-ounce) can beef consommé may be substituted for chicken broth, if desired, when veal is substituted for turkey.

To Roast A Fowl

Prepare a stuffing of bread crumbs, salt, pepper, and seasoning (see directions for force meats, No. 375); fill the crop and breast with this dressing, draw the skin at the neck on to the back, and fasten it to the backbone with a skewer;the body may also be filled with dressing if convenient.Turn the tips of the wings under the back and fasten them with a long skewer, pass a short skewer through the lower part of the legs and then through the tail. It is now ready for cooking. Roast by directions given for roasting beef, being even more particular about basting, as the flavor and excellence of the fowl depend greatly on its being frequently and properly basted. All fowls may be larded. When this is done it is not necessary to baste so frequently. Onions and sage are generally used in dressing geese and ducks. To make the gravy, follow directions given for making gravy for meat, using browned flour for roasted fowls and white flour for boiled. The exact length of time for roasting and boiling fowls cannot be determined; it depends on the size and age of the fowl. The rules given in regard to meat apply to fowls also. Turkeys and chickens are very nice boiled. They are prepared exactly as for roasting, and boiled according to directions for boiling fresh meat. They are served hot with egg sauce. Roasted fowls may be served with giblet gravy, as well as that made by directions for beef gravy.

Instruction in Cooking with Selected Receipts, *1895*

Turkey with Mayonnaise Covering

Yield: 20 to 32 servings

1 (12 to 16-pound) turkey
Favorite stuffing recipe
1 to 2 cups mayonnaise as
   desired
Salt (optional)
Pepper (optional)
2 chicken bouillon cubes
   (optional)
Brandy or water as needed

Remove giblets and neck from body cavity. Rinse turkey and pat dry with absorbent paper. Fill neck cavity loosely with stuffing. Do not pack, as stuffing expands during roasting. Fold neck skin over dressing in cavity opening and fasten securely to back with skewers. Stuff body cavity loosely. Lock wings behind the back (*akimbo*) and tie drumsticks to tail with heavy string.

Coat turkey liberally all over with mayonnaise. Lightly sprinkle with salt and pepper, if desired. Insert meat thermometer into thickest part of thigh muscle. Place in a large heavy paper bag, if desired. (Re-coat with mayonnaise where necessary.) Close and secure bag tightly and place in a large roaster. Or, place mayonnaise coated turkey on a rack in a shallow roasting pan. Add chicken bouillon cubes and about 1 inch of brandy or water to pan. Cover loosely, leaving openings at either end, with aluminum foil (shiny side in). Allow a hole in the foil for the meat thermometer. Roast in a slow oven (325 degrees F.) until done, about 4 1/2 to 5 hours (allow 20 to 25 minutes per pound for roasting); meat thermometer will register 180 to 185 degrees F. Remove foil about 45 minutes before the end of the roasting period to insure even browning of bird. Baste turkey liberally with pan juices.

Cut strings holding legs when two-thirds done. Remove turkey from oven when done and cover tightly with aluminum foil. Allow to rest for 20 to 25 minutes for easier carving. Arrange turkey on heated platter, garnish as desired and serve. Reserve pan juices for gravy; skim off excess fat.

Brown Gravy
Yield: (about 4 cups)
Remove turkey meat from neck. Cut meat and giblets into bite-sized pieces; set aside. Discard neck bones. Blend 1/2 cup flour with drippings from turkey in roasting pan until smooth. Add 2 cups reserved stock or chicken broth or water, 4 chicken bouillon cubes, and 1/8 teaspoon pepper; blend in remaining 2 cups stock or chicken broth or water. Cook over moderate heat until thickened. May add several drops browning sauce, if desired. Stir turkey neck meat and giblets into gravy.

Cheesy Seasoned Bread Stuffing

Yield: about 4 to 5 cups stuffing

6 cups day-old, white or whole wheat bread cubes
1 to 1 1/2 cups shredded sharp Cheddar cheese
3/4 cup chopped celery
1/3 cup minced parsley
2/3 cup hot chicken broth or water
6 tablespoons butter or margarine, melted
3 eggs, beaten
Salt or seasoned salt and pepper to taste

In a large bowl, combine bread cubes, cheese, celery, and parsley. Add hot chicken broth and butter, mixing well. Stir in eggs and seasonings, tossing lightly. Use for stuffing turkey, capon, roast chicken, duck, goose, pork chops or roasts, or fish (see note). Stuffing may be baked separately in a greased 1 1/2-quart casserole, covered, in a moderate oven (375 degrees F.) for 35 minutes, uncover and continue baking for 10 to 15 minutes or until done and top is lightly browned.

Note: Stuffing amount for a 12 to 15 pound turkey needs to be doubled.

Variation: Add 1 teaspoon Worcestershire sauce and 3 to 4 drops hot sauce, if desired. Or, substitute minced fresh dill weed for parsley.

–Updated Old Recipe, circa 1920's
(Source unknown)

Emma Rhodes Neff

But what Mrs. Neff remembers best about her childhood holidays are the family feasts.
"Christmas was always a happy time, because our kin people would ask us to turkey dinner or we'd have one for them."
On the table would be dressing, gravy, mashed potatoes, vegetables canned form the summer garden, homemade pickles and freshly baked bread, all prepared on the kitchen wood stove. For dessert there were sugar cookies, whipped cream pies and cakes. "You had to have coconut cake," Mrs. Neff said. "That's my favorite."

Christine Reid
"Christmas in the 1800's"
Richmond Times-Dispatch, December 23, 1984

Giblet and Mushroom Corn Bread Dressing

Yield: 6 to 8 servings

1 recipe prepared Plantation Corn Bread (see index) (see note)
Goose giblets, including neck, liver, heart, and gizzard (see note)
Boiling water as needed
1 medium onion, peeled and chopped
1 pound small to medium mushrooms, cleaned and quartered
6 to 8 tablespoons butter or margarine, melted
1 cup hot chicken stock or broth
3 tablespoons poultry seasoning
1 tablespoon sage
Salt and pepper to taste

Prepare corn bread 1 to 2 days in advance; allow corn bread to stand, uncovered, at room temperature to become dry. Crumble bread and set aside. In a deep medium heavy saucepan, simmer goose giblets and neck in boiling water to cover thoroughly over low heat for 2 1/2 to 3 hours or until giblets are fork tender and neck meat falls from the bones; add more water as necessary to pan to keep giblets well covered. Drain well; remove meat from neckbones and coarsely chop heart, liver, and gizzard. Discard bones. In a large heavy saucepan, sauté onion and mushrooms in butter until vegetables are tender but not browned. Add chopped giblets, neckmeat, poultry seasoning, and sage. Add crumbled corn bread and chicken stock, mixing well. Season with salt and pepper to taste. Loosely pack into a greased 8x8x2-inch baking pan. Cover with a sheet of oiled waxed paper. Bake in a moderate oven (350 degrees F.) for 1 hour.

Note: A 10 to 12-ounce package of corn bread mix may be prepared according to package directions and used in place of Plantation Corn Bread, if desired.

Note: Turkey or chicken giblets may be substituted.

–Chef Kevin Wade
Gallego's Restaurant
The Omni Hotel

Baked Herbed Sausage Stuffing Balls

Yield: 8 to 10 servings

1 pound mild or hot-spiced bulk pork sausage, crumbled
1/2 cup chopped celery
1/4 cup chopped peeled onion
1 (8-ounce) package herb-

In a medium heavy skillet, cook sausage, celery, and onion over moderate heat, stirring frequently, until sausage is browned and vegetables tender. Drain off excess pan drippings. In a medium bowl, combine sausage mixture and stuffing mix, tossing lightly to mix. Stir in egg, broth, and cranberries, mixing well. Shape mixture into 8 to 10

seasoned stuffing mix
1 egg, beaten
1 cup chicken broth
3/4 cup coarsely ground or chopped cranberries
1/4 cup butter or margarine, melted

equal-sized balls. Arrange stuffing balls in a 15 x 10 x 1-inch baking pan. Brush evenly with butter. Bake, uncovered, in a slow oven (325 degrees F.) for 30 minutes. Serve with desired poultry or pork recipe.

–Linda Bourgeois (Mrs. Bruce)

Nana Fuleihan's Holiday Stuffing

Yield: enough stuffing for a 16 to 18-pound turkey

1 pound sliced bacon, chopped
1 medium onion, peeled and chopped
4 cups chopped celery
1 (15-ounce) package seasoned stuffing mix (see note)
2 to 3 teaspoons poultry seasoning or to taste
2 to 3 teaspoons sage or to taste
Water as needed
Salt and pepper to taste
2 to 3 cups coarsely chopped pecans

In a large heavy skillet, pan-fry bacon over moderate heat until crisp; remove with a slotted spoon, draining well. Drain off a small amount of bacon drippings from pan, leaving about 1/2 cup drippings in pan. In the remaining hot bacon drippings, sauté onion and celery over moderate heat until tender but not browned; *do not* drain. In a large bowl, combine stuffing mix, crisp bacon pieces, onion, and celery mixture, poultry seasoning, and sage, mixing well. Add enough water to achieve desired consistency, mixing well. (Some persons prefer a very moist stuffing, while others like a drier stuffing.)Season with salt and pepper to taste. Stir in pecans. Use stuffing for turkey, roast chicken, capon, duck, goose, or Rock Cornish hen. Stuffing may be baked separately in a greased 2-quart casserole, covered, in a moderate overn (325 degrees F.) for about 50 minutes, or until done and lightly browned.

Note: For roast chicken, capon, domestic duck, or goose, use one-third to one-half the amount of the recipe. For 4 Rock Cornish hens, use one-fourth to one-third the amount of the recipe.

Note: Preferably use Arnold's stuffing mix.

–Ruth Fuleihan (Mrs. Robert)

Calico Brown Rice Stuffing

Yield: about 5 to 6 cups
or enough to stuff a 4 to 6-pound turkey breast
or 5-pound roasting chicken or capon or duck

1 1/4 cups brown rice
2 cups boiling water
3 tablespoons butter or
 margarine, at room
 temperature and divided
Salt to taste
2 chicken bouillon cubes,
 mashed
12 ounces mushrooms,
 thinly sliced or coarsely
 chopped or 1 (6-ounce)
 jar sliced mushrooms,
 drained
1 cup chopped celery
1/2 cup chopped sweet red
 or yellow pepper or 1/4
 cup chopped pimento,
 drained
1/2 cup chopped green
 onion (include some
 green tops)
1/2 cup thinly sliced water
 chestnuts, drained
Pepper to taste

In a large heavy saucepan, combine rice, boiling water, 2 tablespoons butter, and 1/2 to 1 teaspoon salt; cook according to package directions for 30 minutes or until rice is *just* tender and liquid is absorbed. Add remaining butter, chicken bouillon cubes, mushrooms, celery, red or yellow pepper or pimento, green onion, and water chestmuts, mixing well. Add pepper and additional salt, if desired, to taste. Toss lightly to mix. Stuff turkey breast or roasting chicken or capon or duck and bake according to roasting directions for desired poultry. Or, spoon mixture into a greased 1 1/2 to 2-quart casserole. Cover and bake in a moderate oven (350 degrees F.) for 35 to 45 minutes or until vegetables are tender.

Note: 1 beaten egg or 2 slightly beaten egg whites may be added to stuffing mixture as a binder, if desired.

Note: To stuff a 12 to 14-pound turkey, increase recipe ingredients by two times.

Old Richmond Advertisement, date unknown

Crispy Catfish Bake

Yield: 4 to 6 servings

"I get fresh catfish in the area and prepare it with this tasty, but easy recipe. Of course, you need hush puppies to go with it."

1/2 cup grated Parmesan
  cheese
1/4 cup flour
1 teaspoon paprika
1/2 teaspoon salt
1/4 teaspoon pepper
1 egg
1 tablespoon milk
1 1/2 pounds catfish fillets,
  cut into serving pieces
1/4 cup butter or margarine,
  melted, or hot cooking oil
  or bacon drippings
Hush Puppies (see index)
Tartar Sauce (see index)

In a small bowl, combine cheese, flour, paprika, salt, and pepper, mixing well. In a small bowl, beat egg and milk together. Dip fish fillets into egg mixture and then into cheese mixture, coating each piece well. Arrange fish fillets in a greased, foil-lined 12 x 8 x 2-inch baking dish, not allowing fillets to overlap. Drizzle melted butter over fish. Bake, uncovered, in a moderate oven (350 degrees F.) for 20 minutes or until fish is golden brown, crisp on the outside, and flakes easily with a fork.

–Frances Fox (Mrs. Paul)

Oven-Baked Seasoned Blue Fish

Yield: 4 servings

1 medium (Bermuda) onion,
  peeled, thinly sliced, and
  separated into rings
1 to 1 1/3 pounds blue or
  rock fish fillets, cut into 4
  serving pieces
3 to 4 teaspoons lemon
  juice
Seasoned salt and pepper
  to taste
2 to 3 tablespoons butter or
  margarine, at room
  temperature
Paprika to taste
Thin lemon wedges for
  garnish

In a greased 12 x 8 x 2-inch or 9 x 9 x 2-inch baking dish (size of baking dish depends on size of fillets), arrange one half of the onion rings in a single layer across the bottom of the dish. Arrange fish fillets over the layer of onion rings. Evenly sprinkle lemon juice over fillets. Liberally season fish with seasoned salt, pepper, and paprika to taste. Evenly dot fillets with butter. Top with remaining onion rings arranged in a layer. Bake, covered, in a hot oven (400 degrees F.) for 25 minutes; uncover and continue baking for about 10 to 15 minutes or until fish is opaque in color and flakes easily with a fork. Garnish each serving with thin lemon wedges.

–Virginia Cottrell (Mrs. Walker C., Jr.)

The C. F. Sauer Company

The C. F. Sauer Company has been manufacturing flavoring extracts in Richmond for more than one hundred years. The turn-of-the-century red brick corporate headquarters building with its ornate wrought iron interior staircase at the corner of West Broad and Meadow Streets is a landmark for all Richmonders.

Conrad Frederick Sauer Sr., pharmacist by profession, businessman by preference, founded the company on his twenty-first birthday, October 13, 1887. The company has added more products, including herbs and spices, salad dressings, vegetable oils, mustards, peanut products, and gravy, sauce, and seasoning mixes. During the 1940's, C. F. Sauer was a major sponsor of several radio programs originating from Richmond. Today the Company is led by a third generation of Sauers.

Dill and Lemon Fish Bake

Yield: 6 servings

2 tablespoons minced fresh or 2 teaspoons dried dill weed, divided
1 teaspoon grated lemon peel
Pepper to taste
1 1/2 pounds flounder fillet, cut into 6 (4-ounce) serving pieces
Wooden picks (optional)
1 cup water
1/2 cup dry vermouth or apple juice
3 tablespoons lemon juice

In a small bowl, combine one half of the dill weed, lemon peel, and pepper to taste; rub mixture into both sides of each piece of fish, dividing evenly. Starting at the narrow end of each piece of fish, roll pieces jelly-roll style; secure each with a wooden pick, if desired. Arrange fish rolls in a shallow 1 1/2-quart casserole. In a 2-cup measure, combine water, vermouth, lemon juice, and remaining dill weed; pour over fish. Bake, covered, in a moderate oven (350 degrees F.) for 15 to 20 minutes or until fish is opaque in color and flakes easily with a fork. Arrange fish rolls on each of 6 dinner plates and spoon pan liquid over each serving, dividing evenly.

–C. F. Sauer Company
Sauer Spices

234

Flounder Veronique

Yield: 4 servings

1 1/2 pounds flounder, sea or lake trout, or whitefish fillet, cut into 4 (6-ounce) pieces
5 green onions, minced (include some green tops)
3/4 cup unsweetened orange juice (see note)
1 1/2 teaspoons grated orange peel
1/8 teaspoon dry hot mustard
Vegetable cooking spray
Sweet Hungarian paprika to taste
Salt to taste
Freshly ground black pepper to taste
1/4 cup cold water (optional)
2 oranges, peeled, seeded, sectioned, and cut into bite-sized pieces
1 cup seedless green grapes, halved

Arrange fish fillets in a deep medium bowl. In a small bowl, combine onions, orange juice, orange peel, and mustard, blending well; pour over fish fillets. Cover with clear plastic wrap and refrigerate for 2 to 3 hours. Drain fillets; coat each lightly with vegetable cooking spray. Arrange fillets in an 11x7x2-inch baking dish. Pour orange juice mixture over fish. Bake, uncovered, in a moderate oven (350 degrees F.) for 25 to 30 minutes or until fish is done, opaque white in color, and flakes easily with a fork. Baste fish freuqently with sauce. Halfway through baking time, sprinkle fish lightly with paprika, salt, and pepper to saste. If desired, blend cold water and cornstarch together until smooth; blend mixure into orange sauce. Continue baking, spooning mixture over fillets frequently, until fish is almost done. Add orange pieces and grapes to sauce; continue baking for an additional 5 minutes. Do *not overbake* fish. To serve, spoon sauce over each portion, dividing evenly.

Microwave Instructions. Follow previous instructions for marinating fish. Coat each fillet lightly with vegetable cooking spray. Arrange fillets in an 11x7x2-inch glass baking dish. Pour marinade over fish; cover with clear plastic, allowing for steam venting. Microwave at high power for 3 minutes. Blend water and cornstarch together, if desired; uncover fish and blend cornstarch-water into orange juice mixture. Spoon sauce over fillets. Sprinkle lightly with paprika, salt, and pepper to taste. Recover and continue microwaving at high power for 2 minutes or until fish is done, opaque white in color, and flakes easily with a fork. Arrange orange pieces and grapes over fish. Cover and microwave 30 to 45 seconds. Do *not over-microwave.* Add additional cooking time by increments of 30 seconds after first 5 minutes of microwaving. Over-microwaved fish becomes tough.

Baked Fish Packets

Yield: 4 servings

2 tablespoons water
8 ounces mushrooms, chopped
1 1/2 teaspoons minced fresh or 1/2 teaspoon dried oregano
1/4 cup dry white wine
1 tablespoon lemon juice
1 teaspoon onion powder
1/4 teaspoon salt
Pepper to taste
1 pound flounder fillet, cut into 4 (4-ounce) serving pieces
1 tablespoon minced fresh parsley or 1 teaspoon dried parsley flakes, divided
1/4 teaspoon paprika, divided
4 thin lemon slices

In a small heavy skillet, bring water to a boil. Add mushrooms and oregano. Cook, stirring gently, over moderate heat until tender, about 5 minutes. Add wine and lemon juice. Continue cooking, stirring frequently, until almost all liquid is evaporated, about 2 minutes. Stir in onion powder, salt, and pepper. Remove mixture from heat. Lightly grease 4 (12-inch) squares of aluminum foil. Place a piece of fish on each sheet of foil. Top each piece of fish with an equal amount of mushroom mixture. Sprinkle each with parsley, and paprika. Add a lemon slice. Draw edges of foil together, sealing well. Arrange packets on a baking sheet; bake in a hot oven (400 degrees F.) until fish turns opaque in color and flakes easily with a fork, about 15 to 20 minutes. *Do not overcook.*

–C. F. Sauer Company
Sauer Spices

Fish A La Creme

Boil a rock or trout; remove the bones and pick the meat up; mix it with one pint of cream, two tablespoonfuls flour, half-pound of butter, little red pepper and salt; set it on the fire and stir until thick as custard; fill a deep dish with alternate layers of fish and crackers mashed up (not pounded) and cream. Bake twenty minutes.

F. F. V. Receipt Book, *1894*

Picked Fish

Four pounds halibut; cook it and let it cool; shred it, taking out all the bones. Then take one pint cream (with chopped onion in it) and let it heat well; then take out onion, and add butter size of an egg, and a teaspoonful of corn starch; put in a dish with bread-crumbs on top, and bake a light brown.

Mrs. P. H. Mayo
F. F. V. Receipt Book, *1894*

Baked Fish with Herbed Rice Stuffing

Yield: 6 servings

1 (3 to 4-pound) whole
dressed fish, boned, head
and tail in tact (see note)
1/2 cup butter or margarine,
melted and divided
2 tablespoons minced
peeled onion
1 1/2 cups cooked long-
grain rice
1/4 cup breadcrumbs
1 tablespoon lemon juice
1 tablespoon minced
parsley
1 1/2 teaspoons minced
fresh or 1/2 teaspoon
dried basil
3/4 teaspoon minced fresh
or 1/4 teaspoon dried dill
weed
Salt or seasoned salt, and
pepper to taste
Paprika as needed
Metal and wooden skewers
Thin lemon slices sprinkled
with paprika as desired
Parsley sprigs for garnish

Have fish merchant at market prepare fish for baking, if desired.In a medium heavy saucepan, sauté onion in 1/4 cup butter over moderate heat until tender but not browned. Remove from heat; add rice, breadcrumbs, lemon juice, parsley, basil, dill weed,1/2 teaspoon salt, 1/4 teaspoon paprika, and 1/8 teaspoon pepper,mixing well. Fill cavity of fish lightly with stuffing; close cavity and fasten securely with metal or wooden skewers. Arrange some of the lemon slices over the bottom of a greased 12 x 8 x 2-inch baking pan. Arrange stuffed fish over lemon slices (see note). Brush half of the remaining butter over fish. Sprinkle with salt, pepper, and paprika to taste. Bake, uncovered, in a moderate over (350 degrees F.) for 45 minutes or until fish flakes easily with a fork and turns opaque in color. Baste fish frequently with remaining melted butter during the last 15 minutes of baking. Arrange baked fish on a heated platter and garnish with additional lemon slices and sprigs of fresh parsley.

Note: Use a dressed whole sea trout, lake trout, flounder, perch, white fish, pike. or blue fish.

Note: Stuffed fish may be arranged in an attractive curved "C" shape on lemon slices; loosely tie, head and tail together, with heavy string to hold fish in shape during baking. Remove string just before serving presentation.

–Linda M. Bourgeois (Mrs. Bruce)

Baked Fish Continental

Yield: 4 servings

6 tablespoons minced peeled fresh or 2 table-spoons dried minced onion
2 tablespoons cooking oil
1 1/2 tablespoons lemon juice
1 1/2 teaspoons minced fresh or 1/2 teaspoon dried basil
1/2 teaspoon paprika
1/8 teaspoon garlic powder
1 pound fish fillets, cut into 4 (4-ounce) serving pieces (see note)
1 tablespoon minced fresh parsley or 1 teaspoon dried parsley flakes

In a small bowl, combine onion, oil, lemon juice, basil, paprika, and garlic, mixing well. Arrange fish fillets in a greased 10 x 6 x 2-inch baking pan. Evenly pour herb mixture over fish. Bake, uncovered, in a moderate oven (350 degrees F.) for 15 to 20 minutes or until fish turns opaque in color and flakes easily with a fork. Sprinkle each serving with parsley.

Note: Use fresh or thawed frozen fish, as desired.

–C. F. Sauer Company
Sauer Spices

Sturgeon

Sturgeon, sometimes twelve feet in length, were known to inhabit Virginia's waters in early colonial days. Even in nineteenth century cookbooks, recipes appear for ways to prepare sturgeon. Barbecues were popular in colonial Virginia where sturgeons and hogs were roasted over live wood coals. And, of course, from sturgeon comes caviar. Sadly, the sturgeon is now an extinct species in our rivers. Perhaps if our state waters were to be cleaned of pollution, the sturgeon could be reintroduced to Virginia's water and thrive.

Baked Shad with Roe

Yield: 4 servings

1 (5-pound) shad
1/4 cup cider vinegar
Salt and pepper to taste
1/2 cup water
4 tablespoons butter or
 margarine, divided into
 small pieces

Rinse fish with cold running water, inside and outside; dry with absorbent paper. Lightly sprinkle shad, inside and outside, with vinegar, salt, and pepper to taste. Arrange shad, with or without roe, in a medium roaster. Add water to pan, being careful not to pour over fish. Dot shad with small pieces of butter, inside and outside. Cover roaster tightly, being careful cover does not touch fish. Bake in a moderate oven (350 degrees F.) for 1 hour; reduce heat to very slow (250 degrees F.) and continue baking, covered tightly, for 5 hours. Roe may be baked separately in foil, seasoned with vinegar, salt, pepper, and butter, or left in tact in the shad. The roe baked in the shad compliments the fish; roe can be served separately.

Note: For a shad of less weight, decrease the amount of vinegar, water, and butter used. Always use twice the amount of water as vinegar.

–Inger Rice (Mrs. Walter)

Fish

Fish was an important part of the diet, especially for Richmond's poorer people. While many caught their own fish, commercial fisheries, described as "very lucrative," operated on either side of the river at the falls. Herring and shad teemed there in the spring.

Harry M. Ward and Harold E. Greer, Jr.
Richmond During The Revolution, 1775-83, 1977

Sturgeon-No. 160.

In buying sturgeon, always select it from a young, small fish. Unless it is very small, the cut about six or seven inches from the tail is best, but be careful not to get it so close to the tail as to be stringy. Lay the sturgeon in boiling salt and water for one-half hour, before cooking, to extract the oil.

**Instruction in Cooking
with Selected Receipts,** *1895*

Grilled Monkfish with Dill Pesto Sauce

Yield: 6 servings

3 pounds monkfish fillets, cut into serving pieces (see note)
6 tablespoons lime juice
Cooking oil as needed
1 tablespoon *each* fresh minced or 1 teaspoon dried dill weed, thyme, and parsley, mixed together
Dill Pesto Sauce

Rinse fillets in cool running water; pat dry with absorbent paper. Arrange fillets in a 12 x 8 x 2-inch baking dish and sprinkle evenly with lime juice. Allow to stand at room temperature for 15 minutes, turning fillets to absorb lime juice evenly. Drain fillets well; reserve juice. Brush each fillet, both sides, with oil and then sprinkle generously with herb mixture. Arrange fillets on a lightly greased sheet of heavy-duty aluminum foil on a grill rack, 8 to 10 inches above medium coals, (ash gray and glowing). Grill for about 15 minutes depending upon thickness of fish; turn fillets and continue grilling until done, about 12 to 15 minutes more. Fish will be done when flesh has turned opaque in color and flakes easily with a fork. *Do not overcook.* Baste fish several times with reserved lime juice and oil.

Oven Method: Prepare fish fillets for cooking as previously directed. Arrange fillets in a 12 x 8 x 2-inch baking dish. Bake, covered, in a moderate oven (350 degrees F.) for 15 to 20 minutes, depending upon thickness of fish. Baste with reserved lime juice and brush with additional oil. Continue to bake, uncovered, for an additional 15 minutes or until fish is opaque in color and flakes easily with a fork.

Note: 3 pounds Mako shark fillets may be substituted for monkfish.

Dill Pesto Sauce

1 cup coarsely chopped fresh or 1/4 cup dried dill weed
1 cup blanched whole almonds
1 cup grated Parmesan cheese
1/2 cup coarsely chopped parsley

In a food processor or blender container, combine dill weed, almonds, Parmesan cheese, and parsley. Cover and process or blend until mixture is finely ground. Gradually add olive oil, processing or blending thoroughly. Add eggs, lime juice, salt, and pepper, processing or blending until well-mixed and eggs finely ground. Store, tightly covered, in a glass jar in the refrigerator for several days until ready to us.

240

1 cup olive oil (see note)
2 hard-cooked eggs, peeled
   and quartered
1 tablespoon lime juice
1/4 teaspoon salt
1/8 teaspoon pepper

Note: Use a premium quality extra virgin olive oil. Extra virgin refers to the oil
   collected from the first press of the olives.

–Claudia Echols (Mrs. Steven)

Salmon Baked in Shells

Make a roux of one tablespoonful of boiling butter to two of flour; add gradually
a pint of hot milk or boiling water; season with salt and pepper and little
Worcestershire sauce and fine bread-crumbs. Take fresh or canned salmon,
pick it up carefully, and cut it up in small pieces; mix with bread-crumbs, cayenne
pepper, and salt; then mix the seasoning well with the salmon, fill your buttered
shells, and bake for fifteen minutes. Serve hot, with a little of the roux on top
of each shell.

F. F. V. Receipt Book, *1894*

Old Richmond Advertisement, circa 1909

Grilled Tuna with Three Pepper Relish

Yield: 4 servings

Three Pepper Relish

4 shallots, peeled and chopped
1 medium sweet yellow pepper, cored, seeded, and chopped
1 medium sweet red pepper, cored, seeded, and chopped
1 medium green pepper, cored, seeded, and chopped
1 cup dry white wine
Salt and pepper to taste

In a small heavy sauce pan, combine shallots, peppers, and wine; bring to a simmer over moderate heat. Continue simmering until mixture is reduced by half. Add vinegar and reduce again by half over moderate heat. Season with salt and pepper to taste. Cool and then refrigerate for 12 tgo 24 hours before serving.

Grilled Tuna

4 (8-ounce) Yellow Fin tuna steaks (see note)
About 1 to 2 cups salad oil
3 sprigs thyme, minced (see note)
3 sprigs basil, minced (see note)

Place tuna steaks in a deep bowl; add oil to cover and herbs. Marinate tuna for several hours, basting tuna frequently with oil mixture. Remove tuna from marinade, draining well. Arrange on a rack in a broiler pan. Broil, 4 to 6 inches from heat source, until done, golden brown, and fish flakes easily with a fork, about 5 minutes per side. *Do not overcook*. In a small heavy saucepan, bring pepper relish to a simmer over low heat. Arrange grilled tuna steaks on individual dinner plates ans spoon relish atop each portion.

Note: Use fresh or thawed frozen tuna steaks.

Note: If minced fresh herbs are unavailable, 1 teaspoon dried herbs of *each* may be substituted.

–Chef Kevin Wade
Gallego's Restaurant
The Omni Hotel

Dilled Fresh Salmon 'N Mushroom Pie

Yield: 6 to 8 servings

1 pound salmon fillet (see note)
Water as needed
1 pound mushrooms, thinly sliced
1/4 cup chopped peeled onion
5 tablespoons butter or margarine, melted and divided
3 tablespoons flour
1 teaspoon minced fresh or 1/4 teaspoon dried dill weed
1 cup chicken broth
1/2 cup light cream or half-and-half
2 tablespoons lime juice
Salt and pepper to taste
Pastry for Double-Crust Pie (9-inch) (see index)
1 egg white, slightly beaten (optional)

Place salmon in a 9 x 9 x 2-inch baking dish; add water to cover; bake, covered, in a moderate oven (350 degrees F.) for about 20 minutes until fish turns opaque in color and flakes easily with a fork. Drain salmon well; remove any bones and skin. Flake salmon and set aside.

In a medium heavy skillet, sauté mushrooms and onion in 3 tablespoons butter over moderate heat until tender but not browned; set aside. In a medium heavy saucepan, combine flour and 2 tablespoons butter, blending well. Stir in dill weed and mustard. With a wire whisk, gradually add broth and cream, whisking until well blended. Cook, stirring constantly, over moderate heat until sauce is thickened and bubbly hot. Stir in sherry and lime juice. Fold in salmon and mushroom-onion mixture. Season with salt and pepper to taste; set aside.

Roll out half of the pastry into a 10-inch diameter circle; fit rolled pastry into a 9-inch pie plate. Spoon salmon mixture into prepared pastry shell. Roll out remaining pastry into a 9-inch diameter; with a sharp knife, cut rolled pastry into thin strips. Arrange pastry strips in a lattice design over filling. Crimp edge of crust into a fluted ridge. Brush pastry strips with beaten egg white. Bake in a hot oven (425 degrees F.) for 10 minutes; reduce heat to moderate (375 degrees F.) and continue baking for 15 to 20 minutes or until pastry is golden brown and filling is bubbly hot.

Note: A 15 1/2-ounce can of salmon may be substituted for poached fresh salmon. Drain well and remove bones and cartilage. Fresh salmon may be microwaved at MEDIUM (7) power for 6 to 7 minutes or until fish flakes easily with a fork. *Do not overcook.*

–Linda M. Bourgeois (Mrs. Bruce)

The Jefferson Hotel

The Jefferson Hotel, one of the nation's outstanding examples of turn-of-the-century eclectic architecture and designed by the noted firm of Carrere and Hastings,architects of the Ponce De Leon Hotel in St. Augustine, Florida has regained its early regal splendor with its 1987 renovation. Opening its doors Thursday, October 31, 1895, it fulfilled the command of its patron, Richmond philanthropist,Major Lewis Ginter, to the architects to design the finest hotel in America. Aside from architectural merit, the hotel,as originally completed, contained many advanced technological devices such as service telephones, complete electric lighting, central steam heat, and both hot and cold running water for each guest bedroom.

Legend suggests that the Jefferson was "rushed to completion" in order to house the wedding guests and host parties for the social event of the Richmond season ... the wedding of Irene Langhorne, the inspiration for the Gibson Girl, and renowned painter and illustrator, Charles Dana Gibson ... November 7, 1895. Originally scheduled to open November 1st, the celebration was changed as Fridays were considered unlucky days. Wedding guests included "Miss Barrymore," probably Ethel, and Stanford White, noted New York architect, and host of a party for the wedding couple.One of the bridesmaids was Nanny Langhorne, no doubt the bride's sister, Nancy Langhorne, later Lady Astor of England.

Unfortunately, the original Jefferson Hotel was devastated by fire in March, 1901. The present renovation copies the May 6, 1907 restoration. Closed during the late 1970's and early 1980's, the Jefferson has re-opened, minus its famous alligators swimming in The Palm Court pool. The renowned life-size marble statue of Thomas Jefferson sculpted by Richmond sculptor, Edward V. Valentine, again graces the Palm Court Lobby. Once again, the Jefferson takes its place as one of the "Grand Dames" of elegant American Hotels.

Poached Fillet of Salmon with Shallot Sauce and Cucumber Mint Garnish

Yield: 4 servings

Shallot Sauce (see index)
Cucumber Mint Garnish
  (see index)
4 (6-ounce) salmon filléts
Water as needed
1/2 cup dry white wine
3 tablespoons lemon juice
Salt to taste
1 teaspoon minced parsley

Prepare Shallot Sauce and keep warm, covered, in the top of a double boiler, over hot water. Prepare Cucumber Mint Garnish; set aside. In a Dutch oven or large heavy saucepan, arrange salmon filléts in water just to cover. Add wine, lemon juice, and salt to taste. Poach fish over moderate heat (si8mmer but not boiling) for about 6 minutes or until fish is done. Fish will be done when it flakes easily with a fork and turns from a tgranslucent to an opaque pink in color. Remove filléts from hot liquid to a heated platter. Lightly sitr Cucumber Mint Garnish over low heat until thoroughly hot. Spoon garnish over poached fillets and serve with Shallot Sauce. Or, poach slamon in lemon juice-water mixture in a large elctric frypan, covered, over moderate heat (350 degrees F.) for about 6 minutes or until done. Or, poach salmon, covered, in a moderate oven (350 degrees F.) in lemon juice-water mixture for about 20 minutes or until done. Or, microwave salmon, covered with clear plastic wrap (allow for extrea palstic wearp for venting) in a 9x9x2-inch glass baking dish in lemon juice-water mixture. Additional cooking time, if needed, should be added in increments of seconds so that fish will not become overcooked and tough.

–The Jefferson Sheraton Hotel

245

Salmon Gallego

Yield: 6 servings

Salmon and Scallop Mousse

5 1/2 ounces salmon fillets
3 ounces sea scallops
2 egg whites
2/3 cup heavy cream, at room temperature
Salt and white pepper to taste
6 salmon fillets, each about 8 ounces
About 1/4 to 1/2 cup dry white wine

To prepare Mousse, combine 5 1/2 ounces salmon and scallops in a food processor or blender container; cover and process until mixture is a smooth purée. With motor running, add egg whites, one at a time, blending into purée. Add 2/3 cup cream, blending well. Season with salt and white pepper to taste.

Arrange 6 salmon fillets in a lightly greased 13x9x2-inch baking dish. Spread mousse mixture over the top of each fillet, dividing evenly. Add about 1/4 to 1/2 cup wine to baking dish, *just* enough to moisten fish. Bake, uncovered, in a moderate oven (350 degrees F.) for 10 to 12 minutes or until salmon flakes easily with a fork and is opaque in color.

Sauce Vin Blanc

7 shallots, peeled and minced
1 cup dry white wine
1/3 cup heavy cream, at room temperature
2 cups butter, at room temperature (see note)
2 tablespoons minced chives
2 tablespoons minced fresh or 2 teaspoons dried dill weed
Salt and white pepper to taste

While salmon is baking, prepare sauce. In the top of a double boiler, combine shallots and 1 cup wine. Place over moderate to high heat and reduce wine until liquid is almost dry. Add 1/3 cup cream; continue to heat until cream is reduced by three fourths, stirring constantly. Remove from heat. With a wire whisk, blend in butter, whisking in a small amount at a time. Strain. Add chives, dill, and salt and white pepper to taste. Place over hot water to keep warm. Sauce should be kept warm, *not* hot or cold.

To serve, ladle sauce onto each of 6 dinner plates. Arrange a baked mousse topped salmon fillet on each plate over sauce. Serve immediately.

–Chef Kevin Wade
Gallego's Restaurant
The Omni Hotel

Smoked Salmon Potato Pancakes

Yield: 8 pancakes, 4 servings

1 pound medium potatoes
Ice water
1 egg, slightly beaten
1 cup plus 2 tablespoons
  sour cream, divided
3 tablespoons flour, divided
1 very small onion, peeled
  and grated
2 tablespoons cooking oil,
  divided
8 ounces smoked salmon,
  cut into julienne (thin)
  strips
2 to 4 tablespoons capers,
  drained and divided
Watercress or parsley sprigs
  for garnish

Peel and grate potatoes. Immediately place grated potatoes in a large bowl partially filled with ice water. In a large bowl, lightly beat egg; add 2 tablespoons sour cream and 2 tablespoons flour, blending well. Drain potatoes thoroughly and pat dry with absorbent paper. Stir potatoes and onions into egg mixture. Heat 1 tablespoon oil in a large heavy skillet or griddle to medium-high heat, about 375 degrees F. Cook four pancakes at a time. For each pancake, pour about 1/4 cup batter into skillet and spread carefully to make a 3-inch cake. Cook until golden brown on both sides, about 4 to 5 minutes per side, turning once. Transfer pancakes to a heated platter and keep warm in a *very* slow oven (250 degrees F.). Add remaining tablespoon oil to skillet. Repeat cooking process with remaining batter. In a small heavy saucepan, combine 1 cup sour cream and 1 tablespoon flour, blending well. Carefully fold in salmon strips. Stir over low heat until heated through. Arrange two pancakes on each of four luncheon plates. Spoon smoked salmon sour cream sauce over each serving, dividing evenly. Sprinkle 1/2 to 1 tablespoon capers over each serving. Garnish with watercress or parsley sprigs.

–Inger Rice (Mrs. Walter)

Broiled Salmon Steaks with Herbed Sauce

Yield: 6 servings

4 tablespoons butter or
  margarine
1/4 cup dry white wine
1 tablespoon chopped
  parsley
1/4 teaspoon fines herbs
1 garlic clove, sliced
6 salmon steaks (.about 2
  pounds)
1 teaspoon salt

In a small heavy saucepan, combine butter, wine, parsley, fines herbs, and garlic; heat slowly until butter is melted. Let stand for 15 minutes. Sprinkle steaks with salt. Place fish on a greased rack in a broiler pan and brush with sauce. Broil about 3 inches from heat source, about 4 to 6 minutes per side, basting with sauce several times.

Wakefields' restaurant traces its lineage to the former Wakefield Grill, located on West Broad Street across from the legendary dance hall, Tantilla Gardens, vintage 1940 to 1955. In its heyday, the Wakefield Grill was considered the premier restaurant of Richmond, most of the others being of the greasy spoon variety. The chicken specialty, Chicken-in-the-Rough, featuring a secret special seasoning and breading, was the forerunner of today's fare at fast food chicken emporiums. Served with crisp shoestring potatoes and honey, it was indeed "finger lickin' good."

The present owner of Wakefields' restaurant, Jack Terry, became involved by purchasing a descendant of the grill, Wright's Townhouse restaurant, and its recipes from its owner, Mrs. Pearl Wakefield Wright, in 1973. Jack Terry opened Wakefields' Restaurant in 1985, and of course, Mrs. Wakefiled-Wright's wonderful homey recipes accompanied him. Many of those long ago favorites such as the spoon bread, deviled crab, veal dishes, and pies result from the bygone era of the old Wakefield Grill. Today's Wakefields' is the quintessence of a neighborhood eatery, enjoying a following from local residents, as well as a recommendation by the New York Times.

Jack's Grilled Sea Trout Especial

Yield: 6 servings

Marinara Sauce (see index)
1/2 cup chopped peeled
   onion
1/2 cup chopped green
   pepper
1/2 to 1 teaspoon Worces-
   tershire sauce or to taste
1/2 teaspoon sugar to taste
6 sea trout fillets, about 4 to
   6 ounces *each*
Lemon pepper seasoning to
   taste
Celery salt to taste

Prepare Marinara Sauce; add onion, green pepper, Worcestershire sauce, and sugar. Keep warm while preparing trout. Sprinkle each trout fillet liberally with lemon pepper seasoning, celery salt, thyme, cayenne pepper, salt, and pepper to taste. In a large heavy skillet (preferably cast iron), sauté fillets, skin side up, in olive oil over moderate heat until golden brown, opaque in color, and flakes easily with a fork. Spoon 2 to 3 tablespoons Marinara Sauce onto each of 6 dinner plates. Arrange fish fillets over sauce. Garnish each portion with minced dill weed and lemon wedges.

Thyme to taste
Cayenne pepper to taste
Salt and pepper to taste
About 1/3 cup hot olive oil
  (see note)
Minced dill weed and thin
  lemon wedges for garnish

Note: Use a premium quality extra virgin olive oil. Extra virgin refers to the oil
      collected from the first press of the olives.

–Jack Terry, proprietor

Old Virginia Crab Cakes

Yield: 4 servings

*The Hughes-Nielsen family has been serving excellent quality traditional
home-style food to Richmonders for over thirty years. Nielsen's 3N Restaurant,
located since 1969 at 4800 Thalbro Street, formerly was known as the Hughes
House on Broad Street. Martha and Ned Nielsen preside over diners with a
watchful caring eye for their patrons dining pleasure.*

1 pound crabmeat
1 egg, lightly beaten
1 tablespoon cooking oil
1 1/2 to 2 tablespoons
  lemon juice
1/2 teaspoon prepared
  mustard
1/2 teaspoon minced
  parsley
1/8 teaspoon salt or to taste
About 3 to 4 tablespoons
  cooking oil as needed for
  pan-frying
Thin lemon wedges and/or
  Tartar Sauce for garnish
  (optional) (see index)

Pick over crabmeat thoroughly and remove any
remaining shell or cartilage. In a medium bowl,
combine the first 8 ingredients, mixing lightly,
being careful not to break up crabmeat. Shape mixture
into 4 large or 8 small patties. Pan-fry crab cakes
in a large heavy skillet in 2 tablespoons hot oil
over moderate heat until golden brown, about 5
minutes per side. Add 1 to 2 tablespoons additional cooking oil to pan if necessary. Serve with
lemon wedges and/or Tartar Sauce, if desired.

–Martha and Ned Nielsen, proprietors
Nielsen's 3N Restaurant

Butlery Crab and Lobster Cakes

Yield: 6 servings

This marvelous tasting crabcake served at The Butlery, Ltd., located in the River Road Shopping Center is considerably different than the usual Virginia offering. Equally good in flavor as its crab cake cousin, it is light and more French in style and substance.

1 pound lump crabmeat
8 ounces lobster meat, removed from shell and uncooked (see note)
1/4 cup heavy cream, at room temperature
Salt and pepper to taste
1/2 cup clarified butter or margarine, melted (see note)
Sweet Red Pepper Buerre Blanc (optional) (see index)

Pick over crabmeat, removing any remaining shell or cartilage; transfer to a medium bowl. Place lobster meat in a food processor or blender container; cover and process or whiz until lobster is puréed. While motor is running, gradually add cream, blending well. Add salt and pepper to taste. Fold lobster mixture into crabmeat, *being careful not to break up large lumps of crab.* Adjust seasonings to taste, if desired. Form crab mixture into 6 thick patties, each about 4 ounces in weight. In a large heavy skillet, sauté crab-lobster cakes in clarified butter over moderate to high heat until golden brown, about 2 to 3 minutes per side. Arrange crab cakes on a heated platter and keep warm in a *very, very,* slow oven (200 degrees F.), if desired. Serve with Sweet Red Pepper Buerre Blanc and garnish as desired.

Note: 8 ounces uncooked flounder may be substituted for lobster meat, if desired.

Note: To prepare clarified butter, melt butter in a small heavy saucepan over low heat. Pour melted butter into a small bowl and allow to cool to room temperature. Skim off the pure fat collecting at the top of the bowl and discard the remaining solids and water.

–The Butlery, Ltd.

Crab Cakes in Puffed Pastry

Yield: 4 to 6 servings

1 sheet frozen puff pastry
2 pounds backfin crabmeat
3/4 teaspoon baking powder
2 to 3 tablespoons mayonnaise
1 teaspoon Durkee's sauce
1/2 teaspoon seafood seasoning (see note)
6 to 8 drops hot sauce
Seafood Cream Sauce (see index)
Wild Rice with Pecan Basil Butter (see index)

Remove puff pastry from freezer and transfer to the refrigerator for 20 minutes. While pastry is thawing, prepare crabmeat. Pick over crabmeat, removing any remaining shell or cartilage. In a large bowl, combine crabmeat and baking powder, mixing lightly. Add mayonnaise, Durkee's sauce, seafood seasoning, and hot sauce; toss mixture lightly and form into 4 to 6 equal balls. Remove pastry from the refrigerator and cut into pieces about 4 inches square. Place crab balls in center of pastry squares. Fold ends of each pastry square up over each crab ball, pressing ends of pastry together to seal. Arrange pastries on a lightly greased baking sheet. Bake in a hot oven (400 degrees F.) for 25 minutes until pastry is done and golden brown. Serve immediately garnished with Seafood Cream Sauce and accompanied with Wild Rice with Pecan Basil Butter.

–Chef James and Lynn News, proprietors
Mr. Patrick Henry's Restaurant and Inn

Crab Croquettes

1 pint of crab meat, 2 eggs, 1 teacup of stale bread crumbs or cracker crumbs, Salt and pepper to taste, Mix one of the beaten eggs and half of the crumbs with the crab meat. Form into croquettes, and roll the croquettes in the other beaten egg and then in cracker crumbs. Fry in hot, deep fat, and drain.
Nancy Byrd Turner

Famous Recipes From Old Virginia, *1935*

Sam's Crab Imperial

Yield: 2 large or 4 small servings

1 pound lump or backfin
  crabmeat
1 egg, lightly beaten
1/2 cup mayonnaise (see
  note)
Seafood seasoning (see
  note)
2 to 3 drops Worcestershire
  sauce or to taste
Pinch of white pepper
2 to 4 teaspoons butter or
  margarine, melted and
  divided
1/4 to 1/2 cup
  Imperial Sauce

Pick over crabmeat, removing any shell or cartilage. In a medium bowl, combine egg, mayonnaise, and pepper, blending well. Add crabmeat
and *mix very gently, being careful not to break pieces of
crabmeat.* Spoon mixture into 2 to 4 individual
ramekins or casseroles or seafood baking
shells.Pour 1 teaspoon melted butter over each.
Arrange ramekins or baking shells on a baking
sheet; broil, 10 to 12 inches from heat source, for
about 8 minutes. *Watch carefully so crabmeat mixture
doesn't burn.* Remove and spoon 2 tablespoons
Imperial Sauce evenly over each; return to broiler
and continue broiling for 1 to 2 minutes or until
top of each Crab Imperial is lightly browned.
Serve immediately.

Note: Preferably use Old Bay brand seafood seasoning.

Note: Preferably use Hellman's brand mayonnaise. Reduced calorie mayonnaise
  may be used, if desired.

Imperial Sauce
(about 1 cup)
2 egg whites
3/4 cup mayonnaise
Pinch of sugar
Pinch of white pepper

In a deep small bowl, beat egg whites until glossy
stiff, but not dry, peaks are formed. Carefully fold
in mayonnaise,sugar and pepper.

–Sam Miller's Warehouse Restaurant

Old Richmond Advertisement, circa 1909

Blackened Crab Cakes with Stonewall Dirty Rice

Yield: 4 to 6 servings

1 pound crabmeat
1 egg, slightly beaten
1 cup breadcrumbs
1/4 cup mayonnaise
1/4 cup minced parsley
1 teaspoon Worcestershire sauce
1/2 to 1 teaspoon seafood seasoning
1/4 teaspoon dry mustard
Pinch of cayenne pepper or to taste
Salt and pepper to taste
1 to 2 tablespoons butter or margarine, at room temperature
1 to 2 tablespoons cooking oil
1 tablespoon Cajun-style mixed spices
Thin lemon wedges for garnish
Stonewall Dirty Rice (see index)

Pick over crabmeat, removing any shell or cartilage; set a side.In a medium bowl, combine egg, breadcrumbs,mayonnaise,parsley, Worcestershire sauce, seafood seasoning, dry mustard, and cayenne pepper, mixing lightly. Add crabmeat, mixing gently. Season with salt and pepper to taste. Shape mixture into thick patties, about 3 inches in diameter. In a large heavy skillet, combine butter,oil, and Cajun seasoning; bring to moderate to high heat (375 to 400 degrees F.). Sauté crab cakes in hot spiced butter-oil mixture until golden brown and almost blackened, about 2 to 3 minutes per side. Garnish each portion with thin lemon wedges and serve with Stonewall Dirty Rice.

–Chef Nate Johnson
Rick Giovannoni, proprietor
Stonewall Cafe

Fishery

At that period, the resort of shad and herrings to James River was much greater than of late years, and a fishery was attached to the ferry, where fish could be obtained alive and kicking; but of late years their progress has been so much intercepted by the numerous floating and other seines lower down the river, or from some other cause, that few pass up to the falls. Formerly, during the fishing season the rocks in the falls were alive with fishermen casting their nets in the sluices, and catching the finest shad-- such as had strength to stem the torrentof several miles continuance.

Samuel Mordecai
Richmond in By-Gone Days, 1856
Reprint Edition, 1975

Updated Version of Old-Time Crab Croquettes

Yield: 4 servings

1 pound backfin crabmeat
2 eggs, divided
1 cup fine bread or cracker
    crumbs, divided
Salt and pepper to taste
Hot cooking oil as needed
Hollandaise Sauce or Spicy
    Shrimp Sauce (see index)

Pick over crabmeat, removing any remaining shell or cartilage. In a medium bowl, combine crabmeat, 1 egg, 1/2 cup crumbs, and salt and pepper to taste, mixing well. Form mixture into 4 equal-size cone shapes. In a small bowl, lightly beat remaining egg. Dip each crab croquette in beaten egg and then roll in remaining crumbs, coating each well. Pan-fry in about 1/2 to 1 inch of cooking oil in a large heavy skillet over moderate heat until golden brown and crisp on the outside, about 2 to 3 minutes per side. Or, deep-fry in hot cooking oil (375 degrees F.) in a deep fryer for about 2 to 3 minutes or until golden brown.

Variation: Add 1 1/2 teaspoons Worcestershire sauce, 1 teaspoon minced parsley, 1/2 teaspoon dry mustard, 1/4 to 1/2 teaspoon seafood seasoning, and 3 to 4 drops hot sauce to crabmeat mixture.

Chutney-Deviled Crab

Yield: 4 entrées of 6 appetizer servings

1 pound crabmeat, flaked
1 1/2 cups breadcrumbs,
    divided
1/2 cup Bechamel Sauce
    (see index)
2 tablsepoons butter, at
    room temperature
2 tablespoons mango
    chutney
1 tablespoon white wine
    vinegar
1/2 teaspoon dry mustard
Salt and pepper to taste
3 tablespoons butter or
    margarine, melted

In a bowl, combine crabmeat, 1 cup breadcrumbs, 1/2 cup Bechamel Sauce, 2 tablespoons butter, chutney, vinegar, and mustard, mixing well. Add salt and pepper to taste. Spoon evenly into 4 or 6 ramekins or baking shells, mounding lightly. Combine 3 tablespoons melted butter and 1/2 cup breadcrumbs; evenly sprinkle over each serving. Arrange ramekins or baking shells on a baking sheet. Bake in a moderate oven (375 degrees F.) for 20 minutes, then broil, 6 inches from heat source, for 1 to 2 minutes or until top of each serving is golden brown.

Old Dominion Fried Soft Shelled Crabs

Yield: 6 servings

12 soft shelled crabs, cleaned 1 to 1 1/2 cups flour Salt and pepper to taste Hot bacon drippings or cooking oil	Dry crabs with absorbent paper. On a sheet of waxed paper, dredge crabs in flour, coating each well. Sprinkle with salt and pepper to taste. In a large heavy skillet, pan-fry crabs in just enough bacon drippings or oil to keep from sticking until lightly browned,about 5 minutes per side.

Variations: Follow recipe and change as suggested.

Deep-Fat Fried: Place crabs in deep-fat fryer filled with hot bacon drippings or cooking oil (375 degrees F.) for 2 to 3 minutes or until brown.

Soft Shell Crab Almondine: Sauté 1/2 cup slivered blanched or sliced almonds in 2 tablespoonfuls of butter in a small heavy skillet over moderate heat until lightly browned. Remove almonds; panfry crabs in almond butter. Just before removing from skillet, add almonds and serve.

Crabmeat Benedict

Yield: 4 servings

12 ounces backfin crabmeat About 2 tablespoons lemon juice 4 ripe medium tomato slices 2 English Muffins, each split in half and each half toasted Cheese Sauce (see index) Blender Hollandaise Sauce (see index) Paprika for garnish Minced parsley for garnish Thin lemon wedges for garnish	Pick over crabmeat removing any shell or cartilage. Shape crabmeat into 4 equal-sized cakes, about the diameter of an English muffin half. Sprinkle about 1/2 tablespoon lemon juice over each crab cake. Arrange crab cakes and tomato slices on a lightly greased baking sheet; bake in a moderate oven (375 degrees F.) for 5 minutes or until heated through.Remove crab cakes and broil tomatoes 6 to 8 inches from heat source, for about 2 minutes, or until tomatoes are lightly browned. On luncheon plates, arrange tomato slices on toasted English muffin halves; spoon about 1 to 2 tablespoons hot Cheese Sauce over each. Arrange a hot crabcake on each cheese-tomato topped English muffin half. Top each serving with 3 to 4 tablespoons Hollandaise Sauce and sprinkle lightly with paprika and then minced parsley. Garnish each serving with thin lemon wedges.

–Sam Miller's Warehouse Restaurant

255

Lobster Alfredo

Yield: 4 servings

Rudee's on the James opened its doors in a fully restored 1873 brick building located on 12th street in the historic Shockoe Slip area in the spring of 1988. Known for its fresh seafood, Rudee's is an offshoot of the well-known Virginia Beach establishment, Rudee's on the Inlet. Ironically, there was a restaurant housed in the building in 1873. J. T. Johnson, the proprietor, advertised the sale of "oysters, fish, and game." Recently, the establishment changed hands; now it is owned by a group of home towners who are interested in maintaining Rudee's legacy of excellent seafood.

Water as needed
4 (1 1/4-pound) lobsters
4 tablespoons cooking oil, divided
1 teaspoon minced peeled garlic
6 tablespoons brandy
2 1/2 cups heavy cream, at room temperature
1 cup grated Parmesan cheese, divided
Salt and pepper to taste
1 pound fettucine

Arrange a metal rack in a large heavy pot or kettle; add water to just below the level of the rack. Bring water to boiling over high heat; add lobsters, cover, reduce heat to moderate, and steam cook lobsters for 7 to 8 minutes, until lobsters turn bright red-orange in color. While lobsters are steaming, prepare sauce.

In a medium heavy saucepan, heat 1 tablespoon oil over moderate temperature; add garlic and sauté for about 1 minute until garlic is tender, but not browned. Reduce heat, add brandy, and simmer mixture for 3 minutes. Add cream and half of the cheese; stir over low heat until cheese is melted.

Remove lobsters from pot after steaming; extract lobster meat from tails and cut into bite-sized pieces with a sharp knife. Crack claws and reserve for garnish. Extract any remaining edible meat from lobster bodies and cut into bite-sized pieces.

Stir lobster meat into cream sauce. Add salt and pepper to taste. In a large heavy pot, bring about 4 to 5 quarts water to boiling. Add a pinch of salt and fettucine. Cook fresh fettucine for about 1 minute or until *al dente*, tender but firm; cook commercially packaged fettucine according to package directions. Drain pasta well. Arrange fettucine on heated dinner plates, dividing evenly. Stir lobster sauce over low heat for 30 to 60 seconds; spoon mixture over pasta servings, dividing evenly. Sprinkle each portion with 2 tablespoons remaining grated Parmesan cheese and garnish each serving with 2 lobster claws.

–Rudee's on the James

Lobster L'Americaine

Yield: 4 servings

1 pound lump crabmeat
Water as needed
4 (1 1/4-pound) lobsters
1/4 cup chopped peeled
tomato
1/4 cup chopped peeled
shallots
2 teaspoons minced peeled
garlic
1 cup butter or margarine,
melted
1 1/2 cups heavy cream, at
room temperature
Salt and pepper to taste

Pick over crabmeat, removing any shell or cartilage; set aside. Place a rack in a large heavy pot or
steamer; fill pot with water *just* to rack level. Bring
water *just* to boiling; reduce heat and keep at
simmering (small bubbles of water around edge
of pan). Arrange lobsters on rack, cover, and steam
for 3 minutes. Remove lobsters from steamer,
draining well. Place lobsters on a smooth surface
and turn backside down. Remove lobster meat
from tails, claws, and joints. Cut tail meat into 1-
inch pieces. Remove contents of body cavity and
discard; reserve lobster shells. In a small heavy
skillet, sauté tomato, shallots, and garlic in butter
for 1 to 2 minutes. Add lobster, mixing gently;
continue cooking for 1 to 2 minutes. Add crabmeat
and cream, mixing gently. Season with salt and
pepper to taste. Spoon mixture into empty lobster shells, dividing evenly. Arrange lobsters on
heated plates and garnish as desired. Serve
immediately.

–Hugo's
Hyatt Richmond

Boiled Lobster

Yield: 6 servings

These following instructions may sound strange. . . but they are humane!

1/3 cup salt
1 1/2 gallons water
6 live lobsters (1 to 2
pounds each)
Melted butter as needed
Thin lemon wedges

In a large heavy kettle or steamer, add salt to
water, cover, and bring to a boil. Knock lobsters in
between eyes with a hammer and plunge lobsters
into boiling water head first. Reduce heat, cover
and simmer for 8 to 10 minutes or until lobsters
turn red, depending on size of lobsters. Drain,
crack claws, and serve with melted butter and thin
lemon wedges.

Oven Clambake

Yield: 8 to 10 servings

If you can't go to the seashore to take part in the delicious culinary experience of a clambake, bring the clambake to you via the oven!

8 ears of corn, shucked, cut into 3 to 4-inch pieces, and buttered
8 small red-skinned new potatoes, unpeeled
4 medium yams or sweet potatoes, unpeeled and cut in half
Seaweed (optional)
About 25 *little neck* (very small) clams in shell
About 25 *count* (large) oysters in shell
About 8 to 10 tablespoons cooking oil
16 link-style pork sausages or 8 mild spiced Italian-style sausages, cut into 2 to 3-inch pieces
2 (3-pound) frying chickens, cut into serving pieces
Flour
6 parsley sprigs
2 medium onions, peeled and quartered
1 cup coarsely chopped celery (including some leaves)
4 cups boiling water
4 cups dry white wine or beer
1/2 cup lemon juice
1 cup butter or margarine, divided into small pieces, at room temperature
Additional melted butter and thinly sliced seeded lemon wedges

In a large heavy roaster, arrange a layer of buttered corn ears. Lightly grease new potatoes and yams with oil; arrange in layers over corn. Spread a bed of seaweed, if desired, over yams. Arrange raw clams (in shell) and raw oysters (in shell) over seaweed; set aside. In a large heavy skillet, lightly brown sausages, about 1 to 2 minutes per side, over moderate heat. Arrange sausages over oysters. On a sheet of waxed paper, dredge chicken pieces in flour, coating each well. Add remaining oil to skillet. Brown chicken pieces in hot oil, about 3 to 4 minutes per side, over moderate heat. Season with salt and pepper to taste. Arrange chicken pieces over sausages. Place parsley sprigs, onion wedges, and celery in the center of a large square of cheesecloth; close cheesecloth around vegetables and secure with string. Place in roaster. Add water, wine, and lemon juice to pan, being careful *not* to pour over chicken. Evenly distribute pieces of butter over chicken. Cover and bake in a very hot oven (450 degrees F.) for 40 minutes; reduce heat to moderate (350 degrees F.) and continue baking for 1 hour. Transfer chicken, sausage, oysters, clams, and vegetables to individual plates, dividing evenly. Pour pan broth into individual soup cups and accompany with each serving. Discard seaweed and parsley bouquet. Pass additional melted butter and lemon wedges.

Varations: Fish fillets may be added to roasting pan. Arrange fillets on bed of seaweed with clams and oysters. Figure about 3 ounces of fish per person if serving with chicken and about 6 ounces per person if substituting fish for chicken. Use flounder, blue, sea trout, red snapper, cod, haddock, or other firm fish. Or, raw shrimp may be added to roasting pan. Arrange shrimp on bed of seaweed seaweed with oysters and clams.

Figure about 4 ounces of raw unpeeled shrimp per person if serving with chicken and about 8 per person if substituting shrimp for chicken or sausage. Sprinkle 1 to 2 tablespoons seafood seasoning over fish or shrimp, if desired. Add sprigs of additional fresh herbs such as basil, or chervil, or marjoram, or thyme, or rosemary, or tarragon to parsley bouquet garni.

Charcoal Grilling Instructions: Follow preparation instructions previously given; however, arrange layers on 2 large sheets of heavy-duty aluminum foil put together to form a double thickness, shiny side turned in. Bring foil up around layers of food to form a container. Add water, wine, and lemon juice. Evenly distribute pieces of butter over food. Close foil, sealing tightly. Arrange foil package on cooking grill rack about 10 to 12 inches above medium to hot coals. Grill aout 1 to 1 1/2 hours, turing package about every 15 minutes, until vegetables and chicken are tender. Add briquets as necessary to maintain medium hot coals, about 8 to 12 at end of first hour of cooking.

Gas Grill: Preheat gas briguets at high setting, cover closed, for 15 minutes. Reduce temperature thermostate setting to medium. Arrange cooking grill rack 10 to 12 inches from heat source. Proceed as directed for charcoal grilling. Close cover during grilling.

Covered Kettle Style Grill: Follow directions for regular charcoal grilling. Close cover during grilling.

Salt

A letter from a Henrico gentlemen to a friend in Williamsburg, written in 1775 when salt was in short supply and uplanders were raiding the Richmond area for salt, provides some insight into the habits and diets of the poorer people. "...more salt is necessary in the families of the poor and middling sort of people in this part of the country, than in the upper part, for they not having it in their power to raise pork and beef, are obliged to live upon salted fish....If our poor have not salt enough to cure their fish, they must eat bread alone, because they cannot raise meat, and have not money to buy it..."

Harry M. Ward and Harold E. Greer, Jr.
Richmond During The Revolution, 1775-83, 1977

Steamers-In-A-Pot

Yield: 4 servings

6 green onions, thinly sliced
  (including some green
  tops)
1 to 2 ribs celery, minced
2 to 3 cups dry white wine
1/2 cup lemon juice
1 teaspoon minced peeled
  garlic
2 tablespoons minced
  parsley
1 teaspoon seafood seasoning
1/2 teaspoon celery salt
2 to 3 drops hot sauce or to
  taste
Salt and pepper to taste
4 dozen *little neck* (very
  small) clams in the shell
  or 4 dozen mussels in the
  shell
1 to 1 1/2 cups butter or
  margarine, melted, for
  dipping
Additional lemon juice for
  dipping

In an 8 to 10-quart heavy saucepan or Dutch oven, combine the first 12 ingredients. Bring mixture to a boil over moderate heat. Rinse clams and mussels in cool running water. Add clams and/or mussels to boiling wine mixture; reduce heat to simmer, cover tightly, and steam seafood over low heat for about 7 minutes. Shellfish will be cooked when shells are opened. Do *not eat* clams or mussels of which *shells do not open*. Remove steamed shellfish from steamer pot and serve in large shallow soup bowls. Pour broth into cup and serve with "steamers." Add about 1 to 2 teaspoons lemon juice to melted butter and serve with "steamers" in saki cups as a dipping butter.

Varations: Substitute *counts* (large) oysters in the shell for clams or mussels. Or, use a combination of all or two of the shellfish.

Devilled Oysters

Put a layer of raw oysters in a pan, and then a layer of bread-crumbs, black and red pepper, salt, butter, mustard, and al ittle vinegar mixed together. Put alternate layers of each until full, and then bake.

Mrs. Duke
Housekeeping in Old Virginia, *1879*

The U.S. oyster mania, at its peak in the late 1880's through the first decade of the 1900's, records oyster catches of as much as 150 million pounds per year....meat only, not including shell!

Seaside Oysters Linden Row

Yield: 4 servings

1 small to medium onion, peeled and chopped
1 1/2 garlic cloves, peeled and minced
1 1/2 tablespoons olive oil (see note)
9 sun dried tomatoes, soaked in olive oil, drained and chopped
3 tablespoons balsamic vinegar
1 1/2 cup heavy cream
3 ounces fully-cooked smoked Smithfield ham, shaved or minced
1 1/2 tablespoons chopped chives
18 *count* (large) oysters in the shell
Rock salt, or crumpled aluminum foil balls, or dried beans
Additional balsamic vinegar as needed

In a small heavy skillet, sauté onion and garlic in olive oil over moderate heat until tender but not browned; add dried tomatoes and vinegar. Cook until liquid is almost gone. Add cream; bring to a boil and continue to cook until mixture is thickened. Stir in ham and chives. Remove from heat; set aside. Shuck oysters, leaving oyster on the deep side of half shell. Arrange oysters on the half shell over rock salt, aluminum foil balls, or dried beans in a 13 x 9 x 2-inch baking pan. Broil, 6 to 8 inches from heat source, until oysters begin to plump and their edges begin to wrinkle, about 3 to 4 minutes. Remove from heat and splash each oyster with balsamic vinegar. Spoon 2 teaspoons of ham topping over each oyster. Broil for 2 to 3 additional minutes or until topping is bubbly hot. Garnish as desired and serve immediately.

Note: Use a premium quality extra virgin olive oil. Extra virgin refers to the oil collected from the first press of the olives.

—Linden Row Dining Room
Linden Row Inn

261

La Maisonnette Bistro

In the spring of 1989, La Maisonnette took on a new look as La Maisonnette Bistro. Keeping up with the trend in popularity of French bistro-style foods, proprietors Alain and Sandra Vincey began offering more casual food in a French manner. Alain selects "the best seasonal fare to create a variety of daily specials." Open for lunch and dinner, Mondays through Saturdays, the Vinceys recently began serving a delightful Sunday Brunch. Originally opened on St.Patrick's Day in 1981 in a renovated 1930's Carytown residence with a quaint intimate atmosphere, the restaurant has expanded to include al fresco dining on the front patio.

Chef Vincey began his European training at age fourteen, most of which was done in Southern France. His accomplishments are many and include employment at the renowned New York restaurant, Lutece, and even a stint as cook on Jacques Cousteau's ship, the Calypso.

At press time it was learned that La Maisonnette Bistro had, sadly, closed.

Mussels and Fettucine with Garlic and Cream

Yield: 3 to 4 servings

14 ounces fettucine
About 3 quarts boiling
  salted water
3 pounds fresh mussels in
  their shells
5 garlic cloves, peeled
3/4 cup dry white wine
3/4 cup water
2 tablespoons butter or
  margarine
1 medium sweet red pepper,
  cored, seeded, and cut
  into thin 3-inch strips
2 cups heavy cream, at
  room temperature
Salt and pepper to taste

In a large heavy pot, cook fettucine in boiling salted water until tender but firm, *al dente* (see note); drain well, rinse in cold water, and set aside. Clean mussels, but leave them in their shells. In a large heavy pot, combine mussels, garlic, wine, and 3/4 cup water; cover and bring to a boil over moderate heat, stirring occasionally. Reduce heat and simmer, covered, until mussel shells open, about 8 to 10 minutes. Strain mussels and pot liquid; reserve mussels and strain pot liquid a second time through a coffee filter. Reserve garlic. Remove mussels from their shells; set aside. Transfer strained pot liquid to a large heavy saucepan or return to cooking pot. Bring liquid to a boil over moderate heat; continue cooking until liquid is reduced by half. With a sharp knife, mince cooked garlic cloves. In a large heavy saucepan, melt butter over moderate heat; add garlic and red pepper strips, cooking *just* until red pepper is crisp tender but not soft. Add reduced mussel liquid and cream; bring to a simmer over moderate heat. *Do not boil.* Add reserved mussels and fettucine; continue to simmer until mixture is heated through, about 1 minute. Season with salt and pepper to taste. Serve immediately in large shallow soup bowls.

Note: Cook fresh handmade fettucine about 1 1/2 minutes after water returns to a boil. Cook commercial packaged fettucine according to package directions.

–Chef Alain Vincey
La Maisonnette Bristro

> The city faced the constant nuisance of animals running loose in its streets. An ordinance in October 1782 prohibited anyone from allowing a stallion or ridgeling to run free in the limits of the city and established a fine of four shillings for each violation. For each hog or goat running free a fine of five shillings was to be imposed.
> Harry M. Ward and Harold E. Greer, Jr.
> **Richmond During The Revolution**, 1775-83, 1977

Pan-Fried Oysters

Yield: 6 servings

12 ounces fresh or frozen oysters
2 eggs
2 tablespoons light cream
1/4 teaspoon salt
1/3 cup flour
2 cups fine cracker crumbs
1/3 cup butter or margarine, melted (see note)
1/3 cup hot cooking oil or bacon drippings (see note)
Favorite seafood sauce or Tartar Sauce (see index)

Thaw frozen oysters; drain well. Combine eggs, cream, and salt;beat slightly. Dip oysters into egg mixture, then turn into flour. Dip oysters in egg mixture again and roll in cracker crumbs, coating each oyster well. Allow to stand for 5 to 10 minutes before frying. In a large heavy skillet, pan-fry oysters in butter and oil over moderate heat for 5 to 7 minutes or until done and lightly browned, turning once. Serve with favorite seafood sauce or Tartar Sauce.

Note: Amount of butter and oil may be reduced as desired.

Oven-Roasted Oysters in Shells

Yield: 6 servings

3 dozen *count* (large) oysters in shell
1/3 cup butter or margarine, melted
Lemon juice (optional)

Clean oysters thoroughly. Place on a baking sheet. Roast in a hot oven (450 degrees F.) for 15 minutes or until shells begin to open. Serve in shell with melted butter and sprinkle with lemon juice, if desired.

Richmond Way of Pickling Oysters

To one gallon of oysters allow one pint of vinegar, two grated nutmegs, eight blades of mace, three dozen cloves, a dozen and a half of peppers, half a salt-spoonful of Cayenne pepper, a lemon and a half. Put the oysters in hot water, scald them, and, when hot through, drop them into cold water, to plump them; then drain them through a colander. Take a quart and a half of the liquor, let it boil; skim it well, then add the seasoning. Put the oysters in a jar and pour the liquor over them hot.

Virginia Cookery-Book, *1885*

Oysters Rockefeller

Yield: 6 servings

36 oysters on the half shell
(see note)
2 cups torn fresh spinach
leaves, cooked and well-
drained
1/4 cup chopped peeled
onion
2 tablespoons minced
parsley
1/2 teaspoon salt
1/4 teaspoon nutmeg
1/2 teaspoon celery salt
(optional)
6 drops hot sauce
1/3 cup butter or margarine,
melted
1/2 cup fine breadcrumbs
Thin lemon slices for
garnish

Put oysters in their shells on a bed of rock salt in a 15 x 10 x 1-inch baking pan so they will remain upright and not lose their juice. Chop the spinach, onion, and parsley together very fine, or put through a food grinder. Add salt, nutmeg, celery salt, if desired, and hot sauce, mixing well. In a medium heavy saucepan, cook mixture in butter over low heat for 4 to 5 minutes, stirring as needed. Fold in breadcrumbs and spread about 1 tablespoon on each oyster. Bake in a hot oven (400 degrees F.) for 10 minutes or until lightly browned. Garnish with lemon slices.

Note: 2 (12-ounce) cans fresh *select* (medium) oysters may be substituted. Drain oysters, arrange in small baking shells or spread over bottom of a greased shallow baking dish, and top with spinach mixture.

Baked Oyster 'N Cheese Casserole

Yield: 12 servings

6 slices white bread,
buttered and cubed
6 thin slices sharp Cheddar
cheese
1 pint *select* (medium) or
standard (small) oysters
(including liquid) (see
note)
2 eggs
2 cups milk
Salt and pepper to taste

Spread one-half of the bread cubes over the bottom of a greased 13 x 9 x 2-inch baking dish. Arrange cheese slices over breadcubes in casserole. Spread oysters over cheese. In a bowl, combine eggs, milk, salt, and pepper to taste, beating lightly; pour over oysters. Top with remaining bread cubes. Bake, uncovered, in a moderate oven (375 degrees F.) for 1 hour 15 minutes.

Note: 1 1/2 to 2 pounds raw, peeled, deveined shrimp may be substituted.

–Peg Freeman (Mrs. Robert)
Cheese Wedge Committee,
St. Christopher's School

Sea Scallops Virginia

Yield: 4 to 6 servings

Sea Scallops Virginia was created in 1980 while Paul was a member fo the 1980 American Culinary Team competing at the Culinary Olympics in Frankfurt, Germany. The recipe won a gold medal and many accolades for its wonderful flavor and incorporation of native virginia products.

2 pounds large sea scallops
4 tablespoons hot olive oil
2 firm ripe tomatos, peeled, cored, seeded, and chopped
2 sprigs of parsley, minced
1 tablespoon minced peeled shallots
1 teaspoon minced peeled garlic
2 tablespoons butter or margarine, melted and divided
4 ounces fully cooked moked Smithfield-style or other cured ham, cut into a julienne (see note)
2 medium leeks, cut into a julienne

In a large heavy skillet, sauté scallops in olive oil, stirring frequently, until tender, opaque in color, and lightly browned, about 2 to 3 minutes. Do *not overcook* as scallops become tough. Transfer scallops in skillet to a *very very* slow oven (200 degrees F.) to keep warm. In a small heavy saucepan, sauté tomatoes, parsley, shallots, and garlic in 1 tablespoon butter over moderate heat. In a small heavy skillet, sauté ham and leeks in 1 tablespoon butter over moderate heat until leeks are tender. Spoon ham mixture onto 4 dinner plates, dividing evenly. Arrange sautéed scallops over julienne ham and leeks, dividing evenly. Spoon a small amount of hot tomato sauce over each portion. Serve immediately.

Note: To prepare a julienne, cut ham and leeks with a very sharp knife into very thin match-like strips.

–Chef Paul and Marie Antionette Elbling,
La Petite France Restaurant

To Scallop Oysters

Put the oysters in a bowl and wash them out of their own liquor. Strew over them a few bread crumbs and butter, then more oysters, bread crumbs and butter; also add a few celery seed and some nutmeg and bake brown.
The Kitchen Queen, *1893*

Broiled Scallops in Sherry Sauce

Yield: 6 servings

1 1/2 pounds fresh or frozen bay or sea scallops
1/4 cup dry sherry
1/4 cup minced parsley, divided
2 tablespoons thinly sliced green onions (include some green tops)
1 teaspoon Worcestershire sauce
1/2 teaspoon salt
Pinch pepper or to taste
1/4 cup butter or margarine, melted
1 cup reserved hot scallop cooking liquid
1 tablespoon cornstarch
1 tablespoon cold water
Hot buttered toast points

Thaw frozen scallops; rinse and drain well. Cut large scallops in half. In a deep medium bowl, combine sherry, 2 tablespoons parsley, green onion, Worcestershire sauce, salt, and pepper; add scallops to marinade, coating well. Marinate scallops at room temperature for 30 minutes. Drain well, reserving marinade. Arrange a single layer of scallops in a greased broiler pan. Brush scallops with half of the butter and reserved marinade. Broil, 3 to 5 inches from heat source, for 3 to 4 minutes. Turn scallops, brush with remaining butter and marinade; continue broiling for an additional 3 to 4 minutes. Scallops should turn opaque in color and cut easily with a fork when done. Transfer scallops to warm individual ramekins or plates. In a small heavy saucepan, combine cornstarch and cold water, blending until smooth. Stir in reserved hot pan liquid. Cook, stirring constantly, over moderate heat until sauce is bubbly hot. Spoon mixture over scallops, dividing evenly. Sprinkle each serving with 1/2 tablespoon minced parsley and garnish with hot buttered toast points.

Note: Bay scallops are smaller in size and have a sweeter taste than sea scallops.

–Linda M. Bourgeois (Mrs. Bruce)

To Fry Oysters

Take a quarter of a hundred of large oysters, wash them and roll them in grated bread, with pepper and salt, and fry them a light brown; if you choose, you may add a little parsley shred fine. They are a proper garnish for calves-head, or most madedishes.

Mrs. Mary Randolph
The Virginia House-Wife, or Methodical Cook, *1830*

267

Mousse of Sea Scallops with Lemon Dill Sauce

Yield: 6 servings

11 to 12 ounces sea scallops
1 egg
1 tablespoon red port wine
Pinch cayenne pepper or to taste
1 1/2 cups heavy cream, at room temperature
Salt and pepper to taste
6 peeled uncooked medium to large shrimp or 6 tablespoons black or red caviar, divided (optional)
Lemon Dill Sauce

Place scallops in the container of a food processor or blender; cover and process or blend until scallops are puréed. Add egg, port, and cayenne pepper, mixing well. With the motor running at slow speed, gradually add cream in a steady stream until mixture is thoroughly blended. Add salt and pepper to taste; mixture should be quite spicy. Fill 6 buttered small soufflé dishes, 2 inches in diameter, with sea scallop mixture, two-thirds full (see note). Tap soufflé dishes lightly on a flat surface to level scallop mixture. Arrange filled soufflé dishes in a 13 x 9 x 2-inch baking dish; add enough warm water to fill baking dish halfway. Cover soufflé dish lightly with aluminum foil. Bake in a hot oven (400 degrees F.) for 15 to 20 minutes. Unmold mousse onto warmed appetizer plates by inverting a plate over each mousse and then flip over, allowing each mousse to slide onto an individual plate. Spoon a small amount of Lemon Dill Sauce over each mousse.

Note: Soufflé dishes may be filled one-third full with mousse mixture. Then arrange 1 shrimp or spoon 1 tablespoon caviar into center of each mousse, if desired. Fill each souffle dish with additional mousse to fill each dish two thirds full.

Lemon Dill Sauce

2 medium lemons
2 sprigs fresh dill weed, minced
1 medium firm ripe tomato, peeled and chopped
6 tablespoons olive oil
Salt and pepper to taste

Extract juice from lemons. In a small heavy saucepan, combine lemon juice, dill weed, tomato, and olive oil. Season with salt and pepper to taste. Warm mixture over low heat.

–Chef Alain Vincey
La Maisonnette Bistro

Stir-Fried Seafood with Sauce Szechuen-Style

Yield: 4 servings

Most seafood dishes should be prepared at the last minute and served immediately; however, some advance preparation of this recipe may be done to save time. Ketchup and chili sauce were introduced into Chinese cooking during this century. The Chinese find that with the addition of these two sauces food still tastes Chinese but even more flavorful. The sauce is very versatile and may be used as an accompaniment to many meats, fowl, seafood, or vegetables."

2 tablespoons peanut oil
2 garlic cloves, peeled and minced
2 tablespoons minced peeled ginger root
2 tablespoons cut green onions, cut into 1/4-inch pieces
1 pound peeled deveined shrimp or fish fillets, cut into bite-sized pieces (see note)
1 tablespoon dry sherry
1 tablespoon soy sauce (see note)
1 teaspoon sugar
1/2 teaspoon salt or to taste
1 tablespoon ketchup
1 tablespoon chili sauce
1/4 teaspoon crushed dried hot red pepper

In a wok or large heavy skillet, heat oil to moderate high (375 to 400 degrees F.). Add garlic, ginger root, and green onions; stir-fry mixture for 2 minutes. Discard garlic. Add shrimp or fish pieces and continue stir-frying for 1 minute. Add sherry, soy sauce, sugar, and salt; continue stir-frying for 30 seconds. Add ketchup, chili sauce and red pepper, stirring lightly. Serve immediately.

Note: Use a firm fleshed fish such as sea trout or haddock. Or, uncooked boneless chicken breast, cut into bite-sized pieces, may be substituted for shrimp or fish.

Note: Reduced sodium (Lite) soy sauce may be substituted for regular soy sauce. One teaspoon Lite soy sauce contains 100 milligrams of sodium.

–Elizabeth Choi (Mrs. Sung)
Richmond Culinary Guild

Perhaps no city in the United States has been more famous for its brilliant social life than Richmond. Situated on seven hills, above the turbulent, amber rapids of the James river, the city is picturesque and beautiful, and was in "ye olden time," as it is now, the centre of fashion of the State of Virginia a State known widely for its magnificence, courtliness, and hospitality.

Ruth Nelson Robins
The Richmond News Leader, Date unknown

Sautéed Shrimp with Peppers and Green Onions

Yield: 4 servings

This easy to prepare shrimp entrée requires little preparation time and can easily be changed in flavor with the use of different herbs.

12 green onions, slic⸮ ᵈ on the bias and cut into 1 1/2 -inch pieces
1/2 medium sweet red pepper, cored, seeded, and cut into 2 to 3-inch strips
1/2 medium sweet yellow pepper, cored, seeded, and cut into 2 to 3-inch strips
1/4 cup olive oil, divided (see note)
2 to 3 teaspoons minced peeled garlic or 1 to 1/2 teaspoons garlic juice
1 pound jumbo shrimp, peeled, deveined, and butterflied (see note)
1 teaspoon Worcestershire sauce
Several grains cayenne pepper or 5 to 6 drops hot sauce
Salt to taste
Freshly ground black peppercorns to taste
3 tablespoons lemon juice (see note)
2 to 3 tablespoons minced fresh chervil or dill weed or cilantro (coriander) (see note)

In a large heavy skillet or wok, sauté onions and pepper in 2 tablespoons hot olive oil over moderate heat until tender but crisp; remove with a slotted spoon and set aside. Add remaining 2 tablespoons olive oil and garlic to pan. Sauté shrimp in hot oil and garlic over moderate heat for about 2 to 3 minutes or until shrimp begin to turn a coral pink color, turning frequently. Do not overcook. Reduce heat and stir in reserved onions and peppers, Worcestershire sauce, cayenne pepper, and salt. Simmer, uncovered, for 1 to 2 minutes. Grind peppercorns to taste over shrimp and vegetables. Evenly sprinkle lemon juice over shrimp mixture and garnish with minced fresh chervil or dill weed or cilantro. Serve immediately. Do not overcook shrimp as they will become tough or vegetables as they will become limp.

Note: Use a premium quality extra virgin olive oil. Extra virgin refers to the oil collected from the first press of the olives.

Note: To butterfly shrimp, slit each shrimp length wise down the inside center of shrimp with a sharp knife, cutting each almost through. Shrimp will open out flat but remain joined at the center.

Note: Use only freshly squeezed lemon juice. One medium lemon contains about 3 tablespoons lemon juice.

Note: 2 to 3 teaspoons dried chervil or dill weed or cilantro can be substituted for minced fresh herbs.

Grilled Garlic Shrimp

Yield: 4 servings

1 to 1 1/2 pounds large to jumbo shrimp, peeled and deveined
6 garlic cloves, peeled and minced (see note)
1 cup lemon juice
1 cup olive oil (see note)
2 teaspoons minced parsley
1 teaspoon cayenne pepper or to taste
Salt or seasoned salt and pepper to taste (optional)
Thin lemon wedges

Shrimp may be butterflied, if desired. To butterfly, slit the shrimp lengthwise with a sharp knife, almost through. Open each shrimp out flat. In a deep large bowl, combine garlic, lemon juice, olive oil, parsley, and cayenne pepper, blending well with a wire whisk. Add shrimp, coating each well. Cover with clear plastic wrap and refrigerate for 12 hours to blend flavors. Drain shrimp from marinade and arrange on a rack in a broiler pan; brush each shrimp lightly with some of the marinade. Broil, 6 to 8 inches from heat source, about 3 to 4 minutes per side or until shrimp are done and lightly browned. Season with salt or seasoned salt and pepper to taste and garnish each serving with thin lemon wedges. Or, arrange drained marinated shrimp on a lightly greased grill rack, 8 to 10 inches above medium coals (ash gray and glowing); grill for about 4 to 5 minutes per side, brushing shrimp lightly with marinade occasionally. Or, stir-fry drained shrimp in 2 tablespoons of marinade in a wok over moderate heat (350 to 375 degrees F.) until done and lightly browned, about 3 to 5 minutes. Do not overcook as shrimp will shrink in size and become tough.

Notes: 1 tablespoon garlic juice may be substituted for minced garlic.

Note: Use a premium Quality extra virgin olive oil. Extra virgin refers to the oil collected from the first press of the olives.

–Hal Taylor

Old Richmond Advertisement, circa 1895

Shrimp with Cashew Nuts

Yield: 4 servings

The Peking restaurant opened the doors of its first restaurant on the Avenues, at Libbie and Gove, in the fashionable Richmond West End in April, 1978. It was the first restaurant to introduce Szechuan and Mandarin cuisines to the greater Richmond area. Featuring high quality food, attentive service, and elegant atmosphere, the Peking has throughout the past decade received much acclaim from Richmonders. Peking Pavilion opened in April 1984 in the historic Shockoe Slip area and has recently been followed by the opening of the Peking Gourmet in the Southside of Richmond on Midlothian Turnpike.

1 egg white
2 tablespoons cornstarch
1 1/2 teaspoons salt, divided
1 1/2 pounds medium shrimp, peeled and devined
1 cup cashew nuts
About 3 cups soybean oil, divided
20 green onions, each cut 1 inch in length (see note)
16 *very thick* slices peeled fresh ginger root
2 tablespoons rice wine
2 teaspoons sesame oil

In a deep medium bowl, combine egg white, cornstarch, and 1 teaspoon salt, beating lightly with a wire whisk. Add shrimp, coating each well; allow mixture to stand at room temperature for 30 minutes. In a wok, stir-fry cashew nuts in 4 to 6 tablespoons warm (275 to 300 degrees F.) soy bean oil until golden brown, about 3 minutes; drain nuts well on absorbent paper. Increase temperature to very hot (450 degrees F.). Stir-fry marinated shrimp in remaining hot oil in wok for 30 seconds. Remove shrimp; drain on absorbent paper. Drain oil, reserving 1/4 cup in wok. Stir-fry green onion and ginger in moderate to hot (375 to 400 degrees F.) oil until tender but crisp. Add shrimp, rice wine, sesame oil, and 1/2 teaspoon salt to onion-ginger mixture. Stir-fry thoroughly over high heat (400 degrees F.) until shrimp is cooked through, about 1 to 2 minutes. Sprinkle cashews over each portion and serve immediately.

Note: Select young, tender green onions with thin white ends rather than rounded white ends. One inch lengths should include a small amount of green part of onions.

–Peking Restaurant

Shrimp Curry with Parsley Rice

Yield: 6 servings

1 to 1 1/2 pounds cooked, peeled, deveined shrimp
2 tablespoons lemon juice
1/2 cup chopped peeled onion or 6 green onions, thinly sliced (include some green tops)
1/2 cup thiny sliced celery
1/3 cup butter, divided
1/4 cup flour
1 1/2 to 2 teaspoons curry powder or to taste
3/4 teaspoon salt or to taste
1/2 teaspoon sugar
2 cups milk
1 cup half-and-half
1/2 cup dark or golden seedless raisins
1 chicken bouillon cube
1/2 cup slivered blanched almonds
3 tablespoons minced parsley
6 servings hot cooked seasoned rice
Pickled watermelon rind or chutney and coconut (optional)

If large, cut shrimp in half lengthwise. Drizzle lemon juice over shrimp, cover, and refrigerate for 15 to 20 minutes. In a medium heavy saucepan, sauté onion and celery in 1/4 cup butter until onion is tender but not brown. Stir in flour, curry powder, salt, and sugar. Add milk, half-and-half, raisins, and bouillon cube; cook, stirring constantly, until thickened. Add shrimp and heat through. Keep warm in the brazier of a chafing dish. Lightly toast almonds in remaining 1 1/2 to 2 tablespoons butter. Fold parsley into rice and serve with shrimp curry mixture. Sprinkle almonds over shrimp and accompany with pickled watermelon rind or chutney and coconut, if desired.

Old Richmond Advertisement, circa 1895

273

Jambalaya

"Jambalaya! Jambalaya! Jambalaya, crawfish pie, and a filé gumbo..."

-Words and music by Hank Williams, Sr.
Made famous by Hank Williams, Sr.circa late 1940's

Jambalaya is a distinctive "dish" of early New Orleans origin, similar to the Spanish paella, made with ham and rice, and sometimes shrimp or chorizo sausage.

Jambalaya

Yield: 6 to 8 servings

2 medium onions, peeled and thinly sliced or coarsely chopped
2 to 3 tablespoons hot bacon drippings or cooking oil
2 pounds medium shrimp, peeled
1 cup uncooked long-grain white rice (unrinsed)
Boiling water as needed
1/4 cup dry sherry
1 teaspoon Worcestershire sauce
1 teaspoon sweet Hungarian or 1/4 teaspoon hot paprika
1/4 teaspoon celery salt
Salt and pepper to taste
5 to 6 drops hot sauce or to taste
Minced parsley for garnish
Crisp garlic bread and green salad (optional)

In a large heavy skillet or Dutch oven, sauté onions in bacon drippings over moderate heat until tender but not browned. Add shrimp and stir over moderate heat until shell fish are done,about 2 to 3 minutes; remove shrimp and set aside. Shrimp are done when they turn pink or light red in color. *Do not overcook* as shrimp will become tough. Add uncooked rice; cook, stirring constantly, until rice becomes a very light brown in color. Add boiling water to cover. Continue cooking, stirring until the water is reduced by one half in cooking. Gradually add additional boiling water as needed to completely cook rice until tender,about 30 to 35 minutes total. Rice will thicken but will not be done until grains are tender. When rice is tender, add seasonings. Reduce heat and simmer for an additional 8 to 10 minutes. Return cooked shrimp to Jambalaya. Serve garnished with minced parsley and accompanied by crisp garlic bread and a green salad, if desired.

Variation: Brown 6 charizo sausages while sautéeing onions in skillet. Remove sausages and cut into bite-sized pieces. Add sausage pieces and 1 cup cubed fully-cooked smoked Smithfield or Virginia country-style ham, cut into 1/2-inch cubes, to Jambalaya with the rice.

–Frances Fox (Mrs. Paul)

Shrimp or Crab Newburg

Yield: 6 servings

12 ounces cooked peeled
  deveined medium shrimp
  (see note)
1/4 cup butter or margarine,
  melted
2 tablespoons flour
3/4 teaspoon salt or to taste
1/8 teaspoon cayenne
  pepper or to taste
1/8 teaspoon nutmeg
1 1/2 cups half-and-half, at
  room temperature
2 egg yolks, beaten
2 tablespoons dry sherry
'Crisp toast points
Minced Parsley for garnish

Cut each cooked shrimp in half, set aside. In a medium heavy saucepan, blend butter, flour, and seasonings together over low heat. Gradually add half-and-half, blending well. Cook, stirring constantly, over moderate heat until mixture is thickened and bubbly hot. With a wire whisk, blend a small amount of hot sauce into beaten egg yolks; quickly blend egg yolk mixture into remaining hot sauce in saucepan. Over low heat, add shrimp to sauce. Remove mixture from heat and gradually blend in sherry. Serve immediately over crisp toast points and garnish each serving with minced parsley.

Note: Cook 14 to 16 ounces medium fresh or thawed frozen shrimp in 6 to 8 cups lightly salted boiling water for 3 minutes after water returns to a boil or until shrimp turns a bright coral color. Do not overcook as shrimp will become tough. Immediately rinse shrimp in cold water to stop cooking action. Peel, devein, and remove tails of shrimp. Or, 12 ounces crabmeat may be substituted for cooked shrimp.

Variation: Add 1/2 teaspoon prepared Dijon-style mustard and 1/2 teaspoon Worcestershire sauce to sauce, if desired. 2 to 3 teaspoons chili sauce may also be added for a further variation, if desired.

Shrimp and Noodle Casserole

Yield: 6 servings

2 cups narrow egg noodles
Boiling salted water as
  needed
1 teaspoon cooking oil
Salt and pepper to taste
1 1/2 pounds medium
  shrimp
3 tablespoons butter or
  margarine, melted
3 tablespoons flour
1 cup milk
1 cup light or heavy cream
1/2 cup shredded Gruyere or
  Swiss cheese
1/2 cup grated Parmesan
  cheese
4 to 5 drops hot sauce or to
  taste

In a large heavy saucepan, cook noodles in boiling salted water to which 1 teaspoon oil has been added for 8 minutes according to package directions. Drain well; season with salt and pepper to taste. In a large heavy saucepan, cook shrimp in about 3 quarts simmering salted water for 5 minutes. *Do not overcook*. Shrimp will turn pink in color when cooked. When shrimp are cool enough to handle, remove peel, tails, and devein. In a large heavy saucepan, blend butter and flour together to form a smooth paste. Gradually add milk and cream, blending well with a wire whisk. Cook, whisking constantly, over moderate heat until mixture is thickened and bubbly hot. Remove from heat and stir in cheeses, drained noodles, and cooked shrimp. Season with salt and pepper to taste. Transfer mixture to a lightly greased 2 to 2 1/2-quart casserole. Bake, uncovered, in a moderate oven (350 degrees F.) for about 20 minutes, until casserole is bubbly hot and cheese melted.
  –Karen Leidinger (Mrs. William)
  Valentine Museum Guild

Old Richmond Advertisement, circa 1909

Eggs
and
Cheese

Baked Eggs with Smoked Salmon

Yield: 4 servings

4 to 8 ounces thinly sliced smoked salmon
4 to 8 eggs, divided
2 tablespoons butter or margarine, at room temperature and divided
Hollandaise Sauce (see index)
Paprika for garnish
Freshly ground black peppercorns for garnish
Parsley or watercress sprigs for garnish
Buttered toast points

Arrange 1 to 2 ounces of thinly sliced smoked salmon slices in each of 4 greased individual casseroles or ramekins. Crack 1 to 2 eggs into each ramekin atop the salmon, being careful not to break the yolks. Dot each casserole with 1/2 teaspoon butter. Bake, uncovered, in a moderate oven (350 degrees F.) for 15 to 20 minutes, until eggs are desired degree of doneness. Remove from oven and spoon Hollandaise Sauce over each serving. Sprinkle paprika and freshly ground pepper over each, if desired, and garnish with parsley or watercress sprigs. Serve with hot buttered toast points.

Note: A short-cut...Commercially packaged Hollandaise Sauce may be prepared and used in place of the homemade recipe, if desired.

Alternate method of preparation; partially pan-fry eggs in a greased skillet. Bake salmon, covered, in greased individual casseroles for 10 to 15 minutes in a slow oven (325 degrees F.).Transfer partially cooked eggs to salmon-lined casseroles. Dot with butter. Continue baking, uncovered, until eggs are desired degree of doneness. Or, poach eggs in simmering water. Bake salmon as just directed. Top each casserole with poached eggs. Do not bake further, finish as previously directed in main recipe.

–J. Robert Carlton

Eggs for Brunch

Yield: 8 to 10 servings

8 hard-cooked eggs, peeled and halved lengthwise
1/3 cup mayonnaise
1/2 to 1 teaspoon curry powder or to taste
1/2 teaspoon dry mustard
1/2 teaspoon salt
Shrimp 'N Cheese Sauce
1 cup breadcrumbs
1 to 2 tablespoons butter or margarine, melted

Remove yolks from eggs and reserve whites. In a bowl, mash yolks; add mayonnaise, curry powder, mustard, and salt, beating until smooth. Evenly fill egg whites with yolk mixture. Arrange egg halves in a lightly greased 12 x 8 x 2-inch baking pan. Spoon sauce over eggs. In a small bowl, combine breadcrumbs and butter, mixing well; evenly sprinkle over sauce. Bake, covered, in a moderate oven (350 degrees F.) for 15 minutes; uncover and continue baking until breadcrumbs are lightly browned.

Shrimp 'N Cheese Sauce

1 (10 3/4-ounce) can cream
  of shrimp soup, undiluted
1 1/4 cups milk
1/2 cup shredded mild or
  sharp Cheddar cheese

In a small heavy saucepan, combine soup and milk, blending until smooth. Cook over moderate heat until bubbly hot. Reduce heat. Add cheese, stirring until cheese is melted and sauce smooth.

Variation: Fold 1 cup small peeled deveined cooked shrimp into sauce.

Eggs came to be associated with Easter because at one time church law forbade them being eaten during Lent and so they were served in abundance on Easter...

Dyed eggs, were also the forerunners of today's Easter cards. Messages were traced on the eggs with hot wax before they were dyed and, when the wax was removed, the message remained in white. The eggs were then exchanged between friends on Easter morning.

"Easter Symbols Stem From Old folk Tales,"
Richmond Newspaper, Date Unknown

Omlet Soufflé

Two-and-ahalf tablespoonsful of sugar, mixed well with 4 yolks of eggs, and a few drops of Vanilla flavoring. Beat the 4 whites of eggs (always a pinch of salt first) to a stiff froth, and then add in the yholks and sugar. Five to eight minutes is enough in the oven. Dust with powdered sugar, and eat as soon as baked.

-Prof. Blot,
Virginia Recipes, 1890

Eggs Nouvelle

Yield: 4 servings

1 pound backfin crabmeat
2 tablespoons lemon juice
Simmering water as needed
4 drops white vinegar
1/4 cup butter or margarine,
    melted
8 eggs
Nouvelle Sauce
Paprika for garnish

Pick over crabmeat, removing any shell or cartilage. Spoon crabmeat into 4 seafood baking shells or individual ramekins or casseroles, dividing evenly. Sprinkle 1/2 tablespoon lemon juice and then 1 tablespoon melted butter over each. Arrange baking shells on a baking sheet; bake in a moderate oven (375 degrees F.) for 5 minutes or until heated through. While crabmeat is baking, break eggs into a large shallow pan filled halfway with simmering water and vinegar; poach for about 3 minutes or to desired degree of doneness. Remove eggs from water with a slotted spoon; place 2 eggs atop each crabmeat serving. Spoon 3 to 4 tablespoons Nouvelle Sauce over each serving and sprinkle each lightly with paprika.

Nouvelle Sauce

3/4 cup butter or margarine,
    melted
3/4 cup flour
4 cups hot milk
1/2 tablespoon salt or to
    taste
White pepper to taste
1/2 cup dry red wine

In a medium heavy saucepan, combine butter and flour, blending until smooth. Stir over low heat for 2 to 3 minutes until mixture is bubbly. Gradually add milk, blending well. Increase temperature to moderate; cook, stirring constantly, until mixture is thickened and bubbly hot. Season with salt and pepper. Gradually blend in wine, blending well.

–Sam Miller's Warehouse Restaurant

Egg Croquetts

ard boil 8 eggs, and when cold, chop very fine; mix in them 1 tablespoonful of butter, 1 tea-cup of bread-crumbs, 1 teacup of milk, 1 teaspoon of onion chopped fine; make a white sauce with the butter and milk, thickened with a little flour; mix all together and mould; roll in cracker crumbs and bake.

-Mrs. Charles Skiner,
Virginia Recipes, 1890

Bottomley House

Richmond, a city of beautiful homes, is proud to have among
its architectural treasures fifteen houses designed by the renowned early twentieth century American architect, William
Lawrence Bottomley. Synonymous with the best architectur-
ally, Bottomley set the style for many homes built in Richmond
during the first half of this century. Master of neo-georgian
design, he retained an individual style, perfecting what has been
termed his "James River Georgian" architecture. Although
built fifty to seventy-five years ago, his houses are still referred
to with reverence as "Bottomley Houses."

Devilish Scrambled Eggs

Yield: 4 servings

6 to 8 ounces mushrooms, thinly sliced
About 3 tablespoons butter or margarine, melted and divided
6 eggs
2 tablespoons minced parsley
1 teaspoon Worsestershire sauce
1/2 teaspoon dry mustard
3 to 4 drops hot sauce
1/2 cup commercial cream of mushroom soup, undiluted
2 tablespoons milk or half-and-half (optional)
Salt or seasoned salt and pepper to taste
Parsley sprigs for garnish

In a medium bowl, combine eggs, minced parsley, dry mustard, Worcestershire sauce, and hot sauce, beating lightly with a fork. Beat in soup and milk. Season with salt and pepper to taste; set aside. In a medium heavy skillet, sauté mushrooms in butter over moderate heat until tender but not browned. Add remaining butter to skillet, if desired. Pour egg mixture over mushrooms in skillet. Reduce heat and cook until egg mixture begins to set (coagulate) at the bottom and sides of the pan, about 1 minute. With a wooden spoon or fork, turn egg and mushroom mixture in a circular "scrambling" motion. Continue to cook until eggs are cooked through, but still glossy and moist. *Do not overcook.* Serve immediately and garnish each portion with parsley sprigs.

Eggs in a South'rn Manner

Yield: 4 to 6 servings

8 to 12 slices bacon
1 (8-ounce) can herring or other fish roe, drained (see note)
2 to 3 tablespoons hot reserved bacon drippings
8 eggs
1 cup milk
1 teaspoon Worcestershire sauce (optional)
3 to 4 drops hot sauce (optional)
Salt or seasoned salt and pepper to taste (see note)

In a large heavy skillet, pan-fry bacon over moderate heat (325 to 350 degrees F.) until crisp; remove bacon and drain on absorbent paper. Drain off all but 2 to 3 tablespoons bacon drippings from skillet; reduce heat (300 to 325 degrees F.) and add fish roe. Mash roe slightly and cook, stirring or moving as little as possible, for about 2 minutes. In a medium bowl, beat eggs lightly with a wire whisk. Gradually add milk, beating lightly; stir in Worcestershire sauce, hot sauce, salt or seasoned salt, and pepper. Pour mixture over fish roe in skillet; allow mixture to set for a few seconds, then "scramble" gently in a circular motion with a fork or wooden spoon until eggs set (coagulate) and become firm, about 2 to 3 minutes. *Do not overcook or allow egg mixture to become dry; eggs should be glossy and creamy in texture.* Serve at once, accompanied with 2 to 3 crisp bacon slices per portion.

Note: 8 ounces fresh fish roe, such as shad roe, may be substituted for canned fish roe; however, fresh roe will require a few extra minutes of cooking before eggs are added to pan.

–Helen Goode (Mrs. W. A.)

Constable Bros.

Shirt Makers,

MEN'S FURNISHINGS,
HATTERS

No. 419 East Broad Street,
RICHMOND, VA.

Old Richmond Advertisement, date unknown

Eggs represent the new life that returns to nature about Easter time. The custom of exchanging eggs began in ancient times. The ancient Egyptians and Persians often dyed eggs in spring colors and gave them to their friends as gifts. The Persians believed that the earth had hatched from a giant egg ...

In some European countries, people colored eggs red to represent the joy of the resurrection of Christ. In England, friends often wrote messages and dates on the eggs they exchanged...

Elaborate candy eggs with a window in one end and tiny scenes inside were popular gifts in the 1800's. Because the use of eggs was forbidden during Lent, they were brought to the table on Easter Day. This custom is found not only in the Latin but also in the Oriental churches. The custom may have its origin in paganism, for a great many pagan customs, celebrating the return of spring, gravitated to Easter. The egg is the emblem of the germinating life of early spring.

"The Significance Of Eggs At Eastertime," Condensed
Old Newspaper Article, Name and date unknown
Courtesy Valentine Museum

Quiche

According to The New Larousse Gastronomique, the quiche originates in the province of Lorraine in France. Several varieties of quiches are known. Each region of Lorraine o Alsace has its own speciality. An old recipe suggests rolling out bread dough as thinly as possible and laying it in a metal dish. Then small pieces of butter are added to the crust and the dish is filled with thick cream and egges beaten together and seasoned with salt. The quiche is then baked in a very hot oven for 10 minutes. The Dictionary of Gastronomy further defines a quiche as an open-faced flan or tart of ancient origin, originally made of bread dough but replaced gradually through the years with a pastry crust.

Autumn Quiche

Yield: 6 to 8 servings

Unbaked pie shell (9-inch) (see index)
8 ounces medium-spiced bulk pork sausage, crumbled
6 ounces sharp Cheddar cheese, shredded
1 medium tart ripe apple, peeled, seeded, and chopped (see note)
1/2 cup chopped English walnuts
4 eggs
1/2 cup milk
1/2 cup half-and-half or light cream
1/2 teaspoon salt
1/4 teaspoon pepper

Bake pie shell in a hot oven (400 degrees F.) for 7 minutes; remove and cool for 5 to 7 minutes. In a medium heavy skillet, brown sausage thoroughly over moderate heat, about 3 to 4 minutes, stirring frequently; drain well on absorbent paper. Press crumbled sausage and cheese lightly into the bottom of the partially baked pie crust, spreading mixture evenly. Sprinkle apple pieces and nuts over sausage cheese mixture. In a medium bowl, beat eggs lightly. Gradually add remaining ingredients, blending well; pour over sausage mixture in pie crust. Bake in a moderate oven (375 degrees F.) for 40 to 45 minutes or until a silver knife inserted in the center comes out clean. Allow to stand for 5 to 10 minutes before cutting.

Note: Use McIntosh, Winesap, Granny Smith, or other tart variety of apples.

–Dana Gunnels (Mrs. Stephan)

Potato Crust Quiche

Yield: 6 to 8 servings

"As a busy speech language pathologist, I like quick things to prepare. I find a food processor has helped me to be motivated to do some things with shredded potatoes."

3 cups shredded peeled
  potatoes
3 tablespoons cooking oil
3/4 cup crumbled medium-
  spiced bulk pork sausage
1 cup shredded Swiss or
  sharp Cheddar cheese
1/4 cup chopped peeled
  onion
2 eggs
1 cup evaporated milk or
  half-and-half
1/4 teaspoon salt or to taste
  (optional)
1/8 teaspoon pepper
1 tablespoon minced
  parsley

In a large bowl, combine potatoes and oil, tossing lightly to coat potatoes with oil. Press potato mixture over bottom and up sides of a 9-inch pie plate forming a standing ridge. Bake in a hot oven (425 degrees F.) for 15 minutes. In a small heavy skillet, brown sausage over moderate heat; remove with a slotted spoon, drain on absorbent paper, and set aside. Saute onion in hot sausage drippings until tender but not browned; remove with a slotted spoon. Arrange layers of cheese, sausage, and onion in potato crust. In a bowl, with a wire whisk, beat eggs lightly; blend in evaporated milk, salt, if desired, and pepper. Pour over cheese-sausage-onion layers. Sprinkle top with minced parsley. Reduce oven temperature to (375 degrees F.) and continue baking for 30 minutes or until set and top is lightly browned.

–Margaret Bruckhart (Mrs. Robert)

Deviled Eggs

Four hard-boiled eggs, one-eighth teaspoon mustard, one-fourth teaspoon salt, one-fourth teaspoon sugar, dash cayenne pepper, dash paprika, one tablespoon butter or olive oil, one tablespoon vinegar. Cut the hard-boiled eggs in half, length-wise; remove the yolk, being careful not to break the white. Powder the yolks with silver fork, then add the mustard, salt, paprika, sugar, cayenne pepper and vinegar mixed together; add the butter or olive oil; mix smooth and fill the whites.

Virginia Cook Book, 1839

Salmon Quiche

Yield: 8 servings

Unbaked deep dish pie shell (10-inch) (see index)
4 ounces salmon fillet, cut into small pieces
3 to 4 tablespoons butter or margarine, melted and divided
2 cups shredded Swiss or Grùyere cheese
4 eggs
2 cups light cream or half-and-half
3/4 teaspoon salt
1/4 to 1/2 teaspoon pepper or to taste
1/8 teaspoon sugar (optional)
1/8 teaspoon nutmeg
Pinch cayenne pepper

Chill pie shell in refrigerator while preparing filling. In a small heavy skillet, sauté salmon pieces in 2 to 3 tablespoons butter over moderate heat until tender and lightly browned. Lightly brush bottom and sides of chilled pie shell with remaining butter. Lightly press cheese into the bottom of the pie shell; evenly arrange salmon pieces over top of cheese. In a bowl, with a wire whisk, beat eggs lightly; add cream and seasonings, blending well. Pour egg mixture over salmon-cheese mixture. Bake in a hot oven (400 degrees F.) for 12 minutes; reduce heat to slow (325 degrees F.) and continue baking for 25 to 30 minutes until set and top is golden brown. A silver knife inserted in center will come out clean.

Variation: 8 ounces sliced mushrooms or 1 to 2 medium onions, peeled and chopped, sautéed in 2 tablespoons butter may be substituted for salmon. Or, reduce salmon to 2 ounces and add 1 cup sliced mushrooms and 1/2 cup chopped peeled onion sautéed in butter.

–Joy Gerson (Mrs. Martin)
CheeseWedge Committee
St. Christopher's School

How to Test Eggs

In shaking an egg, if it makes a sound it is not good, and should be rejected. The water test consists in putting them in water deep enough to cover; the good eggs will lie flat at the bottom, while the bad eggs will stand upright.

Old Richmond Cookbook
Circa turn of nineteenth/twentieth centuries

Rice Omlet

One cup of boiled rice; pour over it one cup of warm milk, add one tablespoon of melted butter, salt and pepper to taste. Mix well, then add three well-beaten eggs. Put a lump of butter in frying pan and when it begins to boil pour in the omelet and bake in hot oven. When cooked through, fold it double, turn out on a hot dish and serve at onece. Beat eggs separately.

Mrs. D.D. Staley, Richmond
Virginia Cookery Book, *1921*

Spinach Quiche with Fresh Basil and Tomatoes

Yield: 8 servings

1 (12-ounce) package frozen spinach soufflé, thawed
Unbaked pie shell (10-inch)
4 ounces bacon slices, crisp cooked, drained, and crumbled
6 green onions, thinly sliced, include some green tops
1/2 cup chopped fully-cooked smoked ham
1 (4-ounce) package (1 cup) shredded Swiss, provolone, or mozzarella cheese
4 eggs
1 1/2 cups half-and-half
1 tablespoon minced fresh or 1 teaspoon dried basil, divided
Salt to taste
Pinch of nutmeg
1 (4-ounce) package thinly sliced Swiss, provolone, or mozzarella cheese
1 firm ripe medium tomato, thinly sliced

Partially bake spinach soufflé in a moderate oven (350 degrees F.) for 1 hour. Or, microwave at 50% power for 2 minutes; turn container 90 degrees and continue microwaving for 2 minutes. Spread partially cooked soufflé over the bottom and up the sides of pie shell. Alternately layer bacon, green onions, and ham over spinach layer. Top with shredded cheese. In a bowl, combine eggs, half-and-half, one half of the basil, salt, and nutmeg, beating lightly. Pour over mixture in pie shell. Arrange cheese slices over egg mixture in pie shell. Top with tomatoe slices arranged in one layer over cheese slices and sprinkle with remaining basil. Bake in the middle of a moderate oven (350 degrees F.) for 1 hour or until a silver knife inserted in thecenter of the quiche comes out clean.

–Tommie Roberts (Mrs. Joe)

Mile High Crab Soufflé with Hollandaise Sauce

Yield: 6 servings

A soufflé waits for no one...it must be eatn immediately after baking !!

1/3 cup butter or margarine, melted
1/3 cup flour
1 teaspoon seafood seasoning (see note)
1 teaspoon Worcestershire sauce
1/2 teaspoon salt or to taste
1/2 teaspoon sweet Hungarian paprika
1/8 teaspoon dry mustard
1/8 teaspoon white pepper
5 to 6 drops hot sauce
Large pinch saffron
1 1/2 cups milk
1 pound backfin crabmeat, picked and cleaned
6 extra large or jumbo eggs, separated
Hollandaise Sauce (see index)
Parsley sprigs for garnish

In a heavy saucepan, melt butter over low heat. With a wire whisk, blend in flour, seafood seasoning, Worcestershire sauce, salt, paprika, mustard, pepper, hot sauce, and a pinch of saffron. Gradually stir in milk. Cook, stirring constantly, over moderate heat until mixture is thickened and bubbly hot. Remove from heat. Fold in crabmeat. In a large bowl, beat egg yolks until thick and light-colored. Stir a small amount of hot crabmeat sauce into beaten egg yolks. Gradually stir remaining hot crabmeat sauce into beaten egg yolks. In a large, preferably copper bowl, beat egg whites until stiff, glossy, but not dry, peaks are formed. Carefully fold beaten egg whites into crabmeat-eggyolk mixture. Spoon mixture into an ungreased 2 1/2-quart soufflé dish or round casserole or 6 individual soufflé dishes. Run tip of knife about 1 inch deep around casserole 1 inch inside of edge. Set soufflé or dishes in a shallow pan filled halfway with water. Bake large souffle in a moderate oven (350 degrees F.) for 50 to 60 minutes and individual soufflés for 25 to 30 minutes until nicely browned, puffed, and fairly firm to the touch or until a silver knife inserted in center of soufflé comes out clean. Serve at once. Spoon Hollandaise Sauce over each serving and garnish with parsley sprigs.

Note: Preferably use Old Bay brand seafood seasoning.

Hogs running free were the biggest problem, and as fines did not solve it, the Common Hall took more drastic action. The constables, after giving public notice, were instructed to seize and kill any hogs found running at large in the city and to distribute the meat among the poor.
Harry M. Ward and Harold E. Greer, Jr.
Richmond During The Revolution, 1775-83, 1977

Church Hill

Church Hill, located just east of downtown Richmond across the "Bottoms," is the oldest residential district and the second area to have been settled in the city. Some of the existing buildings date from the first decade of the nineteenth century. Taking its name from St. John's Church, of Patrick Henry fame, the area encompasses about forty©five square blocks. Contrary to popular thought, the "hill" is not one but several hills. Many prominent, as well as infamous, persons have resided in the area, including Yankee spy, Elizabeth Van Lew of Civil War infamy. Much o Church Hill is being restored. Through the encouragement of the Historic Richmond Foundation, located in the center of the area in the Elmira Shelton House, nineteenth century home of Edgar Allen Poe's tragic lover, extensive renovations are being made to once dilapidated outdated buildings in Richmond. Picturesque exterior building facades again appear as they did in early Richmond.

Christmas Dinner of 1850

Breakfast was no mean meal either and usually included several kinds of hot breads, Sally Lunn, buckwheat cakes, spoon bread and hot biscuit. Then there were brains with scramble eggs, kidney hash, fried sausage and ham, fried apples and often fried chicken with honey, syrup, jelly, jam and butter, milk, coffee and tea to reinforce the inner man and start Christmas Day right.

Irene Bivens
"Yule Dinners Were Events In Old South,"
Richmond Times-Dispatch, Dec. 25, 1935

Broccoli, Ham, and Cheese Soufflé

Yield: 6 to 8 servings

1/2 (10-ounce) package
frozen chopped broccoli
8 ounces finely grated Swiss
cheese (see note)
Paprika as desired
(optional)
1/2 tablespoon minced
peeled onion
4 tablespoons butter or
margarine, melted and
divided
3 tablespoons flour
3/4 cup milk, scalded
1/2 teaspoon salt
1/8 teaspoon pepper
Pinch of nutmeg or to taste
2 to 3 drops Tabasco sauce
4 egg yolks, at room
temperature (reserve
whites)
1 (4-ounce) can mushrooms,
drained and chopped
1/2 cup minced fully-cooked

Prepare broccoli according to package directions, using only one half the amount of water suggested in the directions; drain well and finely mince with a sharp knife. Combine cheese with two pinches paprika, toss lightly. Sprinkle one-half of the cheese over the bottom of a lightly greased 2 1/2-quart soufflé dish. In a medium heavy saucepan, sauté onion in 1 tablespoon butter over moderate heat until tender but not browned. Add minced broccoli and toss lightly over heat to remove any remaining water from broccoli; set aside. In a 4-quart heavy saucepan, combine 3 tablespoons butter with flour, whisking lightly with a wire whisk over low heat for 1 to 2 minutes. Gradually add scalded milk, blending well with a wire whisk; cook, whisking constantly, over moderate heat until mixture is thickened and bubbly hot. Remove from heat and add salt, pepper, nutmeg, and Tabasco sauce. Add egg yolks, one at a time, whisking well after each addition. Stir in broccoli, mushrooms, ham, and remaining cheese; set aside. Preheat oven to hot (400 degrees F.). In a large deep bowl, beat egg

smoked ham
5 egg whites, at room
    temperature
Additional finely grated
    Swiss cheese for garnish
    (optional)

whites until glossy, stiff, but not dry, peaks are formed. Carefully fold beaten egg whites into broccoli-cheese mixture with a wide rubber spatula. Spoon mixture into prepared soufflé dish. Lightly sprinkle top of soufflé with additional cheese, if desired. Reduce oven temperature to moderate (375 degrees F.) and immediately bake soufflé for 25 to 30 minutes or until soufflé is firm, poofed, and lightly browned. Serve immediately.

Note: Use grated rather than shredded cheese.

-Linda Bourgeois (Mrs. Bruce)

Egg Omelet

Six eggs (beaten separately), one teaspoonful of flour dissolved in one cup of milk. Stir milk mixed with flour into beaten yolks. Fold into stiff sheet, salt to taste and put in long griddle well greased. Roll up as it browns. When it is done put in oven a few minutes with door open. A little grated ham and cheese can be added before omelet is rolled.

This recipe is taken from Mrs. Tyree's recipe book. She was a Virginia housekeeper, granddaughter of Patrick Henry.

Virginia Cook Book, 1839

Cheese Balls

1/2 c. dry bread crumbs
1/4 t. salt
1 c. grated cheese
1/4 t. mustard
1 egg

A few grains cayenne pepper
Mix dry ingredients, add egg, shape in small balls, and fry in deep fat.

Culinary Echoes From Dixie, *1917*

During the Civil War, corn became so scarce in Richmond it sold for fifteen dollars a bushel, while eggs cost a dollar per egg.

Cheese Topped Baked Eggs 'N Canadian Bacon in Toast Cups

Yield: 4 servings

Easy Toast Cups
(8 cups)
8 thin slices white bread
6 tablespoons butter or
  margarine, melted
Paprika (optional)

With a rolling pin, flatten bread slices. Remove crusts. Press a slice of bread into each of 8 greased oven-proof glass baking cups so that corners extend above muffin cups. Press bread against sides of each cup; brush inside of bread cup with butter. Bake in a moderate oven (375 degrees F.) for 10 minutes or until golden brown and crisp. Sprinkle lightly with paprika, if desired. Store in an airtight container; freeze, if desired. Thaw before using.

**Cheese Topped Baked
Eggs 'N Canadian Bacon**
8 thin slices Canadian
  bacon, divided
8 large eggs, divided
1/2 cup shredded sharp
  Cheddar, Swiss, Monterey
  Jack, or jalapeño pepper-
  flavored cheese, divided
Parsley or watercress sprigs
  for garnish
8 fresh strawberries or
  pineapple spears or small
  grape clusters for garnish

Prepare Toast Cups according to recipe. Arrange a slice of Canadian bacon in each toast cup, pressing bacon into cup to fit evenly. Break an egg into each bacon-lined toast cup. Arrange egg-filled glass baking cups on an ungreased baking sheet. Bake in a moderate oven (350 degrees F.) for 12 to 15 minutes. Sprinkle 1 tablespoon shredded cheese over each egg. Continue baking for an additional 3 to 4 minutes or until cheese is melted. *Do not overbake eggs*; yolks should be runny. Remove eggs in cups from oven. With a rubber spatula, loosen each toast cup from baking cups; transfer egg cups to individual plates, two egg toast cups per serving. Garnish each serving with a fresh parsley or watercress sprig and a fresh strawberry or pineapple spear or grape cluster.

Variation: Omit cheese and spoon 1 to 2 tablespoons Hollandaise Sauce (see index) over each baked egg toast cup. Eggs should be baked a total of no more than 20 minutes.

Clam Chowder Scrambled Eggs

Yield: 4 servings

6 eggs, slightly beaten
1 (10 1/2-ounce) can
  Manhattan (tomato-base)
  clam chowder, undiluted,
  or 1 1/4 cups prepared
  clam chowder recipe of
  choice
1 (7 to 8-ounce) can minced
  clams, drained, or 8
  ounces shucked clams,
  drained and minced
1/2 teaspoon
  Worcestershire sauce or
  to taste
1/2 teaspoon salt or to taste
1/8 teaspoon pepper or to
  taste
2 tablespoons butter or
  margarine, melted
Minced parsley for garnish

In a bowl, beat eggs lightly. Add soup, clams, Worcestershire sauce, salt, and pepper, mixing well. Add egg mixture to a heavy skillet coated with melted butter. Cook scrambled egg mixture in a circular motion with a fork over low heat until firm, but not dry. Spoon eggs onto a serving plate and sprinkle with minced parsley.

Variation: 1 undiluted (10 3/4-ounce) can cream of mushroom soup may be substituted for clam chowder. Sauté 8 ounces mushrooms in 3 to 4 tablespoons melted butter and add to egg mixture. Omit clams. Add 4 to 5 drops hot sauce with seasonings.

–Virginia Cottrell (Mrs. Walker C., Jr.)

Tea Dish-"Cheese Fondu"

One cup bread crumbs (very dry and fine), 2 scant cups of milk (rich and fresh), one-half pound dry old cheese,grated, 3 eggs (whipped very light), 1 small tablespoonful melted butter, pepper and salt to taste. A pinch of soda dissolved in hot water and stirred into the milk, soak the crumbs in the milk, beat into these the eggs, butter, seasoning-lately, the cheese. Butter a neat baking dish, pour the fondu into it, strew dry bread crumbs on the top, and bake in a rather quick oven until delicately browned. Serve immediately in the baking dish, as it soon falls.

Mrs. Wm. S. Robertson.
Virginia Recipes, *1890*

293

Cheese Topped Shirred Eggs with Ham

Yield: 4 servings

Easy to prepare and serve, this recipe turns a breakfast or brunch into a special occasion for one or a crowd. Add a fresh fruit cup and homemade muffins or a coffee cake for extra appeal.

4 ounces *very* thinly sliced fully-cooked smoked Smithfield or Virginia country-style ham, divided (see note)
4 to 8 eggs, divided
2 teaspoons butter or margarine, divided
1/4 to 1/2 cup shredded sharp Cheddar or Monterey Jack or Swiss cheese, divided
Pepper to taste (optional)

Arrange 1 ounce of sliced ham in each of 4 lightly greased individual ramekins or casseroles. Crack 1 or 2 eggs into each ham-lined ramekin. Dot each casserole with 1/2 teaspoon butter. Arrange ramekins on an ungreased baking sheet. Bake, uncovered, in a moderate oven (350 degrees F.) for 10 to 12 minutes. Evenly sprinkle 1 to 2 tablespoons grated cheese over each individual egg casserole. Continue to bake, uncovered, for about 5 minutes, or until cheese is melted and bubbly hot. Sprinkle each with pepper to taste, if desired. Serve immediately.

Note: 4 ounces air-dried beef may be substituted for ham.

Variations: A buttered toasted English muffin half or split croissant may be arranged in each ramekin before adding other ingredients. One drained 6-ounce jar of sliced mushrooms may be divided and spooned over ham or air-dried beef before eggs are added. A pinch of cayenne pepper may be sprinkled over grated cheese before baking.

Cheese Dreams

2 t. baking powder
1 tb. shortening
1/2 t. salt
1/3 c. milk
1 c. flour
1/2 c. cheese

Mix and sift in the dry ingredients. Work in the shortening lightly with the tips of the fingers. Add liquid gradually and then sprinkle in the cheese, which has been grated. Toss on floured board, and roll out 1/4 inch in thickness and cut with small cutter. Bake in hot oven 10 minutes and serve hot with salad course.

Culinary Echoes From Dixie, *1917*

Fondue

Fondue, the Swiss specialty, is associated with one or more cheeses melted in a special pottery pot over heat to which wine and flavorings are added. Diners spear pieces of bread on a long two-pronged fork and dip them in the melted cheese, and eat them piping hot. Custom dictates that a person losing his or her bit of bread in the fondue pot must steal a kiss from the person next to him/her!

Other fondues have derived from this specialty. Fondue Bourguignonne is prepared by cooking pieces of meat and vegetables speared on long handled two-prong forks in hot oil. A variety of sauces is served to diners for dipping the cooked pieces of meat and vegetables. Chinese Fondue incorporates much of the same method as the Bourguignonne, except the meat or vegetables are cooked in a simmering stock.

Chocolate Fondue is prepared in much the same way as the cheese fondue with bits of cake, marshmallows, or fruit used as the dippers. Finally, fondue can be applied to a preparation of vegetables cut into thin pieces and cooked slowly in butter until the mixture is a pulp.

Corn and Cheese Soufflé

1 t. butter
1 c. chopped corn
1 t. chopped green pepper
1 c. grated cheese
1/4 c. flour
3 eggs
2 c. milk
1/2 t. salt

Melt the butter and cook the pepper thoroughly in it. Make a sauce out of the flour, milk, and grated cheese; add the corn, chopped yolks and seasonings; cut and fold in the whites beaten stiffly, turn into a buttered baking dish and bake in a moderate oven 30 minutes.

Made with skimmed milk and with butter, this dish has a food value slightly in excess of a pound of beef and a pound of potatoes. Calculated cost about 20 cents.

–Culinary Echoes From Dixie, 1917

295

Cheese Fondue Ham Rolls

Yield: 8 servings

This easy to prepare entreé is a nice change from the usual dunked fondue."

12 ounces Swiss or
   Emmentaler cheese
3 tablespoons flour
2 (10-ounce) packages
   frozen broccoli spears,
   thawed (see note)
8 thin ham slices, each cut
   1/8-inch thick
Wooden picks (optional)
3 cups toasted cubed
   French bread
1 1/2 cups dry white wine
1 teaspoon ground mustard
1/2 teaspoon garlic salt

Combine cheese and flour, mixing well; set aside. Divide broccoli spears evenly and arrange spears on the center of each ham slice; roll each ham slice around broccoli spears, jellyroll-style, securing with wooden picks, if desired. Arrange stuffed ham rolls in a 12 x 8 x 2-inch baking dish. Evenly sprinkle toasted bread cubes over ham rolls; set casserole aside. In a medium heavy saucepan, bring wine to simmer over moderate heat. Add cheese mixture, reduce temperature, and stir over low heat until cheese is melted. Add mustard and garlic salt, blending well. Pour hot cheese sauce evenly over bread cubes in baking dish. Bake, uncovered, in a moderate oven (350 degrees F.) for 30 minutes.

Note: 1 1/2 to 2 pounds of fresh broccoli may be substituted. Remove woody stems from broccoli and cut into spears. Partially cook broccoli in boiling salted water for 4 to 5 minutes after water returns to a boil; drain well.

–Vienna Taylor

French Spiced Cheese

1/2 lb. cream cheese
1/2 c. milk or cream
1 finely chopped tomato
2 tb. olive oil
1 t. paprika
Salt to taste

On a board chop the cheese and work it with a broad kitchen knife into a smooth paste. Add all the ingredients, and work it more with the knife until thoroughly mixed. Garnish with small olives and put on ice. Serve either with rye bread, crackers or toast.

Culinary Echoes From Dixie, *1917*

Goat Cheese Marinated with Rosemary and Lemon

Yield: 6 to 8 appetizer servings

1/2 cup olive oil (see note)
1/4 cup lemon juice
3 tablespoons minced fresh
  or 1 tablespoon dried
  rosemary
11 ounces Chevre or other
  goat cheese, cut in one
  loaf
Whole strawberries and
  small clusters of seedless
  green, red, or black
  grapes for garnish
Thinly sliced French bread
  baguette or assorted
  crackers

In a deep small bowl, combine oil, lemon juice, and rosemary, blending well. Place cheese in mixture, coating well; allow cheese to marinate in mixture at room temperature for 12 hours. Drain cheese from marinade and arrange on a serving plate. Garnish with strawberries and small clusters of grapes. Serve with thin slices of French bread or assorted crackers.

Note: Use a premium extra virgin olive oil. Extra virgin refers to the oil collected from the first press of the olives.

–Chef Kevin Wade
Gallego's Restaurant
The Omni Hotel

Cheese Aigrettes

1/4 c. water
1 c. flour
2 tb. butter
2 small eggs
4 tb. grated cheese
1/2 t. salt
Pinch of pepper

Add butter to boiling water. Stir in flour and beat well until mixture is smooth and leaves pan clean. Cool and add cheese and eggs, salt and pepper. Beat well. Drop mixture by teaspoonfuls into hot fat; it should not be too hot, or cheese will burn. Test: cube of bread should brown in 70 seconds. Fry until a golden brown, cool, drain and sprinkle with grated cheese. Serve hot.

–Culinary Echoes From Dixie, *1917*

Hanover Tavern:
Home of BARKSDALE THEATRE

Originally built as an inn and stagecoach stop in 1723, the historic Hanover Tavern reopened to the public as the Barksdale Theatre in 1954. Ignoring advice to never do serious theatre in the Richmond area, the founders, David and Nancy Kilgore and Muriel McAuley created the first dinner theatre in the United States, naming it in honor of their college friend, Barbara Barksdale, who had died of Multiple Sclerosis. Throughout the last three decades, the Barksdale has received much national critical acclaim for the quality of its presentations.

Along with their theatre work, the Barksdale founders have continued their endless task of restoring the Tavern. From a neglected derelict in 1953, without heat or plumbing, Hanover Tavern today is a Virginia and National Historic Landmark, "a living reminder of our nation's past and a viable home for theatrical creativity."

Here, such historic notables as Thomas Jefferson, the Marquis de LaFayette, and George Washington stopped for a night's rest. Patrick Henry married the daughter of Tavern owner, John Shelton, as his first wife, making the Tavern his home for three years. And from the Tavern, Henry was called to the Courthouse across the road, to strike the first blow against King George III in a case called the Parson's Cause.

In 1781, a message came to the Tavern's crowded tap room that Cornwallis and Tarleton were fast approaching. Legend suggests that the exodus of the assembled patrons was so hasty that the right horses were not returned to the right owners for at least a week. Cornwallis soon after made the Tavern his headquarters for eighteen days, reportedly not paying his bill.

Barksdale Theatre's Brandied Cheese Spread

Yield: about 12 appetizer servings

Homemades by Suzanne prepares the repast served to patrons of the Barksdale prior to theatre performances.

1 (8-ounce) package cream cheese, at room temperature
1 (5-ounce) jar sharp Cheddar cheese food
1/2 cup butter or margarine, at room temperature
1 tablespoon sugar
1/4 teaspoon cayenne pepper
1/4 cup brandy
1/2 cup finely chopped pecans
Bagel chips or assorted crisp crackers, or thin slices of French bead baguette

In a medium bowl, combine the first 5 ingredients, beating until mixture is smooth. Gradually add brandy, beating until well mixed. Stir in pecans. Spoon into a serving bowl, cover, and refrigerate for several hours until flavor "ripens." Allow spread to come to room temperature before serving. Garnish as desired and accompany with Bagel chips, assorted crackers, or thin slices of a French bread baguette.

–Suzanne and Warren Wolstenholme, proprietors
Chef John V. Moore
Homemades by Suzanne

Mexican Rarebit

Use 1 pound of rich, mild cheese grated, 1 tablespoonful of butter, 1 egg, 1/2 cupful of stale beer of milk of preferred, a pinch of salt and from 1 to 2 tablespoonfuls of chili powder. First, put the butter in a saucepan and when melted add the chili powder and salt, stirring until thoroughly mixed; add the cheese and continue to stir briskly until it is thoroughly melted; then slowly add the beer or milk, stirring all the time, and lastly add the egg and stir until the rarebit begins to thicken. Serve quickly on crackers or preferably on hot toast, being sure that your platters are hot.

Culinary Echoes From Dixie, *1917*

Cheese Strata

Yield: 6 to 8 servings

This is a combination strata, soufflé, and quiche and makes into an easy casserole. Strata refers to the layering effect of the food mixture.

12 slices white bread, crusts removed
2 to 3 tablespoons butter or margarine, at room temperature
2 cups cubed fully-cooked smoked ham, cut into 1/2-inch cubes
1 pound fresh asparagus, woody stems removed, partially cooked and drained, or 1 (10-ounce) package frozen asparagus spears, partially cooked and drained (see note)
2 tablespoons chopped peeled onion
1 cup shredded sharp Cheddar, Monterey Jack, or Swiss cheese
6 eggs, beaten
1 (11-ounce) can Cheddar cheese or cream of mushroom soup, undiluted
3 1/2 cups milk
1/2 teaspoon Worcestershire sauce (optional)
1/2 teaspoon dry mustard
1/2 teaspoon or to taste
Few grains cayenne pepper to taste
Cheese or Hollandaise Sauce (optional) (see index)

Evenly butter bread slices; cut into small cubes. Arrange half of the bread cubes in the bottom of a greased 13 x 9 x2-inch baking dish, dividing evenly. Scatter ham over bread layer. Arrange asparagus spears over ham and then top with onions. Evenly sprinkle cheese over onion-asparagus layer. Top with remaining bread. In a bowl, combine eggs, soup, milk, Worcestershire sauce, if desired, mustard, salt, and cayenne pepper, beating well. Pour over layered mixture in baking dish. Bake, uncovered in a moderate oven (350 degrees F.) for 55 to 60 minutes or until a silver knife inserted in the center of the strata comes out clean. Remove from oven and allow to stand at room temperature for 10 to 15 minutes before cutting into squares. Strata servings may be garnished with hot Cheese or Hollandaise Sauce, if desired.

Note: Cook fresh asparagus about 3 to 4 minutes and frozen about 2 to 3 minutes

Pasta, Noodles, and Grains

Chicken Fettucine in Alfredo Sauce

Yield: 4 servings

1 pound boneless chicken breasts, skinned
1/2 cup butter or margarine, melted and divided
1 cup heavy cream
3/4 cup grated Parmesan cheese, divided
1/4 teaspoon salt or to taste
Pinch of nutmeg
8 to 9 ounces fettucine
3 to 4 quarts boiling salted water
1 (13 3/4-ounce) can artichoke hearts, drained and quartered
2 tablespoons minced fresh chervil or parsley

With a sharp knife, cut chicken into bite-sized pieces. In a medium heavy skillet, sauté chicken in 2 to 3 tablespoons butter over moderate heat until lightly browned, about 2 to 3 minutes. Reduce heat, cover, and simmer for an additional 2 to 3 minutes. *Do not overcook.* Remove from heat and set aside. In a medium heavy saucepan, combine remaining butter, cream, 1/2 cup Parmesan cheese, salt, and nutmeg, whisking with a wire whisk over low heat until mixture is smooth and slightly thickened. Cook fettucine in boiling salted water until tender but firm, al *dente* (see note). *Do not overcook.* Drain pasta well. In a large heavy saucepan, combine fettucine, sauce, chicken pieces, artichokes, and chervil or parsley. Toss lightly to mix over low heat. Sprinkle 1 tablespoon of the remaining grated Parmesan cheese over each serving. Serve immediately.

Note: Cook fresh hand made fettucine in boiling salted water for 1 1/2 to 2 minutes after water returns to a boil. Cook packaged noodles according to package directions.

Variation: Reduce cream to 3/4 cup or 3/4 cup plus 1 tablespoon. With a wire whisk, whisk in 3 to 4 tablespoons lemon juice, depending upon intensity of lemon flavoring desired. Omit nutmeg and add 1 1/2 to 2 teaspoons grated lemon peel and pepper to taste. Other herbs such as 1 1/2 to 2 teaspoons minced fresh or 1/2 teaspoon dried dill weed may be added, if desired. Add 1/2 cup toasted coarsely chopped cashews or Macadamia nuts, or blanched almonds if desired.

–Sarah Cardamone McBride (Mrs. Andrew S.)

Old Richmond Advertisement, date unknown

Early Autumn Pasta

Yield: 6 to 8 servings

4 large green or sweet red peppers
2 1/2 pounds whole wheat fettucine
Boiling salted water as needed
1/2 cup fresh basil leaves, rinsed and torn into small pieces
1 cup Calamata olives
1/2 cup olive oil (see note)
1/2 cup red wine vinegar
Pinch minced peeled garlic or to taste
Salt and freshly ground black peppercorns to taste

Evenly roast peppers speared on a long handled two-prong fork over the open flame of a range top gas burner until peel of peppers is charred, turning pepper frequently. Remove peel, scraping off any char; remove core and seeds. Coarsely chop peppers. Or, arrange peppers on a rack in a broiler pan; broil, 6 to 8 inches from heat source, until peppers are charred, turning frequently. Proceed as previously directed. Cook pasta in about 4 to 5 quarts boiling water in a large heavy pot until *just* tender, *al dente*, drain well (see note). In a medium bowl, combine chopped peppers, fettucine, basil, and olives. Add oil, vinegar, and garlic, tossing lightly to mix. Season with salt and pepper to taste. Cover and chill for at least 2 hours in the refrigerator.

Note: Use a premium quality extra virgin olive oil. Extra virgin refers to the oil collected from the first press of the olives.

Note: Cook fresh handmade pasta about 2 minutes after the water returns to a boil.

–Robert Ramsey, proprietor
Bistro Express

To Make Vermecelli

Beat two or three fresh eggs quite light, make them into a stiff paste with flour, knead it well, and roll it out very thin, cut it in narrow strips, give them a twist, and dry them quickly on tin sheets. It is an excellent ingredient in most soups, particularly those that are thin. Noodles are made in the same manner, only instead of strips they should be cut in tiny squares and dried. They are also good in soup.

The Virginia Housewife, 1831

Linguine with Clam Sauce and Mint

Yield: 4 servings

1/2 cup chopped peeled
onion
1/4 cup hot olive oil
3 garlic cloves, peeled and
minced
1/4 cup minced fresh or 2
teaspoons dried basil
1 teaspoon salt or to taste
10 ounces shucked fresh
topneck or *cherry stone*
(small to medium) clams,
including liquid or 1 (10-
ounce) can clams
3 tablespoons minced fresh
or 1 tablespoon dried
mint leaves
1 1/2 cups coarsely peeled
fresh or canned tomatoes
4 ounces linguine (see note)
1 1/2 cups thinly sliced
pitted ripe olives
3 tablespoons lemon juice
2 tablespoons minced
parsley

In a large heavy skillet, sauté onion in olive oil over moderate heat until tender but not browned. Add garlic, basil, and salt; continue to cook for an additional 2 minutes, stirring frequently. Drain clams, reserving juice. Add clam juice and mint to onion mixture; reduce heat and cook, uncovered, for 3 minutes. In a large heavy pot, cook fresh pasta in about 3 quarts boiling water until just tender but firm, *al dente*. (see note). Drain well and transfer to a heated platter. While pasta is cooking, stir clams and tomatoes into sauce mixture; cook for 1 minute. Add olives, lemon juice, and parsley, mixing lightly. Pour sauce over pasta and serve immediately.

Note: Cook fresh hand made linguine for 1 1/2 to 2 minutes after water returns to a boil or until just tender. Cook commercially packaged linguine according to package directions.

–Bobbie Hudson (Mrs. Harvey)

Pasta Fiesta with Clams and Oysters

Yield: 4 servings

8 ounces mushrooms, thinly
sliced
1/2 cup minced sweet red or
yellow or green pepper
2 to 3 tablespoons butter or
margarine, melted
1 chicken bouillon cube,
crumbled
1 cup heavy cream, at room

In a large heavy skillet, sauté mushrooms and sweet red pepper in butter over moderate heat until tender but not browned. Add bouillon cube, heavy cream, and nutmeg. With a wire whisk, blend in 3/4 cup Parmesan cheese; reduce heat and simmer, whisking occasionally, until mixture is slightly thickened. Add clams, oysters, and sour cream, mixing lightly. Continue to simmer until clams and oysters are *just* cooked but tender,

temperature
1/8 teaspoon nutmeg
3/4 cup grated Parmesan
cheese
1 pint (very small) *little neck*
clams, drained
1 pint medium (selects)
oysters, drained
1/2 cup sour cream, at room
temperature
8 ounces linguine or
fettucine
3 tablespoons minced
parsley, divided
Salt to taste
Freshly ground pepper to
taste
Additional grated Parmesan
cheese for garnish

blend in 3/4 cup Parmesan cheese; reduce heat and simmer, whisking occasionally, until mixture is slightly thickened. Add clams, oysters, and sour cream, mixing lightly. Continue to simmer until clams and oysters are *just* cooked but tender, about 2 to 3 minutes. Cook linguine in boiling salted water until tender but firm (*al dente*) about 2 minutes for handmade linguine. (Cook commercially packaged noodles according to package directions.) Drain well, but do not rinse. Fold pasta and 2 tablespoons minced parsley into sauce, mixing well. Add salt and pepper to taste. Serve immediately and garnish each serving with additional grated Parmesan cheese and remaining minced parsley, if desired.

Linguine with Proscuitto and Brie

Yield: 4 to 6 servings

8 ounces brie cheese, cut
into bite-sized pieces
3 to 4 quarts boiling water
About 1/2 cup olive oil,
divided
1 pound linguine
8 ounces proscuitto or fully-
cooked smoked
Smithfield or Smithfield-
style ham, chopped
1 cup grated Parmesan
cheese (see note)
1/4 to 1/3 cup minced fresh
chervil or parsley
Salt and pepper to taste

Allow bite-sized pieces of brie to come to room temperature. In a large heavy pot, combine boiling water and 2 tablespoons olive oil. Add linguine, cook over moderate heat for 2 to 3 minutes after water returns to a boil, or until tender but firm, *al dente.* Drain well, but do not rinse. In a large bowl, combine hot pasta and 6 tablespoons olive oil, tossing well to mix. Add brie cheese, proscuitto, Parmesan cheese, and chervil, tossing again. The mixture may be tossed with the hands to achieveeven distribution of cheeses, proscuitto, and herbs. Season with salt and pepper to taste. Serve slightly warm or at room temperature.

Note: Preferably use freshly grated Parmesan cheese.

Variation: Omit chervil; use only 2 tablespoons minced parsley. Add 2 to 3 tablespoons *each* minced fresh or 2 to 3 teaspoons dried oregano and basil.

–Sarah Cardamone McBride (Mrs. Andrew S.)

Mr. Bojangles

Bill "Bojangles" Robinson, world known dancer and movie actor, remains larger than live in his home town of Richmond, Virginia. Portrayed in a "perpetual stairway stance," his best known dance routine, the nine foot bronze statue atop aluminum steps dominates the Adams and Leight Streets intersection. In the 1930's, Robinson had dedicated the first traffic lights at this busy intersection, paid for by him after learning traffic signals were needed for the protection of neighborhood children.

Born in 1878, Robinson shined shoes and danced in the streets of Richmond as a young boy, earning the nickname of "Bojangles" after an altercation with a Broad Street merchant, Boujassen. He left the area at an early age, dancing his way across America to fame. Throughout his life, though, he fondly considered Richmond his home town. In turn, Richmond, equally proud of this famous dancer, annually observed his birthday. "Mr. Bojangles" died in 1949 at the age of seventy-one.

Mixed-Up Lasagne

Yield: 12 to 16 servings

1 medium zucchini, thinly sliced
1 medium onion, peeled and thinly sliced
2 tablespoons hot olive or cooking oil
1 teaspoon garlic powder or juice
1 pound *lean* ground beef (see note)
1 medium onion, peeled and chopped
1 (16-ounce) can tomato sauce
1 (15 1/2-ounce) jar spaghetti sauce
1 (8-ounce) can sliced mushrooms (including liquid)
3 tablespoons minced fresh or 1 tablespoon dried oregano
1 tablespoon minced fresh or 1 teaspoon dried basil
1 teaspoon hot sauce or to taste
Salt and pepper to taste
3 hard-cooked eggs, peeled and sliced
1 (1-pound) package lasagne noodles
1/2 cup sliced pitted green olives
1 (12-ounce) container creamy-style cottage or ricotta cheese
1 cup shredded mozzarella cheese
1/2 cup dry red wine

In a large heavy skillet, sauté zucchini and sliced onion in oil over moderate heat until tender but not browned; add garlic powder, mixing well. Remove with a slotted spoon; set aside. Brown beef and sauté chopped onions until tender in remaining hot drippings. Reduce heat and add tomato sauce, spaghetti sauce, mushrooms, oregano, hot sauce, basil, salt, and pepper to taste; simmer for 30 minutes. Adjust seasonings.

Spread a layer of meat sauce over the bottom of two 12 x 8 x 2-inch baking dishes. Arrange a layer of uncooked noodles over meat sauce. Sprinkle with a small amount of egg slices, olives, and mozzarella cheese. Dot with cottage cheese and zucchini mixture. Repeat layers, ending with a layer of meat sauce topped by mozzarella cheese.

Bake, covered, in a moderate oven (375 degrees F.) for 35 minutes. Evenly pour red wine over lasagne and bake, uncovered, an additional 20 minutes. Remove and allow to stand for 5 to 10 minutes before cutting.

Note: 1 pound crumbled medium -spiced bulk pork sausage or mild or hot-spiced Italian sausage, removed from casing, may be substituted for beef.

–Ginny Moss (Mrs. John Simpson)

Crab 'N Shrimp Lasagna

Yield: 12 servings

1 pound medium shrimp, cooked, peeled, deveined, and each cut in half
8 ounces crabmeat (see note)
8 lasagna noodles
Boiling salted water as needed
1 cup chopped peeled onion
2 tablespoons butter or margarine, melted
1 (8-ounce) package cream cheese, at room temperature
1 egg beaten
1 1/2 cups ricotta or cream-style cottage cheese
2 tablespoons minced fresh or 2 teaspoons dried basil
1/2 teaspoon salt
1/8 teaspoon pepper
2 (10 3/4-ounce) cans cream of mushroom soup, undiluted
1/3 cup milk
1/3 cup dry white wine
1/4 cup grated Parmesan cheese or to taste (see note)
1/2 cup shredded sharp Cheddar or American cheese or to taste

Prepare shrimp and set aside. Pick over crabmeat, removing any shell or cartilage; set aside. Cook lasagna noodles in boiling salted water according to package directions; drain well. Arrange half of the cooked noodles in the bottom of a greased 13x9x2-inch baking dish. In a small heavy skillet, saute onion in butter over moderate heat until tender but not browned.

In a medium bowl, beat cream cheese until smooth. Add ricotta cheese and egg, blending well. Stir in onions, basil, salt, and pepper. Spread half of the mixture evenly over noodle layer. In a small bowl, combine soup, milk, and wine, blending well. Stir in shrimp pieces and crabmeat. Spread half of the seafood mixture over the ricotta-cream cheese layer. Repeat the layers in order previously given. Evenly sprinkle Parmesan cheese as desired over second seafood layer.

Bake, uncovered, in a moderate oven (350 degrees F.) for 45 minutes. Evenly sprinkle Cheddar or American cheese over lasagna and continue to bake for an additional 4 to 5 minutes or until cheese is melted. Allow baked lasagna to stand, loosely covered, at room temperature for 15 minutes before cutting into squares. Pass additional grated Parmesan cheese, if desired.

Note: A drained 7 1/2-ounce can crabmeat may be substituted for fresh crabmeat.

Note: Preferably use freshly grated cheese.

–Linda M. Bourgeois (Mrs. Bruce)

Macaroni

A form of noodle, laganum, the ancestor of spaghetti,was served in ancient Rome. Often it was served topped with cheese and a fragrant meat or fish sauce.

Thomas Jefferson introduced Neopolitan maccaroni at a formal dinner for the first time in America in 1789. It was served bubbling hot with cheese and butter. Some weeks previous, Jefferson, then secretary of state of our young nation, had sent William Short on a special mission to Naples to learn the process of preparing this delicate strand-like food Americans now call spaghetti.

"Mighty Good" Macaroni 'N Cheese

Yield: 6 servings

3/4 cup macaroni
3 eggs
2 slices day-old bread, cut into 1/2-inch cubes
2 cups milk
2 cups (8 ounces) shredded sharp Cheddar cheese
2 tablespoons butter or margarine, at room temperature

Cook macaroni in boiling salted water according to package directions; drain well. Evenly spread macaroni in the bottom of a greased 13 x 9 x 2-inch baking dish. In a medium bowl, beat egg slightly; stir in bread cubes, milk, and cheese. Evenly spoon mixture over macaroni in baking dish. Dot with butter. Bake, uncovered, in a moderate oven (350 degrees F.) for 1 hour.

–Gladys Antroinen (Mrs. Aaron)

Old Richmond Advertisement, date unknown

309

Macaroni "Pie"

Yield: 6 servings

1 (8-ounce) package
macaroni (1 1/2 cups)
1 1/2 cups shredded sharp
Cheddar cheese, divided
1 1/2 tablespoons butter or
margarine, melted
1/2 teaspoon dry mustard
Salt and pepper to taste
3 eggs, beaten
1 1/2 cups milk

Cook macaroni according to package directions; drain well. In a large bowl, combine macaroni, 1 cup cheese, butter, dry mustard, and salt and pepper to taste, mixing well. Stir in beaten eggs and milk, mixing well. Spoon into a greased 8-inch pie plate or 8x8x2-inch baking dish. Evenly sprinkle remaining 1/2 cup shredded cheese over casserole. Bake, uncovered, in a moderate oven (350 degrees F.) for 30 minutes or until cheese is melted and top is lightly browned.

Variation: Add 1 cup chopped peeled tomato, 1 teaspoon Worcestershire sauce, 4 to 5 drops hot sauce, and seasoned salt to taste to the mixture.

–Ladies' Missionary Society
Great Hope Baptist Church

Broccoli Cappelini

Yield: 4 to 6 servings

3/4 cup water
1 teaspoon salt
1 (10-ounce) package frozen
chopped broccoli
5 ounces cappelini,
vermicelli, or spaghettini
(see note)
4 ounces mushrooms, thinly
sliced
8 tablespoons butter or
margarine, melted
1 cup grated Parmesan
cheese

In a heavy saucepan, combine water and salt; bring to boiling over moderate heat, add broccoli, and cook, uncovered, for 5 to 8 minutes or until tender, but firm. Drain well, reserving cooking water. Cook pasta in reserved cooking water for 30 seconds or until tender, but firm (*al dente*); drain well. In a heavy skillet, sauté mushrooms in 3 tablespoons butter over moderate heat until tender, but not browned. In a large bowl, combine broccoli, pasta, mushrooms, 5 tablespoons remaining butter, and Parmesan cheese; toss lightly to mix. Serve immediately.

Note: Preferably use fresh pasta, but commercially packaged pasta may be substituted; cook according to package directions.

Note: Cappelini may be prepared 1 hour in advance and held, covered, in a warm oven (180 to 200 degrees F.).

–Susan Hayden (Mrs. G. Douglas, Jr.)

> Thalhimers, a landmark Richmond business since its founding in 1842 as a one-room dry goods and notion store, has grown into a multi-chain department store serving customers in Virginia, the Carolinas, and Tennessee. For the past quarter century, preparation and catering delicious food stuffs for Richmonder's parties and functions at the Thalhimers Westmoreland Service Building has been a distinctive part of the business. Surviving the 1857 Money Panic, the devastating 1865 Richmond fire, several relocations and expansions, the community-minded company has joined in the "Richmond Renaissance."

Cheese-Stuffed Spinach Tortellini

Yield: 6 servings

"Tortellini are excellent hors d'oeuvres or as an entrée salad."

7 ounces packaged dry cheese-stuffed tortellini (see note)
2 quarts salted boiling water
1/4 cup lemon juice
1/4 cup minced parsley
3 tablespoons minced fresh or 1 tablespoon dried oregano
3/4 cup olive oil
1/4 cup minced pimento, drained
Salt and pepper to taste

In a large heavy pot, cook tortellini in salted boiling water until *just* tender, but firm (*al dente*), about 20 to 25 minutes; drain well. In a small bowl, combine lemon juice, parsley, and oregano; with a wire whisk, beat in olive oil, adding in a slow steady stream. In a large bowl, combine tortellini and dressing, tossing lightly to coat pasta. Add pimento. Season with salt and pepper to taste; toss again. Cover and chill for 4 to 12 hours.

Note: Cook fresh tortellini for only 4 to 6 minutes.

–Berta Ward
Thalhimers Catering

The Tobacco Company Restaurant

The Tobacco Company Restaurant, in Richmond's historic downtown Shockoe Slip, occupies a stately red brick building at the corner of 12th and Cary Streets. A tobacco warehouse in the 1870's, it is a superb example of elegant renovation. From the bare, brick interior walls to the more than 400 antiques, artifacts, memorabilia, and skylight ceiling over a three-story atrium to the dazzling underground dance floor and bar, the Tobacco Company is one of the most unique entertainment centers in the country. Authentic Tiffany lamps, a nineteenth century mahogany secretary, rare stained glass windows and a turn-of-the nineteenth/twentieth centuries brass elevator are some of the many antiques featured.

Since opening in July, 1977, millions of guests have passed through the beveled glass doors and stepped back into the 19th century. Recently the restaurant has undergone a facelift, adding a black and white marble tiled floor and a look of "neon" to the club area. The Tobacco Company offers lunch, dinner, cocktails, entertainment, dancing, or just relaxing by the fire over a backgammon game.

Crabmeat Raphael

Yield: 4 servings

1 (28-ounce) can Italian-
  style tomatoes, chopped
  (including liquid)
2 medium onions, peeled
  and chopped
2 garlic cloves, peeled and
  minced
1/2 cup grated Romano
  cheese
1/4 cup minced parsley
2 tablespoons basil
3/4 teaspoon crushed dried
  hot red pepper
1/2 teaspoon coarsely
  ground black pepper
1/4 teaspoon oregano
3/4 tablespoon plus 1/4
  teaspoon salt, divided
1 pound crabmeat
12 ounces fresh vermicelli,
  angel hair, or spaghettini
  pasta (see note)
3 quarts boiling water
1 1/2 tablespoons olive

In a heavy saucepan, combine the first 9 ingredients and 1/4 teaspoon salt; simmer over low heat
for 30 minutes, stirring occasionally. *Do not allow
sauce to boil* (see note). Pick over crabmeat, removing any cartilage or shell. As sauce simmers, start
heating water to boiling for pasta; add olive oil
and 3/4 tablespoon salt. Add fresh pasta and cook
for 30 seconds; drain immediately. While pasta is
cooking, add crabmeat to sauce, mixing well;
continue cooking until crabmeat is heated
through. Add pasta, tossing lightly to mix. Serve
immediately.

Note: 1 pound commercially packaged pasta cooked according to package
directions and until tender, but firm (*al dente*) may be substituted.

Note: Sauce may be refrigerated, covered, for up to 5 days.

–The Tobacco Company Restaurant

Macaroni Rarebit

*Boil 2 ounces of macaroni or spaghetti for 1/2 hour. Drain, cover with cold water,
and drain again. At serving time, put 1/2 pound of grated cheese in a saucepan
or chafing-dish, add 1/2 teaspoonful of salt, a tablespoonful of tomato catsup,
a teaspoonful of Worcestershire sauce, and 1 egg, beaten with 2 tablespoonfuls of water. Put over fire and stir continuously until the cheese is melted and
smooth. Add the macaroni cut into inch lengths; heat, and serve at once on
toast or crackers.*

Culinary Echoes From Dixie, *1917*

Spaghetti Supreme

Yield: 8 servings

8 ounces mushrooms, thinly
  sliced
2 garlic cloves, peeled and
  minced
1 large onion, peeled and
  chopped
2 tablespoons butter or
  margarine, melted
2 pounds lean boneless
  beef, cut into bite-sized
  cubes
1 1/2 cups dry red wine
1 (28-ounce) can plum
  tomatoes
1 (20-ounce) can tomato
  sauce
1 (6-ounce) can tomato
  paste
1/2 teaspoon sugar
/4 to 1 teaspoon minced
  fresh or oregano
3/4 to 1 teaspoon minced
  fresh or basil
Salt and freshly ground
  pepper to taste
1 to 1 1/2 pounds spaghetti,
  tagliatelli noodles,
  rigatoni noodles, or
  medium shell pasta

In a large heavy saucepan, sauté mushrooms, garlic, and onion in butter over moderate heat until tender but not browned. Remove with a slotted spoon; set aside. Evenly brown beef cubes in hot pan drippings. Add wine. Blend in tomatoes, tomato sauce, and tomato paste. Add sugar and seasonings. Stir in reserved mushroom mixture. Reduce heat and simmer for 2 hours. Cook spaghetti or pasta in boiling salted water according to package directions until tender, but firm (al dente); drain well. Spoon sauce over each portion of pasta and serve immediately.

—Ginger Levit

Dearie's Pasta with Tomatoes

Yield: 4 to 6 entrée or 6 to 8 side dish servings

"This was a favorite recipe of my grandmother, Mable Tarver Owen, nicknamed Dearie, who was petite in stature but large in heart."

1 (8-ounce) package thin
  spaghetti

Cook commercially packaged spaghetti according to package directions; drain well. Cook fresh

4 slices bacon, cut into 1/2-
  inch pieces
1 medium onion, peeled
  and chopped
1 medium green pepper,
  cored, seeded, and
  chopped
1 (28-ounce) can tomatoes,
  including liquid
1 tablespoon minced fresh
  or 1 to 1 1/2 teaspoons
  dried basil or to taste
  (optional)
Salt and pepper to taste
Freshly grated Parmesan
  cheese for garnish
  (optional)

handmade pasta in 3 to 4 quarts boilind, salted water for about 1 minute after water returns to boil. In a Dutch oven, pan-fry bacon over moderate heat until medium crisp (slightly limp); remove bacon from pan and set aside. Add onion and green pepper to pan; sauté vegetables in hot pan drippings until tender but crisp. Add tomatoes and bacon. Reduce heat and add spaghetti and basil, if desired, mixing well (see note).Season with salt and pepper to taste. Simmer, uncovered, for 45 minutes or until liquid is reduced by one-fourth, mixture is bubbly hot, and flavors are well blended. Serve as an entree or side dish. Garnish each serving with freshly grated Parmesan cheese, if desired.

Note: Cooked spaghetti may be added to sauce after sauce has simmered for those who prefer pasta cooked *al dente*.

–Susan Goode Crone

Serpentine Wall on Sulgrave Road

Pasta with Olive Oil, Garlic, and Fresh Basil

Yield: 4 servings

1 pound spaghetti or linguine
About 5 quarts boiling salted water
10 garlic cloves, peeled and divided
1/2 cup olive oil (see note)
1 tablespoon minced fresh basil
Freshly ground black peppercorns as desired
Freshly grated Parmesan cheese as desired

Cook pasta in boiling salted water until tender but firm, *al dente* (see note); drain well and transfer to a warm serving bowl. While pasta is cooking, thinly slice 5 garlic cloves and mince 5 garlic cloves. Combine garlic and oil in a small heavy saucepan; stir over low heat for several minutes. *Do not allow garlic to brown.* Remove from heat and add basil, mixing well. Pour sauce over pasta, sprinkle with freshly ground black peppercorns, and toss lightly. Serve immediately. Pass Parmesan cheese to sprinkle as desired over each serving.

Note: Use a premium quality extra virgin olive oil. Extra virgin refers to the oil collected from the first press of the olives.

Note: Cook hand made fresh pasta for about 2 minutes after water returns to a boil. *Do not over cook.* Cook commercial packaged pasta according to package directions.

–Jane Hamlin (Mrs. Richard R.)

Noodle Pudding

Yield: 8 to 10 servings

8 ounces medium noodles, 1/4-inch wide
1 (8-ounce) package cream cheese, at room temperature
8 ounces cottage cheese, at room temperature
1 cup sour cream, at room temperature
1/2 cup butter or margarine, at room temperature
6 eggs

Cook noodles according to package directions; drain well. In a large bowl, combine cheeses, sour cream, and butter, beating slightly. Fold in noodles. In a medium bowl, beat eggs lightly; add milk, sugar, and vanilla, blending well. Stir into noodle mixture. Spoon into a greased 12 x 8 x 2-inch baking dish. Bake, uncovered, in a moderate oven (350 degrees F.) for 1 1/2 hours. Serve as an accompaniment to meats.

6 eggs
2 cups milk
1/2 cup sugar
1/2 teaspoon vanilla extract

Note: You may partially bake pudding, cool, cover with aluminum foil, and freeze. When ready to use, thaw and finish baking, uncovered, in a moderate oven (350 degrees F.) for the remaining baking period.

–Janet B. Tutton (Mrs. Roger)

CONFEDERATE GUERRILLAS.

Dinning in "Hotel" Libby,
July 1863

We have tasted of the promised soup: it is boiled water sprinkled with rice, and seasoned with the rank juices of stale bacon; we must shut our eyes to eat it; the bacon, I have no doubt, might have walked into the pot of its own accord. It is brought up to us in wooden buckets, and we eat it, in most cases without spoons, out of tin-cups.

A state of chronic somnolency would be an admirable mental condition in which to pass through the horrors of a protracted captivity; (since) all kinds of hallucinations may be produced on the brain of the sleeper, nothing would be easier than to eat stale bread and imagine it to be sponge-cake; to turn James River water into sparkling champagne; and to convert into "Floating islands" the vapid juices of weak bean soup!

Frederico Fernandez Cavada,
Libby Life, Experiences Of A Prisoner of War In Richmond Va 1863-64

Hominy or hulled corn, was originally an Indian food but became an important staple in the diet of early colonists. Coarse ground hominy or grits is still much appreciated south of the Mason-Dixon line. Grits can be served in place of a potato, pasta, or dish as an accompaniment to the entrée.

Easy Cheese Grits

Yield: 8 servings

3 1/2 cups water
1 teaspoon salt
1/4 teaspoon garlic powder
1 cup quick-cooking white
hominy grits
1/4 cup butter or margarine
1 (5-ounce) jar processed
sharp cheese food spread
2 eggs, beaten slightly
1/2 cup milk
1/4 cup shredded sharp
Cheddar cheese
Paprika

In a saucepan, combine water, salt, and garlic powder; bring to a rapid boil. Add grits in a fine stream and cook, stirring constantly, for 2 to 2 1/2 minutes or until thick. While hot, stir in butter and cheese spread. Combine eggs and milk and stir into grits. Pour into a greased 2-quart round casserole. Bake, uncovered, in a moderate oven (350 degrees F.) for 40 minutes. Sprinkle shredded Cheddar cheese and paprika over top of the casserole 5 minutes before end of baking time.

–Ann Tyler (Mrs. Hal)

..Dark days were in store for Richmond. An incipient bread riot occurred in her streets in April (1863) when a large number of women and children of the poorer class met and marched through Main and Cary streets, attacking and sacking several stores kept by known spectators. President Davis, Governor Letcher, General Elzey, and General Winder, with Mr. Seddon, Secretary of War, met the painful situation by prompt but kind measures and personal appeal. Rations of rice issued by the government aided to calm the disturbance, which left, however, a distressing impression upon all minds....

Harrison
"The Ravages of War (1862-1865),"
Recollections Grave and Gay, 1911

Rice

Rice, not a native of North America, migrated to the American colonies from Madagascar, an island located off the coast of South Africa, via a sea captain stopping in the port of Charleston. Dr. Henry Woodward, one of the founders of South Carolina, was given a small bag of the rice which he planted in his garden where it flourished. It soon was transported to other colonies, including Virginia.

Baked Browned Rice

Yield: 6 servings

1/2 cup butter or margarine
1 cup long-grain rice
1 (10 1/2-ounce) can onion
 soup, undiluted
1 (10 1/2-ounce) can
 consommé, undiluted

Melt butter in a large heavy skillet over moderate heat. Add rice and cook, stirring constantly, until rice is lightly browned. Stir in soups. Transfer mixture to a 1 1/2-quart casserole.Bake, uncovered, in a moderate oven (350 degrees F.) for1 hour or until rice is tender and most of the liquid is absorbed.

Variation: Sauté 1/2 cup chopped peeled onion or thinly sliced green onion in the butter before browning rice. Remove with a slotted spoon; set aside. Add 2 tablespoons minced pimento, 1/2 teaspoon Worcestershire sauce, and sautéed onions with soups to rice. Or, omit pimento, and sauté 1/2 cup chopped sweet red or green pepper with the onion and add to rice with the soups.

–Betty Shipp

319

Seasoned Baked Rice with Cashews

Yield: 8 servings

2 1/2 cups boiling water
1 1/4 cups long-grain brown or white rice
1/2 cup butter or margarine, melted
1/2 cup chopped sweet red pepper
1/2 to 1 teaspoon seasoned salt
1/2 teaspoon minced peeled garlic
5 to 6 drops Tabasco sauce or to taste
2 1/4 cups chicken broth
2 tablespoons minced parsley
1/2 cup cashew nuts

In a large bowl, pour boiling water over rice; cover and allow to stand at room temperature for 30 minutes. Drain well, rinse in cold water, and drain again. In a large heavy skillet, cook rice and sweet red pepper in butter over moderate heat for about 5 minutes or until butter is almost absorbed. Add Worcestershire sauce, seasoned salt, garlic, and Tabasco sauce, mixing well. Turn into a lightly greased 1 1/2-quart casserole; pour chicken broth over rice mixture. Bake, covered, in a slow oven (325 degrees F.) for 45 minutes. Add parsley, mixing well. Evenly sprinkle cashews over casserole. Bake, uncovered, for an additional 10 minutes or until nuts are lightly browned.

Savory Curried Rice

Yield: 4 to 6 servings

3 tablespoons butter or margarine, at room temperature
1 small onion, peeled and chopped
1 teaspoon curry powder or to taste
1 cup long-grain rice
1 1/4 cups chicken broth (see note)
1 1/4 cups water

In a large heavy saucepan, melt butter over moderate heat. Add onion, and cook, stirring frequently, until onion is tender but not browned, about 2 to 3 minutes. Stir in curry powder. Add rice and continue to cook, stirring constantly, until rice turns opaque, about 7 minutes. Add chicken broth and water; increase heat and bring to a boil. Reduce heat, cover, and simmer until liquid is absorbed and rice tender but not mushy, about 20 minutes. *Do not overcook.*

Note: 1 undiluted (10 1/2-ounce) can chicken broth may be substituted for 1 1/4 cups chicken broth.

–Vienna Taylor

Hopping John

Yield: 6 to 8 servings

In the South, Hopping John is traditionally served on New Year's Day to bring luck for the coming year. The name is thought to be derived from the custom of sending children hopping once around the table before the dish was served.

4 slices bacon, chopped
1 cup chopped peeled
  onion
1 cup long-grain rice
2 cups water
1 teaspoon salt
1/4 teaspoon hot sauce
1 (15-ounce) can pinto or
  kidney beans or black-
  eyed peas, drained

Pan-fry bacon and onion in a heavy sauce pan over moderate heat until onion is tender but not brown. Stir in rice, water, salt, and hot sauce. Bring to a boil; reduce temperature, cover, and cook over low heat for about 15 minutes or until done. Stir in beans or peas; cover and heat thoroughly.

Golden Skillet Rice

Yield: 4 to 6 servings

"My friend, Stan Threlfall, who lived in Central America for many years, taught me this Central American method of cooking rice."

1/4 cup chopped peeled
  onion
1/4 cup chopped green
  pepper
3 to 4 tablespoons cooking
  oil, divided
1 1/4 cups long grain rice
2 cups chicken broth or
  water
2 tablespoons butter or
  margarine, at room
  temperature

In a heavy skillet, saute onion and green pepper in 2 tablespoons hot oil over moderate heat until tender but not browned; add rice and remaining oil, spreading over bottom of skillet. Cook, stirring lightly, until some of the rice kernels become opaque and golden in color. Add broth or water; bring to a boil and continue to boil gently for 10 minutes. *Do not stir.* Reduce heat and simmer, cover slightly ajar, for 30 to 35 minutes or until all liquid is absorbed. Remove from heat and add butter, tossing lightly.

Note: It is *very* important *not* to stir rice during the *entire* cooking period.

Variation: Add 1 tablespoon minced parsley and 1 tablespoon minced pimento to cooked rice.

–J. Robert Carlton

The Stonewall Cafe

The Stonewall Cafe, a trendy effervescent restaurant, is located in the English-style basement of the old West End School, 1520 West Main Street (corner of Main and Lombardy Streets), erected in 1886-87. At the time of its construction, the school was built at the extreme western boundary of Richmond, and near Richmond College (now the University of Richmond which has since located farther west) and the new hospital of the Little Sisters of the Poor (now a restored deluxe condominium complex).

With the annexation of land by the city in 1869, the western Richmond boundary was Lombardy Street, an area sorely in need of a school. As the city expanded westward at the end of the nineteenth century, the designated name of the school became superfluous and no longer appropriate. In 1909, the name was changed to the Stonewall Jackson School, honoring the heroic Confederate General. One of the best known landmarks in the Richmond area, the late nineteenth century school survived a century without major alterations to the structure until recently. In the spring of 1990, a major fire devastated the landmark. Today the charming Stonewall Cafe, as well as the entire building, is undergoing major reconstruction and restoration. Plans call for it to reopen in 1991.

Stonewall Dirty Rice

Yield: 6 servings

4 ounces ground pork
1/2 cup minced celery
1/2 cup minced peeled
  onion
1/2 cup minced green
  pepper
2 bay leaves, crumbled
2 tablespoons chicken base
  or chicken bouillon cubes,
  mashed
1 tablespoon minced fresh

In a small bowl, combine pork, celery, onions, green pepper, bay leaves, chicken base, thyme, oregano, cayenne and dried red peppers, garlic, salt, and black pepper, mixing well. Transfer ingredients to a large heavy skillet and cook over moderate heat until pork and vegetables are tender, about 2 to 3 minutes. Add rice and water, mixing well. Reduce heat, cover, and cook for 5 minutes. Remove skillet from heat, allow rice to stand, covered, for about 30 to 35 minutes, or until rice is tender and all liquid is absorbed.

or 1 teaspoon dried
thyme
1 tablespoon minced fresh
or 1 teaspoon dried
oregano
1 teaspoon cayenne pepper
or to taste
1 teaspoon crushed dried
hot red pepper or to taste
2 teaspoons minced peeled
garlic
1 1/2 teaspoons salt or to
taste
1 1/2 teaspoons black
pepper or to taste
3/4 cup converted rice
2 1/2 cups water

–Chef Nate Johnson
Rick Giovannoni, proprietor
Stonewall Cafe

Old Menu:Violet Luncheon, (Cir. 1894),

1. *Grape fruit., Sucre au Rhum., 2. Puree of spinach., 3. Oyster-crab pates served in violet paper chrysanthemums., 4. Breast of chicken with potato croquettes., 5. Sweet-breads and truffles served in violet paper cups, trimmed with violets., 6. Omelette au Rhum., 7. Salad with tomatoes and mayonnaise., 8. Ice-cream in form of eggs, halved, showing yelk., 9. Strawberries and whipped cream., Bonbons, cake, and salted almonds., Cordial and coffee, Champagne served throughout the luncheon.,*

Mrs. George deB. Keim,
F.F.V. Receipt Book, 1894,

Carr's Hill Pineapple Rice

Yield: 8 servings

"Excellent!!! A big hit with everyone."

1 1/3 cups rice
1 cup butter or margarine
1 (20-ounce) can crushed
  pineapple, undrained (see
  note)
1 cup sugar
2 teaspoons nutmeg
2 to 3 tablespoons water as
  needed (optional)

Cook rice according to package directions; drain well. (see note) In a medium heavy saucepan, melt butter over low heat. Add crushed pineapple and sugar; simmer over low heat until mixture is a thin syrup. Remove; stir in nutmeg. Spoon rice and pineapple sauce in alternating layers, ending with a layer of sauce, into a greased 13 x 8 x 2-inch baking dish. Bake, uncovered, in a moderate oven (350 degrees F.) for 30 minutes or until top is lightly browned. If rice begins to get dry before browning, add 2 to 3 tablespoons of water.

Note: Remove rice carefully from pan with a fork so as not to mash the grains. Cooked rice should yield about 4 cups.

Note: Use sweetened or unsweetened pineapple, as desired.

–Eddy Dalton (Mrs. John)
First Lady of Virginia, 1978 to 1982
Virginia State Senator, 1987 to -

Old Richmond Advertisement, date unknown

Wild Rice

A new food to early colonists was wild rice, which is not a true rice, but rather the seed of a tall aquatic grass, zizania aquatica, native to North America and Asia. In pre-colonial days it was an important food of the native Indians.Two-thirds of the world's supply is now grown in the United States in northern Minnesota in the lake region along the Canadian border.

Wild Rice Mushroom Pilaf

Yield: 10 to 12 servings

Wild rice is a costly delicacy, but it makes a magnificent addition to any fowl dinner.

1 (4-ounce) package wild rice
1 cup long grain rice
6 slices bacon, diced
1 cup chopped peeled onion
8 ounces mushrooms, sliced
1 cup chopped green pepper
1 teaspoon salt
1 teaspoon curry powder
1 (13 3/4-ounce) can chicken broth, undiluted

Cook both rices as directed on package labels. In a large heavy skillet, pan-fry bacon until crisp; drain and reserve drippings.Sauté onion in bacon drippings until tender but not brown. Add mushrooms and green pepper and cook until mushrooms are tender and most of the liquid has evaporated. Sprinkle with salt and curry powder. Combine rices, vegetables, and broth, mixing well. Spoon into a greased round 2-quart casserole. Cover and bake in a moderate oven (350 degrees F.) for 25 to 30 minutes. Serve with chicken, duck,or turkey, or in place of potatoes with any favorite entrée.

Mock Macaroni

Break some crackers in small pieces, soak them in milk until they are soft; then use them as a substitute for macaroni.

The Virginia Housewife, *1831*

325

Wild Rice with Pecan Basil Butter

Yield: 6 servings

8 ounces wild rice (see note)

About 2 cups hot chicken stock or broth as needed

1/4 cup chopped green onion (include some green tops)

Salt and pepper to taste

1/2 cup clarified butter (see index)

1 1/2 to 2 tablespoons fresh basil leaves

1/2 cup coarsely chopped pecans

In a large heavy saucepan, bring wild rice and hot chicken stock to boiling over moderate heat. Add green onions and salt and pepper to taste. Continue to cook according to package directions, until wild rice is tender and chicken stock absorbed. In a blender container, combine clarified butter and basil leaves; cover and process until leaves are coarsely chopped. Transfer mixture to a small heavy saucepan; stir over low heat until butter is melted. Add pecans. Pour hot mixture over cooked wild rice and toss lightly with a fork. Adjust seasoning as desired. Serve immediately.

Note: 4 ounces wild rice and 4 ounces long-grain brown rice may be substituted for 8 ounces wild rice.

–Chef James and Lynn News, proprietors
Mr. Patrick Henry's Restaurant and Inn

Bacon and Scrambled Rice

16 Slices Bacon, 4 Cupsful Boiled Rice, 6 Eggs., Fry bacon, carefully making it crisp and attractive, but do not scorch. Arrange sliced around the edges of a platter. Pour off half of the fat from the bacon, leaving remainder in frying pan. Add two cupsful of the boiled rice (separated grains) into which the eggs have been stirred. Stir the rice and the bacon fat until hot, then heap it in the center of the platter.

Old Virginia Cooking, *circa 1909*

Antique Menu(Cir. 1839)

Breakfast, Sliced Oranges, BaconGriddle Cakes, Boiled Eggs, Coffee, Luncheon, Baked Potaoes (served with Butter and Milk), Spring OnionsGluten Gems, Stewed Peaches, Cocoa, Dinner, Lamb Stew (made from ends of Sunday's forequarters), Hash Browned Potatoes, Glazed Carrots, Fresh Tomato Salad, Cafe Frappe

Virginia Cook Book, 1839

Vegetables
and
Side Dishes

Asparagus Mousse with Beurre Blanc

Yield: 6 servings

2 pounds medium asparagus, trimmed and peeled
1/2 cup heavy cream
About 3 eggs, slightly beaten (see note)
1 1/2 teaspoons minced fresh tarragon (optional) (see note)
Salt and white pepper to taste
Butter, at room temperature
2 medium firm ripe tomatoes, peeled, halved, pulp removed, and cut into 1/4-inch slices
Beurre Blanc (see index)
Fresh tarragon or dill leaves for garnish (optional)

Tie asparagus with string into small bundles, about 5 to 6 per bundle. Bring a large heavy, non-aluminum pot of salted water to a boil over high heat. Add asparagus and cook, uncovered, for 3 to 5 minutes or until the tip of a sharp knife pierces the center of an asparagus stalk easily. Drain well and immerse in ice water; allow asparagus to cool thoroughly. Trim 18 asparagus to 3-inch lengths from the tips. Cover asparagus tips with absorbent paper or plastic wrap; refrigerate until ready to use. Transfer trimmings and remaining asparagus to a heavy, non-aluminum saucepan. Add cream; simmer, uncovered, over low heat until asparagus are tender and cream is reduced by one half, about 10 minutes.

Transfer hot mixture to the container of a food blender or processor; cover and blend until mixture is puréed. Press purée through a medium strainer. Allow to cool. Purée should measure about 1 1/2 cups. Stir eggs and tarragon, if desired, into asparagus purée. Season with salt and white pepper to taste.

Thoroughly butter six 2 1/2-ounce heat-proof molds; place molds in freezer for 2 minutes. Butter molds again, then evenly spray each with vegetable cooking spray or line buttered molds with buttered parchment. Spoon asparagus mixture into prepared molds, dividing evenly and filling each to just below the rim.

Arrange filled molds in a roasting pan or a 13 x 9 x 2-inch baking pan; cover molds loosely with buttered parchment. Add enough boiling water to pan to cover about three-fourths of each mold. Bake in a slow oven (325 degrees F.) for 20 to 30 minutes or until a silver knife inserted in center of a mousse comes out clean. Turn molds 90 degrees about halfway through baking.

Invert each mousse onto an individual salad plate. Arrange 3 reserved asparagus tips around each mousse and garnish each with julienne strips of tomato. Spoon Beurre Blanc over one end and to the side of each mousse. Sprinkle each with minced tarragon or dill leaves, if desired.

Note: Use one egg for each 1/2 cup asparagus purée.

Note: Use *only* fresh tarragon.

–The Country Club of Virginia

The early Greeks especially liked asparagus and sometimes decorated their tombs with drawings of the favored vegetable. Julius Ceasar preferred it boiled, granished with butter.

Crunchy Asparagus Casserole

Yield: 8 servings

4 tablespoons flour
1/4 cup butter or margarine, melted
1/2 to 1 teaspoon Worcestershire sauce
4 to 5 drops hot sauce
2 cups milk
Salt and pepper to taste
2 (15-ounce) cans asparagus spears, drained (reserve 1/2 cup liquid) (see note)
2 hard-cooked eggs, peeled and sliced
1 (2-ounce) jar chopped pimentos, drained
8 ounces toasted slivered blanched almonds, lightly toasted
2 cups shredded sharp Cheddar cheese

In a heavy saucepan, blend flour into melted butter until smooth; add Worcestershire and hot sauces. Gradually add milk; cook, stirring constantly, over moderate heat until thickened and bubbly hot. Add salt and pepper to taste. Arrange half of the asparagus spears in a greased 2-quart baking dish. Layer in order: half of the eggs, half of the pimento, and half of the almonds. Sprinkle with half of the cheese. Repeat the process. Add a small amount of reserved asparagus liquid to mixture; evenly spoon white sauce over casserole. Bake, uncovered, in a moderate oven (350 degrees F.) for 25 to 30 minutes or until bubbly hot.

Note: 2 pounds partially cooked fresh or 2 (10-ounce) packages partially cooked frozen asparagus may be substituted. Do not overcook. Reserve 1/2 cup of water in which asparagus are cooked.

–Sue Crowell (Mrs. Robert)

329

> *Although the early colonists were familiar with the broad bean of Europe, the varieties growing naturally in the Americas....wax, pole, navy, lima, kidney, string or snapbeans were new to them. When the beans were first introduced to Europeans with the Spanish returning from Mexican exploration, they were called Haricots, translated from the Aztec name of ayocotl. Haricot verde or verts still refers to tender young green beans. A good test for freshness is to break a bean, listening for a crisp snap.*

Black Bean Cakes with Fresh Tomato Salsa

Yield: 8 servings, about 16 bean cakes

Top these savory Black Bean Cakes with Fresh Tomato Salsa and sour cream and serve with grilled meat as an entrée, or serve unaccompanied as an appetizer.

1 pound dried black beans
Water as needed
3 tablespoons olive oil
2 ounces (about 1/3 cup) chopped bacon
1/3 cup chopped peeled onion
2 beef bouillon cubes, mashed
3/4 teaspoon salt
2 tablespoons chili powder
1 tablespoon minced jalãpeno pepper
1 tablespoon ground cumin
3/4 teaspoon garlic powder or 1 teaspoon garlic juice
Hot cooking oil as needed
Fresh Tomato Salsa (see index)
Sour cream for garnish

In a large bowl, soak beans in water to cover for 4 to 8 hours; drain well. In a Dutch oven or heavy kettle, heat olive oil over moderate heat. Reduce heat and add beans, 6 cups of water, bouillon cubes, and salt. Simmer, uncovered, for about 2 hours or until beans are tender. If much water remains, drain, reserving liquid. Mash beans; place in a blender container, food processor container, or mixing bowl. Cover blender or food processor container; blend or beat until mashed beans are smooth. Add seasonings and jalapeno pepper, mixing well. If bean mixture is too dry, add a small amount of reserved liquid as needed. Cool. Evenly shape mixture into 16 2-ounce patties. In a large heavy skillet, sauté bean "cakes" in a small amount of cooking oil over moderate heat until crisp and heated through, about 2 minutes per side.

–The Tobacco Company Restaurant

330

Cheesy Green Bean Casserole

Yield: 8 servings

2 (10-ounce) packages frozen French-style green beans (see note)
3 tablespoons butter or margarine, melted and divided
2 1/2 tablespoons flour
2 teaspoons sugar
1 teaspoon salt
2 cups shredded Swiss cheese
1 cup sour cream
4 teaspoons minced peeled onion
1 cup cornflakes, finely crushed

Cook green beans according to package directions until beans are *just* tender but firm; drain well. *Do not overcook.* Spread green beans over the bottom of a greased 12 x 8 x 2-inch baking dish. In a small heavy saucepan, blend flour into 2 tablespoons butter until smooth. Stir in sugar and salt. Add cheese, sour cream, and onion, mixing well; evenly spoon over green beans. Combine cornflakes and 1 tablespoon butter, coating cornflakes well; evenly sprinkle over cheese mixture. Bake, uncovered, in a moderate oven (350 degrees F.) for 25 to 30 minutes or until top is golden brown and casserole bubbly hot.

Note: 1 to 1 1/2 pounds whole fresh green beans may be substituted for frozen green beans. Trim ends from beans. Cook in boiling water *just* to cover for 3 to 4 minutes after water returns to boil, until beans are *just* tender but firm; drain well.

–Dotty Stuart (Mrs. Albert)

Old Richmond Advertisement, circa 1909

Virginia Cookery is unique in that it owes its reputation to the fine flavor and unusual taste of simple foods rather than to elaborate presentations of newly created specialties. Yet these plain, substantial Virginia dishes contain a rare quality of goodness unattainable by the average cook unversed in the ways of Virginia Cooking.

Unquestionably, the individual quality of Southern Cooking can be attributed to the Negro mammy of plantation days whose explanation of her art was expressed by, "a handful of dis, an' a pinch of dat." Despite this vague explanation the art has by no means been lost, any visitor to Virginia will attest...

...These old recipes will prove interesting to all gourmets. Especially will the modern cooks marvel at the size of the portions designated in the recipes. Let these present day cooks recall that the cook of the plantation days was daily called upon to serve guests in a number which would tax the capacity of many modern hotels. When you visit old Virginia homes notice the kitchen, usually a large building separate from the main residence — dedicated to the presentation of wholesome food.

Southern Cooking, 1939

Herbed Green Beans

Yield: 4 to 6 servings

1 pound green beans,
  cleaned and tips removed
Salted boiling water as
  needed
1/2 cup minced peeled
  onion
1 garlic clove, peeled and
  minced
2 tablespoons butter or
  margarine, melted
2 tablespoons minced
  parsley

In a heavy saucepan, cook green beans, uncovered, in boiling water to cover for 10 to 15 minutes, just until tender but firm; drain well. In a small heavy saucepan, combine onion, garlic, and butter; simmer over low heat for 5 minutes. Add parsley, rosemary, and basil; cover and continue to simmer for an additional 5 minutes. Add herb mixture to beans; toss lightly, coating beans with herbed butter. Transfer to a heated serving bowl.

3/4 to 1 teaspoon minced
  fresh or 1/4 teaspoon
  dried rosemary
3/4 to 1 teaspoon minced
  fresh or 1/4 teaspoon
  dried basil

–Margaret Bruckhart (Mrs. Robert)

Refried Beans

Yield: 4 to 6 servings

1 cup dried pinto beans
Hot water as needed
1 garlic clove, peeled and
  chopped (see note)
1/2 small onion, peeled and
  chopped
1/2 cup cooking oil or
  shortening (see note)
Salt and pepper to taste

Sort beans, removing any foreign matter. In a large bowl, soak beans in hot water to cover for 8 hours; drain well. Transfer beans to a large heavy saucepan; add hot water to cover, garlic and onion. Simmer, cover ajar, over moderate heat until beans are *very* tender, about 2 hours. Add more hot water as necessary to beans during cooking. Most of the liquid should be absorbed during cooking. In a small heavy saucepan, heat oil or shortening to about 350 degrees F.. Pour hot oil over beans and then mash thoroughly, mixing well. Season with salt and pepper to taste. Stir over low heat until mixture is bubbly hot.

Note: Add more garlic to taste, if desired.

Note: Amount of oil may be reduced, if desired.

Variation: Chill mashed beans thoroughly in refrigerator. Add 1 beaten egg and 2 to 3 drops hot sauce, if desired, mixing well. Shape mixture into 4 to 6 equal-sized thick patties. Dredge patties lightly in flour. In a heavy skillet, pan-fry bean patties in 2 to 3 tablespoons hot oil over moderate to high heat for about 3 minutes per side or until patties are crisp and lightly browned on the outside.

–Michel Zazur Jr., proprietor
La Siesta Restaurant

The Half Way House was built in 1760 by William Hatcher on a grant of land from George II of England by a patent dated 1743. Built as a horse change and rest stop for the Petersburg Coach, the Inn was so named for its location midway between Richmond and Petersburg. While the out buildings are reconstructed, the manor house is original and is furnished in authentic antiques.

Among the Inn's famous guests were Washington, LaFayette, Patrick Henry, Jefferson, Lee, James Whitcomb Riley, and scores of others. As the horse change and rest stop for the coach, everyone who traveled south of Richmond, dating from the Revolution until late in the nineteenth century, stopped for rest and refreshment.

During the spring of 1864 General Butler of the northern Army of the James made the Inn his headquarters while trying to capture Richmond. In mid-May the opposing Union and Confederate forces faced each other on a line running from Centralia to the river, just north of the house. Soon after, Ransom's Division broke through the northern right flank, causing a collapse of the entire northern line and withdrawal of Union troops to Bermuda Hundred.

The Half Way House served the public through the Civil War, closing during the time of Reconstruction. Brydon Tennant. a Petersburg lawyer, purchased and restored the Inn early in the twentieth century, opening it periodically to the public. In November, 1941, Fred and Dorothy Bender purchased it from Mr. Tennant's estate. Opened on March 21, 1942, it has since served the Richmond-Petersburg public as a restaurant.

Half Way House Green Beans

Yield: 8 to 10 servings

6 slices bacon
1 medium onion, peeled and chopped
4 firm ripe tomatoes, peeled

In a large heavy skillet, pan-fry bacon over moderate heat until crisp; remove and drain well on absorbent paper. Crumble bacon and set aside. Sauté onion in hot bacon drippings until tender

and chopped
2 tablespoons sugar
Salt and pepper to taste
2 (16-ounce) packages
   frozen French-style green
   beans, thawed (see note)

but not browned. Add tomatoes and sugar. Season with salt and pepper to taste, mixing lightly. Reduce heat and simmer until tomatoes are tender, about 10 minutes. Add green beans, mixing lightly with sauce; continue to simmer, uncovered, until vegetable mixture is heated through. Sprinkle crumbled bacon over each portion just before serving.

Note: 2 pounds fresh cut or French-cut (sliced one or more times lengthwise) or whole green beans may be substituted for frozen beans. Partially cook beans in a small amount of boiling water for 8 to 10 minutes; drain well.

—Sue and Rick Young, proprietors
Half Way House Restaurant

Cabbage is referred to as man's best friend in the vegetable world. Because of it's high nutritional quality in minerals and vitamins and available varieties, no other vegetable rates as well in comparison.

To the ancient Greeks and Romans, cabbage was not considered in the way we do today. Only the leafy varieties which do not form a head grew well in the Mediterranean climate of ancient Greece, Rome, and Egypt. Such foodstuffs as kale and collard greens, dear to any southerner's heart, were tolerable to the warm climate.

Head-forming cabbages are thought to have arrived in the cooler areas of Europe via the Celts about 600 B.C. Broccoli and cauliflower, more developed forms of the cabbage, are believed not to have made an entrance to the culinary scene until the Middle Ages. Others, however, suggest broccoli was known by the ancient Romans. In fact, the word derives from the Latin bracchium meaning branch or arm. And, of course, Thomas Jefferson grew it at Monticello in the eighteenth century. Plant historians suggest cabbage and its variations were not known in the ancient kingdoms of the far East.

Cabbage Pudding

Take one nice head of cabbage. Scoop out the middle; prepare a rich force-meat made out of cold fowl, or fresh beef chopped up fine; season highly with butter, pepper, and salt; chop six hard-boiled eggs fine, with the force-meat; fill the cavity in the cabbage with this mixture; place a leaf of the cabbage over the hole to keep the meat in; tie it up in a cloth and boil it, serving up with drawn-butter sauce.

Virginia Cookery Book, 1885

I remember something the General said when we began to have parties at clubs, and hotels. "This is all very grand," he observed," and it saves a lot of trouble, but no one is going to ask me to eat chicken hash and batter cakes tomorrow morning."
Helena Lefroy Caperton
"Time Gambols Withal,"
The Richmond News Leader, 1931

Tangy Baked Broccoli 'N Cheese Casserole

Yield: 6 to 8 servings

2 (10 -ounce) packages
frozen chopped broccoli
1 (10 3/4-ounce) can cream
of mushroom soup,
undliuted
1 cup mayonnaise or
commercial cooked salad
dressing
1/2 cup grated shredded
sharp Cheddar or Swiss
cheese
1 tablespoon chopped
peeled onion
Salt and pepper to taste
4 to 5 drops hot sauce
(optional)
1/2 cup buttered bread
crumbs

Partially cook broccoli according to package directions after water returns to a boil for 2 to 3 minutes, or until tender but crisp. Drain well. In a medium bowl, combine broccoli, soup, mayonnaise, cheese, and onion. Season with salt and pepper to taste. Add hot sauce, if desired. Evenly spoon into a greased 2-quart baking dish. Evenly sprinkle bread crumbs over casserole. Bake, uncovered, in a moderate oven (375 degrees F.) for 45 minutes or until bubbly hot and crumbs lightly browned.

–Kimberly Jennings

Buttered Brussels Sprouts with Walnuts

Yield: 4 to 6 servings

1 pound Brussels sprouts
(see note)
Salted boiling water as
needed
1/3 to 1/2 cup chopped
English or black walnuts
2 to 3 tablespoons butter or
margarine, melted
Salt and pepper to taste

Cook Brussels sprouts, cover ajar, in salted boiling water to just cover for 10 to 15 minutes or until tender but crisp; drain well. Add walnuts and butter, tossing lightly to mix. Season with salt and pepper to taste.

Note: 1 pound of Brussels sprouts equals about 4 cups. 1 1/2 to 2 (10-ounce) packages frozen Brussels sprouts may be substituted for fresh Brussels sprouts, if desired; cook according to package directions.

–Elinor Kuhn (Mrs. Frank)
Buffet, catering firm
Richmond Culinary Guild

337

Honey Orange Glazed Carrots

Yield: 4 servings

6 to 7 medium carrots,
   peeled and cut crosswise
   into 1/2-inch thick slices
3 whole cloves
1/3 cup orange juice
3 tablespoons butter or
   margarine, melted
1 tablespoon honey
1/4 teaspoon salt
1 tablespoon minced
   parsley

Prepare carrots for cooking. In a medium heavy saucepan, combine all ingredients except parsley. Cook, covered, over moderate heat for 15 to 20 minutes or until carrots are *just* fork tender. Uncover, remove cloves, reduce heat, and continue cooking until most of the liquid has evaporated. Sprinkle parsley over carrots just before serving.

–Carol Bolinger
Richmond Culinary Guild

Nutty Celery Au Gratin

Yield: 6 servings

3 cups coarsely chopped or
   sliced celery
Boiling water as needed
2 tablespoons flour
2 tablespoons butter or
   margarine, melted
1 cup chicken stock or broth
   (see note)
1/4 cup light cream or half-
   and-half
Salt and pepper to taste
1/2 cup toasted slivered
   blanched almonds
1/2 cup chopped sweet red
   or yellow pepper
   (optional)
1 cup shredded sharp
   Cheddar cheese
1/2 cup buttered bread or
   cornflake crumbs
Paprika for garnish

In a heavy saucepan, cook celery in a small amount of boiling water until tender but crisp, about 5 to 10 minutes after water returns to a boil; drain well. In a heavy saucepan, blend flour into butter until smooth. Gradually add chicken stock and cream; cook, stirring constantly, over moderate heat until thickened and bubbly hot. Season with salt and pepper to taste. Add celery, almonds, sweet red pepper, if desired, mixing well. Spoon into a greased 9 x 9 x 2-inch baking dish. Evenly sprinkle with cheese and then buttered crumbs. Bake, uncovered, in a moderate oven (350 degrees F.) for 20 minutes or until bubbly hot, cheese melted, and crumbs lightly browned. Remove from oven and lightly sprinkle with paprika for garnish.

Note: 1 (10 3/4-ounce) can chicken broth may be substituted.

–Virginia Cottrell (Mrs. Walker C., Jr.)

Southern Corn Pudding

Yield: 4 to 6 servings

1 2/3 cups milk
2 tablespoons sugar
2 tablespoons butter or
  margarine, at room
  temperature
1 teaspoon salt
3 eggs, beaten
1 (8-ounce) can whole-
  kernel corn, drained

In a medium heavy saucepan, bring milk to a scald over moderate heat; milk will form small bubbles around the edge of the pan. *Do not boil.* Add sugar, butter, and salt, stirring with a wire whisk, until butter is melted. Stir a small amount of milk mixture into beaten eggs. Stir egg mixture into remaining milk mixture in pan. Reduce temperature and continue to stir mixture over low heat for 2 minutes. Add corn, mixing well. Spoon mixture into a greased 1 1/2-quart casserole. Bake, uncovered, in a hot oven (400 degrees F.) for 25 minutes or until a silver knife inserted in center of pudding comes out clean.

–Swift Creek Mill Playhouse

Tasty Corn Pudding

Yield: 6 servings

2 (8-ounce) cans whole-
  kernel corn, drained
1 1/2 cups milk, scalded
  (see note)
1/2 cup honey
2 tablespoons butter or
  margarine (see note)
1 teaspoon vanilla extract
Pinch of salt (optional)

In a bowl, combine all ingredients, blending well. Pour mixture into a greased 1-quart casserole. Bake, uncovered, in a moderate oven (375 degrees F.) for 35 to 40 minutes or until a silver knife inserted in the center of the casserole comes out clean.

Note: Ms. McDaniel suggests vegetarians may substitute soy drink for cows milk.

Note: Ms. McDaniel suggests vegetarians use margarine made from soy beans.

–Claudette Black McDaniel
Vice Mayor, 1988 to 1990
Richmond City Council

> Corn is considered the all-American grain. Native to North and South America, it sustained the early colonists when not much else was available to eat.

Country Fresh Corn

Yield: 4 servings

Richmonders thoroughly enjoy the white corn, often the Silver Queen variety, that arrives in early summer fresh from the nearby fields to the fruit and vegetables stands of Richmond. Prepared in a variety of ways, the corn is especially sweet and tender.

4 medium ears white corn, husks removed (see note)
1 cup milk or half-and-half
1 tablespoon butter or margarine
1 tablespoon sugar
1/2 teaspoon salt or to taste
1/4 teaspoon pepper or to taste

Using a very sharp knife, cut kernels from ears of corn (this will yield about 1 1/2 to 2 cups). In a small heavy saucepan, combine corn kernels, milk, butter, sugar, salt, and pepper. Cook, partially covered, stirring occasionally, over moderate heat for 10 to 12 minutes or until corn is tender.

Note: White corn is preferred by Richmonders because it is more tender and sweet than yellow corn; however, the yellow corn may be substituted for the white, if desired. About 1 1/2 to 2 cups frozen corn kernels may be substituted for the fresh corn.

–Vernelle Thomas

> ....The dining room was still in the basement. Probably about 1889 the kitchen was moved from the separate outbuilding to the basement warming room, which was subdivided at one end to provide a narrow pantry.
>
> William Seal
> **Virginia's Executive Mansion: A History of The Governor's House**, 1988

A Mess O' Greens

Yield: 6 servings

No true, self respecting Richmonder will be without a good recipe for "a pot of greens." Sometimes called Créases, referring to the edible leafy green often used in the vegetable combination, a pot o' greens of earlier times with a hunk of country ham thrown in was often the main meal with poor households throughout the South. Now it is considered a culinary delicacy by many. The pot likker, chock full of vitamins, is equally as good to drink.

1 1/2 pounds kale (see note)
1 1/2 pounds turnip greens (see note)
Water as needed
2 to 3 slices bacon, cut into 1/2-inch pieces
1 country ham hock, cut into small pieces
2 tablespoons white vinegar
1 tablespoon sugar
1 tablespoon Worcestershire sauce or to taste
1/2 teaspoon salt or to taste
1/8 teaspoon pepper or to taste
Additional white vinegar as desired
Thinly sliced green onions or chopped peeled yellow onions as desired

In a large heavy pot, combine kale, turnip greens, and enough water to cover. Bring to a boil over moderate heat; reduce and simmer mixture for 30 minutes. Drain well. Return greens to pot; add enough water to cover. Return mixture to a boil; reduce temperature and simmer again for 30 minutes. Drain well. Return greens to pot; add bacon pieces, ham hock pieces, vinegar, sugar, and seasonings; add enough water to just cover. Bring mixture to a boil; reduce temperature and simmer, uncovered, for 2 1/2 to 3 hours. Top each serving with white vinegar and/or sliced green onions or chopped yellow onions.

Note: A mixture of mustard greens, collards, turnips greens, and kale to equal 3 pounds may be used, if desired.

–J. Robert Carlton

Better to serve his accelerated social life, Governor Lee ordered an expansion of the kitchen with the purchase of an iron stove, boilers, cake molds, and various other culinary devices.

William Seal
**Virginia's Executive Mansion:
A History of the Governor's House**, 1988

Ratatouille Nicoise

Yield: 6 servings

"This dish is excellent hot or cold."

3 pounds medium tomatoes
Boiling water as needed
4 medium green peppers, cored, seeded, and cut into 1-inch squares
3 medium eggplant, cut into 1-inch cubes
3 medium zucchini, cut into 1-inch cubes
2 large onions, peeled and cut into thin wedges
Hot olive oil as needed
1 to 2 garlic cloves, peeled and minced
1 bay leaf, crumbled and/or 1 tablespoon minced fresh or 1 teaspoon dried basil
Salt and pepper to taste

Dip tomatoes in boiling water; core and peel. Place tomatoes in a greased 1 1/2-quart casserole; bake, covered, in a slow oven (325 degrees F.) for 15 to 20 minutes or until tender but firm. *Do not overcook* tomatoes. While tomatoes are cooking, saute eggplant in a large heavy skillet in 3 to 4 tablespoons olive oil over moderate heat until tender but firm and not browned; remove and repeat process with zucchini, peppers, and onion, adding olive oil to skillet as necessary. Add vegetables, garlic, bay leaf, and/or basil to tomatoes, mixing well. Season with salt and pepper to taste. Continue to bake, uncovered, for 45 to 50 minutes. *Do not overbake*; vegetables should not be mushy.

–Ann Jenkins (Mrs. Alfred)

....Constance du Pont Darden, called by her husband "Connie,"was a devoted naturalist, interested from childhood in wildlifeand native plants. She kept a "victory garden" in the old kitchenyard, a shaggy lawn where no garden had been planted or chickenskept for forty years at least. Convicts worked it under her direction, and the produce of corn, beans, tomatoes, squash,greens, peppers, and potatoes abounded on the mansion's dinnertable. (circa 1942)

William Seal
Virginia's Executive Mansion:
A History of the Govenor's House, 1988

Baked Onions Au Gratin

Yield: 6 servings

6 medium onions, peeled and cut into thin wedges (see note)
Salted boiling water
2 tablespoons butter or margarine, melted
2 tablespoons flour
1 (5 1/3-ounce) can evaporated milk
1 cup chicken broth (see note)
1/2 cup slivered blanched almonds
1/2 teaspoon salt
1/2 teaspoon pepper
1/2 cup shredded sharp Cheddar or Monterey Jack cheese
1 cup breadcrumbs

In a medium heavy saucepan, partially cook onion wedges in salted boiling water until tender but crisp, about 10 minutes; drain well. In a medium heavy saucepan, combine butter and flour, blending to form a smooth paste. Gradually add evaporated milk and broth, blending well. Cook, stirring constantly, over moderate heat until sauce is thickened and bubbly hot. Fold in onion wedges and almonds. Stir in salt and pepper. Spoon into a lightly greased 1 1/2-quart casserole. Evenly sprinkle cheese over onion mixture and then sprinkle bread crumbs over cheese. Bake, uncovered, in a moderate oven (375 degrees F.) for 30 minutes or until bubbly hot and topping is lightly browned.

Note: Use a mild sweet onion such as the Vidalia variety.
Note: 1 chicken bouillon cube plus 1 cup water may be substituted for chicken broth.
–Frances Fox (Mrs. Paul)

Field Rations For A Civilian Soldier

(At the time of Dahlgren's Raid around Richmond in February-March, 1864) ... all there was to oppose him was a force of local soldiery and a battalion of department clerks. The members of Congress shouldered guns and mounted guard around Richmond. But the small force of department clerks and unskilled soldiers were a match for Dahlgren, and averted the plot he had formed to pour fire upon the devoted capital of the Confederacy. But we soldiers were hungry. I had had nothing to eat all day, and the heartiest meal I ever enjoyed was a piece of dry bread and a raw onion that I asked of an old market woman as she passed me where I was keeping guard. That was the best onion I ever ate in my life.

Thomas J. Semmes
in **XXV Southern Historical Society Papers**

Glazed Baked Onions

Yield: 4 servings

Use a sweet onion such as a Vidalia variety. Oval shaped onions with flat tops and bottoms are also usually more sweet than completely round ones.

4 medium to large yellow or white onions, peeled (see note)

1/4 cup butter or margarine,. melted

1 tablespoon light brown sugar, firmly packed

2 teaspoons Worcestershire sauce

3 to 4 drops hot sauce

1/4 cup honey, divided (optional)

Paprika for garnish (optional)

Remove peel from onions; with a sharp knife, cut a small thin slice from the top and bottom of each onion. Cut onions in half crosswise, or leave whole, as desired. In a 9 x 9 x 2-inch baking dish, combine butter, brown sugar, Worcestershire sauce, and hot sauce. Place onion halves, cut-side down in sauce, coating surface well. Turn onions, cut side up. For whole onions, coat each completely in sauce. Bake, covered, in a moderate oven (375 degrees F.) for 1 to 1 1/2 hours for onion halves and 1 1/2 to 2 hours for whole onions or until fork tender, basting onions frequently with sauce. Remove cover and brush each onion half with 1/2 tablespoon honey or each whole onion with 1 tablespoon honey, if desired. Continue baking, uncovered, for 20 to 25 minutes or until onions are lightly browned andvery tender. To serve, spoon sauce over each portion and sprinkle lightly with paprika, if desired.

...turnpikes bore the highest rank in furnishing the tracks for travel or trade, but not a turnpike road entered Richmond, and the natural ones (so called) were almost impassable in wet seasons and in winter, when the farmers were most at leisure to send their crops to market.

The Brook Turnpike, towards the north, was the first one constructed, then, north-westwardly, the Richmond turnpike, in the line of Broad street; the Westham, in the direction its name indicates, and lastly, the Mechanicsville, north-east-wardly; but neither of these extended beyond eight or ten miles, and some of them soon acquired the name of mud pikes, the demand of toll being the only distinction by which to know them from county roads.

Samuel Mordecai
Richmond in By-Gone Days, 1856
Reprint Edition, 1975

Violet Luncheon
(Cir. 1894)

1. *Grape fruit.*
   Sucre au Rhum.
2. *Puree of spinach.*
3. *Oyster-crab pates served in violet paper chrysanthe mums.*
4. *Breast of chicken with potato croquettes.*
5. *Sweet-breads and truffles served in violet paper cups trimmed with violets.*
6. *Omelette au Rhum.*
7. *Salad with tomatoes and mayonnaise.*
8. *Ice-cream in form of eggs, halved, showing yelk.*
9. *Strawberries and whipped cream.*
   Bonbons, cake, and salted almonds.
   Cordial and coffee

Champagne served throughout the luncheon.

Mrs. George deB. Keim
F.F.V. Receipt Book, 1894

Old Richmond Advertisement, circa 1909

345

Five years have flown past since that otherwise unremark-
able and altogether forgettable Tuesday afternoon in August
when the then editor of these columns gazed upon a hole in
Wednesday's page. That is to say, he measured the column
inches of profundity that would be required to him tomorrow,
and found their number 43; and he measured the galleys of
his wisdom in type and found them 31. He was, in brief, a
foot short.

So our then editor wrote a foot's worth of copy about the
black-eyed pea.

Here the black-eyed pea was described merely as succulent,
superlative, tender, delicious, supremely nourishing, and altogether ravishing. The editorial scarcely got to its merits atall.
It was but the faintest echo of the famous apostrophe delivered
by Dr. George Bagby, late editor of the Lynchburg Virginian:
"Pea, Blessed pea! Thrice-blessed cornfield pea! Sublime
pellet! Celestial molecule! Divine little gob! Oh! Pluperfect
ellipse of vegetable fatness and sweetness! How much is due
thee! All that Virginia is, or has been, or can be, is owed to
thee! Without thee there is no Virginia."

There was a real pea man. Nevertheless, if our own paeon
fell short of Dr. Bagby's, it struck a chord too long silent in our
readers' breasts. The Forum overflowed with tributes to the
Noble Legume, each more fervid than the one before. And
when the then editor suggested that Perhaps a few true believ-
ers in the black-eyed pea might join him for lunch at the John
Marshall, five hundred appeared.

So the Black-Eyed Pea Society of America was born,
flowering in its glory from the 12-inch hole. And the purpose
of this windy reminiscence is to announce that the Society will
sponsor its fourth biennial luncheon at 1 o'clock on the afternoon of Tuesday, September 22, this time at the Hotel Jefferson. The price will shock you: $4.25. It is a terrible commen-
tary on these inflationary times, but it was the best we could
do.

As before, and as always, the perfection of the menu will remain untouched: Ham, cornbread, and all the fresh-picked
black-eyed peas and stewed tomatoes one can eat.

—James J. Kilpatrick
"Return of the Black-eyed Pea,"
The Richmond News Leader, August 31, 1970

Author's update of the Black-eyed Pea Society: James Kilpatrick sadly declares the society to be moribund....just short of the grave. However, he remains Number One Pea and true to his cause. Perhaps the time has come for a revival of the society. All you black-eyed pea lovers unite and carry forth Mr. Kilpatrick's great cause!

Sautéed Black-Eyed Pea Patties

Yield: 4 servings

Many Richmonders do not begin a New Year without eating black-eyed peas to insure their luck throughout the year. These patties are especially good served with stewed tomatoes.

2 cups black-eyed peas
  (about 11 to 12 ounces)
  (see note)
Water as needed
1/2 cup chopped peeled
  onion
1 tablespoon butter or
  margarine, melted
1 egg, beaten
About 1/2 cup plus 2
  tablespoons flour, divided
1 teaspoon minced peeled
  garlic
1 teaspoon Worcestershire
  sauce
1/2 teaspoon seasoned salt
  (optional)
1/8 teaspoon baking powder
3 to 4 drops hot sauce
Salt and pepper to taste
2 tablespoons hot bacon
  drippings or cooking oil

In a large bowl, soak black-eyed peas in 4 to 6 cups water for about 4 hours; drain, rinse thoroughly, and drain again. In a medium heavy saucepan, cook black-eyed peas, uncovered, in about 4 cups water for 30 to 45 minutes or until tender; drain well. While peas are cooking, sauté onion in butter in a heavy skillet over moderate heat until tender but not browned. In a medium bowl, mash one half the cooked peas with a potato masher. In a blender container, place remaining cooked peas; cover and coarsely purée. Add puréed peas to mashed peas. Add sautéed onion, egg, 2 tablespoons flour, garlic, Worcestershire sauce, seasoned salt, baking powder, hot sauce, and salt and pepper to taste to cooked peas, mixing well. Shape mixture into 4 thick patties, about 3 to 4 inches in diameter, dividing evenly. Place patties on a plate or small baking sheet, cover lightly with waxed paper, and refrigerate for at least 1 hour. Dredge patties lightly in remaining 1/2 cup flour. Sprinkle patties lightly with salt and pepper, if desired. In a large heavy skillet, sauté patties in hot bacon drippings or oil over moderate to high heat until golden brown, about 2 to 3 minutes per side. Drain well and serve immediately.

Note: Use fresh, frozen, or drained canned black-eyed peas. Cook frozen black-eyed peas according to package directions.

Mr. Jefferson's Peas

Yield: 4 servings

Mr. Jefferson, a resident of Richmond while he was governor of the Commonwealth in 1779 and 1780, is reputed to have grown over fifty varieties of peas at his home, Monticello, near Charlottesville, Virginia. This recipe is an updated version of one he favored.

1 to 2 tablespoons bacon
  drippings or cooking oil
1 (10-ounce) package,
  frozen very small peas or
2 cups shelled fresh peas
  (see note)
1/2 to 1 ounce fully-cooked
  smoked Smithfield or
  Virginia country-style
  ham, minced (2 to 4 very
  thin slices, about 1/4 to
  1/2 cup minced)
1 1/2 to 2 tablespoons
  minced peeled onion
Pepper to taste

In a medium heavy skillet, heat bacon drippings to about 325 to 350 degrees F.. Break frozen peas into skillet; add ham, mixing well. Stir-fry for 1 to 2 minutes. Add onion, mixing well. Continue to stir-fry for an additional 1 to 2 minutes, or until peas and onion are just tender, and not browned. Do not overcook. Season to taste with pepper. Serve immediately.

Note: 2 cups shelled fresh peas may be blanched or partially cooked in salted boiling water to cover for 2 minutes after water returns to a boil. Drain and sauté as previously directed.

Old Richmond Advertisement, circe 1909

Sautéed Peas and Cucumbers

Yield: 6 servings

Peas have been popular in Virginia since Colonial days. The most famous Virginian to be a devotee of the sweet early spring vegetable was, of course, Thomas Jefferson.

4 medium cucumbers, peeled and cut into 1 1/2-inch chunks
1 1/2 to 2 tablespoons butter or margarine, melted
Salt and pepper to taste
2 cups shelled fresh peas or 1 (10-ounce) package frozen peas, thawed
1/4 cup chicken stock or broth
2 teaspoons minced parsley
1/2 teaspoon minced chives

In a large heavy skillet, sauté cucumber chunks in butter over moderate heat for 5 minutes. Season with salt and pepper to taste. Add peas and stock; continue cooking, uncovered, for 8 minutes for fresh peas and 5 minutes for frozen peas or until cucumbers are translucent. Remove from heat and sprinkle with parsley and chives. Toss lightly to mix. Transfer to a heated serving bowl.

Variation: Add 2 teaspoons drained minced pimento to cooked vegetables with parsley and chives.

–Inger Rice (Mrs. Walter)

William Johnson

For young Johnson, Christmas was a day filled with expectations of "apples and oranges and candy ... and maybe a pair of pants."

Christine Reid
"Christmas in the 1800's"
Richmond Times-Dispatch, December 23, 1984

Baked German Potato "Salad"

Yield: 4 to 6 servings

8 slices bacon
2 to 3 tablespoons reserved hot bacon drippings
1/2 cup chopped celery
1/2 cup thinly sliced green onions (Include some green tops)
1 1/2 tablespoons flour
2/3 cup apple cider or water
1/3 cup cider vinegar
1/3 cup sugar
Salt and pepper to taste
4 cups cubed, peeled cooked potatoes (about 4 medium) (see note)

In a large heavy skillet, pan-fry bacon over moderate heat until crisp; drain bacon well on absorbent paper. Cut one half bacon slices into 1/2-inch pieces; crumble remaining bacon. Sauté celery and onion in reserved bacon drippings over moderate heat until tender but not browned. Sprinkle flour over mixture, blending well; stir in cider or water and vinegar. Cook, stirring constantly, until mixture is thickened and bubbly hot. Stir in sugar, salt, and pepper. Arrange potato cubes and one half of the bacon pieces in a greased 1 1/2-quart casserole. Pour hot sauce over potatoes, mixing lightly. Adjust seasoning, if desired. Bake, covered, in a moderate oven (350 degrees F.) for 20 minutes; uncover, sprinkle remaining crisp crumbled bacon evenly over casserole, and continue baking for 8 to 10 minutes. Serve immediately.

Note: Potatoes should be precooked until just tender. Do not overcook.

Of Judge Marshall I will not presume to say more, than, that his personal appearance and deportment as a citizen were of the most unpretending character—of true republican simplicity—but natural, not assumed—his dress was plain even to negligence, of which he seemed unconscious. He marketed for himself, and might be seen at an early hour returning home, with a pair of fowls, or a basket of eggs in his hand, not with ostentatious humility, but for mere convenience.

–Samuel Mordecai
Richmond in By-Gone Days, 1856
Reprint Edition, 1975

Crusty Au Gratin Potatoes with Bitters

Yield: 6 to 8 servings

4 large or 6 medium baking potatoes (see note)
1/4 cup butter or margarine
4 tablespoons flour
2 cups milk
1 cup shredded sharp Cheddar cheese
Salt and pepper to taste
1 teaspoon Angostura bitters
Pinch of nutmeg or 1/2 teaspoon paprika
About 1/2 cup grated Parmesan cheese

Arrange potatoes on an ungreased baking sheet; bake in a moderate oven (350 degrees F.) for about 50 minutes or until *just* done and tender. Cool, peel, and slice crosswise into medium slices; set aside. In medium heavy saucepan, melt butter over low heat; stir in flour to form a smooth paste. Gradually add milk, blending well. Cook, stirring constantly, over moderate heat until mixture is thickened and bubbly hot. Reduce heat; gradually add cheese, stirring over low heat until cheese is melted. Add salt and blending well. Arrange one half of the potato slices in a greased 2-quart casserole; spoon halfpepper to taste, bitters, and nutmeg or paprika, of the cheese sauce over potatoes in casserole. Arrange remaining potato slices over the first layer; spoon remaining sauce over the second layer of potatoes. Evenly sprinkle Parmesean cheese over the top layer of potatoes. Bake uncovered, in a moderate oven (375 degrees F.) for 20 to 25 minutes or until casserole is bubbly hot and Parmesan cheese is lightly browned.

Note: Use a mealy baking potato such as a russet variety.

–Gladys Antroinen (Mrs. A. P.)

... Beside this liquid refreshment, there was Dabney's boned turkey, boned ham, and bowls of chicken salad. This last was the real thing because the ladies of the household usually cut up the turkey meat and made the mayonnaise themselves. There were hot coquettes, and fried and pickled oysters. In a huge block of ice, scooped out, were raw oysters. There were noble trenchermen in those days with no thought of overweight or calories...

Helena Lefroy Caperton
"Time Gambols Withal"
The Richmond News Leader, 1931

Potatoes Byron

Yield: 6 servings

6 large baking potatoes
Cooking oil as needed
1/4 cup butter or margarine,
   melted
1/2 teaspoon salt or to taste
Pepper to taste
1/2 cup heavy cream
3/4 cup shredded Swiss or
   Emmentaler cheese

Scrub potatoes and rub each lightly with oil; pierce each top with tines of a fork. Arrange on an ungreased baking sheet. Bake in a moderate oven (375 degrees F.) for 1 hour or until potatoes are tender. Remove and cool several minutes until able to handle with the hands. Cut and remove a thin slice horizontally from each potato; scoop out potato pulp and coarsely break up. Add butter, salt, and pepper mixing well; spoon mixture into potato skin shells, dividing evenly. Arrange in a greased 9-inch pie plate or 8 x 8 x 2-inch baking dish; allow to stand for 30 minutes. Pour cream over potato mixture in each shell. Evenly sprinkle each with cheese. Bake in a moderate oven (375 degrees F.) for 20 minutes or until cheese melts and forms crust.

Note: Do not prepare too far in advance

–Priscilla Alexander
Cheese Wedge Committee
St. Christopher's School

Old Richmond Advertisement,
circa 1884

Old Richmond Advertisement,
circa 1884

St. Christopher's School

St. Christopher's School, one of the oldest and most prestigious private schools in Richmond, was founded in 1911 on Grove Avenue as the Chamberlayne School by Dr. Churchill Chamberlayne. Moved to its present location in the Westhampton area of Richmond in 1915, the school was purchased by the Episcopal Diocese of Virginia in 1920 and renamed St. Christopher's. A college preparatory school for boys from kindergarten through the twelfth grade, it presently enrolls nine hundred students. At St. Christopher's, the Mother's Committee Service Auxiliary sponsors many school fund-raising projects throughout the year, one of which was the sale of the Cheese Wedge, a collection of cheese recipes donated by members of the faculty, the auxiliary, and alumni.

Shredded Potato Scallop

Yield: 6 to 8 servings

6 medium potatoes
Boiling salted water as
  needed
2 cups shredded sharp
  Cheddar cheese
1 1/2 cups sour cream
1/3 cup chopped peeled
  onion
1/4 cup butter or margarine,
  melted
1 teaspoon salt or to taste
1/4 teaspoon pepper
2 tablespoons butter or
  margarine, at room
  temperature
Paprika for garnish

In a large heavy saucepan, cook potatoes, covered, in salted boiling water to cover until *just* tender, about 20 to 25 minutes. Drain well, cool, peel, and shred potatoes. In a large bowl, combine cheese, sour cream, onion, melted butter, salt, and pepper. Add shredded potatoes, mixing gently so as not to break or mash potato pieces. Spoon into a lightly greased 2-quart casserole. Evenly dot with remaining 2 tablespoons butter. Bake, uncovered, in a moderate oven (350 degrees F.) for 30 minutes or until casserole is bubbly hot and top is lightly browned. Sprinkle casserole lightly with paprika just before serving.

–Karene Zimmerman

Potato Cake

1 Cupful Butter,
2 Cupsful Franklin Sugar,
4 Well Beaten Eggs,
1 Cupsful Mashed
  Potatoes,
1 Cake Chocolate,
1 Teaspoonful Cloves,
1 Teaspoonful Spice and
  Cinnamon,
1/2 Cupful Milk,
2 1/2 Cupsful Flour,
2 Teaspoonsful Boyd's
  Baking Powder.

Cream together the butter and sugar, add the well beaten eggs, potatoes and melted chocolate, spices, milk and flour into which the baking powder has been sifted. Bake to a delicate brown.

–**Old Virginia Cooking,** circa 1909

Hot Spinach Casserole

Yield: 6 to 8 servings

Although the origin of this casserole is unknown, it is one of the Robb's favorite vegetable recipes and a nice addition to a dinner party menu.

2 (10-ounce) packages
  frozen chopped spinach
Boiling water
2 to 3 tablespoons chopped
  peeled onion
5 to 6 tablespoons butter or
  margarine, melted and
  divided
2 tablespoons flour
1/2 cup evaporated milk
1 teaspoon Worcestershire
  sauce
3/4 teaspoon minced peeled
  garlic
3/4 teaspoon celery salt
Pinch of cayenne pepper
Black pepper to taste
1 (6-ounce) package
  jalapeno-spiced cheese
  food, cut into small
  pieces and melted
1/2 cup coarse breadcrumbs

Cook spinach in boiling water according to package directions; drain well, reserving 1/2 cup cooking liquid. In a small heavy skillet, sauté onion in 4 tablespoons butter over moderate heat until tender but not browned. Add flour, blending well. In a large bowl, combine 1/2 cup spinach liquid, evaporated milk, onion mixture, and seasonings, mixing well. Stir in melted cheese; fold in drained spinach. Spoon into a lightly greased 1 1/2-quart casserole. In a small skillet, sauté breadcrumbs in remaining 2 tablespoons melted butter; do not allow to become too brown. Sprinkle buttered breadcrumbs over casserole. Bake, uncovered, in a moderate oven (350 degrees F.) for 30 minutes or until bubbly hot.

–Lynda Johnson Robb (Mrs. Charles)
First Lady of Virginia, 1982 to 1986

Instruction in cooking with Selected Recipes, circa 1895

355

Baked Seasoned Zucchini Squash

Yield: 4 to 6 servings

4 to 5 medium zucchini or patty-pan squash, thinly sliced crosswise
1 small onion, peeled, cut into thin wedges, and separated into pieces
4 1/2 tablespoons butter or margarine, divided
1 to 1 1/2 teaspoons Worcestershire sauce, divided
Seasoned salt and pepper to taste
2 tablespoons water
1/3 cup fine bread or cornflake crumbs

Arrange one half of the squash and one half of the onion in a 9 x 5 x 3-inch baking dish. Dot with 1 1/2 tablespoons butter and sprinkle with 1/2 to 3/4 teaspoon Worcestershire sauce and seasoned salt and pepper to taste. Arrange remaining squash and onion pieces over first layer of vegetables. Dot with 1 1/2 tablespoon butter and sprinkle with remaining Worcestershire sauce and seasoned salt and pepper to taste. Add water to baking dish. Bake, covered, in a moderate oven (350 degrees F.) for 45 minutes. In a small bowl, combine crumbs and remaining 1 1/2 tablespoons butter, mixing well. With a wooden spoon, lightly mix squash and onions. Sprinkle buttered crumbs evenly over vegetables. Continue baking, uncovered, for 10 to 15 minutes or until squash is tender and crumbs golden brown.

Baked Acorn Squash with Orange Glaze

Yield: 4 to 6 servings

2 to 3 small acorn squash, cut in half crosswise, seeds and pulp removed
Water as needed
6 to 9 tablespoons light brown sugar, firmly packed
1/8 teaspoon nutmeg
Pinch of salt (optional)
2 to 3 tablespoons orange juice
2 to 3 teaspoons butter or margarine, at room temperature and divided

Prepare squash for baking. Arrange squash halves, cut-side turned down, in a 9 x 9 x 2-inch or 13 x 9 x 2-inch baking dish filled with 1/2 inch of water. Bake, covered, in a moderate oven (350 degrees F.) for 1 hour. Add additional water to pan, as necessary. While squash is baking prepare glaze. In a small bowl, combine brown sugar, nutmeg, and salt, mixing well. Gradually add orange juice, blending until mixture is smooth. After the 1 hour baking period, remove squash from oven, drain off water and turn halves in pan, cut side up. Place 1/2 teaspoon butter in the cavity of each squash half. Spoon brown sugar mixture into each cavity, dividing evenly. Bake, uncovered, in a moderate oven (350 degrees F.) for an additional 25 to 30 minutes or until squash is very tender and glaze is lightly browned. Baste surface of the squash halves frequently with the sauce during the last 30 minutes of baking.

Variations: Reduce orange juice by 1 to 2 tablespoons and add 1 to 2 tablespoons orange liqueur or dry sherry to brown sugar mixture. Or, prepare and bake squash as previously directed. Omit brown sugar mixture. Fill each cavity with 2 tablespoons Spiced Cranberries with Port Wine (see index) during the last 30 minutes of baking time

Summer Squash 'N Pepper Sauté

Yield: 4 to 6 servings

6 medium yellow summer squash
Salt as needed
Ice water
3 to 4 tablespoons butter or margarine, divided
1 small onion, peeled and chopped
1 small sweet red pepper, cored, seeded, and coarsely chopped or cut into thin 2-inch strips
3 to 4 tablespoons sour cream
3 to 4 tablespoons grated Parmesan cheese, divided
1/8 teaspoon nutmeg or mace
Pepper to taste
Minced parsley for garnish

Coarsely shred or thinly slice squash crosswise and place in a large glass bowl. Evenly sprinkle with about 1 tablespoon salt, tossing lightly to mix; allow to stand at room temperature for 15 minutes. Rinse thoroughly and return to glass bowl; add ice water to cover. Allow to stand while sautéing onion. In a large heavy skillet, melt 2 tablespoons butter over low heat. Increase temperature to moderate, add onion, and sauté until onion is crisp tender, but firm, about 1 minute. Drain squash and dry thoroughly on absorbent paper. Melt remaining 1 to 2 tablespoons butter in pan with onion. Add squash and pepper strips; sauté over moderate heat until squash and pepper are tender, but crisp and firm, and almost all liquid is absorbed. Reduce heat and stir in sour cream, 2 tablespoons Parmesan cheese, and nutmeg or mace. Add salt if desired, and pepper to taste. Simmer, uncovered, for 1 minute. Sprinkle remaining 1 to 2 tablespoonsful grated cheese over vegetables just before serving. Garnish each serving with minced parsley.

–Laurie Brickham (Mrs. Bruce)

Although used interchangeably in recipes, sweet potatoes and yams are not of the same plant family...sweet potatoes being tubers of a plant of the morning glory family, while yams are edible tubers of another tropical climbing plant.

Sweet potatoes were growing in Virginia when the English colonists arrived, although Columbus had discovered them in the Caribbean islands during his explorations and introduced them to Europeans. He likened the yellow fleshed, sweet flavored vegetable to large radishes, probably because of their shape.

Yams, rounder in shape, with orange colored edible flesh and a sweeter flavor, were first called nyami by black slaves, a Sengalese word for food. The term evolved into yams. Today either root vegetable is available almost year around at the produce departments of nationwide grocery stores. In Virginia, sweet potatoes are a major vegetable crop, grown principally on the Eastern Shore.

Orange-Glazed Sweet Potatoes

Yield: 6 servings

6 sweet potatoes or yams (about 3 pounds) (see note)
1 cup light corn syrup
1 cup sugar
1 cup orange juice
2 tablespoons grated orange peel
2 tablespoons butter or margarine
1 teaspoon salt
1/3 cup toasted slivered blanched or sliced almonds (optional)

Wash the sweet potatoes, but do not peel; cook in boiling water to cover just until tender, about 15 to 20 minutes. Drain, cool, peel, and slice in half lengthwise. Combine the next 6 ingredients in a large heavy skillet; bring to a boil, stirring constantly. Reduce heat and simmer for 5 minutes. Add sweet potatoes and baste with syrup. Cook for 10 to 12 minutes, turning potatoes to glaze evenly. Transfer to a serving dish and spoon glaze over potatoes. Sprinkle with toasted almonds just before serving.

Note: Do not overcook sweet potatoes before glazing. They must be tender but not mushy.

Sweet Potato Croquettes-No. 592

*1 pint mashed sweet
   potatoes,
1/2 teaspoon salt,
1/8 teaspoon pepper,
1 ounce butter,
1 teaspoon sugar,
1/4 teaspoon nutmeg,
3 eggs.*

*To Make: Put the potatoes in a saucepan with
the butter, salt, pepper, nutmeg, and sugar.
When the mixture is hot, stir in one egg; stir until perfectly smooth; set aside to cool. When
cold form into croquettes and finish as directed
(No. 583).*

Author's Note: Dredge croquettes lightly in flour and pan-fry in about 1/2 inch
of hot cooking oil until lightly browned, about 2 to 3 minutes per side. Or, deep
fry in hot cooking oil (375 degrees for about 2 to 3 minutes.

**–Instruction in Cooking
with Selected Receipts,** *1895*

Sweet Potato Pudding

Yield: 6 to 8 servings

*"My mother, Lila Tice, usually serves this recipe as a side dish or vegetable.
However, I usually eat it as a dessert."*

1 cup sugar
1/4 teaspoon salt
Pinch *each* of cinnamon,
   nutmeg, and allspice or to
   taste
1/2 cup butter or margarine,
   at room temperature
3 eggs
1 cup milk
1 teaspoon vanilla extract
1 cup grated peeled raw
   sweet potatoes or yams
3/4 cup pecan halves
1/2 cup flaked coconut

In a small bowl, sift together the sugar, salt, cinnamon, nutmeg, and allspice. In a medium bowl,
lightly beat eggs. Add sugar mixture and butter,
beating well. Add milk and vanilla. Stir in sweet
potatoes, pecan halves, and coconut. Spoon into
a 1 1/2-quart casserole. Bake uncovered, in a
moderate oven (350 degrees F.) for 1 hour or until
a silver knife inserted in the center of the pudding comes out clean.

–Douglas O. Tice, Jr.

Escalloped Sweet Potatoes

Take dry yellow sweet potatoes after having been boiled, and peel and slice them; then cover the bottom of your dish with a layer of potatoes, adding some butter, sugar, and nutmeg, also some grated orange peel; fill the dish in this manner to the top; pour over this a cupful of cream, and set it in the oven and bake until brown.

Virginia Cooking, *1939*

Sliced Sweet Potatoes in Sherry

Yield: 4 servings

2 to 3 medium sweet
   potatoes or yams, peeled
   and cut crosswise into
   1/2 to 1-inch slices
Salted boiling water as
   needed
1/4 cup cream sherry
1 tablespoon butter or
   margarine, melted
   (optional)
Salt to taste

In a medium heavy saucepan, cook sweet potato slices, cover ajar, in enough salted boiling water to cover over moderate heat for 20 to 25 minutes or until potatoes are fork tender but do not fall apart; drain well. Add sherry, butter, if desired, and salt, tossing lightly to coat potatoes. Garnish as desired.

Variations: Add 1/2 cup coarsely chopped cashew nuts to cooked sweet potatoes. Or, add 1 drained (20-ounce) can pineapple tidbits or chunks in unsweetened pineapple juice to cooked potatoes.

–Elinor Kuhn (Mrs. Frank)
Buffet, catering firm
Richmond Culinary Guild

Stuffed Sweet Potatoes

Use shapely potatoes of even size. Scrub well and grease them with lard. Bake and cut in halves lengthwise. Scoop out center, leaving shells whole. Beat pulp smooth, add salt, butter, cream and brown sugar to taste. Beat until smooth then refill skins. Sprinkle with brown sugar and brown in a hot oven.

Virginia Cookery Book, *1921*

Tomatoes

Tomatoes, another favorite vegetable of Americans in the late twentieth century, enjoy an interesting and colorful history. Technically a fruit, but eaten as a vegetable, they were probably first grown in Mexico and South America. In fact, the name tomato results from the Aztec xitomte or xtomatle, although the description of a similar fruit is known from second century A. D. Egypt. The Spanish conquistadors likened the tomato to an apple, because of its shape and called it manzana.

Italians referred to it as the pomo d'oro, yellow apple, as the first tomatoes were yellow in color. According to legend, a Frenchman visiting an Italian asked about the strange "apples" he was served. He was told they were pomi dei Moro or Moor's Apples, referring to the Spanish who were known to the sixteenth century Europeans as Moors. Somewhere in the translation, the Frenchman misinterpreted this to be pommes d'amour or apple of love, which helped to promote the rumor of tomatoes being an aphrodisiac.

Unfortunately, this sweet treasure of summer gardens was also thought to be poisonous by many Europeans, probably because it was listed by an Italian herbalist, Mattioli, as a narcotic herb and a member of the deadly nightshade plant family. Although Thomas Jefferson, considered the United States' first gourmand, grew the delicacy in his garden at Monticello, tomatoes did not begin to gain popularity in America until the mid-part of the nineteenth century.

Smithfield Stuffed Tomatoes

6 whole tomatoes
6 tablespoons ground
   Smithfield ham
6 tablespoons bread
   crumbs
6 tablespoons butter
3 tablespoons celery
Seasoning

Scoop out insides of tomatoes and mix the pulp with tomatoes, bread crumbs, celery or celery seed, ham, pepper, salt, and melted butter. Stuff tomatoes, place in pan and bake until very tender. Half strips of bacon may be laid across tomatoes when they are nearly done.

–De Virginia Hambook, date unknown

361

Baked Cherry Tomatoes with Rum Sauce

Yield: 4 to 6 servings

2 cups very small (cherry) tomatoes
3 tablespoons butter or margarine, melted
3 tablespoons minced parsley
2 tablespoons dark rum
1 teaspoon sugar
1/2 teaspoon salt
1/4 teaspoon pepper

Rinse and dry tomatoes on absorbent paper. In a small deep saucepan, combine tomatoes and butter, stirring gently to coat tomatoes well. Transfer buttered tomatoes to a 10 x 6 x 2-inch baking dish or a 9-inch pie plate. In a small bowl, combine remaining ingredients, blending well;evenly pour over tomatoes. Bake, uncovered, in a slow oven (300 degrees F.) for 15 to 20 minutes, or until tomatoes are hot but still firm. Serve immediately.

–Pat Boschen

In the eighteenth century, John Randolph in his Treatise on Gardening by a Citizen of Virginia, likens the flavor of broccoli stems to eating asparagus and that of the heads to tasting cauliflour.

Crusty Baked Parmesan Tomatoes

Yield: 4 to 6 servings

6 firm ripe small or 4 medium tomatoes
1/2 cup breadcrumbs
1/3 cup grated Parmesan cheese
2 tablespoons butter or margarine, melted
1 tablespoon minced parsley, or chives, or green onion tops
1/2 to 1 teaspoon garlic juice

With a sharp knife, cut a thin slice from the top of each tomato; scoop out a slight depression from the cut area of each tomato. In a small bowl, combine breadcrumbs, cheese, butter, parsley, and garlic juice. Pack crumb mixture into the depression of each tomato, dividing evenly. Arrange tomatoes in an 8 x 8 x 2-inch baking pan. Bake, uncovered, in a moderate oven (350 degrees F.) for 25 to 30 minutes, or until tomatoes are tender but firm and crumb mixture lightly browned. Serve immediately.

Dixie Fried Tomatoes

Yield: 4 to 6 servings

The traditional method of preparation of fried tomatoes is to use green toma-toes or those just about to turn ripe; however, ripe tomatoes may be substi-tuted with equal success. This recipe was one of the first southern dishes I, a former damn Yankee, learned to prepare as a new bride for my Virginian gentleman husband. Usually this tasty delight is served at breakfast, espe-cially on a Saturday or Sunday when one can savor the flavor more leisurely.

3 green tomatoes (see note)
1/2 cup flour
About 1/4 to 1/2 cup bacon drippings
1/2 teaspoon salt or to taste, divided
1/4 teaspoon pepper or to taste, divided
1/4 teaspoon sugar or to taste, divided

Wash tomatoes, core, cut into 1/8-inch slices, and dredge in flour, coating each slice well. Heat bacon drippings in a large heavy skillet to about 375 degrees F. Add tomatoes and sprinkle each slice with one half of the salt, pepper, and sugar. Pan-fry until crisp and golden. Turn, sprinkle tomato slices with remaining salt, pepper, and sugar; continue pan-frying until slices are crispy-crusted and golden brown.

Note: may use tomatoes on-the-turn or those that are ripe but firm.

In her (Elizabeth Seldon McClurg Wickham 1782-1854) early days, tomatoes were scarcely known, and she remem-bered and I believe Papa says when he first remembers toma-toes were used commonly on the table — but he is considera-bly younger than my grandmother, his eldest sister. I knew the man who first introduced them. They were thought dangerous at first, and then to be good for fevers or some such trouble. It was quite a while before they came into general use. In her early days, forks were scarcely used — people ate with their knives as an ordinary thing — and her brother McClurg, who knew my sons when they were babies, always ate with his knife, never having lost his early habit. Then three-pronged forks were introduced, and finally the five-pronged came to be used.

Julis Wickham Procher Wickham
"Family Memoir," begun July 1903
great-grandmother of Elizabeth Seldon McClurg
Wickham and John Wickham

Turnip Cups

Yield: 6 to 8 servings

4 to 5 medium white turnips, peeled and halved crosswise
1 cup water
1/2 cup dry vermouth
2 to 3 tablespoons butter or margarine, at room temperature (optional)
3 tablespoons finely chopped peanuts
Salt and pepper to taste

In a medium heavy saucepan, cook turnips in water and vermouth, covered, over moderate heat for 10 to 15 minutes or until fork tender; drain well. Place turnip halves, flat side down, on a smooth surface. Using a biscuit or round cookie cutter, trim each turnip half. Scoop out center of each turnip half to form a cup. In a small bowl, combine trimmings and scooped-out portion of turnips. Mash thoroughly, removing any remaining lumps or chunks. Add butter, if desired, mixing well. Stir peanuts into mashed turnips; season with salt and pepper to taste. Fill cavities of turnip halves with mashed turnip mixture, dividing mixture evenly. Arrange Turnip Cups on a baking sheet; bake in a moderate oven (375 degrees F.) for 5 to 7 minutes just to reheat turnips thoroughly.

–Elinor Kuhn (Mrs. Frank)
Buffet, catering firm
Richmond Culinary Guild

Mr. Patrick Henry's Baked Granny Smith Apples

Yield: 4 servings

Situated in the historic Church Hill area, Mr. Patrick Henry's Restaurant and Inn is located one block from St. John's Church, site of Patrick Henry's famous "...give me liberty or give me death" speech in 1775. Proprietors James and Lynn News have an extensive previous background in restaurant work. The Inn, housed in nineteenth century buildings, circa 1858, features innovative regional dishes prepared by James and his assistants in the restaurant. Fresh herbs grown in the Inn's garden are used extensively in recipe preparation. The Inn also features a garden area for dining al fresco during pleasant weather and four lovely, recently renovated suites located above the restaurant for bed and breakfast visitors. Mobil Travel Guide has recently added Mr.Patrick Henry's to its recommendation list. Hosts James and Lynn offer pleasant hospitality and good food as their by-words.

4 tart cooking apples (see note)
Apple or currant jelly as needed
Cinnamon as needed
4 teaspoons butter, at room temperature and divided
Japanese breadcrumbs for garnish (see note)

With a sharp knife, cut apples in half horizontally. With a vegetable corer or melon baller, remove core and seeds from center of each apple half. Arrange apple halves in a lightly greased 8 x 8 x 2-inch baking dish. Fill cavity of each apple half with jelly and sprinkle lightly with cinnamon. Top each with 1 teaspoon of butter and sprinkle lightly with breadcrumbs. Bake, uncovered, in a moderate oven (350 degrees F.) for 1 hour or until fork tender. Or, arrange prepared apples on a sheet of heavy-duty aluminum foil on a grill rack opposite ash gray and glowing charcoal and pre-soaked hickory chips in a covered grill or smoker. Smoke for about 1 hour. Or, prepare apples as for baking, except do not top with breadcrumbs. Microwave in a glass dish covered with clear plastic wrap which has been vented at HIGH power for about 6 to 7 minutes, or until fork tender. Additional cooking as needed should be added in increments of seconds. Top each with breadcrumbs and broil, 8 to 10 inches from heat source, for about 2 minutes until breadcrumbs are toasted.

Note: Use McIntosh, Winesap, Granny Smith, or other tart variety of apples.

Note: If Japanese breadcrumbs are unavailable, homemade coarse breadcrumbs may be substituted. Use dry white bread slices and crush coarsely with a rolling pin.

–Chefs James and Lynn News, proprietors
Mr. Patrick Henry's Restaurant and Inn

Pineapples and coconuts were popular food items in the American diet during the nineteenth century, being imported from the West Indies. Oranges, which did not travel well, remained rare treats for the Christmas stocking well into the twentieth century.

365

Piquant Pears

Yield: 8 to 10 servings

1/2 cup dry white wine
3/4 cup Mild Southern
Sweet Pepper Jelly (see
index) or 1 (6-ounce) jar
mild or hot-flavored
pepper jelly, divided
4 to 5 firm ripe medium
pears, cored, peeled and
halved lengthwise
Crisp lettuce leaves for
garnish

In a large heavy skillet, combine wine and 9 tablespoons pepper jelly; stir over low heat just
until jelly is melted. Add pear halves, turning
each to coat with wine mixture. Simmer, covered, over low heat until pears are just tender,
about 15 minutes, turning pears occasionally.
Uncover and continue to simmer until liquid is
almost evaporated. Do not allow pears to become soft.
Remove pears if necessary to serving plate while
liquid is reduced. Arrange pears cut-side up, on
a serving plate lined with crisp lettuce leaves.
Spoon 1 teaspoonful of jelly into the cavity of
each pear half. Serve warm or at room temperature.

–Elinor Kuhn, (Mrs. Frank)
Buffet, catering firm
Richmond Culinary Guild

Saucy Baked Pineapple

Yield: 8 servings

*"Although this recipe is a baked fruit, not vegetable casserole, it is served in
the manner of a vegetable casserole as a side dish to an entrée. It's deli-
ciously different...a favorite of mine from Judy Goss."*

7 slices white bread, cubed
1 (20-ounce) can pineapple
chunks (including juice)
(see note)
4 eggs, slightly beaten
1 cup sugar
1/2 cup butter or margarine,
melted

Evenly spread bread cubes over the bottom of a
greased 1 1/2-quart casserole. In a bowl, combine remaining ingredients, mixing well. Spoon
mixture over bread cubes. Bake, uncovered, in a
moderate oven (350 degrees F.) for 55 to 60 minutes until thickened and bubbly hot.

Note: Sweeteed pineapple or pineapple in-its-
own juice may be used.

Variation: Liberally sprinkle grated Parmesan or shredded sharp Cheddar cheese
over the top during the last 10 minutes of baking.

–Marion Goodloe (Mrs. John Allan, Jr.)

Salads, Dressings, and Sauces

University of Richmond

Although located in a large metropolitan city, the University of Richmond conveys the friendly essence of a charming small town collegiate campus. Long noted regionally for its sound academic program, it is considered to be one of the finest small private universities in the nation. Since its founding in 1830 by the Baptists of Virginia, the university has emphasized quality rather than size.

One of the university's most noted alumni is Earl Hamner, Jr., creator of the television series The Waltons and Falcon Crest. He has remembered his college days both in The Waltons and the novel, Spencer's Mountain. The fictional Boatwright University of The Waltons is patterned after the University of Richmond, so-named for the university's president of half a century, Dr. Frederic C. Boatwright.

Another famous U. of R. alumnus, Dr. Douglas Southall Freeman, was winner of two Pulitzer Prizes for his biographies of Robert E. Lee and George Washington. While editor of the Richmond News Leader, Dr. Freeman kept a sign prominently displayed in his office: "Time alone is irreplaceable. Waste it not." Living by that motto, Dr.Freeman expected others to follow suit. If a visitor to his office disregarded the sign by overextending his visit, Dr. Freeman would rise, grasp the visitor's hand firmly, and declare fervently, "It's been MIGHTY good to see you, suh!"

University of Richmond Ham 'N Raisin Salad

Yield: 4 to 6 servings

Through the years, Ham 'N Raisin Salad has been a favorite luncheon item with students, faculty, and friends at the University of Richmond.

12 ounces boneless fully-
   cooked smoked ham
   (see note)
1/2 cup mayonnaise

With a sharp knife, finely mince ham. Or, grind with the coarse grind of a meat grinder, or mince in a food processor, being careful not to purée ham. In a medium bowl, combine minced ham,

1/4 cup minced peeled
 onion
1/4 cup minced celery
1/4 cup dark seedless
 raisins
Pepper to taste
Crisp greens (optional)

mayonnaise, onion, celery, and raisins, mixing well. Cover and chill thoroughly in refrigerator for at least 1 hour to blend flavors. Spoon onto chilled plates lined with crisp greens, if desired, and garnish as desired.

Note: Fully-cooked smoked Smithfield or Smithfield-style or Virginia country-style ham may be used.

–Anthony Skipper, Catering Chef
University of Richmond
Food Services Department

...Susan Letcher encouraged economy in the kitchen of the mansion. Costs were extremely high, molasses $30 a gallon, apples $25 a bushel, beef $2 a pound, and flour $100 a barrel. Kind friends at home in Lexington sent supplies as often as they could; among these was Mary Anna Jackson, wife of the valiant Stonewall. Salt and meat shortages all fell heavily on life in the capital. Whatever the shortages, and however much the Confederate army might raid the farmers' markets and grocery stores, there were times when the governor had to entertain. One of his guests reported the following: "Governor Letcher received, as usual, on the return of the anniversary that ushered in the year 1862. His guests were welcomed with the broad, good-humored hospitality and dignified courtesy which ever distinguished this gallant son of Virginia. Minus champagne, through the rigid effects of the blockade, the giant punch-bowl was filled with... steaming beverage, the smell of roasted apples betrayed the characteristic toddy, and through the crystal cut-glass gleamed the golden hue of the egg-not, to regale the guests of the Governor." (circa 1862)

–William Seal
Virginia's Executive Mansion:
A History of the Governor's House 1988

Crunchy Autumn Fruit Salad

Yield: 4 to 6 servings

8 ounces black grapes,
  halved and seeded
8 ounces red Tokay grapes,
  halved and seeded or
  8 ounces seedless red
  or green grapes, halved
2 unpeeled firm ripe
  medium bosc or anjou
  pears, cored, seeded, and
  cut into thin strips
2 unpeeled firm ripe tart
  medium apples, cored,
  seeded, and cut into bite-
  sized pieces (see note)
Mary J's Citrus Dressing as
  desired (see index)
4 ounces Roquefort, blue or
  Stilton cheese, crumbled
1/2 to 3/4 cup coarsely
  chopped English walnuts
Crisp butter or bib lettuce
  leaves
Watercress or chervil sprigs
  for garnish

In a medium bowl, combine grape halves, pears, and apples. Add the desired amount of fruit dressing and toss lightly to mix. Cover and refrigerate for at least 1 hour to blend flavors. Add crumbled cheese and nuts, tossing lightly to mix again. Spoon fruit mixture onto chilled individual salad plates lined with crisp butter or bib lettuce leaves, dividing evenly. Drizzle any remaining dressing in bowl over fruit salads. Garnish each salad with watercress or chervil sprigs. Serve immediately.

Note: Use McIntosh, Winesap, Granny Smith, or other tart variety of apples.

Sturgeon Salad-No. 610

Select and prepare the sturgeon as directed (No. 160). Drop in boiling salted water and cook until perfectly tender; take out of the boiling water; drain and drop in cold water for a few minutes. When perfectly cold cut up, rejecting all fat and gristle; dust with celery salt and pepper. Dress each pint of sturgeon with one-half pint of mayonnaise. Serve in crisp lettuce leaves.

**– Instruction in Cooking
with Selected Receipts,** 1895

... Beside this liquid refreshment, there was Dabney's boned turkey, boned ham, and bowls of chicken salad. This last was the real thing because the ladies of the household usually cut up the turkey meat and made the mayonnaise themselves. There were hot coquettes, and fried and pickled oysters. In a huge block of ice, scooped out, were raw oysters. There were noble trenchermen in those days with no thought of overweight or calories...

Helena Lefroy Caperton
"Time Gambols Withal"
The Richmond News Leader, 1931

Fruit Salad-No. 627

2 heads of lettuce,
2 firm bananas,
2 sweet oranges,
1/2 pound white grapes,
2 acid apples,
12 English walnuts,
1/2 pint mayonnaise.

To Make: Wash the grapes carefully; cut each one in half and extract the seed; peel the bananas, apples, and oranges, removing every bit of skin and all seed. Cut all in small pieces. Crack the walnuts and break each kernal in half. Mix all these ingredients together. Select the crispest leaves of lettuce and arrange them upon a cold dish or individual dishes. Pile in each lettuce leaf a large tablespoon of the mixture; cover well with dressing and serve at once.

**–Instruction in Cooking
with Selected Receipts,** *1895*

Waldorf Salad

Oscar Tschirky, better known as Oscar of the Waldorf, major domo of dining at the Waldorf Astoria Hotel at the turn of the nineteeth/twentieth centuries, is credited with the creation of Waldorf Salad, originally a mixture of lettuce, chopped apple, celery, and mayonnaise. A man of the dining room...not the kitchen...Oscar is not credited with other creations bearing his name.

Tuscany Waldorf Salad

Yield: 6 to 8 servings

This recipe was inspired by Julee Rosso's and Sheila Lukins' Waldorf Salad. Since its introduction, Waldorf Salad, in many versions, has been popular with Americans of all regions of the United States, including Richmond.

4 tart ripe large unpeeled apples, cored, seeded, and cubed (see note)
1 large or 2 medium fennel bulbs, cleaned and cut into julienne strips (reserve green tops)
1 cup coarsely chopped pecans
1 cup coarsely chopped pitted dates
3/4 cup chopped dark seedless raisins or dried currants
1 tablespoon minced reserved fennel greens
Tangy Cooked Sour Cream Dressing

In a large bowl, combine apples, fennel strips, pecans, dates, raisins, and minced fennel greens. Add Tangy Cooked Sour Cream Dressing and lime juice; toss lightly to mix. Season with salt to taste, if desired. Cover and refrigerate at least 1 hour. Arrange leaves of radicchio or leaf lettuce on 4 to 6 individual salad plates; if desired. Spoon apple mixture onto radicchio or lettuce-lined plates, dividing evenly. Garnish as desired.

2 tablespoons lime juice
Salt to taste (optional)
Crisp radicchio or leaf
  lettuce (optional)

Note: Use McIntosh, Winesap, or other tart eating apples. Two firm ripe large Bosc
  or Anjou pears may be substitued for two of the apples, if desired.

Variation: Add 1/2 to 1 cup crumbled Stilton, Roguefort, or blue cheese to salad.
  You may also add 1/2 cup crumbled cheese to dressing, if desired. Pour into
  a blender container, cover and whiz until smooth.

Tangy Cooked Sour
  Cream Dressing
(about 1 3/4 cups)
1/4 to 1/3 cup sugar
2 tablespoons flour
1 teaspoon dry mustard
1/8 teaspoon salt
1/2 cup cider or white
  vinegar2 eggs, beaten
1 cup sour cream

In a small heavy saucepan, combine the first 4 ingredients, mixing well. Gradually stir in vinegar. Cook, stirring constantly, over moderate heat until mixture comes to a boil and thickens slightly. Gradually add a small amount of hot mixture to beaten eggs, beating constantly with a wire whisk. Stir egg mixture into remaining hot mixture. Cook, stirring constantly, over low heat for 1 minute. Remove from heat; allow to cool thoroughly. Fold in sour cream.

...One morning she (Elizabeth Montague) went out to borrow a recipe and returned to find a large political delegation waiting for her husband. She went upstairs to the governor, and he descended to meet the callers. When the visitors stayed too long, Mrs. Montague became weary and called crossly down the stairs for the governor to come talk to her. "Just when are those gentlemen planning to go home? Are they trying to spend the night?" "I don't know," he answered, "They are talking to me about nominating me for President of the United States." "Oh," cried Betsie Montague. "They want you to be President? Well, dear, I hope you invited them for dinner and the night!" (circa 1902-06)

—William Seal
Virginia's Executive Mansion:
A History of the Govenor's House, 1988

Spiral Macaroni Salad

Yield: 6 servings

1 (8-ounce) package spiral-shaped macaroni
1 cup fresh peas or 1/2 (10-ounce) package frozen peas, thawed
1 small cucumber, peeled, seeded, and coarsely chopped
1 cup cherry tomatoes, halved
1 cup (4 ounces) shredded sharp Cheddar cheese
2 tablespoons chopped green pepper
2 tablespoons chopped celery
2 tablespoons thinly sliced green onions (include some green tops)
1/4 cup mayonnaise (see note)
1 tablespoon sweet pickle relish
1/2 teaspoon prepared mustard
Pinch of fresh minced or dried dill weed or to taste
Pinch of celery salt or to taste
Pinch of celery seed
Salt and pepper to taste

Cook macaroni according to package directions; drain well, rinse in cold water, and drain again. Cook fresh peas in a small amount of boiling salted water until just tender, about 8 to 10 minutes. Drain well, rinse in cold water, and drain again. Do not cook thawed frozen peas. In a large bowl, combine macaroni, peas, cucumber pieces, tomato halves, cheese, green pepper, celery, and green onion. In a 1-cup measure, combine mayonnaise, pickle relish, mustard, dill weed, celery salt, and celery seed. Pour over macaroni mixture, tossing gently to mix. Season with salt and pepper to taste. Cover and chill for at least 1 hour.

Note: 2 tablespoons sour cream and 2 tablespoons mayonnaise may be substituted for 1/4 cup mayonnaise.

–Pat Boschen

Tortellini Salad with Fresh Basil

Yield: 6 servings

Fresh pasta served in various ways has become increasingly popular in Richmond in the last few years due to the influence of the popularity of pasta from other culinary areas of the United States, notably New York and California. Tortellini is a pasta specialty of Bologna, Italy...also known as the city of three T's...tortellini, towers, and a certain portion of women's anatomy! The pasta is shaped into tiny bishops' hats, filled with meat, cheese, or other delicacies and can be obtained in the traditional egg pasta or often spinach pasta.

1 pound cheese filled
tortellini (see note)
2 to 3 quarts boiling salted
water
4 ounces chunk-style
Parmesan cheese, broken
into bite-sized pieces
6 green onions, thinly sliced
(include some green tops)
1/2 medium sweet red
pepper, cored, seeded,
and coarsely chopped
1/2 medium sweet yellow
pepper, cored, seeded,
and coarsely chopped
1 1/2 to 2 tablespoons
minced fresh or 1 1/2 to 2
teaspoons dried basil
About 1/2 cup Mustard
Vinaigrette Dressing (see
index)
Salt and freshly ground
pepper to taste
4 ounces freshly grated
Parmesan cheese for
garnish

In a large kettle, cook tortellini in about 3 quarts salted boiling water for 6 minutes after water returns to a boil. Draina nd rinse thoroughly in cold water; drain well again. In a large bowl, combine tortellini, bite-sized cheese pieces, green onions, sweet red and yellow peppers, and basil, tossing lightly with two wooden spoons. Add desired amount of Mustard Vinaigrette Dressing and salt and pepper to taste; toss again lightly to mix. Cover and refrigerate until ready to serve. Add grated Parmesan cheese and toss again just before serving.

Note: Preferably choose a fresh handmade tortellini available in many grocery, pasta, and other specialty food stores. Meat, or spinach or seafood filled tortellini may be substituted for cheese filled pasta.

Chilled Curried Rice

Yield: 8 servings

4 cups cooked rice
1 cup thinly sliced celery
1 cup frozen peas, thawed
and uncooked (see note)
1/2 cup mayonnaise
1/2 cup sour cream
5 tablespoons chopped
chutney
2 teaspoons curry powder
1 cup cashew nuts
Crisp lettuce leaves

In a large bowl, combine the first 3 ingredients. Add mayonnaise, sour cream, chutney, and curry powder, mixing well. Cover and refrigerate until thoroughly chilled. Just before serving, add cashews, mixing well. Spoon into a large glass serving bowl or onto individual salad plates lined with crisp lettuce leaves.

Note: 1 cup fresh peas may be substituted. Cook in boiling water for 3 to 4 minutes; drain well.

Variation: Add 2 tablespoons drained chopped pimento to mixture. Substitute 1 cup slivered blanched almonds or pecan or English walnuts halves for cashews.

–Sundra Faber (Mrs. H. B., Jr.)

Far Eastern-style Rice Salad

Yield: 8 to 10 servings

Former First Lady, Jeannie Baliles, declares this to be one of her favorite salads to serve to family and friends.

2 cups rice
2 ribs celery, minced
2 green onions, minced
(include some green tops)
1/2 medium green pepper,
cored, seeded and
chopped
1/2 cup slivered blanched
almonds
2 tablespoons minced
pitted green olives
Curry Dressing

Cook rice according to package directions; drain well. Refrigerate until rice is thoroughly chilled. In a bowl, combine rice, celery, green onions, green pepper, almonds, and green olives. Refrigerate until serving time. Add Curry Dressing, tossing lightly to mix. Spoon into serving bowl and garnish with tomato wedges and parsley sprigs.

Tomato wedges for garnish
Parsley sprigs for garnish

Curry Dressing
1/2 cup mayonnaise
1 tablespoon soy sauce (see note)
1/2 teaspoon lemon juice
1/4 teaspoon curry powder or to taste

In a small bowl, combine all ingredients, mixing well. Store in a small covered container in refrigerator.

Note: Reduced sodium (Lite) soy sauce may be substituted for regular soy sauce. One teaspoon Lite soy sauce contains 100 milligrams of sodium.

–Jeannie Baliles (Mrs. Gerald)
First Lady of Virginia, 1986-1990

Macaroni Seafood Salad

Yield: 6 servings

8 ounces peeled, deveined cooked medium shrimp
8 ounces frozen sea legs, thawed (see note)
1 cup chopped celery
1/2 cup mayonnaise
1/4 cup thinly sliced radishes
3 tablespoons minced fresh or 1 tablespoon dried chives
2 tablespoons Durkee's sauce
2 tablespoons ketchup
2 tablespoons sweet pickle relish
1/2 teaspoon monosodium glutamate (optional)
8 ounces (2 cups) uncooked spiral macaroni
Several grains cayenne pepper
Salt and pepper to taste

In a medium bowl, combine the first 9 or 10 ingredients, mixing gently. Cook macaroni according to package instructions; drain well. Cool. In a large bowl, combine seafood mixture and macaroni. Season with cayenne pepper, salt, and pepper to taste; mix gently. Refrigerate until ready to serve. Garnish as desired.

Note: Sea legs are a combination of Pollack and King crab. 8 ounces cooked lobster meat or blue crab or scallops may be substituted for sea legs. Cut lobster meat into bite-sized pieces and large scallops in half.

–Swift Creek Mill Playhouse

Wild Rice Salad With Tarragon

Yield: 6 servings

"While I was working as a chef in the president's home at the University of Richmond, I found this recipe a wonderful way to utilize leftover wild rice which never seems to taste right when it is reheated for the second time. However, don't hesitate to prepare the recipe with long grain rice rather than the expensive variety."

2 tablespoons chopped
  peeled onion
1 tablespoon hot olive oil
1 cup wild rice or a blend of
  wild rice and long-grain
  rice
3 cups chicken broth
1/4 cup sour cream
1/4 cup mayonnaise
3 tablespoons minced fresh
  or 1 tablespoon dried
  tarragon
1 tablespoon minced
  parsley
2 teaspoons minced peeled
  garlic
Salt and pepper to taste
  (optional)
Very small bunches of
  seedless red grapes and
  sprigs of fresh tarragon
  for garnish

In a large heavy skillet, sauté onion in olive oil over moderate heat until tender but not browned. Add rice to the skillet, stirring well to coat rice with oil. Add chicken broth and bring mixture to a boil. Reduce heat, cover, and simmer for 12 to 15 minutes or until rice is done and tender. Stir rice with a fork. Transfer rice to a large bowl, cover, and cool in refrigerator. When rice is lukewarm (105 degrees to 115 degrees F.), add sour cream, mayonnaise, minced tarragon, parsley, and garlic, mixing well. Season with salt and pepper, if desired. Cover and chill thoroughly in refrigerator. Adjust seasonings. Garnish each serving with a very small (petite) bunch of grapes and a sprig of fresh tarragon.

–Ann Hardy, Catering Chef
University of Richmond
Food Services Department

Old Richmond Advertisement, circa 1909

After supper—not dinner, for that was at 3 o'clock and a custom for which no one can possibly have any regret—with one accord the family moved out onto the porch and sat in the hot twilight in split-bottom rocking chairs....

Before going home with the uncles and grandfather for Sunday dinner, I would be treated to a lemonade. I sat up to the bar with the best of them, sucking through a straw, and passed the time of day with my good friends Judge Samuel Witt, Tom Bolling, Willie Grant, my cousin Sallee Watkins, and many others who were indubitably not imbibing lemonade.

Helen Lefroy Caperton
"Era of Front Porch-Sitting Was Gay,
Happy One in Richmond,"
(turn of nineteenth/twentieth centuries)
Richmond Times-Dispatch, October 16, 1949

Chutney Chicken Salad

Yield: 4 servings

"The English comes out in me with the addition of chutney to chicken salad."

2 hard-cooked eggs, peeled and chopped
1 firm medium apple, cored, seeded, and chopped (see note)
2 cups cubed or slivered cooked chicken
1 cup chopped celery
2 tablespoons chopped chutney or to taste
1 tablespoon chopped sweet pickle, drained
1/2 to 1 cup mayonnaise or to taste
1 teaspoon curry powder or to taste
Salt to taste

In a large bowl, combine eggs, apple, chicken, celery, chutney, and pickle. In a 2 cup measure, combine mayonnaise and curry blending well. Pour over chicken mixture, tossing lightly. Season with salt to taste. Cover and refrigerate until thoroughly chilled.

Note: Apple may be peeled, if desired.

–Alicia Pedersen (Mrs. Paul)

379

du Jour Chicken Salad

Yield: 8 to 10 servings

An often requested specialty of the house at the du Jour restaurant, chicken salad is a uniquely American recipe, originating in colonial days in the southern colonies.

2 (3 to 4-pound) chickens
1 rib celery, chopped (see note)
1/4 cup chopped peeled red onion
3/4 cup mayonnaise
2 tablespoons Dijon-style prepared mustard
2 tablespoons sweet pickle relish
1 1/2 teaspoons salt or to taste
1 teaspoon white pepper
1/2 teaspoon celery salt
1/2 teaspoon minced peeled garlic or to taste
1/2 teaspoon poultry seasoning

Arrange whole chickens on a rack in a large roasting pan. Bake, cover ajar, in a moderate oven (350 degrees F.) for 1 1/2 to 2 hours, or until fork tender. Cool. Remove skin and bones from chicken; discard or reserve for preparing chicken stock or broth. Cut chicken into bite-sized pieces or 1/2 to 3/4-inch cubes. In a large bowl, combine chicken cubes and remaining ingredients, mixing well. Cover and chill thoroughly in refrigerator until ready to serve. Garnish each portion as desired.

–Chef Robert Hamlin, proprietor
Jana Blue Hopper, proprietor
du Jour Restaurant and Caterers

Tropical Chicken and Rice Salad

Yield: 4 large servings

Salad
1 (3-pound) broiler-fryer chicken, cooked, skinned, boned, and cut into bite-sized pieces
4 cups shredded lettuce
2 cups cooked rice, cooled
2 cups fresh or frozen peas, cooked until tender but crisp (see note)
1 cup thinly sliced celery

Prepare chicken; discard skin and bones. Layer shredded lettuce in a straight-sided 2 1/2-quart glass bowl. In a separate bowl, combine chicken pieces, rice, peas, celery, and salt and pepper. In a small bowl, combine mayonnaise, yogurt, curry powder, and onion powder, blending well. Add dressing to chicken mixture, tossing lightly to mix. Spoon mixture evenly over lettuce.

Arrange orange sections and pineapple slice sover salad; cover with colored or clear plastic wrap and chill in refrigerator for several hours. To

1/4 teaspoon salt
Pepper to taste

Dressing
1/2 cup mayonnaise
1/2 cup peach flavored
   yogurt
3/4 teaspoon curry powder
1/4 teaspoon onion powder

Topping
1 (11-ounce) can mandarin
   orange sections, drained
1 (8 1/2-ounce) can
   pineapple slices, drained
   (see note)
Cashew nuts for garnish

serve, spoon some of each salad layer onto luncheon or salad plates. Garnish each with cashew nuts.

Note: Cook fresh peas in boiling salted water to cover until tender but crisp, about 8 to 10 minutes; drain well and rinse in cold water to stop cooking, or use frozen peas cooked for only 4 or 5 minutes, or use uncooked and thawed.

Note: 6 ounces cubed or sliced peeled fresh pineapple, about 1 cup, may be substituted for canned pineapple.

To Microwave Chicken: Arrange chicken pieces in a 12 x 8 x 2-inch glass baking dish with meatiest parts of chicken toward outside edge of dish. If desired, arrange thinly sliced peeled onion over chicken and sprinkle with minced parsley. Cover dish with clear plastic wrap, allowing extra wrap for venting. Microwave at HIGH power for 10 to 14 minutes, turning dish several times while chicken is cooking, or until chicken is fork tender. Cool, remove chicken from bone, and discard bone and skin.

–The Reynolds Wrap Kitchens
The Reynolds Metals Company

The few restaurants that were operating served meals on paper plates. Diners ate with plastic forks and drank soda pop.

–Berry
Richmond Flood, 1972

Islander Chicken Salad

Yield: 6 servings

8 ounces fresh spinach

About 3 cups cooked cubed chicken or turkey, cut into 1/2-inch cubes (see note)

1 (13-ounce) can pineapple chunks, drained

1 (4-ounce) can sliced water chestnuts, drained

1 cup thinly sliced celery

1/4 cup thinly sliced green onions or coarsely chopped peeled onion

Islander Dressing (see index)

5 slices crisp cooked bacon, crumbled

Rinse spinach leaves thoroughly to remove any sand or grit; drain well, dry with absorbent paper, and remove and discard large stems. Tear remaining leaves into bite-sized pieces. In a large bowl, combine spinach, pineapple, water chestnuts, chicken, celery, and green onion. Add desired amount of Islander Dressing, mixing well. Cover and chill in refrigerator until ready to serve. Evenly sprinkle salad with crumbled crisp bacon just before serving.

Note: A cooked 3 to 4 pound chicken will yield about 3 cups cubed cooked chicken and a cooked 2 1/2 pound boneless turkey breast will yield about 4 cups cubed cooked turkey.

Variation: Add 1/2 to 1 cup cashew nuts to salad, mixing well, just before serving. Garnish with watercress sprigs in addition to crumbled crisp bacon.

–Bobbie Hudson (Mrs. Harvey)

In 1984 two well-known restaurants in the historic Shockoe Slip area, Sam Miller's Exchange Cafe and The Warehouse, merged to form Sam Miller's Warehouse. Popular with many Richmonders, the restaurant soon needed expansion. After a complete restoration, the elegant Captain Morgan room, located on the second floor, was opened in 1988, tripling the restaurant's capacity and providing live entertainment Wednesdays through Sundays. Housed in a nineteenth century poultry warehouse, Sam Miller's specializes in fresh Chesapeake Bay seafood dishes, live Maine lobsters, and prime beef. Historic documents and pictures of old Richmond decorate the barn siding and wormy chestnut walls of the casual-style first floor.

Chesapeake Bay Crab Salad

Yield: 4 servings

1 pound backfin crabmeat
3 ribs celery, minced
1/2 small onion, peeled and minced
1 cup mayonnaise (see note)
3/4 tablespoon lemon juice
2 tablespoons minced parsley
1 teaspoon capers, drained
1/2 teaspoon white pepper
Crisp leaf lettuce or other greens (optional)

Pick over crabmeat, removing any shell or cartilage. In a medium bowl, combine crabmeat, celery, onion, mayonnaise, lemon juice, parsley, capers, and pepper, mixing gently, *being careful not to break up crabmeat*. Spoon mixture onto luncheon plates lined with crisp leaf lettuce or other greens, dividing evenly. Garnish as desired.

Note: Preferably use Hellman's brand. Reduced-calorie or cholesterol mayonnaise may be used, if desired.

–Sam Miller's Warehouse Restaurant

383

Shockoe Slip Shrimp Salad

Yield: 4 to 6 servings

1 1/4 pounds small shrimp
1/4 cup mayonnaise (see note)
1/4 cup sour cream
6 tablespoons minced celery
1 1/2 tablespoons minced fresh or 1/2 tablespoon dried dill weed
3/4 tablespoon lemon juice
White pepper to taste
Crisp spinach leaves, cleaned and dried, as needed
1 hard-cooked egg, peeled and thinly sliced, for garnish
1/2 small cucumber, thinly sliced for garnish
1 ripe small tomato, cut into thin wedges, for garnish
1 lemon, cut into thin wedges for garnish
Sprigs of fresh dill weed for garnish

In a large heavy saucepan, cook shrimp in salted boiling water to cover well over moderate heat for about 3 minutes after water returns to a boil or *just* until shrimp have turned opaque and a bright coral color. Rinse immediately in ice water; drain well. Peel and devein shrimp; with a sharp knife cut shrimp into quarters or bite-sized pieces. Or, steam shrimp, covered, on a rack in a large heavy saucepan over a small amount of boiling water for 3 minutes or until opaque and bright coral in color. In a bowl, combine prepared shrimp, celery, mayonnaise, sour cream, minced dillweed, lemon juice, and pepper, mixing well. Cover and chill in refrigerator for 1 hour to blend flavors. Spoon shrimp mixture onto luncheon plates lined with spinach leaves, dividing evenly. Garnish each serving with hard-cooked egg slices, cucumber slices, thin tomato wedges, thin lemon wedges, and a sprig of fresh dill weed.

–Sam Miller's Warehouse Restaurant

ı ı The

Beveridge

Automatic

Cooker.

Old Richmond Advertisement, circa 1895

Hints On Salad Making

Dressings-Salads

1. Never leave the lettuce leaves soaking in cold water. If the leaves are young, this process makes them flabby and tasteless.
2. Only wash the leaves which are gritty.
3. Never cut up the salad, but tear the leaves apart.
4. Use the very best oil or the freshest of mayonnaise."

Virginia Cook Book, *1839*

Author's Note: These rules still apply today.

Potato Salad

Boil well several potatoes (4 large); while hot mash and cream nicely with a little milk, salt, and butter; make a mayonnaise quite thin, and add celery and mix well. Leave half of the mayonnaise for the top; dress with this, and slice hard-boiled egg or parsley.

Mayonnaise Dressing.—Yolk of 1 egg raw, 1 tablespoonful of creamed potatoes, 1 teaspoonful of Worcestershire sauce, a little salt, dry mustard, and sugar; cream all together well; then add olive oil, rubbing in with silver fork a teaspoonful at a time until a thick mass; thin with vinegar to right consistency.

—Mrs. J. W. Wilbur
Receipts for Luncheon and Tea, *1898*

Potato salad, perhaps the Queen of American salads, is a very versatile food. It can be eaten year-round, hot or cold, and with a variety of other foods. The origin of potato salad is somewhat obscure. Potato salads using a mayonnaise dressing were probably not introduced until the latter part of the nineteenth century.

For every potato salad aficionado, there is a recipe or way for preparing the salad. A waxy type of potato rather than a mealy potato should be used to prevent the potato from crumbling in the potato salad preparation. Mayonnaise dressings should be added when the potatoes are cool so that the mayonnaise dosen't separate.

Potato Salad-No. 621.

4 large Irish potatoes,
10 tablespoons olive oil,
3 tablespoons vinegar,
4 tablespoons chopped
    parsley,
2 teaspoons celery salt,
1/2 teaspoon pepper,
    juice of 1 lemon,
1 small onion, if liked.

To Make: Boil the potatoes by directions No. 488, but do not steam them after boiling. When cold cut them into slices or squares; mix with them salt, pepper, parsley, and chopped onion; if you use it, strain over the lemon juice; mix the oil thoroughly through the potatoes, then mix in the vinegar, being careful not to get too much, because if very strong the quantity directed might make the salad too acid. Toss all well together with two forks, and serve in lettuce leaves well chilled. The potatoes may be prepared and dressed with mayonnaise, if preferred. Another nice way to prepare potatoes is to mash them while hot; then, when cold, cut into any form you like. They are probably more digestible this way.

**Instruction in Cooking
with Selected Receipts, 1895**

Picniker's Delight Potato Salad
with Parmesan Cheese

Yield: 8 servings

8 to 10 very small to small
    red-skinned new potatoes
Boiling water
2 1/2 tablespoons white
    wine vinegar
1/2 teaspoon Dijon-style
    prepared mustard
1/4 teaspoon
    Worcestershire sauce
1/4 to 1/2 teaspoon garlic
    juice
1/3 cup salad oil
Salt and pepper to taste
8 green onions, thinly sliced
    (include some green tops)
1 small green pepper, cored,
    seeded, and chopped

In a large heavy saucepan, cook potatoes in boiling water to cover over moderate heat for about 30 minutes or until fork tender; drain well and cool about 30 minutes. While potatoes are cooling, prepare dressing and other vegetables. In a small bowl, combine vinegar, mustard, Worcestershire sauce, and garlic juice. With a wire whisk, beat in oil in a slow steady stream until dressing is slightly thickened and well mixed. Season with salt and pepper to taste. Leaving skins intact, cut potatoes into quarters or eighths, depending upon size. In a large bowl, combine potatoes, green onions, green pepper, and chives. Add mustard dressing and mayonnaise, tossing lightly to mix. Add Parmesan cheese and salt and pepper; toss again lightly. Cover and refrigerate for several hours to blend

3 tablespoons minced fresh
or 1 tablespoon minced
dried chives
1 tablespoon mayonnaise
1/2 cup grated Parmesan
cheese (see note)
5 slices crisp cooked bacon,
coarsely crumbled
(optional)

flavors. Allow potato salad to stand at room
temperature for 15 to 20 minutes before serving.
Add crumbled bacon just before serving, if desired, and toss again.

Note: Preferably use freshly grated Parmesan cheese.

Marinated Green Beans

Yield: 12 servings

3 (16-ounce) cans whole
green beans (including
liquid) (see note)
1 tablespoon bacon
drippings
Salt as needed
1 medium onion, peeled
and chopped
3/4 cup cooking oil
6 tablespoons plus
4 teaspoons white or
cider vinegar, divided
Pepper as needed
3 hard-cooked eggs, peeled
6 tablespoons mayonnaise
2 teaspoons prepared
mustard
Crisp lettuce leaves or curly
endive for garnish
8 slices crisp bacon,
coarsely crumbled for
garnish

In a heavy saucepan, combine green beans, liquid, bacon drippings, and 1/2 teaspoon salt.
Bring to a boil over moderate heat; drain well
and cool. In a large glass bowl, combine green
beans and onion. Combine oil and 6 tablespoons vinegar together, whisking vigorously;
pour over green beans and onions. Add salt and
pepper to taste; toss mixture lightly, coating
green beans and onions well. Cover and refrigerate for 12 hours; drain well. Chop egg white
separately. Mash yolks and combine with mayonnaise, 4 teaspoons vinegar, and mustard, mixing well. Add salt and pepper to taste. Add
dressing to drained beans and onions. Arrange
green beans and onion in a large salad bowl
lined with crisp greens. Sprinkle with chopped
egg white and crumbled bacon.

Note: Salad ingredients may be reduced to one half the amounts for 6 servings.

Note: 3 pounds trimmed fresh whole green beans may be substituted for canned
beans. Cook in salted boiling water to cover. Add bacon drippings and
cook over moderate heat for 2 minutes after water returns to a boil; drain
well. Continue to follow recipe as previously directed.

Note: A pinch of sugar may be added to dressing, if desired.

–Dotty Stuart (Mrs. Albert)

Just north of Richmond in neighboring Ashland, Homemades by Suzanne offers tasty homemade recipes of a variety of cuisines as a catering service, take-out food, and in-house restaurant service. Opened almost a decade ago, Homemades provides the catering needs for diners at the nearby Barksdale Theatre located in the historic Hanover Tavern, as well as at Bloemendahl, in the Lewis Ginter Memorial Gardens. Gourmet picnic baskets may be ordered in advance or the spur of the moment for a repast in the surrounding picturesque countryside. The restaurant is open until 6:00 p.m. Monday through Saturday, opening at 11:00 a.m. om Mondays, 9:00 a.m.on Tuesday through Friday, and at 10:00 a.m. on Saturdays.

Barksdale Theatre's Baby Lima Bean and Country Ham Salad

Yield: 8 servings

2 pounds fresh or frozen
  small lima beans
1/2 cup chopped peeled
  onion
1/4 cup shredded fully-
  cooked smoked country-
  style ham
1/4 cup chopped pimento,
  drained
2 tablespoons chopped
  celery
1 tablespoon sugar
1/2 teaspoon garlic powder
  or 2 medium garlic cloves,
  peeled and minced
1 cup mayonnaise
Salt and pepper to taste

Cook fresh lima beans in salted boiling water to cover until just tender, about 20 to 25 minutes. Cook frozen lima beans according to package directions. Drain beans well, rinse in cold water to stop cooking action, and drain again; allow beans to cool thoroughly. In a medium bowl, combine beans, onion, ham, pimento, celery, sugar, and garlic powder. Add mayonnaise, mixing well. Season with salt and pepper to taste.

–Suzanne and Warren Wolstenholme, proprietors
Chef John V. Moore
Homemades by Suzanne

Horseradish Beet Salad

Yield: 4 servings

1 pound beets, peeled and
  sliced (see note)
Water as needed
1/4 cup mayonnaise (see
  note)
1 tablespoon prepared or 1
  teaspoon freshly grated
  peeled horseradish root
1 teaspoon sugar
Salt and pepper to taste
Crisp greens

Cook beets, uncovered, in a small amount of boiling water for15 to 20 minutes or until fork tender. Drain well, transfer beets to a medium bowl, and allow to cool. In a small bowl, combine mayonnaise, horseradish, and sugar blending well. Season with salt and pepper to taste. Pour dressing over beets, mixing gently. Chill thoroughly in refrigerator. Spoon mixture, dividing evenly, onto chilled salad plates lined with crisp greens.

Note: A drained (16-ounce) can sliced beets may be substituted for fresh beets.

Note: 2 tablespoons mayonnaise and 2 tablespoons sour cream may be substituted for 1/4 cup mayonnaise.

Variation: Add about 2 tablespoons minced fresh or 2 tablespoons dried dill weed or to taste to beet mixture.

–Claudia Echols (Mrs. Steven)

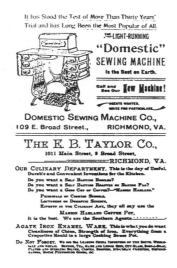

Old Richmond Advertisement, circa late nineteenth century

389

Dinner
(Cir. 1894)

1. *Puree of asparagus.*
2. *Boiled sheep's-head* (Hollandaise sauce).
Potato au gratin
3. *Squab braise with mushrooms.*
4. *Spring Lamb, caper sauce.*
Cucumbers sliced.
5. *Baked sweet-breads, French peas.*
6. *Tomatoes stuffed with celery and mayonaise.*
7. *Fresh strawberries and vanilla ice-cream.*
Cake, cheese, wafers, bonbons.
Coffee and cordials.
Wines served with each course according to rule given.

F.F.V. *Receipt Book,* 1894

Crisp Broccoli, Bacon, and Raisin Salad

Yield: 6 servings

10 ounces sliced bacon
2 1/2 pounds broccoli
1 medium onion, peeled
and coarsely chopped
1/2 cup dark seedless
raisins
3/4 cup mayonnaise
6 tablespoons sugar
1 1/2 cups cider vinegar
Salt and Pepper to taste
(optional)

In a large heavy skillet, pan-fry bacon over moderate heat until crisp, about 7 minutes; drain well on absorbent paper. Or, arrange 5 to 6 bacon slices on a pottery plate lined with absorbent paper, cover with absorbent paper and microwave at HIGH power for 4 minutes. Turn plate 90 degrees and continue microwaving at HIGH power for an additional 30 to 60 seconds until crisp. Drain cooked bacon on additional absorbent paper. Repeat microwave process until all bacon is cooked. Crumble crisp bacon slices. With a sharp knife, remove woody stems from broccoli and discard. Separate broccoli into small florets and slice remaining stems crosswise into small pieces. In a large bowl, combine broccoli florets and stem pieces, crumbled bacon, chopped onion, and raisins. In a small bowl, combine mayonnaise, sugar, and vinegar, blending well. Pour over broccoli mixture, tossing lightly. Season with salt and pepper to taste, if desired. Chill until ready to serve.

–Heilman Dining Center
University of Richmond
Food Services Department

Crunchy Broccoli Salad

Yield: 6 to 8 servings

1 1/4 pounds broccoli, cut into florets and tender stems thinly sliced
1 large red onion, peeled and chopped
1 large sweet red or yellow pepper, cored, seeded, and chopped
12 slices crisp cooked bacon, crumbled
3/4 cup mayonnaise
1/4 cup cider vinegar
2 to 4 tablespoons sugar
Salt and pepper to taste
Crisp butter or leaf lettuce
Thin strips of sweet red or yellow pepper for garnish

In a medium bowl, combine broccoli florets and sliced stems, onion, sweet red pepper, and crumbled bacon. In a small bowl, combine mayonnaise, vinegar, and sugar, blending well; pour mixture over vegetables and bacon. Season with salt and pepper to taste, mixing well. Cover and thoroughly chill in the refrigerator. To serve, spoon mixture onto lettuce-lined chilled salad plates. Garnish each with thin strips of sweet red pepper.

–Leslie Davis Blackwell (Mrs. John D. Jr.)

Old Richmond Advertisement, circa early twentieth century

Coleslaw was introduced into the American colonies in the early eighteenth century by Dutch settlers. The Dutch word for salad, Sla, soon became Americanized; Kohl referred to cabbage, thus coleslaw. It gained in popularity as winter cabbage was often more readily available.

Crunchy Calico Salad

Yield: 4 to 6 servings

1 (15-ounce) can garbanzo beans (chick peas), drained
1 (7 to 8-ounce) can whole-kernal corn, drained or 1 cup fresh whole-kernel corn, cooked and drained
6 to 8 medium green onions, thinly sliced (include some green tops) (about 1/2 cup sliced)
1/2 medium sweet red pepper, cored, seeded, and chopped (about 1/2 cup chopped)
1/2 cup chopped celery
1 tablespoon minced parsley
1/4 cup red wine vinegar
1/2 teaspoon Dijon-style prepared mustad
1/4 to 1/2 teaspoon minced, peeled garlic
1/2 cup salad oil
Salt and pepper to taste
Crisp butter or bib lettuce leaves

In a medium bowl, combine the first 6 ingredients. In a 1-cup measure, combine vinegar and mustard, blending well. With a wire whisk, gradually whisk in oil until mixture is smooth and slightly thickened. Pour dressing over vegetables and mix lightly to coat vegetables. Season with salt and pepper to taste. Cover and refrigerator for at least 4 hours to blend flavors, mixing occasionally. To serve, spoon mixture, with a slotted spoon, draining well and dividing evenly, onto chilled salad plates lined with crisp butter or bib lettuce leaves.

Variation: Add 1 to 2 tablespoons minced fresh or 1 to 2 teaspoons dried oregano or 1 to 2 tablespoons minced cheruil or cilantro.

392

Refrigerator Slaw

Yield: 8 to 10 servings

1 (1 to 1 1/2 pound) cabbage, coarsely chopped
1 large onion, peeled and chopped
1/4 cup chopped green pepper
1/4 cup chopped pimento, drained
1 1/2 teaspoons celery seed
1/2 teaspoon mustard seed
1 cup white vinegar
1 cup sugar
3/4 teaspoon salt

Combine the first 6 ingredients and pack into a clean half-gallon jar. In a 4-cup measure, combine vinegar, sugar, and salt, stirring until sugar and salt are dissolved. Pour over cabbage mixture. Cover and refrigerate 24 hours before serving. This slaw may be kept in the refrigerator for up to one month.

–Dotty Stuart (Mrs. Albert)

Nielsen's Richmond-style Coleslaw

Yield: 6 to 8 servings

1 medium head cabbage (see note)
1 medium carrot, peeled
1 cup sugar
1/4 cup cider vinegar
1 cup mayonnaise
1/2 teaspoon salt or to taste

Remove outer leaves and core of cabbage. Finely shred cabbage and carrot into a large bowl. Add sugar, mixing well. Pour vinegar over cabbage mixture and allow to stand for 15 minutes. Add mayonnaise and salt, mixing well. Cover and refrigerate until ready to serve.

Note: A 1-pound cabbage provides about 3 1/2 to 4 1/2 cups shredded cabbage. Use about a 1 1/2 to 2-pound cabbage.

–Martha and Ned Nielsen, proprietors
Nielsen's 3N Restaurant

Swift Creek Mill Playhouse

Records indicate that Swift Creek Mill was in existence as early as 1663. It is believed to be the oldest grist mill in this country. Henry Randolph I, born in Little Houghton, Northamptonshire, England, migrated to this country about 1640. In 1655, he acquired a large tract of land in Bermuda Hundred on Swift Creek where he erected the present mill. An heir of Henry Randolph I, William Bland Randolph, deeded the mill to William Rowlett on February 20, 1805, and it became known as Rowlett's Mill. In 1852, the Rowlett heirs conveyed the mill to the Swift Creek Manufacturing company.

During the Civil War, on May 9th and 10th, 1864, a battle was fought around the mill when General B. F. Butler's Army of the James attempted to cross Swift Creek. Following the war, the property became Schmidt's Distillery preparing corn whisky. After this, the property changed hands several times. Operated as a grist mill, it became known in 1929 as Swift Creek Mill. It continued to operate as a grist mill until about 1956.

On December 2, 1965, Swift Creek Mill Playhouse opened its doors. To convert the old grist mill into a dinner theatre required an addition to the three-story building to house the kitchen, dressing rooms, and restrooms. Stairways were built leading to upper and lower dining levels, and to the theatre located on the top floor. Much of the old equipment in the mill was refurbished to lend a rustic atmosphere. Swift Creek Mill has been preserved as both an historical landmark and a cultural outlet for the talent of local artists, whose efforts have made possible the artistic achievements of the Mill. The 300 year old Swift Creek Mill has been made a Virginia Historical Landmark and has been listed in the National Register of Historical Places.

Summer Slaw

Yield: 8 to 10 servings

1 medium head cabbage
(about 1 to 1 1/2 pounds)
(see note)
1 medium onion, peeled
and chopped
1 cup sugar
1 cup white or cider vinegar
3/4 cup salad oil
1 tablespoon salt or to taste
1 teaspoon dry mustard
1 teaspoon celery seed

Remove outside leaves of cabbage. Shred cabbage (coarse or fine, as desired) with a shredder; set aside. In a small heavy saucepan, combine sugar, vinegar, oil, salt, mustard, and celery seed; bring to a boil over moderate heat. Combine cabbage and onion in a large bowl. Pour boiling dressing over vegetables, tossing lightly to mix. Spoon mixture into clean quart glass jars. Store, tightly covered, in the refrigerator for up to 1 week.

Note: 1 pound cabbage yields about 3 1/2 to 4 1/2 cups shredded cabbage.

Note: Add 1 each small, cored, seeded, and chopped green and sweet red pepper to slaw, if desired.

Note: For 4 to 6 servings, reduce recipe by half.

–Swift Creek Mill Playhouse

A more ancient and less frequented place of resort for reaction, was the French Garden, of which the name remains, but the site, like that of Troy, has been questionable. A senior cotemporary informs me it was on the hill beyond the city spring, flanked by ravines.

Some refugees from the horrors and massacre of St. Domingo, found their way to Richmond. One of them built a tall thin house, like himself, and, with his co-exiles, laid out a garden in this then remote suburb. Here lemonade, fruits, &c., were served to visitors, and here the worthy man, who had been reduced from wealth and comfort to comparative poverty and to exile, spent his remaining days....

Samuel Mordecai
Richmond in By-Gone Days, 1856
Reprint Edition, 1975

Cauliflower Slaw

Yield: 6 to 8 servings

1 garlic clove, peeled and
   minced (see note)
1 cup mayonnaise
3 tablespoons cider vinegar
1/2 to 1 teaspoon sugar
1/2 teaspoon salt
Pepper to taste
1 medium head cauliflower
   (about 1 1/2 pounds)
1/2 cup thinly sliced celery
1/4 cup thinly sliced green
   onion
Parsley sprigs or minced
   parsley for garnish

In a small bowl, combine the first 6 ingredients, blending well. Remove leaves from cauliflower; clean and break into small florets or cut into thin slices. In a large bowl, combine cauliflower, celery, and green onion. Pour dressing over vegetables, mixing well. Cover and refrigerate for several hours. Garnish with parsley before serving.

Note: 1 peeled crushed garlic clove may be substituted; remove from salad before serving.

–Janet B. Tutton (Mrs. Roger)

"The Critical Cooks"

All gatherings were not frivolous in that winter months fifty years ago. "The Critical Cooks," or the "Company of Cooks," was organized by Misses Minnie Coxe, Florine and Luly Nolting, Ellen and Bland Clarke, Alice Whitcomb, Bettie Deane and Miss Hallie Talcott. Members dressed as cooks in gingham or calico dresses, with the "kettle badge at the corsage," with white kerchiefs,aprons and becoming caps....
                                      Henrietta Crump
                          *"Richmond Society in February, 1889,
                                Was Busy Party-Going,"*
              Richmond News Leader, *February 14, 1939*

Lettuce is thought to have been served on tables of Persian kings in the sixth century B.C. Greeks called it tridax; however, the Romans, who copied much from the Greeks, probably didn't taste lettuce until the first century. The modern word "lettuce" comes from the latin root lactuca. Some authorities suggest lettuce was not introduced into the English diet until the late sixteenth century. In the late twentieth century, lettuce, especially iceberg or head lettuce is the most popular salad ingredient in the American diet.

Seven Layer Salad

Yield: 12 to 15 servings

1 medium head iceberg lettuce, torn into bite-sized pieces
1 large green pepper, cored, seeded, and chopped
1 large red onion, peeled and chopped
1 (10-ounce) package frozen tiny peas, thawed and drained
1 1/2 cups mayonnaise
Salt and pepper to taste
1 pound sliced bacon, crisply cooked and coarsely crumbled
2 cups shredded sharp Cheddar cheese
Crisp lettuce leaves as needed

In a 13 x 9 x 2-inch glass baking dish, layer the first 4 ingredients in the order listed. Evenly spread mayonnaise over peas, completely covering salad. Sprinkle lightly with salt and pepper to taste. Evenly spread bacon over dressing. Top with shredded cheese. Cover and refrigerate for 24 hours. Serve chilled on individual salad plates lined with crisp lettuce leaves.

Note: This salad may be reduced to 6 servings by decreasing the ingredients to one half the given amounts and layering them as previously directed in a 9 x 9 x 2-inch baking dish.

–University of Richmond
Food Services Department

Salad Au Ceasar

Yield: 8 to 10 servings

Created over the July 4th weekend in 1924 by Ceasar Cardini at his restaurant, Ceasar's Place, in Tijuana, Mexico, Ceasar Salad was originally intended as a main course to be eaten with the fingers. Later Cardini shredded the romaine. It became popular with the Hollywood set visiting Tijuana. Today the salad and its many variations is a particular favorite of many Americans, including those in Richmond, Virginia.

2 heads romaine lettuce
1 cup olive oil
2 tablespoons wine vinegar
2 tablespoons lemon juice
5 anchovies, drained
3 garlic cloves, peeled and minced
2 tablespoons Dijon-style prepared mustard
1 egg
2 tablespoons grated Parmesan cheese
1 tablespoon Worcestershire sauce
Freshly ground pepper to taste
Crisp garlic croutons for garnish (optional)

Separate romaine leaves; wash and thoroughly dry between sheets of absorbent paper. Tear romaine into bite-sized pieces and place in a ziplock plastic bag. Refrigerate until ready to serve. Pour olive oil into a large wooden salad bowl; add vinegar and lemon juice. Add anchovies, mashing well. Add garlic and mustard. Hold an egg under hot running water for 2 minutes to coddle; break into olive oil mixture. With a whisk, lightly beat mixture until thick and creamy. Add Parmesan cheese and Worcestershire sauce, mixing well. Add pepper. Allow flavors to blend at room temperature for 1 to 2 hours. Just before serving, add crisp romaine, tossing lightly to coat leaves with dressing. Adjust seasoning as desired. Garnish with croutons, if desired. Serve immediately.

Note: This salad may be reduced to 4 servings by decreasing the ingredients to one half the given amounts. Use 1 egg yolk, or beat 1 whole egg and use only half the amount.

–Ginger Levit

Salads

During the nineteenth century, many people were suspicious of salads and also didn't look too kindly on eating green vegetables.

Crunchy Garden Pea Salad

Yield: 6 to 8 servings

1 (10-ounce) package frozen *very* small peas, thawed and drained or 2 cups shelled fresh peas
Boiling water as needed
5 to 6 slices crisp cooked bacon, crumbled and divided
1 cup shredded sharp Cheddar cheese, divided
1/2 cup minced peeled onion or thinly sliced green onion (include some green tops)
1/4 cup minced sweet red pepper or pimento, drained
1/4 to 1/3 cup mayonnaise
1/4 to 1/3 cup sour cream
1 1/2 tablespoons lemon juice
Seasoned salt and pepper to taste
3 to 4 drops hot sauce (optional)
Crisp lettuce leaves or curly endive

Use thawed frozen peas without additional cooking. Cook fresh peas in boiling water to just cover for 3 to 4 minutes after water returns to a boil or until tender but crisp and firm; drain well. *Do not overcook.* Cool. In a medium bowl, combine peas, one-half of the bacon, 3/4 cup cheese, onion, and sweet red pepper. Add mayonnaise, sour cream, and lemon juice, mixing lightly. Add seasoned salt, pepper, and hot sauce, if desired, mixing again lightly. Cover and chill for at least 1 hour. Spoon pea mixture onto chilled salad plates lined with crisp lettuce leaves or curly endive. Sprinkle each serving with the remaining shredded cheese and crumbled bacon, dividing evenly.

–Virginia Cottrell (Mrs. Walker C., Jr.)

Scorched Linen

To remove slight scorch from linens, sponge them well with cold water and lay in sun for several hours. Or rub them with peroxide until the scorch disappears and then rinse immediately in quantities of cold water.

Barbara Trigg Brown
"Virginia Woman Recalls Christmas Party and Other Events on Franklin Street in the Nineties,"
'Virginia Reel' Had Guests Dancing for Hours
Richmond Times-Dispatch, December 25, 1938

....One day in 1865 Governor Smith heard annoyed voices outside in the entrance hall. The porter was trying to make a caller leave. Smith listened at the door until he heard a female voice, then he appeared out of curiosity, and in his most courtly manner bowed to receive a beautiful woman in faded mourning calico. "I wish to see my governor," she said. "I am your governor," Smith said, "What can I do for you?" "My husband is dead," she said. "I have six children, the oldest not large enough to help me labor. During these years I have cultivated a garden, raised a few fowls, and carted my produce to this city to exchange for necessities of life. Officers have pressed my old horse, soldiers have robbed my coops and garden. I have nothing left and my children are hungry. I have walked seven miles to ask my governor what I am to do." Certainly the state had no recompense to offer. But the governor was affected by the story. He scratched a note to Elizabeth Smith upstairs, asking her to take the woman to the mansion storeroom in the basement and give the caller what she needed. The coachman drove her home in the governor's carriage.

William Seal
Virginia's Executive Mansion: A History of the Governor's House, 1988

Strawberry Spinach Salad

Yield: 8 servings

8 to 12 ounces fresh spinach
1 to 2 pints strawberries
1/2 cup white vinegar
1/2 cup sugar
1 1/2 teaspoons minced peeled onion
1/4 teaspoon Worcestershire sauce
1/4 teaspoon paprika
1/2 cup salad oil

Wash spinach in warm water and remove stems. Tear leaves into small pieces and drain well. Dry between sheets of absorbent paper. Place spinach in a ziplock plastic bag and chill in refrigerator until crisp. Clean, hull, and slice strawberries. Reserve a few whole strawberries for garnish. In a blender container combine vinegar, sugar, poppy seeds, sesame seeds, onion, Worcestershire sauce and paprika. With motor running, gradually add oil, whizzing until

400

2 tablespoons sesame
    seeds
1 tablespoon poppy seeds
Few reserved whole
    strawberries for garnish

well blended. Combine spinach and sliced strawberries in a large salad bowl. Drizzle dressing over mixture, tossing lightly to coat strawberries well. Garnish salad with whole strawberries

—Gladys Antroinen (Mrs. Aaron)

Marinated Vegetable Salad

Yield: 8 to 10 servings

1 (10-ounce) package frozen
    French-style green beans,
    thawed and drained (see
    note)
1 (10-ounce) package frozen
    very small peas, thawed
    and drained (see note)
1 (2-ounce) jar chopped
    pimento, drained
1 small onion, peeled and
    chopped
1 cup chopped celery
1/2 cup white vinegar
1/4 cup sugar
1/2 teaspoon salt
1 cup salad oil
Crisp lettuce leaves as
    needed

In a glass bowl, combine the first 5 ingredients. In a small bowl, combine vinegar, sugar, and salt. With a whisk, beat in oil until mixture is smooth; pour over vegetables. Cover and marinate for 12 hours in the refrigerator. Drain vegetables and spoon into a lettuce-lined serving bowl.

Note: 2 cups shelled fresh peas and 2 cups fresh cut green beans cooked in boiling water to cover for 3 minutes and drained well may be substituted for frozen green beans and peas.

—Virginia Cottrell (Mrs. Walker C., Jr.)

401

Zesty Spinach Salad

Yield: 10 to 12 servings

10 ounces spinach
12 ounces (1 1/2 cups)
  cream-style cottage
  cheese
1 small onion, peeled and
  minced
1 cup sour cream
1/4 cup sugar
3 teaspoons white vinegar
2 teaspoons prepared
  horseradish or to taste
1/2 teaspoon dry mustard
1/4 teaspoon salt
1/2 cup chopped pecans

Wash spinach thoroughly, removing any grit or sand. Remove stems, tear into small pieces, and drain well. Dry on absorbent paper. Store in a ziplock plastic bag in the refrigerator until ready to serve. Combine cottage cheese, onion, sour cream, sugar, vinegar, horseradish, mustard, and salt, blending well (see note). Cover and refrigerate for several hours to blend flavors. Just before serving, place spinach and pecans in a large salad bowl. Add dressing; toss lightly to mix. Serve at once.

Note: For a very smooth consistency to the dressing, pour dressing mixture into a blender container, cover, and blend at medium speed until smooth.

Note: If salad is dry, add additional sour cream and salt to taste.

—Anne Miller (Mrs. Charles)

Only one house that was in Richmond during the time of the Revolution is still standing, the Old Stone House on the north side of Main Street between Nineteenth and Twentieth streets. During the Revolution the house belonged to SamuelEge.

Mount Comfort stood north of Richmond on a four hundred acre estate bordering Shockoe Creek, later designated as the Chestnut Hill and Highland Park sections of Richmond. Mount Comfort, built by 1748, was reported to be the first brick residence in the vicinity and a major social center for the area.

Windsor stood near the river in the area that is today Windsor Farms, named after it.

Harry M. Ward and Harold E. Greer, Jr.
Richmond During the Revolution, 1775-83, 1977

Summer Squash 'N Apple Salad

Yield: 8 servings

1/2 cup dried currants or
 dark seedless raisins
1/4 cup Crème de Cassis or
 Madeira
1 pound zucchini or yellow
 summer squash, thinly
 sliced crosswise
3 tart ripe medium apples,
 cored, seeded, and cut
 into bite-sized pieces
 (see note)
1/3 cup chopped peeled
 onion
3 tablespoons lemon juice
1/3 cup olive oil (see note)
1/4 cup sherry vinegar
Salt to taste
1 cup shredded sharp
 Cheddar or Monterey Jack
 cheese
1/3 cup chopped fresh mint
 leaves
Crisp lettuce leaves (op-
 tional)
Fresh mint sprigs for
 garnish

In a small bowl, soak currants in Crème de Cassis or raisins in Madeira for several hours at room temperature until fruit is plump and liquid is absorbed; drain any remaining liquid. In a medium bowl, combine squash, apples, onion, and lemon juice. Add currants, oil, and vinegar. Toss lightly to mix. Season with salt to taste. Cover and refrigerate for several hours. Just before serving, add cheese and mint leaves, tossing lightly. Allow to stand at room temperature for 10 to 15 minutes before serving. Spoon mixture, dividing evenly, onto individual salad plates lined with crisp greens, if desired. Garnish each serving with sprigs of fresh mint.

Note: Use a premium quality extra virgin olive oil. Extra virgin refers to the oil collected from the first press of the olives.

Note: Use McIntosh, Winesap, Granny Smith, or other tart variety of apples. Use unpeeled or peeled as desired.

–Elinor Kuhn (Mrs. Frank)
Buffet, catering firm
Richmond Culinary Guild

Some of the best tasting tomatoes in the United States are grown just north of Richmond in Hanover county. Experts suggest the superb flavor has something to do with the soil content found in the Hanover area. Many Richmonders are known to start a countdown of days until the Hanover tomatoes come into season about the last week in June, depending upon the weather.

Bloody Mary Aspic Cups

Yield: 6 servings

1 1/4 cups vegetable-tomato juice, divided
1 envelope (tablespoon) unflavored gelatin
1 teaspoon Worcestershire sauce
2 teaspoons lemon juice
4 to 5 drops hot sauce or to taste
Crisp lettuce leaves or curly endive
Celery sticks for garnish

Soften gelatin in 1/2 cup vegetable-tomato juice; allow to stand for 5 minutes. In a small heavy saucepan, combine remaining 3/4 cup vegetable-tomato juice, Worcestershire sauce, lemon juice, and hot sauce; bring to a boil over moderate heat. Remove from heat; add gelatin mixture, stirring until dissolved. Pour into 6 lightly oiled muffin cups (2 3/4 inches in diameter), dividing mixture evenly. Chill until firm. Unmold onto chilled salad plates lined with crisp lettuce leaves. Serve with celery sticks.

–The Reynolds Wrap Kitchens
The Reynolds Metals Company

Layered Fruit 'N Cheese Gelatin Salad

Yield: 8 servings

3 (3-ounce) packages lemon-flavored gelatin
4 cups boiling water
1 tablespoon white vinegar
2 (16-ounce) cans pitted sweet white cherries,

Dissolve gelatin in boiling water; add vinegar, blending well. Set aside 3/4 cup of the mixture. Chill the remaining gelatin mixture until partially set; fold in cherries and pineapple. Spoon one-half of the mixture into a lightly greased 1 1/2-quart mold; chill until firm. Set aside uncon-

404

drained
1 (20-ounce) can crushed
pineapple (including
juice)
1 (20-ounce) can grapefruit
sections, drained and cut
into bite-sized pieces
1 (8-ounce) package cream
cheese, at room
temperature
1 (4-ounce) jar chopped
pimento, drained
1 cup chopped pecans
Crisp lettuce leaves or curly
endive as needed

gealed fruited portion. In a bowl, beat cream cheese until smooth. Add 3/4 cup of reserved unfruited gelatin, beating at low speed of an electric mixer until well-blended. Stir in pimento and pecans. Evenly spoon over firm fruited gelatin layer; chill until firm. Spoon remaining fruited uncongealed gelatin over firm cheese layer; chill until firm. Unmold onto a chilled serving plate lined with crisp greens.

–Betty Wilton (Mrs. E. Carlton)

Grapefruit Lime Aspic

Yield: 6 servings

"This is a favorite recipe which was published in a Richmond newspaper over 20 years ago!"

1 (20-ounce) can grapefruit
sections, drained (reserve
juice)
Water as needed
1 (3-ounce) package lime-
flavored gelatin
2 tablespoons lime or
lemon juice
1/4 teaspoon salt
1 cup heavy or light cream,
chilled
1/2 cup chopped pecans
1/2 cup chopped celery
Crisp lettuce leaves or curly
endive
Mayonnaise
Paprika

Cut grapefruit sections into bite-sized pieces. In a small heavy saucepan, add enough water to reserved juice to measure 1 1/4 cups; heat to boiling. Dissolve gelatin and salt in boiling grapefruit juice mixture. Chill until mixture starts to thicken. Stir in cream, grapefruit, pecans, and celery. Spoon into a lightly oiled 1-quart mold or 6 to 8 individual molds; refrigerate until firm. Unmold onto a chilled lettuce-lined serving plate or individual salad plates. Garnish each serving with a dollop of mayonnaise and sprinkle with paprika.

–Doris Crowell (Mrs. R. E.)

Tomato Jelly

One quart can tomatoes, one-half box gelatine, one-half onion, two bay leaves, small pinch of soda, salt and red, pepper to season well. Cook tomatoes and seasoning about thirty minutes, then add gelatine which has been previously soaked in enough cold water to cover for thirty minutes. Strain through fine sieve in moulds and serve on lettuce leaves with chopped celery and mayonnaise.

Mrs. Starkey
Virginia Cook Book, *1839*

Molded Cranberry Raspberry Gelatin Salad

Yield: 6 to 8 servings

1 (3-ounce) package
  raspberry-flavored gelatin
1 (3-ounce) package lemon-
  flavored gelatin
1 1/2 cups boiling water
1 (16-ounce) can jellied
  cranberry sauce
7 ounces carbonated
  lemon/lime beverage
1 (10-ounce) package frozen
  raspberries, thawed
Crisp greens
Sour cream for garnish
Fresh or thawed frozen
  whole raspberries for
  garnish

In a large bowl, combine the gelatins and boiling water, stirring until gelatin is dissolved. With a whisk, blend in cranberry sauce, mixing well. Whisk until mixture is smooth. Add carbonated lemon/lime beverage. Chill in refrigerator until mixture is partially set; fold in thawed raspberries. Spoon mixture into a lightly oiled 1 1/2-quart mold or individual molds. Chill in refrigerator until firm. Unmold onto a chilled serving plate or individual salad plates lined with crisp greens. Garnish each serving with a dollop of sour cream and whole rasberries.

Old Richmond Advertisement, circa 1909

Pineapple Cheese Gelatin Salad

Yield: 6 to 8 servings

Gelatin salads are a distinctly twentieth-century American innovation. They were especially popular throughout the United States during the first half of the century.

1 (8-ounce) can crushed pineapple (reserve juice)
3/4 cup sugar
1/2 cup reserved pineapple juice
1 envelope (tablespoon) unflavored gelatin
1/4 cup cold water
1 cup shredded sharp Cheddar cheese
1 cup heavy cream, whipped
Crisp lettuce leaves or curly endive as needed

Drain pineapple, reserving juice. In a small heavy saucepan, dissolve sugar in reserved pineapple juice; heat to boiling. While juice is heating, soften gelatin in cold water. Dissolve softened gelatin in hot pineapple liquid; transfer to a large bowl and chill until partially set, but not firm. Add pineapple and cheese. Fold in whipped cream. Spoon into a lightly greased 1 1/2-quart ring mold or 6 to 8 oiled individual molds; refrigerate until firm. Unmold onto a chilled lettuce or endive-lined serving plate or individual salad plates.

Note: This Pineapple Cheese Gelatin Salad is rich and should be served with a meat such as chicken or turkey and also makes a great luncheon salad.

–Sue Crowell (Mrs. Robert)

Immediately following the war, the many lovely young girls visiting the springs were in for disappointment. The beaux were few, either killed in the civil war or too poor to go holidaying. The situation was so desperate that more operatic selections were played than ball music.

Such a condition could not go on for long. Soon came word of fancy mask balls, pink teas, pink dinners, pink germans (everybody and everything wore pink), horse races, champagne dinners, and the beginning of clubs. Dowagers on porches were busy protecting the purity of the Southern belle who was not permitted to step off the piazza after dark nor allowed more than one glass of champagne per party.

Betty Sessler
"Parents Were Quaint, but ... They Had Fun,"
Richmond Times-Dispatch, Nov. 30, 1952

Ribbon Gelatin Salad

Yield: 8 to 10 servings

"This is one of our favorites that was given to us by our friend, Judi Kauffman. It's especially nice to serve at Christmas or Valentine's Day or for a buffet dinner."

1 (6-ounce) package
  raspberry-flavored
  gelatin (see note)
1 1/2 cups boiling water
2 (10-ounce) packages
  frozen raspberries,
  thawed (see note)
1 (13 1/2-ounce) can
  crushed pineapple
  (including juice)
1/4 teaspoon salt
2 cups sour cream, divided
Crisp lettuce leaves or curly
  endive as needed

In a bowl, dissolve gelatin in boiling water. Add raspberries, pineapple, and salt, mixing well. Pour 1 1/2 cups gelatin mixture into a lightly greased 2-quart mold; chill until firm. Allow remaining gelatin mixture to stand at room temperature. Evenly spread 1 cup sour cream over firm gelatin. Spoon one half of the remaining liquid gelatin mixture over sour cream layer. Chill until firm. Evenly spread remaining 1 cup of sour cream over second firm gelatin layer. Top with remaining liquid gelatin mixture. Chill until firm. Unmold onto a chilled serving plate lined with crisp greens.

Note: 1 (6-ounce) package strawberry-flavored gelatin and 2 (10-ounce) packages frozen strawberries may be substituted.

–Mary and Ernie Swartz

Tangy Fruited Ginger Ale Gelatin Salad

Yield: 6 to 8 servings

1 1 (3-ounce) package
  lemon-flavored gelatin
3/4 cup boiling water
1 1/4 cups ginger ale
1 (8-ounce) can fruit
  cocktail, drained
1/2 cup chopped celery
1/2 cup chopped pecans or
  English walnuts
1 tablespoon finely chopped
  crystallized ginger
Crisp lettuce leaves as
  needed
Sour cream, whipped cream,

In a bowl, dissolve gelatin in boiling water. Add ginger ale, blending well. Chill until mixture is partially set, but not firm. Fold in fruit, celery, pecans, and 1 tablespoon crystallized ginger. Spoon into a lightly greased 1-quart mold or into 6 to 8 individual molds; refrigerate until firm. Unmold onto a chilled lettuce-lined serving plate or individual salad plates. Garnish each serving with sour cream, whipped cream, or mayonnaise. Sprinkle lightly with paprika or additional chopped crystallized ginger, if desired.

or mayonnaise for garnish
Paprika for garnish (op-
   tional) or additional finely
   chopped crystallized
   ginger

–Bebe West (Mrs. Eugene, Jr.)

©Eliza B. Askin 1988

In Virginia social affairs consisted mostly of gatherings at the governor's mansion or assemblies held during sessions of court. During these times planters escorted their families to town for the brief period of balls, banquets, and dancing.

As the 17th century advanced, The South enlivened its social life with dinner parties, hunts, dances, and a great deal of visiting. Plantation balls became events of great splendor. In the luxurious homes of Virginia, Maryland, and the Carolinas furnishings from England and France began to appear, paid for from the proceeds of a tobacco-based economic growth.

Visiting in the south was a special event, primarily because the great distances which separated plantations made travel difficult and slow. Having traveled so far the guests needed little coaxing to make themselves at home, and were often quick to agree to a stay much longer than originally anticipated. Records were seldom kept to give us an account of the number of guests at a single time, but we know that on occasions the average mansion might be so crowded as to convince the host that he should direct his guest to the master bedroom and himself sleep on a couch or even the floor!

Adelaide Hechtlinger
"Women in Early America,"
Early American Life , April 1973

Cooked Salad Dressing

Yield: 3 cups

1/2 cup butter or margarine, melted
3 eggs, beaten
1 cup sugar
1/2 cup white or cider vinegar
1/2 teaspoon salt
1 cup cup mayonnaise
1 teaspoon prepared mustard

In the top of a double boiler, melt butter over hot water. With a whisk, blend in eggs, sugar, vinegar, and salt. Cook, stirring frequently, over simmering water until thickened and bubbly hot. Remove from heat and allow to cool. Add mayonnaise and mustard, blending well. Chill thoroughly. Serve with fruit salad, potato salad, and coleslaw. May store in an airtight container in the refrigerator for several days.

–Mary and Ernie Swartz

Aunt Em's Salad Dressing

Yield: about 1 pint

1/4 cup sugar
1/2 tablespoon flour
1 teaspoon dry mustard
1/2 teaspoon salt
2 egg yolks
1 cup light cream or half-and-half
1/3 cup cider vinegar
1 1/2 tablespoons butter or margarine, at room temperature
1 teaspoon lemon juice
Several grains cayenne pepper

In the top of a double boiler, combine the first 4 ingredients, mixing well. Add egg yolks, one at a time, beating well after each addition with a wire whisk or a wooden spoon. Gradually add cream, blending thoroughly with the whisk; then blend in vinegar. Add butter. Cook, stirring constantly, over boiling water until mixture is thickened. Remove from heat; allow to cool. Stir in lemon juice and cayenne pepper. Store, covered, in a glass pint jar in the refrigerator.

–Jane Hamlin (Mrs. Richard R.)

Aunt Dinah's Recipe Book, circa 1914

Crab Louie's Tavern

Crab Louie's Tavern, located in a two hundred year old farmhouse in the Sycamore Square Shopping Center, is thought to be housed in the second oldest building in Midlothian, Virginia, a suburb of Richmond. Known for its marvelous tasting fresh seafood and fish, the restaurant has been restored by the present owner to reflect the mid-nineteenth century Colonial/Greek Revival styles of architecture. The land was developed about 1775 and owned by the Woolridge family who controlled several coal mines. In addition to the sixteen crabmeat entrées and six varieties of fresh fish featured, Crab Louie's also receives raves for its six sweet quick breads and four relishes served at tableside. A second restaurant recently opened north of the James River in the far west end of Richmond at the Gayton Crossing Shopping center.

Crab Louie's Dressing

Yield: about 1 quart

2 cups mayonnaise (see note)
1/2 cup heavy cream
1/2 cup chili sauce
1/2 cup chopped green pepper
1/2 cup chopped green onions (include some green tops)
1/4 cup lemon juice
1 tablespoon Worcestershire sauce
1/2 to 1 tablespoon prepared horseradish
1/2 teaspoon seafood seasoning (see note)

In a medium bowl, combine all ingredients, blending well. Cover and refrigerate for 12 hours to blend flavors. Store, tightly covered, in a clean glass quart jar until ready to use for up to 1 week.

Note: Preferably use homemade mayonnaise (see index), although commercial mayonnaise may be substituted.

Note: Preferably use Old Bay brand seafood seasoning.

–Crab Louie's Tavern

412

Honey Celery Seed Vinaigrette

Yield: about 2 3/4 cups

Since opening in December, 1984, du Jour has become one of the city's "hottest" restaurants. "On the Avenues" of Libbie and Grove, alongside many of Richmond's most exclusive shops, this charming restaurant and sidewalk cafe boasts a dinner menu that changes weekly to feature the freshest seasonal offerings. It has been chosen as one of the best restaurants in Richmond by several local critics and scores of Richmonders.

1/4 cup honey
6 tablespoons tarragon
vinegar
2 tablespoons red wine
vinegar
1 tablespoon celery seed
1 teaspoon salt
1 teaspoon celery salt
1/2 teaspoon minced peeled
garlic
1/2 teaspoon white pepper
1 1/2 cups salad oil

In a small bowl, combine the first 8 ingredients, blending well. Gradually add oil, whisking constantly with a wire whisk, until mixture is thoroughly blended. Store, covered in a clean glass quart jar in the refrigerator for up to 2 weeks until ready to use. Dressing will separate during storage; shake or whisk to remix.

–Chef Robert Hamlin, proprietor
Jana Blue Hopper, proprietor
duJour Restaurant and Caterers

Avenue Shops at Libbey and Grove

Islander Salad Dressing

Yield: About 2 cups

"This dressing is especially good with chicken salad or mixed fresh greens."

1/3 cup catsup or chili sauce
1/3 cup white or cider
vinegar
1/3 cup sugar
2 teaspoons Worcestershire
sauce
1/4 teaspoon curry powder
1 cup salad oil
Salt and pepper to taste
(optional)

In a deep small bowl, combine the first 5 ingredients, mixing well. With a wire whisk, gradually whisk in oil until mixture is smooth and slightly thickened. Or, combine the first 5 ingredients in a blender container; cover and beat for 20 seconds at medium speed. With blender motor at medium speed, gradually add oil in a steady stream until mixture is smooth and slightly thickened. Season dressing with salt and pepper to taste, if desired. Store, covered, in a glass pint jar in the refrigerator for up to 3 weeks.

–Bobbie Hudson (Mrs. Harvey)

French Dressing

Yield: about 1 1/2 cups

"Originally from Charleston, this French dressing recipe has become a family favorite and is delicious for all types of fruit salads."

1/3 cup sugar
1 teaspoon salt
1 teaspoon celery seed
1 teaspoon paprika
1 teaspoon dry mustard
1/4 cup cider or white
vinegar, divided
1/2 teaspoon onion juice
1 cup salad oil

In a small bowl, combine the first 5 ingredients. Add one half of the vinegar and onion juice, blending well. Gradually add oil, beating at medium speed of an electric mixer until smooth and thick. Beat in remaining vinegar. Cover and chill in the refrigerator for several hours to allow flavors to blend.

Note: Dressing should be very thick in consistency.

–Tish Keppel (Mrs. Ernest)

Christmas Come to the Southland During the Late 18th Century
Print from Valentine Museum, circa 1890

Mayonnaise

Yield: about 2 1/2 cups

2 eggs
1/2 teaspoon salt
1 tablespoon sugar
1 1/4 teaspoons dry mustard
1/2 teaspoon paprika
1/4 to 1/2 teaspoon celery
  salt
1/8 teaspoon white pepper
1/3 cup cider vinegar
2 cups salad oil, divided

Combine first 8 ingredients and 1/4 cup oil in blender container. Cover and blend at medium speed for 1 minute. Add remaining oil in a fine stream until thick and smooth.

Poppy Seed Dressing

Yield: about 1 cup

"This dressing is excellent over avocado and mandarin orange salad."

2/3 cup salad oil
1/2 cup sugar
1/4 cup cider or white
vinegar
1 1/2 tablespoons poppy
seeds
1 teaspoon prepared
mustard
1 teaspoon salt

Combine all ingredients together in a clean glass jar; cover and shake vigorously until thoroughly mixed. Store in the refrigerator until ready to use.

–Deubre Anne Crenshaw (Mrs. Gordon)

Sour Cream Fruit Dressing

Yield: about 1 1/4 cups dressing

1/4 cup heavy cream
2/3 cup sour cream
1 1/2 tablespoons honey or
to taste
1 1/2 tablespoons straw-
berry or raspberry liqueur
Pinch salt

In a chilled deep small bowl, beat cream with chilled beaters until stiff peaks are formed. Gradually add sour cream, honey, fruit liqueur, and salt, beating until mixture is smooth. Chill, covered, until ready to serve.

Variation: 1 1/2 to 2 tablespoons strained puréed strawberries or raspberries may be substituted for fruit liqueur.

Dressing For Salad

Break 12 eggs and put raw yolks in a large, flat dish; to that add 3 tea-spoonsful of mustard; stir in very slowly 1quart finest salad oil. After this is all mixed in add salt and vinegar, slowly, to taste, or lemon, if preferred. Mix just before serving, as standing after being mixed causes the celery to wilt and thins the dressing-garnish in any preferred style. A fork is best to use in beating the dressing. Mix with a spoon.

–Mrs. Powhatan Breeden.
Virginia Recipes, *1890*

Salad Dressing

Mix in a cup: one-half teaspoon of mustard, one-half teaspoon of salt, one-half teaspoon of pepper, one tablespoon of flour, one tablespoon of sugar. Mix in a pan: one cup of milk, two well-beaten eggs, mix all in a pan and add a half a cup of vinegar and cook until it thickens.

—Mrs. W. R. Trainham
Virginia Cook Book, *1839*

Sour Cream Roquefort Salad Dressing

Yield: about 2 cups

1 cup sour cream
1/4 cup mayonnaise
1 tablespoon white vinegar
1 teaspoon Worcestershire
  sauce
1 teaspoon sugar
1/2 teaspoon salt or to taste
1/4 teaspoon celery salt
1/4 teaspoon garlic salt
1/4 teaspoon paprika
1/4 teaspoon pepper or to
  taste
4 ounces Roquefort or blue
  cheese, at room temperature and crumbled

In a deep small bowl, combine the first 10 ingredients; beat until mixture is smooth. Carefully fold in crumbled cheese. Store, covered, in a clean glass jar in the refrigerator until ready to use. Serve at room temperature.

—Jane Hamlin (Mrs. Richard R.)

Watercress Dressing

Yield: about 1 1/2 cups

1/2 bunch watercress,
  cleaned and minced
1 garlic clove, peeled and
  minced
1 cup mayonnaise
2 teaspoons lemon juice
Salt to taste

In a small bowl, combine the first 4 ingredients, mixing well. Season with salt to taste. Cover and chill until ready to serve.
—Virginia Cottrell (Mrs. Walker C., Jr.)

417

> Planetary influences were thought to govern the health of both crops and people. Herbs were gathered during certain phases of the moon, and the use of such drugs as were discovered through trial and error to be beneficial for certain disease conditions, was regulated by heavenly configurations.
>
> We can only guess that an adult could resist the ingestion of Venice Treacle once he had tasted it, but an innocent child was probably forced to drink the bitter concoction. It was a gentle blend of viper, white wine, opium, red rose, germander, St. John's wort, juice of rough sloe, dry spices, and twenty more herbs.
>
> Adelaide Hechtlinger
> Childhood in Early America,"
> **Early America Life,** February 1973

Creamy Russian Dressing

Yield: About 2 cups

1 1/4 cups mayonnaise
1/2 cup chili sauce
1 hard-cooked egg, peeled and finely chopped
1 tablespoon lemon juice or vinegar
1 teaspoon minced chives or peeled grated onion
1/2 teaspoon Worcestershire sauce
1/2 teaspoon prepared horseradish
Pinch of cayenne pepper

In a small bowl, combine ingredients in order listed; mix and chill thoroughly.

Mustard Vinaigrette Dressing

Yield: about 1 1/4 cups

1/3 cup red wine vinegar
2 tablespoons balsamic
  vinegar (optional) (see
  note)
1 1/2 teaspoons Dijon-style
  prepared mustard
1/2 to 1 teaspoon garlic
  juice
1/4 teaspoon dry mustard
1/4 teaspoon salt or to taste
1/8 teaspoon white pepper
  or to taste
Pinch sugar (optional)
2/3 cup olive or other salad
  oil (see note)

In a small bowl, combine the first 7 or 8 ingredients, blending well. With a wire whisk, gradually beat in oil until mixture is smooth and well-blended. Store, tightly covered, in a glass container in the refrigerator until ready to use. Just before serving, beat again with a wire whisk.

Note: Balsamic vinegar is available in many grocery and specialty food shops. If balsamic vinegar is not used, the red wine vinegar should be increased to1/2 cup.

Note: Use a high quality, extra virgin olive oil. French olive oil has a sweeter flavor than Italian, Spanish, or Greek olive oil.

19th Century Apple Horseradish Sauce

Yield: about 2 1/2 cups

Serve this updated version of a 19th century Southern horseradish sauce with roast beef or baked ham.

1 cup heavy cream, chilled
1/2 cup unsweetened
  applesauce
2 tablespoons freshly grated
  horseradish or to taste

In a chilled small bowl, beat cream with chilled beaters until stiff peaks are formed. Fold in applesauce and horseradish. Cover and chill thoroughly in the refrigerator. Sauce may be stored in a covered container for up to two weeks.

Traveller's House Dressing

Yield: about 4 cups

Named for Robert E. Lee's famous horse, Traveller's Restaurant, a popular downtown dining establishment, occupies the basement and addition of the small stately house at 707 E. Franklin Street used by General Lee and his family as a residence during the Civil War. Traveller resided in a small barn across the brick patio at the rear of the house. In 1865, when Lee returned home from Appomattox after his surrender to General Grant, he secluded himself in the basement of the house with his invalid wife, seeking solitude from thousands of well-wishers who streamed to the front door during that difficult time. Today the restored building is listed on the National Register of Historic Places.

Traveller's menu is straightforward and uncomplicated. Corn fed prime beef and premium seafood are specialties. Patrons' favorite selections include escargot, onion soup, creamed spinach, sautéed mushrooms, New York-style cheesecake, and a true southern specialty, pecan pie.

1 large or 2 small garlic cloves, peeled and minced
1/2 cup chopped peeled onion
1 1/2 to 2 tablespoons lemon juice
3/4 tablespoon soy sauce (see note)
3/4 tablespoon Worcestershire sauce
1/2 teaspoon salt
1/2 teaspoon pepper
1/2 ounce anchovies, drained and minced
1/2 cup vinegar
1/4 to 1/2 teaspoon Tabasco sauce
1 egg
1 cup grated Parmesan cheese
2 cups salad oil

In a medium bowl, combine the first 7 ingredients. Add anchovies, vinegar, and Tabasco sauce, blending well. With a wire whisk, beat in egg and Parmesan cheese. Gradually beat in oil in a steady stream. Store, tightly covered, in a clean glass quart jar in the refrigerator for up to two weeks.

Note: Reduced Sodium (Lite) soy sauce may be substituted for regular soy sauce. One teaspoon Lite soy sauce contains 100 milligrams of sodium.

–Traveller's Restaurant

Fresh Tomato Salsa

Yield: about 5 cups

Salsa, a spicy fresh tomato relish of Mexican origin, is enjoying a great popularity throughout the United States, including Richmond.

4 cups chopped ripe tomato (see note)
1/2 cup thinly sliced green onion (include some green tops)
1/4 cup minced peeled red onion
1/4 cup minced parsley
1 1/2 tablespoons diced fresh jalapeno pepper
1 1/2 teaspoons minced fresh cilantro
2/3 cup red wine vinegar
1 1/2 teaspoons salt
1 teaspoon coarsely ground black pepper

In a medium bowl, combine the first 6 ingredients. In a 1 cup measure, combine vinegar, salt, and pepper, blending well; pour over tomato mixture. Cover and store in the refrigerator for up to 24 hours until ready to use.

Note: Do not remove peel.

–The Tobacco Company Restaurant

Oriental Orange Sauce

Yield: about 1 1/3 cups

1 garlic clove, peeled and minced
3/4 cup orange marmalade
1/4 cup soy sauce (see note)
1/4 cup dry sherry
2 tablespoons lemon juice
3 to 4 drops hot sauce

In a heavy sauce pan, combine all sauce ingredients; heat until bubbly hot.
Note: Reduced sodium (Lite) soy sauce may be substituted for regular soy sauce. One teaspoon Lite soy sauce contains 100 milligrams of sodium.

–Sarah Cardamone McBride (Mrs. Andrew S.)

French Dressing

Three tablespoons of vinegar, three of olive oil, one-half teaspoon of salt, one-quarter of pepper. Put in salt and pepper, add oil, rub and mix until salt is well in, then add by degrees vinegar. Stir continually for one minute.
Virginia Cook Book, 1839

Standard Homemade Crème Fraîche

Yield: about 1 cup

2/3 cup sour cream, at room temperature
1/3 cup heavy cream, at room temperature

In a small bowl, combine sour and heavy creams; allow to stand uncovered, at 80 degrees F. for 8 to 10 hours. Cover and refrigerate for 48 hours before using.

Note: Brush Crème Fraîche over fish fillets before broiling to seal moisture into the fish.

Old-Fashioned Barbecue Sauce

Yield: 2 quarts

1 (5-ounce) bottle Worcestershire sauce
2 cups ketchup
2 cups cider or white vinegar
1 cup butter or margarine, cut into small pieces
3 tablespoons minced peeled fresh or 1 tablespoon dried onion flakes
1 to 3 tablespoons salt or to taste
1 tablespoon light brown sugar, firmly packed
1 tablespoon hot sauce or to taste
Cayenne and black peppers to taste

In a large heavy saucepan, combine all ingredients. Bring to a boil over moderate heat. Cool. Use immediately with beef, pork, or chicken, as desired. Or, pour into 2 clean quart glass jars. Cover tightly and store in the refrigerator for up to 4 weeks until ready to use.

–Hal Tyler

Tillman's Bar-B-Q Sauce

Yield: 1 1/2 cups

1 egg
1 cup white vinegar
2 1/2 teaspoons salt or to

In a small bowl, lightly beat egg with a wire whisk. Add vinegar, salt, poultry seasoning, and pepper, whisking well to blend. Gradually whisk

taste (optional)
1 1/2 teaspoons poultry
seasoning
1/4 teaspoon pepper
1/2 cup salad oil

in oil until mixture is smooth, slightly thickened, and turns white in color. Marinate chicken in mixture for 2 to 3 hours before cooking or baste chicken liberally with sauce while chicken is cooking.

–Laurie Brickham (Mrs. Bruce)

Grandmother Ervin's Barbecue Sauce

Yield: about 4 cups

1 medium onion, peeled
and chopped
1/2 cup chopped celery
2 tablespoons butter or
margarine, melted
1 cup ketchup or chili sauce
1 cup water
1/4 cup lemon juice
3 tablespoons Worcester-
shire sauce
2 tablespoons bacon
drippings
2 tablespoons light brown
sugar, firmly packed
2 tablespoons cider vinegar
1 tablespoon prepared
mustard
1/8 teaspoon cayenne
pepper

In a heavy saucepan, sauté onion and celery in butter over moderate heat until tender but not browned. Reduce heat and add remaining ingredients, blending well. Simmer for 30 minutes or until sauce is bubbly hot and thickened.

–Maryrita Jackson (Mrs. David)

Tartar Sauce

Yield: 3 cups

2 cups mayonnaise
1/3 cup minced peeled
onion
1/3 cup sweet pickle relish
1/3 cup minced chives
3 tablespoons lemon juice
1/2 teaspoon Worcester-
shire sauce or to taste
Salt and pepper to taste

In a small bowl, combine all ingredients, mixing well. Store in an airtight container in the refrigerator.

–Jane Budwell (Mrs. Leigh)

Basic Cream Sauce (Bechamel)

Yield: about 1 cup

2 tablespoons butter
2 tablespoons flour
1/2 teaspoon salt
Pepper to taste
Pinch of paprika (optional)
1 cup milk or 1/2 cup milk
  and 1/2 cup half-and-half

Melt butter in a small heavy saucepan over low heat; stir in flour and seasonings. Gradually add milk or milk and half-and-half, blending well; cook stirring constantly, over moderate heat until mixture is smooth, thickened, and bubbly hot.

Variations: Thin Cream Sauce: Reduce butter and flour to 1 tablespoon each.

Thick Cream Sauce: Increase butter and flour to 1/4 cup each.

Cheese Sauce: Fold 1 cup (4 ounces) shredded American, Cheddar, or Swiss Cheese into hot sauce and stir until cheese melts. Yield: about 1 1/4 cups.

Horseradish Sauce: Stir in 2 to 3 tablespoons prepared horseradish or 2 to 3 teaspoons grated peeled horseradish root and a drop of hot sauce.

Mustard Sauce: Stir 1 1/2 to 2 tablespoons prepared mustard into sauce. Fold in 1/2 cup sour or whipped cream (optional). Yield: 1 1/2 cups sauce if sour or whipped cream is used.

Blender Bernaise Sauce

Yield: 2 cups

2 eggs
1 1/2 tablespoons lemon
  juice
2 teaspoons minced fresh or
  1 teaspoon minced dried
  tarragon
2 drops Worcestershire
  sauce
2 drops Tabasco sauce
Pinch of mashed chicken
  bouillon cube
3/4 cup clarified butter,
  melted and hot (see
  index).

Break eggs into a blender container; add lemon juice, tarragon, Worcestershire sauce, Tabasco sauce, and chicken bouillon. Cover and whiz at high speed for a few seconds until well blended. With the motor running at high speed, gradually add butter in a steady stream, beating until mixture is thickened. Serve immediately or keep warm, covered, over simmering water.

–Sam Miller's Warehouse Restaurant

Buerre Blanc

Yield: about 1 1/2 cups

3 shallots, peeled and minced
1 cup dry white wine
1/2 cup heavy cream
1 1/2 cups unsalted butter, divided into 24 tablespoons and chilled
Salt and freshly ground white pepper to taste
1 1/2 teaspoons lemon juice (see note)

In a medium heavy non-aluminum saucepan, boil shallots in wine over moderate heat until almost all liquid is evaporated. Add cream and boil mixture until liquid is reduced by half. Remove pan from heat; with a wire whisk, whisk in 2 tablespoons of butter. Place saucepan over low heat and whisk in remaining butter, 1 tablespoon at a time. Remove saucepan from heat briefly if drops of melted butter appear. If sauce breaks down or separates at any time, remove from heat and whisk in 2 tablespoons cold butter. Strain sauce through a fine sieve. Season with salt and white pepper to taste. Stir in lemon juice. Keep warm, covered, in the top of a double boiler over hot water or in a thermos container.

Note: Use only freshly squeezed lemon juice.

Note: Beurre Blanc may be kept warm in a tightly closed thermos for several hours.   –The Country Club of Virginia

Sweet Red Pepper Buerre Blanc

Yield: about 2 cups

Butter sauce dates back to the early part of the nineteenth century with the great French culinary expert, Carême. This recipe is a variation of a butter sauce.

2 tablespoons dry white wine
2 cups unsalted butter, at room temperature
1/3 cup minced sweet red pepper

In a medium heavy saucepan, bring wine to a gentle boil over moderate to high heat; continue to boil until amount of wine is reduced in half. Reduce heat to moderate and gradually add butter in 1-ounce (2 tablespoons) chunks, whisking continually with a wire whisk, until all butter is added. *Do not allow mixture to boil.* Remove from heat and add red pepper, blending well. Serve immediately with desired foods.

–The Butlery, Ltd.

425

Country Gravy

Yield: 2 cups

3 to 4 tablespoons fried
   chicken drippings (see
   note)
3 tablespoons flour
2 cups milk or half-and-half
Salt and pepper to taste

In a medium heavy skillet, blend chicken drippings with flour over low heat until a smooth paste is formed; cook for about 30 seconds. Gradually add milk, blending well with a wire whisk. Increase heat to moderate and cook, stirring constantly, until gravy is thickened and bubbly hot. Season with salt and pepper to taste. Serve with fried chicken or pan-fried pork chops and/or mashed potatoes and/or biscuits.

Note: If serving pan-fried pork chops, substitute hot pork chop drippings for chicken drippings.

Variation: Combine gravy or leftover gravy with about 1/2 to 1 cup minced fully-cooked smoked Smithfield or Virginia country-style ham. Serve over crisp toast points or toasted English muffin halves or hot biscuits.

–J. Robert Carlton

Cheese Sauce

Yield: about 1 1/4 cup

2 tablespoons butter
2 tablespoons flour
1/2 teaspoon salt
   or to taste
Pepper to taste
Few grains of paprika
   (optional)
1 cup milk or 1/2 cup milk
   and 1/2 cup half-and-half
1 cup (4 ounces) shredded
   American, sharp
   Cheddar, Swiss, or
   Monterey cheese

In a medium heavy saucepan, melt butter over low heat; stir in flour and seasonings. Gradually add milk or milk and half-and-half, blending well. Cook, stirring constantly over moderate heat until mixture is thickened and bubbly hot. Reduce heat and fold cheese into hot sauce; stir until cheese melts.

Variation: Add 1/2 teaspoon Worcestershire sauce, 1/4 teaspoon dry mustard, and 3 to 4 drops hot sauce to mixture with other seasonings.

426

Curry Sauce

Yield: About 3 3/4 cups

1 whole clove
2 tablespoons olive oil
1 tablespoon curry powder
1 tablespoon coriander
1 1/2 teaspoons ground
cumin
1 teaspoon minced peeled
garlic
1 teaspoon salt
1 teaspoon ground ginger
1/2 teaspoon white pepper
1/4 teaspoon crushed dried
hot red pepper
1/4 teaspoon nutmeg
2 tablespoons flour
2 cups boiling chicken stock
or broth
1/2 cup dry white wine
1/2 cup sour cream
1/2 (10-ounce) jar chutney,
chopped

In a medium heavy saucepan, combine the first 11 ingredients, mixing well. Cook, stirring occasionally, over low heat for 15 minutes. Gradually add flour, blending until a smooth paste is formed. Continue to cook for 2 to 3 minutes. Gradually add hot chicken stock and wine, blending well. Cook, stirring frequently, over moderate heat until mixture is thickened and bubbly hot. Stir in sour cream. Remove from heat and strain. Add chutney, mixing well. Use with seafood, chicken or turkey, beef, or lamb, as desired.

—Chef Robert Hamlin, proprietor
Jana Blue Hopper, proprietor
du Jour Restaurant and Caterers

A most dilapidated old wooden house on Broad street, west of Sixth, or a portion of it, is now in course of demolition...The cellar was also sometimes a receptacle for rags, besides old iron, broken glass, and other commodities, destined, in regenerated forms, possibly, to aid in the decorations of a palace. Between these upper and lower regions, (the one not tenanted by angels, nor the other by devils,) was the ground floor, on which were shops for the sale of old raiment for the outer man, some of it almost fit for the window blinds of the upper or the bag of the lower tenants; and, for the comfort of the inner man, a cheap repast of cow-heel, tripe, and hoe-cake, or a refreshing dram,whose spirit was not betrayed by its colour.

Samuel Mordecai
Richmond in By-Gone Days, 1856
Reprint Edition, 1975

Basic Brown Sauce

Yield: 2 cups

1/4 cup butter or margarine
1 garlic clove, peeled and
   minced (optional)
1/4 cup chopped peeled
   onion
1/4 cup flour
2 cups beef, or pork, or
   chicken stock, or a
   combination of stocks
   (see note)
1/2 teaspoon Worcester-
   shire sauce (optional)
Salt and paprika to taste

In a medium heavy saucepan, melt butter over low heat. Add garlic, if desired, and onion; increase heat to moderate and sauté mixture until tender and lightly browned. Remove garlic and onion with a slotted spoon, draining butter back into pan. Gradually stir in flour , blending well. Allow mixture to brown lightly over moderate heat, stirring constantly. Gradually add meat stock and Worcestershire, if desired, blending well; cook, stirring constantly, until sauce is thickened and bubbly hot. Season with salt and paprika to taste. Strain before using.

Note: If homemade meat stock is unavailable, 1 1/2 undiluted (10 1/2 or 10 3/4-
   ounce) cans beef broth or consommé or chicken broth may be substi-

Blender Hollandaise Sauce

Yield: 2 cups

2 eggs
1 1/2 tablespoons lemon
   juice
2 drops Worcestershire
   sauce
2 drops Tabasco sauce
Pinch of mashed chicken
   bouillon cube
3/4 cup clarified butter,
   melted and hot (see
   index)

Break eggs into a blender container; add lemon juice, Worcestershire sauce, Tabasco sauce, and chicken bouillon. Cover and whiz at high speed for a few seconds until well blended. With the motor running at high speed, gradually add butter in a steady stream, beating until mixture is thickened. Serve immediately or keep warm, covered, over simmering water.

–Sam Miller's Warehouse Restaurant

Hollandaise Sauce

Yield: 1 3/4 cups

1 cup butter or margarine
3 egg yolks
2 tablespoons hot water
1 tablespoon white vinegar
1 1/2 teaspoons lemon juice
Pinch salt
Pinch white pepper
3 to 4 drops Worcestershire
sauce
3 to 4 drops hot sauce

In a small heavy saucepan, melt butter and keep warm. Combine remaining ingredients in the top of a double boiler; stir over low heat until well-mixed. Place pan over hot water and cook, beating constantly, until thick. Remove from heat. Add melted butter slowly, a tablespoon at a time, beating constantly until thoroughly blended. Keep hot, covered, in the top of a double boiler over simmering water.

Note: If sauce should separate, add a tablespoon or two of boiling water and beat with a hand rotary beater.

Variations:

Lemon Hollandaise Sauce: Omit vinegar and increase lemon juice to 2 tablespoons. Add 1 tablespoon grated lemon peel to sauce.

Lime Hollandaise Sauce: Omit vinegar and add 2 tablespoons lime juice and 1 tablespoon grated lime peel to sauce.

Orange Hollandaise Sauce: Omit vinegar and add 2 tablespoons orange juice and 1 tablespoon grated orange peel to sauce.

Marsala Wine Sauce

Yield: About 2 1/4 cups

2 cups Basic Brown Sauce
(see index)
1/4 cup Marsala wine, or
tawny port, or cream
sherry
Pinch of garlic powder
Salt and pepper to taste

In a small heavy saucepan, combine Basic Brown Sauce, Marsala wine, garlic powder, and salt and pepper to taste. Bring to a simmer over moderate heat.

–Jack Terry, proprietor
Wakefields' restaurant

429

Apple Mustard Sauce

Yield: about 3 1/2 cups

1 tart medium apple,
  peeled, cored, seeded,
  and chopped
1 small onion, peeled
  and chopped
2 tablespoons honey
2 tablespoons cider vinegar
2 cups apple cider
2 tablespoons cornstarch
1/4 cup Dijon-style prepared
  mustard

In a medium heavy saucepan, combine apple, onion, honey, and vinegar; bring to a boil over moderate heat. Reduce temperature and simmer, uncovered, until mixture is slightly thickened. Cool. In a small bowl, blend apple cider into cornstarch with a wire whisk until mixture is smooth; blend mixture into cooled apple mixture. Cook, stirring constantly, over moderate heat, until sauce is thickened and bubbly hot. With a wire whisk, blend in mustard. Serve with Mrs. Pegram's Chicken.

Note: Use McIntosh, Winesap, Granny Smith, or other tart variety of apples.

–Linden Row Dining Room
Linden Row Inn

Marinara Sauce

Yield: about 8 cups

10 canned anchovies,
   drained and minced
6 to 8 green onions, minced
   (include some green tops)
4 to 6 garlic cloves (1 whole
   head), peeled and minced
4 ripe large tomatoes,
   peeled, seeded, and
   chopped
2 medium green peppers,
   cored, seeded, and
   chopped

In a large heavy saucepan, combine all ingredients together. Cook, stirring frequently, over low to moderate heat for 20 to 25 minutes. Do not boil. Store covered in clean quart jars in the refrigerator for up to 1 week. Serve with steamed (shrimp) mussels or clams, cooked pasta, or other desired foods.

2 medium sweet red
   peppers, cored, seeded,
   and chopped
2 bay leaves, crumbled
1 large red onion, peeled
   and minced
3 cups olive oil (see note)
1 cup chopped mushrooms
1/2 cup minced parsley
4 tablespoons minced fresh
   or 2 tablespoons dried
   basil
2 tablespoons tomato paste
2 tablespoons minced fresh
   or 1 tablespoon dried
   oregano
1 tablespoon Tabasco sauce
1 tablespoon Worcester-
   shire sauce
1 tablespoon lemon juice
1 tablespoon salt
1 tablespoon pepper

–Chef Robert Hamlin, proprietor
Jana Blue Hopper, proprietor
du Jour Restaurant and Caterers

Hot Plum Sauce

Yield: 1 3/4 cups

1 1/2 cups red plum jam
1 1/2 tablespoons Dijon-
   style prepared mustard
1 1/2 tablespoons prepared
   horseradish (see note)
1 1/2 teaspoons lemon juice

In a saucepan, combine all ingredients together; stir over low heat until just warm. Serve immediately as a dipping sauce.

Note: 1/2 to 1 tablespoon freshly grated peeled horseradish root may be substituted for prepared horseradish.

Note: For those who like more sauce, prepare twice the amount of the recipe.

Variation: Add 1 to 2 teaspoons soy sauce.

–Ann Tyler (Mrs. Hal)

431

Pineapple Peppercorn Glaze

Yield: 1 1/8 cups

1 (46-ounce) can
  unsweetened pineapple
  juice
2 tablespoons green
  peppercorns, drained and
  crushed

In a heavy non-aluminum saucepan, boil pineapple juice over high heat until juice is reduced to 1 cup. Add crushed peppercorns. Serve hot over roasted or broiled lamb or chicken, and steamed, boiled, or broiled shrimp.

–Chef Robert Hamlin, proprietor
Jana Blue Hopper, proprietor
du Jour Restaurant and Caterers

Provençale Sauce

Yield: 3/4 cup

"This sauce is an excellent choice in which flank or chuck steaks or other less tender cuts of meat may be simmered slowly to ensure tenderness of the cooked meat."

4 ounces mushrooms
3 shallots, peeled and
  minced
1 large garlic clove, peeled
  and minced
1 1/2 tablespoons hot
  cooking oil
1 tablespoon flour
3/4 cup beef stock
3/4 cup dry white wine
About 1 to 2 tablespoons
  bouquet garni (commercial mix)
2 teaspoons tomato paste
Salt and pepper to taste

Trim stems off mushrooms level with the caps; thinly slice caps and mince stems. In a large heavy skillet, sauté mushroom stems, shallots, and garlic in oil over moderate heat until tender and shallots just begin to brown, about 4 minutes. Stir in flour, blending well. Add stock and wine; bring mixture to a boil,stirring constantly. Add bouquet garni; reduce heat and simmer, uncovered, for 20 minutes. Strain mixture. Add tomato paste and sliced mushroom caps to strained sauce. Return mixture to pan and bring to a boil over moderate heat, stirring constantly; reduce heat and simmer, uncovered, for 2 to 3 minutes or until sliced mushrooms are tender.

Note: 3/4 cup undiluted canned beef broth or consommé may be substituted.

–Laurie Brickham (Mrs. Bruce)

Seafood "Cream" Sauce

Yield: about 2 1/2 cups

Actually this sauce recipe is not a typical cream sauce as it has fish stock instead of cream or milk as the liquid ingredient of the sauce.

2 tablespoons butter or margarine, melted
2 tablespoons flour
2 cups strained light fish stock (see index for Court Bouillon)
Salt and white pepper to taste
Several grains cayenne pepper to taste
1 to 2 teaspoons minced parsley (optional)

In a small medium saucepan, combine butter and flour, blending to form a smooth paste. Gradually add fish stock, blending well. Simmer, uncovered, over low heat until slightly thickened. Season with salt, pepper, and cayenne pepper to taste. Add parsley, if desired.

–Chef James and Lynn News, proprietors
Mr. Patrick Henry's Restaurant and Inn

Shallot Sauce

Yield: about 2 cups

4 shallots, peeled and minced
1 teaspoon butter or margarine, melted
1/2 cup dry white wine
3 cups heavy cream, at room temperature
Salt and pepper to taste

In the top of a heavy double boiler, sauté shallots in butter over moderate heat until tender and translucent but not browned. Add wine and continue cooking until wine is reduced in half. Add cream and further reduce mixture by one third. Keep warm, covered, over hot water.

–The Jefferson Sheraton Hotel

433

Spicy Shrimp Sauce

Yield: about 1 1/2 cups

2 tablespoons butter or
  margarine, melted
2 tablespoons flour
1/2 teaspoon Worcester-
  shire sauce or to taste
1/4 teaspoon seafood
  seasoning or to taste
  (see note)
1/4 teaspoon dry mustard
4 to 5 drops hot sauce or
  to taste
1 cup milk
Salt and pepper to taste
1/2 cup peeled cooked
  very small shrimp
1 tablespoon minced
  parsley

In a small heavy saucepan, combine butter and flour, blending until smooth. Stir in Worcestershire sauce, dry mustard, seafood seasoning, and hot sauce. Cook over low heat for 30 to 60 seconds. Gradually add milk, blending well. Cook, stirring constantly, over moderate heat until thickened and bubbly hot. Add salt and pepper to taste. Stir in shrimp and parsley. Adjust seasonings to taste, if desired. Stir over low heat for about 1 minute.

Note: Preferably use Old Bay Seafood Seasoning.

Variation: Add 1 tablespoon seafood sauce to mixture.

Home-Style Fresh Tomato Sauce

Yield: 3 to 4 quarts

The Bistro Express, opened in March, 1989, is a combination French-style pub accommodating fifty people and a Gourmet-Take-Out establishment. Located on far west Broad Street across from the Innsbrook Complex, it is one of the trendy new eateries offering ambiance, as well as good food and wine. The proprietor, Robert Ramsey, has an extensive food preparation background from such places as Monte Carlo, Paris, and Northern Italy.

5 pounds ripe medium
  tomatoes, cored, seeded,
  and chopped
1 1/2 pounds onions, peeled

Prepare tomatoes; set aside. In a large heavy pot, combine onions, ham scrap, and olive oil; sauté over moderate heat until onion begins to brown and starts to become crisp. Add carrots

and coarsely chopped
1 (4-ounce) country ham
  scrap (see note)
2 tablespoons olive oil (see
  note)
2 medium carrots, peeled
  and chopped
1 medium parsnip, peeled
  and chopped
4 cups simmering chicken
  broth
1/2 cup chopped fresh or 2
  1/2 tablespoons dried
  basil
2 tablespoons minced fresh
  or 2 teaspoons dried
  oregano
1 tablespoon minced fresh
  or 1 teaspoon dried
  thyme
Salt and freshly ground
  black peppercorns to
  taste

and parsnip; cook for 5 minutes, stirring frequently. Gradually add broth, stirring and loosening any bits of caramelization in the bottom of the pot. Bring mixture to a simmer; add tomatoes. Reduce heat and cook, uncovered, for 2 to 3 hours until mixture is slightly thickened, stirring occasionally. Add remaining ingredients, except salt. Continue simmering for 30 minutes. Remove from heat; add salt and allow sauce to cool for 30 minutes. Strain sauce; cover and chill in refrigerator for 12 hours to allow flavors to "ripen." Pour into clean pint or quart plastic freezer containers; freeze until ready to use. This sauce is especially good with pasta or Italian recipes.

Note: Use leftover portion of a cooked country-style ham or purchase 4 ounces of fully-cooked smoked country-style ham if leftover scraps are unavailable.

Note: Use a premium quality extra virgin olive oil. Extra virgin refers to the oil collected from the first press of the olives.

–Robert Ramsey, proprietor
Bistro Express

Ann Burwell's Caper Sauce

Ingredients.—One-half pint of melted butter, three tablespoonfuls of capers, tablespoonful of their liquor.

Mode.—Chop the capers twice or thrice, and add them, with their liquor, to one-half pint of melted butter; keep stirring well; let the sauce just simmer, and serve in a tureen. Sufficient to serve with a leg of mutton.

–Beverages and Sauces of Colonial Virginia, *1906*

435

Olive Sauce

Yield: about 5 cups

1/2 cup plus 1 teaspoon
butter or margarine,
melted
1/2 cup flour
3 cups hot duck stock or
chicken broth
1/2 teaspoon garlic powder
1/4 teaspoon bead molasses
(see note)
1/4 cup Madeira or dry
sherry wine
1 cup pitted small black
olives, drained
1 cup pitted small green
olives, drained
Salt and pepper to taste
(optional)

In a medium heavy saucepan, combine butter and flour, blending to form a smooth paste. Cook, stirring constantly, over low heat.Gradually add duck stock or chicken broth, garlic powder, and molasses, blending well with a wire whisk. Increase temperature to moderate and cook, whisking constantly, until mixture is thickened and bubbly hot. Reduce temperature, blend in Madeira, and simmer for 3 to 4 minutes. Add olives, mixing well. Continue to simmer, uncovered, over low heat for 15 to 20 minutes. Adjust seasonings to taste.

Note: Bead molasses is stronger than regular molasses and is available in most grocery stores or specialty Oriental grocery stores.

–Doris Roberts (Mrs. Irving)

Westover Orange Gravy
(For Wild Fowl)

Ingredients.– One-half pint of white stock, one small onion, three or four strips of orange peel, a few leaves of basil, the juice of one orange, salt and pepper to taste, one glass of port wine.

Mode.– Put the onion, cut in slices, into a saucepan, with the stock, orange peel, and basil; let them simmer very gently for one-fourth hour, or rather longer; strain and add to the gravy the remaining ingredients; let the whole heat through, and when on the point of boiling, serve very hot in a sauce tureen which should have a cover to it.

Beverages and Sauces of Colonial Virginia, *1906*

Breads

Biscuits

Biscuits, those small morsels of dough which are kneaded and baked in about 20 minutes, are American baking classics developed by the early colonists.

Flakey Sour Cream Biscuits

Yield: about 16 to 20 Biscuits

3 cups biscuit/baking mix
2/3 cup sour cream
2/3 cup club soda
1 egg white
2 to 3 drops water

In a medium bowl, combine biscuit mix and sour cream, mixing well. Gradually stir in club soda until mixture is pliable.Turn out onto a lightly floured board and knead 8 to 10 times. Roll dough to a 1/4 to 1/2-inch thickness; cut with a floured 2-inch biscuit cutter. Arrange biscuits on greased baking sheets. In a 1-cup measure, combine egg white and 2 to 3 drops water, beating lightly with a wire whisk. Brush tops of biscuits with beaten egg white. Bake in a hot oven (400 degrees F.) for about 15 minutes or until done and golden brown.

–Joy Bray

Paul's Place Buttermilk Biscuits

Yield: about 2 dozen biscuits

4 cups self-rising flour
1 tablespoon baking powder
2 teaspoons sugar
7 tablespoons shortening
3 cups buttermilk
Melted butter or margarine
    as needed

In a large bowl, sift together the first 3 ingredients. With a pastry blender or 2 silver table knives, cut in shortening until mixture resembles coarse meal. Add buttermilk, mixing *just* until dry ingredients are moistened. Turn dough out onto a lightly floured board and knead *lightly* 6 to 8 times. Roll out dough to a 1/2-inch thickness. Cut with a floured 2 to 2 1/2-inch biscuit cutter. Arrange biscuits on ungreased baking sheets. Bake in a very hot oven (450 degrees F.) for 8 minutes, then broil, 8 to 10 inches from heat source, for 6 to 8 minutes or until biscuits are golden brown. Brush biscuit tops lightly with melted butter.

–Paul's Place
Edward, Jackie and Paul Shibley, proprietors

Quick Biscuit Baking Mix

Yield: about 13 1/2 cups

"Use this mixture in place of any commercially prepared pancake/waffle or all-purpose baking mix. This recipe costs less and is more nutritional than the commercial product."

4 cups sifted flour
4 cups sifted whole wheat
  flour
3 cups instant non-fat dry
  milk powder
1 1/2 to 2 cups cooking oil
1/2 cup wheat germ (op-
  tional) (see note)
1/4 cup sugar
5 tablespoons baking
  powder
2 teaspoons salt

In a very large bowl, combine all ingredients with a hand rotary beater or at a low speed of an electric mixer; beat mixture until thoroughly blended and large lumps broken. Store in an airtight container until ready to use.

Note: If wheat germ is added, mixture may be stored unrefrigerated for 1 month or refrigerated for 3 months.

–Fran Lincoln

Horsford's

Bread · Preparation

Is Pure,
Wholesome,
Healthful.

It Excels in Baking Strength and Healthful-
ness, and Produces Biscuit, Cake, &c., that
are Lighter, Sweeter and more Nutri-
tious than those prepared with
ordinary Baking Powders,
Cream Tartar, or
Yeast.

Dr. L. C. BOSHER,
Professor of Anatomy, Med. College of Va., says:
" We have used Prof. Horsford's Bread Preparation
in our house for many years, and it has invariably given
excellent results."

Old Richmond Advertisement, circa 1895

Miss Naomi's Buttermilk Biscuits

Yield: about 15 to 20 biscuits

2 1/2 cups flour
1 1/2 tablespoons baking powder
3/4 teaspoon salt
1/2 teaspoon baking soda
1/3 cup shortening
1 1/2 cups buttermilk

In a medium bowl, sift together the first 4 ingredients. With a pastry blender or two table knives, cut in shortening until mixture resembles coarse meal. Add buttermilk, stirring *just until* dry ingredients are moistened. Turn out onto a lightly floured board and knead lightly 6 to 10 times. Roll out dough or pat to a 1/2 to 3/4-inch thickness. Cut dough with a lightly floured 1 1/2 to 2-inch biscuit cutter. Arrange biscuits on lightly greased baking sheets. Bake in a very hot oven (450 degrees F.) for 10 minutes or until biscuits are done and golden brown.

–Naomi Wilson, Cafeteria Manager
Virginia Museum of Fine Arts

...Thus it is not a wonder that we find a monument of Jefferson guarding the entrance to the hotel that Major Ginter had erected, for Jefferson was the one human he admired most, yet peculiarly enough, the one human he resembled most. Today Valentine's statue of Thomas Jefferson still stands in the lobby of the hotel, the likeness of a statesman, he being too modest and retiring to want a likeness of himself. On the occasion of the opening of the hotel, when he (Major Ginter) heard that some friends were planning to donate a loving cup to him for his outstanding work, he promptly had the idea dismissed, declaring that he would not accept it if it were offered to him. At another time, when he learned that a movement was on foot to erect a likeness of him as a monument in one of the clubs, he immediately had the movement stopped, which was typical of the "Modest Major Ginter."

It was during his travels that his keen foresight awoke to the realization that Richmond was without a first-class hotel, so, single-handed, he undertook to build one that Richmond would justly be proud to call her own.

Moore
Jefferson Hotel, 1940

Golden Sweet 'Tater Biscuits

Yield: about 16 biscuits

Sweet potato or yam biscuits are one of the traditional hot biscuit-style breads served throughout the South.

2 1/2 cups flour
1/4 cup light brown sugar,
   firmly packed, or 1/4 cup
   sugar
2 tablespoons baking
   powder
1 teaspoon salt
1 cup shortening
2 eggs, lightly beaten
1 cup mashed cooked
   peeled sweet potatoes or
   yams (see note)
1/2 cup half-and-half or
   light cream (see note)
1 tablespoon grated orange
   peel (optional)

In a medium bowl, sift together the first 4 ingredients. With a pastry blender or two silver knives, cut in shortening until mixture resembles coarse meal. In a 2 cup-measure, combine eggs, mashed sweet potatoes or yams, half-and-half, and orange peel, blending well. Add mixture all at once to dry ingredients, stirring *just* until dry ingredients are moistened. Turn out onto a lightly floured board and knead lightly 10 to 12 strokes. Roll out dough to a 1/2-inch thickness; cut with a floured 2-inch biscuit cutter. Arrange biscuits on ungreased baking sheets and bake in a hot oven (425 degrees F.) for 10 to 12 minutes or until done and golden brown.

Note: Canned or cooked fresh sweet potatoes, or yams, may be used. To cook fresh sweet potatoes or yams, cook 1 to 2 medium (each about 8 ounces) unpeeled, in boiling water to cover for 20 to 25 minutes or until fork tender. About 1 pound of unpeeled raw yams or sweet potatoes equals 1 cup mashed peeled cooked yams or sweet potatoes.

Note: For a less rich biscuit, milk may be substituted.

441

Almond Lime Loaf

Yield: one loaf

1 (3-ounce) package sliced almonds, divided
1 cup plus 2 tablespoons sugar, divided
5 tablespoons butter or margarine, melted and divided
3 cups sifted flour
3 teaspoons baking powder
1 teaspoon salt
1/4 teaspoon baking soda
2 tablespoons grated lime peel, divided
1 egg, beaten
1 cup milk
3 tablespoons lime juice, divided

In a small bowl, combine 1 tablespoon almonds, 2 tablespoons sugar, and 1 tablespoon butter; set aside. In a medium bowl, sift together flour, 1 cup sugar, baking powder, salt, and baking soda. Add 3/4 cup almonds and 1 tablespoon lime peel, mixing well. Combine egg and milk; stir into dry ingredients. Add 4 tablespoons butter and 2 tablespoons lime juice, mixing just until dry ingredients are evenly moistened. Pour into a lightly greased 9 x 5 x 3-inch loaf pan; spoon butter-almond mixture over batter. Bake in a moderate oven (350 degrees F.) for 1 hour 10 minutes or until a metal tester inserted in center comes out clean. Cool in pan for 5 to 10 minutes, then turn out onto a wire rack to finish cooling. Drizzle remaining 1 tablespoon lime juice over top of Almond Lime Loaf bread and sprinkle with remaining 1 tablespoon lime peel.

–Doris Crowell (Mrs. R. E.)

Breakfast Fruit Bread

Yield: 2 loaves

2 1/3 cups biscuit/baking mix or Quick Biscuit Baking Mix (see index)
1 tablespoon cinnamon
3/4 cup sugar
1/3 cup cooking oil
3 eggs, slightly beaten
1 teaspoon vanilla extract
3 large ripe bananas, peeled and mashed
1/4 cup wheat germ granules
1 cup chopped pecans or English walnuts
1 cup dark seedless raisins, chopped

Sift together the biscuit mix and cinnamon. In a medium bowl, combine sugar and oil, beating well. Add eggs, one at a time, beating well after each addition and vanilla. Stir in mashed banana and wheat germ granules. Add flour, beating just until all ingredients are well-mixed. fold in nuts and raisins. Spoon into two greased 8 x 4 x 2 1/2-inch loaf pans, dividing evenly. Bake in a moderate oven (350 degrees F.) for 55 to 65 minutes or until a metal tester inserted in center of bread comes out clean.

–Fran Lincoln

Sour Milk Banana Nut Bread

Yield: one loaf

1/2 cup soured milk (see note)
2 cups sifted flour
1 1/2 teaspoons baking powder
1/2 teaspoon salt
1/2 teaspoon baking soda
1/2 cup butter or margarine or shortening, at room temperature
1 cup sugar
2 eggs, slightly beaten
3 ripe medium bananas, peeled and mashed
1 cup chopped English walnuts or pecans

Prepare soured milk; set aside. Sift together the next 4 ingredients. In a bowl, cream butter until smooth; add sugar,beating until light and fluffy. Beat in eggs. Stir in bananas.Add dry ingredients, mixing well. Quickly stir in soured milk.Pour into a greased 8 1/2 x 4 1/2 x 3-inch loaf pan. Bake in a moderate oven (375 degrees F.) for 15 minutes, then reduce heat to 350 degrees F. and continue baking for 45 minutes or until done.Cool in pan for 5 to 10 minutes, then turn out onto a wire rack to finish cooling.

Note: To sour milk , add 1 tablespoon lemon juice or vinegar to milk; let stand for 20 minutes.

–Maryrita Jackson (Mrs. David)

Embargo

A large flour mill has been erected at Tredegar, a short distance above the armory, and here grain is ground and cannons are cast in close proximity. This, however, as well as two flour mills, Taliaferro's and Bragg's, on the Manchester side, are all of recent construction, and do not belong to by-gone days; but those do which preceded them and occupied the same ground. Cunningham's, afterwards Rutherford's mill, and also a distillery and a tan-yard, stood where the Tredegar Iron Works are.

Samuel Mordecai
Richmond in By-Gone Days, 1856
Reprint Edition, 1975

Strawberry Bread or Muffins

The Indians were making a kind of strawberry bread in the seventeenth century original American colonies by pounding strawberries and mixing with cornmeal. The colonists invented one of America's favorite desserts, Strawberry Short Cake, from these modest beginnings.

Strawberry Bread or Muffins

Yield: two loaves

Brandy Branch Mill, the home of Mr. and Mrs. Raymond W. Darnell, has a long history. According to recently uncovered records, a mill was built at the locations by Anthony Winston in 1756 and its history is well-substantiated as a gristmill through the years. It has had many owners. In Civil War documents and maps, it was referred to as "Nunnally's Mill." The mill ceased operation in 1941 and stood idle until 1963 when it was purchased by the Darnells, restored, and converted into a home.

3 cups sifted flour
2 cups sugar
1 tablespoon cinnamon
1 teaspoon salt
1 teaspoon baking soda
3 eggs, beaten
1 1/4 cups cooking oil or shortening, melted and cooled
2 (10-ounce) packages frozen sliced strawberries, thawed and well drained
1 1/4 cups chopped pecans
3 to 4 drops red food coloring (optional)

In a medium bowl, sift together the first 5 ingredients. Combine eggs and oil and add all at once to dry ingredients, stirring only enough to moisten dry ingredients. Stir in strawberries, pecans, and red food coloring, if desired. Spoon batter into two greased 8 x 4 x 2 5/8-inch baking pans. Bake in a moderate oven (350 degrees F.) for 1 hour or until a metal tester inserted in center comes out clean. Cool in pans on racks for 10 minutes, then remove loaves from pan and transfer directly to wire racks to finish cooling. Wrap loaves in aluminum foil and allow to stand 12 hours before slicing and serving.

Muffins: Prepare batter as previously directed. Fill greased muffin pans (2 3/4 inches in diameter) two-thirds full. Bake in a moderate oven (350 degrees F.) for 20 to 25 minutes or until done. Cool in pans for 5 minutes and then turn out, wrap in aluminum foil, and allow to stand for 12 hours before serving. Yield: about 15 to 16 muffins.

–Virginia S. Darnell (Mrs. Raymond)

WOMAN'S CHRISTIAN ASSOCIATION,

709-711 Franklin Street, East. RICHMOND, VA.

Boarding-House for Self-Supporting Young Women. Permanent and
. . . . Transient Boarders. . . .

Lunch-Room open from 12 M. to 3 P. M., daily except Sunday, for Ladies and Gentlemen.

Free Circulating Library open
every Friday, 12 M. to 3 P. M.   ❋   Sewing-School for Girls, Saturday, 12 M. to 2 P. M.

DAY NURSERY AND FREE KINDERGARTEN,
Grace and Nineteenth Streets.

Old Richmond Advertisement, circa early twentieth century

445

Toasted Coconut Bread

Yield: one loaf

5 1/4 cups sifted flour
1 cup sugar
4 teaspoons baking powder
1 teaspoon salt
1 cup shredded coconut
1 egg
2 tablespoons peanut oil
1 teaspoon coconut flavoring

Spread coconut in one layer over an ungreased baking sheet; bake in a slow oven (300 degrees F.) for about 8 to 10 minutes or until coconut turns a light gold color. Remove from oven and allow to cool. In a medium bowl, sift flour, sugar, baking powder, and salt; set aside. Stir cooled coconut into dry ingredients. In a small bowl, beat egg slightly. Add milk, oil, and coconut flavoring, beating well. Stir milk mixture into dry ingredients, mixing *just* until dry ingredients are well-moistened. Evenly spoon mixture into a lightly greased 9 x 5 x 3-inch loaf pan. Bake in a moderate oven (350 degrees F.) for about 1 hour or until a metal tester inserted in center comes out clean. Cool in pan for 8 minutes and then turn out onto a wire rack to finish cooling. Wrap in aluminum foil or clear plastic wrap and store in the refrigerator or freezer wrapped in aluminum foil.

–Fanny's Restaurant and Lounge

French Fruit Squares

Yield: about 3 dozen

"These squares are a great accompaniment to morning coffee."

2 1/2 cups sifted flour
1/3 cup plus 1/4 cup plus 1 tablespoon sugar, divided
1 teaspoon salt
1 egg, separated
1 cup margarine, at room temperature
2/3 cup milk
1 (21-ounce) can cherry or blueberry or other desired flavor fruit pie filling
3 to 4 tablespoons butter or margarine, at room temperature

In a medium bowl, sift together the flour, 1/4 cup sugar, and salt. With a pastry blender or 2 silver table knives, cut margarine into dry ingredients until mixture resembles coarse meal. Beat egg yolk. Add beaten egg yolk and milk to dry ingredients, mixing *just* until dry ingredients are thoroughly moistened. Roll out one-half of the dough on a lightly floured surface into a 15 x 10-inch rectangle; carefully fit dough into a 15 x 10 x 1-inch baking pan. Evenly spread fruit filling over dough in pan; dot fruit filling with butter and sprinkle with 1 tablespoon sugar and cinnamon. Roll out remaining dough into a 15 x 10-inch rectangle; fit dough cover over fruit filling. Beat egg white

1/4 teaspoon cinnamon

lightly with a fork; brush top of dough with beaten egg white and then evenly sprinkle with 1/3 cup sugar. Bake in a moderate oven (375 degrees F.) for 35 minutes. Remove from oven and allow to cool for several minutes; cut into squares and serve warm or at room temperature.

–Ann Tyler (Mrs. Hal)

Kugelhopf

Yield: one 9-inch tube cake

My Grandmother Keller, a marvelous German cook, always prepared Kugelhopf, a German coffeecake, for special occasions. This is an updated version of her recipe.

1/3 cup blanched whole almonds
3 1/2 cups sifted flour
3 teaspoons baking powder
1/2 teaspoon salt
1/2 cup butter or margarine, at room temperature
1/2 cup shortening
1 cup sugar
5 eggs
2 teaspoons grated lemon peel
1 teaspoon vanilla extract
1 cup milk
1 cup currants or dark seedless raisins
Sifted confectioners' sugar for garnish

Arrange almonds over bottom of a greased, deep 9-inch tube pan; set aside. Sift together flour, baking powder, and salt; set aside. In a large bowl, cream butter and shortening until smooth. Gradually add sugar, beating until light and fluffy. Add eggs, one at a time, beating well after each addition. Blend in lemon peel and vanilla. Alternately add dry ingredients with milk, beginning and ending with dry ingredients. Fold in raisins. Pour into an almond-lined, greased, deep 9-inch tube pan. Bake in a slow oven (325 degrees F.) for 60 to 75 minutes or until a cake tester inserted in center comes out clean. Cool in pan for 10 minutes, then turn out onto a wire rack to finish cooling. When cold, sprinkle cake with confectioners' sugar.

Note: Cake may be wrapped in heavy-duty aluminum foil and frozen after cooling; thaw and sprinkle with confectioners' sugar before serving.

447

> ## Antique Menu(Cir. 1839)
>
> ---
>
> Breakfast ... Baked Bananas, Cereal and Cream, Ham and Eggs, Rice Pancakes, Coffee ... Luncheon or Supper, Pork and Beans, Cooked Tomatoes and Cheese, Canned Fruit Waters ... Dinner, Oxtail Soup, Fricassee Chicken, Baked Potatoes, Creamed Asparagus, Cucumber Salad, Custard Pudding.
>
> **Virginia Cook Book,** 1839

Nutty Sour Cream Coffeecake

Yield: one oblong or tube cake

Topping

1 cup light brown sugar, firmly packed
3/4 cup chopped pecans
1 teaspoon cinnamon
3 tablespoons butter or margarine, at room temperature

Batter

2 cups sifted flour
1 teaspoon baking soda
1 teaspoon baking powder
1/2 teaspoon salt
1/2 cup butter or margarine, at room temperature
1 cup sugar
3 eggs
1 cup sour cream

To prepare topping, combine brown sugar, pecans, and cinnamon in a small bowl. With a pastry blender, cut in butter; set aside. To prepare batter, sift together flour, baking soda, baking powder,and salt; set aside. In a medium bowl, cream butter thoroughly.Gradually add sugar, beating until light and fluffy. Add eggs,one at a time, beating well after each addition. Alternately stir in dry ingredients and sour cream. Evenly spread one-half the batter in a greased 13 x 9 x 2-inch baking pan. Sprinkle one-half the pecan mixture over batter in pan. Spread remaining batter over nut mixture in pan. Evenly sprinkle remaining pecan mixture over batter. Bake in a moderate oven (350 degrees F.) for 40 minutes or until a metal tester inserted in center comes out clean.

Note: Cake may be baked in a greased 10-inch tube or bundt pan in a moderate oven (350 degrees F.) for 50 minutes or until metal tester inserted in center comes out clean, if desired.

–Judi Kauffman

Flour milling was one of the earliest industries in America and one of the most essential to independent survival. A number of mills existed in the Richmond area at the time of the Revolution. Samuel Overton operated a flour mill on lot no. 741, which he had purchased in the Byrd Lottery in 1772 for 700. The lot, a long triangular tract, extended seven-eighths of a mile along the north bank of the James River from what is today Fourteenth Street. Overton probably established his mill either over the rocks at the foot of Twelfth Street or perhaps farther upriver, where Second and Third streets would reach the river if extended.

In 1777 Overton agreed to provide five hundred barrels of flour to Richard Adams, who was purchasing flour for the state. The fate of Overton's mill cannot be determined. It may have been destroyed in Arnold's raid in 1781, or the mill operated later by David Ross at the foot of Twelfth Street may have been the same as Overton's mill. In January 1784 a flood washed away Ross's mill, which stood over the river, and with it the miller, his assistant, three thousand bushels of wheat, and a quantity of flour.

Harry M. Ward and Harold E. Greer, Jr.
Richmond During The Revolution, 1775-83, 1977

Quik and Easy Cinnamon Ring

Yield: one 10-inch coffeecake

1/2 (3-ounce) package instant butterscotch pudding and pie filling
1/2 cup sugar
1 tablespoon cinnamon
1 cup light brown sugar, firmly packed
1/2 cup butter or margarine, melted
1/2 cup chopped English walnuts or pecans
Butter as needed
About 18 frozen unbaked round dinner rolls

Arrange frozen rolls, evenly spaced, into a lightly greased 10-inch tube or bundt pan. Evenly sprinkle with pudding mix, sugar, and cinnamon. In a small saucepan, combine brown sugar and butter, stirring over low heat until sugar is completely dissolved. Add nuts, mixing well. Evenly pour sauce over rolls. Cover and let rise in a warm place (85 degrees F.) for 8 hours. Bake, uncovered, in a moderate oven (375 degrees F.) for 35 minutes or until done. Immediately invert coffeecake onto a large serving plate, allowing butterscotch mixture to drip over sides of coffeecake. Be careful *not to burn fingers* while handling hot rolls. Pull individual rolls apart and serve with butter.

–Susie Keyser (Mrs. Hugh)

449

Old-Fashioned Coffeecake

Yield: one 10-inch tube cake

This is an updated version of a one hundred fifty-year-old Virginia recipe.

4 cups sifted flour, divided
1 teaspoon ground cloves
1 teaspoon cinnamon
1 teaspoon allspice
1/2 teaspoon salt
1 cup golden seedless
  raisins
1 cup currants
1/2 cup butter, at room
  temperature
1/2 cup margarine or
  shortening, at room
  temperature
2 cups light brown sugar,
  firmly packed
3 eggs
1 cup *very strong* cold coffee
2 teaspoons instant coffee
  crystals (see note)
1/4 cup maple syrup
2/3 cup buttermilk
1 teaspoon baking soda
1 cup chopped English
  walnuts or pecans
Confectioners' sugar for
  dusting cake

Sift together 3 cups flour, cloves, cinnamon, all-spice, and salt;set aside. Combine raisins, currants, and 1 cup flour together,mixing well. In a bowl, cream butter, margarine, and sugar together until light and fluffy. Add eggs, one at a time, beating well after each addition. Add dry ingredients, coffee, coffee crystals, and maple syrup alternately. Combine buttermilk and soda and stir into cake batter. Fold in floured raisins and nuts.Spoon into a lightly greased and floured 10-inch tube pan. Bake in a slow oven (325 degrees F.) for 1 hour 20 minutes or until done. Cool in pan for 10 minutes, then invert on a wire rack to finish cooling. Turn right side up and sift confectioners' sugar over top.

Note: 1/8 teaspoon maple extract may be substituted for 2 teaspoons instant coffee crystals.

The CRACKER

With a

Preference

Wheat-to-Biscuit

Made in
RICHMOND

Virginia Cookery Book, circa 1921

Virginia House

Named for its mistress, Virginia Weddell, the stately mansion located on Sulgrave Road in the Windsor Farms area of Richmond is constructed of stones quarried and shaped in 12th century England. Erected as a religious house in Warwickshire by Henry de Newburg, the first Earl of Warwick, the Priory of St. Sepulchre, as it was known, continued as a monastery for more than four hundred years until royal seizure by Henry VIII. Reconstructed as a manor house by subsequent owner, Thomas Hawkins, a court favorite, the present building bears a window commemorating a visit of Queen Elizabeth I in 1572.

Acquired by Virginia and Alexander Weddell, in 1925, the ancient country house was dismantled and shipped in numbered crates to Richmond to be redesigned by architect Henry Grant into its present form, saving it from demolition. Shortly after completion, Virginia House was conveyed to the Virginia Historical Society with stipulation the Weddells would retain residency during their lifetime. Since 1948, the mansion has been used by the Society for conferences, social events, and the annual membership garden party.

Noted Richmond landscape architect Charles Gillette designed the "pleasances," a series of small terraced gardens, pools, and paths...including a wild garden and wildflower meadow, sanctuary for birds and wild flowers. Completing the colorful charm of the mansion against the backdrop of the meandering James River are furnishings which refelct the Weddell's interests as connoisseurs and collectors of unusual furniture, tapestries, and art objects. The house is open by appointment to individuals and groups.

451

Corn Bread

Corn was an important part of the diet of the Indians and Colonial Americans. Pounded into meal, it was used to make a variety of breads, porridges, cakes, and other foods. Corn bread was one such food. Numerous varieties of corn bread have been developed over the years with such whimsical names as hoecake, ashcake, and Johnny cake. Hoecakes were so christened, because they were actually baked on a hoe over on open fire. Similarly, ashcakes, wrapped in palm or cabbage leaves, were baked in hot ashes. The name "Johnny cake" is an alteration of "Shawnee cake" and is derived from a king of bread made by the shgawnee Indians.

Yankee and Southern corn breads differ because of the type of corn meal used in each locale. Yellow corn was mostly gorwn in New England, while white was predominant in the South. In general, Southern corn bread is richer because plantation cooks used more buttermilk and shortening in their recipes.

Plantation Corn Bread

Yield: 12 to 16 servings

2 cups white corn meal
1/2 cup sifted flour
2 teaspoons baking powder
1 teaspoon salt
1/2 teaspoon baking soda
1 cup buttermilk
1 cup milk
1/4 cup shortening, melted and cooled, or cooking oil
2 eggs, beaten

Five minutes before mixing, place a well-greased 9 x 9 x 2-inch baking pan on the bottom shelf of oven. In a bowl, sift together the first 5 ingredients. Add buttermilk, milk, shortening, and eggs; stir just until dry ingredients are moistened. Pour batter into prepared pan. Bake at once in the top half of a very hot oven (450 degrees F.) for 25 to 30 minutes or until done. Serve hot.

Quick Sour Cream Corn Bread

Yield: about 8 servings

1 (16 to 17-ounce) can
  cream-style corn
1 cup sour cream
1/2 cup cooking oil
3 jumbo or extra large eggs,
  separated
1 (12-ounce) package corn
  muffin mix
Butter or margarine, as
  needed

In a medium bowl, combine corn, sour cream, and oil, mixing well. Beat egg yolks lightly and stir into corn mixture. In deep small bowl, beat egg whites until soft, but not dry, peaks are formed. Stir corn muffin mix into corn-sour cream mixture. Fold in beaten egg whites. Pour batter into a greased 12 x 8 x 2-inch baking pan. Bake in a slow oven (325 degrees F.) for about 45 minutes or until metal tester inserted in center comes out clean. Remove from oven and cool several minutes before cutting into squares. Serve warm or at room temperature with butter.

Variations: Add a drained (8-ounce) can niblet corn to corn-sour cream mixtur
  Fill greased muffin pans (2 3/4 inches in diameter) with batter three-fourths full. Bake in a slow oven (325 degrees F.) for 30 to 35 minutes or until done.

–Joy Bray

Old Richmond Advertisement, circa 1909

Hush Puppies

Yield: about 2 dozen

Folklore tells us that Hush Puppies acquired their whimsical name when fishermen, fishing for catfish, threw their dogs bits of fried bread to keep them quiet, not disturbing the fish or the fisherman's ability to catch the elusive creature. Another story suggests Confederate civilians hiding out from Yankee troops kept their dogs quiet in the same manner admonishing the pups, "Hush, puppy."

2 1/4 cups yellow cornmeal
1 cup plus 2 tablespoons
   flour
2 3/8 teaspoons baking
   powder (see note)
1 1/2 teaspoons salt
1/4 cup chopped peeled
   onion
2 eggs beaten
1 cup milk
2 1/2 tablespoons marga-
   rine, melted (see note)
Hot cooking oil as needed
Hot syrup and/or butter or
   margarine, at room
   temperature (optional)

In a medium bowl, sift together the first 4 ingredi-ents. Add onions, mixing lightly. Combine eggs and milk in a 2-cup measure. Add egg mixture and milk, all at once, to dry ingredients, mixing *just* until dry ingredients are thoroughly moistened. Fill a small scoop (about 1 ounce) with batter; drop mixture into medium hot oil (350 to 375 degrees F.) in a deep fryer. Repeat process, cooking 4 to 5 Hush Puppies at a time. Cook until Hush puppies are golden brown, about 3 to 5 minutes, turning once. Remove and drain on absorbent paper.

Note: If an 1/8 teaspoon measuring spoon is unavailable, use a 1/2 teaspoon measuring spoon; do not fill level, but about three-fourths full.

Note: Margarine is recommended for use rather than butter or shortening.

Note: If a deep fryer is unavailable, Hush Puppies may be pan fried in a deep heavy skillet in about 2 to 3 inches of hot cooking oil.

–Chef W. Keith Pearce

Jenny Lind Bread

1 quart of sifted flour., A lump of butter the size of an egg, 2 teacups of milk., 4 eggs., 1 1/2 teaspoonfuls of soda, 2 teaspoonfuls of cream of tartar. Bake twenty minutes.

Mrs. L.
Housekeeping in Old Virginia, *1879*

Dickens Didn't Like Us

Dickens went on to pay this tribute to liquid refreshments then typical of Virginia: "The mounds of ices and the bowls of mint-julep and sherry cobbler they make in these latitudes are refreshments never to be thought of afterwards, in Summer, by hose who would preserve contented minds."

Jim Walsh
"Dickens Didn't Like Us,"
A Hundred and Ten Years Ago the Great VictorianNovelist
Told Virginia Its Sins and Shortcomings
Richmond Times-Dispatch, *March 2, 1952*

Banana Chocolate Chip Muffins

Yield: 12 muffins

1 1/2 cups sifted flour
1/4 teaspoon nutmeg
1/4 teaspoon salt
3/4 cup semi-sweet chocolate pieces
3/4 cup English walnuts or pecans
1/2 cup butter or margarine, at room temperature
1/2 cup sugar
1 tablespoon hot water
1 teaspoon baking soda
1 egg, lightly beaten
1 cup mashed peeled ripe bananas (about 2 to 3 medium)

In a small bowl, sift together the first three ingredients; add chocolate pieces and nuts, coating each well with the flour mixture. In a medium bowl, cream butter until smooth. Gradually add sugar, beating well. In a 1 cup measure, blend hot water and baking soda together until soda is dissolved. In a small bowl,combine egg, mashed bananas, and soda-water, mixing well; stir into butter mixture. Add flour mixture, mixing *just* until dry ingredients are thoroughly moistened. Fill greased muffin pans (23/4 inches in diameter) two-thirds full. Bake in a moderate oven (375 degrees F.) for 20 minutes or until done.

–Kelly Yuhas (Mrs. Ken)

455

Cracklin' Muffins

Yield: 24 muffins

1 pound pork fatback
3 cups sifted flour
1 1/2 cups yellow or white
  corn meal
3 tablespoons baking
  powder
3 eggs, beaten
6 tablespoons sugar
1 1/4 cups milk
1 cup butter or margarine,
  melted

If fatback is salted, boil in water to cover for 2 minutes; drain well.   Remove skin and cut into 1/2-inch squares. Arrange fatback pieces in a 15 x 10 x 1-inch baking pan; bake in a moderate oven (375 degrees F.) for 50 minutes. Pour off rendered fat and discard.   Drain cracklins on absorbent paper. Sift together flour, corn meal, and baking powder. In a bowl, combine eggs,sugar, and salt, beating lightly. Add milk. Stir in butter and dry ingredients, mixing *just* until dry ingredients are moistened. *Do not overmix.* Fill greased muffin pans (2 3/4 inches in diameter) three-fourths full. Bake in a hot oven (400 degrees F.) for 15 to 20 minutes or until done and lightly browned.

–The Country Club of Virginia

Miniature Date Muffins

Yield: 24 to 27 muffins

This recipe originated with Mary Guthridge, a colorful and philanthropic Richmond lady, who shared many of her recipes with me when I first moved to Richmond many years ago."

2 cups sifted flour
1/4 teaspoon baking powder
1/4 teaspoon salt
1/3 cup butter or margarine,
  at room temperature
1/4 cup light brown sugar,
  firmly packed
1 egg, slightly beaten
4 ounces pitted dates,
  chopped

Sift together the first 3 ingredients; set aside. In a medium bowl, cream butter until smooth. Gradually add sugar,beating until light and fluffy. Add egg, beating well. Stir in dry ingredients and milk, mixing *just* until dry ingredients are thoroughly moistened.   Fold in chopped dates.Fill greased miniature muffin pans (1 1/2 inches in diameter) two thirds full.   Bake in a hot (425 degree oven) for 10 to 15 minutes or until done.

Variation: Fold 1/2 cup chopped pecans or English walnuts into batter with dates.

–Virginia Cottrell (Mrs. Walker)

Crunchy Double Chocolate Pecan Muffins

Yield: 12 muffins

2 cups chopped pecans or
  blanched almonds
1 cup sifted flour
3 tablespoons sifted cocoa
Pinch of salt
2 squares (ounces) un-
  sweetened chocolate
2 ounces semi-sweet
  chocolate
1 cup butter or margarine,
  at room temperature
4 large eggs
1 1/2 cups sugar
1 teaspoon vanilla extract
1/4 teaspoon almond
  extract

Spread pecans or almonds in one layer across a baking sheet;bake in a moderate oven (350 degrees F.) for 15 to 20 minutes, stirring occasionally, until nuts are very hot (pecans should not be any darker in color but almonds will turn a light ivory color). Sift together the flour, cocoa,and salt; set aside. In a heavy 2 1/2 to 3-quart saucepan,combine the chocolates and butter; stir over low heat until completely melted. Remove from heat and stir in eggs, one at a time, sugar, and flavorings. Add dry ingredients, mixing well. Stir in toasted nuts. Fill muffin pans (2 3/4 inches in diameter), lined with paper or foil baking cups, almost full (level with top of baking cups). Bake in a moderate oven (350 degrees F.) for 30 to 35 minutes or until a metal tester inserted in center of muffins come out clean, reversing the muffin pans from the front to the back of the oven halfway during the baking time. *Do not over bake.* Cool muffins in pans for 5 minutes, then turn onto wire racks to finish cooling. The muffins will develop a hard crunchy top crust as they cool.

–Elizabeth Warren (Mrs. E. P.)

Easy Beer Muffins

Yield: 12 to 14 muffins

2 cups biscuit/baking mix
1/4 cup sugar
1 egg, slightly beaten
2/3 cup beer

In a bowl, combine biscuit mix and sugar. Add egg and beer, stirring *just* enough to moisten dry ingredients. If mixture is too dry, an additional tablespoon of beer may be added. Spoon into well-greased muffin cups (2 3/4 inches in diameter) two-thirds full. Bake in a moderate oven (375 degrees F.) for 15 minutes or until done and lightly browned.

–Jaira Cranshaw (Mrs. Ronald)

James Center

The James Center, located between 9th and 12th streets and Cary and Canal streets, adjacent to the restored historic Shockoe area is one of Richmond's newest and most modern office complexes. Completed in 1985-87, it stands on the site of the South's most important industrial center prior to the Civil War. Most of what is now the James Center was once occupied by the turning Basin of the James River and Kanawha Canal.

During the early history of Virginia, the James River was the primary mode of transportation for manufactured goods and food products. Richmond's significant position at the falls of the river turned the city into the major market for the surrounding territory during the 18th and 19th centuries, causing the turning Basin to become the destination and embarkation point for river packets and bateaux (flat bottomed boats). Cargos of tobacco (Virginia Gold), grain and flour, iron ore, coal, exotic food stuff such as oranges and bananas and other goods were loaded and unloaded, resulting in activity daily in the area.

As testimony to those by-gone years, the remains of more than thirty canal boats were excavated during the construction of the complex. Offering tribute to those former days in Richmond's past, sculptor Lloyd Lillie's magnificent bronze sculpture of male figures straining against ropes to hoist three sails dominates the plaza of the Dominion Bank Building, One James Center. Above the figures, the fifty foot high mast, also of bronze, plunges into the smooth brick discs below.

During the Christmas holiday season, faux reindeer, awash with twinkling miniature white lights, stand in mute repose in the plaza, providing delight for those of all ages. Nearby, at the corner of 10th and Cary Streets, the plaza offers Richmonders a place to meet in a tree-lined, flower bedecked park.

An instant landmark, the Clock Tower, fondly known as the "Boatman's Tower," welcomes visitors on the hour and half-hour. Depicting life on the canal from 1785 to 1879. The forty five foot limestone tower, housing a twenty five brass bell carillon, is likened to the charming glockenspiels of old European squares.

Slaves could bring their own provisions to sell in the public market only on Saturday afternoons and Sundays. Even then, a slave had to have written permission from his owner, specifying the articles that he could bring to market. The items could be exposed for sale before sunset on Saturday afternoon and before ten o'clock on Sunday. If not sold by those times, the provisions had to be removed from the city.

Harry M. Ward and Harold E. Greer, Jr.
Richmond During The Revolution, 1775-83, 1977

As the Revolution approached, Richmond was little more than a village of muddy streets and small frame houses. It did have a church, warehouses for tobacco and other trade goods, taverns, and a small courthouse. Main Street, east of Shockoe Creek, was Richmond's major thoroughfare in the time of the Revolution. Along it stood the Henrico courthouse, Henrico County jail, market, Galts's Tavern, and Cowley's Tavern (referred to as Tankard's Ordinary during the war), as well as the shops of some of the city's barbers, tailors, and craftsmen. Across Shockoe Creek to the west, other taverns and Byrd's warehouse fronted on Main Street. Shockoe Hill, future site of the capitol and the public square, was approached by what is today Thirteenth Street, (which becomes Governor Street one block north of Main Street) supposedly following an old Indian trail. Twenty-fifth Street gave principal access to what is today Church Hill.

Roads led out of Richmond to Williamsburg on the east, to Hanover Town and Fredericksburg on the north, to Westham and Charlottesville on the west, and to Petersburg on the south. To Williamsburg, a two-day journey, the road past Bottoms Bridge and New Kent Court House was described by the traveler Schoepf as being "mainly through gloomy forest, only here and there tilled land or a wretched cabin."

Schoepf described the houses in Richmond in 1783 as "almost wholly of wood and scattered irregularly on two heights, divided by the Shokoes, a small brook; the number of them is not large nor are they in themselves of a handsome appearance."

Only one house that was in Richmond during the time of the Revolution is still standing, the Old Stone House on the northside of Main Street between Nineteenth and Twentieth streets. During the Revolution the house belonged to Samuel Ege.

Harry M. Ward and Harold E. Greer, Jr.
Richmond During The Revolution, 1775-83, 1977

Raisin Bran Muffins

Yield: about 4 dozen muffins

2 1/2 cups sifted flour
1 1/2 cups sugar
2 1/2 teaspoons baking soda
1 teaspoon salt
2 eggs, beaten
2 cups buttermilk
1/2 cup cooking oil
1/2 (15-ounce) package
  raisin bran flakes, crushed
Additional 1/2 cup dark
  seedless raisins (op-
  tional)

In a bowl, sift together the first 4 ingredients. In a 4-cup measure, combine eggs, buttermilk, and oil; add to dry ingredients all at once, mixing *just* until dry ingredients are moistened. Fold in bran cereal and additional raisins, if desired. Fill greased muffin pans (2 3/4 inches in diameter) two-thirds full. Bake in a hot oven (400 degrees F.) for 15 to 20 minutes or until done (see note).

Note: Miniature muffin pans (1 1/2 inches in diameter) may be used, if desired. Bake miniature muffins for 10 to 15 minutes or until done. Yield: about 8 to 10 dozen muffins.

–Evelyn Hill (Mrs. S. Winfield)

Six Weeks Refrigerator Raisin Bran Muffins

Yield: about 3 dozen muffins

2 1/2 cups whole wheat
flour, divided
2 1/2 teaspoons baking soda
1 teaspoon cinnamon
1 cup cooking oil or shortening, melted and cooled
1/2 cup sugar
3/4 teaspoon salt
2 eggs, lightly beaten
2 cups buttermilk
1 cup boiling water
3 cups bud-style bran cereal
1 cup dark or golden
seedless raisins

Sift together the 2 cups flour, baking soda, and cinnamon; set aside. In a large bowl, combine oil, sugar, and salt, beating until smooth. Add eggs, beating well. Add buttermilk, boiling water, bran cereal, and flour mixture in order listed, stirring just until well mixed. Do not beat and *do not overmix* as the muffins will become tough. Mix raisins with remaining 1/2 cup flour; fold floured raisins into batter (see note). Cover and refrigerate batter for 4 hours. *Do not stir batter again.* Fill greased muffin pans (2 3/4 inches in diameter), three-fourths full. Bake in a hot oven (400 degrees F.) for 20 minutes or until done. Turn out onto wire racks to cool.

Note: Covered batter will keep in refrigerator for up to 6 weeks.

–Shep Blair (Mrs. John D., III)

Sour Cream Banana Muffins

Yield: 10 to 12 muffins

2 cups sifted flour
1/3 cup sugar or light brown
sugar, firmly packed
1 tablespoon baking powder
1/2 teaspoon salt
1/4 teaspoon nutmeg
(optional)
2 eggs, beaten
1/2 cup sour cream
1/4 cup shortening or butter,
melted and cooled
3 ripe medium bananas,
peeled and mashed
3/4 cup chopped pecans or
English walnuts (op-
tional)

In a medium bowl, sift together the first 4 or 5 ingredients. Combine eggs, sour cream, and short-ening. Add all at once to dry ingredients and stir just enough to moisten dry ingredients. Stir in bananas and nuts, if desired. Do not overmix. Fill greased muffin pans (2 3/4 inches in diameter) two-thirds full. Bake in a hot oven (400 degrees F.) for 20 to 25 minutes or until done and lightly browned.

Southern Batter Bread

Yield: 8 to 10 servings

1 cup boiling water
1 cup white corn meal
2 cups milk
2 tablespoons butter or
  margarine, at room
  temperature
2 eggs
2 teaspoons baking powder
1 teaspoon salt

Preheat a greased 10 x 6 x 2-inch baking dish in a moderate oven (375 degrees F.) while preparing bread. In a medium bowl, pour boiling water over corn meal, mixing well. In a small heavy saucepan, heat milk and butter until milk is hot and butter melted; pour over corn meal, stirring until well mixed. In a small bowl, beat eggs, gradually beating in baking powder and salt until mixture is thick. Add to corn meal mixture, beating well. Pour into prepared hot baking dish. Bake in a moderate oven (375 degrees F.) for 25 to 30 minutes or until puffed and top is golden brown. Cut into squares and serve immediately.

–Margaret Marks (Mrs. Charles)

Old-Time Batter Bread

Yield: 6 to 8 servings

1/2 cup white corn meal
3 teaspoons baking powder
1/2 teaspoon salt
2 tablespoons butter or
  margarine
2 eggs
2 1/2 cups milk

In a medium bowl, sift together the first 3 ingredients. In a hot oven (400 degrees F.), melt butter in an 8 x 8 x 2-inch baking pan. In a small bowl, combine eggs and milk, beating well; add mixture to dry ingredients, stirring *just* until dry ingredients are thoroughly moistened. Pour batter into baking pan containing melted butter. Increase baking temperature to very hot (450 degrees F.) and bake batter bread for about 30 minutes or until lightly browned and done.

–Ollie G. Robinson

463

Spoon Bread

Legend suggests that Indian squaws demonstrated to early colonists a manner of turning corn meal into rounded cakes, appones, baked in hot ashes which became known as "corn pone" throughout Tidewater Virginia. Suppawn or Sappawn, a mush or porridge made from corn meal and water soon became the favored colonial breakfast cereal. One day, so the story goes, a dish of porridge was left for several hours in the fireside oven by accident. The suppawn in an earthenware crock was completely forgotten. When discovered, the porridge had formed a crisp crust over the surface but the inside remained creamy. Of course, the wife was desolate, and her husband remedied the culinary fiasco by lavishly adding butter to the over-cooked concoction. Thus, the birth of one of Virginia's greatest culinary offerings, spoonbread. Later eggs and milk were added. The American cuisine has changed considerably in the last three hundred years since early colonial days, however, there is nothing that tastes better than steaming hot light creamy spoon bread topped with lumps of rich melting butter.

Light 'N High Spoon Bread

Yield: 8 servings

Spoonbread is similar to a soufflé...it waits for no one!

4 cups boiling water
3 cups corn meal
4 eggs
4 cups cold milk
1 cup hot milk
1 cup butter or margarine,
  at room temperature
2 teaspoons sugar
1 1/2 teaspoons salt
2 teaspoons baking powder

In a large heavy saucepan, combine boiling water and corn meal, mixing well; stir over moderate heat until bubbles form around the edge of the pan. With a hand rotary beater or hand electric mixer, beat until mixture is smooth. In a larger bowl, beat eggs and hot and cold milk together; stir into corn meal mixture. Add butter, sugar, and salt, stirring over low heat until butter is melted and incorporated into mixture. Remove from heat and sift baking powder into corn meal mixture, blending *just* until baking powder is evenly distributed. Pour into a greased deep 3-quart casserole or souffle dish. Bake in a very hot oven (450 degrees F.) for 30 minutes. Serve immediately.

–Martha and Ned Nielsen
Nielsen's 3N Restaurant

464

Disappearing Spoon Bread Soufflé

Yield: 6 servings

"The beauty of this recipe is that the hard part is done early, then it can be refrigerated until ready to be baked. It will fall quickly, but that is O.K...it will disappear so fast, no one will notice. It will serve six, if people aren't true spoon bread lovers...otherwise, only three or four!"

3 cups milk, divided
1 cup white corn meal (see note)
2 tablespoons butter or margarine, at room temperature
1 teaspoon salt
1 teaspoon baking powder
5 egg yolks, well beaten (see note)
5 egg whites, stiffly beaten (see note)

In a medium bowl, pour 1 cup milk over corn meal. In a heavy saucepan, scald remaining milk over moderate heat. When milk begins to bubble around the edges of the pan, add corn meal mixture; cook, stirring constantly, for 10 minutes or until mixture is *very* thick. Add butter, salt, and baking powder, stirring until butter is melted. Remove from heat; stir a small amount of hot mixture into beaten egg yolks. Fold a small amount of beaten egg whites into cooked corn meal mixture and then carefully fold corn meal mixture into egg whites. Pour into a greased 2-quart casserole or souffle dish. Bake in a moderate oven (375 degrees F.) for 50 minutes or until puffed and brown. Serve immediately.

Note: Preferably use stone ground corn meal.

Note: 4 egg yolks and whites may be used; however, spoon bread will not rise as high or be as light in texture. Preferably use extra-large eggs.

Note: Batter may be refrigerated after egg whites are added, covered, for several hours until ready to bake.

—Marilyn Smart (Mrs. John)

Picturesque Village

Richmond, "befo' de war," was a charming, picturesque village, with vistas, such as Henry James did not find when he came one snowy winter, for then Richmond was in its ugliest period, that of transition....

Louisa Coleman Blair
"'Little Red Brick Town' In Era of Hoopskirts Was Friendly, Gossipy,"
Richmond Times-Dispatch, *December 7, 1941*

Apple Puffed Pancake

Yield: 4 servings

1 cup flour
3 tablespoons sugar
1/2 teaspoon salt
1/4 teaspoon cinnamon
6 eggs
1 1/2 cups milk
1/2 cup butter or margarine
2 large tart apples, peeled, cored, seeded, and thinly sliced (see note)
2 to 3 tablespoons light brown sugar, firmly packed

Sift together the first 4 ingredients. In a bowl, lightly beat eggs; gradually beat in dry ingredients. Stir in milk. Melt butter in a 12-inch quiche dish or 13 x 9 x 2-inch baking pan in a hot oven (425 degrees F.), coating bottom of pan evenly. Arrange apple slices evenly over bottom of prepared pan. Return to oven just until butter begins to bubble and sizzle. *Do not brown.* Remove pan from oven. Evenly pour batter over apple slices; sprinkle brown sugar over batter. Bake in a hot oven (425 degrees F.) for 20 minutes or until puffy and lightly browned. Serve immediately, cutting into wedges.

Note: Use McIntosh, Winesap, Granny Smith, or other tart variety of apples.

-Gladys Antroinen (Mrs. Aaron)

Canal

The progress of Richmond and of the James River Canal were so intimately connected, that a short notice of the latter may not be amiss.

In 1790 the canal was opened from Westham to a landing, called Broad Rock, a short distance above the city; at which time, or rather on the 29th December, 1789, the legislature were invited to take a trip up the canal and through the locks. In 1795 the canal entered the city, and in November 1800, the water was first let into the basin on trial.

As the charter of the Company required a connection of the canal with tide-water, a contract was entered into with one Ariel Cooley, a cute, uneducated, but practical man, (at least as far as Ariel was interested) for the construction of thirteen locks between the Basin and Mayo's Bridge, for the sum of $49,000. A large excavation was required to be made along the descent of the hill, which Cooley estimated at about $9,000. He stipulated for the use of the water in the basin, if he required it; and he did put it in requisition to some purpose. He cut a small ditch along the centre of the line which the locks were to occupy, and he opened a sluice into it from the Basin. A rapid and increasing sluice it was. In some twenty-four hours or less the water had wrought the $9,000 worth of excavation, and the only difficulty was to prevent its "helping over much." It had wrought an opening for the upper navigation and a contrary effect on the lower one, by washing an immense quantity of earth into the river.

Samuel Mordecai
Richmond in By-Gone Days, 1856
Reprint Edition, 1975

Bread Riot

...On 2 April there occurred an event still referred to as the " Bread Riot." Because speculators had made the situation worse by greatly inflating prices, city residents were running out of food. Accordingly, a group of desperate women met at the Belvidere Baptist Church on Oregon Hill and began a march to the capitol, a distance of over a mile. On the way they looted numerous shops, finally raiding the Confederate commissary. Both the governor and the mayor were called out to quell the disturbance, but it was not until President Davis himself arrived and made ready to have troops fire into the crowd that its members dispersed....

She hurried down the street. The windows swam before her eyes, piled with prayer books and playing cards, umbrellas and rifles, cartridges and groceries. On the sidewalk, near a doorway, a barrel of flour had a sign of $100 and a canteen on top....

She moved around barrels of molasses with "$15 per gal" scrawled on the wood....

"Right from the Valley of Virginia, the first crop of real, native, home-grown apples. Only twenty-five dollars a bushel. Stock up now, ladies and gentlemen, before the speculators raise the prices."....

Then she was at Cary Street, jostled and bumped in the milling mob. She glimpsed the pack of women. Their clothes were tattered and torn, their hair hung disheveled above bestial faces. Her panic shook her as she stared at them, and their animal cries beat at her. Glass was strewn all over the flagstone crossing. Drays and carts swayed in the midst of the women and they shoved and fought over the piles in them. She glimpsed hams and flour barrels and molasses kegs and slabs of pork. The last of the women passed in front of her....

A bent, grayed old woman staggered toward Elizabeth. The men in front of her gave way and stared at the woman. She clutched loaves of bread and a handful of salt herring, and glared out of wide eyes, fever-bright and glassy. She panted like a dog. Dank gray hair tumbled from under her bonnet, half off her head. She came through the lane straight toward Elizabeth, and Elizabeth recognized her family's former dressmaker.

"Mrs. Fitchett," she said weakly. "Mrs. Fitchett!"
The woman stopped and slowly her gaze focused. She shifted as
though she might be ashamed. Then she lowered her eyes.
"What are those women after, Mrs. Fitchett?"
"Bread!"...
"It's all over, Mrs. Paxton," he called cheerfully. "The President
tried talking with them, but one of them threw a loaf of bread
at him. Then Governor Letcher threatened to have the City
Battalion fire into them and they went off, sullen as animals.
I didn't know we had such riffraff in the city."
"What you don't know, apparently," the old aristocrat said
coldly, "is that hunger makes riffraff of us all."...
...The shock of the bread riot, which had gripped her in a
paralysis, broke into its horrible details and she saw again each
hunger-crazed woman. They flashed before her vision like
colored slides. Their bestial screams rang again through her
brain...

Dowdey
Bugles Blow No More (Condensed), 1937

French-Style Pancakes

Yield: 4 small pancakes or 1 large pancake

"Very thin batter...cooks rapidly. Delicious with fruit."

2 eggs whites
1 egg yolk
1 tablespoon flour
Butter or margarine as
  needed, at room temperature
1 tablespoon butter or
  margarine, melted
Sliced strawberries,
  peaches, or nectarines, or
  whole raspberries,
  blackberries, or blueberries, or fruit preserves, or
  warm maple syrup or
  honey

In a bowl, combine the first 3 ingredients, beating well. Batter will be thin. To make pancakes, preheat and lightly butter a 6 to 7-inch crêpe or omelet pan or skillet. Pour in 2 to 3 tablespoons of batter all at once. Tilt pan quickly and rotate to distribute batter evenly over surface. Cook pancakes quickly over moderate heat (350 to 375 degrees F.) until lightly browned on both sides. Remove to a warmed platter; cover. Do not allow butter in pan to become too dark or burn; wipe out pan as necessary between pancake preparation with absorbent paper and add more butter to pan. Repeat process until all batter is used. Brush pancakes with additional butter, if desired, and serve with fresh fruit, preserves, or warm maple syrup or honey.

–Esther D. Shelley (Mrs. Blackwell)

469

Cottage Cheese Pancakes with Blueberry Sauce

Yield: about 14 to 16 pancakes or 6 to 8 servings

"These pancakes are nice to serve as a company breakfast. Hmmm...good."

Sauce
1/4 cup sugar
2 tablespoons cornstarch
Pinch salt
1/2 cup water
1 (16-ounce) package frozen blueberries (see note)
1 teaspoon lemon juice
2 tablespoons blueberry or raspberry liqueur

Batter
3 eggs, slightly beaten
1 (24-ounce) container large curd cottage cheese
2 cups sifted flour
2 teaspoons lemon juice

To prepare sauce, combine sugar, cornstarch, and salt in a small heavy saucepan. Gradually blend in water. Add blueberries and lemon juice, mixing well. Stir in liqueur. Cook, stirring constantly, over moderate heat until sauce is thickened and bubbly hot. Remove from heat, cover, and set aside until pancakes are prepared.

To prepare pancakes, combine all batter ingredients in a large bowl and beat at medium speed of an electric mixer until mixture is smooth. For each pancake, pour about 1/4 cup batter onto a hot, lightly greased griddle or electric griddle set at 375 degrees F.. Turn pancakes when puffed, full of bubbles, and the edges are cooked; cook until done and lightly browned,pressing down slightly with a spatula. Serve immediately and pass Blueberry Sauce.

–Elizabeth Archer

Raisin-Walnut Pancakes

Yield: 8 large pancakes

1 cup whole wheat flour
1 tablespoon sugar
2 teaspoons baking powder
Pinch salt
2 tablespoons wheat germ
granules
1 egg
1 tablespoon butter or
margarine, melted, or
cooking oil
1 teaspoon vanilla
1 cup sour milk or buttermilk
1/2 cup dark seedless
raisins, chopped
1/4 cup chopped English
walnuts or pecans
Warm honey and additional
melted butter or marga-
rine

Sift together the first 4 ingredients. Add wheat germ granules,mixing well. In a bowl, lightly beat egg. Add butter and vanilla, mixing well. Alternately stir in dry ingredients and sour milk, beating well. Stir in raisins and nuts. For each pancake, pour about 1/4 cup batter onto a hot, lightly greased griddle or electric griddle set at 375 degrees F. Turn pancakes when puffed, full of bubbles, and the edges are cooked; cook until done and lightly browned. Serve with warm honey and melted butter.

–Fran Lincoln

Money was so scarce in 1782 that the state began to accept tobacco, hemp, and flour in payment of taxes, making the country responsible for its collection and safekeeping. In March 1782 the court appointed Samuel Ege and Dabney Miller "to receive, safely to keep and to deliver the Hemp and Flour and also to inspect the said hemp, which may be delivered at the Public Inspection in the Town of Richmond as established by Act of Assembly."

Harry M. Ward and Harold E. Greer, Jr.
Richmond During The Revolution, 1775-83, 1977

Waffles

Thomas Jefferson is attributed with introducing waffles to the United States when he was U. S. Minister to France in 1784. During one of his travels to Holland, he encountered waffles and, of course, brought back a waffle iron to Virginia when he returned home.

Quick 'N Easy Waffles

Yield: 3 (9-inch) waffles

2 cups Quick Biscuit Baking Mix (see index)
2 eggs, separated
1 cup water
1 cup blueberries, or chopped dark seedless raisins, or pecans, or English walnuts (optional)

In a medium bowl, combine biscuit/baking mix, egg yolks, and water, mixing well. In a small bowl, beat egg whites until stiff, glossy, but not dry, peaks are formed; fold into batter. Fold in blueberries, raisins, or nuts, if desired. Pour one-third of the batter onto the lower grid of a lightly greased preheated waffle iron; close cover and bake until steaming stops, about 5 minutes. Repeat process until all batter is used. Baked waffles may be kept warm in a *very, very* slow oven (200 degrees F.) until all waffles are prepared.

–Fran Lincoln

Fine 'N Fancy French Toast with Fresh Fruit and Fruit Butter

Yield: 4 servings

4 jumbo eggs
1 1/4 cups light cream or half-and-half
Pinch salt
Pinch nutmeg
8 slices slightly dry (2 to 3 days old) French bread, cut 3/4 to 1-inch thick

In a medium bowl, combine the first 4 ingredients, beating lightly. Soak bread slices, both sides, a few at a time in egg mixture; drain slices over the bowl. Pan-fry bread slices in about 1/4 inch of oil at 325 degrees F. until golden brown, about 1 to 2 minutes per side. Drain on absorbent paper. Arrange on a baking sheet and heat in a hot oven (400 degrees F.) for 3 to 5 minutes or until

Hot cooking oil for pan-
frying
Tasty Fruit Butter
Sifted confectioners' sugar
Fresh fruit of choice (peeled
and sliced peaches or
nectarines, or sliced
strawberries, or whole
blueberries, or raspber-
ries, or blackberries, or
halved pitted sweet dark
cherries for garnish
Mint sprigs for garnish
Warm maple syrup or honey
(optional)

Tasty Fruit Butter
Yield: about 1 1/2 cups
1/2 cup coarse fruit puree (1
medium peach or nectar-
ine, peeled, seeded and
halved, or 1 to 1 1/4 cups
ripe strawberries, halved,
or 1 to 1 1/4 cups whole
blueberries, raspberries,
or blackberries, or 1 cup
sweet dark cherries,
stemmed and pitted)
Ascorbic acid fruit preserving powder (optional)
1 cup butter or margarine,
at room temperature and
divided into medium
pieces
1 to 2 teaspoons honey or
to taste (optional)

toast is puffed. Spread each slice lightly with Tasty Fruit Butter. Arrange 2 slices per serving on heated plates; sprinkle toast with confectioners' sugar and garnish with desired prepared fresh fruit and fresh mint sprigs. Pass warm maple syrup or honey and additional Tasty Fruit Butter.

To prepare fruit pureé, place desired fruit in a blender container; cover and blend at low speed until fruit is a coarse pureé. Sprinkle pureé with fruit preserving powder, if desired. Add butter, one piece at a time, and continue blending at low speed until mixture is smooth. Add honey, if desired, blending well. Spoon into small crock or glass serving dish. Chill in the refrigerator until butter is firm, cover with clear plastic wrap. Butter may be stored in the refrigerator for several days until ready to use. Serve as a spread with French toast, biscuits, rolls, etc.

French Toast

Our French Toast of today is similar to a dessert recipe of ancient Rome. Bread was soaked in milk, fried, and then served topped with honey. The French improved on the recipe and we Americans have borrowed from them in this tasty creation.

> (At the time of Dahlgren's Raid around Richmond in February
> March 1864) all there was to oppose him was a force of local
> soldiery and a battalion of department clerks. The members of
> Congress shouldered guns and mounted guard around
> Richmond. But the small force of department clerks and
> unskilled soldiers were a match for Dahlgren, and averted the
> plot he had formed to pour fire upon the devoted capital of the
> Confederacy. But we soldiers were hungry. I had had nothing
> to eat all day, and the heartiest meal I ever enjoyed was a piece
> of dry bread and a raw onion that I asked of an old market
> woman as she passed me where I was keeping guard. That was
> the best onion I ever ate in my life.
>
> Thomas J. Semmes
> in **XXV Southern Historical Society Papers**

Pineapple Fritters

Yield: about 10 fritters

1 cup sifted flour
1/4 cup sifted confectioners'
    sugar
1 1/2 teaspoons baking
    powder
1/4 teaspoon salt
1/8 teaspoon nutmeg
1 egg, beaten
2/3 cup milk
1 (20-ounce) can sliced
    pineapple, drained
Hot cooking oil as needed
Additional sifted confec-
    tioners' sugar

In a medium bowl, sift together the first five ingredients. In a 1 cup measure, combine egg and milk blending well; stir into dry ingredients all at once, mixing just until dry ingredients are thoroughly moistened. Dip pineapple slices into batter, coating each slice well. Drain off excess batter back into the bowl. Deep-fry fritters in hot oil (375 degrees F.) until crisp and golden brown. Drain each well on absorbent paper, then sift confectioners' sugar liberally over each fritter. Serve warm.

Variation: 2 to 3 ripe tart medium apples may be substituted for the pineapple
    slices. Remove peel, core, and seeds from apples; cut apples into thick
    slices.

Country Oat Waffles with Crème Fraîche and Fresh Strawberries

Yield: 12 to 14 waffles

These waffles have a nutty flavor and are very moist. They're also wonderful served with warm maple syrup or with fresh strawberries or peaches tossed with a little brown sugar.

1 cup flour
1 cup quick cooking rolled oats
1/2 cup white or yellow corn meal
4 1/2 teaspoons baking powder
2 eggs, slightly beaten
2 cups buttermilk
1 cup unflavored yogurt or sour cream
3/4 cup butter or margarine, melted
1 quart strawberries, hulled and sliced
2 tablespoons light brown sugar, firmly packed or to taste
Crème Fraîche (see note)

In a medium bowl, combine flour, oats, corn meal, and baking powder, mixing well. Add eggs, buttermilk, yogurt, and butter, beating well. Allow batter to stand at room temperature for 15 minutes. Pour enough batter to cover two-thirds of the lower grid of a lightly greased preheated waffle iron; close cover and bake until steaming stops, about 5 minutes. Repeat process until all batter is used. Baked waffles may be kept warm in a very, very slow oven (200 degrees F.) until all waffles are prepared. In a small bowl, combine strawberries and brown sugar, tossing lightly to mix. To serve, top each waffle with sweetened strawberries and a dollop of Crème Fraîche. Pass remaining strawberries and Crème Fraîche.

Note: Prepare Crème Fraîche 8 to 12 hours before serving.

Crème Fraîche
(about 1 cup)
1 cup heavy cream, at room temperature
1 tablespoon buttermilk
1 to 2 tablespoons light brown sugar, firmly packed

In a clean glass jar, combine all ingredients, blending well. Cover and secure tightly. Shake mixture and allow to stand at room temperature for 8 to 12 hours until mixture is lightly thickened.

–Elizabeth Archer

Jefferson Lakeside Club

Originally an extension of the Old Jefferson Hotel and named the Jefferson Club, the Jefferson Lakeside Country Club is one of the oldest private clubs in Richmond, having been founded in 1895. Located in the north side of Richmond on Lakeside Avenue in Henrico County near historic Bloemendaal the club grounds were at one time part of a private zoo owned by Lewis Ginter. The present clubhouse was erected in 1940. Although a private club, featuring an eighteen-hole golf course and five tennis courts, the clubhouse facilities are available on a rental basis to non-members for private parties.

Blintz Casserole

Yield: 6 servings

1/2 cup butter or margarine
4 eggs
1/2 cup sour cream
2 tablespoons orange juice
1 teaspoon vanilla extract
Pinch salt
12 prepared Blintz, each rolled jelly roll-style and filled
Cinnamon and sugar as needed

Blintz

Yield: about 12 (6-inch) blintz
3/4 cup sifted flour
2 tablespoons confectioners' sugar
1 teaspoon baking powder
1/2 teaspoon salt

Melt butter in an 11 x 7 x 2-inch baking dish in a moderate oven (350 degrees F.). In a medium bowl, beat eggs lightly. Gradually add sour cream, orange juice, vanilla, and salt, beating until smooth. Arrange rolled blintz in melted butter in preheated baking dish, turning each once. Evenly spoon sour cream mixture over blintz. Lightly sprinkle cinnamon and sugar over top of casserole. Bake, uncovered, in a moderate oven (350 degrees F.) for 1 hour. Arrange two blintz on each plate and spoon a small amount of sour cream sauce over each serving. Sprinkle lightly with additional cinnamon, if desired.

Prepare blintz. In a deep medium bowl, sift together the first 4 ingredients. Add eggs, milk, water, and flavorings, if desired, mixing until smooth. To make blintz, preheat and lightly grease a 6-inch crêpe or omelet pan or skillet. Pour in 2

2 eggs, beaten
2/3 cup milk
1/3 cup water
1/2 teaspoon vanilla extract
    or 1/2 teaspoon grated
    lemon peel
    (optional)

Filling
1 1/2 cups well-drained
    creamy-style or dry
    cottage cheese
1 egg yolk
1 teaspoon butter or
    margarine, at room
    temperature
1 teaspoon vanilla extract or
    1/2 teaspoon grated
    lemon peel
    (optional)

to 3 tablespoons batter. Pan-fry blintz on one side only, until top is bubbly.Carefully remove each blintz with a wide flat spatula to a cloth or absorbent paper, uncooked side up. Prepare filling. In a small bowl, combine cottage cheese, egg yolk, 1 teaspoon butter,and 1 teaspoon vanilla extract or grated lemon peel, if desired. Spoon a small amount of cottage cheese mixture onto each blintz and roll each jelly roll-style. Proceed as directed in Blintz Casserole recipe.

–Chef Frederick Christian, Sr.
The Jefferson Lakeside Club

Old Richmond Advertisement, circa 1909

Soda Bread

Created in Ireland during the nineteenth century and introduced to the United States with the Irish immigrants, sodabread was originally baked in an improvised pot-oven as cooking utensils were scarce in rural cottages. Traditionally served on St. Patrick's Day, soda bread was poor man's bread in past days, being of a heavy coarse texture and using baking soda as the leavening ingredient. When raisins are added to the recipe, it is sometimes called Spotted Dog.

Pan-Fried Crispy Soda Bread

Yield: one loaf

Mrs. Powers gave the following recipe to the children in her 2nd grade religious education class at St. Edward's Catholic Church in suburban Richmond to prepare in class. This recipe is very moist and is unusual because it is pan-fried rather than baked in an oven. Included with Mrs. Powers recipe is (then 7 years old) Andrea Guthrie's short-cut interpretation of her teacher's recipe!

2 cups sifted flour
1 tablespoon sugar
3/4 teaspoon baking soda
1/2 teaspoon salt
6 tablespoons shortening
1/2 to 1 cup dark seedless raisins (see note)
1 tablespoon caraway seeds (optional)
1/2 to 3/4 cup buttermilk
Cooking oil as needed
Butter or margarine, at room temperature

In a medium bowl, sift together flour, sugar, baking soda, and salt. With a pastry blender, cut in shortening until mixture resembles coarse meal. Add raisins and caraway seeds, if desired, mixing well. Gradually add buttermilk, mixing *just* until dry ingredients are thoroughly moistened. The mixture should not be dry. With a rolling pin, roll out dough or pat into a large circle 1 inch in thickness. With a sharp knife, cut dough circle into equal size wedges. Preheat an electric frypan or heavy skillet to moderate (350 degrees F.). Coat frypan or skillet with a small amount of cooking oil. Pan-fry dough wedges, about 5 minutes per side. Reduce heat to low and continue frying until done and golden brown on each side. Remove from frypan and serve warm with butter.

Note: Place raisins in a small bowl; add just enough water to cover. Allow raisins to stand for 10 to 15 minutes to plump; drain well.

\Variation: Omit raisins and add 3/4 cup chopped green onion (include some green tops).

Andrea Guthrie's Interpretation: Get a pot and put flower in it.Put baking stuff in it and half of salt. Mix it. Put a tablespoon of something in it and pour in some milk and mix. Pour into a frypan until it is brown.

–Blanche Powers (Mrs. Timothy)

Yeast Breads

The invention of leavened bread has been attributed to the ancient Egyptians. Through the centuries, white bread, considered of high quality because of the use of white flour, has been associated with the wealthy, while dark bread has been paired with poor folk. The idea of bread being the staff of life traces back to a mid-seventeenth century English saying.

Early American homemakers had to make their own yeast prior to preparing a yeast bread. In the seventeenth century a new method of fermentation was developed, using milk, salt, and beer barm to manufacture finer quality bread loaves. Bread making for the early American homemaker demanded great effort and much time; however, those early cooks took great pride in their bread baking.

During the nineteenth century, a gadget shaped like a milk pail could be screwed to the kitchen table; by turning a crank attached to the rim of the pail, an S-shaped rod inserted vertically through the center of the pail would knead the bread dough. The unique device is the ancestor of what has become known today as the dough hook.

In 1868 commercial yeast became available to consumers in convenient foil-coated little cakes, easing the preparation of the"staff of life." Active dry yeast is a twentieth century invention.

Although most Americans prefer to purchase their bread today at the supermarket, often buying the packaged "thumb print" variety touted by large commercial bakeries, the art of bread making is still revered by many culinary devotees.

479

Petite Angel Biscuits

Yield: about 150 one-inch biscuits

5 cups sifted flour
1/3 cup sugar
1 tablespoon baking powder
2 teaspoons salt
1 cup shortening
1 package active dry yeast
1/4 cup warm water (105 to
115 degrees F.)
1 1/2 cups sour cream or
buttermilk

In a bowl, sift together the first 4 ingredients. Cut in shortening with a pastry blender or two knives until mixture resembles coarse meal. Dissolve yeast in warm water; blend in sour cream. Stir into dry ingredients, mixing well. Turn out onto a lightly floured board and knead lightly, 6 to 10 times. Roll dough to a 1/2-inch thickness. Cut with a lightly floured 1-inch biscuit cutter. Arrange biscuits on ungreased baking sheets. Bake in a hot oven (400 degrees F.) for 5 to 10 minutes or until done and golden brown.

Note: Biscuits may be frozen before or after baking. To freeze, pack biscuits in ziplock freezer bags or wrap in aluminum foil, sealing tightly. Unbaked biscuits should only be frozen for 2 to 3 weeks.

–Sue Crowell (Mrs. Robert)

Southern Yeast Biscuits

Yield: 16 biscuits

2 cups sifted flour
2 tablespoons sugar
2 teaspoons baking powder
1/2 teaspoon salt
1 package active dry yeast
1 cup warm water (105 to
115 degrees F.)
1/4 cup butter or margarine,
melted
Additional melted butter

In a medium bowl, sift together the first 4 ingredients. Add dry yeast, mixing well. In a 2-cup measure, combine water and butter. Be sure water-butter mixture is between 105 to 115 degrees F.. Add to flour mixture, mixing well. Turn out onto a lightly floured board and knead until smooth and elastic. Roll out dough to a 1/2-inch thickness. Cut with a 2-inch floured biscuit cutter. Arrange biscuits in a greased 13 x 9 x 2-inch baking pan. Cover and let rise in a warm place (85 degrees F.) away from drafts for 1 hour or until doubled in bulk. Bake, uncovered, in a slow oven (325 degrees F.) for 15 minutes or until done and golden brown. Remove from oven and brush tops of biscuits with additional melted butter.

–Betty Shipp

Golden Angel Biscuits

Yield: 2 1/2- to 3-dozen biscuits

5 to 5 1/2 cups flour
3 tablespoons sugar
1 tablespoon baking powder
1 teaspoon baking soda
1 teaspoon salt
1/2 cup shredded sharp
  Cheddar cheese
1 cup shortening
1 package active dry yeast
1/4 cup warm water (105 to
  115 degrees F.)
2 cups buttermilk, at room
  temperature
Melted butter or margarine

In a large bowl, sift together 5 cups flour, sugar, baking powder, baking soda, and salt. Add cheese, mixing well. With a pastry blender, cut in shortening until mixture resembles coarse meal. Dissolve yeast in warm water; combine with buttermilk, blending well. Stir into flour mixture; dough will be soft and sticky. Turn mixture out onto a lightly floured board; knead until dough is smooth and elastic, adding up to an additional 1/4 cup flour, 1 tablespoonful at a time, to make dough easier to handle. Roll out dough to a 1/2-inch thickness; cut with a 3-inch floured biscuit cutter. Arrange biscuits on ungreased baking sheets. Bake in a very hot oven (350 degrees F.) for 12 to 15 minutes or until done and golden brown. Brush biscuit tops lightly with melted butter.

–Barbara Kludy (Mrs. Donald)

One of the oldest taverns in town belonged to Abraham Cowley, who received his original license in 1737. His tavern occupied the southwest corner of Main and Twenty-third streets, near the county courthouse. In 1776 Cowley advertised his ordinary for rent, and described it as follows: "...the house is large, very commodious, a good kitchen, dairy, meethouse, new stable, that will contain 74 horses."

The ordinaries were tightly regulated by the county courts and subsequently by the Richmond hustings court. The court issued licenses to tavern keepers, and set all prices for "liquors, diet, lodging, provender, stablage, fodder, and pasturage...." Within one month after they were established, a table of the rates was to be "openly set up in the publick entertaining room of every ordinary."

–Harry M. Ward and Harold E. Greer, Jr.
Richmond During The Revolution, 1775-83,
1977

The Equestrian George Washington in Capitol Square

In 1816, just over 16 years after the first President's death, the Virginia Legislature proposed to erect in Richmond a "suitable" monument to George Washington, including a tomb for his remains. Although Washington's family declined to permit removal of the body from Mount Vernon, plans for the monument continued. However, other than the solicitation of public donations, little was done until 1849 when, after enabling legislation was passed, a plan was selected for a granite and bronze monument designed by Thomas Crawford of Philadelphia.

The laying of the cornerstone for the granite base took place on February 22, 1850, attended by 10,000 enthusiastic citizens and including such notables as President Zachary Taylor and Vice President Millard Fillmore. The bronze equestrian Washington was cast in Munich and arrived at the Richmond dock in November 1857. When the statue, weighing eighteen tons, was being drawn by a struggling team of horses up Main Street, a crowd of four or five thousand men and boys took hold of the ropes and easily moved the "precious burden" up to the Capitol Square. At the entrance, a portion of the iron fence and several trees had to be removed to admit the large monument.

The people of Richmond maintained great interest in the events surrounding preparations for the unveiling. All felt relief when on January 21, 1858, the monument was securely fastened to the base. The formal unveiling was held on Washington's birthday, February 22, 1858. Richmond was ecstatic over the statue; the face of Washington was modeled after the Houdon statue in the Capitol and the horse from "the finest in Queen Victoria's stable." Interestingly, the base of the monument included a tomb, still empty today.

At the time of the unveiling, only two of the lower bronze figures were in place, Patrick Henry and Thomas Jefferson. George Mason was added in 1860, and the rest of the subordinate figures were placed after the Civil War, the last in 1869, finally completing this distinguished monument which symbolizes the City of Richmond.

Douglas O. Tice, Jr., from W. Ashbury Christian,
Richmond Her Past and Present (1912)

WASHINGTON'S STATUE, RICHMOND, VA.

> ..The manufactures of Richmond are various, comprising
> woollen and cotton goods, tobacco factories, and some very large
> iron and steel works; but its chief feature in this respect is the
> manufacture of flour, the largest flour-mills in the United States
> being found here, one of which, when in full play, can turn out
> from 750 to 1,000 barrels of flour per day.
>
> MacKay
> "The People of Richmond Are a PeculiarPeople": **Another**
> **Traveler's View,**
> **Western World,** 1849

Easy-Do Dinner Rolls

Yield: about 4 dozen small rolls

"These rolls are easy to prepare and only one bowl is dirtied."

1 package active dry yeast
1/2 cup warm water (105 to 115 degrees F.)
1/2 cup shortening
1 cup *very* hot (almost boiling) water (200 to 205 degrees F.)
1 egg, beaten
1/4 cup sugar
1 teaspoon (heaping) salt
4 cups sifted flour
Additional melted shortening as needed

In a small bowl, dissolve yeast in 1/2 cup warm water (105 to 115 degrees F.). Place shortening in a large bowl; pour *very* hot water over shortening. Allow mixture to stand at room temperature until shortening melts and temperature cools to 105 to 115 degrees F. Add shortening mixture and egg to dissolved yeast, mixing well. Stir in sugar and salt. Gradually add flour, mixing well. Turn dough out onto a lightly floured board and knead lightly until smooth and elastic. Place dough in a large greased bowl, turning once to grease top. Cover and let rise in the refrigerator until doubled in bulk for 12 hours. Punch down, cover, and let rise again until doubled in bulk in a warm place (85 degrees F.) away from drafts. Roll out dough on a lightly floured board to a 1/2 to 3/4-inch thickness. Cut out dough with a lightly floured 1 1/2 to 2-inch biscuit cutter. Dip cut biscuits in melted shortening and fold each in half. Arrange rolls on ungreased baking sheets. Bake in a very hot oven (450 degrees F.) for 10 to 15 minutes or until done and golden brown.

–Anne Maury Goodloe (Mrs. John Allen)

484

Southern Aristocracy in the Last Winter of the Civil War

...We had little money, little food. It was impossible to draw upon our funds in Washington, and my mother, with a number of ladies, took a situation to go sign bank-notes in the Treasury Department. In what they called "Mr. Memminger's reception-room," she daily met gentlewomen, in whose veins ran the purest currents of cavalier and Huguenot blood. The names written upon those bank-notes might have served to illustrate the genesis of Southern aristocracy.

...This time we had been able to secure only one room in a friend's house, with the use of her drawing-room and dining room and service of her cook, the latter being a nominal one only; our breakfast, at 8 A.M., consisting of corn-bread with the drippings of fried bacon instead of butter, and coffee made of dried beans and peanuts, without milk or sugar. For luncheon we had, day in and day out, bacon, rice, and dried apples sweetened with sorghum. For our evening repast (we) were served cakes made of corn-meal and water, eaten with sorghum molasses, and more of that unspeakable coffee. I cannot remember getting up from any meal that winter without wishing there were more of it. I went once to call upon a family antecedently wealthy, and found father, mother, and children making their dinner upon soup-plates filled with that cheerless compound known as "Benjamin hard-tack," soaked in hot water, sprinkled with salt or brown sugar. It is to be said, however, there was in our community no discussion of diets, fads, or cures, and the health chase of modern society was unknown quantity. People in better physical condition than the besieged dwellers of Richmond, when their cause was beginning to feel the death-clutch at its throat, were certainly not to be found...

Mrs. Burton Harrison (Constance Cary),
Recollections, Grave and Gay, 1916

Everyday Yeast Bread

Yield: three loaves

Artemis emigrated from Greece to the United States about twenty years ago. She makes about ten loaves of bread every two weeks for family and friends.

1 package active dry yeast
2 cups warm water, divided
   (105 to 115 degrees F.)
2 eggs, divided and beaten
1/2 cup sugar
3 tablespoons cooking oil or
   shortening, melted and
   cooled
1 teaspoon salt
About 7 cups sifted flour,
   divided
1 tablespoon milk

In a 2-cup measure, soften yeast in 1 cup warm water (see note). In a large bowl, combine 1 egg, sugar, oil, and salt; stir in water. Add softened yeast, mixing well. Stir in 5 cups flour, beating thoroughly. Add remaining flour, 1/2 cup at a time, mixing well to make a stiff dough.

Turn onto a lightly floured board and knead until smooth and elastic, about 5 minutes (see note). Coat hands lightly with oil; place dough in a large bowl, greasing surface of dough with oiled hands. Cover and let rise in a warm place (85 degrees F.) away from drafts until doubled in bulk, about 1 1/2 to 2 hours. Punch down, turn onto a lightly floured board, and shape into two loaves. Place in greased 9 x 5 x 3-inch loaf pans. Let rise again, covered, in a warm place (85 degrees F.) away from drafts until doubled in bulk, about 1 hour. Or, shape into round rolls, about 2 inches in diameter; arrange on greased baking sheets, 4 inches apart, and let rise until doubled in bulk.

Combine 1 egg and milk, beating lightly with a wire whisk. Brush tops of loaves or rolls with egg mixture. Bake loaves in the lower third of a moderate oven (375 degrees F.) for 30 minutes. Reduce oven to slow (325 degrees F.) and continue baking for 25 to 30 minutes or until golden brown. Remove loaves from pans and cool on wire racks.

Note: To test the yeast, soften in warm water and allow to stand for several seconds; if yeast is properly active bubbles will form at the surface.

Note: To knead correctly, fold dough towards you and then push dough away with the heels of the hands. Repeat action until dough is smooth and elastic. To test dough for proper elasticity, cut a section of dough with a sharp knife; the cut surface will reveal holes in texture suggesting oxygen is incorporated in the dough which is necessary for yeast to act.

Variation: Omit the egg in the dough and increase the water to 2 1/2 cups. This bread will result in a heavier texture.

–Artemis Fulakis (Mrs. Kostas)

Yule in Hanover in 90's Strictly Family Day

Christmas, as we celebrated it in Hanover county during the 1890's, was strictly a family day, yet without a Christmas tree, the Yule log, wassail bowl or boar's head.

A few weeks before the big day, my older sister used to take me to a five-and-dime store on Broad St. to buy presents for the Sunday school....

Our orders would be so big that the store delivered it to Cosby's livery stable on Fifth St., between Marshall and Clay, where we housed old Psyche and the buggy on our trips.

As it was Christmas, we would have a cup of hot chocolate at Shepherd's.

After breakfast and the giving of real presents, preparations for dinner began, to be served at 6 o'clock. Holly had been placed in numerous large vases and over each picture in all the downstairs rooms.

Christmas dinner was a real treat:

First there was soup with wine in it, a rare indulgence. This was followed by turkey, surrounded by link sausages. Then came plum pudding, known to us Britishers as a sweet, followed by a dessert of fruit.

When we came here from England, we brought flags of many countries about three to five inches in color on glazed paper.

My mother was gifted in peeling an orange in such a way that the skin came off in perfect halves. With a sharp knife, she would then ingeniously cut the peel into the most life-like pigs: two pigs to an orange. Unfortunately on one occasion she said to a guest, with the idea of demonstrating her art at the table "Let's all make pigs."

The visitor, never having heard of that type of sculpture, thought she meant for everybody to eat as much as possible. Our guest was obviously very shocked.

—Vera Palmer
"Yule in Hanover in 90's Strictly Family Day,"
The Richmond News Leader, Dec. 23, 1958

Hearty Mixed-Grains Bread

Yield: two loaves

1 cup milk, scalded
3/4 cup boiling water
1 cup white or yellow corn
  meal
1/3 cup butter or shortening
1/4 cup light molasses
1/4 cup brown sugar, firmly
  packed
1 tablespoon salt
2 packages active dry yeast
1/2 cup warm water (105 to
  115 degrees F.)
2 cups whole wheat flour
1 cup rye or buckwheat flour
3/4 cup dark seedless
  raisins
2 to 2 1/2 cups sifted flour

In a large bowl combine milk and boiling water;
stir in cornmeal gradually. Add butter or shortening, molasses, brown sugar,and salt. Cool to
lukewarm. Soften yeast in warm water (105 to 115
degrees F.). Add yeast, whole wheat and rye or
buckwheat flours, and raisins to corn meal mixture. Add enough sifted flour to make a moderately stiff dough.
  Turn out onto a lightly floured board and knead
until smooth and elastic. Place in a greased bowl,
turning once to grease top.Cover and let rise in a
warm place (85 degrees F.) away from drafts until
doubled in bulk, about 1 1/2 to 2 hours. Punch
dough down, turn out onto a lightly floured board,
and shape into two loaves. Place in two greased
8 1/2 x 4 1/2 x 2 5/8-inch loaf pans. Cover and let
rise away from drafts until doubled in bulk,about
1 hour. Bake in a moderate oven (375 degrees F.)
for 40 minutes or until done. Remove from pans
and cool on wire racks.

Fran's Molasses Ginger Oatmeal Bread

Yield: two loaves

"Ginger and molasses add flavor to this nutritious high fiber oatmeal bread."

2 cups milk
1/2 cup molasses
1/4 cup butter or margarine
1 cup rolled oats
2 teaspoons salt
1 teaspoon ground ginger
2 tablespoons active dry
  yeast
1/2 cup warm water (105 to
  115 degrees F.)
2 cups sifted whole wheat
  flour

In a small heavy saucepan, combine milk, molasses, and butter;stir over low heat until mixture is
smooth. Pour mixture over oats in a large bowl;
stir in salt and ginger. Allow mixture to cool.
Sprinkle yeast over warm water in a 1-cup measure; allow to stand until mixture is bubbly, about
10 minutes. Stir into oat mixture. Add whole
wheat flour, mixing well. Stir in 3 cups flour,
mixing thoroughly. Add remaining flour, 1/2 cup
at a time,to make a stiff dough. Turn onto a lightly
floured board and knead until smooth and elastic,
about 10 minutes. Place dough in a large greased

3 1/2 to 4 cups sifted
   unbleached flour, divided
Melted butter as needed
   (optional)

bowl and turn once to coat surfaces. Cover and let rise in a warm place (85 degrees F.) until doubled in bulk, about 1 1/2 to 2 hours. Punch dough down, divide into two equal portions, and knead each piece of dough for several minutes. Let dough rest for 10 minutes. Shape dough into 2 loaves and place each in a greased 9 x 5 x 3-inch loaf pan. (see note). Bake in a moderate oven (350 degrees F.) for 35 to 40 minutes or until done. Loaves will sound hollow when tapped. Remove loaves from pans and cool on racks. Brush tops lightly with melted butter, if desired.

Note: May allow dough to rise again in pans until doubled in bulk, if desired. Texture of bread will be lighter and more delicate.

–Ann Tyler (Mrs. Hal)

Dr. B.C. Holtzclaw

Santa Claus was emphasized, he said, although children did not get as many toys as they do today. "But, we got plenty," he added.

They received games, candy and "plenty of fruit and nuts." His father was "a great believer in fresh fruit," Dr. Holtzclaw said, so the family had fruit nearly all the time.

Christmas was a time for eating turkey; at other times, the family had chicken. He recalls adults saying they were "so tired of turkey and wanted some collard greens."

Dr. Holtzclaw's favorite dessert was bag pudding, a pudding full of plums or raisins cooked in a flour sack in boiled water. "Gelatin and whipped cream and charlotte russe were a hard second."

Christine Reid
"Christmas in the 1800's"
Richmond Times-Dispatch, December 23, 1984

Sally Lunn

*Dlicious served warm with butter and jam, this bread, origi-
nally made as a bun, is also superb when sliced and toated. One
theory about the name comes from the appearance. The golden
tops and white bottoms were throught to resemble the sun and
moon — soleil and lune in French. Both the name and
presentation underwent a significant transformation by the
time the bread was brought to America.*

Grandmother Jackson's Sally Lunn

Yield: 48 small or 36 medium rolls
or one (10-inch) tube bread

*"Lisa Pannill Jackson of Petersburg, my grandmother, gave me this recipe
which has been a family favorite for generations."*

4 cups flour
2 1/2 tablespoons plus 1
 teaspoon sugar, divided
1 teaspoon salt
2 tablespoons shortening
1 package active dry yeast
1/4 cup warm water (105 to
 115 degrees F.)
3 eggs, beaten
Milk

In a large bowl, sift together flour, 2 1/2 tablespoons sugar, and salt. Cut in shortening with a
pastry blender or two table knives until mixture
resembles coarse meal. Dissolve yeast and 1
teaspoon sugar in warm water. Stir yeast mixture
into flour mixture. Add eggs and 1 cup milk,
beating well. Add more milk, as necessary, if
dough is too stiff. Place dough in a large greased
bowl, turning once to grease top. Cover and let
rise in a warm place (85 degrees F.) away from
drafts until doubled in bulk, about 3 to 4 hours.
Punch down, cover, and let rise again until doubled
in bulk. Shape dough into 48 small or 36 medium
rolls. Arrange rolls on lightly greased baking sheets.
Bake in a moderate oven (350 degrees F.) for 10
minutes for small rolls and 20 minutes for medium rolls or until done and golden brown. Or,
place dough in a greased 10-inch tube or bundt
pan. Bake in a moderate oven (350 degrees F.) for
35 to 40 minutes or until done and golden brown.

–Janet Dennis (Mrs. Overton D., Jr.)

In the case of burglary, Daniel Bridgwater and Samuel Thomas were charged with grand larceny for stealing a bag of salt. As no witnesses appeared to give testimony against them, they were acquitted.

Harry M. Ward and Harold E. Greer, Jr.
Richmond During The Revolution, 1775-83, 1977

Cottage Cheese Dill Bread

Yield: one loaf

1 package active dry yeast
1/4 cup warm water (105 to 115 degrees F.)
1 egg, at room temperature
1 cup cream-style cottage cheese, at room temperature
2 tablespoons sugar
2 tablespoons minced fresh or 2 teaspoons dried dill weed
1 tablespoon minced peeled onion
1 tablespoon butter or margarine, at room temperature
1 teaspoon salt
1/4 teaspoon baking soda
2 1/4 to 2 1/2 cups sifted flour

In a large bowl, dissolve yeast in warm water. Add egg, cottage cheese, sugar, dill weed, onion, butter, salt, and baking soda, mixing well. Add flour, 1/4 cup at a time, beating well after each addition, until a stiff dough is formed. Turn onto a lightly floured board and knead until smooth and elastic. Place in a greased bowl and turn once to coat surfaces. Cover and let rise in a warm place (85 degrees F.) away from drafts until doubled in bulk, about 1 1/2 to 2 hours. Punch dough down, transfer to a greased 1 1/2 to 2-quart casserole, cover, and let rise again.Uncover and bake in a moderate oven (350 degrees F.) for 45 to 50 minutes or until done. Cool bread in casserole for 5 minutes,then turn out onto a wire rack. Serve warm or at room temperature.

–Ann Tyler (Mrs. Hal)

491

Orange Butterscotch Date Ring

Yield: one 10-inch tube coffeecake

About 7 1/2 cups sifted
flour, divided
2 teaspoons salt
1/2 teaspoon baking powder
12 teaspoon baking soda
2 cups scalded milk
1/2 cup shortening
1 cup sugar, divided
2 packages active dry yeast
1/2 cup warm water (105 to
115 degrees F.)
1 egg, beaten
1 (8-ounce) jar orange
marmalade (see note)
1 cup butterscotch chips,
divided
1/2 cup chopped pitted
dates
1/4 cup light brown sugar,
firmly packed
1/2 teaspoon cinnamon
2 tablespoons water, at
room temperature
2 tablespoons marshmallow
creme

Sift together 4 cups flour, salt, baking powder, and baking soda. In a very large bowl, combine milk, shortening, and 1/2 cup sugar, blending well; cool to 105 to 115 degrees F.

Soften yeast in 1/2 cup warm water and add to cooled shortening mixture. Beat in egg. Add remaining flour, 1/2 cup at a time, mixing well, to make a stiff dough. Chill, covered, in refrigerator for at least 4 hours and up to 7 days. Allow dough to rest at room temperature on a lightly floured surface for 20 minutes. Roll dough out to 1/16 to 1/8-inch thickness; cut dough into about 10 equal-sized squares.

In a small bowl, combine 1/2 cup butterscotch chips, orange marmalade, dates, brown sugar, and cinnamon, mixing well. Place 1 tablespoon marmalade mixture in the center of each dough square. If any marmalade mixture remains, divide evenly among squares. Fold squares to enclose filling, sealing dough by pressing edges together. Arrange filled dough squares in a greased 10-inch tube pan. Let rise in a warm place (80 degrees F.) away from drafts for 1 hour. Bake in a moderate oven (350 degrees F.) for 25 to 30 minutes, then remove from pan and transfer to a wire rack.

In a small heavy saucepan, combine remaining 1/2 cup sugar and 2 tablespoons water; bring mixture to a boil over moderate heat. Add remaining 1/2 cup butterscotch chips, stirring until mixture is smooth. Stir in marshmallow creme. Drizzle warm topping evenly over warm coffeecake.

Note: Preferably use English-style marmalade which is less sweet in flavor than other marmalades.

Variation: 1 (8-ounce) jar apricot or peach preserves may be substituted for orange marmalade and/or 1 cup peanut butter chips may be substituted for butterscotch chips, if desired.

–Sarah Cardamone McBride (Mrs. Andrew S.)

Pecan Sticky Buns

Yield: 24 buns

Dough

1 cup milk, scalded
1/2 cup butter or margarine
1/3 cup sugar
1 1/2 teaspoons salt
1 package active dry yeast
1/4 cup warm water (105 to 115 degrees F.)
3 eggs
5 1/4 to 5 3/4 cups sifted flour

Filling

1/2 cup butter or margarine, at room temperature, divided
1 cup light brown sugar, firmly packed
2 teaspoons cinnamon
2/3 cup dark seedless raisins or currants
2/3 cup chopped pecans
1 cup dark corn syrup

In a large bowl, combine the first 4 ingredients and stir until butter melts and sugar dissolves. Cool to lukewarm. Soften yeast in warm water; add to liquids. Stir in eggs and enough flour to make a soft, moderately stiff dough.

Turn out onto a lightly floured board and knead until smooth and elastic. Place in a greased bowl, turning once to grease top. Cover and let rise in a warm place (85 degrees F.) away from drafts until doubled in bulk, about 1 1/2 to 2 hours. Turn dough out onto a lightly floured board and divide in half. Roll out each half to a 1/4-inch thickness and into an 18 x 10-inch rectangle.

Spread each rectangle with 1/4 cup butter. Combine sugar and cinnamon and sprinkle half over each rectangle. Scatter half the raisins or currants and nuts over each piece of dough. Butter two 9 x 9 x 2-inch baking pans thoroughly and drizzle 1/2 cup syrup over surface of each. Roll each portion of dough, jelly roll-style, starting at long side. Cut each roll into 12 equal slices and arrange flat in baking pans. Cover and let rise away from drafts until doubled in bulk, about 45 minutes to 1 hour. Bake in a moderate oven (350 degrees F.) for 30 minutes or until done. Immediately turn out of pans onto baking sheets.

Variation: For Maple Sticky Buns, omit dark corn syrup and substitute 1 cup maple syrup.

It was during his (Ginter) travels that his keen foresight awoke to the realization that Richmond was without a first-class hotel, so, single-handed, he undertook to build one that Richmond would justly be proud to call her own.

—*Moore*
Jefferson Hotel, 1940

Swedish Tea Ring (Vetekrans)

Yield: one coffeecake

Dough

3/4 cup warm milk (105 to 115 degrees F.)
1/2 cup plus 1 teaspoon sugar, divided
1 teaspoon salt
2 packages active dry or 2 cakes compressed yeast (see note)
1/2 cup warm water (105 to 115 degrees F.)
2 eggs, slightly beaten
1/2 cup butter or margarine, melted
5 cups sifted flour

Filling

1/2 cup butter or margarine, at room temperature
1/2 cup sugar
3 tablespoons cinnamon
1 cup chopped English walnuts, pecans, or blanched almonds

Frosting

1 cup sifted confectioners' sugar
2 tablespoons water or milk
1 teaspoon vanilla extract

To prepare dough, combine milk, 1/2 cup sugar, and salt in a large bowl, stirring until sugar is dissolved. In a small bowl, dissolve yeast in warm water; add 1 teaspoon sugar. Allow mixture to stand for 5 minutes; it should be foaming. Stir yeast mixture into milk mixture. Add eggs and butter, mixing well. Beat in flour, 1 cup at a time, until dough is dry enough to handle. Dough will be soft and sticky. Turn dough out onto a lightly floured board and knead until smooth and elastic, about 5 minutes. Place dough in a large greased bowl, turning once to grease top. Cover with a clean cloth and let rise in a warm place (85 degrees F.) away from drafts for 1 1/2 to 2 hours or until doubled in bulk. Punch down dough and work dough until smooth. Roll out into a rectangle 24x15 inches on a lightly floured board. Evenly spread dough with butter. Evenly sprinkle 1/2 cup sugar, and then cinnamon over buttered dough. Top with chopped nuts.

Beginning at the wide side of the dough rectangle, roll dough jelly roll-style. Press ends of long "roll" together to seal tightly and form a "ring." Place ring-shaped dough on a greased baking sheet. With kitchen shears, snip dough at 1-inch intervals halfway through "ring" almost to the center. Turn each dough section on its side. Cover with a clean cloth and let rise in a warm place (85 degrees F.) away from drafts for about 1 hour or until doubled in bulk. Bake in a moderate oven (375 degrees F.) for 30 to 35 minutes or until done and golden brown. Remove tearing from oven and transfer to a wire rack to cool. In a small bowl, combine all frosting ingredients, beating until smooth. Spread tea ring with frosting while "ring" is still warm.

Note: Use regular, not fast-acting yeast.

–Anne-Louise Littlefield (Mrs. Donald)

Crispy P 'N J Breakfast Sandwiches

Yield: 6 servings

12 slices white bread
1 (8-ounce) jar fruit preserves, jam, or jelly
3/4 cup crunch-style or creamy-style peanut butter
2 eggs, beaten
3/4 cup milk
1 tablespoon sugar
1/2 teaspoon salt
1/2 teaspoon vanilla extract
1/4 cup butter or margarine, melted
Sifted confectioners' sugar for garnish
Nutmeg for garnish

Evenly spread one side of 6 bread slices with fruit preserves; evenly spread peanut butter over one side of each of 6 remaining slices. Top each jam-coated slice with a peanut butter-coated slice, uncoated side up, forming a "sandwich." In a bowl, combine eggs, milk, sugar, salt, and vanilla, beating lightly. Dip each sandwich quickly into egg mixture, coating each side; drain off excess batter. In a heavy skillet or on a griddle, brown sandwiches, both sides, in butter over moderate heat, turning only once. Sprinkle each with confectioners' sugar and nutmeg. Serve hot.

–Anne Carleton (Mrs. William)

Crusty Baked Herb Bread

Yield: one loaf

1/2 cup butter or margarine, at room temperature
1 teaspoon minced parsley
3/4 teaspoon minced fresh or 1/4 teaspoon dried oregano
1/2 teaspoon garlic salt
1 (1-pound) loaf French or Italian bread
Freshly grated Parmesan cheese

In a small bowl, combine butter, parsley, oregano, and garlic salt, mixing well. With a sharp knife, cut bread into 3/4-to 1-inch thick slices. Evenly spread herb butter over one side of each slice. Reshape slices into a loaf. Arrange loaf on a sheet of aluminum foil; bring foil up around sides of loaf, leaving top uncovered. Evenly sprinkle top of bread with Parmesan cheese. Bake, uncovered, in a hot oven (400 degrees F.) for 10 to 15 minutes or until bread is heated through and lightly browned.

–Gloria Goshow (Mrs. C. L.)

> At our New Year's dinner in 1864, we had to pay $110 for the turkey to grace the feast. It was not such a big dinner in point of courses for we were getting reduced now and money was worth nothing and provisions were high. Nevertheless, it was a good substantial dinner; we had our expensive Confederate turkey, and vegetables and game, and good bread, made at home, and nice desert. We had (Confederate Vice President Alexander H.) Stephens and General Sparrow, and Mr. Garland from our home, and Bishop McGill and dear old Father Hubert to dine with us. I shall never forget that New Year's dinner. We all tried to be gay, but our hearts were inwardly sad. There was the usual visiting, customary in those days on New Year's day, but the old brilliancy and fire were fast ebbing away.
>
> Thomas J. Semmes, in XXV
> **Southern Historical Society Papers**

Hot Herbed Rye Bread

Yield: 8 to 10 servings

3 tablespoons minced parsley
2 tablespoons minced chives
1 teaspoon sage or rosemary
1 teaspoon sweet basil
1 teaspoon marjoram or tarragon
1 teaspoon dry mustard
1/4 teaspoon lemon juice
1 loaf sliced party-style rye bread
1 cup butter or margarine, melted

In a small bowl, combine herbs, mustard, and lemon juice, mixing well; cover with clear plastic wrap and refrigerate for at least 1 hour. Brush rye bread slices, both sides, with butter and sprinkle with herb mixture. Reshape slices into a loaf. Wrap in aluminum foil, securing tightly. Bake in a moderate oven (350 degrees F.) for 10 to 15 minutes or until thoroughly heated. Sprinkle cheese venely over top of loaf, if desired.

Note: Use 1 tablespoon each minced fresh sage or rosemary, and sweet basil and marjoram or tarragon in place of dried herbs, if desired.

496

Sweets

Desserts and Dessert Sauces,
Cakes—Frostings and Fillings,
Pies, Cookies, and Candies

> *Due to the shortage of sugar and molasses during the Revolutionary War, some recipes dictated, "sweeten according to your ideas of economy." This same dictum could be applied today when considering one's caloric intake.*

Flo's Peach Berry Cobbler

Yield: 6 to 8 servings

Filling

1/2 cup sugar
1/2 cup light brown sugar, firmly packed
2 tablespoons cornstarch
1 cup water
2 teaspoons lemon juice
4 cups thinly sliced peeled peaches (about 6 to 8 medium) (see note)
2 cups blueberries (see note)

Topping

1 cup sifted flour
1/2 cup sugar
1 1/2 teaspoons baking powder
1/2 teaspoon salt
1/4 cup butter or margarine, at room temperature
1/2 cup milk
2 tablespoons sugar
1/4 teaspoon nutmeg.

In a medium heavy saucepan, combine the first 3 ingredients. Gradually add water, blending well. Cook, stirring constantly, over moderate heat until mixture is thickened and bubbly hot. Stir in lemon juice. Fold in peaches and blueberries. Turn into a lightly greased 2-quart casserole; set aside. In a medium bowl, sift together 1 cup flour, 1/2 cup sugar, baking powder, and salt. With a pastry blender, cut in butter until mixture resembles coarse meal. Add milk, beating until dough is smooth. Evenly spread topping over filling in casserole. Combine 2 tablespoons sugar and nutmeg, mixing well; sprinkle mixture evenly over topping. Bake, uncovered, in a moderate oven (375 degrees F.) for 40 minutes or until topping is golden brown and filling is bubbly hot.

Note: If using frozen peaches and blueberries, omit the granulated sugar in the filling.

–Jane Hamlin (Mrs. Richard R.)

William's Blackberry Cobbler

Yield: 10 to 12 servings

"During blackberry season, my late husband, Bill Kayhoe, quite a culinary devotee, picked blackberries and prepared his blackberry cobbler, which always won praises from those lucky enough to sample it."

1 1/2 cups sugar
1 1/2 to 2 teaspoons
  cornstarch
8 to 9 cups blackberries
1/4 cup Grand Marnier
  liqueur
1 1/2 tablespoons lemon
  juice
1/4 cup sifted flour
1/4 cup butter or margarine,
  at room temperature
2 cups sifted flour
2 tablespoons sugar
4 teaspoons baking powder
1/2 teaspoon salt
1/2 teaspoon cream of tartar
1/2 cup butter or margarine,
  at room temperature
1/2 cup milk
Sugar as needed
Light cream or vanilla ice
  cream for garnish

To prepare filling, combine 1 1/2 cups sugar and cornstarch. Turn berries into a large bowl; add sugar-cornstarch mixture, tossing lightly. Turn mixture into a lightly greased 12 x 8 x 2-inch baking dish. Evenly sprinkle berry mixture with Grand Marnier and lemon juice. Evenly sift 1/4 cup flour over berries. Dot with 4 tablespoons butter. Set aside. To prepare crust, sift together 2 cups sifted flour, 2 tablespoons sugar, baking powder, salt, and cream of tartar in a medium bowl. With a pastry blender or 2 silver knives, cut in butter until mixture resembles coarse meal. With a fork, quickly stir in milk; form into a ball. Roll out dough onto a lightly floured board into a 12 x 8-inch rectangle, 1/4-inch thick. Carefully fit crust over berry mixture, sealing edges. Cut several 1/2-inch slits in center of crust. Sprinkle liberally with sugar. Bake in a hot oven (400 degrees F.) for 35 to 40 minutes or until crust is golden brown. Serve warm with cream or vanilla ice cream.

–Mary Kayhoe Irvin (Mrs. Julian)

Almond Torte

Yield: 18 servings

"Almond Torte freezes well and is great for picnics as it's not messy."

Crust
2 2/3 cups sifted flour
1 1/3 cups sugar
1 1/3 cups butter or
  margsarine, at room
  temperature
1 egg
1 teaspoon almond extract

To prepare crust, combine flour and 1 1/3 cups sugar in a bowl. With a pastry blender, cut in butter until mixture resembles coarse meal. Add egg and almond extract, mixing well. Form misture into two equal balls; cover one with clear plastic wrap and set aside. Roll out remaining portion into a 9-inch diameter circle between sheets of waxed paper. Remove top sheet of waxed paper and flip into a greased 9-inch spring-form pan, waxed paper side up. Peel off remaining waxed paper.

Filling
1 egg, slightly beaten
1 cup finely chopped
  blanched almonds
1/2 cup sugar
1 teaspoon grated lemon
  peel
Sweetened-flavored
  whipped cream or vanilla
  ice cream for garnish
  (optional)

To prepare filling, combine egg, almonds, 1/2 cup sugar, and lemon peel in a bowl, mixing well. Evenly spread over dough in pan to within 1/2 inch of sides of pan. Roll out remaining dough as previously directed. Place over filling as directed with a lower crust. Remove remaining waxed paper and press top crust lightly into filling. Bake in a slow over (325 degrees F.) for 45 to 50 minutes until crust is a golden brown. Remove from oven and cool in pan for 15 minutes. Remove springform and allow to thoroughly cool. To serve, cut into 18 thin wedges. Garnish with sweetened-flavored whipped cream or vanilla ice cream, if desired.

–Rita Earl (Mrs. Marshall, Jr.)

A Cream Sauce

2 cupfuls of powdered sugar., 2 eggs., 1 cupful of cream., 2 teaspoonfuls of Sauer's Vanilla Extract., Beat the yolks and whites of the eggs separately. Add the powdered sugar to the yolks; then add the stiffly beaten whites; afterwards the well-whipped cream, and, finally, Sauer's flavoring.

C. F. Sauer Company
Sauer Spices, *circa 1920's*

Apple Dumplings

Pare and core five tart apples. Sift into a bowl two cups of flour, two level teaspoons of Rumford Baking powder, one-half teaspoon of salt, rub in lightly four tablespoons of shortening, and add enough milk to hold together. Roll out one-fourth inch thick and cut into squares. Lay an apple on each piece and put in the center a teaspoon of sugar and a quarter of a teaspoon of butter; roll up and press edges lightly together. Place in an agate pan; put a little sugar and a bit of butter on each, cover and bake for thirty minutes. Uncover and bake twenty minutes. Serve hot with hard sauce or cream.

Virginia Cookery Book, *1921*

Helen's Baked Cranberry Apple Dessert

Yield: 12 servings

Filling

3 ripe tart large or 4 small to
   medium red-skinned
   apples, unpeeled, cored,
   seeded, and coarsely
   chopped (see note)
2 cups cranberries
3/4 cup sugar
2 tablespoons water

Topping

1 cup *minus* 2 teaspoons
   quick cooking or regular
   rolled oats
1/2 cup chopped pecans
1/3 cup flour
1/2 cup butter or margarine,
   melted
Sweetened-flavored
   whipped cream for
   garnish

Arrange chopped apples in the bottom of a greased 13x9x2-inch pan. Top with cranberries. Evenly sprinkle sugar and water over fruit; set aside. In a medium bowl, combine rolled oats, brown sugar, pecans, and flour. Add butter, mixing well. Evenly sprinkle or spread over fruit in pan. Bake in a moderate over (350 degrees F.) for 1 hour. Cool. Spoon into dessert dishes and garnish each serving with sweetened-flavored whipped cream, if desired.

Note: Use McIntosh, Winesap, Granny Smith, or other tart variety of apples.

–Helen Hill (Mrs. R.E.)

Greek Festival Showcase

Thousands of Richmonders eagerly look forward to the first weekend in June each year when the Greek Festival Showcase is held, sponsored by Sts. Constantine and Helen Greek Orthodox Cathedral, featuring food and wine, folk dances, arts and crafts, and musical and cultural heritage with a Greek flair. Rain or shine, the four-day festival goes forth. Begun in 1977 to acquaint Richmonders with religious and cultural aspects of the Greek heritage, the celebration has grown in scope and attendance. Over two hundred volunteers begin to assemble food for the festival several weeks, even months, in advance. More than sixty-four thousand pastries...Baklava, Finikin, Galatoboureko, Kourambedes ... and savories...Souvlaki, Tiropita, and Spanakopita...are some of the tantalizing food delicacies offered. Although not originally a fund raising project, the monetary success of the festival now provides proceeds to be donated to various charities.

Galatoboureko

Yield: 20 (2-inch) square servings

"The Greeks traditionally made desserts out of ingredients from the farm...flour from the wheat, honey from the bees...pure, no chemicals."

4 cups milk
1 1/2 cups sugar, divided
2/3 cup farina cereal
1 1/4 cups butter or margarine, divided
8 eggs yolks, well-beaten
1 teaspoon vanilla extract
12 to 16 ounces filo dough
1 cup water
1 medium lemon, slit cut into flesh
1 (3-inch) cinnamon stick

In a heavy saucepan, bring milk to simmering over moderate heat; add 1/2 cup sugar, blending well. Add farina and 1/4 cup butter; cook, stirring constantly, until thickened. Remove from heat and allow mixture to cool to 120 to 140 degrees F. Add egg yolks, mixing well. (The *temperature* of the farina mixture is *very important*...if too high, the egg yolks will be cooked...if too low, the ingredients will not combine properly.) Stir in the vanilla.

In a small heavy saucepan, melt the remaining 1 cup butter over low heat. Arrange one-half of the filo sheets, one at a time, liberally brushing each with melted butter as they are arranged, in a buttered 14x11x2-inch baking pan, stacking buttered filo sheets, one after another, until all are used. Pour the farina mixture over the stacked filo sheets in the pan. Arrange remaining filo sheets, brushed with melted butter as they are arranged, over farina as previously directed. Fold edges of top filo sheets into pan. Liberally brush the top of the dessert with melted butter. Bake, uncovered, in a moderate oven (350 degrees F.) for about 40 to 45 minutes or until pastry is golden brown. Remove pastry from oven and cool thoroughly.

In a small heavy sauce pan, combine 1 cup sugar and water. Squeeze lemon slightly into mixture; insert lemon into liquid. Add cinnamon stick pieces. Bring to a rolling boil. Syrup is ready when a few drops of hot mixture dropped on a plate are not runny but retain shape or stand firm. Discard lemon and cinnamon. Pour over cooled baked dessert, spooning hot syrup over dessert until all syrup is absorbed. Allow dessert to stand for 30 minutes. With a sharp knife, cut into 2x2-inch squares; dessert can be cut into squares prior to baking, if desired.

–Toula Halages (Mrs. John)
Sts. Constantine & Helen Greek Orthodox
Cathedral

...Thus it is not a wonder that we find a monument of Jefferson guarding the entrance to the hotel that Major Ginter had erected, for Jefferson was the one human he admired most, yet peculiarly enough, the one human he resembled most. Today Valentine's statue of Thomas Jefferson still stands in the lobby of the hotel, the likeness of a statesman, he being too modest and retiring to want a likeness of himself. On the occasion of the opening of the hotel, when he (Major Ginter) heard that some friends were planning to donate a loving cup to him for his outstanding work, he promptly had the idea dismissed, declaring that he would not accept it if it were offered to him. At another time, when he learned that a movement was on foot to erect a likeness of him as a monument in one of the clubs, he immediately had the movement stopped, which was typical of the "Modest Major Ginter."

–Moore
Jefferson Hotel, 1940

503

Raspberry Fuzz

Yield: 6 to 8 servings

"This was my invention to utilize the trillions of raspberries my father grows. One could use strawberries, blueberries, or blackberries."

Prepare either Quick Oatmeal or Sweet Almond Crust.

Quick Oatmeal Crust

1 1/2 quick cooking rolled oats
1/2 cup light brown sugar, firmly packed
1/2 cup finely chopped blanched almonds
1/4 cup butter or margarine, melted

Sweet Almond Crust

1 cup sifted flour
1/2 cup ground blanched almonds
1/2 cup sugar
1/2 cup butter, melted

Berry Filling

4 cups fresh red or black raspberries, cleaned and hulled
1 cup sugar
1 envelope (tablespoon) unflavored gelatin
1 tablespoon lemon juice
1 cup heavy cream
1 tablespoon confectioners' sugar
1 teaspoon vanilla extract
Additional sweetened-flavored whipped cream (optional), whole berries and fresh mint sprigs for garnish.

In a medium bowl, combine all ingredients, mixing well. Evenly press mixture over the bottom and up the sides of a lightly greased 9-inch pie plate. Bake in a moderate over (375 degrees F.) for 10 minutes or until lightly browned. Cool

In a bowl, combine berries and sugar, mixing lightly; allow to stand for 1 hour at room temperature. Drain berries, reserving juice and dividing in half. In a small bowl, dissolve gelatin into one-half of the reserved juice. In a small sauce pan, bring remaining juice to boiling over moderate heat; pour over gelatin mixture, blending well. In a large bowl, combine gelatin mixture, lemon juice, and berries, mixing well. Refrigerate until mixture is thickened and almost firm. In a chilled bowl, beat cream until soft peaks are formed; add confectioners' sugar and vanilla, beating well. Fold whipped cream into berry-gelatin mixture. Evenly spoon into baked crust and refrigerate 2 to 4 hours or until filling is firm. Garnish with additional sweetened-flavored whipped cream, if desired, whole berries, and fresh mint sprigs.

Note: Frozen berries may be substituted for fresh. If sweetened berries are used, omit granulated sugar. Thaw and drain berries reserving liquid. Dissolve 1 (3-ounce) package raspberry, blackberry, or strawberry-flavored gelatin in 1/2 cup boiling water. Add reserved, drained berry liquid to gelatin mixture in place of cold water. Omit lemon juice and continue to follow recipe as previously directed.

–Carol Nance
Assistant Attorney General
State of Virginia

Old Richmond Advertisement, circa turn of nineteenth/twentieth centuries

Ribbon Blanc-Mange

1 quart of milk., 1 cupful of
  sugar
2 tablespoonfuls of arrowroot
3 eggs (whites only)
1/2 teaspoonful of salt
1 square unsweetened
  chocolate
1/2 cupful chopped nut
  meats
1 teaspoonful of Sauer's
  Vanilla Extract
1 teaspoonful of Sauer's
  Strawberry Extract
Sauer's pink vegetable
  coloring

Dissolve the arrowroot in a portion of the milk, then add it to the remainder of the milk while boiling, with the sugar and salt. Stir until the mixture begins to thicken and add the well-beaten whites of the eggs; cook for about a minute longer, then remove from the fire, and divide into three equal parts. Flavor one with Sauer's Vanilla Extract; flavor the second part with Sauer's Strawberry Extract, and add a little Sauer's pink vegetable coloring; melt one square of chocolate and stir it into the third portion, adding the nutmeats. Arrange in a mould in alternate layers, keeping the three colors distinct. Serve with whipped cream, well sweetened.

C. F. Sauer Company
Sauer Spices, circa 1920's

Apple Pudding

3 cupfuls of chopped
  apples
2 cupfuls of sugar
7 eggs
1 cupful of butter
2 teaspoonfuls of Sauer's
  Vanilla Extract

Line a deep dish with a rich and flaky pastry crust. Fill with a mixture composed of the apples, sugar, butter, Sauer's flavoring extract, and the well-beaten yolks of the eggs. Bake until done, then cover the top with a thick meringue composed of the whites of the eggs sweetened with powdered sugar; brown, and serve hot.

C. F. Sauer Company
Sauer Spices, circa 1920's

Sponge Pudding

One quart flour, one pound raisins, six eggs, a little salt, milk to make a thick batter; flour raisins well; boil two hours and serve with hard butter sauce. SAUCE.--Half-pound pulverized sugar, quarter-pound butter, wine, and nutmeg to taste.

Mrs. J. G. C.
The Kitchen Queen, 1893

Empandidas De Piña (Pineapple Flipovers)

Yield: About 24 pastries, 24 servings

"Just before the beginning of the school season in September, the Food Services Department invites the 'head' resident staff to a special dinner at the Heilman Dining Center. Each year a different theme is used. For some occasions, lobsters have been flown from Maine and steaks served hot off charcoal grills. Every meal is planned as a special event. In September, 1988, the dining center was turned into a small cafe in Mexico for a traditional Mexican meal. The Empandidos De Pina was one of the desserts served."

Pastry

2 (3-ounce) packages cream cheese, at room temperature
1 cup margarine, at room temperature (see note)
2 cups flour

In a medium bowl, cut cream cheese and margarine into flour with a pastry blender or two silver knives until mixture resembles coarse meal. Form dough into 2 balls, cover with clear plastic wrap, and chill in refrigerator for 30 minutes. While dough is chilling, prepare filling.

Filling

1 cup canned yams or sweet potatoes, drained and mashed
1/2 cup canned crushed pineapple, drained
1/2 cup sugar
1/2 teaspoon salt
1/2 cup shredded coconut
1 egg yolk
1 teaspoon water
Sifted confectioners' sugar as needed

In a medium bowl, combine mashed yams or sweet potatoes, crushed pineapple, sugar, and salt, mixing well. Fold in coconut, set mixture aside. Roll each dough ball out onto a lightly floured surface to a 1/8-inch thickness. With a cookie cutter, cut dough into 6-inch diameter circles (see note). Place 2 rounded teaspoonfuls of filling on each dough circle. Fold one-half of each pastry circle over filling; press edges of pastry together, sealing with the tines of a fork. In a small cup, lightly beat egg yolk and water together with a wire whisk. Arrange pastries on ungreased baking sheets; brush each lightly with egg yolk wash. Bake in a moderate oven (350 degrees F.) for 15 minutes or until pastries are golden brown. Sprinkle each with confectioners' sugar.

Note: Do not use butter in this pastry crust as crust will be too short and hard to handle.

Note: Smaller pastries may be prepared by cutting out dough into 3-inch diameter circles. Allow two small pastries per serving.

–Marna Seal
University of Richmond
Food Services Department

Meringue Topped Apple Pudding

Yield: 6 servings

This early 20th century recipe from the C. F Sauer Company has been updated for late 20th century cooks.

1/2 recipe for Extra-Flaky Pie Crust (Double-Crust) (see index)
7 eggs, separated
3 cups chopped peeled tart cooking apples (see note)
2 cups sugar
1 cup butter or margarine, at room temperature
2 teaspoons vanilla extract
3/4 cup sifted confectioners' sugar

Roll out pastry to fit a deep 1 1/2-quart casserole; line a casserole with pastry crust. In a large bowl, beat egg yolks. Add sugar, butter, and 1 teaspoon vanilla, mixing well. Prepare apples and fold into egg-yolk mixture; spoon mixture into pastry- lined casserole. Bake, covered, in a moderate oven (375 degrees F.) for 35 minutes; uncover and continue baking for 10 minutes or until apples are tender and sauce thickened and bubbly hot. In a bowl, beat egg whites with cream of tartar until foamy; gradually add confectioners' sugar and 1 teaspoon vanilla, beating until stiff glossy, but not dry, peaks are formed. Spread meringue evenly over top of apple pudding, sealing meringue to edges of crust. Bake in a moderate oven (375 degrees F.) for 15 to 20 minutes or until meringue is lightly browned. Cool for 5 to 10 minutes, then serve warm.

Note: Use McIntosh, Winesap, Granny Smith, or other tart variety of apples.

–C. F. Sauer Company
Sauer Spices

Wine Jelly

Take 4 calves feet, & wash them well without taking off the hoofs, (or instead of that 1 oz. isinglass, or 1 oz. of deers horns) These feet must be well boiled the day before they are wanted. Let them cool in order to take off the greese (sic). After taking off the greese put the jelly in the casserolle. Put there 4 oz. sugar, cloves, nutmeg. Boil all together. Take 6 whites of eggs, the juice of 6 lemons, a pint of milk, a pint of maderia. Stir all together. Pour it into the jelly and boil it. Taste it to see if sweet enough if not, add powdered sugar. Strain it 2 or 3 times thru flannel till clear. Put it in glasses or moulds.

Thomas Jefferson's manuscript, Library of Congress
First Ladies Cook Book, *1965*
Courtesy of Wilton Museum House

Brown's Island Dam

Bread Pudding Custard

Yield: 6 servings

"This is an old-fashioned bread pudding custard...a perfect   quick dessert. Friends declare it the best they've ever eaten."

·2 eggs, beaten
3 cups hot (not boiling) milk
1 1/2 cups fine breadcrumbs
2/3 cup sugar
1 tablespoon cooking oil
1/2 teaspoon vanilla extract
1/4 teaspoon salt
1/2 cup chopped English
  walnuts or pecans or dark
  seedless raisins
Sweetened-flavored
  whipped cream for
  garnish

In a medium bowl, combine the first 7 ingredients, beating well. Stir in nuts or raisins. Pour into a greased 1 1/2-quart casserole. Bake in a moderate oven (350 degrees F.) for 35 to 40 minutes or until a silver knife inserted in center comes out clean. Cool thoroughly. Garnish each serving with sweetened-flavored whipped cream.

–Margaret C. Kittell

Baked Colonial Fruit Pudding

Yield: 6 servings

"This is one hundred fifty years old...a never-fail recipe used in Richmond with fruit available according to seasons. We would call it a deep dish fruit pie today."

2 cups favorite fresh fruit
1 1/2 cups sugar, divided
1 cup sifted flour
1 tablespoon baking powder
1 tablespoon butter or margarine, at room temperature
1/2 cup milk
1 cup boiling water

Peel fruit and remove seeds as necessary; chop or slice fruit as desired. In a bowl, combine fruit and 1 cup sugar, tossing lightly to mix; set aside while preparing batter. Sift together flour and baking powder. In a bowl, combine 1/2 cup sugar and butter, beating until light and fluffy. Stir in dry ingredients and milk, mixing well. Spread batter over the bottom of a greased 12 x 8 x 2-inch baking pan or 2-quart casserole. Spoon fruit over batter; pour boiling water over fruit. Baked, uncovered, until crust rises to top and is a golden brown, about 30 minutes. Cool for at least 10 to 15 minutes before serving warm or at room temperature.

Note: Try thinly sliced peeled tart apples or peaches or whole strawberries, blackberries, blueberries, raspberries, or pitted tart cherries.

–Elizabeth C. Britton (Mrs. H. Douglas)

Tapioca Pudding

1 pint of milk., 2 eggs., 2 tablespoonfuls of tapioca., 1/2 cupful of sugar., 1/2 cupful of hot water., 1/2 saltspoonful of salt., 2 teaspoonfuls of Sauer's Vanilla, or Lemon Extract. Soak the tapioca in the water until all is absorbed; add the milk, and cook in a double boiler until the tapioca is soft. Then add the well beaten yolks of the eggs, the sugar, and the salt; cook about five minutes; add Sauer's flavoring extract, and fold in the well-whipped whites of the eggs. Serve cold.

C. F. Sauer Company
Sauer Spices, *circa 1920's*

Stanley Pudding

Half-pound flour, six ounces butter, four ounces sugar, three eggs, six ounces fruit, half-gill grape wine, quarter of a nutmeg; boil as plum pudding.

Mrs. George M. West
The Kitchen Queen, *1893*

Crunchy French Custard

Yield: 4 servings

2 cups light cream
4 egg yolks
2 1/2 tablespoons sugar
Pinch of salt
1 teaspoon vanilla extract
2 tablespoons light brown
   sugar, firmly packed

In a small heavy saucepan, scald cream over moderate heat (a light film will form over cream and small bubbles will form in cream around edge of pan but cream will not boil). In a medium bowl, beat egg yolks until thick and light in color. Gradually beat in sugar and salt. Very gradually stir scalded cream into egg mixture with a wire whisk, being careful not to curdle egg mixture. Stir in vanilla. Pour mixture into a 1-quart casserole or soufflé dish; place casserole in a large pan filled with about 1 to 1 1/2 inches of hot water. Bake in a moderate oven (350 degrees F.) for 1 hour or until a silver knife inserted in the center of the custard comes out clean. Evenly sift brown sugar over top of baked custard; broil, 4 to 5 inches from heat source, until brown sugar melts and becomes slightly hard and crunchy. Remove from oven, cool, and then refrigerate for at least 1 to 2 hours

–Elizabeth Warren (Mrs. E. P.)

Virginia Spinsters' Whipt Cream

Mode.—Take a quart of thick cream and the whites of eight eggs beaten with one-half pint of sack; mix it together, and sweeten it to your taste with double refined sugar. You may perfume it, if you please, with some ambergris tied in a piece of muslin, and steeped a little in the cream; whip it up with a whisk, with a bit of lemon peel tied in the middle of the whisk. Take the froth with a spoon, and lay it in your glasses.

Beverages and Sauces of Colonial Virginia, *1906*

Peach Noodle Pudding

Yield: 12 servings

(8-ounce) package wide noodles
3 eggs
1 cup creamy-style cottage cheese
1 cup sour cream
1/2 cup sugar
1/2 cup butter or margarine, at room temperature
1 teaspoon salt
1/2 teaspoon cinnamon
1/8 teaspoon ground cloves
1 (20-ounce) can sliced peaches, drained and cut into bite-sized pieces

Cook noodles according to package directions; drain well and set aside. In a large bowl, combine eggs, cottage cheese, sour cream, sugar, butter, salt, cinnamon, and cloves. Fold in noodles and peaches. Spoon into a greased 13 x 9 x 2-inch baking pan. Bake in a moderate oven (350 degrees F.) for 1 hour. Cool on a wire rack. Cut into squares. Serve warm or at room temperature or chilled.

Note: Pudding freezes well covered in aluminum foil.

–Joy Gerson (Mrs. Martin)
Cheese Wedge Committee
St. Christopher's School

Old Richmond Advertisement, date unknown

Mrs. Black's Old-Time Rice Pudding

Yield: 6 servings

"A family favorite, this recipe was handed down to me from my mother, Mrs. Leo C. Black. The origin is obscure today."

1 cup long-grain rice
1 cup dark seedless raisins
Water as needed
2 eggs, lightly beaten (see note)
1 cup milk, scalded
1/2 cup light brown sugar, firmly packed
1 tablespoon vanilla extract
1 teaspoon nutmeg or to taste
Pinch of salt (optional)

Cook rice according to package directions; drain well. In a small bowl, soak raisins in water to cover for about 15 minutes or until raisins have plumped; drain off remaining liquid. In a medium bowl, combine eggs, milk, brown sugar, vanilla, nutmeg, and salt, if desired. Stir in cooked rice and plumped raisins. Pour mixture into a 1 1/2-quart casserole. Bake, uncovered, in a hot oven (400 degrees F.) for 45 to 55 minutes or until a silver knife inserted in center of pudding comes out clean. Serve warm or at room temperature.

Note: Ms. McDaniel suggests vegetarians may substitute soy drink for cow's milk.

–Claudette Black McDaniel
Vice Mayor 1988 to 1990,
Richmond City Council

English Plum Pudding

1 Pound Flour, 1 Pound Currants, 1 Pound Franklin Sugar, 1 Pound Raisins, 5 Ounces Candied Lemon Peel, 1 Pound Suet, 1 Teaspoonful Boyd's Baking Powder, 1 Nutmeg, 1 Pinch Ground Cinnamon, Milk or Water., Chop lemon peel very fine and suet very fine, mix and add baking powder, nutmeg and cinnamon. Sift the flour, baking powder and salt together. When thoroughly mixed add a sufficient quantity of cold milk or water to make a batter barely thick enough to spoon into the mold, filling about two-thirds full, leaving room to rise. Cover closely and boil for five hours.

Old Virginia Cooking, *circa 1909*

Paul's Place Baked Rice Pudding

Yield: 12 servings

Paul's Place, a folksy old-fashioned fountain-style grill restaurant reminiscent of the '30's and 40's, is located in the Westhampton Pharmacy adjacent to the shopping avenues of Libby and Grove and the fashionable St. Catherine's School. Specializing in homemade food and serving breakfast and lunch, Eddie, Jackie and son, Paul, opened the neighborhood eatery in 1984, naming it for Paul. People come from as far away as Charlottesville and Williamsburg to sample the delicious homemade biscuits, hash browns, cakes, salads, and soups. One of the best sellers is the Old-Fashioned Club sandwich which is made in the same manner as the one prepared by Eddie's father forty years ago. Homemade daily specials include spaghetti, lasagne, and oven-fried chicken. Paul's Place Baked Rice Pudding is the hands-down favorite dessert request. For those who don't want to cook breakfast on Saturday mornings, Paul's Place is the place to be seen ... best breakfast in town!

1 cup uncooked rice
6 eggs
4 cups milk
2 cups sugar
1 teaspoon lemon extract
1 teaspoon vanilla extract
1 teaspoon cinnamon
1 teaspoon nutmeg
1 cup dark seedless raisins
Light cream or half-and-half
   (optional)

Cook rice according to package directions, drain well and set aside. In a large bowl, beat eggs at medium speed of an electric mixer for 2 minutes. Add milk, lemon and vanilla extracts, cinnamon, and nutmeg, blending well. Stir in cooked rice and raisins. Pour into a greased 3-quart casserole. Bake in a moderate oven (350 degrees F.) for 40 minutes or until a silver knife inserted in center comes out clean. Cool and then refrigerate until ready to serve. Each portion may be served plain or with light cream or half-and-half, if desired.

Note: The recipe may be halved and baked in a greased 1 1/2-quart casserole for 30 to 35 minutes or until a silver knife inserted in the center comes out clean.

–Paul's Place
Edward, Jackie and Paul Shibley, proprietors

Miss Pidgeon's Caramel Pudding

2 cups sugar, 4 eggs, 1 quart milk, 1 teaspoon vanilla, Brown one cup of sugar in skillet. Have milk boiling hot, and when sugar turns to syrup pour into milk. (Have milk in large vessel, as it boils up very high when sugar is poured in.). Put in eggs, well beaten, saving out one or two whites. Pour into pudding dish, put in vanilla, and remainder of sugar. Bake in oven until a knife blade stuck in middle comes out clean, placing the pudding dish in pan of hot water. Make meringue of whites of eggs, and cover top of pudding. Serve cold with or without cream.

Virginia Cookery Book, *1921*

Heavenly Chocolate Pudding

Yield: 8 to 10 servings

1 pound sweet baking chocolate
1 ounce (square) un- sweetened chocolate
1 cup strong coffee
4 eggs, separated
Sweetened-flavored whipped cream for garnish

In a heavy saucepan, melt chocolates in coffee over low heat, stirring until smooth. Cool. Beat egg yolks until light and thick; stir into cooled chocolate mixture. Beat egg whites until stiff peaks are formed; fold into chocolate mixture. Spoon into a large glass serving bowl and chill for at least 3 hours. Garnish each serving with sweetened- flavored whipped cream.

–Esther D. Shelley (Mrs. Blackwell)

Banana Pudding

Fill a pudding dish with alternate layers of sponge cake and sliced bananas. Pour a boiled custard, flavored with Sauer's Vanilla Extract, over them, and cover all with a meringue composed of the whites of the eggs used in making the custard. Serve very cold.

C. F. Sauer Company
Sauer Spices - *Circa 1920's*

Macaroon Puddin'

Yield: 8 to 10 servings

My husband, a Virginia gentleman, enjoyed macaroon pudding as a boy, especially at holiday time. After many attempts which did not pass inspection, I have finally come up with what he remembers from his childhood. However, I omit the whipped cream and cherry garnish; no frills for him! For my son, who doesn't like almond macaroons, I substitute thin vanilla or chocolate wafers and add grated semi-sweet chocolate as a garnish.

About 1 pound small almond macaroons (see note)
Soft custard (see index)
Sweetened-flavored whipped cream
Chopped red and green maraschino cherries, drained well (optional)

Reserve 15 to 20 macaroons; store in an airtight container until ready to use. Allow remaining macaroons to stand, uncovered, for 24 hours. Between sheets of waxed paper, with a rolling pin, roll dried macaroons into coarse crumbs. Line a 1 1/2-quart glass serving bowl with reserved whole macaroons. Spoon one-half of the custard into macaroon-lined bowl. Sprinkle one half of the crumbs over custard in bowl. Spoon remaining one half of the crumbs over custard in bowl. Spoon remaining custard over crumb layer and top with remaining crumbs. Chill in the refrigerator until ready to serve. Garnish with sweetened-flavored whipped cream and chopped red and green maraschino cherries, if desired.

Note: 1 pound vanilla wafers or 2 (8-ounce) packages chocolate wafers may be substituted for almond macaroons.
Note: If the bowl is deep, arrange two stacked rows, one on top of the first row of macaroons, around inside of bowl to form a standing ridge.

"As soon as the housekeeping was done, my mama began preparing for a week of feasting. Four four days the smells were wonderful ... goose, ham, pies, cakes, cabbage and all kinds of vegetables, one after another."

To stave off her brood from the Christmas foods, Mrs. Lucas said her mother would make ash cakes, a bread roll that was baked on the hearth around the ashes. It was a 19th-century treat equivalent to licking the brownie mix bowl."

Christine Reid
"Christmas in the 1800's"
Richmond Times-Dispatch, December 23, 1984

Zabaglione Cream

Yield: 6 servings

Zabaglione, of Italian origin, is a light dessert to serve for festive occasions or warm weather dining.

1/2 cup sugar, divided
1 teaspoon unflavored gelatin
1/2 cup dry sherry (see note)
6 eggs, separated, plus 3 egg whites
1 tablespoon Amaretto liqueur
1 teaspoon vanilla extract
1 cup heavy cream
1/8 teaspoon cream of tartar
Dash salt
Fresh strawberries, or raspberries, or blueberries, or blackberries, or sliced fresh peeled peaches, or nectarines, or chocolate curls

Combine 1/3 cup sugar and gelatin in the top of a double boiler; stir in sherry. Beat egg yolks until very light, fluffy, and lemon-colored. Add to double boiler and cook over gently boiling water until thickened, stirring constantly. Remove from heat and cool. Stir in brandy and vanilla. Whip cream and fold into egg mixture. Combine 9 egg whites, cream of tartar, and salt, beating until whites are foamy. Add remaining sugar and continue beating until whites are stiff, but not dry. Fold into custard. Spoon into tall dessert dishes. Chill thoroughly (at least 1 hour). Garnish with strawberries, or raspberries, or blueberries, or blackberries, or sliced fresh peeled peaches, or nectarines, or chocolate curls.

Note: Marsala wine or brandy may be substituted for Amaretto liqueur, if desired.

–Sarah Cardamone McBride (Mrs. Andrew S.)

Apricot Brandy Ice Cream

Yield: 4 servings

1 to 1 1/2 pounds peaches or apricots, peeled and thinly sliced (see note)
2 tablespoons sugar
1 pint peach ice cream, at room temperature
1/2 cup apricot brandy

In a blender container, combine peaches or apricots and sugar; cover and blend for 30 to 60 seconds until mixture is a coarse, thick puree. In a bowl, combine fruit puree and ice cream, mixing gently. Quickly stir apricot brandy into fruit mixture. Cover and refreeze in bowl or spoon into parfait or sherbet glasses, cover, and freeze until ice cream is firm.

Note: 1 (10-ounce) package thawed frozen peaches or apricots may be substituted for fresh peaches or apricots. Omit sugar.

–Marilyn Smart (Mrs. John)

517

Butter Pecan Tortoni

Yield: 18 individual servings

Two years after the end of World War II, in 1947, the Reynolds Metals Company, based in Richmond, introduced the revolutionizing kitchen helper, aluminum foil. Since its introduction, company home economists have been developing and testing new recipes and uses for new products, including oven cooking bags, freezer paper, foilware, paper and foi bakecups, waxed paper, and reclosable plastic bags. Recently, colored plastic wrap in rose, blue, green, and yellow, was introduced in the new product line. The Reynolds Wrap Kitchens, opened at Company headquarters in 1976, continue to develop new recipes and educational material helpful to consumers.

2 cups loosely-packed coconut macaroon cookie crumbs (about 10 2-inch cookies)
1/4 cup apricot preserves
1/2 teaspoon almond extract
1/2 gallon butter pecan ice cream, slightly softened
18 Maraschino cherries, well drained
1/2 cup thinly sliced almonds

Line muffin pans (2 3/4-inches in diameter) with aluminum foil baking cups. In a medium bowl, combine cookie crumbs, preserves, and almond extract, stirring lightly with a fork until crumbs are coated. Press one rounded tablespoon of crumb mixture into the bottom of each foil cup. Spoon one rounded scoop of ice cream into each bake cup. Top each with a Maraschino cherry and sliced almonds. Freeze until serving time. For freezer storage, overwrap each frozen dessert with heavy duty aluminum foil.

–The Reynolds Wrap Kitchens
The Reynolds Wrap Company

Gingerbread Apple Pudding

Leftover ginger bread., 1-2 cups raisins., 1-4 cup mixed candied peels, if desired., 2 1-2 cups (No. 2 can) apple sauce., 2 tablespoons butter., 1-4 cup sugar., 1-2 cup water., Slice gingerbread thin and arrange in layer in bottom of buttered pudding dish. Dot with butter and sprinkle with raisins and fruit. Cover with apple sauce, add more raisins, etc., and top with second layer of sliced gingerbread. Dot with butter, sprinkle with sugar and add water or left-over fruit syrup. Bake 45 minutes in moderate oven, 375 degrees F. Serve hot with hardsauce or cool with cream.

Irene Bivens
"Yule Dinners Were Events In Old South,"
Richmond Times-Dispatch, *Dec. 25, 1935*

Coconut Sherbet

Yield: 6 to 8 servings

"Serve this easy-to-prepare sherbet as the dessert for your next dinner party and accompany with Lacy Oatmeal Crisps."

1 cup sugar, divided
1 envelope (tablespoon)
  unflavored gelatin
1 cup milk
2 (8-ounce) cans coconut
  juice
1 cup flaked coconut
2 teaspoons vanilla extract
2 egg whites
Mint sprigs for garnish
Lacy Oatmeal Crisps
  (optional) (see index)

In a small heavy saucepan, combine 3/4 cup sugar and gelatin. Gradually add milk, blending well; stir over low heat until sugar and gelatin dissolves. Stir in coconut juice, coconut, and vanilla. Turn mixture into a shallow pan and freeze in freezer until mixture is solid. In a deep small bowl, beat egg whites until foamy. Gradually add remaining 1/2 cup sugar, beating until stiff, but not dry, peaks are formed. Turn sherbet into a large bowl; beat until mixture is light and fluffy. Fold in beaten egg whites. Spoon into a 2-quart bowl, cover, and freeze in freezer until firm. Serve in chilled sherbet glasses, garnish with mint sprigs, and accompany with Lacy Oatmeal Crisps, if desired.

–Carole Ackell (Mrs. Edmund F.)

Claret Sherbet

Half-gallon water, two-and-a-half-pounds sugar, whites of five eggs, one quart of claret, six to eight lemons; rub the rinds of two lemons in sugar and freeze.
The Kitchen Queen, *1893*

....In Virginia, it was celebrated very much as in old England, with the bringing in of a Yule log, decorations of holly and mistletoe, feasting, dancing, and drinking. There was no thought of work on Christmas Day. Each house was hospitably open for guests, some of whom stayed a week or more. Great bowls of eggnogg were prepared and served to all who came. The slaves or servants usually appeared at the great house for their share as soon as Christmas Day dawned. Cannon or smaller arms were fired on the lawn as greetings to friends on other plantations. Communion services were held in the churches. The boar's head, roast beef, roast goose, plum pudding, and mince pie were among the traditional Christmas viands. Gifts were exchanged, but the Christmas tree was unknown....

"Christmas in Colonial Days,"
Richmond News Leader, October 11, 1939

Nectarine Custard Ice Cream

Yield: 1 1/2 quarts

2 eggs, slightly beaten
1 1/2 cups milk
1 cup sugar
1/8 teaspoon salt
1 1/2 cups light cream
1 1/2 teaspoons vanilla
extract
1/4 teaspoon almond
extract
4 large ripe nectarines
Crushed ice
Coarse salt

In a heavy saucepan, combine eggs, milk, sugar, and salt. Cook, stirring constantly, over low heat until mixture lightly coats a metal spoon. Remove from heat; stir in cream, vanilla, and almond extract. Cool. Blanch nectarines in boiling water for 1 minute. Peel, slice, and mash with a fork or press through a coarse sieve to make at least 1 1/2 cups coarse puree. Stir into custard mixture. Pour into a 2-quart freezer container; cover. Combine crushed ice and salt (8 parts ice to 1 part salt), mixing well; pack around ice cream freezer container in an ice cream freezer bucket. Proceed according to ice cream freezer manufacturer's directions until turning the paddle is difficult. If ice cream is not to be eaten immediately, repack for ripening following manufacturer's instructions. If to be eaten soon, cover top of freezer container and bucket with a heavy cloth until ready to eat.

–Glad Applegate (Mrs. William)

Ambrosia

"In Greek mythology, ambrosia was the food of the gods on Olympus, their drink being nectar. According to Hesiod and the poets who followed him, the immortals inhabiting the Olympian mansions fed on the pure and bloodless food of ambrosia, and drank only of nectar, a distillation of refined dew. The word signifies 'immortal' and the drink was a balsamic one designed to preserve immortality. It could bestow immortality to humans who were permitted to partake of it. Mortals who drank of the nectar also gained in beauty and strength, becoming in some measure akin of the gods. "The word has also been applied to various sweet fruit salads which are supposed to have something of the glory of the fabled celestial drink of the gods."

Andre L. Simon & Robin Howe 1978

"Mac Mac's" Holiday Ambrosia

Yield: 12 to 16 servings

"My grandmother, Fannie Belle Rice McNeeley, of Shelby, North Carolina, received her unusual nickname, Mac Mac, from me, her first grandchild, when I was very young and could not pronounce her name correctly. Like many pet names, it stayed with her for he rest of her life."

8 chilled oranges, peeled, seeded, and thinly sliced crosswise
1/2 cup fresh coconut, shell removed, grated, or 1 cup flaked
1/2 cup sifted confectioners' sugar
Orange liqueur as needed (optional)

Arrange a single layer of orange slices in a large clear glass (preferably cut glass) bowl. Thickly sprinkle coconut over orange layer. Sprinkle lightly with confectioners' sugar. Repeat layers until bowl is filled and all ingredients used. Drizzle orange liqueur over fruit, if desired. Serve shortly after layering.

–Louis Mahoney
Food Editor
The Richmond News Leader

Dooley Mansion at Maymont

Maymont, the magnificent late nineteenth century estate of Richmond philanthropist, James A. Dooley, was named for Mr. Dooley's wife, the former Sallie May. Overlooking the James River in Richmond's fashionable West End, Maymont became a showplace, "the likes of which Richmond had never seen before."

Dooley designated in his will that the property be turned over to the city after Sallie's death. Accordingly, just six months after her passing, Maymont was opened in Spring 1926 to an awed public.

Historical accounts suggest the Dooleys, though extremely wealthy, entertained on a small scale. One exception was a grandiose party to which five hundred guests attended. The dining table for this occasion was "decorated with a candy cabbage as large as a great pumpkin, with candy rosebuds reposing on the leaves, each of which was to be plucked from the foundation."

Major Dooley is said to have done some of the grocery shopping, frequenting A. Eichel & Company, a wholesale/retail specialty grocer. He was known to have a taste for Italian food, acquired form his extensive European travels. No doubt his cook, Frances Walker, attended a cooking school, "which was often the case in well-to-do homes," to be able to cater to Dooley's continental tastes.

Mrs. Walker indicated to her great-great niece that "everything was elaborate and very proper." Invoices from R.L. Christian and W.C. Gray's indicate traditional Southern fare was purchased. Another anonymous account portrays Major Dooley "with great dignity" requesting a servant to "give Mrs. Dooley some of those jigger cakes."

"Although Mrs. Dooley was not above stepping into her kitchen to make oatmeal cookies for picnics in Hollywood Cemetery, the cook, of course, prepared daintier creations for tea." Small custard filled cakes and edible nasturtium sandwiches are recalled in remembrances of two Dooley guests.

Rice Dainty

1 pint of cream., 1 cupful of cold boiled rice., 2 tablespoonfuls of gelatine., 2 teaspoonfuls of Sauer's Vanilla Extract., Dissolve the gelatine, and when cool mix it with the well-whipped cream. Add the sugar and Sauer's flavoring extract, and stir into the freshly boiled rice. Mix both cream and rice, and serve, very cold, in individual glasses garnished with chopped nut meats and bits of candied fruits.

C. F. Sauer Company
Sauer Spices, circa 1920's

Grapefruit Jelly

Put three tablespoonfuls of gelatin into a saucepan; add one and one-half cupfuls of cold water, one-half cupful of sugar, and three cupfuls of grapefruit juice and pulp; stir over the fire until almost boiling, then strain and one tablespoonful of lemon juice. Divide into small wet glasses and place in the refrigerator until firm. Decorate with marshmallow topping or whipped and sweetened cream and cocoanut.

Old Recipe, Date Unknown

523

Southern Christmas Angel Hash

Yield: 18 to 24 servings

"After trying dozens of recipes in as many musty-smelling cookbooks over the past decade, I'd given up on Angel Hash, my grandmother's holiday recipe, as a reality, and filed it with other memories that I could treasure but never relive. I could still smell it, though. Thanks to the magic provided by one Fairy Godmother, also known as Aunt Margaret, I have finally obtained Mac Mac's recipe. My Fairy Godmother does not quite fit the frilly aproned June Cleaver image. Some kin consider her a mite eccentric just because she's spending her retirement doing things like square dancing in Christmas parades or flying in from the Coast got up as a chartreuse mini-skirted, pink spiked-haired punk rocker. I consider her wonderful, but you can see why it never occurred to me to ask her about Mac Mac's Angel Hash. She's had the recipe ever since Mac Mac spent her only Christmas … her last … away from North Carolina. That year Mac Mac celebrated with Aunt Margaret in California. Aside from the incomparable fragrance, one of the best parts of eating Christmas dessert at Mac Mac's was that I got to layer the Coconut Cake, Ambrosia, and Hash all on one plate. At least I did until I grew up and moved from the breakfast room grandchildren's table to the dining room adults' table."

1 pound marshmallows (see note)
2 cups sugar
About 1/2 cup white vinegar
3 eggs, well-beaten
1 (15 1/2-ounce) can crushed pineapple in its own juice, well-drained
2 cups heavy cream, whipped
8 ounces sliced almonds, toasted and divided (see note)

With kitchen shears, cut marshmallows into quarters; set aside. Place sugar in the top of a double boiler. Pour just enough vinegar into pan to moisten sugar. Add eggs, mixing well. Cook, stirring over simmering water, until mixture is a thick smooth custard, about 20 to 30 minutes. Remove from heat and allow to cool to room temperature. In a bowl, combine cooled custard, pineapple, marshmallow pieces, whipped cream, and half of the almonds. Spoon mixture into a large glass compote. Chill in the refrigerator until serving time. Just before serving, top with remaining almonds.

Note: Miniature marshmallows may be substituted for quartered regular marshmallows, if desired; however, the texture of the dessert is better with regular-size marshmallows.

Note: To toast sliced almonds, evenly spread almonds on a baking sheet; bake in a slow oven (300 degrees F.) for about 10 minutes or until nuts are lightly browned.

–Louis Mahoney,
Food Editor,
The Richmond News Leader

Enticing Chocolate Torte

Yield: 24 (2-inch) square servings

"This is a winner...especially with men."

Crust
1 cup sifted flour
1 cup finely chopped pecans
3/4 cup butter or margarine,
  at room temperature

Filling
2 (8-ounce) packages cream
  cheese, at room temperature
1 cup sifted confectioners'
  sugar
1 (16-ounce) container plus
  1 cup frozen non-dairy
  whipped topping, thawed
  and divided (see note)
1 (3-ounce) package instant
  chocolate pudding and
  pie filling
1 (3-ounce) package instant
  vanilla pudding and pie
  filling
3 cups milk
3/4 cup chopped pecans for
  garnish
1 (4-ounce) bar semi-sweet
  or sweet milk chocolate,
  grated, for garnish

In a bowl, combine flour and 1 cup pecans. With a pastry blender, cut in butter until mixture resembles coarse meal. Evenly press mixture over the bottom of a 12 x 8 x 2-inch baking dish. Bake in a moderate oven (350 degrees F.) for 10 to 15 minutes or until golden brown. Cool thoroughly. In a bowl, beat cream cheese until smooth. Gradually add confectioners' sugar, beating until light and fluffy. Fold in 1 cup whipped topping. Evenly spread over cooled crust. Chill while preparing pudding mix. In a bowl, combine pudding mixes and milk. Prepare according to package directions. Spoon over cream cheese layer. Chill for 15 minutes. Spread the 16-ounce container whipped topping over pudding layer. Evenly sprinkle remaining pecans and then grated chocolate over torte. Chill for several hours. To serve, cut into 2-inch squares.

Note: An equal amount of sweetened-flavored whipped cream may be substituted for frozen non-dairy whipped topping.

–Becky White Williams

To Whip Cream Delicately

Beat the white of one egg thoroughly; then gradually add the cream, whipping it continually; when quite stiff commence to beat in the sugar, continuing the beating until all has been blended. Finally, add the necessary quantity of Sauer's flavoring extract.

C. F. Sauer Company
Sauer Spices, *circa 1920's*

Gâteau âu Magnifique

Yield: 8 to 10 servings

1 cup butter or margarine, at room temperature
1/2 cup sugar
3 eggs, separated
1 square (ounce) un-sweetened chocolate, grated or 3 tablespoons sifted cocoa (see note)
1 cup toasted chopped blanched almonds
1 teaspoon vanilla extract
1 cup milk
1/4 cup cognac or dark rum
2 (3-ounce) packages lady fingers, each separated in half lengthwise (about 24) or 5 ounces vanilla wafers (about 40)
Additional toasted chopped blanched almonds

In a medium bowl, cream butter until smooth. Gradually add sugar, beating until light and fluffy. Add egg yolks, one at a time, beating well after each addition. Add chocolate or cocoa, almonds, and vanilla, mixing well. In another bowl, beat egg whites until stiff, but not dry peaks are formed; fold into butter mixture. In a shallow bowl, combine milk and cognac or rum, blending well. Dip lady finger halves or vanilla wafers into milk-cognac mixture. Arrange a single layer of dipped cookies in an 8 x 8 x 2-inch baking dish. Spread one-half of butter mixture over cookies in dish. Arrange a second layer of cookies over butter mixture in pan. Spread remaining almond mixture over second layer of cookies. Evenly sprinkle additional toasted chopped almonds over dessert. Refrigerate for several hours until dessert is thoroughly chilled.

Note: Because the texture and flavor of grated unsweetened chocolate and cocoa is quite different, the use of one versus the other will result in a slightly different flavored and textured gateau.

–Debbie Destounis

Lemon Spongette Dessert

Yield: 10 to 12 servings

"This recipe dates back to 1932."

8 graham crackers, finely crushed, divided
1 cup sugar
3/4 cup water
1/4 cup lemon juice
2 teaspoons grated lemon peel

Evenly sprinkle one half of the graham cracker crumbs over the bottom of an 11 x7x2-inch baking pan; set aside. In a small heavy saucepan, combine sugar, water, lemon juice, and peel; bring to a boil over moderate heat and continue boiling for 2 minutes. In a bowl, combine lemon gelatin and boiling liquid, blending well. Cool. Refrigerate until partially thickened. In a bowl, chill

1 (3-ounce) package lemon-flavored gelatin
1 (13-ounce) can evaporated milk

evaporated milk until ice crystals begin to form around edge of bowl. With chilled beaters, beat evaporated milk until soft peaks are formed. Fold beaten evaporated milk into gelatin mixture. Evenly spoon half of the lemon filling over prepared crumb-lined pan. Sprinkle half of remaining crumbs over top. Evenly spoon remaining filling over first layer and sprinkle with remaining crumbs. Refrigerate for several hours. To serve, cut into squares.

–Luma Merritt (Mrs. Randolph)

Food was served to this room (dining room) from the two-story brick kitchen in the side yard, a whole story lower than the main floor of the house. There was no roof over the walkway that connected the kitchen to the main house, so the governor's meals were carried across an open dirt yard—perhaps on a brick walk—into the basement and up the service stairs to the dining room.

Keeping the food hot was a chore and a science. Meals were served in courses; all serving dishes had tops. Servants used a fireplace in the basement to heat the food enroute from kitchen to table. Dinner plates were warmed in a tin warmer before the dining-room fireplace, and, while no cooking was done there, water for coffee and tea was boiled over coals raked out on the hearth. Finishing touches might be put on any number of dishes after the food reached the dining room, the butler performing his skills at the sideboard. After dinner the usable leftovers were kept in wire "safes" in the basement, rather than being returned to the kitchen outside

...Long after a dinner or ball was over, the governor's wife stood by the door counting with the butler the silver knives and forks and the plates and other china as they were brought up from the dining room, where they had been washed. A full accounting was required at the administration's close.

William Seal
Virginia's Executive Mansion:
A History of the Governor's House, 1988

Divine Chocolate Mousse

Yield: 8 servings

"This mousse serves 12 to 16 persons. It is the simplest of desserts. The secret is to make it in a blender and the whole thing takes 15 to 20 minutes to prepare."

8 ounces semi-sweet chocolate pieces
3/4 cup butter or margarine, at room temperature
1 1/2 cups sugar
3 eggs, separated
1 tablespoon Amaretto liqueur or brandy
1/2 teaspoon almond extract
1/4 cup toasted slivered blanched almonds
2 cups heavy cream, whipped
Additional sweetened-flavored whipped cream for garnish
Shaved bittersweet chocolate or curls for garnish

In the top of a double boiler, melt chocolate pieces over hot water. Cool slightly. In a bowl, cream butter thoroughly. Gradually add sugar, beating until light and fluffy. Beat in egg yolks, Amaretto or brandy, and almond extract. Add cooled chocolate and almonds, mixing well. Beat egg whites until stiff, glossy, but not dry peaks are formed; fold into chocolate mixture. Fold in whipping cream. Spoon into a 2-quart glass serving bowl or souffle dish. Chill in the refrigerator or cover and freeze in freezer until firm. If mousse is frozen, allow to stand at room temperature for 30 minutes before serving. Garnish with additional sweetened-flavored whipped cream and bittersweet chocolate curls.

–Jane Pendleton Wootton (Mrs. J. Percy)

The Richmond German on a Monday evening in February, 1889, was led by "Mr. Stern," the same Colonel Jo Lane Stern who continued to lead the "Monday" until almost up to the time of his death in 1932. Among the chaperones were Mrs. C. U. Williams, Mrs. Meredith Montague, Mrs. Thomas Rutherfoord and Mrs. Virginius Newton.

The refreshments were "coffee, sandwiches and bouillon" served during the evening, but two private suppers were given after the German, one by Mrs. William Talbott and the other by Mrs. Bronson.

Henrietta Crump
"Richmond Society in February, 1889, Was Busy Party-Going,"
Richmond News Leader, February 14, 1939

Flaming Cherries Jubilee

Yield: 4 servings

3/4 cup butter or margarine, at room temperature
1 cup sugar
6 tablespoons Kirschwasser liqueur
1/2 cup orange juice
1 (20-ounce) can pitted dark sweet cherries, drained
1 to 2 pints vanilla ice cream, divided

In a sauté pan or medium heavy skillet, melt butter over moderate heat. Blend in sugar and stir over heat until sugar is carmelized and turns a light golden color. Add Kirschwasser and ignite carefully. When flame is extinguished, add orange juice, blending well. Add cherries, stirring gently. Spoon ice cream into 4 sherbet dishes and ladle hot cherry sauce over each, dividing evenly.

–Chef Kevin Wade
Gallego's Restaurant
The Omni Hotel

Easy-Do Fresh Strawberry Mousse

Yield: 4 servings

1 pint (about 1 1/2 cups mashed) *ripe* strawberries, hulled, cleaned, and dried
1 (3-ounce) package strawberry-flavored gelatin
1 cup boiling water
1/2 tablespoon lemon juice
1/4 cup sugar
Pinch salt
1/4 cup strawberry liqueur or brandy (optional)
1 cup heavy cream
Additional sweetened-flavored whipped cream for garnish
Additional whole strawberries for garnish
Fresh mint sprigs for garnish (optional)

Slice strawberries and then coarsely mash with a potato masher; set aside. In a small bowl, dissolve gelatin in boiling water. In a large bowl, combine strawberries, lemon juice, sugar, and salt. Add dissolved gelatin and strawberry liqueur, if desired, mixing well. Chill in the refrigerator until mixture is the consistency of unbeaten egg whites. In a chilled small heavy bowl, beat cream with chilled beaters until stiff peaks are formed. Fold whipped cream into chilled gelatin mixture. Spoon mousse into individual sherbet glasses or dishes or a 1-quart mold; chill in the refrigerator for several hours until mousse is set. Garnish each serving with additional sweetened-flavored whipped cream, if desired, a whole strawberry, and a fresh mint sprig, if desired.

Variation: 1 pint fresh raspberries may be substituted. Pureé and strain berries. Raspberry liquer may be used.

529

Orange and Lemon Crêpes

Yield: about 10 crêpés

3/4 cup sifted flour
1 tablespoon confectioners' sugar
Pinch salt
2 eggs plus 1 egg yolk
About 1 1/2 cups milk
2 teaspoons grated orange peel
2 teaspoons grated lemon peel
1 1/2 teaspoons vanilla extract
Clarified butter (see index)

In a medium bowl, sift together the first 3 ingredients. In a small bowl, beat eggs and egg yolk together lightly. Stir eggs into dry ingredients. Gradually blend in one-half of the milk with a wire whisk. Gradually add remaining milk, whisking until smooth (see note). Strain through a fine sieve, if necessary, to remove any lumps. Stir in orange and lemon peels and vanilla. Cover and allow to stand at room temperature for 2 hours. Batter may be refrigerated for up to 24 hours before using, if desired. Heat an 8-inch crêpe pan or heavy skillet over moderate heat; brush liberally with clarified butter. Remove pan from heat. Stir batter; ladle 3 tablespoons into a corner of the crêpé pan, tilting so batter *just* coats the bottom of the pan. Return excess batter to bowl. Cook over moderate heat until bottom of crepe is lightly browned, loosening edges with a knife or narrow rubber spatula, about 1 to 2 minutes. Turn crêpe and continue cooking until second side is lightly browned, about 1 minute. Slide crepe out of pan onto a serving plate. Repeat process until all the batter is used. Crêpes may be prepared in advance, layered, and separated with clear plastic wrap, and stored in the refrigerator for up to 3 days or separated with clear plastic wrap, covered tightly, and stored in the freezer for up to 2 weeks.

Note: Batter should be runny but will coat a silver spoon.

Variation: To prepare Chocolate Crêpes, omit the vanilla extract and the orange and lemon peels and add 2 to 3 tablespoons of chocolate syrup.

–The Country Club of Virginia

Eliza B Ashni 1990

Country Club of Virginia

The Country Club of Virginia was founded in 1908 "to promote open air and indoor games and sports," as well as "to keep hounds, maintain kennels, keep horses, operate a private race track...." Although the hounds and horses are now gone, the Club boasts fifty-four holes of championship golf. Twenty-two tennis courts, three swimming pools, and two clubhouses are also a part of the complex which has become a social hub of Richmond. Land that now comprises the Club grounds is the former site of a quaint town, Rio Vista, which disappeared around World War I. What was considered "way out in the country" at the turn of the century is now the center of the ever-expanding West End of Richmond. Club land adjoining the University of Richmond formerly was Westhampton Park, a project of the Richmond Street Railway Company which declared bankruptcy in 1903.

Raspberry Crêpe Soufflé

Yield: 10 servings

1 pound raspberries or 1 1/2
  (10-ounce) packages
  frozen raspberries,
  thawed (see note)
1 cup water
1 cup plus 1 tablespoon
  water, divided
About 2 tablespoons
  raspberry liqueur
About 1 1/2 tablespoons
  lemon juice (see note)
1 cup milk or half-and-half
1/4 cup minced vanilla bean
3 egg yolks
1/4 cup sifted flour
6 egg whites, at room
  temperature
1/4 teaspoon cream of tartar
10 Orange and Lemon
  Crepes (see index)
Sifted confectioners' sugar

In a medium heavy non-aluminum saucepan, combine raspberries, water, and 3/4 cup sugar, bring mixture to a boil over moderate heat. Reduce temperature and simmer for 7 minutes. Pour mixture into a blender or food processor container; cover, and blend until mixture is puréed. Strain purée through a fine sieve to remove seeds. Remove 1 cup of sauce; cover and refrigerate until ready to use, for up to two days. Return remaining sauce to saucepan; cook over low heat until mixture is the consistency of jam or reduced to about 3/4 cup. Stir in raspberry liqueur and lemon juice. Cool thoroughly, then cover and refrigerate until ready to use, for up to two days. (Jam must be rewarmed before using.) In a medium heavy saucepan, combine 2 tablespoons sugar, milk, and vanilla bean; bring to a boil over moderate heat. In a medium bowl, combine eggs and 2 tablespoons sugar, whisking lightly with a wire whisk, blend in flour and then milk mixture. Return mixture to saucepan and cook, whisking constantly, over moderate heat until thickened, about 2 minutes. Remove from heat and whisk in raspberry jam. Place buttered plastic wrap directly on surface of raspberry cream. Refrigerate for up to 24 hours until ready to use. Whisk raspberry cream over low heat before using. In a medium bowl, beat egg whites until foamy. Gradually add cream of tartar, beating until soft peaks are formed. Beat in remaining 1 tablespoon sugar. Fold one-fourth of the beaten egg whites into warm raspberry cream. Fold raspberry cream into remaining egg whites. Arrange prepared crêpes on a buttered baking sheet. Spoon 1/2 cup soufflé mixture over one-half of each crêpé. Fold remaining half of each crepe over souffle mixture. Bake, uncovered, in a moderate oven (375 degrees F.) until souffles are puffy and crepes lightly browned, about 10 minutes. Sprinkle each with confectioners' sugar and garnish with reserved raspberry sauce.

–The Country Club of Virginia

The Feature of Entertaining
Visitors Attracted to the Races--The Balls and
Some of Those Who Attended Them--The
Changes That Came With the War.

Perhaps no city in the United States has been more famous for its brilliant social life than Richmond. Situated on seven hills, above the turbulent, amber rapids of the James river, the city is picturesque and beautiful, and was in "ye olden time," as it is now, the centre of fashion of the State of Virginia a State known widely for its magnificence, courtliness, and hospitality.

About half a century before the war Virginia was in its prime, and Richmond was at the height of its social brilliance. In the winter many of the opulent planters would leave their stately homes in the counties of Virginia, and bring their families to Richmond for a month or more, thus swelling the ranks of society with beauty and wealth....

Race-week was always a carnival, and one of its most brilliant features was the race-ball. This ball was opened by one of the managers and the lady he most desired to honor, with a stately minuet de la cour. The gentlemen wore "shorts and silks," pumps, and powdered hair, while the ladies, in the glory of multi-colored brocades and satins, looked like a gorgeous tulip-bed swaying in the wind. After the profound stateliness of the minuet the more lively reel was danced, and, after that, the contra dances. Probably the ball would end with a jig, or hornpipe....

Ruth Nelson Robins
The Richmond News Leader, Date unknown

Holiday Plum Pudding

Yield: 10 to 12 servings

Plum pudding remains as much a part of the Christmas tradition as the glittering tree, fragrant evergreen wreath, and lighted candles in the windows. Its origins are remote; however, it is thought to have begun in merry old England as made from mutton stock, currants, raisins, and sherry. Later, bread was added to the soup as a thickening agent which then became plum porridge. Eventually, meat, suet, and spices were included. Our English ancestors introduced Plum Pudding to the new world when the colonists settled here. An old English superstition suggests "whoever eats plum pudding on each of the twelve days between Christmas and Epiphany, January 6th, making a wish on the first mouthful of pudding each day, will be blessed by luck and fulfillment during the next twelve months. But, bad luck attends the greedy who nibble plum puddings before the Christmas feast."

1 cup sifted flour, divided
1/4 teaspoon salt
1/4 teaspoon baking soda
1/4 teaspoon allspice
1/4 teaspoon cinnamon
1/4 teaspoon nutmeg
1/4 teaspoon ground cloves
1 1/4 cups dark or golden
   seedless raisins
1 1/4 cups dried currants
1/2 cup chopped English
   walnuts
2 eggs
1/2 cup finely chopped suet
1/4 cup light molasses
1/4 cup buttermilk
1/4 cup brandy or un-
   sweetened pineapple
   juice
1 cup breadcrumbs
4 to 5 tablespoons warmed
   brandy for igniting,
   divided
Hard Sauce (see index)

Sift together 1/2 cup flour, salt, baking soda, and spices. In a medium bowl, combine remaining 1/2 cup flour, raisins, currants, and nuts. In a large bowl, beat eggs well. Add suet, molasses, buttermilk, and 1/4 cup brandy. Stir in dry ingredients, floured fruit and nuts, and breadcrumbs, mixing well. Spoon into a greased 1 1/2-quart mold. Cover mold lightly with a sheet of aluminum foil and arrange on a rack in a deep heavy kettle or Dutch oven. Add boiling water to about 1 inch below the cover of mold. Cover kettle and steam for 1 1/2 to 2 hours or until metal tester inserted in the center of the pudding comes out clean. Remove from steam kettle. Cool *just* until easy enough to handle, then unmold onto serving plate. Garnish as desired and served flamed and accompanied with Hard Sauce. To flame pudding, pour 3 to 4 tablespoons warmed brandy over pudding. Ignite an additional tablespoon of brandy and add to pudding. When the flame is extinguished, cut into slices and serve. Pass Hard Sauce.

–Updated old Richmond recipe
date and origin unknown

Sippet Pudding

Cut a loaf of bread as thin as possible, put a layer of it in the bottom of a deep dish, strew on some slices of marrow or butter, with a handful of currants or stoned raisins; do this till the dish is full; let the currants of raisins be at the top; beat four eggs, mix with them a quart of milk that has been boiled a little and become cold, a quarter of a pound of sugar, and a grated nutmeg--pour it in, and bake it in a moderate oven--eat it with wine sauce.

Mrs. Mary Randolph
The Virginia House-Wife, or Methodical Cook, *1830*

Hot Brandy or Cognac Sauce

Yield: about 2 1/3 cups

1/2 cup butter or margarine, at room temperature
2 cups sifted confectioners' sugar
2 egg yolks
1/2 cup heavy cream
3 tablespoons brandy or cognac

In a medium bowl, cream butter until light and fluffy. Add sugar gradually, beating constantly. Add egg yolks and beat until thick and lemon-colored. Add cream slowly, beating constantly. Turn into the top of a double boiler. Place over gently simmering water for 5 to 6 minutes, stirring constantly. Stir in brandy or cognac and serve warm over desired desserts.

Hot Fudge Sauce

Yield: 1 2/3 cups

1/2 cup half-and-half
1 (6-ounce) package semi-sweet chocolate pieces
1 cup miniature marshmallows
1/4 teaspoon salt
1 teaspoon vanilla extract

In a heavy saucepan, stir half-and-half over low heat until bubbles form around edge of pan. Stir in chocolate pieces, marshmallows, and salt. Heat, stirring constantly, until chocolate and marshmallows are melted. Remove from heat and stir in vanilla. Serve over ice cream, cake, or brownies, or use for dipping.

Microwave Directions:
In a 2-quart glass bowl, heat half-and-half at 50% power for 5 minutes, stirring halfway through cooking time. Stir in chocolate pieces, marshmallows, and salt. Cover with clear plastic wrap, allowing for venting, and microwave at 50% power for 5 minutes or until melted, stirring every 2 minutes.

535

Hard Sauce

Yield: 2 1/2 cups

1/2 cup butter or margarine, at room temperature
1 1/2 cups sifted confectioners' sugar
1 tablespoon light cream or half-and-half
1 teaspoon vanilla extract
1/2 teaspoon lemon extract
1 to 1 1/2 teaspoons grated orange or lemon peel

In a small bowl cream butter until light and fluffy. Gradually add sugar gradually and continue creaming. Add cream, vanilla extract, lemon extract, and peel, blending thoroughly. Cover and chill thoroughly in refrigerator. Serve with heated plum pudding or other desserts.

Variation: Brandy or Rum Hard Sauce: Omit last 4 ingredients and add 2 to 3 tablespoons brandy or rum to mixture.

...After the cakes came custards--the sweet potato custards, cocoanut custards--delightful individual pies. I wonder if there is a pie line that runs along with the Mason and Dixon? So many Virginia pies seem to be called by another name. However, nothing could be as sweet, or as indigestibly interesting, as our citron puddings. I happened on the recipe in an old cook book dated 1853. "Yolks of eight eggs, three-quarters of a pound of sugar, one-quarter of a pound of butter, two tablespoonfuls of cracker, soaked in a teacup of new milk and a glass of wine and a little nutmeg; all well-beaten and poured over sliced citron in a rich paste." There you are; and may you be "unpainedly thankful."

Catherine Copeland
"OLD VIRGINIA CHRISTMAS"
"Yule Feast at Old Home Was Biggest Event of Year; Gay 90's Christmas Recalled,"
Richmond Times-Dispatch, Date unknown

Brandon Brandy Sauce

Mode.--To a teaspoonful of baked flour add three ounces of fresh butter, and work them well together with a wooden spoon, stir in one and one-half gills of boiling water, a tablespoonful of moist sugar, boil gently for ten minutes; add a wine glass full of French brandy.

Beverages and Sauces of Colonial Virginia, *1906*

Hot Lemon Sauce

Yield: about 1 1/2 cups

1/2 cup sugar
2 tablespoons cornstarch
1/4 teaspoon salt
1 cup water
3 tablespoons lemon juice
1 1/2 tablespoons butter or
  margarine
1 1/2 teaspoons grated
  lemon peel

In a small heavy saucepan, combine sugar, corn-starch, and salt. Stir in water. Cook over low heat until mixture thickens and becomes clear, stirring constantly. Stir in lemon juice, butter, and lemon peel. Serve hot or warm over bread pudding or gingerbread.

Variation: Reduce lemon juice to 1 tablespoon, omit peel, and stir in 3 table-spoons rum with butter.

Hot Buttered Rum Sauce

Yield: about 2 1/2 cups

1 cup sugar
1 tablespoon cornstarch
1/4 teaspoon salt
3/4 cup boiling water
1/2 cup lemon juice
1 1/2 teaspoons grated
  lemon peel
1/3 cup butter or margarine
1/8 to 1/4 teaspoon grated
  nutmeg
1/2 cup light rum

Combine the first 3 ingredients in a medium heavy saucepan. Stir in boiling water. Cook, stirring constantly, until mixture starts to thicken. Add remaining ingredients and cook, stirring constantly, until thickened and bubbly hot. Serve hot over bread pudding or hot mince pie or plum pudding or other desired desserts.

537

Brandied Nectarine Sauce

Yield: about 1 quart

7 to 8 firm ripe medium nectarines, peeled, seeded and thinly sliced
1 2/3 cups water
1 cup light brown sugar, firmly packed
1 cup sugar
1/3 cup brandy
Pinch of salt
1 tablespoon cornstarch

Prepare nectarines; set aside. In a medium heavy saucepan, combine water, brown sugar, sugar, brandy and salt, blending well. Bring to a boil over moderate heat. Add sliced nectarines and continue to cook until mixture returns to a boil and nectarines are tender but firm. Remove sauce from heat; allow to cool. Stir cornstarch into cooled sauce, blending well to remove lumps. Stir over moderate heat until sauce is bubbly hot and slightly thickened. Store, covered, in a clean quart glass jar in the refrigerator. Serve hot or at room temperature over ice cream, pound cake, cheesecake or other desired desserts.

Variation: Firm ripe peaches may be substituted for nectarines.

Raspberry Sauce with Framboise

Yield: 8 to 10 servings

1 (10-ounce) package frozen red raspberries, thawed, or
3 (1/2 pints) fresh red raspberries (see note)
3/4 cup sugar
3 teaspoons lemon juice
3 tablespoons Framboise or other raspberry liqueur or to taste
Fresh mint leaves for garnish (optional)

Combine the first 3 ingredients in a blender container; cover and blend until sugar is dissolved and puree is thick. Add Framboise, blending well; cover and chill until ready to use. Serve over Raspberry Mousse or other desserts, as desired. Garnish with fresh mint leaves, if desired.

Note: If using frozen raspberries, sugar may be decreased slightly.

Banana Fiesta Cake

Yield: one two-layer 9-inch cake

"This banana-flavored cake originated in a recipe insert tucked into a box of cake flour marketed forty years ago, in 1949."

2 cups sifted cake flour
1 1/3 cups sugar
1 teaspoon baking powder
1 teaspoon baking soda
3/4 teaspoon salt
1/2 cup sour milk or butter-
    milk, divided (see note)
1 teaspoon vanilla extract
1/2 cup shortening or butter,
    at room temperature
1 cup mashed peeled ripe
    bananas (about 2 to 3
    medium)
2 eggs
1/2 cup chopped English
    walnuts or pecans
1 cup heavy cream, whipped
1 tablespoon minced
    Maraschino cherries,
    drained
3 medium bananas, peeled
    and cut crosswise into
    1/4-inch slices
Whole or Maraschino cherry
    halves for garnish

In a medium bowl, sift together the first 5 ingre-dients. In a 1-cup measure, combine sour milk and vanilla. In a large bowl,cream shortening until smooth. Sift in dry ingredients. Add 1/4 cup sour milk mixture and bananas, mixing until dry ingredients are moistened; then beat at low speed of an electric mixer for 2 minutes. Add eggs, nuts, and remaining sour milk mixture; beat at low speed for an additional 1 minute. Spoon batter into two greased 9-inch round layer pans, dividing evenly. Bake in a moderate oven (375 degrees F.) for 25 minutes or until a cake tester inserted in the center of each layer comes out clean. Cool in pans on wire rack for 5 min-utes, then turn out onto wire racks,right side up, to finish cooling completely. Fold minced cher-ries into one-third of the whipped cream; evenly spread cherry whipped cream over one layer. Arrange one half of banana slices over cherry whipped cream mixture. Top with second cake layer. Spread whipped cream over second layer and around sides of stacked layers. Garnish top of cake with remaining banana slices and whole or half Maraschino cherries just before serving.

Note: To sour milk, add 1 1/2 teaspoons of lemon juice or white vinegar to milk; let stand for 10 minutes.

Variation: Omit whipped cream, banana slices, and Maraschino cherries. Prepare Citrus Butter Cream Icing (see index); spread icing between layers and over top and sides of cake. Garnish with well drained mandarin orange sections or candied orange peel or slices.

–Dorothy Parker (Mrs. Walter)

Blackberries were first called brambleberries in colonial America, growing among the brambles, and were considered a nuisance. Beginning in the 1830's, they became quite popular and were used in making desserts such as cake, pie, and a molded dessert called a flummery.

Blackberry Jam Cake
with Buttermilk Caramel Icing

Yield: two 9-inch round layers or one 9-inch tube cake

Blackberry Jam Cake was especially popular during the nineteenth century. This recipe was a favorite of Frances Fox's mother, Mrs. W. W. Beasley, of Alabama.

3 cups sifted cake flour
1 tablespoon cocoa
1 teaspoon cinnamon
1 teaspoon baking soda
1/2 teaspoon nutmeg
1/2 teaspoon ground cloves
1/2 teaspoon allspice
1 cup butter or margarine,
  at room temperature
2 cups sugar
4 eggs
1 cup seedless blackberry
  jam
1 teaspoon vanilla extract
1 cup buttermilk
Buttermilk Caramel Icing
  (see index)

Sift together the first 7 ingredients. In a large bowl, cream butter thoroughly. Gradually add sugar, beating until light and fluffy. Add eggs one at a time, beating well after each addition. Stir in blackberry jam and vanilla. Alternately add dry ingredients and buttermilk, mixing well, beginning and ending with dry ingredients. Pour batter into two lightly greased and floured 9-inch round layer pans, dividing evenly. Or pour batter into a greased and floured 9-inch tube pan. Bake layer pans in a moderate oven (350 degrees F.) for 25 to 30 minutes. Or, bake tube cake in a slow oven (325 degrees F.) for 30 minutes; increase heat to moderate (350 degrees F.) and continue baking for 55 minutes. Cool in pans or pan for 10 to 15 minutes, then turn out on a wire rack to finish cooling. Frost and fill cake as desired with Buttermilk Caramel Icing.

–Frances Fox (Mrs. Paul)

Fruit Cake

Three pounds flour, three pounds sugar, three pounds butter, thirty eggs, six pounds currants, well washed and dried; three pounds stoned raisins, one pound citron, one pound blanched almonds, one ounce mace, one ounce cinnamon, one ounce nutmeg, one-quarter ounce cloves, one-quarter ounce allspice, half-pint brandy. Beat the butter with the hand to a cream. Add the sugar, then the whites, then the yolks (these having been beaten separately till perfectly light); to which add the fruit and spices; stir in the flour without beating; bake six hours in a moderate oven. The above should either be baked in a barrel-hoop or divided into two.

–Mrs. George M. West
The Kitchen Queen, *1893*

English Spiced Fruitcake

Yield: one 10-inch tube cake

"We serve this every Christmas...the recipe originated with my family in England and was for three, five pound cakes."

2 cups sifted flour, divided
3/4 teaspoon nutmeg
1/2 teaspoon cinnamon
1/4 teaspoon mace
1/4 teaspoon allspice
1/4 teaspoon ground cloves
8 ounces dark seedless
  raisins
8 ounces dried currants
8 ounces candied mixed
  fruit
1 cup butter or margarine,
  at room temperature
1/2 cup sugar
3 eggs
1 tablespoon water
1/4 teaspoon baking soda
1/2 cup dark molasses
1/4 cup brandy (see note)
Orange juice or milk
8 ounces chopped pecans
  or slivered blanched
  almonds
Additional brandy (see
  note)

Line a greased 10-inch tube pan with waxed paper; grease again. Reserve 1/2 cup flour to mix with fruit. Sift together 1 1/2 cups flour, nutmeg, cinnamon, mace, allspice, and cloves. Combine 1/2 cup reserved flour, raisins, currants, and candied mixed fruit, mixing well. In a large bowl, cream butter thoroughly. Gradually add sugar, beating until light and fluffy. Add eggs, one at at time, beating well after each addition. Dissolve baking soda in water; stir molasses into soda mixture. Alternately stir dry ingredients and molasses mixture into butter mixture. Stir in brandy. Add a small amount of orange juice or milk if batter is too stiff (see note). Fold in floured fruits and nuts. Spoon into prepared pan. Bake in a *very* slow oven (250 degrees F.) for 4 hours or until a cake tester inserted in center comes out clean. Cool in pan for 30 minutes, then turn out and remove waxed paper. Finish cooling, right side up, on a wire rack. Wrap cake in cheesecloth soaked in brandy and store in an airtight container. Add more brandy to cheesecloth, as desired.

Note: Use an excellent quality of brandy.

Note: Wooden spoon should stand up in batter.

–Alicia Pedersen (Mrs. Paul)

541

At Table a Long Time

How restless and squirmy children of today would be if they were compelled to sit the long hours at the dinner table that we endured. At 2 o'clock my father drove home in his buggy, and we sat down to a long course dinner. Breakfast had been eaten at 8:15, a bountiful repast with fruit, cereal, bacon and eggs, cornbread, biscuits and every morning a third kind of "fancy" bread, in turn Sally Lunn, shortcake, muffins, waffles, or griddle cakes (which later my father called "stack of browns"). As soon as school was over at noon we children had brown sugar on bread and glasses of milk to sustain us until 2 o'clock found us ravenous again. Otelia, in stage whispers—when there were no guests present—as she passed behind our chairs, warned us of some infraction of good table manners. For a time we had my Uncle "Major's" butler, Tom, who stood behind my father's chair and waved the great branch of peacock feathers to frighten off any stray fly that might wander into the room. Tom was well known to all the gentlemen who came to the family dinners. He knew by heart all of the Major's best stories, and would warn him. "You knows I jes' got to bust out laffing if you tells that joke I al'ays laffs at."

Barbara Trigg Brown
"Virginia Woman Recalls
Christmas Party and Other
Events on Franklin Street in the Nineties,"
'Virginia Reel' Had Guests
Dancing for Hours
Richmond Times-Dispatch, December 25, 1938

King's Cake

Yield: one 10-inch tube cake

Of English and German origin, King's Cake is traditionally served during the Christmas holidays on Twelfth Night, January 6th, the beginning of the Feast of Epiphany. When the cake is served, a man receiving a piece of cake containing a bean is chosen king for the festivities. A woman receiving cake containing a pea is chosen queen for the evening.

1/4 cup dark seedless raisins
1/4 cup golden seedless raisins
1/4 cup dried currants
1/4 cup chopped candied orange or lemon peel
About 1/3 cup brandy
5 cups sifted cake flour
2 tablespoons baking powder
2 cups butter or margarine, at room temperature (see note)
2 cups sugar
10 eggs, separated
1 teaspoon grated lemon peel
1 teaspoon vanilla extract
1/2 cup heavy cream (see note)
1/3 cup cognac (see note)
1 dried navy or other bean (optional)
1 dried pea (optional)
1 teaspoon lemon juice

In a medium bowl, combine raisins, currants, and candied orange or lemon peel. Pour brandy over fruit, cover, and allow to stand at room temperature for 12 hours. Fruit should absorb all of the liquid. Sift together the flour and baking powder. In a large bowl, cream butter thoroughly. Gradually add sugar, beating until light and fluffy. Add egg yolks, one at a time, beating well after each addition. Add lemon peel and vanilla extract, mixing well. Alternately add dry ingredients, cream, and cognac, mixing well. Stir in brandied fruit, bean, and pea, if desired. In a large bowl, beat egg whites until frothy; add lemon juice. Continue to beat egg whites until stiff, but not dry, peaks are formed. Fold beaten egg whites into cake batter. Evenly spoon batter into a greased and floured 10-inch tube pan with a removable bottom. (Cake pan will be almost full of batter but will not overflow pan during baking.) Bake in a slow oven (300 degrees F.) for 3 hours or until metal tester inserted into the center of the cake comes out clean. Check cake after 2 hours but do not disturb batter. Cool cake in pan for 15 minutes, then turn out onto a wire rack to finish cooling. Store in an airtight container.

Note: Margarine or hydrogenated shortening used as shortening will produce a cake of greater volume than one made with butter. 1 cup butter and 1 cup shortening or margarine may be substituted for 2 cups butter, if desired.

Note: Cream may be reduced to 1/3 cup and cognac increased to 1/2 cup, if desired.

–Elinor Kuhn (Mrs. Frank)
Richmond Culinary Guild,
Buffet, catering firm

Brandied Fresh Pear Cake

Yield: one 10-inch tube cake

3 cups sifted cake flour
1 teaspoon baking soda
1 teaspoon salt
2 cups sugar
1 1/2 cups cooking oil
1/3 cup brandy
1 teaspoon vanilla extract
3 jumbo eggs
3 cups chopped peeled firm ripe pears
1 1/2 cups chopped English walnuts or pecans
Hot Buttered Brandy Sauce

Sift together the first 3 ingredients. In a large bowl, combine sugar, oil, brandy, and vanilla, beating at high speed of an electric mixer for 2 to 3 minutes. Add eggs, one at a time, beating well after each addition. Stir in dry ingredients. Fold in chopped pears and nuts, mixing well. Evenly spoon into a greased 10-inch tube pan. Bake in a moderate oven (350 degrees F.) for 70 to 75 minutes or until a cake tester inserted in center comes out clean. Allow cake to cool in pan for 20 minutes, then turn out, top side up, onto a sheet of aluminum foil. Pour Hot Buttered Brandy Sauce over cake. Bring sides of foil up around cake. Allow cake to cool completely.

Hot Buttered Brandy Sauce

1/2 cup butter or margarine
1 cup sugar
1/3 cup brandy

In a small heavy saucepan, melt butter over low heat. Add sugar and brandy, mixing well. Bring mixture to a boil over moderate heat; reduce heat and simmer for 2 to 3 minutes.

Porcupine Cake

Cut a sponge cake thin horizontally, spread each section with fruit jelly, except the top piece. Put them smoothly one on the other, then pour over it wine enough to moisten it. Make a rich custard; cut into it a handful of blanched almonds. Put the cake on the dish on which it is to be served. Take 1/2 pound of blanched almonds, cut them in three lengthwise pieces. Stick them thickly over the cake and pour the custard over it.

—Mrs. M. D. Burrall
Receipts for Luncheon and Tea, *1898*

Lila Tice's Pineapple Upside Down Cake

Yield: one 10-inch skillet cake

Upside Down Cake is one of those cakes that just happened. Necessity causes creativity. Early American cooks needed to use seasonal ripe fruit before it spoiled. Berries and cherries were used long before pineapple as the designated fruit, as pineapple was not imported to the United States from Cuba until the mid-nineteenth century.

Topping
1/2 cup light brown sugar, firmly packed
1/4 cup butter or margarine, melted
1 (8-ounce) can crushed pineapple, including juice

Batter
1 1/4 cups sifted cake flour
3/4 cup sugar
1 1/4 teaspoons baking powder
1/4 teaspoon salt
1/4 cup butter or margarine, at room temperature, or shortening
2 eggs, well beaten
1 teaspoon vanilla extract
1/2 cup milk

To prepare topping, combine in a small heavy saucepan 1/2 cup sugar and 1/4 cup melted butter; stir over low heat until sugar is thoroughly dissolved. Spread mixture over the bottom of a greased 10-inch oven proof round heavy iron or other oven-proof skillet; evenly arrange prepared fruit in butter-sugar mixture. Sift the first 4 batter ingredients together. In a medium bowl, cream 1/4 cup butter thoroughly. Add eggs, vanilla, dry ingredients, and milk, mixing well; then beat hard by hand or at high speed of an electric mixer for 1 minute. Evenly spread batter over fruit mixture in skillet. Bake in a moderate oven (350 degrees F.) for 50 minutes or until cake tester inserted in center of cake comes out clean. Cool cake in skillet on a wire rack for 15 minutes. Loosen edges of cake from skillet with a knife or rubber spatula; invert serving plate over cake and flip plate and skillet over to turn out cake.

Note: Any desired fruit may be used, such as pitted fresh, or thawed frozen, or drained canned sour cherries, or blueberries, or blackberries, or crushed or sliced fresh or drained canned pineapple. Use about 1 3/4 cups prepared fruit.

–Douglas O. Tice, Jr.

Rueger's Restaurant,

Ninth and Bank Streets,

RICHMOND.   -   VIRGINIA.

Old Richmond Advertisement, date unknown

The Cake Even A Man Can Bake

Yield: one 13 x 9-inch cake

1 (15-ounce) can crushed pineapple (including juice)
2 eggs
3 cups sugar, divided
2 cups sifted flour
1 teaspoon vanilla extract
1 teaspoon baking soda
1/2 teaspoon salt
1/2 cup butter or margarine
1/2 cup evaporated milk
1 cup chopped pecans
1 cup flaked coconut

In a bowl, combine pineapple, eggs, 2 cups sugar, flour, vanilla, baking soda, and salt, mixing well with a wooden spoon. Pour into a greased and floured 13 x 9 x 2-inch baking pan. Bake in a moderate oven (350 degrees F.) for 30 minutes. During the last 5 minutes of baking, melt butter in a heavy saucepan over moderate heat. Add 1 cup sugar and evaporated milk, blending well. Cook, stirring constantly, until bubbly hot. Stir in pecans and coconut. Remove cake from oven, and with the tines of a fork, poke holes in the surface of the cake every two to three inches. Immediately pour hot pecan-coconut mixture over cake, spreading evenly. Cut into squares and serve hot or at room temperature.

–Carol Nance
Assistant Attorney General
State of Virginia

Cake flour is always a better choice than all-purpose flour to use with cakes, as it comes from a softer wheat which contains less gluten, thereby giving a more delicate product.

Apple Sauce Cake

2 cupfuls of flour
1 cupful of granulated sugar
1/2 cupful of butter
1 cupful of apple sauce
1 cupful of raisins
1 heaping teaspoonful of soda
3 teaspoonfuls of Sauer's Cinnamon Extract

Stir the soda into the apple sauce while it is still hot. Cream the butter and sugar; add the other ingredients, and bake in a single loaf. Cover with a boiled icing.

C. F. Sauer Company
Sauer Spices, *circa, 1920's*

Virginia Spice Cake with Caramel Glaze

Yield: one 10-inch tube cake

"Early nineteenth century cakes were heavy, dense cakes, well spiced, glazed to preserve freshness, heavily sugared if the family could afford it, and beaten one hour. This cake will give you a nineteenth century taste without all the hard work. As one nineteenth century cook observed, this keeps well only if you lock it up!"

3 cups sifted cake flour
2 teaspoons cinnamon
2 teaspoons nutmeg
2 teaspoons ground cloves
1 teaspoon salt
1 teaspoon baking soda
1 cup chopped pecans
1/2 cup chopped pitted
  dates
1/2 cup dark or golden
  seedless raisins
1 (16-ounce) can un-
  sweetened applesauce
2 cups sugar
1 cup cooking oil
Caramel Glaze (see Index)

In a large bowl, sift together the first 6 ingredients. Add pecans, dates, and raisins, mixing well. Stir in applesauce, sugar, and oil, mixing well. Spoon into a greased and floured 10-inch tube pan. Bake in a slow oven (325 degrees F.) for 1 hour or until cake tester inserted in center comes out clean. Cool in pan for about 20 minutes before turning out onto a wire rack to finish cooling. Prepare glaze and immediately pour over cake arranged on a serving plate. Allow glazed cake to completely cool before cutting.

–Kathryn Marshall Arnold

Cheesecakes of a sort are thought to have been served in second century Greece. Some cheesecake recipes were made of flour and sesame seeds as the pastry crust which held a soft cheese mixture. Some were baked, some fried, and others were boiled in oil (deep fat fried). Others were moulded and chilled in snow and still others contained no cheese. An ancient Roman cheesecake was a simple sweetened custard of milk and eggs. Small cheesecakes were also know in merry olde England, often known as Maids of Honor. Anne Boleyn is said to have tempted Henry VIII with them.

Present day cheesecakes in the United States result form those confections prepared by Jewish and Italian immigrants living at the turn of the nineteenth/twentieth centuries in New York's lower East side. Sometimes called New York-style cheesecake, the delicacy preferred by the Jewish heritage contained a smooth creamy filling of cream cheese, while the Italians used ricotta cheese. Rumor suggests that more cheesecake is eaten today in the United States than elsewhere in the world.

Prize Winning Cheesecake

Yield: one 9-inch cake

Mrs. Robb's cheesecake won a first prize and the Corning Creative Cookery Award presented by the Corning Glass Works at a March of Dimes 1987 fund raising gala in Washington, D.C.. Simple in its preparation, this cheesecake is smooth in texture and superb in flavor. Not one crumb will remain for leftovers! Serve it ungarnished or embellish it with Brandied Nectarine Sauce for a special party.

Crust

2 cups fine graham cracker crumbs

6 tablespoons sugar

1 teaspoon cinnamon

1/2 cup butter or margarine, at room temperature

To prepare crust, combine crumbs, sugar and cinnamon, mixing well. Mix butter into crumbs with a pastry blender until crumbs are evenly coated. Press crumbs evenly over bottom and 1 1/2 to 2 inches up sides of a 9-inch spring-form pan (see note). Place crust in the freezer while filling is being prepared.

Filling

3 (8-ounce) packages cream cheese, at room temperature

1 1/2 cups sugar

4 jumbo eggs, at room temperature and separated

1 cup sour cream, at room temperature

1 teaspoon vanilla extract

Sifted confectioners' sugar for garnish

Brandied Nectarine Sauce for garnish (optional) (see index)

In a large bowl, beat cream cheese until smooth. Add sugar 1/2 cup at a time, beating well at low speed of an electric mixer. Add egg yolks, one at a time, beating well after each addition. Stir in sour cream and vanilla. In a medium bowl, beat egg whites until stiff, but not dry, peaks are formed. Fold beaten egg whites into cream cheese mixture. Spoon batter into cold prepared crust. Bake in a slow oven (300 degrees F.) for 1 hour 15 minutes. Turn off oven, door closed, allowing cake to remain in oven for 1 hour 15 minutes. *Do not open oven door.* Thoroughly cool on a wire rack. Lightly sift confectioners' sugar over cheesecake before serving. Cheesecake may be served at room temperature or chilled. Store cheesecake, loosely covered, in refrigerator. A small amount of warm Brandied Nectarine Sauce may be spooned over each serving if desired.

Note: The easiest and least messy method of pressing crumbs is to press crumb mixture firmly with a flat bottomed 2 to 3-inch diameter glass.

–Lynda Johnson Robb (Mrs. Charles)
First Lady of Virginia, 1982 to 1986

Elegant Cheesecake

Yield: one 9-inch cake

Crust
1 1/2 cups fine graham
cracker crumbs
1/4 cup sifted confectioners'
sugar
1 teaspoon allspice or 1/2
teaspoon cinnamon and
1/4 teaspoon each
nutmeg and allspice
1/3 cup butter or margarine,
melted

To prepare crust, combine crumbs, confectioners' sugar, and spices in a bowl, mixing well. With a pastry blender, mix in butter until crumbs are evenly coated. Press crumbs evenly over bottom and 1 1/2 inches up sides of a 9-inch spring-form pan; set aside.

Filling
2 (8-ounce) packages cream
cheese, at room tempera-
ture
1 cup sugar
5 egg yolks
1 tablespoon vanilla extract
5 egg whites, at room
temperature

To prepare filling, beat cream cheese in a bowl until smooth. Gradually add 1 cup sugar, beating well. Add egg yolks, one at a time, beating well after each addition, and 1 tablespoon vanilla. In a bowl, beat egg whites until soft peaks are formed; fold in egg yolk mixture. Pour into prepared crust. Bake in a very slow oven (275 degrees F.) for 50 minutes or until filling is set. Cool cake for one hour away from drafts.

Topping
2 cups sour cream
1/3 cup sugar
1 tablespoon vanilla extract
Cinnamon for garnish
Slivered blanched almonds
for garnish

To prepare topping, combine sour cream, 1/3 cup sugar, and 1 tablespoon vanilla in a bowl, blending well. Spoon over cooled cake. Sprinkle lightly with cinnamon and almonds. Bake in a very slow oven (275 degrees F.) for 7 minutes or until sour cream topping sets. Cool thoroughly in pan, then chill.

–Esther D. Shelley (Mrs. Blackwell)

During colonial days, the use of sugar in food preparation became a standard of measurement of the excellence of food offered in a household.

Fresh Peaches 'N Cream Cheesecake with Brandied Peach Sauce

Yield: one 10-inch cheesecake

Crust

2 cups fine vanilla wafer crumbs
1/3 cup sugar
1/8 teaspoon salt
1/3 cup butter or margarine, melted

Combine crumbs, sugar, and salt, mixing well. Add butter, mixing well with a pastry blender. Press crumbs evenly over bottom and 1 1/2 to 2 inches up sides of a 10-inch spring-form pan; set aside.

Filling

3 (8-ounce) packages cream cheese, at room temperature
1 1/2 cups sugar
1 envelope (tablespoon) unflavored gelatin
5 jumbo eggs
1 cup sour cream
1 cup heavy cream
2 tablespoons brandy (optional)
1 teaspoon almond extract
3 cups fresh coarse peach puree (see note)
Brandied Peach Sauce

In a bowl, beat cream cheese until smooth. Add sugar, 1/2 cup at a time, and gelatin, beating well at low speed of an electric mixer. Add eggs, one at a time, beating well after each addition. Stir in sour cream, heavy cream, brandy, if desired, and almond extract, blending well. Fold in peach pureé, blending until smooth. Bake in a slow oven (300 degrees F.) for 1 hour 15 minutes. Turn off oven; with door slightly ajar, cool in oven for 1 to 1 1/2 hours. Thoroughly cool cake on a wire rack, then chill in the refrigerator until ready to serve. Spoon a small amount of Brandied Peach Sauce over each serving.

Note: Use about 4 to 5 medium peaches to make pureé. Remove seeds and cut unpeeled peaches into thick slices or pieces. Place peaches in a blender container; cover and blend at medium speed until peaches are puréed. Nectarines may be substituted, if desired.

Brandied Peach Sauce
Yield: 2 cups
3/4 cup sugar
2 tablespoons cornstarch
4 to 6 large peaches, peeled, seeded, and thinly sliced
1 large peach, unpeeled, seeded, and pureéd (see note)

In a medium heavy saucepan, combine sugar and cornstarch. Add peaches and peach pureé, stirring until cornstarch is lump free. Cook over low heat, stirring constantly, until clear and thickened. Stir in butter and then brandy.

1 tablespoon butter or
  margarine, at room
  temperature
2 tablespoons peach brandy

Note: To purée peach, place unpeeled fruit in a blender container. Cover and blend at medium speed until peach is pureéd.

Note: Fresh nectarines and nectarine liqueur may be substituted for peaches. Or (10-ounce) package thawed frozen sliced peaches and juice may also be substituted for fresh peaches. Peach pureé may be eliminated.

During the Civil War, corn became so scarce in Richmond it sold for fifteen dollars a bushel, while eggs cost a dollar per egg.

Chip 'N Cherry Cake

Yield: one loaf cake

1 1/2 cups sifted flour
1 1/2 teaspoons baking
  powder
1/4 teaspoon salt
2 cups chopped English
  walnuts or pecans
1 cup chopped pitted dates
1 cup chopped red candied
  cherries
3/4 cup semi-sweet choco-
  late pieces
3 eggs, beaten
1 cup sugar

Line a greased 9 x 5 x 3-inch loaf pan with waxed paper; grease again. Sift together the first 3 ingredients; add nuts, dates, cherries, and chocolate pieces, mixing well. In a bowl, combine eggs and sugar, beating until thick and light yellow in color. Fold in flour-fruit-nut mixture. Spoon into prepared pan. Bake in a slow oven (325 degrees F.) for 1 1/2 hours. Cool in pan for 10 minutes, then turn out onto a wire rack to finish cooling.

Note: There is no shortening in the cake. It is more like a torte and keeps well.

Variation: 1 cup chopped candied citron or 1/2 cup chopped pitted dates and 1/2 cup chopped citron may be substituted.

–Sue Crowell (Mrs. Robert)

Key Lime Cheesecake

Yield: one 10-inch cake

Crust

2/3 cup graham cracker crumbs
1/4 cup sugar
2 1/2 tablespoons butter or margarine, melted

To prepare crust, combine crumbs and sugar in a medium bowl. Add butter, mixing well with a pastry blender. Press crumbs evenly over bottom of a 10-inch spring-form pan; chill in freezer for 10 to 15 minutes.

Filling

4 (8-ounce) plus 2 (3-ounce) packages cream cheese, at room temperature
1 3/4 cups sugar
4 eggs
1 1/3 cups sour cream
2/3 cup Key lime juice (see note)
2 tablespoons grated lime peel
Very thin slices of Key or Persian limes for garnish

In a bowl, beat cream cheese until smooth. Add sugar, 1/2 cup at a time, beating well at low speed of an electric mixer. Add eggs, one at a time, beating well after each addition. Stir in sour cream, lime juice, and lime peel. Pour filling into chilled prepared crust. Bake in a slow oven (300 degrees F.) for 1 hour 35 minutes. Turn off oven. With door closed, cool cheesecake in oven for 1 hour 15 minutes. Garnish with very thin slices of fresh Key or Persian limes. Store in refrigerator.

Note: Use fresh or bottled Key lime juice. If Key lime juice is not available, Persian lime juice may be substituted; however, the flavor will be slightly different.

–Chef Kevin Goodrich
The Berkeley Restaurant
The Berkely Hotel

Chocolate Applesauce Cupcakes with Caramel Frosting

Yield: 8 cupcakes

2 squares (ounces) un-
sweetened chocolate
1 3/4 cups sifted flour
1 teaspoon baking soda
1 teaspoon cinnamon
1/2 teaspoon salt
1/2 teaspoon allspice
1/4 teaspoon nutmeg
1/8 teaspoon ground cloves
1/2 cup shortening
1 cup sugar
1 egg
1 1/4 cups unsweetened
applesauce
Caramel Frosting

In the top of a double boiler, melt chocolate over hot water; allow to cool slightly. Sift together flour, baking soda, cinnamon, salt, allspice, nutmeg, and cloves. In a bowl, cream shortening thoroughly. Gradually add sugar, beating until light and fluffy. Beat in egg. Stir in chocolate. Alternately add dry ingredients and applesauce, mixing well after each addition. Fill greased muffin pans, 2 3/4 inches in diameter, individually lined with paper baking cups, two-thirds full. Bake in a moderate oven (375 degrees F.) for 20 minutes. Remove and cool thoroughly on a wire rack. Frost with Caramel Frosting.

Variation: Fold in 1 cup chopped English walnuts or pecans, or 1 cup semi-sweet chocolate pieces, or 1/2 cup nuts and 1/2 cup chocolate pieces into batter.

Caramel Frosting
1/2 cup butter or margarine
3/4 cup dark brown sugar,
firmly packed
1/3 cup half-and-half or
light cream
1 1/2 teaspoons vanilla
extract
1/4 teaspoon salt
3 1/2 to 4 cups sifted
confectioners' sugar

In a heavy saucepan, combine butter and brown sugar. Cook over moderate heat until mixture bubbles around edges of pan, then simmer slowly for 1 minute. Transfer to a bowl and cool for 10 to 15 minutes. Stir in half-and-half, vanilla, and salt. Stir in confectioners' sugar, one-third at a time, adding sugar as needed until smooth and of desired spreading consistency. Frost on thoroughly cooled cupcakes.

Buttermilk Cake

One pound of flour, one pound sugar, half pound butter, five eggs; dissolve half teaspoonful soda in half-pint of buttermilk, season with little mace, or any spice you like, add one cup of chopped raisins, and bake in little tin shapes.
F. F. V. Receipt Book, *1894*

Chocolate Raspberry Supreme

Yield: one 10-inch cake

This sinful, but delicious gâteau is easy to prepare and does not require flour. Serve it topped with Chocolate Raspberry Fudge Icing for chocoholics or with Raspberry Sauce with Framboise for others.

Butter for greasing, at room temperature
10 1/2 ounces semi-sweet chocolate pieces
5 1/2 tablespoons strained raspberry puree (see note)
6 jumbo eggs, separated (see note)
1 cup minus 1 tablespoon butter or margarine (15 tablespoons)
1/2 cup plus 1 tablespoon raspberry liqueur (9 tablespoons)
Pinch salt
3/4 cup sugar
3/4 cup potato starch (see note)
Chocolate Raspberry Fudge Icing or sifted confectioners' sugar and Raspberry Sauce with Framboise (see index)
Fresh raspberries for garnish

Chocolate Raspberry Fudge Icing
2 1/2 squares (ounces) unsweetened chocolate
3/4 cup butter
5 tablespoons raspberry pureé
1/4 teaspoon salt

Line the bottom of a 10-inch round cake pan with waxed paper. Butter sides of pan thoroughly; set aside. In the top of a double boiler, melt chocolate in raspberry pureé over simmering, but not boiling, water. Remove from heat; beat egg yolks lightly and then blend into the chocolate mixture. Cook over simmering water for 2 to 3 minutes. Remove from heat; blend in butter and raspberry liqueur. In a large bowl, beat egg whites with salt until foamy. Gradually add sugar and continue beating until stiff, glossy, but not dry, peaks are formed. Beat in starch. Gradually fold in chocolate mixture, blending well. Evenly spoon batter into prepared pan. Bake in a moderate oven (375 degrees F.) for 30 minutes or until a cake tester inserted in center comes out clean. Remove and cool in pan for about 30 minutes; loosen edges of cake, invert onto a wire rack, tap bottom of pan all over with handle of a table knife, and *carefully* turn out onto a wire rack to finish cooling. Frost cake with Chocolate Rasberry Fudge Icing and garnish with fresh rasberries. Or, sift confectioners' sugar over top of cake. Garnish cake with fresh rasberries. Spoon Rasberry Sauce with Framboise over each serving of the gâteau topped with confectioners' sugar, if desired.

Combine the first 4 ingredients in a heavy saucepan; melt chocolate and butter over low heat, stirring until smooth. Remove from heat and beat in confectioners' sugar as necessary until smooth and of desired spreading consistency. Add raspberry liqueur, beating until smooth. Spread warm frosting over top and sides of cake.

About 1 (1-pound) box
  confectioners' sugar
  (about 4 1/2 cups), sifted
About 2 1/2 tablespoons
  raspberry liqueur

Note: To Make rasberry pureé, spoon the contents of a thawed frozen (10-ounce package rasberries into a blender container; cover and blend at medium speed until berries are pureéd. Strain through a fine sieve to remove seeds. Any remaining pureé may be used for Chocolate Rasberry Fudge Icing or Rasberry Sauce with Framboise.

Note: If medium to small eggs are used, increase to 7.

Note:9 tablespoons cornstarch may be substituted for potato starch if potato starch is unavailable.

Mrs. Ward remembers pound cakes, jelly cakes and fruit cakes at Christmas. There were pumpkin and apple pies that her mother made and pea pie that her older sister made from black-eyed peas.

There was always plenty of chicken, turkey and ham, and home-canned vegetables for Christmas dinner.

Her family raised all its food and every year her father killed four hogs and one cow for the winter's meat. The food was cooked in a fireplace.

Christine Reid
"Christmas in the 1800's"
Richmond Times-Dispatch, December 23, 1984

Chocolate Cake

Grate or cut fine half cake Baker's chocolate; add one egg, one cup sugar, half cup milk, and cook until it get hot through; set that aside to cool; then cream half cup butter with one cup sugar and half cup of milk, mix this with yolks of three eggs; beat light; then add the well-beaten whites; add slowly two cups sifted flour and two teaspoonfuls of baking powder; when chocolate gets perfectly cold, mix with this batter. Bake in three deep layer-pans; put one and a half pints granulated sugar, half-pint water in sauce-pan, and cook until it candies; then pour in the well-beaten whites of three eggs; season with vanilla, and beat until stiff enough to spread on cake.

–Mrs. R. W. Powers
F. F. V. Receipt Book, *1894*

Devil's Food Cake

Possibly the devil knows the origin of Devil's Food Cake ... there are many theories but few facts to date its beginning. Some suggest it is a variation of an old chocolate cake with a modern name. Martha Washington is said to have served it to her guests. Others speculate that with the invention of angel food cake, there had to be a Devil's Food cake! Still others declare there was no mention of Devil's Food cake until the turn of the twentieth century, and some sources suggest that it is an improved Spanish creation. One Chicago hostess of the late 1880's, Mrs. Wm. Vaughn Moody, known for her chocolate cakes in Chicago and London, wins the most votes as the originator of this "devilishly good-tasting" cake. Choose your theory ... only the devil knows. There's even an argument as to the icing ... chocolate or white!

Red Devil's Food Cake with Old-Fashioned 7-Minute Frosting

Yield: one three-layer 9-inch cake

1 cup sour milk (see note)
3 cups sifted cake flour
3 teaspoons baking powder
1 teaspoon salt
3 squares (ounces) un-
  sweetened chocolate
1 cup boiling water
1/2 cup shortening
2 cups sugar
2 eggs plus 2 egg yolks (see
  note)
2 teaspoons vanilla extract
2 teaspoons baking soda
Old Fashioned 7-Minute
  Frosting (see index)

Prepare sour milk; allow to stand at room temperature for 10 minutes. Sift cake flour, baking powder, and salt together; repeat process twice more. In the top of a double boiler, melt chocolate over hot water; quickly blend in boiling water, stirring until smooth. Allow mixture to cool to room temperature. In a large bowl, cream shortening thoroughly. Gradually add sugar, beating until mixture is light and fluffy. Add eggs and egg yolks, one at a time, beating well after each addition; stir in vanilla. Alternately add dry ingredients and sour milk, mixing well after each addition. Combine cooled chocolate/water and baking soda, stirring until mixture is thickened, then quickly stir into cake batter. Pour into three

556

greased 9-inch round layer pans. Bake in a moderate oven (375 degrees F.) for 25 minutes or until a cake tester inserted in center of layers comes out clean. Cool in pans for 10 minutes and then turn out onto wire racks to finish cooling. Spread Old-Fashioned 7-Minute Frosting between layers and over top and sides of cake.

Note: To make sour milk, add 1 tablespoon of lemon juice or white vinegar to 1 cup milk.

Note: Reserve 2 egg whites for the Old-Fashioned 7-Minute Frosting

–Dorothy Parker (Mrs. Walter)

Virginia Cookery Book, circa 1921

Sour Milk Chocolate Sheet Cake with Nutty Chocolate Frosting

Yield: one 15 x 10 x 1-inch cake

"This delicious tasting cake is very moist. It is also very easy to prepare because one doesn't have to wait for the cake to cool before frosting."

2 cups sifted cake flour
2 cups sugar
1 teaspoon baking soda
1 teaspoon cinnamon (optional)
1 cup cold water
1/2 cup cooking oil
1/2 cup butter or margarine, at room temperature
1/4 cup sifted cocoa
2 eggs
1/2 cup sour milk (see note)
Nutty Chocolate Frosting (see index)

In a large bowl, sift together the first 3 or 4 ingredients. In a medium heavy saucepan, combine water, oil, butter, and cocoa. Bring cocoa mixture to a boil over moderate heat; remove from heat and set aside. To dry ingredients, add eggs, one at a time, beating well after each addition. Add sour milk and hot cocoa mixture, mixing well. Pour into a lightly greased 15 x 10 x 1-inch baking pan. Bake in a hot oven (400 degrees F.) for 18 minutes or until a metal cake tester inserted in the center comes out clean. Frost the hot cake evenly with hot frosting. Allow frosted cake to cool in pan thoroughly before cutting into squares.

Note: To sour milk, add 1 1/2 teaspoons lemon juice to milk; allow to stand for 10 minutes.

–Rachel Koppenhaver (Mrs. Ronald)

Sour Cream Pound Cake

Yield: one 10-inch tube cake

3 cups sifted cake flour
1/2 teaspoon baking soda
1 cup butter or margarine, at room temperature
3 cups sugar
6 eggs
2 teaspoons vanilla extract
1 teaspoon lemon or almond extract
1 cup sour cream
Vanilla Frosting (see index)

Sift together flour and baking soda. In a large bowl, cream butter until smooth. Gradually add sugar, beating well. Add eggs, one at time, beating well after each addition. Beat in flavorings. Alternately add dry ingredients and sour cream, starting and ending with dry ingredients, mixing well. Spoon into a greased and floured 10-inch tube pan. Bake in a slow oven (300 degrees F.) for 1 1/2 hours. Cool in pan for 10 minutes, then turn out onto a wire rack, top side up, to finish cooling. Frost top and sides of cake with Vanilla Frosting.

–Susie Keyser (Mrs. Hugh)

Chiffon cake, hailed as "the first really new cake in a hundred years" when it was introduced in the 1940's, owes its creation to a professional baker named Harry Baker who had been tempting Hollywood celebrities with his cakes for years to great acclaim. Harry sold his recipe with its secret ingredient, cooking oil as the shortening, to General Mills for thousands of dollars.

Fresh Lemon Chiffon Cake

Yield: one 10-inch tube cake

1 2/3 cups sifted cake flour
2/3 cup sugar
2 1/4 teaspoons baking powder
1/2 teaspoon salt
6 extra large eggs, separated and at room temperature
1/3 cup plus 1 tablespoon cooking oil
1/3 cup plus 1 tablespoon water
1/4 cup lemon juice
1 1/2 teaspoons grated lemon peel
1/2 teaspoon cream of tartar
1 1/3 cups sifted confectioners' sugar
Lemon Cream Frosting (see index) or additional sifted confectioners' frosting

Sift together the first 4 ingredients into a large mixing bowl. In a medium bowl, beat egg yolks until thick and light yellow in color. Add oil, water, lemon juice, and peel to beaten egg yolks, blending well. Add egg yolk mixture to dry ingredients, beating until smooth. *Do not overmix.* In a large bowl, beat egg whites until they are foamy; beat in cream of tartar. Gradually add confectioners' sugar, beating until stiff, but not dry, peaks are formed. Carefully fold beaten egg whites into batter. Spoon batter into an ungreased 10-inch tube pan. Bake in a moderate oven (350 degrees F.) for 40 to 45 minutes or until cake tester inserted in center of cake comes out clean. Invert cake on a wire rack until cold. Loosen cake from sides of pan and around tube with thin-bladed knife or spatula. Remove cake from pan. Frost with Lemon Cream Frosting or sprinkle sifted confectioners' sugar over cake.

–Heilman Dining Center
University of Richmond
Food Services Department

Gingerbread Cake

Yield: one 10-inch tube cake

"This cake, which we always referred to simply as 'gingerbread,' was one of my favorite desserts when I lived at home."

2 1/2 cups sifted flour
2 teaspoons baking powder
1 teaspoon cinnamon
1 teaspoon ground ginger
1 teaspoon cloves
1/2 cup butter or margarine,
  at room temperature
1/2 cup sugar
2 eggs
1 cup dark corn syrup
1 cup milk

Sift together the first 5 ingredients. In a medium bowl, cream butter thoroughly. Gradually add sugar, beating until light and fluffy. Add eggs, one at a time, beating well after each addition. Alternately add dry ingredients with corn syrup and milk, mixing well. Spoon into a greased 9 or 10-inch tube pan. Bake in a moderate oven (350 degrees F.) for 45 minutes or until a cake tester inserted into center of gingerbread comes out clean. Cool in pan for 10 minutes, then turn out onto a wire rack to finish cooling. Serve warm or at room temperature.

–Douglas O. Tice

Molasses Cake

Take one cup of butter or lard and mix well with one cup of sugar, then beat in three eggs. Add two cups of molasses, one cup of sour milk alternately with three and one half cups of flour sifted with two teaspoons of soda, one half teaspoon of salt and one tablespoon of ginger. Bake in a slow oven in a greased tin

(Old Recipe, Richmond, Virginia, circa 1840)
The Williamsburg Art of Cookery, 1938

Cheese Gingerbread No. 1

1 cup molasses
2 cup flour
4 ounces cheese
2 teaspoon ginger
1 teaspoon soda
1/2 teaspoon salt

Heat the molasses and cheese in a double boiler until the cheese is melted. Add the soda and stir vigorously. Mix and sift dry ingredients and add them to the molasses and cheese alternately with water. Bake 15 minutes in small buttered tins.
Culinary Echoes From Dixie, 1917

Usually in the eighteenth and nineteenth centuries, baking was done once a week. Glazes helped preserve the moistness of the cake in the days before protective wraps.

Black Walnut Pound Cake

Yield: one 10-inch tube cake

3 1/4 cups sifted cake flour
1/2 teaspoon baking powder
1/8 teaspoon salt
1 cup butter or margarine, at room temperature
1/2 cup shortening
3 cups sugar
5 eggs
2 teaspoons vanilla extract
1 cup milk
1 1/2 cups chopped black walnuts

Sift together the first 3 ingredients. In a large bowl, cream butter and shortening thoroughly. Gradually add sugar, beating until mixture is light and fluffy. Add eggs, one at a time, beating well after each addition, and vanilla extract. Sift dry ingredients into butter mixture alternately with milk, mixing well. Spoon batter into a greased and floured 10-inch tube pan. Bake in a slow oven (300 degrees F.) for 1 1/2 hours or until a cake tester inserted in center of cake comes out clean. Turn cake out onto a wire rack to cool thoroughly.

–Beverly Black Tice (Mrs. Douglas O. Jr.)

Loaf Cake

1 Pound Flour,
1 Pound Franklin Sugar,
3/4 Pound Butter,
2 Pounds Currants,
1 Pound Raisins,
1 Cupful Milk,
1 Teaspoonful Soda,
1 Ounce Mace,
6 Eggs.

Use your own good judgement in handling the ingredients, properly bake and you will have a nice cake.

-Old Virginia Cooking, circa 1909

Pound Cake

1 pound of sugar
1 pound of flour
1 pound of butter
12 eggs
1 tablespoon of Sauer's Lemon, or Vanilla Extract

Cream the butter and flour together. Beat the yolks of the eggs, and add the sugar. Mix the flour and butter with the eggs and sugar, and beat thoroughly. Then add the stiffly beaten whites of the eggs and Sauer's flavoring extract; beat again. Bake slowly in a moderately hot oven.

C.F. Sauer Company
Sauer Spices, *circa 1920's*

Five-Flavor Pound Cake

Yield: one 10-inch tube cake

3 cups sifted cake flour
1/2 teaspoon baking powder
1 cup margarine or butter, at room temperature
1/2 cup cooking oil
3 cups sugar
1 teaspoon vanilla extract
1 teaspoon lemon extract
1 teaspoon rum extract
1 teaspoon coconut flavoring
1 teaspoon butter flavoring
5 extra large eggs
1 cup milk
Five-Flavor Glaze

Sift together flour and baking powder. In a bowl, cream margarine and oil until smooth. Gradually add sugar, extracts, and flavorings, beating until light and fluffy. Add eggs, one at a time, beating well after each addition. Alternately add dry ingredients and milk, beginning and ending with dry ingredients, mixing well. Spoon into a greased and floured 10-inch tube pan. Bake in a slow oven (325 degrees F.) for about 1 1/2 hours or until a cake tester inserted in center comes out clean. Cool in pan for 15 minutes, then turn out, top side up, onto a wire rack placed over a sheet of waxed paper. Pour hot Five-Flavor Glaze over cake while warm, allowing glaze to drip down sides of cake.

Five-Flavor Glaze
1/2 cup sugar
1/4 cup water
1/2 teaspoon vanilla extract
1/2 teaspoon lemon extract
1/2 teaspoon rum extract
1/2 teaspoon almond extract
1/2 teaspoon coconut flavoring
1/2 teaspoon butter flavoring

In a small heavy saucepan, combine all ingredients; stir over moderate heat until mixture is bubbly hot. Immediately pour over warm cake.

–Virginia S. Darnell (Mrs. Raymond)

Great-Grandmother's Pound Cake

Yield: one 8-inch cake

"This recipe was printed in a Chicago paper during Abraham Lincoln's administration as his wife's favorite pound cake. My mother had the yellowed copy of the printed recipe which her grandmother had saved, but it was washed away in the 1954 hurricane that hit Cape Cod so badly. Fortunately, she had a copy of it so we can enjoy it today."

This cake was possibly also called Election Cake. Mary Todd Lincoln was considered quite a talented baker and must have loved her "sweets." Records indicate she purchased great quantities of sugar in 1859 and certainly served considerable plates of cake and cups of coffee.

Mary was frequently criticized for her southern sympathies during the Civil War. Her family were southerners from Lexington, Kentucky. Interestingly, ancestors had migrated from the northern part of Ireland to Pennsylvania to Virginia and finally to Kentucky in 1775. Her great great-uncle was pastor of the old Providence Church in the Gum Springs area of Virginia.

2 cups sifted flour
1/4 teaspoon mace
1 cup butter or margarine,
  at room temperature
1 2/3 cups sugar
5 eggs

Line a greased 8 x 8 x 2-inch baking pan with parchment paper; grease again. Sift together flour and mace. In a bowl, cream butter thoroughly. Gradually add sugar, beating well after each addition. Add eggs, one at a time, beating well after each addition. Stir in dry ingredients, mixing well. Spoon into prepared pan. Bake in a slow oven (300 degrees F.) for 1 hour 15 minutes or until a cake tester inserted in center comes out clean. Cool in pan for 10 minutes, then turn out onto a wire rack to finish cooling

–Sue Crowell (Mrs. Robert)

On November 11, 1920, the anniversary of the W. W. I armistice, one hundred thousand Richmonders turned out to cheer Marshall Ferdinand Foch visiting the capitol of the Old Dominion. As part of the festivities, Governor and Mrs. Westmoreland Davies treated the great French general to "an old southern menu" featuring the cook's specialties of spoon bread and southern-style vegetables. Indians from a Virginia reservation were asked to cook game for the luncheon. Charlotte Russe, served for dessert topped with a miniature French flag, paid homage to the general's home country.

"Mac Mac's" Holiday Coconut Cake

Yield: 8 or 9-inch round three layer cake

"Mac Mac, my grandmother, was a marvelous cook and certainly an enigma in her day. She was a working mother before the 1930's Depression, owning and managing a ladies wearing apparel business. Her career coincided with her style of cooking which was very fashionable.

"Mac Mac's Coconut Cake always was flanked by a bowl of Ambrosia and a compote of Angel Hash on the Christmas sideboard. I helped her make the cake enough times to know exactly how she did it. The project was a grandchild's delight...countless bowls, pots, pans, spatulas, and spoons to lick for three nights. The first night, she'd open, drain, and grate two coconuts and refrigerate the juice and the coconut separately. The next night, she'd bake her pound cake batter in three layer pans. When the layers were in the oven, she'd make a double batch of Lemon Curd, cool it, and refrigerate it. While the cake layers were still warm, she poked holes all over them with a fork and poured coconut juice (chilling since the night before) over them, very, very slowly until it all soaked in. On the third night, she made two batches of Old Fashioned 7-Minute Frosting. Sometimes she added a drop of lemon extract, other times, just the vanilla specified in the recipe. Then, the fun began.

"By now, the cake layers were so moist and so rich that the only way to hold them together on the cake stand was with wooden toothpicks. First, we put strips of waxed paper, which could be slipped out carefully after they caught all the messes we made during construction, around the stand. While the soaked cake layers were still cold, we cut each horizontally in half with her long bread knife. Then we started building...cake, frosting, coconut, lemon curd, frosting, coconut, cake...

"When Mac Mac's Coconut Cake was finished, it took up the whole top shelf of the refrigerator in the back hall where it waited...under sheets of waxed paper that barely touched it...for Christmas dinner."

2 fresh coconuts
One recipe favorite pound cake (see index)
Old-Fashioned 7-Minute Frosting, recipe doubled (see index)
1 cup Lemon Curd Filling, well chilled (see index)

Puncture coconut shells with a sharp knife or ice pick; allow juice to drip into container. Strain juice into a clean glass jar, cover, and refrigerate. Crack coconut and remove shell. Cut coconut meat into finger-sized pieces. Shred 'meat' in small batches in a food blender or processor fitted with a metal blade. Place shredded coconut in a ziplock plastic bag; refrigerate until ready to use. Prepare pound cake according to recipe directions. Spoon batter into three greased and floured 8- or 9-inch round layer pans, dividing evenly. Bake in a moderate oven (350 degrees F.) for 25 to 35 minutes or until done. Cake layers are done when layers spring back when pressed lightly in center and begin to pull away from sides of pans. Cool in pans for 5 minutes, then turn out onto wire racks to cool completely. With the tines of a fork, evenly poke holes over cake layers. Slowly pour coconut juice over each layer, dividing juice evenly. Cover each layer in clear plastic wrap; refrigerate until ready to use. Just before assembling cake, prepare Old-Fashioned 7-Minute Frosting. Evenly cut each cold cake layer horizontally in half with a sharp serrated knife. Place one half layer on a cake stand. In order, spread cake layer with icing, sprinkle with coconut, sprinkle with lemon curd, spread with icing, sprinkle with coconut, and top with next half cake layer. Repeat sequence until all cake layers are assembled. Finish by frosting top and sides of cake with remaining Old-Fashioned 7-Minute Frosting. Evenly press remaining coconut over top and sides of frosted cake.Cover cake loosely with waxed paper and refrigerate for about 12 hours.

Note: Refrigerate any leftover cake. Because of the moisture in the cake layers, the consistency of the lemon curd, and the amount of the icing, wooden picks may be used to hold cake layers together. Guests should be warned before eating cake if wooden picks are used.

–Louis Mahoney
Food Editor
The Richmond *News Leader*

Company for Sunday Dinner

Sunday, we suspect, was rather a dull affair. It was enlivened a little by company to dinner....

As no war since the Revolution had much troubled the comfort of Richmond, the transforming conditions of 1861-65 poured upon our people rains of fiery hail, which would have swamped a people less English, less stable, less resolutely brave.

Gone was thought of personal self-indulgence. The daughters of a Major had two roast potatoes for their dinner. I knew of one family, who, hearing that a battalion from the South had arrived at the Capitol Square, took all the food the family had on their storeroom shelves and sent it to the soldiers on the square. Old women, little boys, everybody, thought only of the boys in gray, who fought to give us political liberty. Like Carthage of old, the siege of Richmond called out a heroism hardly believable....

Louisa Coleman Blair
"'Little Red Brick Town' In Era of Hoopskirts
Was Friendly, Gossipy,"
Richmond Times-Dispatch, December 7,1941

Spiced Carrot Cake with Cream Cheese Icing

Yield: two-layer 9-inch cake

This cake is a favorite enjoyed by staff and visitors to the Virginia Museum of Fine Arts cafeteria.

2 1/2 cups sifted cake flour, divided
2 1/2 cups sugar
2 1/2 teaspoons cinnamon
2 1/2 teaspoons baking soda
1 teaspoon salt
1/2 cup dark seedless raisins, chopped (optional)
1 3/4 cups cooking oil
4 eggs
3 1/2 cups grated peeled carrots
Cream Cheese Icing
1 1/2 to 2 cups coarsely chopped pecans (optional)

Sift together 2 cups of flour, sugar, cinnamon, baking soda, and salt. In a small bowl, combine remaining 1/2 cup flour and raisins, mixing lightly to coat raisins with flour. In a large bowl, combine oil and eggs, beating well. Add dry ingredients, beating at medium speed of an electric mixer for 4 minutes. Stir in carrots and floured raisins, mixing well. Pour into two greased 9-inch round layer pans. Bake in a moderate oven (350 degrees F.) for 35 to 40 minutes, or until a cake tester inserted in center comes out clean. Cool in pans for 10 minutes, then turn out onto wire racks to finish cooling. Fill and frost layers with Cream Cheese Icing. Press chopped pecans over top and around sides of frosted cake, if desired.

Cream Cheese Icing

Yield: Fills and frosts top and sides of two-layer 9-inch cake

1 (8-ounce) package cream cheese, at room temperature
1/2 cup butter or margarine, at room temperature
1 (1-pound) box confectioners' sugar (about 4 1/2 cups), sifted and divided
1 teaspoon vanilla extract
Half-and half or milk as needed (optional)

In a medium bowl, beat cream cheese and butter until smooth. Gradually add confectioners' sugar and vanilla, beating well. Continue to add confectioners' sugar, beating well until mixture is of desired spreading consistency. Add a few drops half-and-half if mixture becomes too stiff.

–Renee King, pastry baker
Virginia Museum of Fine Arts

Coca Cola Cake

Yield: one 15 x 10-inch cake

2 cups sifted flour
2 cups sugar
1 cup cooking oil
1 cup cola
1/2 cup butter or margarine, at room temperature
3 tablespoons cocoa
2 eggs
1/2 cup buttermilk
1 teaspoon baking soda
1 teaspoon salt
1 cup miniature marshmallows
Special Icing
1 cup chopped English walnuts, or pecans, or slivered blanched almonds for garnish

In a large bowl, combine flour and sugar, mixing well. In a heavy saucepan, combine oil, cola, butter, and cocoa; bring to a boil over moderate heat, stirring constantly. Remove from heat and stir into flour mixture. Add eggs, buttermilk, baking soda, and salt, beating well with a wooden spoon. Fold in marshmallows. Pour into a greased 15 x 10 x 1 1/2-inch baking pan. Bake in a slow oven (325 degrees F.) for 40 to 50 minutes or until a cake tester inserted in center comes out clean. Remove and frost in pan with Special Icing while cake is hot. Garnish with walnuts, pecans, or almonds. Allow cake to cool before cutting into squares.

Special Icing

1/2 cup butter or margarine
6 tablespoons cola
3 tablespoons cocoa
1 (1-pound) box confectioners' sugar (about 4 1/2 cups), sifted

In a heavy saucepan, melt butter over low heat. Add cola and cocoa; bring to a boil over moderate heat. Remove from heat and gradually beat in confectioners' sugar until smooth and creamy.

–Marion Goodloe (Mrs. John Allan, Jr.)

The first English colonists to Virginia brought with them such items as dates, raisins, cured beef and pork, olive oil, and Spanish sherry.

Happy Cake

Yield: one 10-inch tube cake

1 cup butter or margarine,
   at room temperature
1 3/4 cups sugar
5 eggs
1 teaspoon vanilla extract
2 cups sifted cake flour
1 (8-ounce) jar Maraschino
   cherries, drained and
   quartered
1 (3 1/2-ounce) can flaked
   coconut
1 cup finely chopped pecans

In a large bowl, cream butter thoroughly. Gradually add sugar, beating until light and fluffy. Add eggs, one at a time, beating well after each addition, and vanilla. Stir in flour, cherries, coconut, and pecans, mixing well. Spoon into a lightly greased 10-inch tube pan. Bake in a *very* slow oven (250 degrees F.) for 1 1/2 hours or until a cake tester inserted in center comes out clean. Cool in pan for 10 minutes, then turn out onto a wire rack to finish cooling.

–Inger Rice (Mrs. Walter)

Nutty Oatmeal Cake

Yield: one 13 x 9-inch cake

"This cake is very moist and filling. I have my children crack the nuts on a cold rainy day with the promise of a special treat later."

2 cups sifted cake flour
2 teaspoons salt
2 teaspoons cinnamon
1 1/2 teaspoons baking soda
1 1/2 cups rolled oats
2 cups boiling water
1 1/2 cups sugar
3/4 cup light brown sugar,
   firmly packed
2/3 cup cooking oil
3 eggs
1 cup chopped filberts, or
   pecans, or English or

Sift together the first 4 ingredients. Place oats in a small bowl; add boiling water and allow mixture to stand for 10 minutes. Stir oatmeal into dry ingredients. In a bowl, combine sugars and oil, beating well. Add eggs, one at a time, beating well after each addition. Stir in oatmeal mixture, mixing well. Stir in nuts. Spoon batter into a greased 13 x 9 x 2-inch baking pan. Bake in a slow oven (325 degrees F.) for 50 to 60 minutes or until cake tester inserted in center of cake comes out clean. Cool cake in pan for 10 minutes, then turn out onto a heavy cardboard rectangle cut to fit cake. Immediately frost top and sides of cake.

black walnuts
Nutty Coconut Frosting

Place frosted cake on a baking sheet; broil, 6 to 8 inches from heat source, for 2 to 4 minutes or until frosting is lightly browned. To serve, cut cake into squares.

Nutty Coconut Frosting

1/4 cup butter or margarine, at room temperature
1/2 cup light brown sugar, firmly packed
1/4 cup evaporated milk
1/2 teaspoon vanilla extract
1/2 cup chopped filberts, or pecans, or English or black walnuts
1/2 cup flaked coconut

In a small bowl, cream butter thoroughly. Add brown sugar, beating until light and fluffy. Stir in evaporated milk and vanilla. Fold in nuts and coconut.

–Linda M. Bourgeois (Mrs. Bruce)

Sunshine Cake

Whites of 11 eggs, yolks of 6, 1 1/2 cupfuls of granulated sugar; measure after sifting once; 1 cupful of flour, also measured after sifting, 1 teaspoonful of cream of tartar, 1 teaspoonful of orange extract. Beat the whites of eggs to a stiff froth, and gradually beat in the sugar. Beat the yolks in a similar manner, and add to them the whites and sugar, and flavor, then stir in the flour. Mix quickly and well. Bake fifty minutes in a slow oven using a pan that has little legs at the top corners, so that when the pan is turned upside down on the table after baking a current of air will pass under and over it. If you have no pan of this kind set 3 tumblers under the pan and it will answer same purpose.
Mrs. G. E. Caskie
Receipts for Luncheon and Tea, *1898*

Pork Cake

Cut fine one pound of salt pork and pour over it two cups of boiling water. Add two cups of molasses, one cup of brown sugar. Sift together seven cups of flour, two tablespoons each of cinnamon and allspice, two teaspoons each of cloves, nutmeg and soda, and beat well into the batter. Add one pound of well-cleaned currants and one and one half pounds of raisins (which have soaked overnight in one cup of brandy if you choose). Bake in three large loaf-pans in a very slow oven about one hour.
(Old Recipe, Highland Springs, Virginia, date unknown)
The Williamsburg Art of Cookery, *1938*

1898 Sunshine Cake

Yield: one 10-inch tube cake

This cake is similar to one my grandmother made for me as a child. Grandma Keller was known as a wonderful cook and her mile-high Sunshine and Angel Food cakes were legendary. Of course, she didn't follow a recipe nor divulge her baking secrets!

6 jumbo egg yolks, at room temperature
1 teaspoon orange extract
11 jumbo egg whites, at room temperature
1 teaspoon cream of tartar
Pinch salt
1 1/2 cups sugar
1 cup sifted cake flour
Sifted confectioners' sugar or Citrus Butter Cream Icing
   (see index)

In a medium bowl, beat egg yolks until thick and lemon-colored. Beat in orange extract. In a large bowl, combine egg whites, cream of tartar, and salt, beating until egg whites are foamy. Gradually add sugar, beating until egg whites form stiff, but not dry, peaks. Carefully fold in beaten egg yolk mixture and then flour. Spoon into an ungreased 10-inch removable bottom tube pan. Bake in a moderate oven (350 degrees F.) for 50 minutes or until a cake tester inserted in center comes out clean. Turn cake in pan upside down on a wire rack and cool thoroughly. Remove cake from pan when cooled and sift confectioners' sugar over cake or frost top and sides with Citrus Butter Cream Icing.

Cookbooks of the late nineteenth century offer many varieties of the Robert E. Lee Cake: However, the following recipe donated at the early part of the twentieth century by a Miss Edmo Lee of Fredericksburg is reputed to be Mrs. Lee's original recipe, Robert E. Lee's favorite cake.

Mrs. Lee's Cake

Twelve eggs, their full weight in sugar, a half weight in flour. Bake it in pans the thickness of jelly cakes.
Take two pounds of nice "A" sugar, squeeze into it the juice of 5 oranges and three lemons together with pulp. Stir it in the sugar until perfectly smooth, then spread it over the cakes as you would do jelly—putting one above another till the whole of the sugar is used up.

Virginia Cookery, Past and Present, 1921

Updated Version of Mrs. Lee's Cake

Yield: three 9-inch layers

1 1/4 cups sifted cake flour
3/4 cup sugar, divided
1/2 teaspoon salt
6 jumbo eggs, divided
1 teaspoon vanilla (op-
tional)
1/2 teaspoon cream of tartar
About 3/4 cup sifted
confectioners' sugar
About 1/2 cup orange juice
2 tablespoons lemon juice
2 teaspoons grated orange
peel (optional)
1 to 2 teaspoons grated
lemon peel (optional)

Sift together the flour, 1/4 cup sugar, and salt. In a medium large bowl, beat egg yolks and vanilla until egg yolks are thick and light yellow in color. Gradually add dry ingredients, mixing well. In a large bowl, beat egg whites and cream of tartar until foamy. Gradually add remaining 1/2 cup sugar, beating until stiff, glossy, but not dry, peaks are formed. Carefully fold egg yolk mixture into beaten egg whites. Spoon batter into 3 ungreased 9-inch round layer pans. Gently cut through batter with a knife to break up any air pockets. Bake in a moderate oven (350 degrees F.) for 15 minutes or until cake tester inserted in center comes out clean. Place cake layers in pans upside down on wire racks until cake layers are cool. Remove from pans. In a small bowl, gradually add orange and lemon juices to confectioners' sugar, beating until smooth and desired spreading consistency. Stir in orange and lemon peels, if desired. Spread one-fourth of the mixture over a layer; place a second layer over the frosted layer. Repeat procedure until all cake layers are frosted and stacked. Allow frosting of top layer to drizzle down the sides of the cake.

Variation: Prepare cake as previously directed and fill layers with Lemon Curd Filling (see index) and frost top and sides of cake with Citrus Butter Cream Icing (see index).

Sponge Cake

Fifteen eggs; their weight in sugar; weight of eight in flour; two fresh lemons; beat eggs separately till a stiff froth; add sugar, then flour, juice and grated rind of lemons. Bake in moulds in quick oven.

Mrs. William P. Braxton
The Kitchen Queen, *1893*

Spice Cake

Take one cup of brown sugar and beat it well with one fourth pound of butter. Add well beaten yolks of two eggs. Sift together one and one fourth cups of flour, one half teaspoon each of cloves, cinnamon, nutmeg and baking powder, add this to your mixture alternately with one half cup of sour milk in which you have mixed one half teaspoon of soda. Pour your batter in a small well-greased square pan, and spread it with a meringue made by beating the two egg whites with one cup of sifted brown sugar. Sprinkle with one third cup of chopped English wlanuts. Bake in moderate oven about thirty-five minutes. This may be served warm.

(Old Recipe, Richmond, Virginia, date unknown)
The Williamsburg Art of Cookery, *1938*

Buttermilk Caramel Icing

Yield: fills and frosts two 9-inch round layers
or a 9-inch tube cake

2 cups sugar
1 cup buttermilk
1/2 cup butter or margarine,
   at room temperature
1/2 teaspoon baking soda
1 teaspoon vanilla extract

In a large heavy saucepan, combine the first 4 ingredients. Stir over moderate heat until sugar is dissolved and butter melted. Bring mixture to a boil; reduce heat, cover, and cook for 3 minutes. Uncover, insert candy thermometer into mixture, increase heat to moderate and boil mixture rapidly, stirring constantly, until candy thermometer registers 232 degrees F. Remove from heat, allowing candy thermometer to remain in hot caramel mixture; allow icing to cool to luke warm (110 degrees F.). Remove thermometer; add vanilla, beating until icing becomes like fudge in consistency. Immediately frost and fill cake layers or frost the top and sides of a tube cake.

–Frances Fox (Mrs. Paul)

Caramel Glaze

Yield: glaze for 1 10-inch tube cake

1/2 cup butter or margarine,
   at room temperature
1 cup light or dark brown
   sugar, firmly packed
1 tablespoon milk
1 teaspoon vanilla extract

In a medium heavy saucepan, melt butter over low heat. Stir in brown sugar, blending well. Add milk or water. Cook, stirring constantly, over moderate heat until bubbly hot. Remove from heat and stir in vanilla.

–Kathryn Marshall Arnold

Nutty Chocolate Frosting

Yield: enough to frost one 15 x 10 x 1-inch cake

1/2 cup butter or margarine,
   at room temperature
1/4 cup sifted cocoa
6 tablespoons milk
1 (1 pound) box confectioners' sugar, sifted
1 teaspoon vanilla extract
1/2 cup chopped pecans, or
   English or black walnuts,
   or cashew or filbert nuts

In a medium heavy saucepan, combine the butter, cocoa, and milk; bring to a boil over moderate heat. Remove mixture from heat. Gradually beat in confectioners' sugar until mixture is the desired spreading consistency. Beat in vanilla. Stir in nuts. Immediately frost cake before frosting "sets".

–Rachel Koppenhaver (Mrs. Ronald)

Chocolate Icing

One cake chocolate, add two cups sugar, one cup milk, Cook about twenty-five minutes.

F. F. V. Receipt Book, 1894

Citrus Butter Cream Icing

Yield: fills and frosts a two-layer 9-inch cake

1/4 cup orange juice
1 tablespoon grated orange
   peel
2 teaspoons lemon juice
1/2 teaspoon grated lemon
   peel
3 tablespoons butter or
   margarine, at room
   temperature
1 egg yolk
About 3 cups confectioners'
   sugar, sifted

In a small bowl, combine orange and lemon juices, add orange and lemon peels. Allow to stand at room temperature for 10 minutes. In a medium bowl, cream butter until smooth; add egg yolk, beating well. Gradually beat in half of the confectioners' sugar. Add half of the juice and peel. Gradually add remaining confectioners' sugar and juice and peel, beating until mixture is of spreading consistency.

–Dorothy Parker (Mrs. Walter)

Fare of Our Ancestors
The Evolution of the Fork

"In the Tenth century colloquy of Archbishop Alfric," says Mr.
Carew Hazlett, "the boy is made to say that he is too young to
eat meat, but subsists on cabbages, eggs, fish, cheese, butter
and beans," and the drink, which was rarely ale, was usually
water. The nursery rhyme tells us of King Alfred's "bag pudding of barley meal, with raisins and meat." The frying pan,
Mr. Hazlett says, preceded the grill, "just as the fork lagged
behind the spoon, from which it is a seeming evolution." For
centuries in England there was a prejudice against the fork,
which displaced the fingers, and forks at first were the privilege
only of kings. When Coryat employed one after his visit to
Italy, where the instrument originated in the Eleventh century,
he was nicknamed Furcifer. It took six hundred years, or until
the Seventeenth century, to establish it in England, and even
then it did not attain general use. A country boor "still eats his
bacon or his herring with his fingers, just as Charles XII of
Sweden buttered his bread with his royal thumb."

It is said that the origin of washing the hands before eating
arose from the fact that food at first was eaten wholly—all
around the table dipping into one dish—with the hands. Now,
with the finger bowl, an ablution ends as well as precedes the
meal. Carving knives, like the fork, were at first a luxury, and
as late as the close of the Fifteenth century were confined to
kings' tables and those of the nobility.

Joel Benton in New York Herald
Old Richmond Newspaper, date unknown

Ivory Satin Frosting

Yield: Fills and frosts a three-layer 9-inch cake

1 cup light brown sugar, firmly packed
1/2 cup water
1/3 cup dark corn syrup
1/8 teaspoon cream of tartar

Combine first 4 ingredients in a heavy 3-quart saucepan. Bring syrup to 230 to 232 degrees F. on a candy thermometer (syrup spins a thread 2 inches long when dropped from spoon or fork). Beat egg whites until they form stiff peaks. Pour

3 egg whites, at room
  temperature
1 teaspoon vanilla extract

syrup slowly in a fine stream into beaten egg whites, beating constantly at medium speed of an electric mixer. Add vanilla and beat at high speed until mixture forms stiff peaks.

Variations:

White Satin Frosting: Substitute 1 cup granulated sugar, and use light corn syrup.

Chocolate Swirl Frosting: Melt 2 squares (ounces) unsweetened chocolate. Cool slightly and fold carefully into White Satin Frosting or Old-Fashioned 7-Minute Frosting (see index) just until frosting is streaked with chocolate swirls. Be careful not to overbeat.

Coconut Marshmallow Frosting: Fold 3/4 cup miniature marshmallow halves and 1/2 cup flaked or shredded coconut into White Satin Frosting or Old-Fashioned 7-Minute Frosting(see index).

Lord Baltimore Cake Frosting: Prepare White Satin Frosting or Old-Fashioned 7-Minute Frosting (see index) and substitute1/2 teaspoon each orange and lemon extract for vanilla. Fold in 1/4 cup each chopped candied red cherries, blanched almonds, pecans,and macaroon crumbs (optional). Fills and frosts top and sides of two-layer 9 inch cake.

Mint Frosting: Tint White Satin Frosting or Old-Fashioned 7-minute Frosting (see index) a pale green with green food coloring (optional). Substitute 1/2 teaspoon mint extract for 1/2 teaspoon vanilla and fold in 1/2 to 3/4 cup crushed after-dinner mints.

Peppermint-Stick Frosting: Prepare White Satin Frosting or Old-Fashioned 7-Minute Frosting (see index) and substitute1/2 teaspoon peppermint extract for vanilla. Tint frosting a delicate pink with red food coloring (optional) and fold in 1/3 cup crushed peppermint-stick candy. Garnish cake with additional crushed candy or chocolate curls.

Chocolate Frosting

Yield: fills and frosts a three-layer 9-inch cake

1/2 cup butter or margarine,
  at room temperature
4 cups sifted confectioners'
  sugar
3 squares (ounces) un-
  sweetened chocolate,
  melted
2 egg yolks
2 teaspoons vanilla extract
1/3 cup half-and-half or
  light cream

Cream butter and 1/2 cup sugar. Add chocolate, egg yolks, and vanilla; beat thoroughly. Stir in remaining sugar and half-and-half or cream as needed until smooth and of desired spreading consistency.

575

Lemon Cream Frosting

Yield: fills and frosts a two-layer 9-inch cake

1/2 cup butter or margarine, at room temperature
1 (1-pound) box confection-ers' sugar (about 4 1/2 cups), sifted and divided
1 egg yolk
1/4 teaspoon salt
2 teaspoons grated lemon peel
2 tablespoons lemon juice

Combine butter, 1 cup sugar, egg yolk, salt, and grated lemon peel. Add remaining sugar and 1 tablespoon lemon juice, beating until smooth. Add remaining lemon juice as needed, tea-spoonful at a time, until smooth and of desired spreading consistency.

Lemon Curd Filling

Yield: about 2 cups

1/3 cup butter or margarine, melted
1 cup sugar
1/3 cup lemon juice
1/4 cup grated lemon peel
1/4 teaspoon salt
3 eggs, beaten

Melt butter in a small heavy saucepan. Add sugar gradually, stirring constantly until sugar dissolves. Stir in lemon juice, lemon peel, and salt. Stir a small amount of hot mixture into eggs. Stir egg mixture into hot mixture. Cook over low heat until mixture coats a silver spoon, stirring constantly. Cool, stirring occasionally.

Boiled Icing

3 cupfuls of sugar
3 eggs (whites only)
Water, as necessary

Dissolve the sugar by boiling it in the water, and cook until it threads, When the whites of the eggs have been beaten to a stiff froth pour the hot syrup over them; beating continuously. Flavor with either of Sauer's flavoring extracts. When the icing begins to thicken, spread.

C. F. Sauer Company
Sauer Spices, circa 1920's

576

Old Fashioned 7-Minute Frosting

Yield: fills and frosts top and sides of one three-layer 9-inch cake

1 1/2 cups sugar
1/4 teaspoon baking powder
Pinch of salt
2 egg whites
6 tablespoons water
1 teaspoon vanilla extract

Combine the first 3 ingredients together in the top of a double boiler, mixing well. Add egg whites and water. Place over boiling water and beat rapidly with an electric mixer for 5 to 7 minutes, or until mixture forms stiff peaks. Remove from heat and beat in vanilla.

–Dorothy Parker (Mrs. Walter)

Vanilla Frosting

Yield: fills and frosts one 10-inch tube cake

Vanilla Frosting
1/2 cup butter or margarine, at room temperature
1 egg white
4 1/2 cups sifted confectioners' sugar
1/2 teaspoon cream of tartar
1 teaspoon vanilla extract
2 to 4 tablespoons water

In a bowl, cream butter until smooth. Add egg white, confectioners' sugar, and cream of tartar, beating at high speed of an electric mixer for 5 minutes. While beating, gradually blend in vanilla and enough water until smooth and of desired spreading consistency.

–Susie Keyser (Mrs. Hugh)

In the South, small square houses were built over cool springs to store food. Rooms or holes constructed underground served as ice houses. Ice was shipped from the North, packed in straw or sawdust, then wrapped in flannel and held in place between stone slabs.

Mimi's White Chocolate Fudge Frosting

Yield: fills and frosts a two-layer 9-inch or one 13 x 9-inch cake

2 squares (ounces) white chocolate
1/2 cup butter or margarine, at room temperature
5 tablespoons half-and-half or milk
1/8 teaspoon salt
1 (1-pound) box confectioners' sugar (about 4 1/2 cups), sifted
1 teaspoon vanilla extract
1/2 cup chopped pecans or English walnuts (optional)

In a large heavy saucepan, combine the first 4 ingredients. Stir over low heat until butter and chocolate are melted and bubbles begin to form around the edge of the pan. Continue to stir over heat for 30 seconds. Remove from heat; gradually add confectioners' sugar, beating until mixture is smooth and begins to lose its gloss. Beat in vanilla. Stir in nuts, if desired. Immediately spread hot frosting quickly over a hot 13 x 9-inch cake or fill and frost a hot 9-inch round two-layer cake.

–Marion Peeschla (Mrs. Ralf)

Christmas In Virginia Hundred Years Ago

...But it was the Christmas dinner that formed the chief event of the day — a gargantuan, amazing dinner that had kept the servants busy for a week and had puzzled the mind of the lady of the house. Some of the menus of those good old days have come down to us, and their content is enough to make one's mouth water even now. As many of the Richmond people had estates in the country, they received farm products and game in this way; those less fortunate purchased them from the hunters and the fishermen who came to town and peddled their wares. There was, of course, a turkey, preferably a wild one, shot in the woods the week before and kept hanging until the feast. Then there was a roast pig, a ham, a great baked fish, a saddle of venison, a dish of birds — one is positively staggered at the store of meat. Of cakes and pies, there was abundance, and after the dishes were removed — the wine ...

Old Richmond Newspaper, date unknown
Courtesy Valentine Museum

Pies

Pie making flourished in America during the nineteenth century when the use of more efficient sugar-processing machinery and larger plantations in Louisiana reduced sugar prices. Lard, used as shortening, made very flaky pie crusts. Vents cut in the top crust, allowing steam to escape, helped to prevent the crust from becoming soggy.

Cheddary Apple Pie

Yield: One 9-inch deep dish pie

Pastry for Double-Crust Pie (deep dish 9-inch) (see index)
1 1/4 cups sugar
3 tablespoons flour
1/2 to 1 teaspoon cinnamon
1/4 teaspoon nutmeg
1/4 teaspoon salt
6 cups peeled, cored, seeded and thinly sliced tart cooking apples (about 2 pounds) (see note)
2 tablespoons lemon juice
1 cup shredded sharp Cheddar cheese, or processed cheese food divided
2 tablespoons butter or margarine, at room temperature
Milk or half-and-half (optional)
Additional sugar (optional)

Prepare crust and line a deep dish pie plate with pastry. Combine sugar, flour, spices, and salt, mixing well. Prepare apples, place in a large bowl, and sprinkle with lemon juice. Add flour mixture to apples, mixing lightly to coat fruit. Arrange one half of the apple slices in prepared pie plate. Sprinkle one half of the cheese evenly over apples in pastry. Top first layer with remaining apple-flour mixture. Sprinkle evenly with remaining cheese. Dot with butter. Top with crust, fluting edges as directed for a double-crust pie. Brush top crust lightly with milk or half-and-half and sprinkle lightly with sugar. Bake in a hot oven (400 degrees F.) for 60 minutes, or until apples are tender. Cool on a wire rack. Serve warm or at room temperature.

Note: Use McIntosh, Winesap, Granny Smith, or other tart variety of apples.

Miller & Rhoads Chocolate Silk Pie

Yield: 8 servings/one 8 or 9-inch pie

Making its debut in the 1950's, Miller & Rhoads Chocolate Silk Pie originated with Charlie Watson, baker for the Tea Room for thirty-five years.

Crust

1/2 cup butter or margarine, at room temperature
1/2 cup sugar
About 2 cups fine graham cracker crumbs

Filling

1/2 cup unsalted butter or margarine, at room temperature
3/4 cup confectioner's sugar
1 square (ounce) unsweetened chocolate, melted and cooled
1 teaspoon vanilla extract
Pince of salt
3 eggs
2 cups sweetened whipped cream for garnish
Shaved semi-sweet chocolate for garnish

To prepare crust, cream 1/2 cup butter thoroughly. Gradually add sugar, beating until light and fluffy. Add *just* enough graham cracker crumbs to form a slightly crumbly paste. Evenly press crumb mixture into a chilled 8 or 9-inch pie plate. Bake in a moderate over (350 degrees F.) for 5 minutes. Cool to room temperature.

To prepare filling, cream 1/2 cup unsalted butter thoroughly. Gradually add confectioners' sugar, beating until light and fluffy. Stir in unsweetened chocolate, vanill, and salt. Add eggs separately, beating for 5 minutes, *no less*, after each addition. Chill in refrigerator for 24 hours. Just before serving, garnish pie with sweetened whipped cream and top with shaved semi-sweet chocolate.

-Miller & Rhoads Tea Room

Mary Randolph has been suggested to have written "the most influential American cookbook of the nineteenth century." A member of the prominent Randolph family of Virginia, Mary resided in Richmond for a time during the early part of the century. Due to financial reversals, she opened a boarding house, where her food became famous. Her Virginia Housewife or Methodical Cook, first published in 1824, is still referred to by Southern cooks of today.

Randolph combined a knowledge of English cooking with native Indian food influences. She reflected her know-how by combining the use of regional nuts and vegetables with overall cooking techniques and social graces. Further, she introduced into her recipes the use of African food ingredients, knowledge gained from servants.

One-crust pies, often with a custard base, are favored in the South, while two-crust pies are more popular in other areas of the U.S.A.

A private "Starvation Club" in Richmond Society, 1863

Now was instituted the "Starvation Club," of which, as one of the original founders, I can speak with authority. It was agreed between a number of young women that a place for our solider visitors to meet with us for dancing and chat, once a week, would be a desirable variation upon evening calls in private homes. The hostesses who successively offered their drawing-rooms were among the leaders in society. It was also decided that we should permit no one to infringe the rule of suppressing all refreshment, save the amber-hued water from the classic James. We began by having piano music for the dances, but the male members of the club made up between them a subscription providing a small but good orchestra. Before our first meeting, a committee of girls waited on General Lee to ask his sanction, with this result to the spokeswoman, who had ended with: "If you say no, general, we won't dance a single step!" "Why, of course, my dear child. My boys need to be heartened up when they get their furloughs. Go on, look your prettiest, and be just as nice to them as ever you can be!

We had constant demands to admit new members, and all foreigners and general officers who visited Richmond were presented to our club, as a means of viewing the best society of the South.

Mrs. Burton Harrison (Constance Cary),
Recollections, Grave and Gay, 1916

Grandma's Creamy Fruit Pie

Yield: one 9-inch deep dish pie

Unbaked Deep Dish Pie Shell (9-inch) or Unbaked Deep Dish Double-Crust Pie Shell (9-inch) (see index)
6 cups peeled, cored, seeded, thinly sliced tart apples (see note)
2 tablespoons lemon juice
1 to 1 1/4 cups light brown or granulated sugar, firmly packed
3/4 cup heavy cream
3 tablespoons flour
1/4 to 3/4 teaspoon cinnamon
1/4 teaspoon nutmeg
1/4 teaspoon salt
Milk (optional)
Additional granulated sugar (optional)
Crumb Topping (optional)
Wedges of sharp Cheddar or gouda cheese (optional)
Whipped cream or vanilla ice cream (optional)

Prepare crust and line a deep dish 9-inch pie plate with pastry. Prepare apples and sprinkle with lemon juice. Arrange one-half of the apple slices in prepared pie plate. In a chilled medium bowl, combine brown sugar, heavy cream, flour, cinnamon, nutmeg, and salt; beat with chilled beaters until mixture is *very* thick. Spoon one-half of cream mixture over apples in pie plate. Arrange remaining apple slices over first apple layer. Spoon remaining cream mixture over top layer of apples. Arrange top pastry crust over pie, fluting edges as directed for double-crust or lattice pies. Brush top lightly with milk and sprinkle with small amount of sugar. With a sharp knife, cut 5 small slashes in the top crust to allow steam to escape. Bake in a hot oven (400 degrees F.) for 60 minutes until apples are tender. If top crust begins to brown too much, cover loosely with a sheet of aluminum foil, shiny side turned in. Cool pie to lukewarm on a wire rack. Serve warm or cold, plain, or with wedges of sharp Cheddar or gouda cheese, whipped cream, or vanilla ice cream.

Note: If a deep dish (9 1/2- or 10-inch) pie shell is used, prepare one and one-half recipes of filling.

Note: Use McIntosh, Winesap, Granny Smith, or other tart variety of apples.

Variations: For Crumb Topped Creamy Apple Pie, omit top pastry crust. Bake pie in a *very* hot oven (450 degrees F.) for 10 minutes. Reduce oven temperature to moderate (350 degrees F.) and bake for 30 minutes. Evenly sprinkle Crumb Topping over the pie filling. Continue baking for an additional 15 to 20 minutes or until topping is done and pastry is lightly browned. Serve warm or at room temperature.

Thinly sliced peeled peaches or nectarines may be substituted for the apples. Omit cinnamon; increase the nutmeg to 1/2 to 1 teaspoon and add 1/2 to 1 teaspoon almond extract to cream mixture.

Peach Custard Pie

Yield: one 9-inch pie

Unbaked Pie Shell (9-inch) (see index)
1 1/2 to 2 cups sliced peeled ripe peaches (about 4 medium) or 1 (16-ounce) can sliced peaches, drained
4 eggs
1/2 cup light brown sugar, firmly packed (see note)
1/4 cup sugar
2 teaspoons vanilla extract
1/8 teaspoon salt
1 1/2 cups milk
Cinnamon and/or nutmeg to taste (optional)

Arrange well-drained peaches in the unbaked prepared pie shell. In a medium bowl, beat eggs thoroughly. Gradually add brown sugar, sugar, vanilla extract, and salt, beating well. Stir in milk; pour mixture over peaches in crust.Sprinkle filling lightly with cinnamon and/or nutmeg, if desired. Bake in a hot oven (400 degrees F.) for 30 minutes; reduce heat to moderate (350 degrees F.) and continue baking for an additional 15 minutes or until filling is set and a silver knife inserted into the center of the pie comes out clean. Transfer pie to a wire rack to cool thoroughly.

Note: 3/4 cup firmly packed light brown or granulated sugar may be used in place of the 1/2 cup light brown and 1/4 cup granulated sugar.

Variation: Ripe nectarines or plums may be used in place of peaches.

—Ann Tyler (Mrs. Hal)

Caramel Pudding, or Pie

Cream together 1 cup of butter and 1 cup of sugar, add 5 eggs, whites and yolks beaten separately, and 1 cup of damson preserves (seeds removed). Cream butter and sugar, add beaten yolks, then stiffened whites. Season with vanilla. Bake on pie-crust.

Mrs. Dibrell
Virginia Recipes, *1890*

Currant Pie

1 1/2 Pounds Currants,, 1 Cupful Franklin Sugar,, 3 Table-spoonsful Butter,, 3 Table-spoonsful Apple Jelly,, Cinnamon., Boil currants with enough water to cover well, letting boil till water has boiled off; fill pie tins with the currants, adding the sugar, butter, and apple jelly. Sprinkle with cinnamon and bake with two crusts.

Old Virginia Cooking, *circa 1909*

Glazed Fresh Strawberry Pie

Yield: one 9-inch pie

The month of May and early June is strawberry season in the Old Dominion for this homegrown delicacy. There is nothing better tasting than a fresh strawberry pie prepared with sweet Virginia berries.

5 cups ripe firm strawberries, washed, hulled, and drained
1 cup sugar
3 tablespoons cornstarch
Pinch of salt
3/4 cup water
3 tablespoons light corn syrup
Red food coloring as desired (optional)
Baked Pie Shell (9-inch) or Vanilla Cookie Crust (see index)
1 1/2 cups sweetened flavored whipped cream
Finely chopped pistachio nuts or mint sprigs for garnish (optional)

Crush 1 cup of the smaller, less perfect berries and reserve.In a medium heavy saucepan, combine sugar, cornstarch, and salt; stir in water, corn syrup, and crushed berries.Cook over low heat, stirring constantly, until thickened and bubbly hot. Tint a strawberry color with a few drops of food coloring, if desired. Spread a small amount of sauce over the bottom of prepared crust. Arrange strawberries in the pie shell and spoon remaining sauce over berries. Cool thoroughly. To serve, garnish with a border of whipped cream and pistachio nuts or a few mint sprigs.

History, art, and landscape architecture are combined in the magnificent setting of Hollywood Cemetery, perched on the bluffs along the James River in Richmond. No better view of the skyline of Richmond, from ground level at the picturesque falls of the James, can be seen in the city. Headstones read as a who's who of the Confederacy.

By the late 1840's, the city-owned cemetery, Shockoe, was approaching its capacity and the older graveyard located on the grounds of St. John's Church had long been full. Noted Philadelphia architect, John Notman, was selected to design a natural cemetery located on forty-two acres of land puchased from the Harnie family, adjacent to the James River. Notman's original plan of retaining the area's natural beauty accompanied by winding scenic roads and planted with ornamental shrubs and flowering trees still prevails almost one hundred and fifty years later. One of the finest collections of mortuary art, which flourished for a century from about 1830 to 1930, is found here. After serious opposition from some towns people was over come, Hollywood Cemetery was formally dedicated in June 1849.

Named for the many holly trees located on the premises, James Monroe, John Tyler, and Confederacy President Jefferson Davis were buried here. More than eighteen thousand Confederate and Union soldiers are laid to rest in this lonely setting.

Much of Richmond's nineteenth century German population, who had come to work in the flour mills located in the area during the 1840's and 50's, residing in the nearby Jackson Ward district, chose Hollywood as their final resting place. Scores of other 19th and 20th century Richmond citizens are interrned at Hollywood Cemetery as well.

Cranberry Chiffon Pie

Yield: one 9-inch pie

1 envelope (tablespoon) unflavored gelatin
1/2 cup cold water
2 cups (about 8 ounces) cranberries
3 egg whites, divided
1 cup plus 1 tablespoon sugar, divided
1 tablespoon lemon juice
1/4 teaspoon salt
Baked Pie Shell (9-inch) (see index) or Graham-Cracker Crumb Crust (see index)
1 cup heavy cream, chilled
Additional cranberries for garnish
Additional sugar for coating berries

In a small bowl, soften gelatin in cold water. In a medium heavy saucepan, combine cranberries and softened gelatin. Bring to boiling over moderate heat; reduce temperature and simmer for 5 minutes, stirring frequently. Cool. In a large bowl, combine 2 egg whites, 1 cup sugar, lemon juice, and salt. Stir in cooled cranberry mixture. Beat at high speed of an electric mixer until glossy firm, but not dry, peaks are formed. Spoon mixture into a baked pie shell or graham-cracker crust, piling high. Chill in refrigerator for 4 to 5 hours. In a deep small bowl, beat cream with chilled beaters until soft peaks are formed. Beat in 1 tablespoon sugar. Spoon flavored whipped cream around the edge of the cranberry filling. Chill pie until ready to serve. Dip additional cranberries in lightly beaten egg white and then roll in additional sugar on waxed paper, coating cranberries well. Allow sugar coated cranberries to dry. Garnish whipped cream edge of pie with glace cranberries just before serving.

–Linda M. Bourgeois (Mrs. Bruce)

White Russian Pie

Yield: one 9-inch pie

Crust
1 (10-ounce) package shortbread cookies
2 tablespoons sugar
1/2 cup butter or margarine
1 tablespoon coffee liqueur

With a rolling pin, crush cookies into fine crumbs between sheets of waxed paper. In a small bowl, combine crumbs and 2 tablespoons sugar. In a small heavy saucepan, melt butter over low heat *just* until butter begins to brown; remove from heat and add 1 tablespoon coffee liqueur. Add butter mixture to crumbs, mixing well. Reserve 1/2 cup crumbs. Press remaining crumbs over the bottom and up the sides of a buttered 9-inch pie

Filling
1 envelope (tablespoon)
  unflavored gelatin
1/4 cup cold water
3 large eggs, separated
7 tablespoons sugar,
  divided
1/4 cup coffee liqueur
3 tablespoons vodka
1/2 cup heavy cream, chilled

Topping
1 cup heavy cream, chilled
3 tablespoons coffee liqueur
Coarsely grated sweet white
  or semi-sweet baking
  chocolate

plate. Chill crust thoroughly in the refrigerator.

To prepare filling, sprinkle gelatin evenly over cold water in the top of a double boiler; allow mixture to stand for 5 minutes to soften. Place pan over very hot water to dissolve gelatin completely. In a medium bowl, beat egg yolks, gradually adding 4 tablespoons sugar until thick and light yellow in color. Gradually add dissolved gelatin, beating well. Stir in 1/4 cup coffee liqueur and vodka. In a medium bowl, beat egg whites, gradually adding 3 tablespoons sugar, until stiff, but not dry, peaks are formed. Carefully fold beaten whites into gelatin mixture. In a chilled deep small bowl, beat 1/2 cup cream with chilled beaters until soft peaks are formed. Fold into gelatin mixture. Chill filling for several minutes until it begins to mound on a spoon when tested. Turn half of the mixture into the chilled crust. Evenly sprinkle reserved crumbs over filling in crust. Spoon remaining filling over crumb layer. Chill pie for 8 to 12 hours. Just before serving, prepare topping.

In a chilled deep small bowl, beat remaining 1 cup cream with chilled beaters until soft peaks are formed. Beat in remaining 3 tablespoons coffee liqueur, 1 tablespoon at a time, and continue beating until stiff peaks are formed. Evenly spread mixture over pie. Garnish the top of the pie with grated sweet white or semi-sweet dark chocolate, if desired.

–John Tyler

Rhubarb Pie

2 Pints Rhubarb,, 1 1/4 Pints Franklin Sugar,, 1 Lemon (Juice), 1 Cupful Water., Peel and chop the rhubarb, add the sugar and lemon juice, also the water. Stew until tender, fill the bottom crust, cover and bake. Serve cold with whipped cream.

Old Virginia Cooking, *circa 1909*

Chocolate Chess Pie with Cinnamon

Yield: two 9-inch pies

A form of custard pie or pye was served in England since before Queen Elizabeth I. Of course, the recipes were brought with the colonists and adapted to cooking in Colonial America. One story suggests a nineteenth century Southern cook when asked what was her delicious pastry, replied, "Why tha's jest pie!". Another story suggests the name came from the pies made with large quantities of sugar which could be stored in a pie chest. Still another legend implies the name came from the English lemon curd ... or cheese. Somehow the name evolved into chess pie. This recipe is wonderfully and sinfully rich.

5 squares (ounces) un-sweetened chocolate
1 1/4 cups butter or margarine, at room temperature
2 1/4 cups sugar
1 teaspoon cinnamon
5 large eggs
3 tablespoons milk
1 tablespoon vanilla extract
2 Unbaked Pie Shells (9-inch) (see index)
Kahlua flavored whipped cream for garnish

In the top of a double boiler, melt chocolate and butter over hot water. While chocolate is melting, sift together sugar and cinnamon; stir into melted chocolate mixture. With a wire whisk or wooden spoon, blend in eggs, milk, and vanilla, beating lightly. Pour filling into two unbaked pie shells. Bake in a moderate oven (350 degrees F.) for 20 to 25 minutes or until a silver knife inserted in the center of the pies comes out clean (see note). Cool. Garnish with flavored whipped cream, if desired.

Note: Center of pie will rise while baking and fall after being removed from oven. Pies baked for 20 to 25 minutes will have a filling which is fudge-like in consistency while pies baked 25 to 30 minutes will have a filling more cake-like in consistency. These pies may be baked in tart shells for 15 to 20 minutes or until filling is done.

–Linda Leftwich (Mrs. Leonard Largen)
Richmond Culinary Guild

The social disposition of Mr. Darmsdadt brought him into society, even the best. His own entertainments were given daily.

Samuel Mordecai
Richmond in By-Gone Days, 1856
Reprint Edition, 1975

Lemon Chess Pie

Yield: two 9-inch pies

1/2 cup butter or margarine, at room temperature
3 cups sugar
1/4 cup flour
6 eggs
6 tablespoons lemon juice
2 Unbaked Pie Shells (9-inch) (see index)
1 to 2 teaspoons nutmeg

In a bowl, cream butter until smooth. Combine sugar and flour and gradually add to butter, beating until light and fluffy. Add eggs, one at a time, beating well after each addition. Stir in lemon juice. Sprinkle unbaked pie shells evenly with nutmeg; pour filling into shells. Bake in a moderate oven (350 degrees F.) for 30 minutes or until a silver knife inserted in center comes out clean.
—Winifred M. Peebles (Mrs. William B.)

Mecklenburg County Lemon Chess Pie

Yield: one 9-inch pie

1/2 cup butter or margarine, at room temperature
1 3/4 cups sugar
2 tablespoons flour
4 eggs, well-beaten
6 tablespoons lemon juice
1 tablespoon grated lemon peel
Unbaked Pie Shell (9-inch) (see index)

In a medium bowl, cream butter thoroughly. Gradually add sugar and flour, beating well. Add eggs, lemon juice, and peel, mixing well. Pour mixture into prepared pie shell. Bake in a moderate oven (350 degrees F.) for 40 minutes or until metal tester inserted in the center of the pie comes out clean.

—Jane Rowe (Mrs. A. Prescott)

Nutty Chocolate Chess Pie

Yield: one 9-inch pie

1 1/4 cups sugar
1/4 cup sifted cocoa
2 eggs
1 (5 1/3-ounce) can evaporated milk
1/4 cup butter or margarine, melted
1/2 cup chopped English walnuts or pecans (optional)
Unbaked Pie Shell (9-inch) (see index)

In a bowl, combine sugar and cocoa, mixing well. Add eggs, evaporated milk, and butter, beating lightly and until well-mixed. Stir in nuts, if desired. Pour into an unbaked pie shell. Bake in a slow oven (325 degrees F.) for 45 minutes or until a silver knife inserted in center comes out clean. Cool on a wire rack. Serve warm or at room temperature.

—Virginia Harding (Mrs. William)

Old Southern Chess Pie

Yield: two 9-inch pies or
40 (2 1/2-inch) tartlettes

"This recipe was given to me by a Florida friend who said it was truly an old Southern recipe for Chess Pie."

1 cup butter or margarine, at room temperature
2 cups sugar
1 tablespoon plus 1/2 teaspoon flour
4 eggs, slightly beaten
1/2 cup light cream or half-and-half
1 tablespoon vanilla extract
2 Unbaked Pie Shells (9-inch) (see index)

In a bowl, cream butter until smooth. Gradually add sugar, beating well. Stir in flour. Add eggs, cream, and vanilla, blending well. Pour into two 9-inch unbaked pie shells or 40 (2 1/2-inch) unbaked tartlette shells. Bake in a moderate oven (350 degrees F.) for 30 minutes for 9-inch pies or 12 minutes for tartlettes or until a silver knife inserted in center comes out clean. Cool on wire racks.

–Jo Almond (Mrs. J. Lindsey, Jr.)
First Lady of Virginia, 1958 to 1962

Black Forest Cherry Pie

Yield: one 10-inch deep dish pie

This sinful delicious pie is a variation of the famous cake.

Chocolate Curls
6 squares (ounces) semi-sweet chocolate
Chocolate Cookie Crust
1 3/4 cups fine chocolate wafer crumbs
3 tablespoons sugar
1/3 cup butter or margarine, melted
Chocolate Filling
8 squares (ounces) semi-sweet chocolate
2 envelopes (tablespoons) unflavored gelatin
1/4 cup cold water
1/3 cup milk, lukewarm
4 tablespoons sugar
1 (8-ounce) package cream

To prepare chocolate curls, melt 6 ounces semi-sweet chocolate and paraffin in the top of a double boiler over hot water. Pour into a small lightly greased square container; allow to cool at room temperature. Chocolate should be almost firm, but not hard. Turn out of container. Prepare chocolate curls with a vegetable peeler. Using steady strokes, slice across edge of chocolate bar. Arrange chocolate curls on a tray and refrigerate until needed.

To prepare cookie crust, combine the crumbs and sugar in a bowl. Add butter and blend thoroughly. Pack crumbs evenly over bottom and up sides of a deep dish 9 1/2 or 10-inch pie plate, making a standing rim. Bake in a moderate oven (350 degrees F.) for 7 minutes. Cool and then chill while preparing fillings.

590

cheese, at room temperature
1 3/4 cups heavy cream, whipped (see note)

Cherry Filling
1 (16 1/2- to 17-ounce) can pitted dark sweet cherries
2 1/2 tablespoons cornstarch
2 tablespoons sugar
2 to 3 tablespoons Kirsch liqueur

Topping
1 1/2 cups heavy cream
1/3 cup sifted confectioners' sugar
Use fresh sweet dark or Maraschino cherries for garnish.

To prepare chocolate filling, in the top of a double boiler, melt 8 ounces semi-sweet chocolate over hot water. Cool. Soften gelatin n cold water; gradually add warm milk, stirring until dissolved. In a bowl, beat sugar into cream cheese until smooth. Add cooled chocolate mixture, then gelatin mixture, beating well. Fold in whipped cream, beating at low speed of an electric mixer.

To prepare cherry filling, drain cherries and reserve syrup. Combine cornstarch and sugar in a heavy saucepan. Gradually blend in syrup. Cook, stirring constantly, over moderate heat until sauce is thickened. Fold in cherries; stir in 2 to 3 tablespoons Kirsch. Cool.

To assemble pie, spoon chocolate filling into chilled cookie crust. Chill until firm. Spread cherry filling over chocolate mixture. Chill while preparing topping.

To prepare topping, combine 1 1/2 cups heavy cream confectioners' sugar, and Kirsch. Chill thoroughly in freezer. In a deep bowl, whip with chilled beaters until cream mixture holds stiff peaks. Spread over chilled pie, securely sealing to the edges of the crust. Press chocolate curls over top. Garnish with fresh sweet dark cherries or Maraschino cherries.

Note: 3 1/2 cups thawed frozen whipped topping may be substituted for heavy cream.

...Not all Richmond women knew self-denial and there was a group — that ever present "fast set" in any society — that was acquainted with only military balls and profiteering. To be sure, there were parties also for those unsung heroines, those one-time "gentle creatures" whose flower-like beauty once had ben caught up in ballads. But they were called "starvation parties," parties where walnuts and hickory nuts, apples and cider, sorghum, roasted sweet potatoes and Irish potatoes were delicacies...
"Superb Gallantry of Women In Wartime Displayed Here,"
Richmond Times-Dispatch, September 18, 1937

Triple Chocolate Mousse Pie

Yield: One deep dish 9-inch pie

Chocolate lovers will be in Chocolate Heaven eating this dessert. It is also delicious served without the crust as a mousse in sherbet glasses. Don't count calories...this treat is for splurging occasions!

1 (12-ounce) package semi-sweet chocolate pieces
1/4 cup cognac, brandy, orange liqueur, or light rum
3 tablespoons instant coffee powder or crystals
2 tablespoons boiling water
Pinch of salt
1/2 cup unsalted butter, at room temperature
6 jumbo eggs, separated
Chocolate Cookie Crumb Crust (9-inch deep dish) (see index)
1/2 cup heavy cream, whipped
Sweetened whipped cream flavored with vanilla or desired liqueur for garnish (optional)
Shaved unsweetened chocolate or bittersweet chocolate curls for garnish

Place chocolate pieces, cognac, instant coffee, boiling water, and salt in a blender container; cover and whiz at high speed until mixture is smooth. Add butter and egg yolks, one at a time; cover and continue beating until thick and smooth. In a large bowl, beat egg whites until stiff, but not dry, peaks are formed. Carefully fold chocolate mixture into beaten egg whites. Spoon two-thirds of mixture into a prepared Chocolate Cookie Crumb Crust. Chill for 10 minutes. Fold whipped cream into remaining one-third chocolate mixture; spoon over first chocolate mixture. Refrigerate until ready to serve. Garnish with additional flavored sweetened whipped cream and/or shaved unsweetened chocolate or bitter sweet chocolate curls.

Note: This dessert is very rich; cut into 10 to 12 thin servings.

Peach Custard Pie

One cup of sugar, quarter-cup of butter, 3 eggs, half-cup of sweet milk, 1 full cup of peaches mashed with a silver fork; season with ess. lemon; more sugar may be used. Reserve the whites of 2 eggs for meringue. This quantity fills 2 pies.
Mrs. J. B. Winston
Virginia Recipes, *1890*

Jane's Easy Chocolate Pie

Yield: one 9-inch pie

Pâté Sucre Brisé Crust

2 cup flour
1 teaspoon salt
1/2 cup plus 2 tablespoons
  butter or margarine, at
  room temperature
1 egg
1 1/2 to 2 tablespoons ice
  water

Filling

2 squares (ounces) semi-
  sweet chocolate
1/2 cup butter or margarine,
  at room temperature
3 eggs
1 (5 1/3-ounce) can evaporated milk
1 3/4 cups sugar
1 1/2 teaspoons vanilla
  extract

In a bowl, sift flour and salt together. Cut in butter with a pastry blender or 2 knives until mixture resembles coarse meal. Add egg, mixing well. Sprinkle water evenly over surface, 1 tablespoon at a time, mixing lightly with a fork. Or, prepare crust in a food processor. Shape into a ball,wrap in waxed paper or clear plastic film and chill in refrigerator for at least 30 minutes. On a board, roll out between sheets of lightly floured waxed paper into a circle 1/8-inch thick and 1 1/2 inches larger in diameter than inverted 9-inch pie plate. Remove top layer of waxed paper;fit crust into pie plate, waxed paper side up. Peel off remaining waxed paper. Fold edge under and flute into a high-standing edge. Chill in refrigerator for 30 minutes.

In a heavy saucepan, melt chocolate and butter over low heat;cool. In a food processor or blender container, combine chocolate mixture, eggs, evaporated milk, sugar, and vanilla; cover and process or blend until smooth. Allow to stand while crust is chilling. Pour into crust. Bake in a moderate oven (350 degrees F.) for 35 minutes or until filling is set. Cool slightly and serve warm or at room temperature.

—Ginny Moss (Mrs. John Simpson)

Orange Custard Pie (Very Nice)

Juice and grate rind of one orange, three-fourths of a cup of sugar, one cup of water, one heaping table-spoonful of flour mixed in a little of the water, four well-beaten eggs, reserving the whites of two for frosting; fill into crust and bake. For the frosting beat the whites of the reserved eggs to a stiff froth, with two table-spoonfuls of powdered sugar; spread evenly over top of pie, and return to the oven till slightly browned.

Virginia Cookery-Book, *1885*

Potion of Love Pie

Yield: one 9-inch pie

Fanny's Restaurant and Lounge, located in the Holiday Inn at I-64 and West Broad Street, has been a Richmond dining choice for over a decade. Named after a legendary, fun loving, mischievous, turn-of-the-century woman, fond of sampling the world's best food,the restaurant takes pride in its style of cuisine and service.

Crust
1 cup flour
1/2 cup butter or margarine, at room temperature
3/4 cup chopped pecans

Filling
1 (8-ounce) container thawed frozen non-dairy whipped topping
1 (8-ounce) package cream cheese, at room temperature
3/4 cup sifted confectioners' sugar
1 (3-ounce) package instant chocolate pudding and pie filling
1 (3-ounce) package instant vanilla pudding and pie filling
3 cups milk
2 tablespoons Kahlúa liqueur
2 tablespoons Amaretto liqueur
1 teaspoon vanilla extract

Additional thawed frozen non-dairy whipped topping for garnish
Additional chopped pecans for garnish

To prepare crust, cut butter into flour with a pastry blender in a small bowl until mixture resembles coarse meal. Add pecans,mixing well. Press mixture over the bottom and up the sides of a greased 9-inch pie plate, forming a standing rim around the edge of the pie plate. Bake in a slow oven (325 degrees F.) for 20 minutes or until done and lightly browned. Cool.

In a medium bowl, combine whipped topping, cream cheese, and confectioners' sugar, beating *only* until smooth. Evenly spread over the bottom of the cooled baked pie shell. Chill in the refrigerator until cheese mixture is firm. In a bowl, combine pudding mixes, milk,liqueurs, and vanilla, beating lightly according to package directions. Pour mixture over cream cheese layer in pie shell. Chill until pudding mixture is set. Garnish each serving with additional whipped topping and chopped pecans.

–Fanny's Restaurant and Lounge

Old Colonial Pie

Yield: one 10-inch deep dish pie

6 jumbo or extra large eggs
2 1/4 cups sugar
6 tablespoons butter or
  margarine, melted
2 1/2 tablespoons white or
  cider vinegar
1 1/2 teaspoons vanilla
  extract
Pinch salt
Unbaked Pie Shell (10-inch)
  (see index)
Sweetened-flavored
  whipped cream and
  chopped pecans or
  English walnuts for
  garnish (optional)

In a large bowl, lightly beat eggs. (Do *not over beat* as a foam will form.) Stir in sugar, butter, vinegar, vanilla, and salt, mixing until mixture is smooth. Pour into unbaked pie shell. Bake in a moderate oven (350 degrees F.) for about 1 hour or until a silver knife inserted in center comes out clean. Remove from oven and cool on a wire rack. Pie may be served plain or garnished with sweetened-flavored whipped cream and chopped nuts, if desired, just before serving.

Coconut Pie

Yield: two 9-inch pies

2 cups sugar
1/4 cup flour
4 eggs
2 cups milk
4 teaspoons butter or
  margarine, melted
4 teaspoons lemon extract
2 cups flaked coconut
2 Unbaked Pie Shells (9-
  inch) (see index)

Sift sugar and flour together. In a medium bowl, beat eggs lightly. Add sugar-flour mixture, milk, butter, and lemon extract, beating well. Stir in coconut. Pour into unbaked pie shells, dividing evenly. Bake in a moderate oven (350 degrees F.) for 30 minutes or until a silver knife inserted in the center of pies comes out clean. Cool on wire racks.

–Lucretia Powell

Almost all our citizens, in those days, went early to market, to furnish their larders...

Samuel Mordecai
Richmond in By-Gone Days, 1856
Reprint Edition, 1975

Impossible Pie

Yield: two 9-inch pies

"The crust forms as the pies bake."

4 eggs
2 cups milk
1 3/4 cups sugar
1/2 cup self-rising flour
1/4 cup butter or margarine,
 melted
1 teaspoon vanilla extract
2 (3 1/2-ounce) cans flaked
 coconut

In a bowl, combine the first 6 ingredients, beating well. Fold in coconut. Pour into 2 greased and floured 9-inch pie plates, dividing evenly. Bake in a moderate oven (350 degrees F.) for 30 to 35 minutes or until filling is set.Cool on wire racks. To serve, cut in wedges.

–Frances Fox (Mrs. Paul)

> ...The household items reveal a kitchen stove at $15.00; coffee grinder 45 cents — and you roasted and ground your own coffee, and glazed the beans with egg whites when it was parched. Two stone jar, $.35 cents, followed...
>
> Lucy Cole Durham
> "Diary of Young Matron Reveals Strange Notations,"
> **Richmond Times-Dispatch** (Condensed), February 13, 1938

Kentucky Derby Pie

Yield: one 9-inch pie

1 cup semi-sweet chocolate
 pieces
1/2 cup butter or margarine
2 eggs, lightly beaten
1 cup sugar
1 teaspoon vanilla extract
1/2 cup sifted flour
1 cup chopped pecans or
 English Walnuts
Unbaked Pie Shell (9-inch)
 (see index)
Sweetened-flavored
 whipped cream for
 garnish

In the top of a double boiler, melt chocolate and butter over hot water. Cool. In a medium bowl, combine chocolate mixture, eggs,and sugar, and vanilla, beating lightly. Stir in flour. Fold in nuts. Spoon into unbaked pie shell. Bake in a moderate oven (350 degrees F.) for 30 minutes or until pastry is lightly browned.Cool thoroughly on a wire rack. Garnish with sweetened-flavored whipped cream just before serving.

–Linden Row Dining Room
Linden Row Inn

Tackey Pie Party

You are invited to attend
A Tackey Pie Party in the far West End,
At half-past eight on Thursday night,
The 28th of May, at "Leonard Heights."
Our costumes all must tacky be,
Our refreshments also, as you will see;
But listen, boys, and shut your eyes:
All the girls shall bring some lovely pies;
So bring your quarters, nickels and dimes,
And we will have some good old times.
The pies at auction shall be sold;
The proceeds therefrom we shall hold,
And with these and other pennies that we save,
We will a summer outing have.
So come on, boys—eat your fill,
We hope that the pies will not kill;
But don't you come unless you wear
Tacky clothes and tacky hair,
Tacky head and tacky face;
We'll have everything tacky about the place.
We shall have a judge to give the prize
To the tackiest tacks with the tackiest eyes,
And we all will have the tackiest time,
If you come in response to this tacky rhyme.
The car leaves promptly at half-past eight,
So don't you tarry for the car won't wait
For anyone, whoer'er he may be,
If he is hero, hobo or R. S. C.

R. Care Maddox
"Big Chief."
Source unknown, 1908

597

Old-Fashioned Sweet Potato Pie

Yield: one 9-inch pie

Frequently, sweet potato or yam pie is served in place of pumpkin pie in Richmond as well as other parts of the South.

5 medium sweet potatoes
  or yams
Boiling salted water as
  needed
2 eggs
1 cup sugar
1/4 cup butter or margarine,
  at room temperature
1 teaspoon cinnamon
1 teaspoon nutmeg
1 teaspoon vanilla extract
Pinch of salt
1 cup milk
Unbaked Pie Shell (9-inch)
  (see index)

In a large heavy saucepan, cook sweet potatoes or yams, covered, in boiling salted water to cover over moderate heat for 35 to 40 minutes or until fork tender; drain well. Cool, peel, and mash thoroughly. In a medium bowl, combine mashed sweet potatoes or yams, eggs, sugar, butter, cinnamon, nutmeg, vanilla, and salt, beating well. Gradually stir in milk, blending well. Pour into pie shell. Bake in the lower third of a moderate oven (350 degrees F.) for 30 to 35 minutes or until a silver knife inserted in the center comes out clean. Cool on a wire rack.

–Vernelle Thomas

Caramel Pecan Pumpkin Pie

Yield: one 9-inch pie

1 1/2 cups light brown
  sugar, firmly packed,
  divided
1/2 cup sugar
1 tablespoon flour
1/2 teaspoon salt
1/2 teaspoon cinnamon
1/2 teaspoon nutmeg
1/2 teaspoon ground
  allspice
2 1/2 cups mashed cooked
  pumpkin, fresh or canned
1/4 cup heavy cream
2 eggs, slightly beaten
1/2 teaspoon lemon extract
1/2 teaspoon vanilla extract
1 tablespoon butter or
  margarine, melted

In a small bowl, combine 1/2 cup brown sugar and the next 6 ingredients together, mixing well; set aside. In a large bowl, combine pumpkin, cream, and eggs, blending well. Add sugar-spice mixture, lemon and vanilla extracts, and 1 tablespoon melted butter, stirring slowly so air will not be incorporated. Pour into pie shell. Bake in the lower third of a hot oven (425 degrees F.) for 10 minutes. Reduce heat to moderate (350 degrees F.) and continue baking for 40 minutes or until a silver knife inserted in center of pie comes out clean. While pie is baking, prepare topping. In a small bowl, combine pecans, 1 cup brown sugar, and remaining butter, blending well. Spread mixture over the top of the baked pie. Place pie under broiler, 4 inches from heat source, and broil until topping is caramelized. Remove and cool on a wire rack.

1 cup pecan halves
5 tablespoons butter or
    margarine, at room
    temperature
Unbaked Pie Shell (9-inch)
    (see index)

Note: May garnish with whipped cream, if desired.

Light N' Luscious Lemon Pie

Yield: one 9-inch pie

"You'll receive raves for this recipe...very light, low calorie, and melts in your mouth."

Crust

1 cup fine corn flake crumbs
2 tablespoons sugar
1/3 cup butter or margarine, melted (see note)

Filling

3 eggs, separated
1/2 cup sugar, divided
1/3 cup lemon juice
1 tablespoon grated lemon peel
2 envelopes artificially sweetened reduced calorie whipped topping mix
1 cup *very* cold milk

To prepare crust, combine crumbs and sugar. Add butter or margarine, mixing well. Press mixture firmly over the bottom and up sides of a 9-inch pie plate, forming a standing rim around the edge of the pie plate. Chill in refrigerator while preparing filling. In a large bowl, beat egg yolks lightly; gradually add 1/4 cup sugar, beating until thick and lemon-colored. Stir in lemon juice and peel. In a medium bowl, beat egg whites until foamy; gradually add remaining 1/4 cup sugar, beating until stiff, glossy, but not dry, peaks are formed. Fold beaten egg whites into egg yolk mixture. In a medium bowl, combine whipped topping mix and milk, beating until thickened; fold into egg mixture. Spoon into chilled pie shell and freeze for 6 to 8 hours.

Note: Reduced calorie margarine may be substituted for butter or margarine.

–Elizabeth Archer

Frozen Mincemeat Ice Cream Tarts

Yield: 8 tarts

"A marvelous dessert at holiday time."

1 quart vanilla or French
   vanilla ice cream, slightly
   softened
1 cup prepared mincemeat
   (see note)
1 teaspoon grated orange
   peel
8 (3-inch) baked pastry or
   graham-cracker crust tart
   shells
1/2 cup heavy cream

In a bowl, combine ice cream, mincemeat, and orange peel, mixing well. Evenly spoon mixture into each tart shell. Freeze until firm. Just before serving, garnish each tart with sweetened-flavored whipped cream and sprinkle with toasted almonds.

Note: Homemade or commercially prepared mincemeat may be used.

Variation: Stir 2 tablespoons brandy into ice-cream mixture before spooning into tart shells.

–Susie Keyser (Mrs. Hugh)

...In the times when "Needle, needle, who's got the needle" was the mere expression from a child's game, food was far more important than fashion. Especially in families where there were little children. There wa at least one Christmas dinner — the Christmas before the surrender — that consisted of pumpkin pie made with sorghum but without eggs and a small piece of sparerib.

"That Christmas," a woman of the Confederacy related, "I filled my children's stockings with apples, walnuts, hickory nuts, sweept potatoes and sorghum candy..."

"Superb Gallantry of Women In Wartimes Displayed Here,"

Richmond Times-Dispatch, *Spetember 18, 1937*

Southern Pecan Pie

Yield: One 9-inch pie

3 eggs
2/3 cup sugar
1/8 teaspoon salt
1 cup dark corn syrup
1/3 cup butter or margarine,
   melted
1 cup pecan halves
Unbaked Pie Shell (9-inch)
   (see index)

In a bowl, beat eggs lightly. Blend in sugar and salt and continue beating lightly. Stir in syrup and butter or margarine. Fold in pecans. Pour into pie shell. Turn pecans rounded side up. Bake in moderate oven (350 degrees F.) for 50 minutes, or until pie crust is golden brown and filling is firm.

–Maryrita Jackson (Mrs. David)

Paulette's Authentic Key Lime Pie

Yield: one 9-inch pie

Unbaked Pie Shell (9-inch)
4 large or 3 jumbo eggs,
   separated
1 (14-ounce) can sweetened
   condensed milk
1/2 cup Key lime juice (see
   note)
1/2 teaspoon cream of tartar
1/4 cup sugar
Very thin Key lime or
   Persian lime slices for
   garnish

Prebake pie shell in a hot over (425 degrees F.) for 12 to 15 minutes or until golden brown. Remove and cool on wire rack. In a medium bowl, beat egg yolks until foamy. Add sweetened condensed milk, beating well. Stir in lime juice; set filling aside. In another medium bowl, beat egg whites with cream of tartar until foamy. Gradually add sugar, beating egg whites until stiff, glossy, but not dry, peaks are formed. Fold one-fourth of the meringue into the reserved filling. Spoon filling into baked pie shell, spreading evenly with a rubber spatula; gently spread meringue over the top of the pie, sealing to crust edges. With a teaspoon, make swirl designs in the top of the meringue. Bake in a moderate oven (350 degrees F.) for about 15 minutes or until meringue is golden brown. Turn off oven, and with oven door ajar, allow pie to cool thoroughly before serving. Store any remaining pie in the refrigerator.

Note: Key lime juice may be obtained from fresh Key limes or it is also available commercially bottled in many grocery and food specialty stores. Key limes are different from Persian limes usually seen in grocery stores. Grown on the Florida Keys, Key limes are a smaller, rounder, and more acid variety of lime.

601

Regal Mince Pie

Yield: one 9-inch pie

Pastry for Double-Crust Pie
(9-inch) (see index)
3 cups homemade or
commercially prepared
mincemeat
1 cup peeled, finely
chopped apples
2 tablespoons flour
1/4 cup brandy, apple juice,
apple cider, or syrup from
watermelon or peach
pickles
Hard Sauce or Brandy Sauce
(see index)

Prepare crust and line pie plate with pastry. In a large bowl, combine remaining ingredients, mixing well. Spoon mixture into prepared pie plate. Top with remaining crust and flute edges as directed for double-crust pies. Bake in a hot oven (400 degrees F.) for 40 to 45 minutes or until crust is browned. Serve slightly warm with Hard Sauce or Brandy Sauce.

Real Spirit of Christmas

Even during the War Between the States, when purses were lighter than were the hearts of many Virginians, Christmas was the gala season of the year...

What work Christmas meant to the women in those days! Picture the tables laden with roasted fowls (goose, duck, guinea, wild turkey or even, maybe, venison), with home-made cakes (pound-cake taking the honors, with horse-cake, lady-cakes, coffee-cakes and molasses cakes), which had to be baked without the vanilla or lemon extracts so indispensable to the modern cook. Oranges and bananas were not available, of course, but the home-grown apple appeared in all its manifestations, from the original polished fruit as centerpiece to the brimming dish of brown apple-butter and the ever-present bowl of cider. Topping the menu there was a pudding. It might be made of Irish or sweet potatoes, or it might be made of rice, and the children ate it with a relish as they washed it down with an imitation coffee concocted either from wheat or parched meal.

The Richmond News Leader, *December 14, 1939*

Grandma's Shoo-Fly Pie

Yield: two 9-inch pies

"The top of the pie will be a bit crumbly while the center is similar to cake and the bottom will be some what gooey.If you like sweets, you'll love this one!"

Crust
3 cups flour
1 1/2 teaspoons salt
1 1/3 cups shortening
3 tablespoons *ice* water

Filling
1 cup molasses
1 cup light brown sugar,
   firmly packed
3 eggs, beaten
1 1/2 teaspoons baking
   powder
2 cups warm water

Topping
3 cups flour
1 cup light brown sugar,
   firmly packed
1/2 cup shortening

In a bowl, combine flour and salt, mixing well. With a pastry blender or 2 silver knives, cut in shortening until mixture resembles coarse meal. Evenly sprinkle ice water over dough; toss lightly with a fork to mix. Shape pastry mixture into 2 balls. Roll out each ball between sheets of waxed paper into 2 circles 1/8-inch thick and 1 1/4 inches larger in diameter than inverted pie plate. Remove top layer of waxed paper; invert pie plate over crust and flip pie crust and plate over so that crust falls easily into pie plate. Remove remaining layer of waxed paper. Carefully fit crust into pie plate. Trim crust edge, leaving a 1/2-inch overhang. Turn edges of crust under and flute with fingers or times of a fork; set aside.

To prepare filling, combine molasses and brown sugar in a medium bowl, blending well. Combine eggs and baking powder. Stir into molasses mixture. Add warm water, mixing well. Pour into unbaked pie shells, dividing evenly.

To prepare topping, sift the flour and brown sugar together in a medium bowl. With a pastry blender, cut in shortening until mixture resembles coarse meal. Sprinkle mixture over each pie, dividing evenly. Bake pies in a hot oven (400 degrees F) for 15 minutes. Reduce oven temperature to moderate (350 degrees F.) and continue baking for an additional 25 minutes. Remove pies from oven and cool on wire racks.

–Fran Lincoln

Raisin Pie

Half pound of raisins, seeded and stewed until tender, add tablespoonful of vinegar, and sweeten to taste. Dredge with flour, and bake between pie-crust.
Mrs. T. H. Brown
Virginia Recipes *1890*

Hattie Lassiter

...Christmas was a simple and principally religious holiday, with much praying and feasting with family and friends.

...Her mother raised chickens, ducks and turkeys for eggs and meat to complement the hogs and cows her father raised and butchered. At Christmas time, a turkey would be killed. Mrs.Lassiter remembers plucking the feathers. "It was a hard job,"she said.

...As gifts, each family member would prepare a stocking. Inside would be an orange--often mushy but still a treat at a time when citrus was not readily available--and apples, nuts, hand-knit gloves, a muffler or hat or something similar.

Christine Reid
"Christmas in the 1800's,"
Richmond Times-Dispatch, December

Lemon Pie

Three eggs, 1 cup of brown sugar, the juice and grated rind of 1 lemon, 3 teaspoonsful of sifted flour, quarter of a teacup of milk. Beat yolks and sugar together, add lemon juice and rind, then the flour, beaten to a smooth paste, with the milk; beat all until light, and bake in pastry. A meringue of the 3 whites and 3 tablespoonsful of powdered sugar, beaten light, put on cooked pie, and returned to the oven to brown.

Mrs. James
Virginia Recipes, 1890

Meringue Topped Cider Vinegar Pie

Yield: one 9-inch pie

Eighteenth and nineteenth century cooks were ingenious. When lemons were scarce, which happened frequently, cooks substituted vinegar for the lemon juice used in lemon pies, achieving a similar flavor.

1 cup sugar
1/4 cup cornstarch
1/4 teaspoon salt
3 eggs yolks, slightly beaten

In a heavy saucepan, combine sugar, cornstarch, and salt. Add egg yolks and vinegar; mix well. Stir in boiling water. Cook over low heat, stirring constantly until thick. Remove from heat; stir in

1/4 cup cider vinegar
1 3/4 cups boiling water
3 tablespoons butter or
  margarine, at room
  temperature
1 teaspoon lemon extract
Baked Pie Shell (9-inch)
  (see index)
Basic 3-Egg Meringue (see
  index)

butter and lemon extract. Pour into a baked pie shell. Prepare meringue flavored with lemon extract; spread carefully over filling sealing it to edges of crust. Bake in a moderate over (375 degrees F.) about 12 to 15 minutes or until meringue is attractively browned. Cool on a wire rack.

> Before the female province of pastry making was subdued by the countrymen of Napoleon, there flourished in Richmond a lady of the dark aristocracy, Mrs. Nancy Byrd, a name that carries its own passport of distinction. No dinner nor supper party could be complete unless she had a finger in the pie. She held undisputed sway over the dessert, with the rolling-pin for her sceptre; and considered herself as forming the under-crust of gentility along with her compeers.
>
> Samuel Mordecai
> **Richmond in By-Gone Days,** 1856
> Reprint Edition, 1975

Creamy Date Walnut Pie

Yield: one 10-inch pie

1 cup sugar
2 tablespoons flour
1 1/4 teaspoons cinnamon
1/2 teaspoon nutmeg
1/2 teaspoon salt
1/4 teaspoon ground cloves
3 eggs, slightly beaten
1 1/2 cups heavy cream
2 teaspoons vanilla extract
1 cup chopped pitted dates
1/2 cup chopped English
  walnuts
1/2 cup flaked coconut
Unbaked Pie Shell (10-inch)

In a large bowl, combine the first 6 ingredients. In a medium bowl, mix together eggs, cream, and vanilla. Add sugar mixture, blending thoroughly. Fold in dates, nuts, and coconut. Pour into an unbaked pie shell. Bake in a hot oven (400 degrees F.) for 15 minutes. Reduce temperature to slow (325 degrees F.); continue baking for 30 to 35 minutes or until silver knife inserted in center comes out clean. Cool.

Note: Coconut may be omitted and dates increased to 1 1/2 cups.

Low Calorie Windowpane Pie

Yield: one 9-inch pie

3 tablespoons sugar (optional)
2 teaspoons unflavored gelatin
1 cup chilled unsweetened pineapple or apple juice, divided (see note)
Artificial sweetener to equal 8 teaspoons sugar (see note)
1 cup sliced *ripe* strawberries (see note)
1 cup sliced peeled nectarines (see note)
1 cup seedless green grapes (see note)
Graham-Cracker Crumb Crust (see index)

In a small heavy saucepan, combine sugar and gelatin. Stir in 1/2 cup apple juice, softening gelatin. Stir over low heat until gelatin and sugar are dissolved. Stir in artificial sweetener and remaining apple juice. Pour into a small bowl; chill in freezer for 8 to 10 minutes, until mixture is consistency of syrup. Prepare fruit while gelatin mixture is chilling. Arrange the fruit in the Graham-Cracker Crumb Crust, in random clumps of color. Do not mix fruits together. Gently pack fruits down. When gelatin mixture is the consistency of syrup, evenly spoon over the fruit in the pie shell. Chill pie in refrigerator for several hours until gelatin is firm.

Note: Unsweetened orange juice or artificially sweetened cranberry juice may be substituted for pineapple or apple juice.

Note: Use artificial sweeteners sparingly as they often leave a bitter after taste. The proportionate amount of individual artificial sweetener used to the amount sugar is not always the same. Follow recommended proportion of artificial sweetener versus sugar of individual branded products.

Note: Any combination of fresh fruits including raspberries, blueberries or blackberries, sliced peaches or pears, seedless red grapes, thinly sliced peeled bananas, kiwi fruit, seedless peeled and sectioned oranges, seeded and thinly sliced unpeeled apples may be used. Do *not* use fresh pineapple as it will cause the gelatin to not gel and become firm.

–Glad Applegate (Mrs. William)

Dixie Peanut Pie

Yield: one 9-inch pie

There is nothing more southern in cooking or better tasting than luscious, crunchy peanut or pecan pie. Made famous by slave cooks of plantation days, peanuts and pecans were readily available in the South. Today this marvelous confection is still a favored dessert with Southerners. Don't count the caloris ... you don't want to know ... just enjoy!!

3 eggs
3/4 cup light brown sugar, firmly packed
2 tablespoons flour
1/2 teaspoon salt
1 cup dark corn syrup
2 tablespoons butter or margarine, melted
1 1/2 teaspoons vanilla extract
1 1/4 cups coarsely chopped salted peanuts
Unbaked Pie Shell (9-inch) (see index)
Sweetened whipped cream for garnish (optional)

In a medium bowl, beat eggs slightly. Blend in sugar, flour and salt; beat slightly. Stir in syrup, butter or margarine and vanilla extract; fold in pecans. Pour into pie shell; turn pecans rounded side up. Bake in center of hot oven (400 degrees F.) for 10 minutes. Reduce heat to slow oven (325 degrees F.) and bake 35 to 40 minutes or until pie crust is a golden brown color and filling firm. When pie is just the right color, loosely cover with a tent of foil and finish baking. Cool. Serve plain or topped with whipped cream.

Variations: Pecans may be sutbsituted in any of the following variations.
   Bourbon Peanut Pie: Substitute 3 tablespoons bourbon for the vanilla extract.
   Chocolate Peanut Pie: Melt 2 squares (ounces) unsweetened chocolate and add with butter.
   Deep-South Peanut Pie: Use 1/2 cup light molasses and 1/2 cup dark corn syrup.
   Honey Pecan Pie: Use granulated sugar and substitute honey or light corn syrup for dark corn syrup.
   Southern Pecan Pie: Substitute 1 1/4 cups pecan halves for the peanuts.

Mince-Meat-No. 683.

1 pound chopped beef, 1/2 pound chopped beef suet, 1 pound citron, 1 pound brown sugar, 2 pounds chopped apples, 1 quart good brandy, 1 pint wine, 1 teaspoon salt, 2 pound seeded raisins, 2 pounds cleaned currants, 1 grated nutmeg, juice and rind of 2 oranges, juice and rind of 1 lemon, 1 teaspoon ground cloves, 2 teaspoons ground mace, 1 teaspoon ground cinnamon. To Make: Cook the meat, cool, and chop it fine. Chop the suet. Slice the citron into small pieces. Mix all the dry ingredients together. When perfectly mixed add the grated rind and juice of the oranges and lemon. Mix again and pack in a stone jar; pour over the brandy and wine; cover closely and put in a cold place. This will keep all the winter. When ready to use take out the quantity needed; thin with cider or wine; put in the lined pie plates; cover with the crust; make a small opening in the top; press the crust well together around the edges of the plate and bake.

Instruction in Cooking with Selected Receipts, *1895*

Sour Cream Black Walnut Pie

Yield: one 10-inch pie

5 eggs, slightly beaten
3/4 cup sugar
3/4 cup light brown sugar,
  firmly packed
3/4 cup sour cream
1/2 cup butter or margarine,
  melted
1/3 cup light corn syrup
1 to 2 teaspoons vanilla
  extract
1 cup chopped black or
  English walnuts, or
  pecans
Pastry for Unbaked Pie Shell
  (10-inch) (see index)

In a large heavy sauce pan, combine eggs, sugar, brown sugar, sour cream, butter, and corn syrup together. Cook over low heat, stirring constantly for 6 minutes. Remove from heat; stir in vanilla extract and nuts. Pour into an unbaked pie shell. Bake in a moderate oven (350 degrees F.) for 55 to 60 minutes or until filling is set and crust is golden brown.

Variation: Use 1 1/2 cups light brown sugar in place of granulated and brown sugar.

Old Richmond Advertisement, date unknown

In April 1783 *the* Hustings Court *decreed the following*
rates for Richmond taverns:
For Breakfast or Supper   *two shillings*
For Dinner   *two shillings and six pence*
For one night's lodging   *one shilling*
For a Servant's Diet   *one shilling*
For a quart of Madeira Wine   *six shillings*
For a Quart of port Wine   *four shillings*
For a quart of Rum Punch
    made with loaf sugar   *two shillings and six pence*
For a quart of Rum or Brandy Toddy   *one shilling*
                                               and six pence
For a jill of Rum or French Brandy   *six pence*
For a jill of common Brandy and Whiskey   *four pence*
For a Gallon of Corn or Oats   *ten pence*
For a pound of Hay or Fodder   *two pence*
For stablage or pasturage for one horse.   *seven pence*
                           half penney for one night
Harry M. Ward and Harold E. Greer, Jr.
Richmond During The Revolution, 1775-83, 1977

Rueger's Restaurant,

Ninth and Bank
Streets,

RICHMOND,   -   VIRGINIA.

Basic 3-Egg Meringue

Yield: topping for 9-inch pie

3 egg whites
1/4 teaspoon cream of tartar
1/4 teaspoon lemon or
    orange extract or
    1/2 teaspoon vanilla
1/3 cup sugar

Combine first 3 ingredients in beater bowl and beat until egg whites are foamy. Add sugar gradually, 1 tablespoon at a time, and beat until sugar is dissolved and whites are stiff, glossy, and hold soft peaks. Spread carefully over a hot or warm filling, sealing it securely to edges of crust or baking dish. Bake in a moderate oven (375 degrees F.) about 12 to 15 minutes, or until meringue is attractively browned. Cool on wire rack away from drafts.

609

Chocolate Cookie Crumb Crust

Yield: one 9-inch deep dish pie crust

1 1/2 cups fine chocolate
   wafer crumbs
3 tablespoons sugar
1/2 cup butter or margarine,
   melted

In a bowl, combine crumbs and sugar, mixing well. Add butter; blend thoroughly. Pack crumbs evenly over bottom and up sides of a 9-inch deep dish pie plate, forming a standing rim. Bake in a moderate oven (350 degrees F.) for 7 to 8 minutes. Cool, then chill in refrigerator for 15 to 20 minutes.

Variation: Vanilla or gingersnap cookie crumbs may be substituted for chocolate wafer crumbs.

Graham-Cracker Crumb Crust

Yield: one 9-inch pie crust

1 1/2 cups fine graham-
   cracker crumbs (18 to 20
   crackers)
1/3 cup sugar
3/4 teaspoon cinnamon
1/8 teaspoon nutmeg
   (optional)
1/2 cup butter or margarine,
   melted

Combine the first 4 ingredients. Add butter and blend thoroughly. Pack crumbs evenly over bottom and sides of a 9-inch pie plate, forming a standing rim. Bake in a moderate oven (350 degrees F.) for 5 minutes; cool, then chill.

Variation: Substitute 1 1/2 cups fine vanilla, chocolate wafer, or gingersnap cookie crumbs for graham-cracker crumbs. Omit spices and reduce sugar to 3 tablespoons and melted butter to 1/3 cup.

Good Pastry

4 level tablespoons lard, 1 1/2 cups sifted flour, 1/2 teaspoon salt, 1/4 cup ice water, Mix flour, lard and salt light with silver knife, not too fine, then sprinkle in ice water and stir together with silver fork. Throw on a floured board and roll out as lightly as possible one-fourth inch think. Bake in hot oven.

Mrs. B. O. James
Virginia Cookery Book, *1921*

Pastry for Double-Crust Pie

Yield: crust for one 9-inch pie

2 cups sifted flour
1 teaspoon salt
3/4 cup shortening, at room temperature
About 5 to 6 tablespoons *very* cold water (approximate)

In a bowl, sift together flour and salt. Cut in shortening with a pastry blender or two knives until mixture resembles coarse corn meal. Sprinkle water evenly over surface, 1 tablespoon at a time, mixing lightly with fork until particles hold together and leave sides of bowl. Shape into a ball and divide in half. Cover each half with clear plastic wrap or waxed paper and let stand at room temperature for 5 to 10 minutes.

On a lightly floured board, roll out half the dough into a circle 1/8-inch thick and 1 1/4 inches larger in diameter than inverted pie plate. Carefully fit crust into pie plate. Trim crust edge, leaving a 1/2-inch over hang. Pour filling into shell.

Roll out remaining dough into a circle 1/8-inch thick and 1 inch larger in diameter than top of inverted pie plate. Cut small designs or slits in center of crust for steam vents. Moisten edges of lower crust. Cover with top crust and press edges together. Trim crust 1/2 inch beyond edge of pie plate and press edges together to seal. Fold edges under bottom crust and flute with fingers or tines of a fork. Bake as directed for filling used.

Note: For a Deep Dish Pie Shell, increase recipe ingredients by one and one-half the amounts given.

"Foundation Pastry"-No. 645

1 quart of flour,, 1 teaspoon of salt,, 10 ounces butter and lard mixed,, ice water enough to mix., To Mix: Sift the flour and salt together; make a hollow in the middle of the flour; put in the lard and butter, cover the shortening with the flour, and with a knife and fork, or two knives, chop the shortening until it is thoroughly mixed with the flour; wet with a little ice water, and mix with your hands as quickly and lightly as possible. Put on a floured board, divide into as many parts as you intend using,

Instruction in Cooking with Selected Receipts, *1895*

Pastry for Unbaked Pie Shell

Yield: one 9-inch pie crust

1 1/2 cups sifted flour
1/2 teaspoon salt
9 tablespoons shortening or butter, at room temperature
About 3 tablespoons *very* cold water
Few drops white vinegar (see note)

In a bowl, sift together flour and salt. Cut in shortening or butter with a pastry blender or two knives until mixture resembles coarse corn meal. Sprinkle water and vinegar evenly over surface,1 tablespoon at a time, mixing lightly with fork until particles hold together and leave sides of bowl. Shape into a ball, cover with clear plastic wrap or wrap in waxed paper, and let stand at room temperature for 5 to 10 minutes.

On a lightly floured board, roll out dough into a circle1/8-inch thick and 1 1/2 inches larger in diameter than inverted pie plate. Carefully fit crust into pie plate. Trim crust edge,leaving a 1-inch overhang. Fold edge under and flute with fingers or tines of a fork into a high standing edge. Bake as directed for filling used.

Note: For a Deep Dish Pie Shell, increase recipe by one and one-half.

Note:Vinegar added to pastry helps to make it more flakey.

Variation: For a baked pie shell (9-inch) prick deep holes close together on bottom and sides of crust, using a 4-tined dinner fork. Bake in a very hot oven (425 degrees F.) for 10 to 12 minutes or until golden. Check crust after 5 minutes and prick any bubbles that have appeared. Cool on a wire rack before filling.

... Mr. Pizzini would arrive with his minions, go into the dining room and lock the door. When we were allowed to enter, the table would have become a veritable fairy land of spun sugar, upon which the candles glittered like the wedding of Cinderella and the Prince. On one end there would be a pyramid of candied Malaga grapes, on the other one of peeled orange sections, on the four corners ... nougat baskets, and over all a pale golden bridal veil of spun sugar. Then there were the gigantic bowls of egg nog and of a punch that perhaps fortunately exists no longer...

Helena Lefroy Caperton
"Time Gambols Withal"
The Richmond News Leader, 1931

Chewy Banana Bars

Yield: about 2 dozen bars

"No eggs are included in these moist, chewy bars."

1 1/2 cups sifted flour
1 1/2 teaspoons baking powder
1/2 teaspoon salt
1/4 cup shortening
1 cup light brown sugar, firmly packed
1/2 teaspoon vanilla extract
1/2 teaspoon lemon extract
1 cup mashed peeled *very ripe* bananas
1/2 cup chopped English walnuts or pecans
1/3 cup sifted confectioners' sugar
1 teaspoon cinnamon

Sift together the flour, baking powder, and salt. In a medium bowl, cream shortening thoroughly. Gradually add brown sugar, beating until light and fluffy. Add vanilla and lemon extracts. Beat in mashed bananas. Stir in dry ingredients and then nuts, mixing well. Spoon into a greased 11 x 7 x 2-inch baking pan, spreading evenly. Bake in a moderate oven (350 degrees F.) for 30 to 35 minutes or until a metal tester inserted in center of dough comes out clean. On a sheet of waxed paper, combine confectioners' sugar and cinnamon, mixing well. Remove baked dough from oven and cut into bars. Gently roll bars in cinnamon sugar mixture, coating each lightly.

–Vienna Taylor

Scotch Shortbread

Yield: about 4 dozen bars

"Scotch Shortbread was a favorite recipe of my parents, Jean and Tom Pryde, who were born in Scotland. My dad used to make and sell these very buttery short cookies to The Three Bears gift shop (not the storybook bears!) at the Medical College of Virginia, which in turn sold the cookies to hospital personnel and visitors."

2 cups butter or margarine, at room temperature
1/4 cup sugar
4 to 4 1/2 cups sifted flour

In a large bowl, cream butter thoroughly. Gradually add sugar, beating well. Stir in flour. Knead dough lightly until the mixture holds together. Pat cookie dough into a 15 x 10 x 1-inch baking pan; prick the surface, every 1/2 inch, with the tines of a fork. Bake in a *very* slow oven (250 degrees F.) for 1 hour. Cut into small triangles or bars while shortbread is hot. Allow cookies to cool completely in pan before removing. Store in an airtight container.

–Carole Ackell (Mrs. Edmund F.)

Cookie is an Americanized interpretation of the word Koekjes, referring to the sweet biscuits baked by the Dutch in colonial Nieuw Amsterdam.

Lemon Melt Aways

Yield: 16 cookies

1 cup butter or margarine, at room temperature
1 1/2 cups sugar
1 egg, beaten (reserve 1 tablespoon)
1 teaspoon grated lemon peel
1 teaspoon lemon extract
1/4 teaspoon salt
2 1/2 cups sifted flour

In a medium bowl, cream butter thoroughly; gradually add sugar, beating until light and fluffy. Add egg, lemon peel and extract, and salt, beating well. Stir in flour, mixing well. Knead dough lightly, then press into a greased 8 x 8 x 2-inch baking pan. Brush top of dough evenly with 1 tablespoon reserved beaten egg. Bake in a moderate oven (350 degrees F.) for 40 to 45 minutes or until done and golden brown. Cool in pan for about 25 to 30 minutes. Cut into diamond shapes or squares or bars or other desired shapes. Cookies harden as they cool. Store in an airtight container.

–Vienna Taylor

Rosegill Tea Room
(Mrs. Horace Welford Jones)
20 West Franklin Street
Richmond, Va.

Almond Cookies

1/2 pound of butter
1/4 pound of sugar
3/4 pound of flour
1 tablespoonful of Sauer's Almond Extract
1 teaspoonful of Sauer's Vanilla Extract

Mix all the ingredients together and knead thoroughly. Roll thin, cut with cookie cutters, and bake in a slow oven.

C. F. Sauer Company
Sauer Spices, circa 1920's

P and J Bars

Yield: about 3 dozen

"Children will delight with these as a lunch box trezt."

1 1/4 cups sifted flour
3/4 teaspoon baking soda
1/2 teaspoon baking powder
1/2 cup shortening
1/2 cup creamy or crunch-
style peanut butter
1/2 cup sugar
1/2 cup light brown sugar,
firmly packed
1 egg
1/2 to 1 cup seedless grape
or raspberry jam, or
cherry or strawberry
preserves
Glaze

Sift together the first 3 ingredients. In a medium bowl, cream shortening and peanut butter until mixture is smooth. Gradually add sugars, beating until mixture is light and fluffy. Add egg, beating well. Reserve 1 cup cookie dough; evenly press remaining dough in an ungreased 13 x 9 x 2-inch baking pan. Spread dough in pan evenly with jam or preserves. Crumble remaining 1 cup dough and evenly sprinkle over jam layer. Bake in a moderate oven (350 degrees F.) for 20 minutes or until golden brown. Cool. Drizzle glaze evenly over baked dough. Cut into 2 x 1 1/2-inch bars.

Glaze
1/2 cup sifted confectioners'
sugar
1 tablespoon butter or
margarine, melted
1/2 teaspoon vanilla extract
1/2 to 1 tablespoon hot
water

In a small bowl, combine confectioners' sugar, butter, and vanilla, beating well. Add hot water, 1/2 teaspoon at a time, beating until glaze is desired consistency and smooth.

–Linda M. Bourgeois (Mrs. Bruce)

Picturesque Village

Richmond, "befo' de war," was a charming, picturesque village, with vistas, such as Henry James did not find when he came one snowy winter, for then Richmond was in its ugliest period, that of transition....

Louisa Coleman Blair
*"'Little Red Brick Town' In Era of Hoopskirts
Was Friendly, Gossipy,"*
Richmond Times-Dispatch, December 7, 1941

615

New Year's Entertaining

But when I look back on the post-bellum days in Richmond, with their steady, sturdy bravery, their cheerful spirit, although our young men were stunted in body from overwork and want of athletics, I rejoice that I witnessed such a courageous generation, the finest I have ever known, and the picture that comes most lovingly to mind is that of the young men in their old evening or borrowed clothes, the girls in home-made simple dresses, dancing with vim in the low-pitched, simple little hall of the City Water Works below Hollywood.

Louisa Coleman Blair
"'Little Red Brick Town' In Era of Hoopskirts Was Friendly, Gossipy,"
Richmond Times-Dispatch, December 7, 1941

Jumbals

Put one pound of nice sugar into two pounds of flour; add pounded spice of any kind, and pass them through a sieve; beat four eggs, pour them on with three quarters of a pound of melted butter, knead all well together, and bake them.

Mrs. Mary Randolph
The Virginia House-Wife, or Methodical Cook, *1830*

Mrs. Beasley's Pecan Squares

Yield: 25 (1 1/2-inch) squares

"This old recipe was one of my mothers' favorite cookies."

1 cup sifted flour
2 teaspoons cinnamon
1 1/2 teaspoons baking powder
1/2 teaspoon allspice
1/4 teaspoon ground cloves
1/8 teaspoon salt

Sift together the first 6 ingredients. In a medium bowl, beat eggs lightly. Gradually add sugar, beating until mixture is thick and light yellow in color. Fold dry ingredients into beaten egg mixture. Fold in pecans. Pour batter into two greased 9 x 9 x 2-inch baking pans. Bake in a moderate oven (350 degrees F.) for 20 minutes. Do *not*

616

4 eggs
2 1/4 cups dark brown sugar,
firmly packed
2 cups chopped pecans
Sifted confectioners' sugar

overbake. Remove from oven, dust top of cookies with sifted confectioners' sugar, and cut into squares while cookies are still hot. Allow squares to remain in pan until cool.

Note: Squares should be very moist.

–Frances Fox (Mrs. Paul)

Fudge-Filled Oatmeal Bars

Yield: about 6 dozen bars

2 1/2 cups sifted flour
1 teaspoon baking soda
1 teaspoon salt, divided
1 cup butter or margarine,
at room temperature
2 cups light brown sugar,
firmly packed
2 eggs
2 teaspoons vanilla extract,
divided
3 cups rolled oats, quick
cooking or regular
1 (14-ounce) can sweetened
condensed milk
1 (12-ounce) package semi-
sweet chocolate pieces
2 tablespoons butter or
margarine
1 cup chopped English
walnuts or pecans

Sift together the flour, baking soda, and 1/2 teaspoon salt. In a large bowl, cream 1 cup butter until smooth. Gradually add brown sugar, beating mixture until it is light and fluffy. Add eggs, one at a time, beating well after each addition, and 1 teaspoon vanilla. Stir in flour mixture and oats, mixing well. Reserve 1/3 cup of oatmeal mixture; press remaining mixture evenly in a greased 15 x 10 x 1-inch baking pan. In a 2-quart heavy saucepan, combine sweetened condensed milk, chocolate pieces, 2 tablespoons butter, and 1/2 teaspoon salt; stir over low heat until chocolate pieces and butter are melted. Remove from heat and stir in 1 teaspoon vanilla and chopped nuts. Spread hot chocolate mixture evenly over oatmeal mixture in pan. Drop reserved oatmeal mixture by rounded teaspoonfuls evenly over chocolate mixture in pan. Bake, uncovered, in a moderate oven (350 degrees F.) for 25 to 30 minutes or until done and topping is lightly browned. While baked dough is warm, cut into 2 x 2-inch bars. Cool thoroughly.

–Linda M. Bourgeois (Mrs. Bruce)

Mansion Fudge Brownies

Yield: about 16 brownies

These tempting confections were a specialty served at the Virginia Executive Mansion while Eddy Dalton was First Lady of Virginia.

2 squares (ounces) unsweetened chocolate
1/2 cup butter or margarine
2 eggs, beaten
1 cup sugar
1 teaspoon vanilla extract
Pinch of salt
1/4 cup sifted flour
2/3 cup chopped English or black walnuts, or pecans, or cashews, or peanuts (optional)
Sifted confectioners' sugar as needed

In a small heavy saucepan, melt chocolate and butter over low heat; cool. In a medium bowl, combine chocolate mixture, eggs, sugar, vanilla, and salt, beating well. Stir in flour, mixing well. Fold in nuts, if desired. Spoon into a lightly greased 9x9 x 2-inch baking pan, spreading evenly. Bake in a moderate oven (350 degrees F.)for 25 to 30 minutes or until a cake tester inserted into the center of the brownies comes out clean. *Do not overbake.* Cool in pan 10 minutes; sprinkle top of brownies with confectioners' sugar and cut into squares.

–Eddy Dalton (Mrs. John)
First Lady of Virginia, 1978 to 1982
Virginia State Senator, 1987 to ___

Jumbles

(This formula may be utilized in disposing of the egg-yolks left after making cakes like angel food.)

1 cupful of butter
2 cupfuls of sugar
2 1/2 cupfuls of flour
8 eggs (yolks only)
1 teaspoonful of baking powder
2 teaspoonfuls of Sauer's Orange, Lemon or Vanilla Extract.

Cream the sugar and butter; add the egg yolks, well beaten; then add the flour, into which the baking powder has previously been sifted. Finally, add Sauer's flavoring extract. Roll thin, and cut with a regular jumble cutter. When baked, sugar the tops.

C. F. Sauer Company
Sauer Spices, circa 1920's

> ....When Winston Churchill came to dinner, the servant
> who took his coat and hat was drunk and in the course
> of outlandish fumbling dropped both. Dismissed, the
> servant reappeared on bended knees, begging extravagantly
> for his job. He won it from a forgiving Tuck (governor),
> who could appreciate good showmanship. (circa late 1940's)
>
> William Seal
> **Virginia's Executive Mansion:**
> **A History of the Governor's House, 1988**

Nutritious Delicious Carrot Cookies

Yield: about 3 dozen medium-size cookies

1 1/2 cups sifted flour
1 teaspoon nutmeg
1/2 teaspoon baking powder
1/2 teaspoon baking soda
1/8 teaspoon salt (optional)
1/2 cup shortening
1/2 cup corn oil margarine,
 at room temperature
1 cup light brown sugar,
 firmly packed
2 eggs
1 teaspoon vanilla extract
2 cups rolled oats, quick
 cooking
1 cup finely grated peeled
 carrots
1 cup chopped English
 walnuts or pecans
1 cup shredded coconut
 (see note)

Sift together the first 5 ingredients. In a large bowl, cream shortening and margarine together until smooth. Gradually add sugar, beating until light and fluffy. Add eggs and vanilla, and continue beating until smooth. Stir in flour mixture and rolled oats, mixing well. Stir in carrots, walnuts, and coconut. Drop by rounded teaspoonfuls, 2 inches apart, onto greased baking sheets. Bake in a moderate oven (350 degrees F.) for 12 to 15 minutes or until cookies are lightly browned. *Do not overbake.* Cookies should be moist and chewy.

Note: 1 cup chopped dark or golden seedles raisins may be substituted for coconut or use 1/2 cup of each.

–Elinor Kuhn (Mrs. Frank)
Buffet, catering firm
Richmond Culinary Guild

Scottish Shortbread

Yield: about 16 to 36 squares

3/4 cup plus 1 1/2
 tablespoons butter or
 margarine, at room
 temperature
1/2 cup sugar
2 1/3 cups sifted flour

In a bowl, cream butter thoroughly. Gradually add sugar, beating until light and fluffy. Stir in dry ingredients, mixing well. Mixture will be crumbly and have the appearance of corn meal. Press mixture firmly into a shortbread mold or 8x8x2-inch baking pan, packing tightly. If using a short-bread mold, rap mold sharply 2 or 3 times to loosen shortbread from mold. Arrange pan on an ungreased baking sheet. Bake in a moderate oven (350 degrees F.) for 20 minutes or until bottom edges are golden brown; reduce heat to *very* slow (250 degrees F) and bake an additional 20 min-utes or until top is golden brown. If baking in a pan, bake until golden brown. Cut shortbread into 2x1/2-inch bars immediately upon removal from oven. *Shortbread cannot be cut cold.*

–Barbara Cole
The Scottish Society of Richmond

Market Has Changed Little

Crowds of haggling shoppers, holly thick with berries, the scents of pine and cedar, and competent, warmly-wrapped vendors weave Christmas spells in Richmond's Sixth Street Market....

It's not unusual to see Mrs. Emily Royal slice sweet potatoes into a pan over the coals, then produce several small skillets and pots in which she cooks pork chops and coffee. (Hot food tastes good on mornings when the temperature dips to 10 degrees.)....

Katherine Whaley
"Market Has Changed Little,"
Old Richmond Newspaper, Date Unknown

Every one of distinction brought letters of introduction to Mr. Wickham whose attainment, grace of manner and great wealth placed him at the head of society in Richmond which then could boast of a highly cultivated and refined circle ... Mr. and Mrs. Wickham entertained grandly. All strangers of distinction from abroad or at home were entertained at his house for he was at the head of society in Richmond and as distinguished for his grace of manner as for the charm of his conversation-- No one of note came to Richmond without letters of introduction to the Wickhams — and were entertained at dinner or in the evening ...

Miss Harley Graham's account of the Wickhams,
April 11, 1890

Lombardy Park

621

Miniature Fruit Cake Drops

Yield: (about 5 1/2 dozen cookies)

8 ounces candied
  pineapple, chopped
4 ounces candied red
  cherries, quartered
4 ounces candied green
  cherries, quartered
4 ounces candied orange
  peel, chopped
2 cups pecans or walnuts
  chopped1 cup dark
  seedless raisins
1 cup chopped pitted dates
1 1/2 cups flour, divided
1 teaspoon baking soda
1/2 teaspoon cinnamon
1/2 teaspoon nutmeg
1/4 teaspoon ground cloves
1/2 cup butter or margarine,
  at room temperature
1/2 cup light brown sugar,
  firmly packed
2 eggs
1/4 cup bourbon whisky or
  brandy

In a large bowl, combine fruits and nuts; dredge with 3/4 cup flour, stirring well. Set mixture aside. Sift remaining 3/4 cup flour with baking powder and spices, mixing well; set aside. Cream butter thoroughly in a large bowl; gradually add sugar, beating well at medium speed of an electric mixer. Add eggs, mixing well. Stir in flour and spice mixture, mixing well. Add bourbon whisky or brandy. Fold fruit and nut mixture into batter. Drop by rounded teaspoonfuls onto greased baking sheets, about 2 inches apart. Bake in a slow oven (325 degrees F.) for 13 to 15 minutes or until done. Cool on wire racks.

Variation: Fill miniature muffin pans (1 1/2 inches in diameter) lined with paper baking cups almost full of batter. Bake in a slow oven (325 degrees F.) for 18 to20 minutes or until a cake tester inserted in center comes out clean.

Old Richmond Advertisemetn, date unknown

622

Fudge Crackles

Yield: about 6 dozen cookies

"My boys call these confections, 'Cracked Chocolate Cookies'."

2 cups sifted flour
2 teaspoons baking powder
1/2 teaspoon salt
4 squares (ounces) unsweetened chocolate
2 cups sugar
1/2 cup cooking oil or shortening, melted and cooled
4 eggs
2 teaspoons vanilla extract
1 cup sifted confectioners' sugar

Sift together the first 3 ingredients. In the top of a double boiler, melt chocolate over simmering water; cool. In a large bowl, combine sugar and oil, beating well. Stir in chocolate. Add eggs, one at a time, beating well after each addition, and vanilla. Stir in dry ingredients, mixing well. Cover and chill in the refrigerator for several hours. Drop dough by rounded teaspoonfuls into confectioners' sugar spread on a sheet of waxed paper, coating each well. Shape coated dough pieces into balls. Arrange balls, 2 inches apart, on greased baking sheets. Bake in a moderate oven (350 degrees F.) for 10 to 12 minutes. *Do not overbake.* Cool slightly and then transfer to wire racks to finish cooling.

–Linda M. Bourgeois (Mrs. Bruce)

Chocolate Coconut Macaroons

Yield: about 1 1/2 dozen cookies

1 1/2 squares (ounces) unsweetened chocolate
2/3 cup sweetened condensed milk
1 1/2 cups shredded coconut
1/4 cup sifted flour
1/2 teaspoon vanilla extract

In the top of a double boiler, melt chocolate over hot water. Remove from heat and blend in sweetened condensed milk. Stir in coconut, flour, and vanilla, mixing well. Drop by rounded teaspoonfuls onto greased baking sheets. Bake in a moderate oven (350 degrees F.) for 15 minutes. *Do not over bake.* Remove cookies immediately from baking sheets and transfer to wire racks to cool thoroughly.

–Ladies' Missionary Society
Great Hope Baptist Church

Fabulous Nutty White Chocolate Morsels

Yield: 5 1/2 to 6 dozen cookies

Inspired by the original Toll House cookie recipe of a half century ago, these cookies include the popular food stuffs of the late twentieth century, Macadamia nuts and white chocolate. The Toll House Cookie (chocolate chip) which is every American's idea of what a cookie should be, originated at a charming wayside inn in Massachusetts. Ruth Wakefield, mistress of the Toll House, began serving these crisp little cookies filled with bits of semi-sweet chocolate during the 1940's. She generously shared her recipe with visitors, causing a "run" on semi-sweet chocolate bars at local grocery stores, emptying the shelves.

2 1/4 cups sifted flour
1 teaspoon baking soda
1 teaspoon salt
1 cup butter or margarine, at room temperature (see note)
3/4 cup sugar
3/4 cup light brown sugar, firmly packed
2 eggs, beaten
1 teaspoon vanilla extract
2 cups sweet white chocolate baking pieces
1 cup coarsely chopped Macadamia nuts or pecans

Sift together the first 3 ingredients. In a medium bowl, cream butter until smooth. Gradually add sugar, beating until light andf luffy. Beat in eggs and vanilla. Stir in dry ingredients, mixing well. Fold in chocolate pieces and nuts. Drop dough by rounded teaspoonfuls, 2 inches apart, onto ungreased baking sheets. Bake in a moderate oven (375 degrees F.) for 10 minutes, or until done. Do *not overbake.* Transfer cookies to wire racks to cool. Cookies will be soft upon removal from oven and will firm upon cooling. Store in an airtight container.

Note: Cookies made with butter will tend to be flatter and the dough will spread out more readily as they bake than those made with margarine which tend to puff up and hold their shape. The flavor of butter, however, can not be duplicated.

Kisses

We can thank Elizabeth I of England for the popularity of the petite meringue confections we call kisses! These sweets were usually served to the queen by her chief lady-in-waiting. Kneeling before her sovereign , the lady would kiss the "faire cloth" that held the treats before presenting them to the queen to be tasted.

Chocolate Tipped Meringue Kisses

Yield: about 4 dozen

Meringues are easy, but somewhat tricky to prepare. They are greatly affected by humidity. For best results, prepare them on a dry, low humidity day.

4 egg whites
1 teaspoon vanilla extract
1/2 teaspoon vinegar
1/4 teaspoon cream of tartar
1/4 teaspoon salt
1 cup sugar
1 cup finely chopped black
  or English walnuts,
  pecans, or toasted
  almonds
1 (12-ounce) package semi-
  sweet chocolate pieces
1/2 ounce (1 tablespoon)
  parrafin

Cover 4 baking sheets with heavy brown paper (not paper grocery bags) or parchment (or use Teflon-lined pans). Brush liberally with cooking oil. Beat together the first 5 ingredients until egg whites are white and foamy. Add sugar, 1 table-spoon at a time, and continue beating until sugar is entirely dissolved and egg whites stand in *very stiff*, glossy, firm peaks. Fold in nuts. Drop by tablespoonfuls or teaspoonfuls onto oiled paper, about 2 inches apart. Bake in a very slow oven (250 degrees F.) for 45 minutes, or until kisses are dry and a light ivory color. Turn off heat. Remove meringues from paper, transferring to a wire rack, and return to oven to cool. In the top of a double boiler, melt semi-sweet chocolate pieces and paraffin together over boiling water. Dip one edge of cooled kisses in hot melted chocolate mixture. Cool on a sheet of waxed paper.

Polka Dot Macaroons

Yield: about 3 dozen

3 egg whites
1/2 teaspoon salt
3/4 cup sugar
1 teaspoon vanilla extract
3 cups cornflakes
1 (6-ounce) package semi-
  sweet chocolate pieces

In a bowl, beat egg whites and salt until foamy. Gradually beat in sugar and vanilla, beating until soft, glossy, but not dry, peaks are formed. Fold in cornflakes and chocolate pieces. Drop by rounded teaspoonfuls, 2 inches apart, onto lightly greased baking sheets. Bake in a moderate oven (350 degrees F.) for 15 minutes or until lightly browned. Allow macaroons to cool on baking sheets for 1 to 2 minutes. Transfer to wire racks to finish cooling.

Surprise Meringues

Yield: about 3 dozen

2 egg whites
1/4 teaspoon vanilla extract
1/8 teaspoon cream of tartar
1/8 teaspoon salt
3/4 cup sugar
1 (6-ounce) package semi-
  sweet chocolate pieces
1/4 cup chopped pecans

Line baking sheets with heavy brown paper (not paper grocery bags) or parchment (or use Teflon-lined pans). Brush liberally with cooking oil. In a bowl, combine egg whites, vanilla, cream of tartar, and salt; beat until foamy. Gradually add sugar, 1 tablespoon at a time, beating until sugar is completely dissolved and whites form stiff, glossy, but not dry peaks. Fold in chocolate pieces and pecans. Drop by rounded teaspoonfuls, 2 inches apart, onto oiled paper. Bake in a slow oven (300 degrees F.) for 25 minutes or until meringues are a light ivory color and can be easily lifted from paper. Transfer to wire racks to cool.

The gay social whirl reached its height last week. The entertainments were many and they were varied. There were lunches, suppers, dinners, teas, receptions and dances, and the fortunate people who went have but one voice. All were elegant, and some—including the reception given by Mrs. Gideon Davenport—were so brilliant as to rival any private entertaining here for many years....

On Monday night Mr. and Mrs. Edgar Freeman entertained practically the same party at an elegant dinner given in the beautiful Green dining-room at the Westmoreland Clubhouse...

"Society,"
The Times-Richmond Va., January 30, 1898

Revitalized Main Street

Crunchy Cranberry Nut Drops

Yield: about 5 dozen cookies

1 1/2 cups sifted flour
1/2 teaspoon baking powder
1/4 teaspoon salt
1/8 teaspoon baking soda
1/4 cup butter or margarine,
   at room temperature
1/2 cup sugar
1/3 cup plus 1/2 tablespoon
   light brown sugar, firmly
   packed
2 tablespoons milk
1 tablespoon orange juice
1 egg yolk
1 1/4 cups chopped or
   coarsely ground
   cranberries
1/2 cup chopped pecans or
   English walnuts

Sift together the first 4 ingredients. In a large bowl, cream butter thoroughly. Gradually add sugars, beating until light and fluffy. Add milk, orange juice, and egg yolk, beating well. Stir in dry ingredients, mixing well. Stir in cranberries and nuts. Drop dough by rounded teaspoonfuls, 2 inches apart, onto greased baking sheets. Bake in a moderate oven (375 degrees F.) for 10 to 15 minutes or until done. Transfer to wire racks to cool thoroughly.

–Linda M. Bourgeois (Mrs. Bruce)

627

Old-Fashioned Mincemeat Cookies

Yield: about 8 dozen

These are similar to Grandma's fat old-fashioned style of cookies. They don't last long.

3 1/4 cups sifted flour
1/2 teaspoon salt
1 cup butter or margarine,
  at room temperature
1 1/2 cups sugar
3 eggs
3 tablespoons brandy or
  orange juice
1 teaspoon baking soda
1 1/2 cups mincemeat (see
  note)
1 cup chopped English
  walnuts
2 tablespoons grated
  orange peel
Brandy or Orange Glaze
  (optional)

Sift together flour and salt. In a large bowl, cream butter and sugar until light and fluffy. Beat in eggs. Combine brandy or orange juice and baking soda, stirring until well dissolved. Stir one-half of the flour mixture and all of the soda mixture into the batter. Add remaining flour mixture, mincemeat, and nuts, mixing well. Drop by rounded teaspoonfuls, 2 inches apart, onto greased baking sheets. Bake in a moderate oven (350 degrees F.) for 10 to12 minutes or until golden brown. Transfer cookies from baking sheets to wire racks to cool while cookies are still soft. Store cookies in an airtight container. Frost cookies with Brandy or Orange Glaze, if desired.

Note: Commercial or homemade mincemeat may be used.

Brandy or Orange Glaze

1/4 cup butter or margarine,
  at room temperature
2 cups sifted confectioners'
  sugar
3 to 4 tablespoons *warmed*
  brandy or orange juice

In a small bowl, cream butter thoroughly. Gradually add confectioners' sugar, beating well. Add enough brandy or orange juice to achieve desired spreading consistency. Glaze will be slightly runny.

–Updated Old Richmond Recipe, circa 1920's
Source unknown

Old Richmond Advertisement, date unknown

Frosted Orange Drops

Yield: about 4 dozen

2 cups sifted flour
1/4 teaspoon baking powder
1 (3-ounce) package cream
  cheese, at room
  temperature
1/2 cup shortening
1 cup sugar
2 eggs
1 tablespoon grated orange
  peel
1 teaspoon vanilla extract
1/2 cup frozen orange juice
  concentrate, thawed
Creamy Orange Frosting

Sift together flour and baking powder. In a large bowl, beat cream cheese and shortening together until smooth. Gradually beat in sugar until mixture is light and fluffy. Beat in eggs. Add orange peel and vanilla. Alternately stir in dry ingredients and orange juice concentrate, mixing well. Drop by rounded teaspoonfuls, 2 1/2 inches apart, onto lightly greased baking sheets. Bake in a moderate oven (375 degrees F.) for 10 minutes or until done and lightly browned. *Do not overbake.* While cookies are baking, prepare frosting. Transfer to wire racks to cool. Frost cookies while still warm.

Creamy Orange Frosting
1 (3-ounce) package cream
  cheese, at room
  temperature
3 to 4 tablespoons orange
  juice concentrate, thawed
About 4 cups sifted
  confectioners' sugar
1/2 teaspoon vanilla extract
1 teaspoon grated orange
  peel (optional)

In a medium bowl, beat cream cheese until smooth. Gradually beat in confectioners' sugar and orange juice concentrate to achieve desired spreading consistency. Beat in vanilla. Stir in orange peel, if desired.

"Biscuits Au Rhum."

The whites of three eggs, a small cup of powdered sugar, 1 dozen macaroons, 1 quart of sweet cream, a large wine glass and a half of rum; beat eggs to a stiff froth, gradually incorporate the sugar, pound and roll macaroons until they are as crumbs, then add to the eggs and sugar; when well mixed make into biscuits or small round cakes, and slightly brown; now whip the cream, sweeten slightly and season with rum. When ready to serve, line a glass dish with the biscuits and entirely cover with the whipped cream. Decorate the top with conserves.

–Mrs. Clarence T. Boykin
Receipts for Luncheon and Tea, *1898*

Grandmother's Pennsylvania Dutch Sugar Cakes

Yield: about 2 dozen

4 cups sifted flour
3 teaspoons baking powder
2 teaspoons baking soda
1 cup butter or margarine,
  at room temperature
2 cups sugar
3 eggs
1 1/2 teaspoons vanilla
  extract
1 cup buttermilk

Sift together the first 3 ingredients. In a bowl, cream butter until smooth. Gradually add sugar, beating until light and fluffy. Add eggs, one at a time, and vanilla, beating well after each addition. Alternately add dry ingredients and buttermilk, mixing well. Cover and refrigerate for 24 hours. Drop by rounded teaspoonfuls, 2 1/2 inches apart, onto greased and floured baking sheets. Bake in a moderate over (375 degrees F.) for 7 minutes or until golden brown. Remove from baking sheets and cool on wire racks. Store in layers between sheets of waxed paper in an airtight container.

–Sundra Faber (Mrs. H. B., Jr.)

Walnut Clusters

Yield: 2 1/2 dozen

1/2 cup sifted flour
1/2 teaspoon salt
1/2 teaspoon baking powder
2 squares (ounces)
  unsweetened chocolate
1/4 cup butter or margarine,
  at room temperature
1/2 cup sugar
1 egg
1 1/2 teaspoons vanilla
  extract
2 cups coarsely chopped
  English walnuts

Sift together the first 3 ingredients. In the top of a double boiler, melt chocolate over *hot* water; cool slightly. In a bowl, cream butter thoroughly. Gradually add sugar, beating until light and fluffy. Beat in egg and vanilla. Add chocolate. Stir in dry ingredients. Fold in walnuts. Drop by rounded teaspoonfuls, 1 inch apart, onto greased baking sheets. Bake in a moderate oven (350 degrees F.) for 10 minutes (*no longer*). Remove from oven and transfer to wire racks to cool.

–Virginia Cottrell (Mrs. Walker C., Jr.)

Whoopie Pies

Yield: about 2 1/2 dozen

2 3/4 cups sifted flour
1 teaspoon baking soda
1 teaspoon baking powder
1/2 teaspoon salt
1/2 cup hot water
1/2 cup sifted cocoa
1/2 cup shortening
1 1/2 cups sugar
1 teaspoon vanilla extract
2 eggs, well beaten
1/2 cup sour milk (see note)
Cream Filling

Sift together the first 4 ingredients. In a small bowl, stir hot water into cocoa until well blended and a smooth paste is formed. In a medium bowl, cream shortening thoroughly. Gradually add sugar, beating well. Add vanilla and eggs, beating well after each addition. Alternately add dry ingredients with sour milk and cocoa paste, mixing well. Drop by tablespoonfuls, 2 inches apart, onto greased baking sheets. Bake in a moderate oven (350 degrees F.) for 15 minutes or until done. Transfer to wire racks to thoroughly cool. Liberally spread filling over 15 cookies, dividing evenly. Top each with a second cookie.

Note: Add 1 1/2 teaspoons lemon juice to 1/2 cup milk; allow to stand for 10 minutes to sour.

Cream Filling
1/2 cup cold milk
2 1/2 tablespoons flour
1/2 cup shortening
1/2 cup sugar
1 teaspoon vanilla extract
Pinch of salt

In a small heavy saucepan, gradually stir milk into flour, blending well. Cook, stirring constantly, over moderate heat until mixture is thickened and bubbly hot. Cool. In a small bowl, cream shortening thoroughly. Gradually add sugar, beating well. Add vanilla and salt. Beat in cooled cooked milk-flour mixture.

–Laurie Brickham (Mrs. Bruce)

Empire Biscuits

Sift well six heaping tablespoons of flour, four tablespoons of sugar, one teaspoon of cinnamon. Cut into this one fourth of a pound of butter. Knead together lightly, roll out thin. Prick all over with a fork and cut with small round cutters. Bake in moderate oven on greased papers about twenty minutes. Cool. Put currant jelly between two biscuits, spread the top with a flavored white icing then decorate with candied angelica or cherries.

Old Recipe, Richmond, Virginia, date unknown
The Williamsburg Art of Cookery, 1938

Agecroft

Agecroft Hall, a fifteenth century English Tudor house, located on twenty-three acres adjacent to the James River in the elegant Windsor Farms area of Richmond, includes an interesting Elizabethan herb garden featuring eighty-five culinary and physic varieties. Transported from Lancashire, England in the 1920's, the manor house has been restored and furnished with authentic period antiquities. Now open as a lifestyle museum, Agecroft affords visitors a magnificent view of the meandering James River.

Nutty Ice Box Cookies

Yield: about 6 to 8 dozen

3 1/2 cups sifted flour
1 teaspoon baking soda
1/2 teaspoon salt
1 cup butter or margarine,
  at room temperature
2 cups light brown sugar,
  firmly packed
2 eggs
1 teaspoon vanilla extract
1 cup chopped black
  walnuts or pecans

Sift together the first 3 ingredients. In a large bowl, cream butter thoroughly. Gradually add brown sugar, beating until light and fluffy. Add eggs and vanilla, beating well. Stir in dry ingredients, mixing well. Stir in nuts. Form dough into two long rolls, dividing evenly. Wrap in waxed paper and refrigerate for at least 12 hours. With a sharp knife, cut each cookie roll into thin slices. Arrange cookie slices on lightly greased baking sheets. Bake in a hot oven (400 degrees F.) for 7 to 8 minutes or until browned. *Do not overbake.* Transfer to wire racks to cool.

–Dorothy Parker (Mrs. Walter)

Thumbprint Cookies with Mild Southern Sweet Pepper Jelly

Yield: 3 dozen cookies

"Serve these cookies at holiday time to create a nice surprise."

2/3 cup butter or margarine,
  at room temperature
1/2 cup light brown sugar,
  firmly packed
1 egg, separated
1/2 teaspoon vanilla extract
1 1/2 cups sifted flour
1 cup finely chopped pine
  nuts, Macadamia nuts,
  pecans, pistachio nuts, or
  English walnuts
About 2/3 cup red or green
  Mild Southern Sweet
  Pepper Jelly (see index)
  or 1/3 cup red and 1/3 cup
  green pepper jelly.

In a medium bowl, cream butter thoroughly. Gradually add brown sugar, beating until light and fluffy. Add egg yolk and vanilla, beating well. Stir in flour, mixing well. Shape dough into balls, each about 3/4 to 1-inch in diameter. Dip balls into egg white, drain, and them roll in nuts on a sheet of waxed paper, coating dough ball well. Arrange balls, 1 inch apart, on ungreased baking sheets. With the thumb, make a depression in the center of each ball. Bake in a moderate oven (350 degrees F.) for 10 minutes. Remove from oven and press thumb or handle end of a wooden spoon into each depression. Quickly fill depressions with red and/or green pepper jelly. Bake cookies an additional 5 to 10 minutes, until jelly in cookie depressions melts. Transfer cookies to wire racks to cool. Store in an airtight container.

–Vienna Taylor

633

> Our Hessian citizen (Joseph Darmsdadt) established himself
> in Richmond, not long after he renounced his foreign alle-
> giance. He was a shrewd man, and as the valley beyond the
> Blue Ridge was settled by Germans, his knowledge of the
> language enabled him to attract the custom of the farmers,
> who drove their wagons to Richmond, laden with the prod-
> ucts of the dairy, the mill, the forest and the chase.
>
> The social disposition of Mr. Darmsdadt brought him into
> society, even the best. His own entertainments were given
> daily. Almost all our citizens, in those days, went early to
> market, to furnish their larders; and Mr. D. would have a
> large coffee-pot before his fireplace, of the contents of which,
> prepared by himself, many of his friends, judges, lawyers,
> doctors and merchants, partook, whenever they were so
> inclined—particularly on wet or cold mornings; and here the
> chit chat of the day was first heard, and much news was
> circulated from this social coffee-house. Its proprietor re-
> tained it and its customers some thirty or forty years, until his
> death.
>
> Samuel Mordecai
> **Richmond in By-Gone Days,** 1856
> Reprint Edition, 1975

Chocolate Tipped Nut Slices

Yield: about 6 1/2 dozen cookies

2 cups sifted flour
1 1/2 teaspoons baking
  powder
1/2 teaspoon salt
2/3 cup butter or margarine,
  at room temperature
1 cup sugar
1 egg
1 teaspoon vanilla extract
1/2 teaspoon almond

Sift together the first 3 ingredients. In a large bowl, cream butter thoroughly. Gradually add sugar, beating until light and fluffy. Add egg and flavorings, beating well. Add dry ingredients, mixing well. Transfer 3/4 cup dough into a small bowl. Add 1/4 cup nuts and 2 to 3 drops food coloring (red for almonds, pecans, and walnuts, green for pistachio nuts), mixing well. Form dough into a roll 10 inches in length; cover in clear plastic wrap.

extract (optional)

1 cup finely chopped or
coarsely ground blanched
almonds, or pecans, or
black or English walnuts,
or pistachio nuts, divided

1 (6-ounce) package semi-
sweet chocolate pieces

Form remaining dough into a 10 x 4 1/2-inch rectangle; cover in clear plastic wrap. Refrigerate both cookie dough roll and rectangle for 1 hour. Place nutty dough roll in the center of dough rectangle; carefully mold uncolored cookie dough around colored dough. Cover in clear plastic wrap and refrigerate until dough is very firm, about 8 to 12 hours.

With a sharp knife, cut roll into 1/8-inch thick slices. Arrange cookie slices, 2 inches apart, on ungreased baking sheets. Bake in a moderate oven (375 degrees F.) for 8 to 10 minutes or until lightly browned.

Transfer cookies to wire racks to cool completely. In the top of a double boiler, melt chocolate over hot water. Spread edges of cooled cookies with melted chocolate, then carefully roll the edge of each cookie in the remaining nuts. Refrigerate cookies until chocolate is firm. Store in airtight containers.

–Nancy Scoggins (Mrs. Robert)
Valentine Museum Guild

Tavern Biscuit

To one pound of flour, add half a pound of sugar, half a pound of butter, some mace and nutmeg powdered, and a glass of brandy or wine; wet it with milk, and when well kneaded, roll it thin, cut it in shapes, and bake it quickly.

Mrs. Mary Randolph
The Virginia House-Wife, or Methodical Cook, *1830*

...The kitchen, wholly modernized by Governor Davis, was entirely rebuilt beneath the dining room....The reborn kitchen house served, and still serves, many purposes beyond housing guests and overflow from the household.
(circa 1926)

William Seal
**Virginia's Executive Mansion:
A History of the Governor's House,** 1988

Lacy Oatmeal Crisps

Yield: about 5 dozen cookies

1 cup whole wheat flour
1 teaspoon baking soda
1 teaspoon cinnamon
1/2 teaspoon salt
1/2 cup toasted wheat germ
  granules
1 cup butter or margarine,
  at room temperature
1 cup light brown sugar,
  firmly packed
1/4 cup sugar
2 eggs, beaten
1 teaspoon vanilla extract
1 1/2 cups rolled oats, quick
  cooking or regular
1 cup chopped English
  walnuts
Granulated sugar as needed

Sift together the first 4 ingredients; add wheat germ, mixing well. In a large bowl, cream butter thoroughly. Gradually add sugars, beating until mixture is light and fluffy. Add eggs, one at a time, and vanilla, beating well after each addition. Stir flour mixture into butter mixture, mixing well. Stir in rolled oats and walnuts. Cover and chill in the refrigerator for 2 hours. For each cookie, shape 1 tablespoon dough into a ball. Arrange balls, 4 inches apart, on greased baking sheets. Generously butter the bottom of a flat bottomed glass. For each cookie, dip the bottom of the glass into granulated sugar and then press dough balls with sugar coated glass; flatten each to a 1/4-inch thickness. If the dough sticks to the glass, coat glass bottom with additional butter. Bake in a moderate oven (375 degrees F.) for 5 minutes or until done. *Do not overbake.* Transfer warm cookies to wire racks to cool. Store in an airtight container.

–Carole Ackell (Mrs. Edmund F.)

Peppered Biscotte (Biscuits)

Yield: about 30 to 36

1 3/4 cups sifted flour
1/2 teaspoon baking powder
1/2 teaspoon baking soda
1 teaspoon coarsely ground
  black pepper
1/2 cup butter or margarine,
  at room temperature
1 cup sugar
2 eggs
1 tablespoon grated lemon
  peel
1 teaspoon vanilla extract
1/2 teaspoon almond
  extract

Sift together the first 3 ingredients; add pepper, mixing well. In a medium bowl, cream butter thoroughly; gradually add sugar, beating until light and fluffy. Add eggs, one at a time, beating well after each addition. Stir in lemon peel and flavorings. Add dry ingredients, mixing well. Stir in nuts. Chill dough, covered, in the refrigerator for 12 hours. Divide dough into thirds. Shape each dough portion into a long roll, about 1 1/2 inches in diameter. Arrange each dough roll on an ungreased small baking sheet. Bake rolls in a moderate oven (350 degrees F.) for 20 minutes or until done. Remove rolls from oven and cool slightly. With a sharp knife, diagonally cut roll

1 cup coarsely chopped toasted pecans or blanched almonds (see note)

into 1/2-inch thick slices. Arrange cookie slices on baking sheets and continue to bake for an additional 10 to 15 minutes or until lightly browned. Transfer cookies to metal racks to cool thoroughly. Store in an airtight container.

–Elinor Kuhn (Mrs. Frank)
Buffet, catering firm
Richmond Culinary Guild

Soft Ginger Cakes

Cream together one cup sugar, one half cup of lard. Add one cup black molasses. Dissolve one teaspoon soda in one cup sour milk. Add enough flour to make butter stiff. Sift with flour, one teaspoon ground ginger, one teaspoon cinnamon. Drop from spoon. Bake in moderate oven on greased tins.

Old Recipe, Richmond, Virginia, date unknown
The Williamsburg Art of Cookery, *1938*

Morning Visits to Market

In the morning everyone went to market (or wanted to), elderly, gentlemen, grown girls, open willow market-basket on the arm. It was considered necessary to inspect what was to be used for the household's food, although Richmond's market was good and varied—tender meats, seafood of the best, sturgeon (then looked down upon), venison, sora, partridges, squabs, squirrels, lucious melons and vegetables from Hanover County.

Many people with large lots had their own gardens and fruit trees. Their produce was generously shared with neighbors. Guests from the country brought barrels of apples and pears, fine old hams and game.

Richmond then was still a village—"The little red brick town," as Mary Johnston called it. There was delightful space for its people and much variety in its architecture....

Louisa Coleman Blair
"'Little Red Brick Town' In Era of Hoopskirts Was Friendly, Gossipy,"
Richmond Times-Dispatch, December 7, 1941

Abbie's Sugar Cookies

Yield: 3 dozen cookies

"My Grandmother Abbott always had the dough for these cookies waiting in the freezer for me to cut into Santas, stars, and Christmas trees. She didn't seem to mind that I got more of the red and green sugar sprinkles on the floor than on the cookies."

1 1/2 cups sifted flour
2 teaspoons baking powder
1/2 cup butter or margarine, at room temperature
1 cup sugar
2 eggs
1 teaspoon vanilla extract
Granulated sugar or colored sugar sprinkles or finely chopped nuts, or chopped or halved red or green candied cherries for decoration

Sift together the flour and baking powder. In a medium bowl, cream butter until smooth. Gradually add sugar, beating until light and fluffy. Add eggs and vanilla, beating well. Cover and thoroughly chill dough in refrigerator for 2 to 3 hours. Roll out dough very thin, about 1/8-inch thickness, on a lightly floured surface; cut into desired shapes with lightly floured cookie cutters. Arrange cookies on ungreased baking sheets; decorate each with sugar, colored sugar sprinkles, nuts, or candied cherries. Bake in a hot oven (400 degrees F.) for about 7 to 10 minutes or until cookies are done. *Do not burn cookies.* Transfer cookies to wire racks to cool.

Note: Dough may be covered in aluminum foil, sealed, and frozen. Small portions of dough may be removed, thawed, rolled out and cut into cookies. Unused portion of frozen dough may be returned to freezer immediately. Dough left at room temperature will become *very* sticky.

–Jann Malone
Food Editor
Richmond Times-Dispatch

Almond Gingerbread Santas

Yield: 6 dozen cookies (2 inches high)

3 1/2 cups sifted flour
1 1/2 teaspoons cinnamon
1 teaspoon finely crushed cardamom seeds
1/2 teaspoon nutmeg
1/2 teaspoon baking soda
1/2 teaspoon salt

Sift together the first 6 ingredients. In a large bowl, combine almond paste, honey, and sugar, mixing well. Add eggs, one at a time, beating well after each addition. Stir in dry ingredients. Fold in candied fruit and peel, and walnuts, mixing well. Cover and refrigerate dough for 12 hours. Roll out one fourth of the dough on a lightly

REFRIGERATOR COOKIES/ROLLED and SHAPED

6 ounces commercial
  almond paste
1 cup honey
1/2 cup sugar
3 eggs
4 ounces minced mixed
  candied fruits and peels
1 cup chopped English
  walnuts
1 egg white, slightly beaten
1 tablespoon water
1/2 cup sifted confectioners'
  sugar
1 tablespoon butter or
  margarine, at room
  temperature
1 to 1 1/2 tablespoons hot
  lemon juice

floured board to a 1/8-inch thickness. Cut out cookies with a lightly floured Santa Claus cookie cutter. Arrange cookies, 2 inches apart, on ungreased baking sheets. Combine egg white and water, beating lightly with a wire whisk. Brush mixture lightly over the top of each cookie. Bake in a moderate oven (350 degrees F.) for 12 to 15 minutes or until done. *Do not overbake.* Transfer cookies to wire racks to cool thoroughly. In a small bowl, combine confectioners' sugar and butter, beating until smooth. Add lemon juice, blending well. Spread over each Santa cookie, dividing glaze evenly.

–Nancy Scoggins (Mrs. Robert)
Valentine Museum Guild

Granny's Peanut Butter Cookies

Yield: About 6 dozen

In the late twentieth century, the production of peanuts in Virginia annually tops over 200,000,000 pounds, accounting for about 6.6% of the United States' yearly production.

1 1/2 cups sifted flour
1 teaspoon baking powder
1 teaspoon salt
1/2 cup butter or margarine,
  at room temperature
3/4 cup light brown sugar,
  firmly packed
1 egg, beaten
1/4 cup honey
1 1/2 teaspoons vanilla
1 cup creamy or crunch-
  style peanut butter

Sift together the first 3 ingredients. In a large bowl, cream butter thoroughly. Add brown sugar, 1/4 cup at a time, beating well after each addition. Mix in egg, honey, and vanilla. Stir in peanut butter, then dry ingredients. Shape rounded teaspoonfuls of dough into balls. Arrange balls, 2 inches apart, on greased baking sheets. Flatten balls crisscross fashion, using tines of a dinner fork dipped in flour. Bake in a slow oven (325 degrees F.) for 10 to 12 minutes. Cool cookies slightly on baking sheets, then transfer to wire racks to finish cooling.

Miniature Peanut Butter Surpirse Drops

Yield: 48 cookies

1 (20-ounce) package
refrigerated peanut butter
cookie dough
2 (14-ounce) packages
miniature chocolate
covered peanut butter
candies

With a sharp knife, cut dough roll into slices according to package directions; cut each slice into 4 equal pieces. Place a pice of dough into each of 48 greased miniature muffin cups (1 1/2-inches in diameter) or muffin pans lined with miniature paper baking cups. Bake in moderate over (350 degrees F.) for 10 minutes; dough will puff up. While cookies are baking, unwrap miniature candies. Remove cookies from oven and insert a piece of candy into the center of each cookie. Allow cookies to cool in muffin pans for about 45 minutes; loosen cookies around the edge of each muffin cup with a knife; remove from cups.

Note: 1 recipe of Granny's Peanut Butter Cookie dough (see index) may be substituted for commercial refrigerated cookie dough.

–Laura Daly

Nannie's Cookies

Yield: about 7 to 8 dozen

This is an old recipe of the Top Knot Nursery School, circa 1931 to 1947, operated by Miss Virginia Withers and located adjacent to Mary Wingfield Scott's house on Roselawn Road in Richmond. Whenever a child had a birthday, he or she was taken across the yard to Miss Scott's kitchen to help prepare the cookies as a birthday treat. Miss Withers and Miss Scott, well-known Richmond author and historian, shared living quarters in Miss Scott's home. Many children who attended the school enjoyed preparing the cookies long after the school closed.

4 cups sifted flour
1 tablespoon mace
1 tablespoon nutmeg
1 tablespoon cinnamon
1/2 cup boiling water
1 teaspoon baking soda
1/2 cup butter or margarine,
   at room temperature
2 cups sugar
1 cup light brown sugar,

Sift together the first 4 ingredients. Dissolve baking soda in boiling water; allow to cool. In a medium bowl, cream butter thoroughly. Gradually add sugars, beating until light and fluffy. Add eggs, one at a time, beating well after each addition. Stir in dry ingredients and soda water, mixing well. Cover and refrigerate dough for several hours. Remove small amounts of dough at a time; refrigerate remaining dough. Roll out dough *very, very* thin, about 1/16-inch thickness,

firmly packed
3 eggs

on a lightly floured surface. Cut different shapes as desired with cookie cutters. Arrange cookies on lightly greased baking sheets. Bake in a moderate oven (375 degrees F.) for 8 to 10 minutes or until cookies are lightly browned. *Do not overbake.* Remove and transfer cookies to wire racks to cool.

Variation: Omit spices. Melt 4 squares (ounces) unsweetened chocolate over hot water; cool. Stir cooled chocolate into cookie dough. Butter may be reduced by 2 to 3 tablespoons, if desired.

–Elizabeth Reed (Mrs. Stanley)

Phyllis' Ginger Cookies

Yield: 3 to 4 dozen

Phyllis White was the talented cook at the Virginia Executive Mansion during Governor John Dalton's tenure. These wonderfully tasting ginger cookies were given to each visitor during the Christmas season open house tours while Governor and Mrs. Dalton lived in the mansion.

2 1/2 cups sifted flour
2 tablespoons ground
  ginger (see note)
2 teaspoons baking soda
1/2 teaspoon salt
1/2 teaspoon cinnamon
1/2 teaspoon ground cloves
1/2 cup shortening (see
  note)
1/4 cup butter or margarine
  (see note)
1 cup sugar
2 eggs
1 cup molasses

Sift together the first 6 ingredients. In a small heavy saucepan, melt shortening and butter over low heat; cool. In a large bowl, combine shortening mixture, sugar, and eggs, beat mixing well. Stir in dry ingredients. Add molasses, mixing well. Cover lightly and refrigerate for at least 1 hour until dough is thoroughly chilled. Roll out dough on a lightly floured board, one third at a time, to an 1/8-inch thickness or less. Cut out dough with assorted cookie cutters. Arrange cookies, 2 inches apart, on lightly greased baking sheets. Bake in a moderate oven (350 degrees F.) for 10 minutes or until done. *Do not overbake.* To prevent "sweating", lift cookies with a spatula while they're hot; leave loose cookies in place on baking sheets to cool. Store in an airtight container.

Note: For a less gingery flavor, ginger may be reduced to 1 to 3 teaspoons, if desired.

Note: Amount of shortening and butter may be reversed, using 1/2 cup butter and 1/4 cup shortening, if desired.

–Eddy Dalton (Mrs. John)
First Lady of Virginia, 1978 to 1982
Virginia State Senator, 1987 to____

Tipsy Rum Raisin Cookies

Yield: about 2 dozen

"I fill tins of these 'yummies' to give as gifts at Christmas."

1 cup dark rum
2 cups golden or dark
  seedless raisins
4 cups sifted flour
1/2 teaspoon salt
1/2 teaspoon baking
  powder
2 cups butter or margarine,
  at room temperature
1 cup sifted confectioners'
  sugar

In a medium heavy saucepan, warm rum slightly over low heat; add raisins, mixing lightly. Bring raisins to a boil, remove from heat, cover, and allow to stand at room temperature for 30 minutes. Raisins will absorb most of the liquid. Drain well. While raisins are soaking, sift flour, salt, and baking soda together. In a large bowl, cream butter thoroughly; gradually add sugar, beating until light and fluffy. Stir in dry ingredients and then plumped raisins, mixing well. Chill dough, covered, for at least 1 hour. With a rolling pin, roll out half of the dough on a floured board to a 1/8-inch thickness. Cut rolled dough with a 2 1/2-inch diameter cookie cutter. Decorate cut-out cookies with a cookie stamp or press. Repeat procedure with remaining cookie dough. Arrange cookies, 2 inches apart, on ungreased baking sheets. Bake in a moderate oven (375 degrees F.) for about 20 minutes or until done and lightly browned. Transfer cookies immediately to wire racks to cool.

–Linda M. Bourgeois (Mrs. Bruce)

Springerle Cookies

Yield: about 4 dozen

This holiday cookie has been made by cooking enthusiasts at Christmas time in Richmond for many decades. Traditionalists suggest Springerles were never meant to be soft inside as the cookies were meant to be dunked.

4 cups sifted flour
1/4 teaspoon salt
2 teaspoons ground anise
  seeds
4 eggs
2 cups sugar

Sift the first 3 ingredients together. In a medium bowl, beat eggs at high speed of an electric mixer for 5 minutes. Gradually add sugar and continue beating for about 15 minutes or until eggs are very thick, light lemon yellow in color, and almost hold soft peaks. Gradually add the dry ingredients, stirring until a stiff dough is formed. Roll out dough on a lightly floured surface to 3/8-inch thickness. Press well floured Springerle molds deeply enough into dough to form a clear impression. Or, roll out dough with a well floured Springerle roller to form designs. With a sharp knife, cut out formed cookie rectangles. Arrange cookies, 2 inches apart, on ungreased baking sheets; allow cookies to stand in a cool dry place for 12 hours to dry and set springerle designs. Bake in a moderate oven (375 degreesF.) for 3 minutes; reduce temperature to slow (325 degrees F.) and continue baking for an additional 12 minutes. Cookies should be a light straw color. *Do not overbake.* Transfer to wire racks to cool.

Note: If the dough is difficult to handle and the Springerle molds or roller stick after flouring well, sift extra flour over the top of the dough before pressing. Brush or blow off extra flour from cookies after removing mold or roller.

–Updated old Richmond recipe
date and origin unknown

Swedish Broomstick Cookies

Yield: about 3 dozen

The name originates from the act of rolling the cookies around a broomstick handle immediately after baking.

2/3 cup chopped blanched almonds
1/2 cup butter or margarine, at room temperature
1/2 cup sugar
1/4 cup sifted flour
2 tablespoons light cream

In a medium heavy saucepan, combine all ingredients; stir over moderate heat until bubbles begin to form. Remove from heat and stir briskly for a few minutes. Drop mixture by teaspoonfuls, 4 inches apart, onto greased and lightly floured baking sheets. Bake in a moderate oven (375 degrees F.) for 5 to 6 minutes. *Bake only 5 to 6 cookies at a time.* Remove cookies from oven and cool for 2 minutes on baking sheets. *Carefully* remove cookies from baking sheets with a spatula and place over a narrow rolling pin or clean broom handle until cookies are cool. If cookies should harden before they are removed from the baking sheets, they should be reheated in a *very* slow oven (200 degrees F.) for a few seconds to soften.

–Ann Tyler (Mrs. Hal)

643

Glazed Chocolate Pecan Thumbprints

Yield: about 3 1/2 dozen

1 2/3 cups sifted flour
1/2 cup sifted cocoa
1/4 teaspoon baking powder
1/4 teaspoon baking soda
1/4 teaspoon salt
3/4 cup butter or margarine, at room temperature
3/4 cup sugar
1 egg
1 1/2 teaspoons vanilla extract
About 40 pecan halves
1 (6-ounce) package semi-sweet chocolate pieces
2 tablespoons half-and-half or strong coffee (see note)

Sift together the first 5 ingredients. In a medium bowl, cream butter thoroughly. Gradually add sugar, beating well. Beat in egg and vanilla. stir in dry ingredients, mixing well. Shape mixture into 1-inch balls; arrange balls 1 to 2 inches apart on ungreased baking sheets. Press a pecan half into center of each ball. Bake in a moderate oven (350 degrees F.) for 8 to 10 minutes or until done. Transfer to wire racks to cool. In the top of a double boiler, melt chocolate pieces over hot water. Stir in half-and-half or coffee until mixture is smooth. Spread a small amount of chocolate mixture over each cookie, including pecan half. Allow glaze to set. Store cookies in an airtight container.

Note: 2 tablespoons of desired flavored liqueur such as orange, raspberry, strawberry, or mint may be substituted for half-and-half or coffee.

Mocha "Pillows"

Yield: about 3 dozen

3 ounces semi-sweet chocolate
1/2 cup butter or margarine
2 eggs
3/4 cup sugar
1 tablespoon brandy
1/2 teaspoon instant coffee crystals
1/2 cup sifted flour
1/2 cup chopped English walnuts or pecans
36 English walnut or pecan halves

In a small heavy saucepan, melt chocolate and butter over low heat. In a medium bowl, beat eggs and sugar until light and fluffy. Gradually add chocolate mixture, beating well. In a cup, combine brandy and coffee crystals, partially dissolving coffee; add to chocolate mixture. Add flour, stirring until smooth. Fold in chopped nuts. Spoon batter into miniature muffin pans, 1 1/2 inches in diameter, lined with paper baking cups, dividing batter evenly. Top each with an English walnut or pecan half. Bake in a moderate oven (350 degrees F.) for 18 to 20 minutes or until metal tester inserted in center of cookies comes out clean. Cool thoroughly. Store in an airtight container.

Note: If paper baking cups are not used, muffin pans *must be greased.*

–Elinor Kuhn (Mrs. Frank)
Buffet, catering firm
Richmond Culinary Guild

Fabulous Chocolate Nut Fudge

Yield: about 30 pieces

Many favorite American fudge recipes have originated in the test kitchens of evaporated milk companies where recipes were developed to help market evaporated milk to the public.

16 marshmallows or 1 cup
  marshmallow creme
2 1/4 cups sugar
1 cup evaporated milk
1/4 cup butter or margarine,
  at room temperature
1/4 teaspoon salt
1 (6-ounce) package semi-
  sweet chocolate pieces
1 teaspoon vanilla extract
1 cup coarsely chopped
  English or black walnuts,
  pecans, Macadamia nuts,
  cashews, or peanuts
About 30 nut halves of
  desired flavor (optional)

In a heavy 3-quart saucepan, combine the first 5 ingredients;bring to a boil over moderate heat, stirring constantly.Continue to boil and stir for an additional 5 minutes.Remove from heat, stir in chocolate pieces and vanilla,mixing well until chocolate is completely melted. Stir in nuts. Evenly spread mixture into a greased 9 x 9 x 2-inch or 8 x 8 x 2-inch baking dish. Lightly press nut halves into top of fudge, arranging evenly, if desired. Store in an airtight container in refrigerator.

–Elizabeth Warren (Mrs. E. P.)

Sugared Popcorn

Make a syrup boiling together 2 cups granulated sugar and 1 cup water. Boil until the syrup strings from the spoon or hardens when dropped into cold water. Pour over 6 quarts of freshly popped corn and stir well.

Culinary Echoes From Dixie, *1917*

Chocolate Peanut Butter Fudge

Yield: about 36 pieces

1 (14-ounce) can sweetened
  condensed milk
3 squares (ounces) un-
  sweetened chocolate
1 cup creamy-style peanut
  butter
1 teaspoon vanilla extract
1 to 1 1/2 cups chopped
  peanuts (optional)

In a medium heavy saucepan, combine the first 3 ingredients; stir over low heat until chocolate and peanut butter are melted. *Do not boil*. Immediately remove from heat and stir in vanilla. Fold in peanuts, if desired. Spoon into a buttered 8x8x 2-inch baking dish, spreading evenly. Allow fudge to cool and become firm. With a sharp knife, cut into small squares.

Monument made of James River Granite
in Honor of Confederate Dead at Hollywood Cemetery

Chocolate Candy

1/4 lb. unsweetened chocolate2 teaspoons vanilla2 cups white sugar1/2 teaspoon salt1 cup sweet milk1 tablespoon butterMelt chocolate slowly in half of milk, stir till smooth, then add sugar, salt and the remainder of milk. Stir constantly while cooking. When nearly done add butter. Beat a little while after taking from stove. Add vanilla. Pour a thin stream slowly on a marble slab, stir until stiff enough to knead with the hands, shape into long rolls and cut about half an inch long.

Miss Annie Tucker
Virginia Cookery Book, 1921

Jiffy Fudge

Yield: 36 to 40 pieces

1 (12-ounce) can evaporated skim milk (see note)
3 cups sugar
1/2 cup butter or margarine, at room temperature
1 teaspoon salt
6 squares (ounces) semi-sweet chocolate pieces
1 (6-ounce) jar marshmallow creme
2 tablespoons creamy-style peanut butter

In a heavy saucepan, combine the first 4 ingredients; bring to a boil over moderate heat and continue to boil for 5 to 7 minutes. Remove from heat and add chocolate pieces, marshmallow creme, and peanut butter; beat by hand for several minutes. Pour into a buttered 15 x 10 x 1-inch pan. Cool slightly and cut into squares; cover and refrigerate.

Note: Preferably use MILNOT brand (cholesterol free vegetable oil blend).

–Maryrita Jackson (Mrs. David)

Meme's Creamy Pralines

Yield: about 2 dozen candies

"When my Grandmother Malone lived in New Orleans, she learned to make pralines. Her version is creamy as opposed to another type that has a sugary texture. These are very rich, so it is best to make them small. Both varieties are sold in New Orleans. If you ever want to buy some, pronounce them `prawleens,' not`praylines'...no one will know you're a tourist."

3 cups sugar
1 cup buttermilk
1 teaspoon baking soda
1 1/2 cups coarsely chopped pecans or pecan halves
1 teaspoon vanilla extract
2 1/2 to 3 tablespoons butter or margarine, at room temperature

Place sugar in a heavy 3-quart saucepan. In a 2-cup measure, combine buttermilk and baking soda, blending well; add to sugar, mixing well. Cook mixture, stirring constantly, over moderate heat until candy thermometer registers 234 degrees F. (syrup forms a soft ball in cold water). Just before mixture reaches 234 degrees F., stir in pecans. When the mixture registers 234 degrees F., remove from heat; add vanilla and butter, mixing well. Allow mixture to cool for several minutes, then vigorously stir until mixture begins to stiffen. Drop mixture by rounded teaspoonfuls onto waxed paper. Allow candies to cool and firm. Store in an air-tight container at room temperature.

–Jann Malone
Food Editor
Richmond Times-Dispatch

647

Rules for Candy Making

Never stir syrup after the sugar is dissolved, the only object in stirring being to prevent the sugar from settling and burning when first put on the stove.

Never shake or move the kettle while syrup is boiling or the mass may grain.

Feather or soft ball degree means that when a little of the mixture is dropped in cold water it will make up into a soft ball.

Soft crack degree is reached when the mixture dropped in cold water cracks between the fingers, but if held a moment forms into a hard ball again.

The crack has been reached when the mixture dropped in cold water becomes crisp and just too hard to form a ball.

Hard crack is reached when the mixture dropped into water andt hen taken out will crack between the fingers like an egg shell.

Hard ball is reached when the candy dropped into water forms a firm and rather hard ball between the fingers.

The thread degree is reached when a bit of syrup taken between the thumb and fingers after dipping them in cold water threads they are drawn apart and then breaks and settles on one of them.

C. F. Sauer Company
Sauer Spices, circa 1920's

Microwave Chocolatey Chocolate Fudge

Yield: 36 pieces

1 (14-ounce) can sweetened condensed milk
1 (12-ounce) package semi-sweet chocolate pieces
1 teaspoon vanilla extract
1 cup chopped English or black walnuts, or pecans,

In a medium glass bowl, combine condensed milk and chocolate. Loosely cover with clear plastic wrap, allowing space for venting; microwave at HIGH power for 3 minutes. Uncover, stir until chocolate mixture is well blended. Stir in vanilla and then nuts. Pour into an aluminum foil-lined 8 x 8 x 2-inch baking dish. Allow to cool until firm.

or cashews, or Macada-
mia nuts

With a sharp knife, cut fudge into equal-sized squares. Store in an air-tight container in a cool place.

–Terry Beistel (Mrs. Eric)

Sea Foam

Boil together one and one-half cups of water, one and one-half cups of sugar, and teaspoon of vinegar. Boil until it will harden in cold water. Remove from fire and beat briskly after adding white of an egg beaten to a stiff froth. Nuts may be added if desired. Have buttered plates ready and drop into them, forming cakes.

Miss McGehee
Virginia Cook Book, *1839*

Nutty Special-Occasion Fudge

Yield: about 5 pounds

"The secret to preparing smooth creamy fudge is in the beating."

1 (12-ounce) can evaporated milk
4 1/2 cups sugar
1/8 teaspoon salt
3 (6-ounce) packages semi-sweet chocolate pieces
1 square (ounce) un-sweetened chocolate
1 cup butter or margarine, at room temperature
2 teaspoons vanilla extract
2 cups chopped pecans, English or black walnuts, blanched almonds, cashews, or Macadamia nuts

In a 4-quart heavy saucepan, combine evaporated milk, sugar, and salt. Bring to a boil over moderate heat and continue boiling for 8 minutes, stirring constantly. Temperature should register about 236 degrees F. on a candy thermometer (syrup forms a soft ball in cold water). Remove from heat and add chocolate pieces and square, butter, and vanilla extract. Beat at high speed of an electric mixer until mixture is smooth and creamy. Fold in nuts. Pour into a buttered 13 x 9 x 2-inch baking dish and spread quickly into an even layer. Cool and cut into 1-inch squares.

–Mary Jo Banton (Mrs. Thomas)

Grandmama Coleman's Easter Egg Fudge

Yield: about 12 eggs

"My husband's mother, Grandmama Coleman, was a most unique energetic woman. Often she would accompany her husband, Dr. Coleman, in a horse and buggy on his patient rounds. Sometimes she would wait in the buggy while he delivered a baby. She delighted me and my daughter, Elizabeth, with these eggs every Easter until she died. We loved them!"

Grandmama Coleman must have also had great patience and dexterity, as these wonderful eggs do require both talents from the person preparing these eggs! However, the effort is well worth the work with the finished product. A late twentieth century shortcut method is to fill hollow colored plastic eggs, which easily open, with the hot confection.

3 cups sugar
3/4 cup sifted cocoa
1 cup plus 2 tablespoons
    evaporated milk, undi-
    luted
6 tablespoon water

10 to 12 colored plastic eggs which open into 2 halves or about 12 medium egg shells (see note) In a heavy sauce pan, combine sugar, cocoa, evaporated milk, water, and corn syrup; stir over low heat until sugar dissolves. Increase temperature and cook over moderate heat until candy thermometer registers 234 degrees to 236 degrees F. (syrup forms a soft ball in cold water). Remove from heat; stir in vanilla and salt. Set saucepan in cold water and cool to lukewarm (110 degrees F.) without stirring. Beat vigorously until candy molds its shape and begins to lost its gloss. Spoon into plastic egg shells filling both halves. Allow chocolate to harden and then close halves together to form a whole egg. It using regular egg shells, do not beat. Spoon hot mixture carefully into holes of egg shells with a long-handled iced tea spoon. Set eggs into egg cartons and allow chocolate to harden.

Note: To blow out egg shells, prick each end of egg with a pin and *very carefully* made an 1/8 to 1/4-inch diameter hole. Hold egg *very gently* with both hands and blow into one hole, drawing the yolk and white into a bowl through the opposite hole. You may with to run a straw from a broom carefully through the holes to draw egg yolk and white out more rapidly. Color egg shells with food coloring or Easter egg dye if desired.

–Janet Coleman (Mrs. Custis L.)

Fondant Candy

3 1/2 lbs. white sugar, 1 tablespoon vinegar, Whites of 2 eggs, 1 1/2 pts. water, Put sugar, vinegar and water in sauce pan and cook until 238 degrees, then remove from stove and pour on marble slab. When cool enough to lay the back of your hand on put on the stiff beaten whites and work until creamy. You can the cover brazil nuts, cherries, or flavor in any way desires., When you have made your fondant and wish to cover with chocolate take:, 1/4 lb. bitter chocolate And a little parafin, 1/2 lb. sweet chocolate in a double boiler, and when melted dip your fondant balls in same, and place on waxed paper to harden.

Virginia Cookery Book, *1921*

Butter-Scotch

1 cup brown sugar 1 dessertspoon vinegar 1/2 cup water. Piece of butter size of walnut. Boil about twenty minutes. With a teaspoon drop on a marble slab. Flavor if desired.

Virginia Cookery Book, *1921*

Sinful Fudge Tidbits

Yield: 36 to 42 pieces

2 ounces (squares) un-
sweetened chocolate
2 cups light brown sugar,
firmly packed
1/2 cup butter or margarine,
at room temperature
6 tablespoons milk
2 teaspoons light corn syrup
1 teaspoon baking powder
1 teaspoon vanilla extract

In a large heavy saucepan, combine the first 5 ingredients; cook, stirring constantly, over moderate heat until chocolate melts and mixture is smooth. Continue cooking, stirring occasionally, until candy thermometer registers 234 to 236 degrees F. (syrup forms a soft ball in cold water). Remove from heat; stir in baking powder and vanilla. Set saucepan in cold water and cool to lukewarm (110 degrees F.) without stirring. Beat vigorously until candy holds its shape and begins to lose its gloss. Drop mixture by rounded teaspoonfuls, 2 inches apart, onto lightly buttered sheets of waxed paper. Allow candies to firm. Store in an airtight container.

Variations: Add 1 to 2 tablespoons cherry or orange, or coffee-flavored liqueur to hot candy mixture.

–Dotty Stuart (Mrs. Albert)

651

Chocolate Dipped Strawberries

Yield: about 3 dozen

2 pints *ripe* strawberries (see note)
12 ounces milk or dark bitter-sweet chocolate, broken into pieces (see note)
1 1/2 teaspoons corn oil
1/2 ounce paraffin

Wash and pat dry whole strawberries with absorbent paper, leaving stems intact. Allow strawberries to stand for at least 30 minutes on absorbent paper. In the top of a double boiler, combine chocolate pieces, corn oil, and paraffin. Heat over boiling water until chocolate and paraffin are melted, blending with a wooden spoon until smooth. Dip each strawberry into melted chocolate mixture, liberally coating strawberry, except stem. Place chocolate-covered strawberries on waxed paper; allow to stand at least 1 hour or until set. Store in a cool dry place. *Do not refrigerate.*

Note: Strawberries are perishable and should be eaten within 48 hours. Chocolate dipped strawberries should not be refrigerated as the chocolate containing paraffin will turn an undesirable mottled color.

Note: Use any high quality chocolate.

Orange Pecan Dandies

Yield: about 36 to 40 pieces

3 cups sugar, divided
1 cup hot evaporated milk
1/4 cup hot orange juice
1/4 cup butter or margarine, melted
1/4 teaspoon salt
6 tablespoons freshly grated orange peel
1 cup coarsely chopped pecans

Grease a 9 x 9 x 2-inch pan or have ready sheets of waxed paper. In a heavy saucepan, melt 1 cup sugar over moderate heat until light brown in color. Blend in milk, orange juice, and butter. Add remaining 2 cups sugar and salt, stirring until sugar is dissolved. Cook until candy thermometer registers 234 to 236 degrees F. (syrup forms a soft ball in cold water), stirring frequently. Remove from heat and blend in grated orange peel. Set saucepan in cold water and cool to lukewarm (110 degrees F.) without stirring. Beat until mixture is creamy and starts to lose its gloss and stiffen. Stir in pecans. Pour at once into prepared pan and spread quickly into an even layer. Cool and cut into squares. Or, drop mixture by teaspoonfuls onto waxed paper.

Variation: Dip Dandies into 1 (12-ounce) package semi-sweet chocolate pieces, melted over boiling water and combined with 1/2 ounce paraffin.

Chocolate Creams

To make the insides, mix two cups sugar, one cup water, and one and a half tablespoonfuls of arrowroot. Let them boil from five to eight minutes, stirring all the time. After this is taken from the fire, stir or beat until it comes to a cream. When it is nearly smooth add one teaspoonful extract vanilla and make the cream into balls. The cream, when cooked exactly right, should be of the substance of putty. For the outsides, melt one-half pound of Baker's chocolate, but do not add water to it. Roll the cream balls into the chocolate while it is warm. One cup grated cocoanut poured into the cream as it is cooling improves them. The cream is used for nut candies of all kinds; also cream dates.

Miss Gertie Sydnor
Virginia Cook Book, 1839

Martha's Rum Soaked Chocolate Truffles

Yield: 12 to 18 large
or 40 to 50 small truffles

7 ounces semi-sweet baking chocolate
1 ounce (square) un-sweetened baking chocolate
1/4 cup dark rum
2 tablespoons strong liquid coffee
1/2 cup unsalted butter or margarine, cut in 1-inch pieces
3/4 to 1 cup gingersnap crumbs
1/2 cup sifted cocoa
1/4 cup instant coffee crystals

Break chocolate into small pieces. In the top of a double boiler, combine chocolate, rum, and liquid coffee. Cover and place over bottom of double boiler containing boiling water. Remove double boiler from heat. When chocolate has melted, beat in butter, a small amount at a time. Blend in gingersnap crumbs. Chill mixture for several hours. Combine cocoa and instant coffee crystals; spread on a plate. With a tablespoon or teaspoon, shape chilled chocolate mixture into rough shaped balls. Roll each ball in cocoa-coffee mixture. Place each truffle on a paper candy cup and refrigerate until ready to serve. Truffles may be stored in an airtight container in the refrigerator for several weeks.

Coconut Bar

4 c. sugar1/2 grated coconut1 c. water1 t. flavoring1/2 t. cream tartarHeat the first three ingredients, stirring until the sugar is dissolved. Cook without stirring until it forms a soft ball. When tried in cold water remove from the fire and cool.Beat until it thickens, adding coconut and flavoring. Pour into buttered pans. Cool slightly and cut into bars.

Culinary Echoes From Dixie, *1917*

Peppermint Drops

Yield: 1 1/2 dozen candies

Peppermint Drops, an old recipe of the C. F. Sauer Company, circa 1920, has been updated with variations for twentieth century use.

1 1/2 cups sugar
1/2 cup boiling water
1 tablespoon white vinegar
1 tablespoon butter or
    margarine, at room
    temperature
1/4 teaspoon baking soda
1 to 2 teaspoons pepper-
    mint extract

In a heavy saucepan, combine sugar and water; bring to a boil over moderate heat. Add vinegar and butter and continue to cook for 3 to 4 minutes. Add baking soda and continue to cook until candy thermometer registers 230 to 233 degrees F.(syrup spins a thread 2 inches long when dropped from a spoon.) Cool mixture to 100 degrees F. in pan which has been placed in ice water and stir in peppermint extract. Beat with an electric hand mixer at high speed until mixture is thick and creamy, about 10 to 15 minutes. Drop by rounded teaspoonfuls onto waxed paper or greased baking sheets. Allow candies to become firm.

Variation: 1 to 2 teaspoons butterscotch or maple flavoring or extract may be substituted for peppermint extract.

–C. F. Sauer Company
Sauer Spices

White Chocolate Crunch

Yield: About 54 1 1/4-inch square pieces

20 ounces white chocolate
    (see note)
2 cups crisped rice cereal

Melt chocolate in the top of a double boiler over hot water,or microwave, loosely covered with clear plastic wrap, at HIGH power in a large glass bowl for 1 to 2 minutes or until melted. Fold cereal into melted chocolate. Spoon into an 11 x 7 x 3/4-inch baking pan. Allow to cool until candy is firm. Cut into squares or bars as desired.

Note: White confectioners' bar or almond bark may be substituted for all or part of the white chocolate. Use 16 ounces confectioners' bar plus 4 ounces of white chocolate or 20 ounces of the white confectioners' coating or almond bark.

Variations: 1 cup chopped blanched almonds, pecans, or other nuts may be substituted for 1 cup of the crisped rice cereal. Or, 2 cups finely crushed hard peppermint candy may be substituted for 2 cups crisped rice cereal.

–Marion Peeschla (Mrs. Ralph)

No account of an old time Virginia household would be complete without mention of the negro servant. In the court end of Richmond, Mr. Wickham's Bob was as widely known as Mr. Wickham himself, and his fame as a julep mixer among the members of the "Barbecue club" was only second to that of his master himself, as a member of the bar.

Bob's wife as a famous cook, and Mr. Wickham thought so highly of them both that he provided them with a comfortable and tiny home of their own. Here parties of gentlemen were wont to partake of the game suppers cooked by Bob's wife, and while the feast was being prepared, to indulge in a little game of cards. Sometimes, when they lacked one of the number required to make up the game, Bob himself would be asked to take a hand. On one such, one of the party, thinking to have a little sport, openly cheated. The rest of the gentlemen pretended not to see it, but Bob promptly informed the joker that he was detected. A little later Mr. Blank cheated again, and again Bob remonstrated. A third time he cheated. This was too much for Bob, who, rising haughtily, declared that the only thing for a "gentleman" to do when there was persistent cheating, was to withdraw from the game.

Mr. Blank was highly offended, but his companions upheld Bob, and said that the gentleman was but justly punished for so ugly a piece of practical joking...

Mary Baker Newton Stanard
"The Wickham House,"
Richmond News, *Saturday supplement, 1900*

655

Chocolate Truffles

Yield: 30 candies

These delicious candies were served at a special dinner hosted by the Women's Committee of the Richmond Symphony following a special musical recital for patrons of the Richmond Symphony.

1 cup minus 1 tablespoon
  heavy cream
1/4 cup light corn syrup
5 squares (ounces) un-
  sweetened chocolate,
  broken into small pieces
1/4 cup Framboise,
  Frangelica, or Grand
  Marnier liqueur
30 hollow semi-sweet
  chocolate truffle shells

In the top of a double boiler, heat cream and corn syrup until *very hot*, but not boiling, over hot water. Remove from heat; add chocolate and stir until chocolate is melted and mixture very smooth. Add liqueur of choice and continue to stir until mixture is cool enough not to melt a chocolate shell when filled. Fill pastry bag fitted with a number 3 plain tip with chocolate *ganache* mixture; rapidly press mixture into chocolate shells. Top each truffle with extra *ganache* until all *ganache* is used and chocolate shells completely filled. Smooth each top with a small narrow spatula.

–Ridgewell's Catering Firm
As used for the Women's Committee of the
Richmond Symphony Fund Raising Dinner

The Evacuation

....By daylight, on the 3d, a mob of men, women, and children, to the number of several thousands, had gathered at the corner of 14th and Cary streets and other outlets, in front of the bridge, attracted by the vast commissary depot at that point; for it must be remembered that in 1865 Richmond was a half-starved city, and the Confederate Government had that morning removed its guards and abandoned the removal of the provisions, which was impossible for the want of transportation...
Clement Sulivane, Captain, C.S.A.
"The Fall of Richmond,"
Battles and Leaders, 1887-88

Pickles, Relishes
and Preserves

Boiling Water Bath

Processing is the name given to cooking covered jars in a covered bath of boiling water, with the water completely covering the jars. Adjust jar covers as manufacturer suggests and place filled jars on a rack in a kettle containing boiling water to a depth of one or two inches over tops of glass jars (do not pour boiling water directly over the tops of glass jars). Cover the kettle and begin to count processing time specified in recipe. Add additional boiling water, if necessary, to keep jars covered. Remove jars immediately when processing is over, tighten seals, if necessary, and set upright on a wire rack, a few inches apart, to cool.

Dilly Beans

Yield: 7 to 8 pints

4 pounds small to medium whole green beans, cleaned and stemmed
8 garlic cloves, peeled and halved, divided
3 1/2 to 4 teaspoons mustard seed, divided
3 1/2 to 4 teaspoons dill seed, divided
1 3/4 to 2 teaspoons crushed dried hot red pepper, divided
5 cups white vinegar
5 cups water
1/2 cup un-iodized salt
Boiling Water Bath (see index)

Cut beans into lengths to fit pint jars. Pack into hot sterilized jars; add 2 garlic clove halves, 1/2 teaspoon mustard seed, 1/2 teaspoon dill seed, and 1/4 teaspoon red pepper to each jar. In a large heavy saucepan, combine vinegar, water, and salt; bring to a boil over moderate heat. Pour boiling liquid into each jar, filling to within 1/2 inch from top. Seal and process in Boiling Water Bath for 5 minutes after water comes to a boil.

–Ann Jennings (Mrs. Joseph)

Sweet Pickled Ginger (Amazu Shoga)

Yield: 12 to 16 ounces

"Amazu Shoga is a 'go with' for sushi such as we associate mustard with hot dogs. It is served at the corner of a sushi tray and is meant to be eaten between sushi courses to refresh the palate. As a garnish, not a salad, pickled ginger should be eaten a slice at a time."

8 to 12 ounces young ginger root (see note)
Salt as needed
Boiling water
3/4 cup rice vinegar
5 tablespoons water
2 1/2 tablespoons sugar
Red food coloring (optional)

With a sharp knife, remove peel and cut peeled ginger root into *very* thin transparent slices. Place ginger in a glass or ceramic bowl and sprinkle with 2 teaspoons salt; allow to stand at room temperature for 24 hours. Rinse thoroughly in cold water to remove excess salt. In a medium heavy saucepan, cook ginger in boiling water to cover for 5 minutes; drain well. Prepare vinegar marinade. In a deep medium glass or ceramic bowl, combine rice vinegar, 5 tablespoons water, sugar, pinch of salt, and red food coloring, if desired. Add hot cooked ginger to marinade, set aside. Ginger will turn a pale pinkish orange as it cools. Store, covered, in a glass jar for up to several weeks in the refrigerator.

Note: Young ginger root may be distinguished by its pale pink color.

–Elizabeth Choi (Mrs. Sung)
Richmond Culinary Guild

Always use un-iodized salt in canning. Iodized salt will impart an undesirable color to products

---

Chili Sauce

Ten onions, twenty-seven green peppers, ninety-six peeled tomatoes chopped fine; one salt-spoon Cayenne pepper chopped, fifteen tablespoons salt, sixteen tablespoons sugar, sixteen cups cider vinegar. Boil three hours.
–Miss Anne Blair
The Kitchen Queen, *1893*

Saffron Onions

Yield: about 4 cups

4 1/2 to 6 cups thinly sliced peeled onions (see note)
About 3/4 cup olive oil, divided
1/8 to 1/4 teaspoon saffron

In a heavy saucepan or skillet, cook onions, covered, in 6 to 9 tablespoons hot olive oil over moderate heat until tender but not browned. Add 3 to 6 tablespoons additional olive oil, if necessary. Blend in saffron and cook several more minutes. Remove and drain on absorbent paper. Onion mixture may be refrigerated or frozen for later use.

Note: Use a sweet variety of onion such as a Vidalia.

Old Richmond Advertisement, circa 1895

Spiced Gingery Preserved Seckel Pears

Yield: about 8 pints

Seckel pears are a very small, very sweet, firm variety similar to a Bosc pear. The skin is a dull green to a brownish color with a red blush often coloring the sides.

2 (3-inch) cinnamon sticks, broken into pieces
2 tablespoons whole cloves
1/4 cup chopped crystalized ginger
5 cups light brown sugar, firmly packed
2 cups white vinegar
4 quarts (about 60 to 70) *very small* Seckel pears, peeled, stems intact (do not remove core or seeds) (see note)

Arrange cinnamon stick pieces and cloves in the center of a square of cheesecloth; bring up sides of cheesecloth and secure tightly. In a large heavy pot, combine the spice bag, brown sugar, vinegar, and chopped ginger; bring to boiling over moderate heat. Add prepared pears to mixture, coating well with syrup. Reduce heat and simmer, uncovered for 3 to 5 minutes. Pears should remain firm and not become soft or mushy. Pack pears into hot sterilized pint jars. Add syrup to each jar, filling to within 1/2 inch from top of the jars. Seal and process in Boiling Water Bath for 5 minutes after water comes to a full boil.

Note: Small Bosc, Anjou, or firm just ripe Bartlet pears may be substituted. Peel, core, and remove seeds from these pears, and then cut in half lengthwise. Quart jars may be required to fit pears into jars. Prepare as previously directed for Seckel pears.

....*A favorite evening pastime was the game of "Loo," which was played by both sexes, but especially loved by the ladies. After a "dish of tea" the card-table was brought out, and in the excitement of winning and losing the fair ones were often brought to tears. This amusement became so unpleasant that George Tucker, under the name of Hickory Cornhill, made such an attack on it thatit gradually disappeared....*
Ruth Nelson Robins

The Richmond News Leader, Date unknown

Crisp Bread 'N Butter Pickles

Yield: about 8 pints

"These pickles are quite crisp and not too sweet in flavor."

25 to 30 thinly sliced medium cucumbers (about 16 cups)
8 small white onions, peeled, sliced, and separated into rings
1 large green pepper, cored, seeded, and cut into thin strips, each about 4 inches in length
1 large sweet red pepper, cored, seeded, and cut into thin strips, each about 4 inches in length
1/2 cup un-iodized salt
Cracked ice as needed
5 cups sugar
5 cups white vinegar
2 tablespoons mustard seed
2 teaspoons celery seed
1 1/2 teaspoons turmeric
1/2 teaspoon ground cloves

In a large ceramic crock or *very* large glass or ceramic bowl, arrange cucumber slices, onions, and pepper strips. Add salt. Cover mixture with a thick layer of cracked ice; mix thoroughly. Allow mixture to stand at room temperature for 3 hours; rinse and drain well. Combine remaining ingredients in a large heavy kettle. Add drained cucumber mixture. Bring to a boil over moderate heat. Spoon into hot sterilized pint jars to within 1/2 inch from top of the jars, dividing evenly. Seal and process in a Boiling Water Bath for 5 minutes after water returns to a boil.

–Frances Fox (Mrs. Paul)

Old-Fashioned Bread and Butter Pickles

Yield: 6 to 8 pints

30 medium cucumbers, unpeeled
10 to 12 medium onions, peeled
1/2 cup un-iodized salt
5 cups white vinegar
4 cups sugar
2 tablespoons celery seed
2 tablespoons ground ginger

Slice cucumbers and onions thinly. Place in a large glass bowl and sprinkle with salt; weight down with a ceramic plate and set aside for 1 hour, then drain. Combine remaining ingredients in a large kettle; bring to a boil and boil for 10 minutes. Add cucumbers and onions and return to a boil. Spoon into sterilized jars and seal. Cool.

2 tablespoons white
   mustard seed
1 tablespoon turmeric   –BeBe West (Mrs. Eugene, Jr.)

Pepper Vinegar

Get one dozen pods of pepper when ripe, take out the stems, and cut them in two; put them in a kettle with three pints of vinegar, boil it away to one quart and strain it through a sieve. A little of this is excellent in gravy of every kind, and gives a flavour greatly superior to black pepper; it is also very fine when added to each of the various catsups for fish sauce.

Mrs. Mary Randolph
The Virginia House-Wife, or Methodical Cook, *1830*

Easy Refrigerator Pickles

Yield: 1 gallon

12 to 15 cups thinly sliced
   medium cucumbers
4 cups thinly sliced peeled
   onion
3 cups white or cider
   vinegar
1 teaspoon un-iodized salt
1 teaspoon mustard seed
1 teaspoon celery seed
1 teaspoon turmeric
3 cups sugar

Place thinly sliced cucumbers and onions in a 1-gallon glass jar; set aside. In a heavy saucepan, combine vinegar, salt, mustard seed, celery seed and turmeric; bring to a boil. Add sugar, stirring until dissolved. Pour mixture over cucumbers and onions; cool, cover tightly, and refrigerate for 48 hours. Pickles may be stored in the refrigerator for up to 4 to 6 weeks.

–Bill Guthrie

Raspberry Vinegar

Put a quart of ripe red raspberries in a bowl; pour on them a quart of strong well flavoured vinegar—let them stand twenty-four hours, strain them through a bag, put this liquid on another quart of fresh raspberries, which strain in the same manner—and then on a third quart: when this last is prepared, make it very sweet with pounded loaf sugar; refine and bottle it. It is a delicious beverage mixed with iced water.

–Mrs. Mary Randolph
The Virginia House-Wife, or Methodical Cook, *1830*

Fourteen Day Pickles

Yield: about 16 pints

About 60 small cucumbers, unpeeled and thinly sliced
Boiling water as needed, divided
2 cups un-iodized salt
2 tablespoons pickling alum
1 ounce (3 tablespoons) pickling spice
1 ounce (about 4 to 5) (3-inch) cinnamon sticks, broken
1/2 ounce (about 2 tablespoons) celery seed
Cheesecloth square
16 cups white vinegar
10 to 13 cups sugar or to taste, divided

Place sliced cucumbers in 2 clean one gallon or 4 clean one-half gallon jars, dividing evenly. Add salt to 1 gallon boiling water and pour over cucumbers. Allow cucumbers to stand in solution, covered, for 7 days; shake mixture thoroughly once each day.

On the 8th day, drain salt water from cucumbers. Pour 1 gallon fresh boiling water over cucumbers; allow to stand, covered, for 24 hours. On the 9th day, drain cucumbers. Add alum to 1 gallon boiling water; pour over cucumbers and allow mixture to stand, covered, for 24 hours. On the 10th day, drain cucumbers. Add 1 gallon fresh boiling water to cucumbers; allow to stand, covered, for 24 hours.

On the 11th day, drain cucumbers. Combine pickling spice, cinnamon sticks, and celery seed in a cheesecloth bag, securing tightly. In a heavy pot, combine spice bag, vinegar, and 11 cups sugar; bring to a boil over moderate heat. Pour boiling spice mixture over drained cucumbers.

On the 12th day, taste vinegar solution for sweetness. Add additional sugar to taste to solution, if desired. Pour vinegar solution from cucumbers into a large heavy pot; add spice bag and bring to a boil over moderate heat. Pour mixture over cucumbers. Repeat process on 13th day.

On the 14th day, drain cucumbers. Pour vinegar solution into a heavy pot; add spice bag and bring mixture to a boil over moderate heat. Pack cucumber slices into hot sterilized pint jars, filling jars to within 1/2 inch of top. Seal and process in Boiling Water Bath for 5 minutes after water comes to a boil.

—Sylvia Reynolds (Mrs. A. Wayne)

Crisp Watermelon Rind Pickles

Yield: 14 pints

"Watermelons vary in water content so sometimes you'll have excess syrup; but most of the time, you may have to prepare a bit more of the vinegar-sugar-spice mixture."

10 pounds prepared watermelon rind
1 1/2 cups pickling lime powder
Water as needed
2 to 3 tablespoons un-iodized salt
16 to 17 cups sugar (8 pounds)
8 cups white or cider vinegar
1/2 (1 1/4-ounce) box pickling spice (dried red peppers removed)
Boiling Water Bath (see index)

To prepare the rind, cut away all of the outside green and pink edges from melon and cut into 1-inch squares. Measure and place in a large ceramic crock or ceramic or glass bowl. Add water to cover; stir in lime powder, blending well. Allow to stand for 12 hours. Drain and rinse in cold water. Place in a large kettle and add water to cover; stir in salt. Bring to a boil over moderate heat and continue boiling for 20 minutes; drain well, rinsing in cold water. Return rind to kettle and add cold water to cover; bring to a boil and continue boiling for 20 minutes. Drain well, rinsing in cold or ice water. In a large kettle, combine sugar and vinegar. Tie pickling spices (without dried hot red peppers) in a cheesecloth bag, securing tightly; add bag to vinegar mixture. Bring mixture to a boil over moderate heat; add watermelon rind, reduce heat, and simmer for 1 hour or until rind is translucent. Pack hot pickles loosely into hot sterilized jars. Cover with boiling syrup to within 1/2 inch from top. Seal and process in Boiling Water Bath for 5 minutes after water comes to a boil.

–Winifred M. Peebles (Mrs. William B.)

Old Richmond Advertisement, circa 1898

Old-Time Watermelon Rind Pickles

Yield: about 12 pints

"This is an old family recipe. Watermelon rind will keep a long time in refrigerator as you collect eight pounds ... or just cut the recipe in half."

8 pounds watermelon rind
1 cup pickling lime powder
Water as needed
16 to 18 cups sugar (8 pounds)
8 cups white vinegar
2 tablespoons mixed pickling spices
2 tablespoons whole cloves
1 tablespoon celery seed
1 lemon, thinly sliced and seeds removed
Boiling Water Bath (see index)

To prepare the rind, cut away all of the outside green from melon, leaving a small bit of pink edge. Cut into 1-inch squares. Combine 1 gallon (16 cups) water and lime powder, blending well. Place rind in a large crock or glass or ceramic bowl; pour lime water over rind and allow to stand for 12 hours. Drain and rinse thoroughly in cool water; drain again. Place rind in a large kettle and add water to cover; bring to a boil and continue to boil for 20 minutes. Drain well. Return rind to kettle; add sugar and vinegar, mixing well. Combine pickling spices, cloves, and celery seed in a cheesecloth bag, securing tightly. Add spice bag and lemon slices to rind mixture. Bring to a boil over moderate heat; reduce temperature, cover, and simmer for 1 to 1 1/2 hours or until watermelon rind is translucent and wooden pick can easily be inserted into rind. Remove spice bag and lemon slices. Pack pickles loosely into hot sterilized jars and cover with hot syrup to within 1/2 inch from top. Seal and process in Boiling Water Bath for 5 minutes after water comes to a boil.

–Joe Benedetti

Mustard Pickles

Yield: 2 cups

Mustard Pickles were traditionally served with the Missouri Club Sandwich, another Miller & Rhoads Tea Room specialty. Some suggest they were first served during the sixties in Roanoke, Virginia.

1 pint mixed sweet pickles
5 to 6 tablespoons sugar
3/4 teaspoon ground cloves
2 tablespoons prepared

Thoroughly drain pickles of liquid; pat dry between sheets of absorbent paper. Place pickles in a deep medium bowl; sprinkle evenly with sugar and cloves. Toss mixture lightly to blend.

yellow mustard

Add mustard, blending well. Cover and refrigerate for 12 hours to allow sugar to dissolve thoroughly. Stir again before serving. Pickles may be stored, covered, in the refrigerator for up to 3 weeks.

–Miller & Rhoads Tea Room

Note: The Missouri Club Sandwich recipe may be found in *Richmond Recipts*.

Race-week was always a carnival, and one of its most brilliant features was the race-ball. This ball was opened by one of the managers and the lady he most desired to honor, with a stately minuet de la cour. The gentlemen wore "shorts and silks," pumps, and powdered hair, while the ladies, in the glory of multi-colored brocades and satins, looked like a gorgeous tulip-bed swaying in the wind. After the profound stateliness of the minuet the more lively reel was danced, and, after that, the contra dances. Probably the ball would end with a jig, or hornpipe ...

Ruth Nelson Robins
The Richmond News Leader, *date unknown*

PIN-MONEY · PICKLES.

SOLD BY Leading

Grocers

Everywhere!

Mrs. E. G. KIDD,

RICHMOND, VA.

Old Richmond Advertisement, circa 1895

Shenandoah Easy Apple Butter

Yield: 11 pints

6 pounds tart cooking apples, peeled, cored, and sliced (about 5 quarts sliced) (see note)
4 cups sweet apple cider or water
5 cups sugar
1 1/2 to 2 teaspoons cinnamon
1/2 to 1 teaspoon ground cloves
1/2 to 1 teaspoon allspice
Boiling Water Bath (see index)

Combine apples and cider or water in a large heavy Dutch oven or saucepan and simmer gently, covered, *just* until apples are tender. Press apples through a sieve or food mill or put into a blender container, a small amount at a time, cover, and blend just until smooth. Turn apple mixture into a large heavy roasting pan or Dutch oven or saucepan or kettle. Combine sugar and spices and stir into apples. Bring to a boil, stirring occasionally. Place, uncovered, in a slow oven (325 degrees F.) for about 1 1/2 to 2 hours or until apple butter is a rich amber color and very thick. Stir every 15 to 20 minutes. Pour into hot sterilized 1/2-pint or pint jars, filling jars to within 1/4 inch from top. Seal and process in Boiling Water Bath for 10 minutes after water comes to a boil.

Note: Use McIntosh, Winesap, Granny Smith, or other tart variety of apples.

Note: If the apples used fail to produce an amber-colored apple butter, stir in just a few drops of food coloring, if desired.

Variation: For peach or pear butter, use the same ingredients, substituting 4 cups of peach syrup or pear nectar for the apple cider.

Mince Meat

This rule is an old one and was used in the Custis Family. Mrs. Washington made famous mince pies.

Two pounds beef, two pounds currants, two pounds raisins, one pound citron, two pounds suet, one and one-half pounds of lemon peel, four pounds apples, two pounds sultana raisins, two pounds sugar, two grated nutmeg, one quarter ounce cinnamon, one quarter ounce cloves, one teaspoonful salt, two lemons, juice and rind,t wo oranges, juice and rind. Simmer meat until tender. When perfectly cold chop it fine; seed the raisins, shred the citron, pare, core and peel the apples.Mix the dry ingredients, then add the juice of the lemons and oranges. Pack in jars, cover well and cool. This will keep all winter.

Old Southern Receipts, *1930*

668

Virginia Apple Relish

Yield: 10 to 11 pints

30 tart apples, peeled, cored, and seeded (see note)
12 medium onions, peeled and chopped
4 cups coarsely ground celery
1/2 cup minced pimento or sweet red pepper
6 tablespoons un-iodized salt
7 1/2 cups sugar
6 cups cider vinegar
1 1/2 tablespoons celery seed
1 1/2 teaspoons cinnamon
1 1/2 teaspoons ground cloves
1 to 2 teaspoons crushed dried hot red pepper
Boiling Water Bath (see index)

Coarsely shred apples. (May wish to sprinkle with lemon juice or powdered fruit freshener to keep fruit from turning brown). In a large glass bowl or pottery crock, combine apples, onions, celery, and pimento. Add salt, mixing well. Weight down with a ceramic plate and allow to stand for 1 hour. Rinse thoroughly and drain well. In a large kettle, combine remaining ingredients. Bring vinegar mixture to a boil. Add drained apple mixture, reduce temperature and simmer over low heat for 7 minutes. Spoon into hot sterilized jars, seal and process in Boiling Water Bath for 5 minutes after water comes to a boil.

Note: Use McIntosh, Winesap, Granny Smith, or other tart variety of apples.

Old Richmond Advertisement, circa 1895

Cranberry Orange Conserve

Yield: 7 to 8 (1/2 pints)

Another favorite to give as a gift at holiday time.

1/2 cup *very* thin strips orange peel, cut 1-inch long
1/2 cup *very* thin strips lemon peel, cut 1-inch long
Water as needed
1 (12-ounce) package cranberries (6 cups)
3 cups orange juice
2 cups sugar
3 (3-inch) cinnamon sticks, broken
1/4 teaspoon ground cloves
1 1/2 cups coarsely chopped pecans or English walnuts
Boiling Water Bath (see index)

In a heavy saucepan, combine orange and lemon peels in water to cover. Bring to a boil; reduce temperature and simmer over low heat until tender, about 30 minutes. Drain well. In a large heavy saucepan, combine cooked peel, cranberries, orange juice, sugar, cinnamon sticks, and cloves, mixing well. Quickly bring to a boil and cook until mixture is thick and registers 215 degrees F. on a candy or jelly thermometer, about 20 minutes. Remove from heat, stir in nuts, and ladle into hot sterilized 1/2-pint jars, filling to within 1/2 inch from top. Seal and process in Boiling Water Bath for 5 minutes after water comes to a boil.

Brandied Applesauce

Yield: about 7 pints

20 to 24 medium cooking apples, peeled, cored, seeded and cut into large pieces (see note)
4 cups water
2 cups light brown sugar, firmly packed or to taste
1 teaspoon salt or to taste
3 (3-inch) cinnamon sticks, broken into pieces
1 cup brandy
Boiling Water Bath (see index)

In a large heavy pot, combine apples, water, brown sugar, and salt. Bring to a boil over moderate heat. Reduce heat, add cinnamon stick pieces, and simmer, uncovered for 1 1/2 hours. Add brandy and continue simmering for 30 minutes or until mixture is a lumpy purée, thickened, and reduced by one-third. Remove cinnamon stick pieces. Spoon applesauce into hot sterilized pint jars. Seal and process in Boiling Water Bath for 5 minutes after water comes to a full boil.

Note: Use McIntosh, Winesap, Granny Smith, or other tart variety of apples.

Variations: Omit brandy. One cup additional water may be added to mixture if needed. Or, substitute 4 cups orange juice for 4 cups water. Add 2 to 3 tablespoons grated orange peel to mixture, if desired.

Aunt Effie's Old Dominion Chili Sauce

Yield: about 14 (12-ounce) jars

6 medium sweet red or green peppers or 3 sweet red and green peppers, cored, seeded, coarsely ground, and drained

3 medium onions, peeled, coarsely ground, and drained

9 cups coarsely chopped peeled tomatoes (about 18 medium)

8 cups coarsely chopped peeled seeded peaches

8 cups coarsely chopped peeled seeded tart apples (see note)

3 cups coarsely ground celery, drained

10 cups sugar (see note)

7 cups white vinegar

4 (3-inch) cinnamon sticks, broken

1 (1.25-ounce) can pickling spice, tied in cheesecloth

2 tablespoons un-iodized salt

Boiling Water Bath (see index)

Combine the first 6 prepared ingredients in a large stainless steel pot or ceramic crock or large glass or ceramic bowl. Add sugar and vinegar, mixing well. Place cinnamon sticks and cheesecloth bag of pickling spice in mixture. Stir in salt. Cover and allow mixture to stand for 24 hours. Bring mixture to a boil in a large heavy pot. Reduce heat and simmer for 2 1/2 to 3 hours, stirring occasionally, until mixture is reduced by one-third, slightly thickened, and mahogany in color. *Do not burn mixture.* Remove spice bag and cinnamon sticks. Ladle hot mixture into sterilized jars to within 1/2 inch of top. Seal and process in Boiling Water Bath for 5 minutes after water comes to a boil.

Note: Use McIntosh, Winesap, Granny Smith, or other tart variety of apples.

Note: For a less sweet, more tart tasting product, reduce amount of sugar to 7 or 8 cups.

Piedmont Corn Relish

Yield: about 4 (12-ounce) jars

1 tablespoon cornstarch
1 teaspoon turmeric
1 cup plus 1 tablespoon
  white vinegar
8 ounces white onions,
  peeled and chopped
4 ribs celery, chopped
2 green peppers, cored,
  seeded, and chopped
2 sweet red peppers, cored,
  seeded, and chopped
2 large tomatoes, peeled
  and chopped
1 large cucumber, peeled,
  seeded, and chopped
2 large ears fresh white or
  yellow corn, husks
  removed and kernels cut
  from cob
1 1/4 cups sugar
1/4 teaspoon mustard seed

In a large kettle or pot, blend cornstarch and turmeric with a small amount of vinegar. Add remaining vinegar and mix in all of the remaining ingredients. Bring to a boil; reduce heat and simmer, uncovered, for 50 to 60 minutes or until thick. Pour into hot sterilized 12-ounce jars and seal.

Note: Relish may also be cooled and poured into refrigerator or freezer containers. Refrigerate for immediate use or freeze for future serving.

Mushroom Catsup

Take the flaps of the mushrooms from the stems, wash them add some salt and crush them; then boil them some time, strain them through a cloth, put them on the fire again with salt to your taste; a few cloves of garlick, quarter-ounce cloves pounded to one peck mushrooms; boil it till reduced to less than half the original quantity. Bottle and cork it well.

The Kitchen Queen, 1893

Spiced Cranberries with Port Wine

Yield: about 1 quart

This unique-flavored and versatile cranberry sauce was featured for a special holiday gourmet dinner, A Holiday Culinary Journey, sponsored by the Womens' Committee of the Richmond Symphony and benefiting the Richmond Symphony, November 21, 1988.

1 pound cranberries
2 cups sugar
1 cup orange juice
1 cup red port wine
2 (3-inch) cinnamon sticks, broken

Pick over cranberries, removing any stems or blemished berries. Rinse thoroughly and dry on absorbent paper. In a deep medium heavy saucepan, combine all ingredients. Bring to a simmer over moderate heat; continue to simmer (*do not boil*) until all cranberries have burst their skins. Spoon mixture into a medium glass bowl or quart jar. Cover and refrigerate until ready to serve for up to one week. Remove cinnamon sticks just before serving.

–Chef Kevin Wade
Gallego's Restaurant
The Omni Hotel

Old Richmond Advertisement, circa 1909

673

Tomatoes and Cucumbers with Yogurt

Yield: 6 to 8 servings

"Tomatoes and Cucumbers with Yogurt is a refreshing dish originating from the northern area of my native country, India, which is often served as a relish with curried meats or rice dishes."

1 large cucumber, peeled, seeded, and cut into small cubes
1 teaspoon salt
2 medium tomatoes, peeled, and coarsely chopped or cut into small cubes
1 teaspoon sugar (optional)
1/2 teaspoon cumin
1/8 teaspoon pepper
1 (16-ounce) container unflavored yogurt
Paprika to taste
Cooked rice

In a medium bowl, combine cucumber cubes and salt, mixing well. Allow to stand at room temperature for 10 minutes; drain well. Add tomatoes, sugar, if desired, cumin, and pepper, mixing well; cover and chill in the refrigerator for 1 hour. About 8 to 10 minutes before serving, drain thoroughly and then add yogurt, mixing well. Spoon into a serving bowl and sprinkle mixture lightly with paprika. Serve with cooked rice.

–Harsha Patel

The twenty-four hours from Sunday morning, 2 April 1865, to that of Monday, 3 April, are the most horrifying and traumatic in all of Richmond's history. President Jefferson Davis had been at his pew in St. Paul's Church when the fateful message arrived from Lee: the lines at Petersburg could no longer be held, the capital must be evacuated....Because Richmond had been the first city of the Confederacy in every way that is meaningful and measurable, it was ironically appropriate that precisely one week after her fall, General Lee surrendered at Appomattox.

"The Fall of Richmond,"
Battles and Leaders, 1887-88

Tomato Tart

Yield: 7 pints

"Delicious as an accompaniment to turkey or ham, Tomato Tart is an old Scottish recipe that has been given a Southern accent."

7 pounds ripe tomatoes, peeled and finely chopped

7 large, tart apples, peeled, seeded, and finely chopped (see note)

2 large onions, peeled and finely chopped

3 pounds light brown sugar, firmly packed

2 cups cider vinegar

2 ounces whole mixed pickling spices, tied in cheesecloth

1 tablespoon un-iodized salt

1 teaspoon cayenne pepper

Combine all ingredients in a 4-quart kettle and bring to a boil. Reduce heat and simmer for 1 1/2 to 2 hours or until slightly thickened. Remove spice bag. Pour into sterilized jars and seal.

Note: Use McIntosh, Winesap, Granny Smith, or other tart variety of apples.

–Crist Brown (Mrs. B. B.)

Tomata Catsup

Gather a peck of tomatas, pick out the stems, and wash them; put them on the fire without water, sprinkle on a few spoonsful of salt, let them boil steadily an hour, stirring them frequently; strain them through a colander, and then through a sieve; put the liquid on the fire with half a pint of chopped onions, half a quarter of an ounce of mace broke into small pieces; and if not sufficiently salt, add a little more—one table-spoonful of whole black pepper; boil all together until just enough to fill two bottles; cork it tight. Make it in August, in dry weather.

Mrs. Mary Randolph
The Virginia House-Wife, or Methodical Cook, *1830*

Calamondin Marmalade

Yield: 4 to 6 12-ounce jars

"Calamondins are a very small-type of orange, and if unavailable, other oranges may be substituted; but Calamondins make the best marmalade."

35 to 45 Calamondin oranges, halved and seeded

3 Temple oranges, peeled, seeded, and cut into bite-sized pieces (remove as much of the white membrane from fruit as possible)

4 cups water

5 cups sugar

Boiling Water Bath (see index)

Coarsely grind seeded Calamondin halves. In a large heavy saucepan, combine ground Calamondins, orange pieces, and water. Bring to a boil over moderate heat; reduce temperature and simmer for 20 minutes. Remove from heat and set aside for 12 hours. Measure liquid from Calamondin mixture. Add enough water, if necessary, to measure 5 cups. Combine Calamondin mixture, 5 cups Calamondin liquid and sugar in a large heavy saucepan. Bring to a boil over moderate heat and cook until mixture is thick and registers 220 degrees F. on a candy or jelly thermometer, about 20 to 25 minutes. Remove from heat, skim and ladle into hot sterilized 12-ounce jars, filling jars to within 1/2 inch from top. Seal and process in Boiling Water Bath for 5 minutes after water comes to a boil. Cool.

–Alicia Pedersen (Mrs. Paul)

Peach Chips

Slice them thin and boil them till clear in a syrup make with half their weight of sugar, lay them on dishes in the sun and turn them till dry, pack them in pots with powdered sugar sifted over each layer. Should there be syrup left continue the process with other peaches.

The Kitchen Queen, 1893

Old Richmond Advertisement, date unknown

Clementine or Tangerine Marmalade

Yield: about 7 (12-ounce) jars

Imported from Mediterranean countries and becoming very popular in Richmond, Clementines are usually available from November to February in the city. A hybrid of the tangerine and Seville (bitter) orange, created by Pere Clement in Algeria during the first decade of the twentieth century, Clementines are small in size, easy to peel, juicy, and sweet in flavor. They are wonderful to eat out of hand or to prepare into preserves or marmalades, liqueurs, or assorted confections.

10 cups sugar
6 cups cut clementine
 sections, peel, white
 membrane, and seeds
 removed (see note)
4 cups thinly sliced
 clementine peel, cut into
 2 to 3-inch thin strips,
 white membrane removed
3 cups water
1/4 teaspoon baking soda
2 (3-ounce) envelopes or 1
 (6-ounce) bottle liquid
 pectin

In a large pot or Dutch oven, combine all ingredients. Bring mixture to a boil over moderate heat; reduce temperature and simmer, cover ajar, for 30 minutes. Return mixture to a rolling boil over moderate heat and continue boiling for 1 minute,stirring constantly. Remove from heat and quickly stir in liquid pectin. Ladle into sterilized jars and seal at once with hot paraffin. Cool thoroughly.

Note: About 20 medium or 30 small clementines equal 6 cups prepared cut-up fruit.

Note: Addition of baking soda omits foaming.

Varations: reduce water to 2 1/2 cups and add 1/2 cup Irish, scotch or bourbon whisky or orange liqueur to fruit mixture. Or, 20 medium or 16 large tangerines may be substituted for clementines.

Pineapple Preserves

Take whole pineapples and set them around in a porcelain kettle. Put water to them, and par-boil until tender. Lift them out by the leaves, and as soon as they are cool enough to handle, peel and slice them. Weigh, and to a pound of fruit allow a pound of sugar. Make a syrup; drop in the fruit and cook.
Mrs. L. V. Breeden.
Virginia Recipes, *1890*

Crist's Citron Preserves

Yield: 4 to 5 pints

"Citron Preserves is an old Virginia recipe that has been handed down from generation to generation. I grew up on a farm near Amherst, Virginia. My father used to grow citron melon, and Mother used to make these wonderful preserves."

4 pounds citron melon, peeled, seeded, and cut into small pieces
16 cups cold water, divided
1 tablespoon un-iodized salt
9 cups sugar
1 lemon, thinly sliced
1 teaspoon ground ginger or cloves
1 teaspoon cinnamon

Place citron in a 4-quart kettle and add 8 cups cold water and salt. Let stand for 1 hour; drain thoroughly. Return to kettle and add remaining 8 cups cold water. Bring to a boil and continue to boil for 10 minutes. Remove from heat; drain thoroughly, reserving 1 cup citron water for syrup. Add sugar, lemon, and spices to the reserved 1 cup citron water. Pour over citron and again bring to a boil. Lower heat and simmer until mixture is the consistency of honey. Pour into sterilized jars and seal.

–Crist Brown (Mrs. B. B.)

Best-Ever Concord Grape Jam

Yield: about 8 (1/2-pint) jars

Preparation of this recipe is fool-proof and easy to do...better yet, wonderful to taste.

About 3 1/2 pounds Concord grapes
6 cups sugar
1/2 teaspoon butter or margarine (see note)
1 (3-ounce) package liquid pectin
Paraffin, melted, as needed

Remove skins from grapes. Place skins in a blender container; cover and blend until skins are puréed and smooth. Purée should measure about 2 cups; set aside. Place grape pulp with seeds, including juice, in a medium heavy saucepan. Bring to a boil over moderate heat; continue boiling for 1 to 2 minutes until seeds begin to separate from pulp. Strain pulp through a medium sieve, removing all seeds. Pulp may need to be pressed through a sieve with a wooden spoon. Pick out any remaining seeds in sieve. Place all pulp and juice in a Dutch oven or large heavy saucepan. Stir in grape skin purée, sugar, and butter, blending well. Bring to a full rolling boil over high heat, stirring constantly.

678

Quickly add liquid pectin to grape mixture and return to a full boil, stirring constantly. Continue to boil mixture for 1 minute, stirring and removing any foam with a slotted spoon. Remove jam from heat and ladle into sterilized 8-ounce jelly jars to within 1/2-inch of the jar tops. Seal at once with hot melted paraffin.

Note: Butter or margarine added to grape jam mixture before heating decreases the amount of foam formed while boiling the jam mixture.

Note: A double batch of the jam may be prepared, if desired. Larger quantity batches should not be attempted as the results may not be as full-proof without the recipe being reworked.

Nectarine Preserves with Red Port Wine

Yield: 7 to 8 (12-ounce) jars

These preserves are excellent as an accompaniment to hot biscuits, toast or pancakes. Serve them also with roasted meats and poultry for a unique flavor combination.

9 to 10 firm ripe medium nectarines (see note)
10 3/4 cups sugar
1 cup red port wine
1/2 cup lemon juice
1 (3-ounce) package liquid pectin

Peel, seed, and cut nectarines into bite-sized pieces to equal 6 cups prepared fruit. In a large heavy pot or Dutch oven, combine prepared fruit, sugar, port, and lemon juice. Cook, stirring frequently, over moderate heat for 25 to 30 minutes, until mixture comes to a full rolling boil. Continue to cook at a rolling boil for 1 minute. Remove from heat and quickly stir in liquid pectin, blending well. Return to heat and cook for an additional 1 minute. Remove from heat and skim foam from surface. Ladle hot preserves into hot sterilized jars to within 1/2 inch from top. Seal with hot paraffin.

Note: Ripe peaches, pears, or plums may be substituted, if desired.

Mild Southern Sweet Pepper Jelly

Yield: about 14 1/2 pints

Pepper jelly is a favorite recipe in the South but but this one is not quite as hot in flavor as some pepper jellies—besides, there is no messing with the peppers!

8 large sweet red or green bell peppers
1/3 cup water
5 pounds sugar (about 10 3/4 cups) (see note)
3 cups white vinegar
1 3/4 teaspoons hot sauce or to taste
4 (3-ounce) packages liquid pectin
Few drops red or green food coloring (optional)
Boiling Water Bath (optional) (see index)

Wash peppers, cut out stems, and remove seeds. Cut into large pieces; put pepper pieces and water into blender container, cover, and purée. Dissolve sugar in vinegar in a large kettle. Add peppers, bring to the boiling point, and boil for 5 minutes. Remove from heat (strain, if desired, to remove any unpuréed pepper pulp), skim top, and stir in hot sauce; blend in liquid pectin and a few drops food coloring, if desired. Continue boiling for 1 minute; stirring well. Pour into sterilized jars and seal with paraffin or apply canning lids and screw bands and process in Boiling Water Bath for 5 minutes after water comes to a boil.

Note: 1/2 cup additional sugar or to taste may be added to taste if desired.

To Preserve Figs

Soak the figs three days in salt water, changing the water every day; then soak them three days in fresh water, changing the water twice each day. Cut a slit in each fig before putting in salt water. On the seventh day boil the figs 4 hours in alum water. To 1 pound of fruit add 1 1/2pounds of sugar. Make a syrup and boil seven hours. Boil white ginger with this. when cold, add a lemon if you like. Slices of lemon peel preserved with the figs give a nice flavor.

Mrs. Anne E. Grant.
Virginia Recipes, *1890*

D. S. McCarthy.

Andrew L. Haynes.

McCarthy & Haynes,

627 E. Broad Street,

Richmond, Virginia.

Family Grocers....

Potables

Rudee's Ruckus

Yield: 4 servings

"Limit!! Two per customer, please!!"

2 ounces vodka, divided
2 ounces light or dark rum, divided
2 ounces gin, divided
2 ounces Blue Curaco, divided
4 ounces sour or collins mix, chilled and divided
4 ounces unsweetened pineapple juice, chilled and divided
Bacardi 151 or other rum
4 pineapple cubes, fresh, frozen, or canned for garnish
4 Maraschino cherries with stems for garnish
Wooden picks for garnish
Mint sprigs for garnish

In each of 4 10 to 12-ounce glasses, pour 1/2 ounce vodka, 1/2 ounce rum, 1/2 ounce gin, and 1/2 ounce Blue Curaco. Add a splash (about 1 ounce) of sour or collins mix and a splash of pineapple juice to each glass; stir or shake well. Fill glasses with ice cubes and top each with a float of Bacardi 151 or other rum. Garnish each with a pineapple cube and Maraschino cherry secured with a wooden pick and a mint sprig.

Note: Other orange liqueur may be substituted.

–Rudees's on the James

Wes Booth's Two-Fisted Bloody Mary

Yield: about 2 quarts

1 (46-ounce) can vegetable-tomato or tomato juice
2 cups vodka or gin
2 tablespoons lemon or lime juice
1 tablespoon prepared or 1 teaspoon freshly grated horseradish

In a large pitcher, combine the first 6 ingredients; add celery and seasoned salts, and pepper to taste, blending well. Cover lightly and chill mixture in refrigerator for several hours. Just before serving, coat the rim of each serving glass lightly with egg white mixed with a few drops of water. Quickly dip egg-white coated glasses into seasoned salt before egg white dries, coating the rim

1 teaspoon Worcestershire
  sauce or to taste
Celery salt, seasoned salt,
  and pepper to taste
1 egg white, lightly beaten
  with a few drops of water
Seasoned salt to coat rims
  of glasses
Ice cubes as needed
Celery stick stirrers
Seeded thin lemon or lime
  wedges for garnish

of each glass well. Add ice cubes to glasses; pour vegetable-tomato or tomato juice mixture over ice cubes. Garnish each serving with celery sticks and thin lemon or lime wedges.

Virgin Mary Variation: Omit vodka or gin. Lemon or lime juice may be increased to 3 tablespoons, if desired.

Grapefruit Gin Fizz

Yield: 10 to 12 servings

3 egg whites
3 cups pink or ruby red
  grapefruit juice (see note)
1 cup gin
2 tablespoons sugar or to
  taste
Ice cubes as needed
Fresh mint sprigs for
  garnish

In a blender container, combine egg whites, grapefruit juice, gin and sugar; cover and whiz at high speed for about 30 seconds. Pour over ice cubes in tall glasses and garnish each with a mint sprig.

Note: Strain juice if fresh grapefruit juice is used.

Gin Punch

Peel of half lemon; juice of one lemon; three-quarters pint gin; one glass sherry; ice well.

F. F. V. Receipt Book, 1894

Irish Coffee

Yield: 6 servings

Irish Coffee, an import from Ireland via the Shannon Airport Restaurant, has become a favorite after dinner drink of late twentieth century Americans.

6 teaspoons sugar, divided
4 to 6 cups strong hot
  coffee, divided (see note)
6 (1 1/2-ounce) jiggers Irish
  whisky, divided
Softly whipped cream for
  garnish (see note)

Warm glasses (goblets, cups, or mugs). Hold bowl of metal spoon near the bottom of serving glass; pour hot water into spoon and then into glass. Empty glass and repeat with each serving glass. Add 1 teaspoon sugar to each glass. Fill glasses one fourth full with coffee. Stir until sugar dissolves. Add a jigger of whisky to each glass and fill glass to within 1 inch of top with coffee. Top with softly whipped cream. Do not stir. Serve at once.

Note: Amount will vary depending on size of goblet, cup, or mug.

Note: Cream should be whipped lightly until it just starts to mound but does not hold peaks.

Frozen Whisky Sours

Yield: 8 to 10 servings

1 (6-ounce) can frozen
  orange juice concentrate
1 (6-ounce) can frozen
  lemonade concentrate
3/4 to 1 cup bourbon
  whisky
About 3 cups crushed ice
1 medium seedless orange,
  thinly sliced and cut into
  half slices, for garnish
Stemmed Maraschino
  cherries for garnish

Partially thaw fruit juice concentrates. In the container of a blender, combine the first 4 ingredients, cover and whiz at high speed until mixture is a thick frappé. Pour into chilled footed whisky sour glasses and garnish each with a thin orange slice and a stemmed Maraschino cherry.

Variation: Add 3/4 cup club soda to mixture. Bourbon may be increased to taste.

—Marion Peeschla (Mrs. Ralf)

The Westmoreland Club

....One social organization of particular interest that arose during the time in question was the Westmoreland Club. The forerunner of the present-day Commonwealth Club, it was founded by Confederate veterans and was named for the county of General Lee's birth....

....Its house had been the home of Poe's "Helen," the beautiful Mrs. Stanard; and in its garden, like a green fountain, was a weeping willow grown from one at Mount Vernon, in turn grown from one over Napoleon's grave. Many of the senior Westmorelanders, veterans of The War, liked to sit around the bar and talk about "battles long ago," to the boredom of the younger members, including Father and my uncles....

Uncle Bob said. "How'd you like to see the bloodiest battlefield in the whole War?...Fine! I'll pick you up at noon tomorrow."

Naturally, I expected a jaunt to Cold Harbor, Seven Pines, the Crater, Yellow Tavern, or some other nearby field where (as I quoted to myself with tingling scalp) "superstition nightly hears the neighing of chargers, and still sees with heated fancy the rushing squadrons of spectral war." But where Uncle Bob took me was to the Westmoreland, downstairs, to the door of the bar.

"Here it is, son," he said. "Gaze your fill! Right here, in this very room, more Yankees have been slaughtered than at Bull Run, Fredericksburg and Gettysburg put together!"

Considering that the Westmoreland had been founded by Confederate officers and named for General Lee's native county, that it had held its first meeting in his former Richmond home,and that its first nonresident member was Capt. Robert E. Lee, I felt that the elders were well within their rights when they reminisced about The War—that, indeed, any other topic would have been inappropriate, unbecoming, and even downright indecent....

Whenever Major Hunter was invited time Cousin Jim and his guests felt that they had fittingly celebrated his brother Bev's ordination as Bishop of Southern Virginia....

Well, the Westmoreland disbanded in 1936; its library, silver and portraits were dispersed; and the building was torn down. Where it stood, a parking garage stands now. The old warriors are gone. Their place is empty forever. But I will be forever grateful for the privilege of having known them and listened to them.

Bryan
The Sword over the Mantel (Condensed), 1960

A Southern Tradition....the Mint Julep

The mint julep is indeed a Southern institution—about as Southern as one can find. Wherever there is a mint julep, there resides a bit of the Old South. It is part romance, ceremony, tradition, and regional nostalgia, as well as a bit of flavor, taste, and aroma. With a history that is quite elusive, the julep has been the subject of poets and a scene prop of novelists.

An early form of the julep was served in ancient Persia. Prepared as a non-alcoholic fruit drink or a potable flavored with sweet wine, that julab bears little resemblance to its more famous cousin. Early English mint juleps were often made with Spanish sherry. Even rum was used by those in the colonies.

For we Americans though, the mint julep as we know and enjoy it, originated in the Northern Virginia tidewater area. It was first made with rye, the locally grown spirit. The julep of antebellum Virginia may have had some brandy added to it. After Captain George Thorpe's invention in seventeenth century Jamestown of converting corn mash into bourbon became a Kentucky specialty in the early nineteenth century, a good julep was only prepared with bourbon whisky. The availability to southerners of only locally grown ingredients after the Civil War may have also contributed to this standard.

Juleps are not to be obliterated by adding garnishes of fruit salads to the julep glass or goblet. Two things can ruin any julep...too much sugar...and...too little whisky!!

...Your health ladies and gentlemen as I raise my silver Jefferson cup in eager anticipation of savoring the golden spirit.

Old Virginia Mint Julep

The strength and degree of sweetness of the Julep are matters of taste, but the advice is offered, "do not use too little liquor nor too much sugar."

Who would dwell in Virginia and not be acquainted with mint julep? And who would come to Virginia and not seek its acquaintance? The Virginia garden, as a matter of course, has its bed of fragrant mint, flourishing luxuriantly in some shady corner. Even in winter, under sheltering branches, the mint will remain green and aromatic, to be plucked early in the morning while the dew it on it, and be careful not to bruise it. The true julep is served in a silver goblet, covered with frost. The goblet is garnished by moistening the rim, and dipping it into about a quarter of an inch of powdered sugar. Ice is washed and then crushed in a clean towel; there will be no silvery frost if this process is reversed. Two jiggers of old whiskey in which a teaspoonful of sugar has been dissolved is poured over the ice. Into the goblet are thrust sprigs of mint, their lower leaves first crushed, bruised leaves more fragrant are, and the goblet is buried in ice for at least ten minutes. Thus is concocted the nectar of Virginia.

Virginia Cooking, 1939

The Jefferson Hotel Restoration, circa 1903

The Jefferson's Mint Julep

Yield: 4 servings

In the Old Dominion, Virginia Gentleman brand would be the choice of bourbon.

Mint leaves as desired
  (about 12)
8 teaspoons sugar
6 ounces bourbon whisky
Crushed ice as desired
Additional fresh mint sprigs
  for garnish
Short straws as desired

Crush or coarsely chop mint leaves. In a 2-cup measure, combine mint leaves and sugar blending into a coarse paste. Add bourbon, blending well. Add crushed ice as desired to chilled julep cups or 6 to 8-ounce glass tumblers. Pour bourbon mixture over crushed ice in each glass, dividing evenly. Garnish each with a fresh mint sprig and a short straw. Serve immediately. Cheers!!
-The Jefferson-Sheraton Hotel

687

A place of great public resort during many years after about 1810, for politicians, guidnuncs, stock jobbers, and in general those who had nothing else to do, was Lynch's Coffee House, two doors below the Globe, which Mr. Lynch had vacated. Here all the news, foreign and domestic, rumours true or false, scandal and tittle-tattle centered, and from hence it was diffused, with increased vigor at each corner round which it circulated. Here windy talkers would blow their bellows, and tedious ones tire their listeners.

Samuel Mordecai
Richmond in By-Gone Days, 1856
Reprint Edition, 1975

Mollie's Infamous Old-Fashioneds

Yield: 4 servings

Mollie Mitchell is as well known to many Richmonders as the elegant, prestigious, men's club where she gracefully presides over the ladies bar on the first floor....an area of the club in which women are allowed!!! Mollie began work in 1953 at the old Rotunda Club, housed for many years in the Jefferson Hotel. When the club closed in 1976 and its membership was incorporated into the elite Commonwealth Club, Mollie went along, tending bar to this day with her "wicked" concoctions and delightful charm.

4 teaspoons Angostura bitters, divided
1/2 cup Heavy Syrup, divided
Ice cubes or crushed ice as desired
8 ounces Scotch or bourbon whisky, divided
1 teaspoon lemon juice, divided
Thin orange half-slices and

Into each of 4 Old-Fashioned glasses, (6-ounce short tumblers), add 1 teaspoon bitters. Blend in 2 tablespoons Heavy Syrup into each. Add ice cubes or crushed ice. Pour 2 ounces Scotch or bourbon over ice in each glass. Add 1/4 teaspoon lemon juice. Stir lightly and garnish each with a thin orange half-slice and a Maraschino cherry. Serve immediately.

688

Maraschino cherries for
garnish

Heavy Syrup: In a small heavy saucepan, combine 3/4 cup sugar and 1/2 cup
water; bring to boiling over high heat. Cool thoroughly before using.
Store in a tightly covered clean glass jar at room temperature for several
days.

–Mollie S. Mitchell

Cherry Bounce (My Father's)

*Four quarts of morello cherries, four quarts of red hearts, three pounds of
sugar, one gallon of good whiskey, one pint of brandy. Mash the cherries, and
break the stones; then mix them with the sugar and whiskey. Put into a cask;
cork tightly and let stand for two weeks; then strain and bottle. This will keep
for years.*
An after dinner cordial to be served with black coffee.

Virginia Cooking, 1939

Ice Cream Brandy Alexander

Yield: 4 servings

*"This is a drink for those who prefer dessert to drink. A traditional brandy
alexander is made from equal parts of brandy, creme de cacao, and sweet
cream. The ice cream version replaces the cream with a liberal portion of
good quality vanilla ice cream. In our family, Breyers, with its distinctive vanilla
flavor, is the brand of choice. Of course, other flavors of ice cream may be
used, but nut flavors should be avoided."*

1/4 cup brandy
1/4 cup Crème de cacao
2 cups vanilla ice cream,
slightly softened

In a bowl, combine all ingredients, blending just
enough to retain the consistency of a milk shake.
Serve in chilled wine or champagne glasses.

–Douglas O. Tice, Jr.

689

George Washington's Eggnog

George Washington had his own "invented" recipe for Christmas eggnog still popular in the South at Christmas night. This somewhat soupy libation is a descent from the old, innocuous sillabub of England, devoted largely to maiden aunts and adolescents. Washington's eggnog recipe called for:

One quart milk   One quart cream
One dozen eggs   One dozen teaspoonfuls sugar
One pint brandy   One half-pint rye
One quarter pint   One quarter pint sherry
Jamaica rum

And the father of his country had his own special technique, all of which is to be found written down in his own hand. The liquor was mixed first of all and then the other ingredients were ingeniously "folded in" with much whipping and beating. The eggnog was made several days before Christmas and was put in "a cool place" to become duly aromatized.

The Richmond Times-Dispatch, date unknown

Summertime Sangria

Yield: 12 to 15 (4-ounce) servings

Sangria, the fruity wine punch traditionally served in Spain and Mexico, is a refreshing chilled drink to serve to guests on a hot day as an aperitif before serving brunch or luncheon. Careful ... this libation is potent!

1 (4/5-quart) dry red Burgundy wine
3 ounces cognac
2 ounces banana liqueur
2 ounces Triple Sec liqueur
2 ounces light rum
2 ounces peach or pineapple brandy
1 medium lime, thinly sliced
1 medium orange, thinly sliced
1 medium lemon, thinly sliced
1 medium apple, cored, seeded, and chopped
1 medium banana, peeled and chopped
12 fresh strawberries, stemmed and halved
1/2 fresh pineapple, peeled, cored, and cut into chunks
13 to 20 ounces club soda, chilled
Crushed ice or cubes as needed

Combine wine and liqueurs in a 2 1/2- to 3-quart pitcher. Add fruit and chill for one hour to blend flavors. Add soda to taste and ice just before serving. Spoon a small amount of fruit into each serving glass and pour in Sangria.

...At the mansion the door was open all day, the punch bowl filled with spirits for the delegates. (circa 1829-30)
—William Seal
Virginia's Executive Mansion:
A History of the Governor's House, 1988

General Lee's Favorite Wines

Robert E. Lee's historical image would have us believe he avoided all things alcoholic. However, his foremost biographer, Douglas Southall Freeman, acknowledges that in spite of an intense aversion to hard spirits Lee was known to drink wine, even if "rarely and in small quantities."

General Lee, who was a man of simple tastes, may have preferred homemade wines. That such wines were available in his home is suggested by the publication in 1879 of three of Mrs.Lee's wine recipes and attributed to "Mrs. Gen. R. E. Lee" in Housekeeping In Old Virginia, a compilation of receipts and domestic advice.

—Condensed from **Housekeeping in Old Virginia,**
1879 and **R. E. Lee,** Douglas Southall Freeman,
Vol I and IV, Edited by Douglas O. Tice, Jr.

Fox Grape Wine

To every bushel of fax grapes add twenty-two quarts of water. Mash the fruit and let it stand twenty-four hours. Strain through a linen or fine sieve that willprevent the seed from getting through. To every gallon of juice add two pounds of brown sugar. Fill the cask not quite full. Let it stand open fourteen days, and then close the bung. —Mrs. Gen. R.E. Lee

Marion Cabell Tyree
Housekeeping in Old Virginia, *1879*

Blackberry Wine

Fill a large stone jar with the ripe fruit and cover it with water. Tie a cloth over the jar and let them stand three or four days to ferment; then mash and press them through a cloth. To every gallon of juice add three pounds of brown sugar. Return the mixture to the jar and cover closely. Skim it every morning for more than a week, until it clears from the fermentation. When clear, pour it carefully from the sediment into a demijohn. Cook tightly, set in a cool place. When two months old it will be fit for use.-Mrs. Gen. R.E. Lee

Marion Cabell Tyree
Housekeeping in Old Virginia, *1879*

Currant Wine

Put three pounds of brown sugar to every squeezed gallon of currants. Add a gallon of water, or two, if juice is scarce. It is better to put it in an old wine-cask and let it stand a year before you draw if off.-Mrs. Gen. R.E. Lee
Marion Cabell Tyree

Housekeeping in Old Virginia, 1879

Wassail Bowl

Yield: 12 (4-ounce) servings

Of English background, the tradition of serving Wassail at the Christmas holidays was brought to Virginia by the early colonists. Not as popular today, it is still a festive beverage to serve for a party.

6 lady apples or small red apples
3 tablespoons water
2 whole cloves
2 whole allspice
2 cardamon seeds, coarsely broken
1 (3-inch) cinnamon stick, broken into 1/2-inch pieces
1 (28-ounce) bottle ginger ale, divided
1/2 teaspoon nutmeg, divided
1 cup sugar
2 cups dry sherry
3 eggs, separated

Place apples in a shallow baking pan, add water, and cover with aluminum foil. Bake in a moderate oven (350 degrees F.) for 15 minutes or until apples are tender but hold their shape (see note). Remove apples from the pan carefully; set aside. Tie whole and broken spices in a small double-thick cheesecloth bag. Combine one-half of the ginger ale, nutmeg, and spice bag in a large heavy saucepan; simmer gently for 10 minutes. Remove the spice bag. Stir in remaining ginger ale, sugar, and sherry. Heat slowly, but do not boil. In a medium bowl, beat egg whites until stiff beaks are formed. In a very large bowl, beat egg yolks in a separate bowl and fold in whites. Slowly whisk or stir in hot ginger ale mixture until smooth. Pour mixture into a large punch bowl carefully and float apples on top. Serve in warmed mugs or punch cups.

Note: Washed and polished fresh apples are a bit more attractive and may be substituted for cooked ones, if preferred.

Note: Apples may be microwaved in a glass baking dish, loosely covered with plastic wrap, for 2 to 3 minutes at high power.

The Wickham-Valentine House and Museum

In 1812, John Wickham, prominent Richmond citizen and noted lawyer, built his neo-classical style residence at Eleventh and Clay streets in Richmond's fashionable Court End area. Designed by Alexander Parris of Boston, the house remains one the the United States' most lovely examples of Greek Revival architecture. Excellent wall paintings similar to fresco work, and the only known examples of this type of work of the time in the United States, have recently been uncovered in the drawing rooms, dining room, and library of the main floor.

An invitation to the Wickham home was a coveted social plum for visitors to Richmond in the early decades of the nineteenth century. Among the famous men who were enterained were Henry Clay, whose booming voice asking for Mrs. Wickham could be heard throughout the house; Daniel Webster; John C. Calhoun; and John Randolph, who read Sir Walter Scott's Marmion to Mrs. Wickham and her daughter, Julia Wickham Leigh, when it was first published. General Winfield Scott of Mexican war fame, was much remembered by the younger Wickham children for his plumed hat while he waited for their mother, Elizabeth Wickham, as she regally swept down the oval staircase.

Founded as a private museum in 1892 through the will of Mann S. Valentine II, only four owners resided in the house during the nineteenth century. Prominent Richmond hotelier John Ballard purchased the house in 1854, promptly modernizing the fireplaces and lighting, adding touches of the Victorian era. Unfortunately, bankruptcy took its toll of Mr. Ballard and the house was again sold in 1858 to James Brooks. More than two decades later, the ownership again changed hands to Mann Valentine.

The Wickham-Valentine House opened its door as a museum in 1898 to reveal Valentine's personal art and archaelogical treasures. Thirty years after the museum's opening, adjacent buildings were acquired and renovated as exhibit areas for the museum. The house was restored to display different periods of the decorating arts and interior design of the early and later nineteenth century. Other building additions and funding of the late twentieth century have added to the size and scope of the museum, now Richmond's repository of the city's history.

Eliza B. Askin 1990

Presently undergoing a vast renovation, the Wickham-Valentine House in the 1990's will again be in the pristine condition of its early nineteenth century grandeur. For those who visit the grande dame, one can capture the magic from afar of the handsome, witty, John Wickham and his lovely wife, Elizabeth, entertaining the aristocracy of early Richmond at dinner in the flickering candlelight.

Rum Shrub

Yield: about 2 quarts

2 1/2 cups water
1 1/2 cups sugar
4 cups dark rum
1 cup lime juice
Thin lime slices for garnish
Fresh sprigs of mint for
garnish

In a 2-quart container, combine water and sugar, stirring to dissolve thoroughly. Add rum and lime juice. Pour into a freezer container; freeze until mixture is the consistency of slush. Spoon into punch cups and garnish each with a thin lime slice and a fresh mint sprig.
–The Valentine Museum

Robert's Whisky Sours

Yield: 1 serving

Robert Dandridge is a Richmonder of fame, distinction, and warm regard. Born in the historic Church Hill area of Richmond in 1910, Robert began work as a bartender at the old Westmoreland Club in 1930. Sadly, the historic men's club closed June 1, 1937. The next day, Robert began work at the well-known Commonwealth Club, a private professional men's social club, dating from 1890 where the elite civic, business, and banking leaders of Richmond meet. With affection and gratitude, the Club issued a proclamation of appreciation to Robert when he celebrated his golden anniversary with the club, June 2, 1989. Members look forward to a "chat" with Robert. He is much loved and fondly described as a "low keyed listener and soft spoken counselor, all the while illuminating the lives of those he has touched." No doubt, as in the code of all excellent bartenders, there are many interesting tales Robert has heard over the years that will never pass his lips to the ears of others.

2 ounces bourbon
2 tablespoons sour mix, chilled (see note)
Crushed or shaved ice
A thin orange half slice and a Maraschino cherry with stem for garnish

In a cocktail shaker, combine bourbon and sour mix; stir, or cover and shake vigorously. Add crushed or shaved ice as desired to chilled whisky sour glass. Pour bourbon mixture over ice into glass. Garnish with an orange half slice and a Maraschino cherry. Serve immediately.

Note: Preferably use Langhorne Sour Mix.

Dacquiri variations: Substitute 2 ounces light Bacardi rum for 2 ounces bourbon. Omit orange slice and cherry and garnish with a thin lime slice. For a *straight-up* Dacquiri, omit ice and serve in a chilled Dacquiri or other stemmed glass. For a *Dacquiri-on-the-Rocks*, place ice in a 6-ounce short tumbler; pour rum mixture over ice. Serve immediately.

–Robert Dandridge

...Gradually, some order came out of the chaos of over-tasked hospital service. The churches gave their seat cushions to make beds; the famous old wine-cellers of private houses sent their priceless Madeira, port, sherry, and brandy; everybody's cook was set to turning out dainties, and for our own men we begged unblushingly until they were fairly well supplied...

Harrison
"The Ravages of War (1862-1865),"
Recollections Grave and Gay, 1911

Mulled Wine

Yield: 12 servings

4 cups dry red Burgundy
  wine or claret
3 tablespoons grated
  orange peel
2 teaspoons grated lemon
  peel
6 whole cloves
1 (3-inch) cinnamon stick,
  broken
1 whole nutmeg
1 tablespoon sugar
12 (3-inch) cinnamon sticks
  for stirrers (optional)

In a medium heavy saucepan, combine the first 6 ingredients; bring to simmering over moderate heat and continue simmering for 5 to 10 minutes. Strain and serve hot in mugs. Garnish each with a whole cinnamon stick as a stirrer, if desired.

–The Valentine Museum

....According to the principles of a general equality was the behavior at our tavern, which in its arrangements was very like an eastern caravansery (sic). Mr. Formicola, a Neapolitan by birth, was the landlord here. The entire house contained but two large rooms on the ground-floor, and two of the same size above, the apartments under the roof furnished with numerous beds standing close together, both rooms and chambers standing open to every person throughout the day. Here, no less than in most of the other public-houses in America, it is expected that rooms are to be used only as places for sleeping, eating and drinking. The whole day long, therefore, one is compelled to be among all sorts of company and at night to sleep in like manner;....

Schöpf
"Of Coaches There Were None":
A German Traveler Visits the Emerging
City at the Falls,
Travels in the Confederation,
trans. and ed. Morrison (Condensed), 1911

Champagne Apricot Punch

Yield: 30 (4-ounce) servings

2 (4/5-quart) bottles
   champagne, chilled
4 cups apricot nectar,
   chilled
3 cups apple juice, chilled
2 cups orange juice, chilled
Thin orange slices and fresh
   mint sprigs for garnish

In a large chilled punch bowl, just before serving, combine the first 4 ingredients, blending well. Add ice cubes and orange slices; float mint sprigs on top.

Citrus Wine Cooler

Yield: 10 to 12 (6-ounce) servings

1 bottle (28 to 32 ounces)
   dry white wine
1 (12-ounce) can frozen
   orange juice concentrate,
   thawed
1 liter bottle (33.8 ounces)
   club soda or sparkling
   water, chilled
Ice cubes, as needed
Thin orange half-slices and
   fresh mint sprigs for
   garnish

In a large pitcher or other container, combine wine and orange juice concentrate, blending well. Cover and chill until ready to serve. Add club soda to mixture just before serving. Fill 10 to 12 glass tumblers with ice cubes as desired; pour chilled wine cooler mixture into each glass to within 1/2 inch of the top of each glass. Garnish each serving with an orange half-slice and a fresh mint sprig.

Variations: Omit orange juice concentrate and orange slices. Add 1 (12-ounce) can thawed frozen lemonade or limeade concentrate to wine. Or, add 1 (6-ounce) can of thawed frozen orange juice concentrate and 1 (6-ounce) can thawed frozen unsweetened pineapple juice concentrate. Proceed as previously directed.

Cranberry Fruit Sparkler

Yield: 20 to 25 (4 to 5-ounce) punch cup servings

1 (6-ounce) can frozen
   orange juice concentrate,
   thawed

In a large glass pitcher, combine cranberry juice, orange juice concentrate, and sugar, blending until sugar is dissolved; chill thoroughly in refrig-

698

8 cups cranberry juice (see note)

1/4 cup sugar or to taste

2 cups vodka (optional) (see note)

2 cups club soda or sparkling water, chilled

Ice cubes as needed or fruited ice ring (optional)

Thin orange slices for garnish

erator. Just before serving, add vodka, if desired, blending well. Pour mixture into a small punch bowl, gradually pour club soda down the side of the bowl. Add ice cubes or a fruited ice ring and garnish with thin orange slices.

Note: Use artificially sweetened cranberry juice if, desired.

Note: May use gin or other alcoholic spirits, if desired. If a non-alcoholic punch is desired, use 2 cups additional fruit juice such as pineapple juice.

–Helen Winston Pinder (Mrs. John)

Dottie's Marguerita Punch

Yield: 40 (4-ounce) punch cup servings

3 (12-ounce) cans frozen limeade concentrate, thawed

1 (12-ounce) can frozen lemonade concentrate, thawed

3 cups tequila

2 cups water

1 cup Triple Sec liqueur

3 to 4 egg whites, slightly beaten (optional)

Few drops water (optional)

Salt as needed (optional)

2 (32-ounce) bottles sparkling water or club soda, chilled

Ice cubes as desired

Thin lime slices for garnish

In a pitcher, combine limeade and lemonade concentrates, tequila, water, and Triple Sec, blending well. Cover and chill thoroughly. In a small bowl combine egg whites and a few drops of water. Dip the rim of each punch cup into egg white wash and then into salt (placed in a bowl or mounded on a sheet of waxed paper), coating the rim of each glass well, if desired. Allow salt coating to dry. Just before serving, pour chilled tequila mixture into a punch bowl. Add sparkling water or club soda; stir gently. Add ice cubes, if desired. Garnish punch bowl with thin lime slices.

POTABLES, ALCOHOLIC and NON-ALCOHOLIC

Roman Punch

Make Two quarts lemonade rich with pure juice of lemon fruit; add one tablespoonful Sauer's extract of lemon; work well and freeze juice before serving. Add for each quart of ice one-half pint of Jamaica rum; mix well and serve in high glasses; as this makes what is called a semi or half ice.

Old Richmond Recipe
Circa turn of nineteenth/twentieth centuries

Power House Punch

Yield: about 50 punch cup servings

3 (6-ounce) cans frozen limeade concentrate, thawed
1 (46-ounce) can unsweetened pineapple juice, chilled
1 (46-ounce) can apricot nectar, chilled
3 (28-ounce) bottles ginger ale or sparkling water, chilled
1 fifth (25.4 ounces) vodka
Fresh whole strawberries, fresh pineapple cubes, and thin lime slices (optional)
Ice ring (optional)

Combine limeade concentrate, pineapple juice, and apricot nectar together in a punch bowl or other container. Just before serving, add ginger ale or sparkling water and vodka; stir to mixt horoughly. Float a few fresh strawberries, fresh pineapple cubes, and lime slices and/or an ice ring in punch, if desired.

–Maryrita Jackson (Mrs. David)

...The Westmoreland's standard drink was not champagne but "Mountain" (i.e., bourbon), taken need, by the "dram," and reverently. Venerable Westmorelanders have not forgotten the vehemence, becoming violence, with which Major S. protested that his dram "reeked" of turpentine. The house committee traced the dram to a bottle on the bar, and the bottle to a barrel in the cellar, and the barrel to a vat in the distillery. One of its oaken staves had split, they found, and had been ignorantly replaced with a stave of pine...

Bryan
The Sword over the Mantel, 1960

Power Packed Virginia Tea Punch

Yield: About 32 4-ounce punch cups

"This mixture tastes like a potent whisky sour. Stand back...it's powerful! An ice ring filled with red and green Maraschino cherries may be floated in the punch as a colorful garnish."

4 cups prepared hot strong tea
2 cups sugar
2 cups orange juice
1 cup lemon juice
1 fifth (25.4 ounces) bourbon whisky
1 quart (32 ounces) ginger ale, chilled
An ice ring filled with red and green Maraschino cherries for garnish (optional)
Thin orange and lemon half slices for garnish (optional)

In a 2-quart container, combine tea, sugar, orange, and lemon juices; stir until sugar is completely dissolved. Cover and thoroughly chill in the refrigerator. Just before serving, pour mixture into a punch bowl. Add bourbon and ginger ale, blending well. Float an ice ring filled with red and green Maraschino cherries and thin orange and lemon half slices in punch if desired.

–Jane Roe (Mrs. A. Prescott)
The Valentine Museum Guild

Sunday Callers

When callers dropped in, the ladies gravitated to the parlor, the gentlemen always being asked to "step this way." This way was the sideboard in the back hall where gurgles from decanters and tinkle of ice could be heard, and my grandfather presided, his rich voice telling so good a story that delighted shouts of male laughter rang through the house.

None of the ladies even considered participating in this refreshment, not even to a glass of sherry....

Old Richmond newspaper, date unknown

Mrs. J. Ambler Johnston's Eggnog

Yield: 18 to 20 servings

4 cups light cream or half-and-half
2/3 cup sugar
6 eggs, separated
1 3/4 cups whisky
1 cup heavy cream
Nutmeg for garnish

In a medium bowl, combine light cream and sugar stirring to dissolve sugar; allow mixture to come to room temperature. In a large bowl, beat egg yolks until thick and lemon yellow in color. Gradually add whisky, drop by drop, beating the liquor into egg yolks in a steady stream. Stir in light cream mixture. Strain mixture into a clean large bowl. In another large bowl, beat egg whites until stiff, glossy, but not dry peaks are formed; carefully fold beaten egg whites into egg yolk mixture. Cover and refrigerate for 24 hours to "*ripen*" flavors. In a chilled, small deep bowl, beat heavy cream with chilled beaters until stiff peaks are formed; fold whipped cream into egg mixture. Pour into punch bowl and sprinkle lightly with nutmeg. Serve in punch cups.

—Elise Wright (Mrs. Wesley)

Our Favorite Egg-Nog

18 eggs
1 quart XX cream
1 quart whiskey
1/2 pint rum
18 rounded tablespoons sugar

Beat the yolks and whites separately and thoroughly, then trickle the liquor into the yolks, beating as you do so. Add sugar, beating until thoroughly dissolved. Add the rum, and then the cream, which should be well whipped. Last, add the whites and stir all together. Set in a cool place or pack in ice until ready to serve.

Mrs. Stuart McGuire
Famous Recipes From Old Virginia, *1935*

Milk Punch

Sweeten a glass of milk to taste and 2 or 3 tablespoonsful of best brandy.

Virginia Recipes, *1890*

George Washington's Christmas Nog

Yield: about 4 quarts

Everyone in the Old Dominion has his or her favorite recipe for eggnog, a winter holiday tradition since colonial days. This eggnog is an updated version of a recipe reputed to have been favored by Martha and George Washington. Mind you...it is wonderfull, but very potent!

2 cups brandy
1 cup rye whisky
1/2 cup Jamaican rum
1/2 cup dry sherry
12 eggs, separated
3/4 cup sugar
4 cups milk
4 cups half-and-half or light cream

In a 4-cup measure, combine the first 4 ingredients. In a very large bowl, beat egg yolks lightly, add sugar gradually, and beat until light and lemon-colored. Add 1 cup liquor mixture, a drop at a time, beating slowly. Add remaining liquor gradually, beating slowly. Stir in milk and half-and-half. In a large bowl, beat egg whites until soft peaks are formed; fold into egg yolk mixture. Chill.

Egg Liqueur

Yield: about 16 (3-ounce) servings

This German-style liqueur is similar to eggnog...rather potent and delicious!

6 egg yolks
2 1/4 cups sifted confectioners' sugar
1 teaspoon vanilla extract
1 cup heavy cream
1 cup milk
1/2 cup grain alcohol or to taste

In a medium bowl, beat egg yolks until light in color. Gradually add sugar and vanilla, beating until thickened and tripled in volume. Beat in cream and milk. Serve in chilled punch cups or wine or claret glasses.

Note: Egg liqueur may be prepared in a blender at high speed.

–Marion Peeschla (Mrs. Ralf)

Old Richmond Advertisement, date unknown

> During Mr. Jefferson's tenure as governor of Virginia in 1781, the British destroyed the precious wine cellar contents of America's first gourmand.

Kahlúa Liqueur

Yield: about 1 1/2 quarts

4 cups sugar
4 cups boiling water, divided
3/4 cup instant coffee crystals
2 cups 100-proof vodka
1 vanilla bean, cut diagonally

In a large container, dissolve sugar in 3 cups boiling water, Dissolve instant coffee crystals in 1 cup boiling water. Cool mixtures thoroughly. In a clean glass gallon jar, combine cooled liquids; add vodka and vanilla bean; cover lightly. Allow mixture to stand in a cool, dark, dry area for 2 weeks. Pour mixture into clean glass bottles, seal, and store in a dark, cool, dry area.

–Linda M. Bourgeois (Mrs. Bruce)

No institution was more important in the social life of early Richmond than its taverns—also called inns or ordinaries, with the three terms used interchangeably. Men of the community gathered to eat or drink, to politick, to gossip, to play billiards, and to hear the latest news from travelers. After the capital was moved to Richmond, the local taverns increased in importance, providing board for members of the General Assembly and for other people who had business with the state. The Henrico County Court and the Richmond hustings court licensed fifteen men and one woman to keep taverns in Richmond during the years 1781,1782, and 1783.

Galt's Tavern, referred to in later years as City Tavern, opened in 1775 and reported among its customers respectively, Arnold, Simcoe, Cornwallis and Lafayette, who made the tavern their headquarters. The Continental officer Feltman described in his journal playing billiards as Galt's Tavern and dining "very sumptuously upon Rock fish."

Harry M. Ward and Harold E. Greer, Jr.
Richmond During The Revolution, 1775-83, 1977

Kir Royale

Yield: 4 servings

Serve Kir Royal in place of cocktails at your next dinner party for a delightful and different before-dinner drink.

4 ounces Crème de Cassis (black currant liqueur)
Ice cubes, if desired
16 to 24 ounces chilled brut champagne
4 thin lemon slices

Pour 1 ounce Crème de Cassis into each of 4 chilled champagne glasses. Add 1 to 2 ice cubes to each glass, if desired. Pour 4 to 6 ounces chilled champagne into each glass. Float a lemon slice in each glass for garnish.

Blackberry Cordial

Mix two ounces of cloves, allspice, cinnamon, with half bushel of berries; mash all well together and boil for half an hour; then strain through a cotton bag, and add best brandy, allowing one quart of a gallon; bottle and keep for sickness, although it is a delicious drink.

F. F. V. Receipt Book, *1894*

After Dinner Cordials, Served With Black Coffee

Half teaspoonful of maraschino, half teaspoonful creme de menthe, half teaspoonful yellow chartreuse, half teaspoonful green chartreuse, half teaspoonful French brandy; all must be carefully poured one over the other and served without mixing.

F. F. V. Receipt Book, *1894*

Strawberry Acid

Mix nine ounces tartaric acid with one gallon water andt wenty-four quarts of strawberries; let it stand for forty-eight hours; then strain it and add as many pints of sugar as you have juice; let this stand two days, stirring it often until the sugar is well dissolved; bottle and cork it but not too tight. Serve mixed with a little water and crushed ice.

F. F. V. Receipt Book, *1894*

Iced Coffee Punch

Yield: 32 punch cup servings

3/4 cup plus 1 1/2
  tablespoons sugar
1/2 cup plus 1 tablespoon
  instant coffee crystals
Pinch salt
1 cup boiling water
8 cups milk
1 quart vanilla ice cream, at
  room temperature

In a heat-proof pitcher or other container, combine sugar, coffee crystals, and salt. Add water, stirring until well blended. Cover and set aside to steep and cool. Pour milk into a punch bowl or other large container; add coffee mixture, stirring well. One half hour before serving, spoon ice cream into coffee-milk mixture; blend well as ice cream melts. Serve in punch cups.

–Ida Mae Leatherman

(Old-Fashioned) Coffee

Mix 1 teacup of ground coffee with a gill of cold water, and pour on it 1 1/2 pints of boiling water; let it boil 10 minutes; strain through a piece of yellow cotton into a second pot; add some white of egg to the cold water and coffee, if the coffee has not been glazed. Three-quarters of a pound of coffee will make 1 gallon. Three-quarters each of Mocha, Java, and Laguyra.

Virginia Recipes, *1890*

Café Frappe

1 egg (white)
1/2 c. cold water
1/2 c. ground coffee
4 c. boiling water

Beat white of egg slightly, add cold water, and boil 1 minute; place on back of range 10 minutes; strain, add sugar, cool, and freeze to a mush, using equal parts ice and salt. Serve in frappe glasses, with whipped cream, sweetened and flavored.

Culinary Echoes From Dixie, *1917*

Fruited Tea Punch

Yield: about 36 punch cup servings

2 (6-ounce) cans frozen
  orange juice concentrate
2 (6-ounce) cans frozen
  lemonade concentrate
8 cups *freshly brewed* strong
  tea, at room temperature
6 cups unsweetened
  pineapple juice, chilled
2/3 cup lemon juice, chilled
Sugar to taste (optional)
Ice cubes or fruited ice ring
Thin orange half slices
  and/or pineapple cubes

Allow frozen juice concentrate to thaw. In a punch bowl, combine orange juice and lemonade concentrates. Add tea, and pineapple and lemon juices. Stir in sugar to taste, if desired. Add ice cubes or fruited ice ring, if desired. Garnish with orange half slices and/or pineapple cubes.

Age of Innocence Cup

Yield: 60 punch cup servings

4 cups *freshly brewed* tea,
  cooled
8 cups cold tea
6 cups sweetened or
  artificially sweetened
  cranberry juice
4 cups orange juice
Ice cubes as needed
1 quart ginger ale
About 2 cups Heavy Syrup

Prepare freshly brewed tea; allow to cool. Combine fresh tea, cold tea, cranberry juice, and orange juice in a punch bowl. Add ice cubes as desired. Gradually pour ginger ale over ice cubes. Sweeten to taste with heavy syrup. Garnish as desired.

Heavy Syrup: In a small heavy saucepan, combine 2 cups sugar and 1 cup water. Bring to a boil over moderate heat and continue boiling for about 3 to 4 minutes.

–The Valentine Museum

Tangy Fruit Punch

Yield: 25 punch cup servings

2 (6-ounce) cans frozen grapefruit juice concentrate, thawed
2 (6-ounce) cans frozen orange juice concentrate, thawed
2 (6-ounce) cans frozen limeade concentrate, thawed
Ice cubes or fruited ice ring
2 liters (33.8 ounces) club soda or sparkling water, chilled
2 medium seedless oranges, thinly sliced into half-slices

In a pitcher, combine the first 3 ingredients. Chill until ready to serve. Pour citrus mixture into a small punch bowl; add ice cubes or fruited ice ring, as desired. Add club soda; blend well. Garnish punch with orange half-slices.

Excellent Cool Summer Beverages

Lemonade is the quickest and the easiest thing to make on impromptu occasions, and this popular beverage may be varied ad infinitum, according to the housewife's resources. Raspberry or strawberry juice and some of the whole fruit may be added; a few sprigs of mint make a pleasant flavor and a very refreshing drink of ordinary lemonade. A bottle of ginger ale added to a quart of lemonade will add to its quality as well as its quantity.

The best lemonade is made by boiling the sugar and water together to a syrup and adding it to the strained lemon juice when cool. Then the mixture is placed in the ice chest to be poured over cracked ice at serving time.

Mrs. Caroline B. King
Culinary Expert of the Evening Telegraph
Virginia Cook Book, *1839*

Safe 'N Sane Virgin Mary Cocktail

Yield: 6 servings

3 1/2 cups tomato or
   vegetable-tomato juice
3 to 4 tablespoons lemon or
   lime juice
2 to 3 teaspoons
   Worcestershire sauce or
   to taste
1 teaspoon bottled steak
   sauce
Hot sauce to taste
Seasoned salt or salt and
   pepper to taste
Celery salt to taste
Ice cubes as needed
6 celery ribs
6 thin lemon or lime slices

In a large pitcher, combine tomato or vegetable-tomato juice, lemon or lime juice, Worcestershire and steak sauces, blending well. Add hot sauce, celery salt, seasoned salt or salt and pepper to taste. Pour into 6 tall glasses containing ice, dividing evenly. Add a celery rib and lemon or lime slice to each glass and sprinkle wih celery salt and/or seasoned salt, if desired.

Note: Glass rims may be dipped in lightly beaten egg white and then dipped in seasoned salt, if desired. Allow glasses to stand for several minutes to dry egg white before pouring tomato cocktail into glasses.

Triple Fruit Juice Cooler

Yield: 6 to 8 servings

1 (6-ounce) can frozen
   grapefruit juice
   concentrate, thawed
1 (6-ounce) can frozen
   lemonade concentrate,
   thawed
3 cups unsweetened
   pineapple juice
1/4 cup grenadine syrup
Ice cubes as desired
Thin orange half slices

In a large pitcher, combine the first 4 ingredients, blending well. Chill thoroughly. Add ice cubes as desired to tall glass tumblers; fill glasses with fruit juice mixture. Garnish each serving with an orange half slice.

Iced tea, now a staple of American beverages, was invented by accident by an exasperated visiting Englishman at the 1904 St. Louis International Exposition trying to demonstrate the value of hot tea on a sweltering humid summer day to the indifferent visiting crowds. In desperation, Richard Blechynden threw ice chunks into the tea urn...instant acceptance by the crowds and one of America's favorite non-alcoholic beverages was born.

Refreshing Citrus Fruit Tea

Yield: 8 servings

1 quart cold water
3 teaspoons grated lemon peel
1 to 1 1/2 cups sugar or to taste
2 cups medium to strong tea
1/4 cup lemon juice
1 teaspoon vanilla extract
2 cups cold water
Lemon slices for garnish (optional)
Fresh mint sprigs for garnish (optional)

In a medium saucepan combine the lemon peel, 1 quart water, and sugar. Boil together for 5 minutes. Add tea; cool. When mixture is cool, add lemon juice, vanilla, and 2 cups cold water. Stir well; chill. Fill glasses with ice cubes and pour fruit-tea mixture to within 1/2 inch of top of glass. Garnish each with a lemon slice and a mint sprig.

Variation: Omit grated lemon peel and juice and substitute 3 teaspoons grated orange peel and juice from 3 oranges. Add 1 (3-inch) cinnamon stick to boiling fruit mixture, if desired. Proceed as directed above.

–Marion Peeschla (Mrs. Ralf)

Spiced Milk

Yield: 2 (8-ounce) servings

1/2 teaspoon cinnamon
1/2 teaspoon nutmeg
1/4 teaspoon sugar
Pinch of salt
2 cups milk or half-and-half, chilled

In a pitcher, combine the first 4 ingredients. Add milk or half-and-half and stir until sugar dissolves. Serve cold.

Menus

Winter Holiday Breakfast

Chilled Rosé Brut

Wassail Bowl
(page 709)

Sparkling Wine

Oven Roasted Oysters in Shells
(page 280)

Sis's Mushroom Torte
(page 38), or
Salmon Quiche
(page 302)

Clam Chowder Scrambled Eggs
(page 310), or
Devilish Scrambled Eggs
(page 298)

Jewel Glazed Holiday Ham
(page 163)
or
Old Virginia Sausage Patties
(page 170)

Brandied Applesauce
(page 670)

Toasted Coconut Bread
(page 446), or
Sour Cream Banana Muffins
(page 478)

Pecan Sticky Buns
(page 509)

Quick and Easy Cinnamon Ring
(page 465)

Strawberries and Pineapple in Champagne
(page 59)

Coffee

Tea

Cold Weather Repast by the Fire

Oven Beef Stew with Guiness 'N Prunes
(page 102)
or
Red Hot Chili
(page 132)
Sour Cream, Chopped Onions, Shredded Sharp Cheddar or
Monterey Jack Cheese, Minced Chives, Coarsely Chopped
Avocado, Freshly Grated Parmesan Cheese

Crusty Baked Herb Bread
(page 511)
or
Sour Cream Corn Bread
(page 469

Refrigerator Slaw   Crisp Bread N' Butter Pickles
(Page 409)   (Page 678)

Mrs. Beasley's Pecan Squares
(page 632), or
Chewey Banana Bars
(page 629)

Tea   Coffee
Chilled Guiness Stout
Chilled Mexican Beer with Lime
Chilled Assorted Soft Drinks

Elegant Dinner for Friends

Crab Streudel
(page 32)

Quick 'N Easy Company Tomato Soup
(page 76)

Apple and Apricot Stuffed Veal Loin
with
Madeira Sauce
(page 173)

Wild Mushroom Pilaf   Herbed Green Beans
(page 341)   (Page 348)

Strawberry Spinach Salad
(page 416)

Easy-Do Dinner Rolls
(page 500)
Butter Curls

Chocolate Raspberry Supreme
(page 554)

Irish Coffee   Expresso
(page 700)

Cellar Temperature Beaujolais

Take-A-Long Party
at the Strawberry Hill Races

Zesty Curry Dip with Vegetable Crudités
(page 48)

Cocktail Nibbles
(page 36)

Southern Fried Chicken
(page 211)

Barbecued He-Man Beef Brisket
with
He-Man Barbecue Sauce
(page 121)
Kaiser or Onion Rolls

Spiral Macaroni Salad   Crunchy Broccoli Salad
(page 390)   (page 407)

Strawberry Bread or Muffins
(page 444)

Old-Time Watermelon   Dilly Beans
Rind Pickles   (page 674)
(page 682)

Black Walnut Pound Cake   Nutty Oatmeal Cake
(page 561)   (page 684)

Chocolate Dipped Strawberries
(page 668)

Citrus Wine Cooler   Chilled Virginia Chardonnay
(page 714)
Chilled Draft Beer
Chilled Assorted Soft Drinks

Garden Week Brunch

Wes Booth's Two-Fisted
Bloody Mary
(page 698)

Safe 'N Sane
Virgin Mary
(page 725)

Spinach Quiche with Fresh Basil and Tomatoes
(page 304)

Creamed Turkey with Toasted Almonds
'N Raisins over Toast Points
(page 224)

Orange Glazed Sweet Potatoes
(page 374)

Fresh Fruit Squares
(page 462)

Kugelhopf
(page 463)

Raisin Bran Muffins
(page 477)

Grapefruit Lime Aspic
(page 421)

Easy Refrigerator Pickles
(page 679)

Virginia Apple Relish
(page 685)

Five Flavor Pound Cake
(page 578)

Thumbprint Cookies
with Mild Southern Sweet
Pepper Jelly
(page 649)

Lemon Meltaways
(page 696)

Nutty Special Occasion Fudge
(page 665)

Coffee

Tea

Chilled Virginia Riesling

Cocktail Nibbles and Sweets

Chinese Chicken Walnut Fingers
with Oriental Orange Sauce
(page 29, 421)

Baked Crab Puffs
(page 43)

Zesty Baked Artichoke Dip
(page 26)

Party-Time Triple Cheese Ball   Salmon Mousse
(page 50)   (page 53)

Crisp Assorted Crackers

Creamy Orange Fruit Dip
(page 47)
with
Assorted Fresh Fruits

1898 Sunshine Cake
(page 586)

Polka Dot Macaroons   Mocha Pillows
(page 641)   (page 660)

Nutty Ice Box Cookies
(page 649)

Chilled Spanish Semi-Secco
Chilled Sparkling Water
Chilled Sparkling Wine with Lime Wedges
Power House Punch
(page 716)

Graduation Celebration Buffet

Chilled Domestic or Foreign Sparkling Wine
for Toasting

Avocado and Watercress Dip
with Chilled Shrimp
(page 45)

Crumb Topped Country Ham In A Bag
(page 166), or
Pungent Pork Tenderloin
(page 152)

Easy Chicken Divan   Cheese Stuffed Spinach Tortellini
(page 197)   (page 327)

Baked Cherry Tomatoes with Rum Sauce
(page 378)

Salad Au Ceasar
(page 414)

Golden Sweet 'Tater Biscuits
(page 457), or
Southern Yeast Biscuits
(page 406)

Fresh Peaches 'N Cream Cheesecake
with Brandied Peach Sauce
(page 566)

Southern Pecan Pie
(page 617)

Fruited Tea Punch   Iced Coffee Punch
(page 723)   (page 722)

Chilled Italian Pinot Grigio

July 4th Celebration

Dottie's Marguerita Punch
(Page 715)

Frozen Whisky Sours
(page 700)

Festive South-of-the-Border Dip
(page 146)

Jewell's Mushrooms
(page 33)

Crab Stuffed Cherry Tomatoes
(page 55)

Gazpacho Blanco
(page 68)
or
Chilled Easy Blender Fresh Asparagus Soup
(page 75)

Grilled Monkfish with Dill Pesto Sauce
(page 256), or
Grilled London Broil Teriyaki
(page 113)

Baked Brown Rice
(page 335)

Marinated
Vegetable Salad
(page 47)

Summer
Slaw
(page 411)

Piedmont Corn Relish
(page 688)

Grandmother Jackson's Sally Lunn
(page 490), or
Quick Sour Cream Corn Bread
(page 469)

Almond Cookies
(page 614)

Nectarine
Custard Ice Cream
(page 536)

Lacy Oatmeal Crisps
(page 652)

Iced Tea

Chilled Beer
Chilled Assorted Soft Drinks
Chilled Sauvignon Blanc
or
Cellar Temperature Pinot Noir

Easy Fixins for a Summer's Eve

Mexican-Style Tomato Gazpacho
(page 69), or
Chilled Curried Cucumber Soup
with Tarragon
(page 67)

Thinly Sliced Smithfield
or
Virginia Country-Style Ham
(page 165, 167)

Islander Chicken Salad
(page 398), or
Hot and Spicy Skewered Chicken
(page 204)

Tortellini Salad with Fresh Basil
(page 391), or
Wild Rice Salad with Tarragon
(page 394)

Mr. Jefferson's Peas
(page 348)

Crusty Herb Bread
(page 511)

Easy-Do Fresh Strawberry Mousse
(page 545), or
Apricot Brandy Ice Cream
(page 533), or
Butter Pecan Tortoni
(page 534)

Iced Tea   Coffee
Summertime Sangria
(page 707)

Urban Seashore Dinner

Curried Sesame Dip
(page 56)
Assorted Crudités or Crisp Corn Chips

Wild Mushroom Strudel
(page 40)
Roquefort Cheese Ball
(page 52)
Assorted Crackers

Oven Clambake
(Clams, oysters, shrimp, chicken, sausage,
small new red skinned potaoes,
yams or sweet potaoes,
corn-on-the-cob)
(page 274)

Bloody Mary Aspic Cups
(page 420)

Fourteen Day Pickles   Cranberry Orange Compote
(page 680)   (page 686)
Hush Puppies
(page 470)

Lemon Chess Pie   Spiced Carrot Cake
(page 605)   with Cream Cheese Icing
(page 566)

Chilled Dry Spanish White Wine   Chilled Draft Beer
Assorted Soft Drinks
Coffee   Tea

Early Autumn Picnic at Westover

Goat Cheese Marinated with Rosemary and Lemon
(page 313)

Smoked Salmon Pâté   Russian-Style Eggplant Butter
(page 49)   (page 51)

Thinly Sliced French Baguette

Mediterranean-Style Roasted Chicken
(page 198)

Picniker's Delight Potato Salad
with Parmesan Cheese
(page 402), or
Early Autumn Pasta
(page 303)

Marinated Green Beans   Tuscany Waldorf Salad
(page 403)   (page 388)

Tomato Tart   Brandied Applesauce
(page 691)   (page 686)

Miss Naomi's Buttermilk Biscuits
(page 456)

Nectarine Preserves   Tangerine
with Red Port Wine   Marmalade
(page 695)   (page 693)

Sour Milk Chocolate Sheet Cake   Granny's Peanut Butter Cookies
with Nutty Chocolate Frosting   (page 655)
(page 574)

Tangy Fruit Punch   Chilled Seyval Blanc
(page 724)

Hot Coffee in a Thermos

Late Supper After the Opera

Crabmeat Soufflé Spread   Easy Brie Appetizer
(page 48)   (page 54)
                    Crisp Assorted Crackers

Shrimp and Noodle Casserole
(page 292)

Baked Chicken Breasts
with Apple Brandy
(page 194)

Buttered Brussels Sprouts
with Walnuts
(page 353)
Ribbon Gelatin Salad   Piquant Pears
(page 408)   (page 368)
                    Miniature Date Muffins
                    (page 472)

Fresh Lemon Chiffon Cake
(page 575)
or
Prize Winning Cheesecake
(page 564), with
Brandied Nectarine Sauce
(page 554)

Coffee   Tea

            Chilled California Gewürtztraminer

After-the-Game Party for Teens

Thumprints   Pretzels
(page 44)

Cocktail Nibbles   Piquant Fiesta Spread
(page 27)   (page 28)
Crisp Assorted Crackers, or
Melba Toast Rounds

Super Maid Rites   Easy Oven Barbecued Beef
(page 128)   (page 119)
Toasted Buttered Kaiser or French Rolls
or
Hearty Mixed-Grains Bread
(page 188)
Chopped Onions, Shredded Monterey Jack or Sharp Cheddar Cheese

Refried Beans Patties
(page 333)

Nielsen's Richmond-Style Coleslaw
(page 409)

Crunchy Autumn Fruit Salad
(page 370)

Chocolate Applesauce Cupcakes with Caramel Frosting
(page 569)
White Cholocate Crunch
(page 670)
Meme's Creamy Pralines   Jiffy Fudge
(page 663)   (page 663)

Age of Innocence Cup   Chilled Assorted Soft Drinks
(page 723)

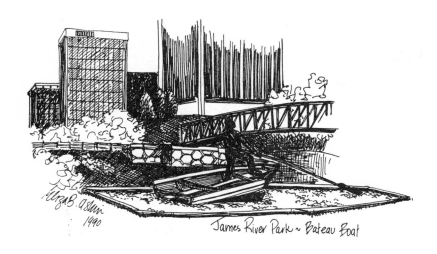

James River Park ~ Bateau Boat

James River Park

James River Park, begun in 1968, is composed of five different areas in the city of Richmond, adjacent to the meandering James River. Made up of uninhabited grass and woods space located at Huguenot Woods, the Pony Pasture, the Great Shiplock Park, North Park (nicknamed Texas Beach), the main section of park runs parallel to the river from the Boulevard east to the Lee Bridge and along five miles of river rapids. Additionally, the infamous Belle Island ... known in the early nineteenth century as a "men's pleasure island ... horse racing, high living, gambling and houses of ill repute" ... and later during the Civil War for its prison incarcerating enlisted Yankee soldiers ... will open officially in 1991 as a part of the park.

Until recently a handsome representation of a bateau man steering a bateau, created in fiberglass by artist Paul Dipasquale, stood on Brown's Island in the main park area as a tribute to the long-ago boatmen of the James. Unfortunately, vandalism caused its demise. In the near future, this silent sentinel will be reconstructed to once again stand watch over the James. An important part of Richmond history and its river traffic, the bateau men maneuvered their precious cargo of Virginia gold (tobacco stored in "hogs heads") via their flat bottomed boats over the canals and rapids of the James River during the early nineteenth century.

Today the river area at the 42nd Street entrance of the Pony Pasture is considered the best place to swim and innertube in the city. Further, some of the finest small mouth bass fishing can be found in the waters of the James at the rapids. And white water boating over the James rapids, a sport with many Richmond enthusiasts, is the only activity of its kind to be found within the confines of an urban environment.

725

Virginia-Style Thanksgiving Dinner

Virginia Peanut Soup
(page 100), or
Savory Pumpkin Soup
(page 88)
Toasted Parmesan Crunchies

Holiday Roast Goose
(page 218), or
Roasted Turkey with Mayonnaise Covering
(page 226)
Nana Fuleihan's Holiday Stuffing
(page 231), or
Baked Herbed Sausage Stuffing Balls
(page 228)

Giblet Gravy

Whipped Potatoes   Sweet Potato Pudding
(page 361)

Baked Onions Au Gratin   Half Way House Green Beans
(page 359)   (page 334)
Spiced Cranberries with Port Wine
(page 368)

Light 'N High Spoon Bread   Miss Naomi's
(page 480)   Buttermilk Biscuits
(page 456)
Miniature Butter Molds

Molded Cranberry Raspberry Gelatin Salad
(page 422), or
Tangy Fruited Gingerale Salad
(page 424)

Crisp Assorted Relishes

Old-Fashioned Sweet Potato Pie   Frozen Mincemeat Ice Cream Tarts
(page 614)   (page 616)
"Mac Mac's" Holiday Coconut Cake
(page 580), or
Brandied Fresh Pear Cake
(page 560)
Seafoam   Fabulous Chocolate Nut Fudge
(page 665)   (page 661)

Demitassé

Chilled Virginia or California Dry Blush

Shockhoe Founatin in Historic Shockhoe Area

New Year's Eve Buffet

Cheesey Mushroom Sticks
(page 36)

Crab Streudel
(page 32)

Zesty Baked Artichoke Dip
(page 26)

Caviar Pie
(page 56)

Roquefort Cheese Ball
(page 53)

Crisp Assorted Crackers

Hot and Spicy Skewered Chicken
(page 204)

Aprcot Glazed Ham
(page 62)

Golden Angel Biscuits
(page 497)

Miniature Sautéed
Black Eyed Pea Patties
(page 364)

Stewed Tomatoes

Hopping John
(page 321)

"Mac Mac's" Holiday Ambrosia
(page 537)

English Spiced Fruitcake
(page 557)

King's Cake
(page 543)

Devil's Food Cake
with Old-Fashioned 7-Minute Frosting
(page 536)

Springerle Cookies
(page 658)

Walnut Clusters
(page 646)

Miniature Fruit Cake Drops
(page 638)

Peppered Biscotti
(page 652)

Martha'sRum Soaked
Chocolate Truffles
(page 669

White Chocolate
Peppermit Crunch
(page 670)

Champagne Apricot Punch
(page 669)

Tangy Fruit Punch
(page 724)

Mrs. J. Ambler Johnston's Eggnog
(page 718)
Chilled Virginia, California or French Sparkling Wine
Chilled White Merlot

View of Richmond for **Tombs History of the South**
1866, Steel plate done in 1863

Glossary of Cooking Terms

À la king Served in rich cream sauce

Appetizer A foodstuff of a light consistency served as the first course at a dinner to excite the palate

Aspic A savory jelly made from stock or tomato juice containing sufficient gelatin to hold its shape when cold

Au gratin Foods creamed or moistened with milk or stock....the food is placed in a casserole or baking dish, covered with crumbs, butter or cheese, and baked or boiled until the top is brown

Au jus Meat served with its natural unthickened juices

Au lait With milk or cooked in milk

Au natural Applied to food cooked plainly and in a simple fashion

Bake To cook by dry heat, usually in the oven....when applied to meats,the process is called roasting

Barbecue To roast or broil on a rack or revolving spit over or under a source of cooking heat....the food is usually basted with a highly seasoned sauce

Baste To moisten with liquid or food juices while cooking

Beat To make a mixture smooth by rapid, regular motion that lifts it upand over....an electric mixer, hand rotary beater, wire whisk, or mixing spoon may be used

Bechamel A foundation white sauce

Bisque A creamy soup usually made of shellfish

Blanch To cook in boiling water for a short time....then plunge into cold water to chill quickly

Blend To mix well

Boil To cook in water at a temperature of 212 degrees F. at sea level

Bombe An ice cream dessert, usually frozen in a mold

Bordelaise A basic brown sauce using Bordeaux wine for part of the liquid

Bouillabaisse A stew containing several varieties of fish and shellfish

Bouillon A clear soup or strong broth

Bouquet garni A small bunch of fresh or dried herbs tied in cheesecloth and used to flavor stocks and stews....usually consisting of parsley, thyme, tarragon, bay leaf, marjoram, and chervil

Bourguignonne Food cooked in a rich sauce containing burgundy wine, braised onions, and often mushrooms

Braise To brown, then to cook, tightly covered, with a small amount of liquid

Bread To coat the surface of food with fine dry bread, cracker, or cereal crumbs, or to coat with crumbs, and then dip in diluted eggs or milk, and again coat with crumbs

Breadcrumbs Available in two varieties....as dry breadcrumbs which are of a fine texture and commercially prepared and as soft breadcrumbs which are prepared by crumbling day-old bread

Bread Flour Flour which has a higher protein (gluten) content and which will be slightly more granular than regular all-purpose flour

Brochette, en Cooked or served on a skewer

Broil To cook under direct heat, as in a broiler or over hot coals, as on a grill

Broth Beef or chicken stock or bouillon....in some cases refers to liquids in which vegetables are cooked

Brush To spread butter or margarine, (usually melted), eggs, etc., on top of food with a brush, paper towel, or cloth

Café Coffee

Café au lait Equal parts of hot coffee and hot milk

Canapé A savory appetizer on a base of bread, toast, or crisp cracker

Candy When applied to fruit and fruit peels, it means to cook in a heavy sugar syrup until transparent....then drip and dry....the second meaning applies to vegetables that are cooked in a sugar syrup to give a coating or glaze.

Capers The unopened flower buds of the caper plant preserved in vinegar

Capon An emasculated male chicken

Caramel, or Caramelize Sugar cooked almost to the burning point or to a deep brown syrup

Charlotte A dish of custard

Chasseur Hunter's style or with a robust tomato, garlic, and mushroom sauce, often containing red wine

Chill To refrigerate food until cold, not frozen

Chop To cut food into small pieces with a knife or meat grinder

Clarify As applied to liquid food or fat, it means to render clear....to separate the solids from liquid, as in clarified butter

Coat To roll, shake, or sprinkle foods until well covered with flour, meal, breadcrumbs, beaten egg, or a combination of these ingredients

Coat a spoon Indicates the thickness of a custard sauce....a metal spoon dipped in thickened sauce will be thoroughly covered with a thin film

Compote Fruits stewed in a light syrup

Coddle To simmer gently in liquid over low hftwo knives, a pastry blender, or fork

Condiments Spices, herbs, and spiced and highly flavored relishes and sauces

Consommé A clear soup made from meat or poultry and vegetables

Cool To let stand at room temperature until no longer warm to the touch

Coquille A French term for a scallop....or a term usually applied to a recipe in which scallops are the main ingredients

Court bouillon Liquid in which fish is cooked, usually containing water, white wine, vegetables, herbs, salt, and peppercorns

Cream To mix shortening until light and fluffy

Crimp Used in pastry making....applies to formation of decorative edge on crust

Croustades Various shapes of fried bread used for serving or garnishing meat, poultry, or fish entrees

Croutons Small cubes of fried bread used to garnish soups and other recipes

Cube To cut food into small squares larger than dice or chop

Cut in To distribute a solid shortening through dry ingredients by using two knives, a pastry blender, or fork

Dash A scant 1/8 teaspoon of dry ingredients or liquid

Deep-fat fry To cook in a deep container in enough hot fat to cover food

Dice To cut into 1/4-inch cubes

Dissolve To combine a dry substance with a liquid so that they merge and the dry substance liquifies

Dredge To cover completely with a dry ingredient....but not thickly

Dress To prepare for cooking

Dumpling A small ball of dough which is steamed in liquid or baked.... sometimes filled with minced meats or vegetables

Dust To sprinkle lightly with flour or sugar

Few drops Less than 1/8 teaspoon of liquid ingredient

Few grains Less than 1/8 teaspoon of dry ingredient

Entrée Usually referred today as the main course of a luncheon, dinner, or supper menu

Filé A powder made from ground tender leaves of sassafras, added to a stew or gumbo just before serving as a thickening agent

Filet The tenderloin of meat

Fillet A slice of fish without bones

Fines herbes A mixture of finely chopped fresh or dried herbs, usually consisting of tarragon, dill, chives, chervil, and parsley

Flake To break up into small pieces with a fork

Flambé To cover or combine food with alcoholic spirits and burn with a flame

Flan An open custard, fruit, or cream tart...or may be a set cream such as Crème Caramel

Florentine A method of cooking used mainly with fish and eggs which always includes spinach....often creamed

Fluting An edging for pastry....dough is pressed around the rim of a pie plate into a standing rim and then formed into a fluted edge with thefingertips

Fold in To combine a delicate ingredient such as whipped cream or beaten egg whites with a solid mixture such as batter, using a gentle under-and-over motion with a wire whisk or rubber spatula

Fricassée A stew of chicken, rabbit, or veal in a white sauce

Fritter A food dipped in batter or in a beaten egg and crumbs and fried or deep-fat fried

Fry To cook, uncovered, in hot fat or shortening

Garnish To decorate a serving plate or platter attractively

Glacé A French term for glaze. Also referring to ice cream or ices

Glaze To make food shiny or glassy or to add lustre either with egg, water, and sugar....to coat with sugar, syrup, or melted jelly, either during or after cooking....or a strong meat gravy or bone stock reduced by long boiling to a brown syrup which sets firm when cold

Grate To rub on a grater to produce small particles

Gratiner To place under the broiler briefly or to salamander (heat with a hot food iron) a prepared recipe sprinkled with breadcrumbs or grated cheese to give the finished product a golden color

Grease To rub a cooking utensil with a fat such as shortening or butter before filling with food

Grill Another term for broiling

Grind To put through a food chopper

Hors d'oeuvre A relish, light food, or dainty sandwich served as an appetizer before the regular courses of a meal

Hull To remove or strip off outer covering or stems of certain fruits and vegetables

Jardiniere Prepared or garnished with young vegetables

Julienne To cut food into narrow, lengthwise, match like strips

Knead To place dough on a flat surface and to work it by pressing down with the knuckles, folding over, and repeating the actions as often as needed

Lard To insert strips of fat bacon into lean meat....also to cover with bacon or salt pork....or purified and solidified fat from a pig used as shortening for pastry making and frying or deep-fat frying foods

Level Applied to measurements of dry or solid ingredients in cooking....ingredients should come to the top of the measuring utensil and then be leveled off with a straight-edged spatula or knife

Lukewarm In cooking, means the liquid or solid food is moderately warm to the touch (about 110 degrees F.)

Lyonnaise A garnish or style of cooking in which fried shredded onion is

733

a main ingredient

Marinade A savory mixture in which food is soaked

Marinate To soak in savory mixture of wine, vinegar, and spices

Mash To make a soft or pulpy mass of food

Mask To cover a food completely with sauce, jelly, aspic, mayonnaise, or whipped cream

Mayonnaise A thick oil and egg sauce (emulsion)

Meringue A sweet cake or cookie made of beaten egg whites and sugar....also a beaten egg white and sugar topping for pies and pastries

Mince to cut or chop into very fine pieces

Monrnay A rich sauce containing melted cheese

Mousse A light frothy mixture containing either whipped cream or beaten eggs whites; may be sweet or savory

Pan-broil To cook, uncovered, in a hot skillet, pouring off fat as it accumulates

Pan-fry To cook in a small amount of fat in a hot skillet

Parboil To boil in a liquid until partially ooked

Pare To cut away the outer surface of vegetables and fruits with a knife or other utensil

Pâté The French term for pastry or pasta

Or, a mixture of any finely ground meat, liver, game etc. seasoned, flavored and baked

Peel To strip off the outer covering of certain vegetables and fruits. . . also, the rind or skin or certain fruits

Phyllo or Phylo A plain, paper-thin flour and water pastry used in Greek and Turkish sweet and savoury pastries

Pickling A process of flavoring or preserving meat, fish, vegetables,fruits, and other foods in brine, vinegar or lemon juice, beer, wine, and spices

Pie A dish of meat, fish, fruit, vegetables, custards or creams, or other foods baked in a pastry crust....and sometimes not baked but chilled or frozen

Pilaf A rice dish flavored with saffron or turmeric....often consisting of rice, onions, raisins, and spices to which meat, poultry, or vegetables are often added

Pinch The amount of a spice, herb, or condiment that can be held between the thumb and the forefinger

Pipe To decorate foods with a decorating tube

Piquant A sharp flavor

Pit To remove pits or seeds from fruit

Poach To cook in liquid that is barely simmering

Potable A beverage

Potage A thick soup

Pot roast To cook by braising, usually over direct heat

Precook To simmer for a short time in water before cooking by some other method (see Parboil)

Provencale Recipes originating in the region of France known as Provencale and containing garlic, olive oil, tomatoes, and black olives....often containing spices marjoram, oregano, thyme, and savory

Purée To press food through a fine sieve or a food mill

Quenelles A type of dumpling made of finely ground raw meat or fish mixed with eggs, shaped into ovals and poached

Ragoût A rich white or brown stew containing meat, fish, or vegetables

Ramekin A small heat-proof individual serving dish or casserole....also a savoury made of cheese and egg and baked like a cheese custard

Remoulade A cold mayonnaise sauce flavored with herbs and mustard

Render To heat fat, such as suet or salt pork, until melted, with only the crisp part (called cracklings) remaining

Rice A starchy grain grown in a warm climate....also a term used to describe pressing food through small holes

Roast To cook by dry heat, usually in the oven

Roll To spread flat with a rolling pin, as rolling out pastry....or to roll up, as with a jelly roll....or a small piece of yeast dough baked in any of numerous forms

Roux A mixture of melted butter and flour cooked together over a low heat and used in making sauces and gravies

Sauce Usually a semi-liquid mixture served with a food to add flavor or interest

Sauté To cook in a small amount of hot fat in a skillet

Savory A rather bitter herb vaguely tasting like thyme

Savoury A piquant morsel served as the last course at dinner

Scald To heat to just below boiling or 196 degrees F.

Score To make cuts in an edge or surface

Scramble To stir or mix gently while cooking

Sear To brown quickly over high heat

Season To add salt, pepper, and other herb s and spices to taste

Set Until firm enough to hold its shape....usually applies to gelatin dishes

Shred To cut or tear into long, narrow pieces

Sift To put one or more dry ingredients through a fine sieve

Simmer To cook in liquid just below the boiling point

Singe To remove or burn off small down (feathers) from a plucked bird by holding and turning it over a flame

Skewer To hold in place with metal or wooden picks

Slit To make a shallow incision or cut in the surface, as in pie crust or meat

Sliver To cut into very thin slices

GLOSSARY

Snip To cut with a knife or scissors into small pieces
Soak To submerge in liquid....usually water
Soufflé A light puffed mixture containing eggs, which may be sweet or savoury
Steam To cook on a rack above boiling water in a tightly closed container....also to cook in a double boiler
Steep To soak in hot or cold liquid
Stew To cook in liquid over low heat
Stir To blend with a circular motion
Supreme The most delicate....the choice piece of chicken or meat or a cream sauce enriched with egg yolks
Tart or tarte Generally tarts are considered those dishes with an undercrust only and no crust covering the filling....or a term to describe a sharp caustic flavor
Tenderize To make meat tender by pounding, marinating, or using a meat tenderizer
Toast To brown by direct heat in a toaster or the oven
Torte An open pie or rich cake....sometimes a cake made of many thin layers
Toss To tumble ingredients lightly with a fork and spoon
Truffle A fungus, similar to a mushroom, which grows under the roots of young oak trees....also, a type of candy
Truss To fasten the leg and wing joints of fowl with skewers or twine before cooking
Virgin olive oil Oil from the first pressing of the olive, much preferred over extractions from the second and third pressings...often referred to as *extra virgin*
Vinaigrette A sauce of vinegar, oil, salt, pepper, and herbs
Whip To beat rapidly with a hand rotary beater, electric mixer, or wire whisk to incorporate air and increase volume
Whisk A wire beater for eggs, cream, or other ingredients and used to beat or whip to a froth....also meaning to beat
Zest The oil from the outer thin yellow or orange peel (rind) of citrus fruits

INDEX

INDEX

Brandied Applesauce, 670
Chili Sauce, 659
Crisp Bread 'N Butter Pickles, 662
Crisp Watermelon Rind Pickles, 665
Dilly Beans, 658
Easy Refrigerator Pickles, 662
Fourteen Day Pickles, 664
Fresh Tomato Salsa, 421
Mince Meat, 668
Mushroom Catsup, 672
Mustard Pickle, 666
Old-Fashioned Bread and Butter Pickles, 662
Old-Time Watermelon Rind Pickles, 666
Pepper Vinegar, 663
Piedmont Corn Relish, 672
Raspberry Vinegar, 663
Saffron Onions, 660
Spiced Cranberries with Port Wine, 673
Spiced Gingery Preserved Seckel Pears, 661
Sweet Pickled Ginger (Amazu Shoga), 659
Three Pepper Relish, 242
Tomata Catsup, 675
Tomatoes and Cucumbers with Yogurt, 674
Tomato Tart, 675
Virginia Apple Relish, 669
Pies
About, 579, 581, 590
Black Forest Cherry Pie, 590
Bourbon Pecan Pie, 606
Caramel Pecan Pumpkin Pie, 598
Caramel Pudding, or Pie, 583
Cheddary Apple Pie, 579
Chess Pie, 588
Chocolate Chess Pie with Cinnamon, 588
Chocolate Pecan Pie, 606
Coconut Pie, 595
Cranberry Chiffon Pie, 586
Creamy Date Walnut Pie, 605
Currant Pie, 583
Deep-South Pecan Pie, 607
Dixie Peanut Pie and variation, 606
Frozen Mincemeat Ice Cream Tarts, 600
Fruit Pies, 579, 583, 584, 586, 587, 589, 590, 593, 599, 601, 603, 605
Glazed Fresh Strawberry Pie, 583
Grandma's Creamy Apple Pie, 582
Grandma's Shoo-Fly Pie, 603
Honey Pecan Pie, 607
Impossible Pie, 596
Jane's Easy Chocolate Pie, 593

Kentucky Derby Pie, 596
Lemon Pie, 604
Lemon Chess Pie, 589
Light 'N Luscious Lemon Pie, 599
Low Calorie Windowpane Pie, 606
Mecklenburg County Lemon Chess Pie, 589
Meringue Topped Cider Vinegar Pie, 604
Miller & Rhoads Chocolate Silk Pie, 580
Mince Meat for Pies, 668
Mince-Meat-No. 683, 608
Nutty Chocolate Chess Pie, 589
Old Colonial Pie, 595
Old-Fashioned Sweet Potato Pie, 598
Old Southern Chess Pie, 590
Orange Custard Pie (Very Nice), 593
Paulette's Authentic Key Lime Pie, 601
Peach Custard Pie, 583
Potion of Love Pie, 594
Raisin Pie, 603
Regal Mince Pie, 602
Rhubarb Pie, 587
Sour Cream Black Walnut Pie, 608
Southern Pecan Pie, 601
Tacky Pie Party, 597
Triple Chocolate Mousse Pie, 592
White Russian Pie, 586
Pilaf, 325
Pineapple
Carr's Hill Pineapple Rice, 324
Empandidas De Piña (Pineapple Flipovers), 507
Lila Tice's Pineapple Upside Down Cake, 545
Pineapple Cheese Gelatin Salad, 407
Pineapple Fritters, 474
Pineapple Peppercorn Glaze, 432
Pineapple Preserves, 677
Saucy Baked Pineapple, 366
Southern Christmas Angel Hash, 534
Strawberries and Pineapple in Champagne, 59
Plum
Holiday Plum Pudding, 534
Hot Plum Sauce, 431
Pork (see Meats, Pork)
Potables (see Beverages)
Potatoes
Baked German Potato "Salad," 350
Cheesey Potato Cabbage Soup, 91
Crusty Au Gratin Potatoes with Bitters, 351
Escalloped Sweet Potatoes, 362
Grandmother Garrett's Tomato-Potato

About the Author

Well-known television personality and certified home economist, Jan Carlton, has had over twenty-five years' experience as a culinary expert and public relations specialist. She has attended Simone Beck's French Cooking School in Mougins, France, and Marcella Hazan's classes for Italian cooking in Bologna, Italy.

As a docent and tour guide, she is active in the Virginia Museum of Fine Arts, as well as a member of the Valentine Museum Guild and the Women's Committee of the Richmond Symphony, for whom she edited *Apron Strings*, a cookbook featuring some of her favorite recipes, as well as those of other committee and symphony members.

Apron Strings won the Tastemaker Award, first runner-up, for the best soft-cover cookbook published in 1983 (The Tastemaker Award is the only award given annually for the best cookbooks published during the year.) She is the author of three best-selling cookbooks. *The Old-Fashioned Cookbook*, Holt, Rinehart & Winston; and *A Festival of Meat Cookery*, Golden Press; both chosen among the best cookbooks published in 1975 and 1971, respectively. Her recent cookbook, *Richmond Receipts*, published in 1987, sold over 20,000 copies and was recommended by *Bon Appetit* magazine.

She has served two Virginia governors as a consumer education specialist and as Mrs. Iowa, she promoted United States savings bonds. Presently, Mrs. Carlton appears as a regular culinary guest of "Thirteen Live," WVEC-TV, in Norfolk, Virginia, as well as in Richmond and other cities of the United States. Additionally, Mrs. Carlton is the mother of two boys, Andrew and Jeff McBride and grandmother to Stephanie and Ian McBride.